Stress &
Well-Being
at Work

Assessments and Interventions for Occupational Mental Health

Edited by
James Campbell Quick
Lawrence R. Murphy
Joseph J. Hurrell, Jr.

American Psychological Association, Washington, DC

Published by the
American Psychological Association
750 First Street, NE
Washington, DC 20002

First printing July 1992
Second printing April 1993

Copies may be ordered from the
APA Order Department
P.O. Box 2710
Hyattsville, MD 20784

This book was typeset in Century by Easton Publishing Services, Inc., Easton, MD.

Printer: Braun-Brumfield, Inc., Ann Arbor, MI
Cover designer: Berg Design, Albany, NY
Technical editor and production coordinator: Cynthia L. Fulton

Library of Congress Cataloging-in-Publication Data

Stress and well-being at work: assessments and interventions for occupational mental health/James Campbell Quick, Lawrence R. Murphy, and Joseph J. Hurrell, Jr., editors.
    p. cm.
    Companion v. to: Work and well-being/edited by Gwendolyn Puryear Keita, and Steven L. Sauter. 1992.
    Includes bibliographical references and index.
    ISBN 1-55798-175-2 (acid-free paper)
    1. Industrial psychiatry—Congresses. 2. Job stress—Congresses.
I. Quick, James C. II. Murphy, Lawrence R. III. Hurrell, Joseph J. IV. Work and well-being.
    [DNLM: 1. Occupational Diseases—prevention & control—congresses. 2. Occupational Health Services—Congresses. 3. Psychology, Industrial. 4. Stress, Psychological—prevention & control—congresses. 5. Work—psychology—congresses. WA 495 S913]
RC967.5.W67 1992b
158.7—dc20

                                 92-10497
                                    CIP

Printed in the United States of America

Contents

Contributors

Michael W. Boye, *London House, Park Ridge, IL*

Mark Braverman, *Harvard University School of Medicine and Crisis Management Group, Inc., Watertown, MA*

Pascale Carayon, *Department of Industrial Engineering, University of Wisconsin—Madison*

Cary L. Cooper, *Institute of Science and Technology, University of Manchester, United Kingdom*

David M. Corey, *Wolf-Corey, Inc., Napa, CA*

Katherine Ellison, *Department of Psychology, Montclair State College*

William A. Erickson, *Department of Design and Environment Analysis, Cornell University*

Terence E. Fitzgerald, *University of Rochester School of Medicine and Dentistry*

Sheila C. Gehlmann, *American Psychological Association, Washington, DC*

Martin M. Greller, *College of Business, University of Wyoming*

Stephen J. Guastello, *Department of Psychology, Marquette University*

Alan Hedge, *Department of Design and Environmental Analysis, Cornell University*

Michael A. Hitt, *Department of Management, Texas A&M University*

Joseph J. Hurrell, Jr., *National Institute for Occupational Safety and Health, Cincinnati, OH*

John W. Jones, *London House, Park Ridge, IL*

Ellen Kirschman, *Palo Alto Police Department, Palo Alto, CA*

Karl W. Kunhert, *Department of Psychology, University of Georgia*

H. Luczak, *Institut fur Arbeitswissenschaft, Technische Universitat Berlin*

Beryce MacLennan, *George Washington University Medical School*

Carol Marcy, *Montgomery County Police Department, MD*

Steven E. Markham, *Management Department, Virginia Polytechnic Institute and State University*

Eugene V. Martin, *Washington, DC*

Gail H. McKee, *Department of Business and Economics, Roanoke College*

Debora R. D. Mitchell, *School of Psychology, Georgia Institute of Technology*

Lawrence R. Murphy, *National Institute for Occupational Safety and Health, Cincinnati, OH*

Margaret H. Mushinski, *Metropolitan Life Insurance Company, New York, NY*

Debra L. Nelson, *Department of Management, Oklahoma State University*

Dusty Orman, *Department of Management, University of Texas at Arlington*

Charles K. Parsons, *School of Management, Georgia Institute of Technology*

Roy L. Payne, *Manchester Business School, University of Manchester, United Kingdom*

Sally B. Philips, *Metropolitan Life Insurance Company, New York, NY*

James Campbell Quick, *Department of Management, University of Texas at Arlington*

Lillian Robbins, *Department of Psychology, Rutgers University—Newark*
Irvin Sam Schonfeld, *Department of Social and Psychological Foundations, City College of New York and Department of Psychiatry, Columbia University*
K. Dow Scott, *Management Department, Virginia Polytechnic Institute and State University*
Ellen Scrivner, *National Institute of Justice, Washington, DC*
Lois E. Tetrick, *Department of Psychology, Wayne State University*
Robert J. Vance, *Center for Applied Behavioral Sciences, Pennsylvania State University*
Gordon D. Wolf, *Wolf-Corey, Inc., Napa, CA*

Foreword

Psychologists have a long history of involvement in the study of human behavior in organizations and in mapping the field of stress. Hugo Munsterberg, American Psychological Association (APA) president in 1898, conducted pioneering studies of industrial safety and accidents. Robert Yerkes, APA president in 1917, conducted ground-breaking work in the field of stress in collaboration with Walter B. Cannon, while also enjoying his friendship as a neighbor in their New Hampshire retreats. Although psychologists continue to work on problems of occupational stress, safety, and health, such problems have not been given the attention that is warranted in a rapidly expanding area of research and practice.

Improved training, better job design, and reduction of stress in the workplace can contribute significantly to the promotion of health and well-being and the prevention of work-related psychological disorders. The APA welcomes the opportunity of working with the National Institute of Occupational Safety and Health (NIOSH) and with psychologists and colleagues in other key professions in making the world a better place to work. A committee of the U.S. Senate has recently noted the value of this collaboration and urged a continued focus on understanding job stress, its related social and economic costs, and ways to control stress such as job redesign.

This is the second of two volumes to result from a national conference on work and well-being that was convened in Washington, DC, in November 1990 under the joint sponsorship of NIOSH and the APA. The first volume, titled *Work and Well-Being: An Agenda for the 1990s*, reported the results of work done by expert panels on occupational stress. This companion volume is a collection of selected papers that were presented at the conference.

Only a decade ago, Joseph Matarazzo, APA president in 1989, recognized behavioral health as a new interdisciplinary specialty within behavioral medicine and identified a unique role for psychology within this specialty, which he labeled *health psychology*. Together with J. Donald Millar, director of NIOSH, and Patrick DeLeon, APA Recording Secretary, Matarazzo was instrumental in stimulating the collaborative effort that resulted in a highly successful NIOSH/APA conference. Matarazzo was also primarily responsible for creating and providing effective leadership for the APA Science Directorate Task Force on Health and Behavior.

Although industrial and health psychology are the two most obvious fields within our discipline with direct relevance for workplace wellness and occupational stress, other specialties within psychology continue to make contributions to the health and well-being of our nation's workers. Researchers in behavioral medicine and personality have identified variables that influence vulnerability to stress, such as Type-A characteristics, hostility, and hardiness. Clinical and counseling psychologists treat employees experiencing stress and psychological disorders in the workplace. And social psychologists have demonstrated the importance of stress buffers, such as social support, job role ambiguity, and the psychological climate of the workplace. Most of these stress-related conditions are examined in the chapters of this volume.

We are indebted to the many fine researchers, clinicians, practitioners, and scholars who presented their work at the conference. Unfortunately, our effort to achieve a manageable volume meant that some excellent papers presented at the conference could not be included. The decision process for doing this was not an easy one given the quality of work presented.

For their role in organizing this conference, I would like to acknowledge the effective leadership of Gwendolyn Puryear Keita, Associate Executive Director of the APA Public Interest Directorate, and Steven L. Sauter of the NIOSH Division of Biomedical and Behavioral Sciences. I would also like to thank Sonja Preston for her skill and dedication in coordinating the conference activities.

Charles D. Spielberger, PhD
President, American Psychological Association
Director, Center for Research in Behavioral
Medicine and Health Psychology

Preface

Stress is a natural and inevitable characteristic of work and life. It is neither inherently bad nor destructive. It is, in fact, one of a person's best assets for achieving peak performance and managing legitimate emergencies. However, it does have the potential for turning into distress, or strain, due to a variety of reasons. It is this latter manifestation of stress that is individually and organizationally destructive. The purpose of this volume is to present a series of chapters addressing assessment and intervention approaches aimed at enhancing stress management and occupational well-being in the workplace. This is important because psychological disorders in the workplace have been identified as being among the 10 leading work-related diseases and injuries (National Institute for Occupational Safety and Health [NIOSH], 1988).

In 1982, at the direction of J. Donald Millar, Director of NIOSH, a list of leading work-related diseases and injuries was developed by the scientific leadership of NIOSH (Millar, 1984). Three criteria were used to select conditions or disorders for inclusion in the list: (a) the frequency of the condition, (b) the severity of the condition in the individual case, and (3) the "preventability" of the condition. NIOSH leadership identified 10 disorders that met these criteria, and psychological disorders was one of the 10. The "top ten" list was intended to encourage deliberation and debate, to assist in setting national health priorities, and to disseminate the concerns of the NIOSH leadership and the focus of the institute (Millar, 1984).

In 1985 and 1986, symposia were held to establish national prevention strategies for the leading work-related diseases and injuries. Psychological disorders were addressed at the 1986 symposium held in Cincinnati, Ohio. It was one of five areas of occupational safety and health subjected to a panel review by experts in the field at this symposium. Over 400 professionals from industry, business, trade unions, voluntary organizations, academia, and the professions attended. A prevention strategy for psychological disorders was reviewed and refined during the symposium. The final document addressed four major areas: job design, surveillance, education and training, and mental health services (NIOSH, 1988).

In 1989, the American Psychological Association (APA), in collaboration with NIOSH, developed the APA/NIOSH Work and Well-Being Project, which used the NIOSH (1988) psychological disorders prevention document as its point of departure. This collaboration, to date, has resulted in a national Work and Well-Being Conference convened in November, 1990; two volumes published by the APA, of which this is one (see also Keita & Sauter, 1992); the development of an APA initiative for enhancing occupational mental health and preventive stress management; and plans for an international conference in the fall of 1992.

This book is based on the 1990 Work and Well-Being Conference. The underlying structure for this national conference was a set of three core panels of interdisciplinary experts drawn together to address stress and job design, the surveillance of occupational stress and psychological disorders, and enhancing occupational mental health (see Keita & Sauter, 1992). Paper and poster sessions were developed around the core panels reporting theoretical and empirical work in a wide diversity of topics concerned with work and well-being. The chapters in this book were derived from these sessions.

Acknowledgments

A book such as this would not be possible without substantial contributions to the Work and Well-Being Conference from a number of individuals. First and foremost, we thank J. Donald Millar, Director of NIOSH, for providing the thrust toward prevention research at NIOSH, for supporting and then defending the inclusion of psychological disorders as a leading work-related disorder amidst no small controversy, and for his provision of resources and encouragement for the Work and Well-Being Conference.

The editors would like to thank the following critical reviewers for their helpful comments: Dan Ganster, Stevan E. Hopfoll, Janet J. Johnston, Sharon Alise Lobel, and Chaya Piotrkowski. Although these reviewers provided needed help for revisions, any remaining errors or shortcomings of this book are the responsibility of the editors, not these reviewers.

James Jones, director of APA's Public Interest Directorate, was responsible for initially mobilizing APA behind this effort, and Charles D. Spielberger, APA President, and Ray Fowler, APA CEO, provided encouragement and ensured a high level of APA support throughout the entire process, from the early planning phase to the present. Steven L. Sauter of NIOSH and Gwendolyn Puryear Keita of APA served as co-chairs of the conference and shouldered the lion's share of the day-to-day work and planning necessary to successfully "pull off" a conference of this size and scope. Naturally, a great deal of thanks is due to the contributors to this volume, who not only prepared papers for the conference but endured several series of postconference reviews conducted by APA, NIOSH, and the editors.

The editors would also like to thank a number of people who assisted in the development of this volume. These people assisted in a variety of ways, including manuscript and figure preparation, translations aand styling assistance, and a number of essential yet unglamorous tasks. Thanks go to Beverly Antilley, Beverly Gilbert, Gayle Hussey, and Sonja William.

James Campbell Quick
Lawrence R. Murphy
Joseph J. Hurrell, Jr.

References

Keita, G. P., & Sauter, S. L. (Eds.). (1992). *Work and well-being: An agenda for the 1990s*. Washington, DC: American Psychological Association.

Millar, J. D. (1984). Letter to the editor. *Journal of Occupational Medicine, 26*, 340–341.

National Institute for Occupational Safety and Health. (1988). *Proposed national strategies for the prevention of leading work-related diseases and injuries—Psychological disorders*. Washington, DC: U.S. Department of Health and Human Services.

Part I

Introduction

1

James Campbell Quick, Lawrence R. Murphy,
Joseph J. Hurrell, Jr., and Dusty Orman

The Value of Work, the Risk of Distress, and the Power of Prevention

Psychological disorders in the workplace have been identified as being among the 10 leading work-related diseases and injuries in the United States (National Institute for Occupational Safety and Health, 1988). The purpose of this chapter is to present an overview of the value of work in the life experience; to identify the risks of distress within the framework of the public health notions of disease; and to argue the case for the power of prevention as the platform for advancing stress-management skills and enhancing psychological well-being in the workplace.

Work ... and Love

Freud was once asked what he thought a "normal" person should be able to do well. He is reported to have said "Lieben und arbeiten" ("to love and to work"; Erikson, 1963 (p. 265). In addressing the evolution of culture, Freud (1930) argued as follows: "The life of human beings in common therefore had a twofold foundation, *i.e.* the compulsion to work, created by external necessity, and the power of love" (p. 68). According to Erikson, Freud's meaning of love is an erotic love that is a process of supreme mutual experience of two beings. Our interpretation of Freud's work also suggests that his definition of love includes more than just a physical process and is instead an ultimate experience of psychological intimacy between individuals. Often, it is through one's family that love-related needs are gratified. Although families are a central source of psychological intimacy for an individual, they may not necessarily be the only source.

Freud's own intense work ethic was a testament to the value he placed on the notion of work. According to Jones (1963), "in Vienna, Freud's life consisted of little besides work" (p. 347). Intellectually, Freud (1930) argued that work had a more powerful effect than any other aspect of human life to bind a person to reality. Thus, "in his work he is at least securely attached to a part of reality, the human community" (Freud, 1930, p. 34). Therefore, Freud's call for a normal person to love and to work can be interpreted as an emphasis on work and family for normal psychological functioning.

Erikson's (1963) own theory of the eight ages of human development also addresses the themes of love (intimacy vs. isolation) and work (industry vs. inferiority). Erikson saw the capacity for work and industriousness beginning in childhood. However, this stage of development, as with each of his stages of development, has an effect through adulthood and the entire life cycle. Erikson (1963) suggested in his discussion of intimacy versus isolation that children must have the capacity to commit themselves to concrete affiliations and partnerships in order to establish a sense of identity. He also suggested that children "must begin to be a worker and a potential provider" (pp. 258–259) in his discussion of industry versus inferiority. He went on to suggest that children need more than just work in their lives to develop a sense of identity.

Hazan and Shaver (1990) proposed a functional parallelism between love and work in adulthood with attachment and exploration in infancy and early childhood. Although there is an intractability between attachment and exploration, both aspects of human behavior are essential to development. Theoretical arguments by Maslow (1954), as well as research evidence from investigators such as Vaillant (1977), suggest that Freud's early proposition that both work and love are essential ingredients for healthy psychological functioning was correct.

A person's work and occupational stature may play an important role in an individual's sense of identity, self-esteem, and psychological well-being. For most individuals, work is the central and defining characteristic of life. For such individuals, it is through the work role that life achieves its primary meaning and value. This is illustrated in the case of Dr. Faust (J. C. Quick & Quick, 1990), who did not want to leave the community in which his 65–70 year professional life had been spent because it would have meant a shift in his primary identification from his professional role (Dr. Faust) to a familial role (father). Although a range of familial, avocational, self-defined life roles may complement one's identity at work, the work role may be the key role. In such cases, the complementary roles one adopts add supplementary meaning and value to the life experience.

Locke (1976) outlined six conditions that lead to job satisfaction for a worker: (a) Work is mentally stimulating, providing challenges with which workers can cope successfully. (b) Work includes physical exertion and activity but is not over-tiring. (c) The rewards of work are viewed as just, fair, and indicative of performance. (d) The work environment facilitates work goals and is physically compatible with worker needs. (e) Work enhances self-esteem and enriches self-identity in the work force. (f) Work leaders and supervisors facilitate the work process and work goal attainment.

Work may have intrinsic value, instrumental value, or both. Intrinsically, the value of work is found in its central role as one important aspect of a person's psychological well-being. The intrinsic value of work is the value an individual finds in performing the work, in and of itself, outside of its utilitarian function. Instrumentally, the value of work is found in its identity-defining characteristic; its basis for providing the necessities of life; its role in giving meaning and structure to the adulthood years; and serving as a channel for the individual's talents, abilities, and knowledge.

Although work has the capacity to enhance the identity and psychological well-being of the individual, it also has important meaning and value for the culture in which it is accomplished. Work organizations may well be the dominant organi-

zational form of Western civilization. The purpose of each of these work organizations is to produce a product or deliver a service to the society. The extent to which
work organizations are effective and efficient in doing so will determine their contribution to the collective well-being of the culture.

There are individuals for whom the familial or avocational life roles are the
defining ones. In these cases, one's work identity becomes a complement to the
primary role as parent, spouse, child, sports enthusiast, and so forth. Unfortunately,
there is evidence that work may be a very meaningless human activity for large
segments of adults in the United States (Kasl, 1978). The work role becomes less
salient in the maintenance of self-concept and self-identity as workers engage in
processes of impoverishment, psychological withdrawal, and surrender to unsatisfactory jobs.

Scott (1967) argued that the dichotomization, or split, in a person's work and
family or home identities dates back to the Industrial Revolution. It was then that
it became necessary for a person to leave the home to "go to work," effectively
bifurcating the individual's experience and identity. In examining the allocation of
investment in work and family roles, Lobel (1991) proposed that social identity
theory provides a different set of predications than when one uses a utilitarian
approach. She offered social identity theory as a basis for approaching integration
and work–family balance, or the stress-free management of work and family roles.

Work and family investments need not necessarily be at odds with each other
(Lobel, 1991). According to Kanter (1977), knowledge of how tension and illness-
producing features of one system, either work situations or family systems, affect
a member's successful adjustment to the other system is critical if clinicians and
researchers are to extend their understanding of the barriers to well-being and their
ability to intervene to produce greater levels of health. It seems clear that most
workers do not leave the pressures of the job behind after leaving work. Indeed,
there is increasing evidence of a "spillover" effect of work-related stress to the home
environment (Bacharach, Bamberger, & Conley, 1991; Burke 1986), resulting in
distress for family members. Kanter (1977) suggested that the effects of the work
system on the family system vary considerably. Depending on the nature of the
family system, various work situations affect family systems in different ways.
Preventive interventions can have immense benefits for the psychological well-being
of family members.

Although the focus of this book is on work, the second central theme of love in
theories of psychological well-being should not be forgotten. Work alone is not
enough for the individual or the society. Love may be viewed as one of the coun-
terbalances to productive, effortful activity. Just as the child who is engaged in
exploration of the world must have a secure attachment figure to which to retreat
in threatening circumstances, the adult who is engaged in productive work must
have a network of secure relationships through which renewal may occur by the
gratification of deeper psychological and emotional needs. Although the purpose of
this book is not to consider the theme of love, we consider it important to recognize
the theme here as a counterpoint to the theme of work, for both are intertwined in
the psychological well-being of the individual.

Although work and love are essential to full psychological functioning and well-
being, each carries with it risks, complications, and dilemmas. Neither carries with

it the *guarantee* of happiness or salvation. In the case of work, the 1990s and 21st century will be stressful and risky because of daily workplace demands coupled with international competitive challenges and corporate-restructuring activities. Although we do not examine the risks associated with love, we do address the risks of distress associated with work.

Distress: The Risk of Work

Beginning during the Industrial Revolution in Germany, Prince Otto Edward Leopold von Bismarck, first chancellor of the German Empire (1871–1890), believed that workers should have some form of medical care and wage supplement to assist them during periods following an on-the-job injury (Adams, 1987). This policy explicitly recognized the accidental injury risks associated with industrial work as well as the company's need to accept some responsibility for the worker subject to accidental injury. In the case of physical injury, such as the loss of limbs, the evidence of damage is both graphic and visible. Thus, the tradition of attention to physical occupational health risks, in the form of toxins, falling objects, and dangerous machinery, has been well established. Although these risks are the most visible and the most measurable of the health risks in any work environment, they are not the only ones.

Levi (1981), in his examination of work stress, gave attention to the psychosocial as well as physical demands of the work environment that trigger the stress response. He devoted particular attention to the various aspects of modern technology and automation that create high-risk situations in the work environment. In addition, he discussed populations within the workplace, such as young and older individuals, women, and physically challenged people, who may be at physical or psychological high-risk of specific disorders because of peculiar vulnerabilities.

Although Levi (1972) was among the first authorities to draw attention to the risks of psychosocial demands in the workplace, he was not alone. Levinson (1969) drew attention to the emotional toxicity of the work environment. In addition, two forces played critical roles in the growing recognition of the psychosocial risks of work. The first force followed the discovery of the stress response by Walter B. Cannon circa 1915 (Benison, Barger, & Wolfe, 1987). This discovery gave rise to a long stream of medical, psychological, and behavioral stress research throughout the rest of the century that drew attention to the role stress may play in people's health as well as in their diseases. Levi (1981), Selye (1976), and J. C. Quick and Quick (1984) have all drawn a clear distinction between stress and distress; it is the latter that is a health problem.

The second force was the shift in health-care risks during the 20th century from acute and infectious diseases to the chronic and debilitating diseases (Foss & Rothenberg, 1987). This is important because stress and psychosocial factors play a far more central role in the chronic disorders than they do in the acute diseases (Pelletier, 1977). As a consequence, both employees and employers have become increasingly aware of the deleterious effects of work-related stress. A recent nationwide survey by the Northwestern National Life Insurance Company (1991), for example, showed that nearly 46% of American workers felt that their jobs were very or somewhat stressful, whereas nearly 27% reported that their jobs were the single greatest source of stress in their lives. Nearly 72% of those surveyed experienced frequent stress-related physical and mental conditions. Perhaps more alarming, this same study found that the proportion of stress-related disabilities had doubled over the past 9 years from 6% to 13%. Although a wide range of health-care providers have focused increasing attention on the psychosocial dimensions of disease, organizational psychologists have focused greater attention on psychosocial risk factors in the work environment (see Ilgen, 1990).

In a chapter on work design, Landy (1992) drew attention to four categories of psychosocial demands in the workplace that may pose health risks for workers. These demands were (a) the lack of control over the work and the workplace; (b) the presence of uncertainty, either with regard to employment or the workplace; (c) the existence of dysfunctional conflict in the workplace (Landy clearly stated that not all conflict is dysfunctional); and (d) the more general set of task and work demands.

Although Landy (1992) did not prioritize the risk factors, the issue of job control has received the most attention and research examination over the past two decades. Sauter, Hurrell, and Cooper (1989) attempted to draw coherence to the domain of job control and worker health through a series of theoretical, review, and empirical chapters. Originally linked to exhaustion, depression, sick days, pill (tranquilizers and sleeping pills) consumption, and dissatisfaction both at work and home, lack of job control has more recently been linked to higher incidence of cardiovascular illness (Karasek & Theorell, 1990). Although the Zeitgeist concerning job control and worker health has swept occupational health communities in both Sweden and the United States, important operational and measurement issues still linger. Therefore, Sauter et al. (1989) presented a critical review and reappraisal that addressed three basic questions: (a) On the basis of current research evidence, how important is job control to worker health? (b) What is the theoretical basis for understanding job control and the mechanisms whereby it affects worker health? (c) What are the implications of current research and theory for modern work practices?

Turning to *uncertainty*, Jackson (1989) defined it from an organizational perspective as inadequate knowledge about an event that requires action or resolution. An appropriate illustration would be the uncertainty associated with engineering test results in the defense industry. In a study of the U.S. Navy's major weapon systems project managers, Bodensteiner, Gerloff, and Quick (1989) found inferential evidence that perceived environmental uncertainty led to increased levels of psychological distress for the project managers. They also found that psychological distress was linked to physiological distress and to burnout. Hence, uncertainty may have adverse impacts at the psychological, emotional, and physiological levels within the person.

Although the relation between lack of job control or environmental uncertainty with work distress appears to be relatively linear in nature, the relation between conflict and work distress is somewhat more complex. In their classic study of organizational stress, Kahn, Wolfe, Quinn, Snoek, and Rosenthal (1964) found a range of dysfunctional consequences of role conflict and ambiguity. These included increased distrust in working relationships, disruptions of communication relationships, and increased distance in interpersonal relationships. This line of research examined the adverse impact of conflict in the work environment. More recent work by Tjosvold (1991) suggested that there are positive dimensions to conflict within an organization. Specifically, he showed how well-managed conflict actually contributes to problem solving, strengthened morale, performance improvement, and increased competitive advantage. The implication of this line of work and reasoning is that certain types, categories, or varieties of conflict may need to be stimulated in the workplace if they are not already present. Hence, the relation between conflict and distress in the workplace does not appear to be as straightforward as does the relation between either lack of control or uncertainty and distress.

Another mental health risk that emerged in the 1980s had its basis not so much in objective working conditions as in worker perceptions of those objective conditions: HIV (human immunodeficiency virus) and AIDS (acquired immunodeficiency syndrome). All available evidence indicates that although occupational exposure to HIV and AIDS (via blood and other bodily fluids) does occur in certain occupations (e.g., surgeons, phlebotomists, nurses, dentists), the risk of occupational HIV transmission is very low (approximately 0.3%). Despite this low risk, and the wide dissemination of educational materials by the Centers for Disease Control (1987, 1988), fear among workers of contracting the HIV at work remains high. For example, 56% of emergency medical service professionals believed their risk of occupational HIV infection to be "somewhat" to "very high" (Smyser, Bryce, & Joseph, 1990). Also, although 80% of residency-program house officers stated their actual chances of acquiring the HIV based on patient contact (i.e., 1 in 10,000 or less), 48% expressed "moderate" or "high" personal concern about acquiring AIDS from patients (Link, Geingold, Charap, Freeman, & Shelov, 1988). These perceptions and concerns regarding uncertainty may affect workers' psychological well-being.

People should expect work to be challenging and difficult because it requires productive as well as effortful activity. Therefore, one should expect work to be demanding and stressful by definition. The challenging, difficult, and demanding aspects of work elicit better performance from people while enhancing their self-esteem and enriching their self-identity (Locke, 1976; Locke & Latham, 1990). What one should *not* expect is for work to be *di*stressful. Although stress is one of the natural, inevitable characteristics of life in general and worklife in particular, *di*stress is neither a natural nor inevitable consequence of life or work. Given this premise, the question becomes one of how to experience or create the natural stress that leads to achievement while avoiding the psychological, emotional, and physiological distress that all too often occurs in work environments.

The Power of Prevention: Enhancing Occupational Mental Health

Life expectancies in the United States have advanced over 50% during this century, from a life expectancy at birth of just under 50 years in 1900 to just over 75 years in 1990 (Department of Health and Human Services, 1985; United Nations, 1986). That is a 25-year increase in life expectancy in just 90 years. On the basis of such an advance in life expectancy, the acid test of success in managing stress, it is erroneous to say "STRESS: The Test Americans are Failing," as did *Business Week* (Staff, 1988).

The basis for this dramatic increase in life expectancy is found in the prevention practices within public health, first advocated by visionaries such as President Eliot of Harvard University (Benison et al., 1987). It was he who put pressure on the Harvard Medical School to develop a "preventive" orientation in their medical education just after the turn of the century. Others followed in his footsteps throughout the century.

From this beginning, three waves of prevention practices have swept North America during the 20th century, with the first of these being the public sanitation and personal hygiene programs of the very early part of the century. These prevention initiatives led the battle against the infectious and acute diseases (J. C. Quick, 1989).

The second wave was the emergence of a wide range of vaccines and "miracle" drugs that targeted the infectious and acute diseases. Rather than minimizing the health risks, as occurred through public sanitation, the second wave of prevention practices strengthened the host's defenses against disease and supplemented the natural healing powers of the mind–body system. It is within this prevention initiative that alleopathic medicine has made its most powerful and therapeutic contribution to the health of the nation.

The third wave of prevention practices encompassed a wide range of life-style redesign initiatives, such as exercise, relaxation, cognitive–behavioral interventions, and self-regulatory activities (e.g., biofeedback). The hallmark of this third wave has been behavioral change and individual responsibility for one's own well-being. The effects of these three complementary waves of prevention practices are history and a testament to the power of the public health notions of prevention.

Prevention rests on a three-tiered approach of primary prevention, secondary prevention, and tertiary prevention. According to Last (1988), epidemiology and preventive medicine authorities do not agree on the precise boundaries between these three levels of prevention, nor were the notions originally developed in the domain of stress. J. C. Quick and Quick (1984) originally presented the transference of a prevention framework into a work stress context, later presenting a comparison of the preventive medicine context with the organizational stress context (J. D. Quick, Quick, & Horn, 1986, p. 21). It is this basic preventive stress-management framework that we have used to frame the present work. Figure 1 presents our framework of prevention for enhancing occupational mental health, psychological well-being, and stress management. The three key elements in the framework are (a) occupational mental health risks, (b) individual stress responses and early warning signs, and (c) organizational and individual distress. In addition, the figure includes the three levels of preventive intervention for enhancing occupational mental health and averting psychological distress.

First, occupational mental health risks are work demands and stressors that place the person at risk psychologically. Lack of control, uncertainty, and conflict, discussed in the last section, fall in this risk category. Individuals subject to these occupational mental health risks do not necessarily develop occupational mental health disorders but are vulnerable to them based on the risk exposure. Second, there will be individuals who develop early warning signs of distress. These will

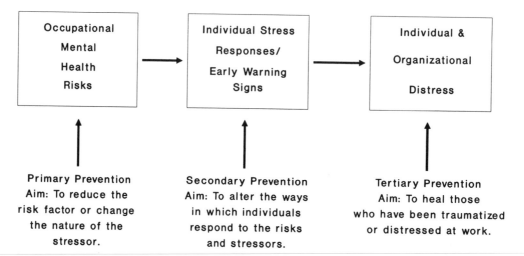

Figure 1. A model for occupational well-being, mental health promotion, and distress prevention.

result from the exposure to the occupational mental health risks, personal vulnerabilities and personality predispositions, or both. For example, rapid talking and spells of quiet sullenness may be early warning signs of psychological distress exhibited by combat soldiers. Third, early stages of psychological distress may turn into full-blown traumatic crises for specific individuals or groups. The individual and the organization both pay a price for advanced stages of distress. For example, individuals exposed to traumatic disasters, such as airline crashes, may exhibit posttraumatic stress symptoms at some point following the disaster.

Preventive intervention is, in fact, an integrated set of three levels of action. Primary prevention is the preferred point of action. Elimination or amelioration of the occupational mental health risk minimizes the need for using either secondary or tertiary prevention, although both must be available. The basic notion in primary prevention is embodied in the following ancient proverb: "An ounce of prevention is worth a pound of cure." It must be noted that primary prevention efforts at work, in the form of job or task redesign or modifications of organizational structure or function, can themselves create stress in workers. This can occur for two reasons: (a) change of any kind, even positive change, produces new demands that require adaptation on the part of the worker (Selye, 1956); and (b) changes made at one level in the organization often have unintended and negative consequences at other levels (Alderfer, 1976). The point is that, in organizational settings, secondary prevention plays a role in easing the adjunctive stress effects of primary prevention efforts (Murphy, 1984). Likewise, regardless of how aggressively primary prevention is pursued, there are individuals who will exhibit some early warning signs of distress as well as unique stress responses.

Tertiary prevention or treatment is for individuals in distress. Even in circumstances in which the adverse effects of occupational mental health risks are minimized and individuals' awareness levels as well as strengths are enhanced, unanticipated crises occur or peculiar individual vulnerabilities are exploited by environmental events. Hence, mental health practitioners and stress experts must be prepared to heal those in distress through a range of treatment and therapeutic interventions. It is important to keep in mind that tertiary prevention is always the last resort in the sequence of preventive actions. We are not aware of any disease epidemic in human history that has been stopped through treatment. Treatment is always a last resort for advancing public health, whether that be medically or psychologically.

In practice, tertiary prevention programs in the workplace are far more common than primary prevention programs, with secondary prevention programs intermediate in frequency (Murphy, 1988). Tertiary prevention programs, usually in the form of an employee assistance program (EAP), traditionally have offered counseling for alcohol-related and personal problems, but in the 1980s they became broader and expanded their programs to include stress-management programs. However, these EAP-based stress-management programs typically do not seek to identify organization-centered problems, in part because EAP counselors lack training in organizational behavior and occupational stress. Rather, EAP-based programs offer counseling techniques used in community programs that emphasize personal or individual solutions to stress reduction.

The Present Book

We have organized the chapters in this book into three major sections that parallel the three prevention levels in Figure 1. Within each of the major sections, there are chapters that address assessment and chapters that address intervention. The assessment chapters are primarily concerned with the diagnostic assessment or measurement of occupational mental health risks; early warning signs and individual stress responses; and indicators of individual and organizational distress, respectively.

The intervention chapters concern individual or organizational programs of preventive change that will modify or eliminate the mental health risks; modify or enhance the individual's responses to inevitable risks; and heal individual and organizational distress. The organization of the book and chapters are broad; the details of the chapters can be found in a brief page section introduction for each of the three major sections.

In the concluding section of this book there are two chapters. In chapter 22, we discuss directions for future research. Although much is already known, researchers need to continue to advance the frontiers of knowledge through a wide variety of natural scientific and idiographic research programs. Chapter 23 provides an international perspective on the issues. Cooper and Payne compare societal and cultural differences between North America and the European Community that may account for different theoretical paradigms, research questions, and modes of inquiry.

Although these are the dominant themes that are developed in this book, there are some additional themes that are also covered. For example, the issues of women and workplace stress, which have received recent attention, are intertwined in the context of two chapters. In addition, there are population groups, as Levi (1981) pointed out, that are at higher risk than others. Police forces and health-care professionals are among such high-risk populations. Several chapters report empirical data concerning these high-risk populations.

References

Adams, G. T., Jr. (1987). Preventive law trends and compensation payments for stress-disabled workers. In J. C. Quick, R. S. Bhagat, J. E. Dalton, & J. D. Quick (Eds.), *Work stress: Health care systems in the workplace* (pp. 235–245). New York: Praeger.

Alderfer, C. P. (1976). Change processes in organizations. In M. Dunnette (Ed.), *Handbook of industrial and organizational psychology* (pp. 1591–1638). Chicago: Rand McNally.

Bacharach, S. B., Bamberger, P. B., & Conley, S. (1991). Work-home conflict among nurses and engineers: Mediating the impact of role stress on burnout and satisfaction at work. *Journal of Organizational Behavior, 12,* 39–53.

Benison, S., Barger, A. C., & Wolfe, E. L. (1987). *Walter B. Cannon: The life and times of a young scientist.* Cambridge, MA: Harvard University Press.

Bodensteiner, W. D., Gerloff, E. A., & Quick, J. C. (1989). Uncertainty and stress in an R & D project environment. *R & D Management, 19,* 309–323.

Burke, R. J. (1986). Occupational and life stress and family: Conceptual frameworks and research findings. *International Review of Applied Psychology, 35,* 347–369.

Centers for Disease Control. (1987). Recommendations for prevention of HIV transmission in health-care settings. *Morbidity and Mortality Weekly Report, 36* (Suppl. 2S).

Centers for Disease Control. (1988). Update: Universal precautions for the prevention of human immunodeficiency virus, hepatitis B virus, and other bloodborne pathogens in health-care settings. *Morbidity and Mortality Weekly Report, 37,* 377–382, 387–388.

Department of Health and Human Services. (1985). *Vital statistics of the United States, 1985, life tables* (Vol. 2, Section 6, DHHS Publication No. PHS 88-1104). Washington, DC: U.S. Government Printing Office.

Erikson, E. H. (1963). *Childhood and society* (2nd ed.). New York: Norton.

Foss, L., & Rothenberg, K. (1987). *The second medical revolution: From biomedical to infomedical.* Boston: New Science Library.

Freud, S. (1930). *Civilization and its discontents.* London: Hogarth Press.

Hazan, C., & Shaver, P. R. (1990). Love and work: An attachment-theoretical perspective. *Journal of Personality and Social Psychology, 59,* 270–280.

Ilgen, D. R. (1990). Health issues at work: Opportunities for industrial/organizational psychology. *American Psychologist, 45,* 273–283.

Jackson, S. E. (1989). Does job control job stress? In S. L. Sauter, J. J. Hurrell, Jr., & C. L. Cooper (Eds.), *Job control and worker health* (pp. 25–53). New York: Wiley.

Jones, E. (1963). *The life and work of Sigmund Freud.* Garden City, NY: Anchor Books.

Kahn, R. L., Wolfe, D. M., Quinn, R. P., Snoek, J. D., & Rosenthal, R. A. (1964). *Organizational stress: Studies in role conflict and ambiguity.* New York: Wiley.

Kanter, R. M. (1977). *Work and family in the United States: A critical review and agenda for research and policy.* New York: Russell Sage Foundation.

Karasek, R., & Theorell, T. (1990). *Healthy work: Stress, productivity, and the reconstruction of working life.* New York: Basic Books.

Kasl, S. V. (1978). Epidemiological contributions to the study of work stress. In C. L. Cooper & R. Payne (Eds.), *Stress at work* (pp. 3–48). New York: Wiley.

Landy, F. J. (1992). Work design and stress. In G. P. Keita & S. L. Sauter (Eds.), *Work and well-being: An agenda for the 1990s* (pp. 119–158). Washington, DC: American Psychological Association.

Last, J. M. (1988). *Dictionary of epidemiology* (2nd ed.). New York: Oxford University Press.

Levi, L. (1972). Stress and distress in response to psychosocial stimuli. *Acta Medica Scandinavia, 191* (Suppl. 528).

Levi, L. (1981). *Preventing work stress.* Reading, MA: Addison-Wesley.

Levinson, H. (1969). Emotional toxicity of the work environment. *Archives of Environmental Health, 19,* 239–243.

THE VALUE OF WORK 13

Link, R. N., Geingold, A. R., Charap, M. H., Freeman, K., & Shelov, D. D. (1988). Concerns of medical and pediatric house officers about acquiring AIDS from their patients. *American Journal of Public Health, 78*, 455–459.

Lobel, S. A. (1991). Allocation of investment in work and family roles: Alternative theories and implications for research. *Academy of Management Review, 16*, 507–521.

Locke, E. A. (1976). The nature and causes of job satisfaction. In M. D. Dunnette (Ed.), *Handbook of industrial and organizational psychology* (pp. 1297–1349). Chicago: Rand McNally.

Locke, E. A., & Latham, G. P. (1990). *A theory of goal setting & task performance.* Englewood Cliffs, NJ: Prentice-Hall.

Maslow, A. (1954). *Motivation and personality.* New York: Harper & Row.

Murphy, L. R. (1984). Occupational stress management: A review and appraisal. *Journal of Occupational Psychology, 57*, 1–15.

Murphy, L. R. (1988). Workplace interventions for stress reduction and prevention. In C. L. Cooper & R. Payne (Eds.), *Causes, coping, and consequences of stress at work* (pp. 301–339). New York: Wiley.

National Institute for Occupational Safety and Health. (1988). *Proposed national strategies for the prevention of leading work-related diseases and injuries—Psychological disorders* (DHHS [NIOSH] Publication No. 89-13). Washington, DC: U.S. Department of Health and Human Services.

Northwestern National Life Insurance Company. (1991). *Employee burnout: America's newest epidemic.* Minneapolis, MN: Author.

Pelletier, K. (1977). *Mind as healer, mind as slayer: A holistic approach to preventing stress disorders.* New York: Delcorte.

Quick, J. C. (1989). An ounce of prevention. *Stress Medicine, 5*, 207–210.

Quick, J. C., & Quick, J. C. (1984). *Organizational stress and preventive management.* New York: McGraw-Hill.

Quick, J. C., & Quick, J. D. (1990). The changing times of life: Career in context. In J. D. Quick, R. E. Hess, J. Hermalin, & J. D. Quick (Eds.), *Career stress in changing times* (pp. 1–24). Binghamton, NY: Haworth Press.

Quick, J. D., Quick, J. C., & Horn, R. S. (1986). Health consequences of stress. *Journal of Organizational Behavior Management, 8*, 19–36.

Sauter, S. L., Hurrell, J. J., Jr., & Cooper, C. L. (1989). *Job control and worker health.* New York: Wiley.

Scott, M. (1967). The bifurcation of work and family life. Seminar on the church and the world of work. Chicago: Presbyterian Institute of Labor and Industrial Relations at McCormick Seminary.

Selye, H. (1956). *The stress of life.* New York: McGraw-Hill.

Selye, H. (1976). *Stress in health and disease.* Boston: Butterworths.

Smyser, M. S., Bryce, J., & Joseph, J. G. (1990). AIDS-related knowledge, attitudes, and precautionary behaviors among emergency medical professionals. *Public Health Reports, 105*, 496–504.

Staff. (1988, April 18). Stress: The test Americans are failing. *Business Week*, pp. 74–76.

Tjosvold, D. (1991). *The conflict-positive organization: Stimulate diversity and create unity.* Reading, MA: Addison-Wesley.

United Nations. (1986). *Demographic yearbook* (Vol. 164, pp. 162). New York: Author.

Vaillant, G. E. (1977). *Adaptation to life.* Boston: Little, Brown.

Part II

Occupational Mental Health Risks

Introduction

We noted in Chapter 1 that the distinctions between the stages of prevention, and even between the processes of assessment and intervention, are not always clear (Last, 1988). Unraveling occupational mental health risks from individual responses, either psychologically or behaviorally, to the risks may be no easier in some cases than distinguishing between early warning signs of possible distress from full-blown distress. At what point is the line drawn? Thus, the model we proposed in Figure 1 (Chapter 1) to frame the present work has the same limitation as any model. Specifically, it is a simplification of the reality it attempts to represent. In a similar way, it may not always be easy to distinguish assessment from intervention. When do we stop measuring or examining a person or organization in terms of his or her experience of stress and begin to intervene or change the person or organization in an effort to enhance health and well-being?

It seems to us that the emphasis in the six chapters in part 2 is largely on the stressors and occupational mental health risks, as opposed to indicators of distress and strain. However, the chapters do include data on and address issues related to strain. It is simply not possible to pull the stressor or health risk entirely apart from the response to it, as Lazarus, DeLongis, Folkman, and Gruen (1985) pointed out. Therefore, the effort is made to focus attention at one point or another in an interrelated process.

Assessment Chapters

The three assessment chapters in this section examine the impact of various risk factors and stressors, from job design variables in chapter 2 to job insecurity in chapter 4, on a range of strain and distress indicators. These relations contribute to the establishment of such stressors as risk factors. Chapter 2, by Carayon, reports a 3-year study of 122 office workers from a public service organization. She examines the relations between nine job design variables and eight worker strain variables. Her cross-lagged analyses suggest that job design variables contribute to worker strain. Particular attention is drawn to job control as well as task clarity, supervisory support, and future job ambiguity. Boredom, distress, tension/anxiety, anger, and distress are adversely affected by the design of a worker's job.

Chapter 3, by Greller, Parsons, and Mitchell, reports a study of 72 officers in a large metropolitan police organization. They found organizational stressors to have a main, adverse impact on police officer strain. Although they suggest that positive family and co-worker relationships may compensate for job stress, they found no indication that these supportive relationships had a buffering effect in the job stress–strain relation.

Chapter 4, by Kuhnert and Vance, reports a study of 262 White blue-collar employees in a large U.S. manufacturing organization. They examined the relation between job insecurity and six psychological indicators of adjustment. Occupational mobility and work orientation were found to moderate the job insecurity–employee health relation. In addition, job type differences helped explain some of the discrepant research findings.

Intervention Chapters

The three intervention chapters in this section either report the impact of a specific intervention (chapter 4), propose strategies for modifying specific occupational mental health risks (chapter 5), or present a standard for the way work should be designed to avert distressful outcomes (chapter 7).

Chapter 5, by Corey and Wolf, reports the implementation of a network of strategies in five public-sector organizations. The strategies are designed to change the organization's approach to hiring, orientating, training, and managing employees, as well as the early response to mental or physical work-related injuries. Mental stress claims declined in these five organizations from 7.8 claims per 1,000 public-service workers (preintervention) to 1.2 claims per 1,000 (postintervention). This compares with 1.7 claims per 1,000 public-service workers statewide.

Chapter 6, by MacLennan, reports an examination of work stressors in the banking industry, the federal government, and the transportation industry. She categorizes the stressors and recommends solutions in environmental, managerial, and interpersonal categories. Differences in stressors, strains, and recommended solutions were found across industries.

Chapter 7, by Luczak, reports an ergonomic, industrial engineering perspective on the design of work. Taking a "mentofacturing" framework, he examines characteristics of "good" work that meet engineering expectations for effective, efficient use of technology and automation while not violating human nature. His is primarily an ecological approach in which the emphasis is redesigning the work in a suitable way to fit the worker.

The reader should keep in mind that the focus of primary prevention is always on the risk factor or stressor: How can it be changed, altered, eliminated, or in other ways rendered innocuous? The first step in primary prevention is always to isolate the risk factor and then to devise strategies or approaches to eliminate or manage it. Each of these six chapters in one way or another contributes to the isolation of an occupational mental health risk, proposes strategies for eliminating or managing the risks, or reports of the effectiveness of a particular primary prevention strategy. If there is one conclusion to draw at this point it is that significantly more work is needed in the realm of primary prevention, both in the isolation of occupational mental health risks and in the evaluation of prevention strategies for addressing these risks once they are identified.

References

Last, J. M. (1988). *Dictionary of epidemiology*. New York: Oxford University Press.
Lazarus, R. S., DeLongis, A., Folkman, S., & Gruen, R. (1985). Stress and adaptational outcomes: The problem of confounded measures. *American Psychologist, 40*, 770–779.

2

Pascale Carayon

A Longitudinal Study of Job Design and Worker Strain: Preliminary Results

The purpose of this study is to examine the relations between job design and worker strain over time. Many cross-sectional studies of these relations have been conducted (Cooper & Marshall, 1976; Smith, 1987). However, very few studies have examined such relations in a longitudinal manner (Kasl, 1987), and the need for longitudinal studies has been emphasized by many (Eaker, 1988; Kasl, 1978, 1987). Although there are a few epidemiological studies of the long-term effects of job design on worker health (e.g., Haynes & Feinleib, 1980; House, Stretcher, Metzner, & Robbins, 1986; Karasek, 1979), very few longitudinal organizational- or occupational-level studies of the work environment and worker strain have been conducted. However, the job-design measures used in those epidemiological studies have usually been very limited (except for studies by Karasek). Therefore, our knowledge of the relations between job design and worker strain is incomplete. Job-design factors are occupational mental health risks that can influence individual distress or worker strain. This study will examine whether the relations between occupational mental health risks and individual distress are stable over time.

Miles (1975) studied the causal inference between (a) role conflict and role ambiguity (b) and job-related tension and job satisfaction. Data were collected at two points in time, over a 4-month period, from 202 professionals of nine organizations. The correlations of role conflict and role ambiguity with the outcomes were stable over time. Cross-lagged correlations suggested that role ambiguity could be a causal factor for job satisfaction. Causal direction could not be inferred for role conflict or for job-related tension.

Rose, Jenkins, and Hurst (1978) studied a group of air-traffic controllers for a period of 3 years, taking measurements every 9 months. This study examined the nature and extent of health changes in the air-traffic controllers and the factors that could predict these health changes. The measures of satisfaction and one measure of workload (paceload) were stable over time. The 9-month test–retest reliability coefficients were between .67 and .69 for satisfaction and between .49 and .50 for workload. The 18-month reliability coefficients were between .51 and .63 for satisfaction and was .49 for workload. The 9-month stability was relatively high for the mood states (McNair, Lorr, & Droppleman, 1971), ranging from .38 for fatigue to .57 for vigor. Relations between workload and a range of outcomes were examined at each of the three rounds. The correlations between workload and the outcomes were very similar across the three rounds. The scores for workload were averaged over the 18-month study period and were then correlated to the outcomes. No cross-lagged correlation analysis was conducted to examine the effects of workload on the outcomes over time.

Chadwick, Chesney, Black, Rosenman, and Sevelius (1979) studied a group of managers for 1 year, taking measurements every 4 months. Measures of the work environment (e.g., job control and workload) were taken at the baseline examination. Psychological and physiological measures of stress were taken at the baseline examination and at each repeat examination. The average of the stress measures taken over the entire study period was correlated to the baseline measures of the work environment. Social support and job control were negatively related to physiological measures of stress. Work pressure was related to psychological and physiological measures of stress.

Haynes and Feinleib (1980) examined the effects of psychosocial factors on the development of coronary heart disease (CHD) in a sample of men and women 8 years after their involvement in the Framingham Heart Study. Clerical working women had a much higher CHD rate than did housewives and nonclerical working women. The most significant predictors of CHD among clerical working women were suppressed hostility, having a nonsupportive boss, and decreased job mobility. Frese (1985) used data from a longitudinal study of 90 blue-collar workers to examine the causal relation between psychological work-related stressors on psychosomatic complaints. The correlations between psychological stressors and psychosomatic complaints for the two rounds of data were similar. Results from the cross-lagged panel correlation design suggested that stressors contributed to psychosomatic complaints, and not the reverse.

Several studies have examined the effect of select job-design factors on blood-pressure change (Aro, 1984; Howard, Cunningham, & Rechnitzer, 1986; Jenner, Puddey, Beilin, & Vandongen, 1988; Kawakami, Haratani, Kaneko, & Araki, 1989; Theorell, Knox, Svensson, & Waller, 1985; Theorell et al., 1988). Howard et al. (1986) studied 217 managers over a period of 2 years. Measures of role ambiguity and job satisfaction along with physiological measures such as blood pressure were taken at the beginning and end of a 3-year period. The change in blood pressure was related to the change in role ambiguity: This relation was positive for Type A individuals, whereas it was negative for Type B individuals. Theorell et al. (1985) found that subjects classified as hypertensives with "strain" occupations had more marked elevations of systolic blood pressure after a ten-year period than other subjects. Theorell et al. (1988) studied a sample of 73 men and women working in six different occupations for a period of 1 year. The spontaneous variations in job strain (determined as the self-reported ratio between demands and job-decision latitude) were related to changes in systolic blood pressure during working hours but not to changes in diastolic blood pressure or in systolic blood pressure during leisure time.

Studies that have examined the impact of job design on job satisfaction in a longitudinal manner can provide some understanding of the relations between job design and worker strain if job satisfaction is assumed to be related to worker strain (Caplan, Cobb, French, Harrison, & Pinneau, 1975). Szilagyi (1977) examined the causal relations of role ambiguity and role conflict with satisfaction with work and performance. Two-hundred and twenty-five employees from a hospital participated in a 6-month study. The results suggested that role ambiguity was a source of causal inference for satisfaction with work for administrative employees and professionals, whereas role conflict was a source of causal inference for satisfaction with work for professionals and service employees. With regard to performance, only role ambiguity had a causal effect only for administrative employees. The relations of role ambiguity and conflict with work satisfaction and performance were stable over time. Greenberger, Strasser, Cummings, & Dunham (1989) conducted two separate longitudinal studies with two data-collection points to examine the link between job control and job satisfaction. The first study included 149 nursing-service employees, whereas the second study included 400 clerical workers. In both studies and in both rounds of data, increased job control was consistently related to increased job satisfaction.

The purpose of the current study is to examine the relations between job design and worker strain over time. I expected these relations to be stable; that is, the job design variables related to worker strain would be similar across two rounds of data. I will also examine the causality between job design and worker strain: I expected that job design was the cause of worker strain.

Method

Sample

A group of office workers from a midwestern public service organization participated in a 3-year longitudinal study of job design and worker strain. The response rate was 85% at Time 1 ($n = 177$), whereas it was 65% at Time 2 ($n = 136$). The response rate for the first round was high but dropped slightly in the second round. A subset of the sample ($n = 122$) participated in the two rounds of data collection. Comparisons on select demographic variables and on the job-design and worker-strain variables were performed between subjects who participated in both rounds and subjects who did not participate in one of the two rounds. There was a higher proportion of part-time or nonpermanent employees among subjects who participated in Round 1 but not in Round 2, as compared with subjects who participated in both rounds. Comparisons on the job-design variables showed that subjects who participated in both rounds reported less supervisor social support than did subjects who participated in only one of the two rounds. Comparisons on the worker-strain variables showed that subjects who participated in Round 1 but not in Round 2 reported less fatigue and boredom. Only 5 of the 43 comparisons performed between subjects who participated in both rounds and subjects who participated in only one of the two rounds were statistically significant. Thus, the differences between participants in both rounds of data and subjects who participated in one of the two rounds were minor. Reported here are only the demographics for the sample of subjects who participated in both rounds of data.

The majority (70%) was female. Forty-eight percent were married, 37% single, 12% separated or divorced, and 2% widowed. Only 10% were either part-time or nonpermanent employees. Employees had been working for this organization for

9.6 years on average (*SD* = 6.2 years) and in their current position for 6.0 years on average (*SD* = 5.4 years). The average age was 37.8 years (*SD* = 9.9 years), whereas the average number of years of schooling was 14.7 years (*SD* = 2.3 years). The sample included clerical workers such as data-entry operators and secretaries (63%), professionals such as accountants and systems programmers (27%), and a few supervisors and middle-level managers (10%).

Measures

Measures of job design and worker strain were obtained by means of a questionnaire that included questions from Caplan et al. (1975); Smith, Cohen, and Stammerjohn (1981); Sauter, Gottlieb, Rohrer, and Dodson (1983); and Piotrkowki, Coray, and Cohen (1987). The following variables were measures of job design: (a) quantitative workload, (b) attention, (c) work pressure, (d) utilization of skills, (e) task clarity, (f) job control, (g) social support from supervisor, (h) colleague support, and (i) job future ambiguity. The scales of quantitative workload and skill utilization were taken from Caplan et al. (1975). Twenty-eight items taken from Smith et al. (1981) and Piotrkowki et al. (1987) were factor analyzed using principal component analysis with Varimax rotation and yielded the other seven measures of the work environment (Carayon, in press; Sainfort, 1990). Cronbach alphas for the nine measures of job design varied between .67 and .89 at Round 1 and between .62 and .92 at Round 2.

The following indicators of worker strain were used: (a) boredom (Caplan et al., 1975), (b) workload dissatisfaction (Caplan et al., 1975), (c) tension/anxiety (McNair et al., 1971), (d) depression (McNair et al., 1971), (e) anger (McNair et al., 1971), (f) fatigue (McNair et al., 1971), (g) daily life stress (Reeder, Schrama, & Dirker, 1973), and (h) an index of health complaints (Piotrkowki et al., 1987). Similar to Piotrkowki et al., a measure of health complaints was constructed by summing up 12 items from the NIOSH health checklist (Smith). This measure included items such as back pain, pain or stiffness in neck/shoulders, burning eyes, and headaches. Piotrkowki et al. reported a coefficient alpha of .91 for the health complaints index. Cronbach alphas for the eight measures of worker strain varied between .84 and .92 at Round 1 and between .82 and .94 at Round 2.

The only variables that were not normally distributed were the four measures of mood states (tension/anxiety, depression, anger, and fatigue). The distributions were skewed to the left, that is, toward reporting low levels of strain. Square-root transformations of these variables were performed and yielded normal distributions. The square-roots of tension/anxiety, depression, anger, and fatigue were used in the correlation and regression analyses.

Procedures

One midwestern organization had agreed to participate in a longitudinal study of office automation. The target population of this study was all office workers such as clerical workers, professionals, supervisors, and middle-level managers but not top-level managers. The list of names of potential participants was provided by management. All potential participants were asked to participate in the study, and among them 85% participated in Round 1 and 65% in Round 2. Potential participants were told the purpose of the study and then were asked to participate. A questionnaire survey was part of the longitudinal study. The questionnaire asked a range of questions on working conditions, job characteristics, and worker health status, behaviors, and attitudes. Most of the questionnaires were handed out in person and collected by a researcher. Other data-collection methods included having a contact person who distributed and collected questionnaires (sealed in envelopes), and leaving the questionnaire in the participant's mailbox and having him or her return the questionnaire by mail in a sealed envelope. The questionnaire took about 90 min to complete and was administered into two 45-min segments that were given 1 week apart. Participants in Round 1 and potential new subjects were asked to participate in a second round of data collection 1 year later. In Round 2, subjects were given the same questionnaire to fill out as they were in Round 1.

Statistical design

Cross-sectional relations between job design and worker strain were examined using correlation and regression analyses. Longitudinal relations were examined using cross-lagged correlations. A cross-lagged panel correlation analysis was used to examine the causal direction between job design and the strain indicators (Markus, 1979; Pelz & Andrews, 1964). Frese (1985) has used a similar approach to examine the causal direction between a global measure of job stressors and psychosomatic complaints. Results suggested that the causal direction was from stressors to psychosomatic complaints and not the reverse. The procedure used to examine causal direction followed Frese (1985). A similar procedure has been used by Bateman and Strasser (1983) to examine the relations between various facets of job satisfaction and job-related tension in a sample of 129 nursing employees.

The influence of demographic variables on worker strain was examined using correlation and regression analyses. Only a few demographic variables were related to a few worker strain variables. The statistical analyses were performed with and without demographic variables, and similar results were found. I will present the results of the analyses without demographic variables for sake of simplicity.

Two rounds of data were analyzed. The third round of data is currently being analyzed, and results will be reported later.

Results

Relations Between Job Design and Worker Strain at Rounds 1 and 2

To test relations between job design and worker strain, correlation and regression analyses were conducted. The regression analyses were conducted to understand the concomitant effect of the job-design variables on various indicators of worker strain.

Pearson correlations were computed to examine the relations between job design and worker strain. Table 1 displays the Pearson correlations between job design and worker strain for both rounds of data. Results of Round 1 show that job control was related to six of eight measures of worker strain. Quantitative workload was related to four of eight measures of worker strain, and attention and work pressure were related to three measures of worker strain. Task clarity and colleague social support were related to two measures of worker strain, and skill utilization and job future ambiguity were related to only one measure of worker strain (i.e., boredom). Results of Round 2 show that supervisor social support and job future ambiguity were related to all of the worker strain measures, and task clarity was related to all of them except health complaints. Quantitative workload was related to four of eight measures of worker strain. Job control and attention were related to three of eight indicators of worker strain. Work pressure and skill utilization were related to only two measures of worker strain, and colleague social support was related to

Table 1. Pearson Correlations Between Job Design and Worker Strain

Variable	BOREDOM	WLDIS	TENANX	DEPR	ANGER	FATIG	DSTRESS	HEALTH
CQWL	−.34***	.48***	−.09	−.01	−.02	.01	.35***	.30**
	−.21***	.32***	.07	−.07	−.02	.08	.39***	.29**
ATTEN	−.40***	.11	−.14	.13	.01	−.09	.29**	.21*
	−.36***	.05	−.05	−.11	−.13	.01	.25**	.24**
PRESS	−.28**	.47***	−.12	.00	−.09	−.06	.34***	.18
	−.15	.46***	.09	.00	.03	.09	.36***	.16
SKILL	−.38***	−.08	−.08	−.02	−.05	.01	.12	.07
	−.44***	−.14	−.18*	−.16	−.13	−.12	.02	.17
CLARITY	−.19*	−.17	.03	.01	.04	−.01	−.21*	−.09
	−.33***	−.32***	−.32***	−.30***	−.27**	−.25**	−.28**	−.10
CONTROL	−.32***	−.26**	−.22*	−.27**	−.16	−.15	−.18*	−.20*
	−.27**	−.30***	−.11	−.04	.06	−.07	−.11	−.28**
SUPSS	−.22*	−.34***	.07	−.04	.05	−.12	−.32***	−.15
	−.30***	−.43***	−.22*	−.21*	−.24**	−.25**	−.31***	−.28**
COLLSS	.09	−.05	.00	−.04	.04	−.02	−.27**	−.19*
	.23*	−.11	−.15	−.07	−.07	−.11	−.16	−.14
FUTURE	.31***	.05	.09	.04	.02	.06	.15	.10
	.39***	.31***	.27**	.28**	.22*	.20*	.20*	.26**

Note. Round 1 correlations are given above Round 2 correlations. BOREDOM = boredom; WLDIS = workload dissatisfaction; TENANX = tension/anxiety; DEPR = depression; ANGER = anger; FATIG = fatigue; DSTRESS = daily life stress; HEALTH = physical health complaints. CQWL = quantitative workload; ATTEN = attention; PRESS = work pressure; SKILL = skill utilization; CLARITY = task clarity; CONTROL = job control; SUPSS = supervisor social support; COLLSS = colleague social support; FUTURE = future ambiguity.
*$p < .05$. **$p < .01$. ***$p < .001$.

only one. Twenty-eight of the 47 correlations (60%) that were nonsignificant at Round 1 were nonsignificant at Round 2. Nineteen of the 25 correlations (76%) that were significant at Round 1 were significant at Round 2. A total of 47 (28 + 19) out of 72 correlations (65%) were consistent over time.

Regression analyses with the worker strain measures as dependent variables and the job design measures as independent variables were performed to examine the concomitant effect of job-design factors on worker strain. At Round 1, the job-design factors explained a significant proportion of the variance of three of eight worker strain variables: boredom, workload dissatisfaction, and daily life stress. Table 2 shows the results of the regression analyses for Round 1. At Round 2, the job-design factors explained a significant proportion of the variance of six of eight indicators of worker strain: boredom, workload dissatisfaction, tension/anxiety,

Table 2. Regression Analyses of Worker Strain

	Round 1							
Variable	BOREDOM	WLDIS	TENANX	DEPR	ANGER	FATIG	DSTRESS	HEALTH
CQWL	−.05	.39***	.08	.09	.29	.27	.21	.31*
ATTEN	−.33***	−.18	−.18	.11	−.05	−.24*	.11	.10
PRESS	−.15	.20	−.03	−.13	−.20	−.29*	.05	−.13
SKILL	−.17	−.12	.00	−.04	−.05	.11	.03	.00
CLARITY	.06	−.06	.06	.17	.03	.19	−.04	.05
CONTROL	−.30**	−.22*	−.32**	−.27*	−.29*	−.21	−.06	−.06
SUPSS	−.21*	−.19*	.10	−.10	.08	−.19	−.18	−.02
COLLSS	−.01	.00	.03	.05	.01	.02	−.20*	−.21*
FUTURE	.09	−.17	.07	.04	.01	.13	.12	.13
Adjusted R^2	36%	33%	3%	3%	0%	6%	22%	7%
p	.000	.000	.228	.228	.411	.092	.000	.074
	Round 2							
CQWL	−.11	.10	−.08	−.30	−.11	.04	.22	.20
ATTEN	−.30**	−.33**	−.03	.03	−.10	−.01	.15	.08
PRESS	.06	.41***	.13	.13	.10	.00	.08	−.15
SKILL	−.14	.08	−.11	.04	.06	−.05	−.06	.25*
CLARITY	−.11	−.14	−.25*	−.26*	−.21	−.13	−.21*	.08
CONTROL	−.15	−.18	.00	.01	.07	.13	.18	−.12
SUPSS	−.11	−.19	−.09	−.19	−.22	−.20	−.15	−.19
COLLSS	−.09	−.03	−.06	.01	.05	−.07	−.07	−.05
FUTURE	.18	.10	.10	.04	.08	.11	.09	.24*
Adjusted R^2	31%	35%	10%	9%	6%	3%	19%	18%
p	.000	.000	.022	.040	.090	.218	.001	.001

Note. BOREDOM = boredom; WLDIS = workload dissatisfaction; TENANX = tension/axiety; DEPR = depression; ANGER = anger; FATIG = fatigue; DSTRESS = daily life stress; HEALTH = physical health complaints; CQWL = quantitative workload; ATTEN = attention; PRESS = work pressure; SKILL = skill utilization; CLARITY = task clarity; CONTROL = job control; SUPSS = supervisor social support; COLLSS = colleague social support; FUTURE = future ambiguity.
*p < .05.   **p < .01.   ***p < .001.

depression, daily life stress, and health complaints. Table 2 shows the results of the regression analyses for Round 2.

Relations Between Job Design and Worker Strain Over Time

Table 3 displays the correlations between any one variable at Round 1 with that same variable at Round 2. The correlations for the job-design factors were between .45 and .80, indicating that the job-design factors were very stable over time. Colleague social support and job future ambiguity were relatively less stable compared with other job-design factors. The over-time correlation for colleague social support was .45, whereas it was .54 for job future ambiguity. The correlations for worker strain showed that mood states (tension/anxiety, depression, anger, and fatigue) were not stable over time. The over-time correlations for these variables were between $-.26$ and $-.11$. The other worker-strain measures were very stable over time: boredom (.66), workload dissatisfaction (.66), daily life stress (.51), and health complaints (.76).

A cross-lagged panel correlation design similar to that used by Frese (1985)

Table 3. Cross-Lagged Correlations

Variable	Cross-lagged correlation
Job design	
CQWL	.69***
ATTEN	.71***
PRESS	.74***
SKILL	.65***
CLARITY	.69***
CONTROL	.76***
SUPSS	.80***
COLSS	.45***
FUTURE	.54***
Worker strain	
BOREDOM	.66***
WLDIS	.66***
TENANX	$-.21$*
DEPR	$-.11$
ANGER	$-.26$**
FATIG	$-.18$
DSTRESS	.51***
HEALTH	.76***

Note. CQWL = quantitative workload; ATTEN = attention; PRESS = work pressure; SKILL = skill utilization; CLARITY = task clarity; CONTROL = job control; SUPSS = supervisor social support; COLLSS = colleague social support; FUTURE = future ambiguity; BOREDOM = boredom; WLDIS = workload dissatisfaction; TENANX = tension/anxiety; DEPR = depression; ANGER = anger; FATIG = fatigue; DSTRESS = daily life stress; HEALTH = physical health complaints.
*$p < .05$.   **$p < .01$.   ***$p < .001$.

Table 4. Cross-Lagged Correlation Design

Variable pair	r(JD, WS) Round 1	r(JD, WS) Round 2	Stability JD	Stability WS	r(JD1, WS2)	r(JD2, WS1)	r(JD1, WS2) given WS1	r(JD2, WS1) given JD1
BOREDOM, CQWL	-.34***	-.21***	.69***	.66***	.13	-.36***	.14	-.15
BOREDOM, ATTEN	-.40***	-.36***	.71***	.66***	-.33***	-.39***	-.10	-.14
BOREDOM, SKILL	-.38***	-.44***	.65***	.66***	-.35***	-.46***	-.15	-.29**
BOREDOM, CLARITY	-.19*	-.33***	.69***	.66***	-.32***	-.15(.099)	-.27**	-.03
BOREDOM, CONTROL	-.32***	-.27**	.76***	.66**	-.29***	-.30***	-.11	-.08
BOREDOM, FUTURE	.31***	.39***	.54***	.66***	.40***	.23**	.28**	.09
WLDIS, CQWL	.48***	.32***	.69***	.66***	.36***	.28**	.07	-.07
WLDIS, PRESS	.47***	.46***	.74***	.66***	.43***	.36***	.18**	.01
WLDIS, CONTROL	-.26**	-.30***	.76***	.66***	.26**	-.27**	-.12	-.11
WLDIS, SUPSS	-.34***	-.43***	.80***	.66***	-.36***	-.29**	-.19**	-.02
DSTRESS, CQWL	.35***	.39***	.69***	.51***	.30***	.33***	.15	.15
DSTRESS, ATTEN	.29**	.25**	.71***	.51***	.17(.060)	.29***	.02	.14
DSTRESS, PRESS	.34***	.36***	.74***	.51***	.26**	.26***	.10	.00
DSTRESS, CLARITY	-.21*	-.28**	.69***	.51***	-.24**	-.19*	-.14	-.05
DSTRESS, SUPSS	-.32***	-.31***	.80***	.51***	-.31***	-.25**	-.17(.078)	.02
HEALTH, CQWL	.30**	.29**	.69***	.76***	.32***	.29**	.21*	.10
HEALTH, ATTEN	.29**	.25**	.71***	.76***	.18*	.18(.057)	.06	.06
HEALTH, CONTROL	-.20*	-.28**	.76***	.76***	-.18*	-.16(.090)	-.04	-.03

Note. JD = job strain; WS = worker strain; BOREDOM = boredom; WLDIS = workload dissatisfaction; DSTRESS = daily life stress; HEALTH = physical health complaints; CQWL = quantitative workload; ATTEN = attention; PRESS = work pressure; SKILL = skill utilization; CLARITY = task clarity; CONTROL = job control; SUPSS = supervisor social support; FUTURE = future ambiguity.

$*p < .05.$ $**p < .01.$ $***p < .001.$

was used to analyze the relations between job design and worker strain over time. In the cross-lagged panel correlation design, only those variables that were stable over time were examined. In addition, I examined only the relations between job design and worker strain that were consistent (and statistically significant) over time (i.e., assumption of stationarity; Rogosa, 1980). The cross-sectional relations between job design and worker strain had to be similar at the two time periods. A total of 18 relations were examined: 6 relations between boredom and job design, 4 relations between workload dissatisfaction and job design, 5 relations between daily life stress and job design, and 3 relations between health complaints and job design.

Table 4 shows the results of the cross-lagged panel correlation design. Columns 2 and 3 include the correlations between job design and worker strain at Rounds 1 and 2. Columns 4 and 5 include the stability scores for job design and worker strain. The zero-order cross-lagged correlations between job design at Round 1 and worker strain at Round 2 and between job design at Round 2 and worker strain at Round 1 are given in Columns 6 and 7, respectively. Columns 8 and 9 include the partial cross-lagged correlations between job design at Round 1 and worker strain at Round 2 given strain at Round 1 and between job design at Round 2 and strain at Round 1 given job design at Round 1. Because the stability scores can influence the cross-lagged correlations (Rogosa, 1980), partial cross-lagged correlations were computed by partialing out the effect of the stabilities.

Seven of the cross-lagged correlations between job design at Round 1 and strain at Round 2 were greater than the cross-lagged correlations between job design at Round 2 and strain at Round 1. The reverse was true for four relations. In the rest of the seven relations, the cross-lagged correlations were very close. The partial cross-lagged correlations between job design at Round 1 and strain at Round 2 were statistically significant in five relations (and one borderline, $p > .05$ and $p < .10$), whereas only one partial cross-lagged correlation between job design at Round 2 and strain at Round 1 was statistically significant (boredom/skill utilization).

Discussion

The cross-lagged correlation analyses show that the measures of job design were stable over time. The cross-lagged correlations were between .45 and .80. The lowest cross-lagged correlations were for colleague social support (.45) and job future ambiguity (.54). The 1-year time lag between the two data-collection rounds was long enough to show that the measures of job design are reliable and that job design does not vary much over time. Four of the eight measures of worker strain were stable over time: boredom (.66), workload dissatisfaction (.66), daily life stress (.51), and health complaints (.76). The other four measures were not stable over time: tension/anxiety $(-.21)$, depression $(-.11)$, anger $(-.26)$, and fatigue $(-.18)$. Because the time frame for these mood states was the "past week," it was expected that the stability of mood states would vary. However, in a study of air-traffic controllers, Rose et al. (1978) found that mood states were very stable across a period of 9 months.

Further studies are needed to determine what measures of worker strain can be used in longitudinal studies. If mood states fluctuate a lot over time, they may not be good measures to examine the long-term effects of job design on worker strain. However, fluctuations in worker strain could help identify workers who are under constant strain. House et al. (1986) used a similar strategy to study the "cumulative" effect of stressors on strain.

Overall, 65% of the correlations between job design and worker strain were consistent over time. However, results showed that the job-design factors that correlated with worker strain at Round 1 were different from those that did so at Round 2. In Round 1, the main job-design contributor to worker strain was job control; whereas in Round 2, the main contributors were task clarity, supervisor social support, and job future ambiguity. This is a surprising result given that past longitudinal studies have found consistent relations between job design and worker strain (Frese, 1985; Miles, 1975).

The lack of consistency over time may be due to the fact that some measures of worker strain are not stable over time. The four measures of mood states (tension/anxiety, depression, anger, and fatigue) were not stable over time. The cross-lagged correlations for these four measures were between − .26 and − .11. At Round 1, job control was related to two of these variables (tension/anxiety and depression). At Round 2, task clarity, supervisor social support, and job future ambiguity were all related to mood states. However, there was a similar, but weaker, trend for the other worker-strain measures. Job control was related to boredom, workload dissatisfaction, and health complaints at both rounds but with daily life stress only at Round 1. Task clarity was related to boredom and daily life stress at both rounds but to workload dissatisfaction only at Round 1 and not to health complaints at either round. However, the correlations between task clarity and each of boredom and daily life stress were higher at Round 2 than at Round 1. Job future ambiguity was related to boredom at both rounds but to workload dissatisfaction, daily life stress, and health complaints at Round 2 only. Thus, even with the stable measures of worker strain, there seems to be some inconsistencies regarding the job-design factors that are related to worker strain.

A different explanation for this lack of stressor−strain consistency could be that in November, 1988, the local election produced a change in the top management of the organization. The second round of data collection occurred in the fall of 1988, some occurring right before and some right after the local election. This election could have affected the results of this study. The job-design factors that contributed to worker strain at Round 2 could all have been related to such an occurrence as this event, which could have created an organizational climate in which uncertainty and lack of information became important factors. Task clarity, supervisor social support, and job future ambiguity have in common the idea of uncertainty and information flow. McGrath (1976) argued that "uncertainty of outcomes" is important in determining physiological and behavioral stress reactions. Experienced stress does not result from a misfit between the perceived demand the perceived ability to cope with it but rather from the uncertainty of meeting the demand. Jackson (1989) recently proposed an uncertainty framework for examining stress in organizational settings. Uncertainty at different levels seems to be a key factor for understanding worker strain. Task clarity, supervisor social support, and job future ambiguity could all be conceptualized as sources of uncertainty.

Another possibility is that work environments and people are flexible. The job-design factors that contribute to worker strain are not static: They change over time. Most theories of worker strain have in common the implicit assumption that relations between job design and worker strain are stable over time. If, in fact, these relations are variable over time, then we need to reevaluate the theories of job design and worker strain to take into account that variety. Examination of the third round of data will shed light on the stability of relations between job design and worker strain. We need to develop theories that take into account the work environment's flexibility. This dynamic view of the stressor–strain relation has been emphasized in the same manner by Frese and Zapf (1988).

The results of this study suggest that the job-design factors that contribute to worker strain change over time. This has some implications for primary interventions. The effectiveness of primary interventions that focus on a few job-design factors selected a priori might be limited. They might reduce worker strain in the short-term but not in the long-term because other job-design factors might later have a determinant influence on worker strain. This suggests the need for continuous improvement. In that perspective, monitoring of work-related stressors and strain effects is important because it allows managers to know what job-design factors need to be changed. The results of this study suggest that primary interventions that have a limited scope in terms of content and time frame might be less effective than interventions that emphasize continuous monitoring and improvement.

The cross-lagged panel correlation design suggested that job design was the cause of worker strain, and not the reverse. The evidence was relatively weak. Furthermore, cross-lagged panel correlation can suggest causal influence but does not guarantee it (Rogosa 1980). Controlled experimental studies are necessary to provide further evidence that job design influences worker strain.

This study has some weaknesses that may limit the generalizability of the results. The data originated from only one organization with a predominantly female sample. Thus, generalizations to other organizations must be made with caution. In addition, the amount of variance explained by the job-design factors is relatively small: It was less than 10% for the measures of mood disturbances, slightly higher for the measures of daily life stress and health (from 7% to 22%), and much larger for boredom and workload dissatisfaction (around 35%). Given the variety of factors that can influence worker strain and the complexity of measuring stressors and strain variables, I expected the amount of variance explained by the job-design factors to be small. Frese and Zapf (1988) argued that even low amounts of variance explained are important to examine who is more likely to experience strain and consequent health problems. In addition, more research is needed to further understand the stressor–strain relation. Individual differences, moderating effects, and other stressors can play an important role in the stressor–strain relation. Understanding the role of these variables can help improve the amount of explained variance of the strain outcome.

In summary, this study showed that relations between stressors and strain may be variable over time. Job-related stressors that influence worker strain at one time may not influence worker strain at another time. Therefore, the results of cross-sectional studies might not be reliable. Longitudinal studies that collect repeated data on worker strain, but also on job design, are necessary to further understand the relations between workers and their work environment (House et al., 1986). Different time models of the stressor–strain relation could be tested with longitudinal data. Frese and Zapf (1988) have proposed several time models that could be compared one against the other, given that the right longitudinal data is collected. For instance, collecting data before and after introduction of a new stressor could provide information on the short- and long-term effects of the stressor on worker strain. Economic, social, and technological changes are happening at an increasing rate. Occupational stress research needs to integrate a dynamic, flexible view in the development and application of theories and methodologies.

References

Aro, S. (1984). Occupational stress, health-related behavior, and blood pressure: A 5-year follow-up. *Prevention Medicine, 13,* 333–348.

Bateman, T. S., & Strasser, S. (1983). A cross-lagged regression test of the relationships between job tension and employee satisfaction. *Journal of Applied Psychology, 68,* 439–445.

Caplan, R. D., Cobb, S., French, J. R. P., Harrison, R. V., & Pinneau, S. R. (1975). *Job demands and worker health.* Washington, DC: U.S. Government Printing Office.

Carayon, P. (in press). *Stressful jobs and non-stressful jobs: A cluster analysis of office jobs. Ergonomics.*

Chadwick, J. H., Chesney, M. A., Black, G. W., Rosenman, R. H., & Sevelius, G. G. (1979). *Psychological job stress and coronary heart disease.* Menlo Park, CA: SRI International.

Cooper, C. L., & Marshall, J. (1976). Occupational sources of stress: A review of the literature relating to coronary heart disease and mental ill health. *Journal of Occupational Psychology, 49,* 11–28.

Eaker, E. D. (1988). Use of questionnaires, interviews, and psychological tests in epidemiological studies of coronary heart disease. *European Heart Journal, 9,* 698–704.

Frese, M. (1985). Stress at work and psychosomatic complaints: A causal interpretation. *Journal of Applied Psychology, 70,* 314–328.

Frese, M., & Zapf, D. (1988). Methodological issues in the study of work stress: Objective vs subjective measurement of work stress and the question of longitudinal studies. In C. L. Cooper & R. Payne (Eds.), *Causes, coping and consequences of stress at work* (pp. 375–411). New York: Wiley.

Greenberger, D. B., Strasser, S., Cummings, L. L., & Dunham, R. B. (1989). The impact of personal control on performance and satisfaction. *Organizational Behavior and Human Decision Processes, 43,* 29–51.

Haynes, S. G., & Feinleib, M. (1980). Women, work and coronary heart disease: Prospective findings from the Framingham Heart Study. *American Journal of Public Health, 70,* 133–141.

House, J. S., Stretcher, V., Metzner, J. L., & Robbins, C. A. (1986). Occupational stress and health among men and women in the Tecumseh Community Health Study. *Journal of Health and Social Behavior, 27,* 62–77.

Howard, J. H., Cunningham, D. A., & Rechnitzer, P. A. (1986). Role ambiguity, Type A behavior, and job satisfaction: Moderating effects on cardiovascular and biochemical responses associated with coronary risk. *Journal of Applied Psychology, 71,* 95–101.

Jackson, S. E. (1989). Does job control control job stress? In S. L. Sauter, J. J. Hurrell, Jr., & C. L. Cooper (Eds.), *Job control and worker health* (pp. 25–53). New York: Wiley.

Jenner, D. A., Puddey, I. B., Beilin, L. J., & Vandongen, R. (1988). Lifestyle- and occupation-related changes in blood pressure over a six-year period in a cohort of working men. *Journal of Hypertension, 6* (Suppl. 4), 605–607.

Karasek, R. A. (1979). Job demands, job decision latitude and mental strain: Implications for job redesign. *Administrative Science Quarterly, 24,* 285–306.

Kasl, S. V. (1978). Epidemiological contributions to the study of work stress. In C. L. Cooper & R. Payne (Eds.), *Stress at work* (pp. 3–48). New York: Wiley.

Kasl, S. V. (1987). Methodologies in stress and health: Past difficulties, present dilemmas, future directions. In S. V. Kasl & C. L. Cooper (Eds.), *Stress and health: Issues in research methodology* (pp. 307–318). New York: Wiley.

Kawakami, N., Haratani, T., Kaneko, T., & Araki, S. (1989). Perceived job-stress and blood pressure increase among Japanese blue collar workers: One-year follow-up study. *Industrial Health, 27,* 71–81.

Markus, G. B. (1979). *Analyzing panel data.* Newbury Park, CA: Sage.

McGrath, J. E. (1976). Stress and behavior in organizations. In M. D. Dunnette (Ed.), *Handbook of industrial and organizational psychology* (pp. 1251–1395). Chicago: Rand McNally.

McNair, D., Lorr, M., & Droppleman, L. (1971). *Profile of mood states.* San Diego, CA: Educational and Industrial Testing Service.

Miles, R. H. (1975). An empirical test of causal inference between role perceptions of conflict and ambiguity and various personal outcomes. *Journal of Applied Psychology, 60,* 334–339.

Pelz, D. C., & Andrews, F. M. (1964). Detecting causal priorities in panel study data. *American Sociological Review, 29,* 836–848.

Piotrkowki, C. S., Coray, K. E., & Cohen, B. G. F. (1987). *The relationship of working conditions to health and well-being among women office workers* (Technical Report Order No. 86-71437). Cincinnati, OH: National Institute for Occupational Safety and Health.

Reeder, L. G., Schrama, P. G., & Dirker, J. M. (1973). Stress and cardiovascular health: An international cooperative study. *Social Science Medicine, 7,* 753–784.

Rogosa, D. (1980). A critique of cross-lagged correlation. *Psychological Bulletin, 88,* 245–258.

Rose, R. M., Jenkins, C. D., & Hurst, M. W. (1978). *Air traffic controller health change study.* Washington, DC: U.S. Department of Transportation, Federal Aviation Administration, Office of Aviation Medicine.

Sainfort, P. C. (1990). Perceptions of work environment and psychological strain across categories of office jobs. *Proceedings of the Human Factors Society 34th Annual Meeting,* 849–853.

Sauter, S. L., Gottlieb, M. S., Rohrer, K. M., & Dodson, V. N. (1983). *The well-being of video display terminal users.* Madison, WI: Department of Preventive Medicine, University of Wisconsin—Madison.

Smith, M. J. (1987). Occupational stress. In G. Salvendy (Ed.), *Handbook of human factors* (pp. 844–860). New York: Wiley.

Smith, M. J., Cohen, B. G., & Stammerjohn, L. W., Jr. (1981). An investigation of health complaints and job stress in video display operations. *Human Factors, 23,* 387–400.

Szilagyi, A. D. (1977). An empirical test of causal inference between role perceptions, satisfaction with work, performance and organizational level. *Personnel Psychology, 30,* 375–388.

Theorell, T., Knox, S., Svensson, J., & Waller, D. (1985). Blood pressure variations during a working day at age 28: Effects of different types of work and blood pressure level at age 18. *Journal of Human Stress, 11,* 36–41.

Theorell, T., Perski, A., Akerstedt, T., Sigala, F., Ahlberg-Hulten, G., Svensson, J., & Eneroth, P. (1988). Changes in job strain in relation to changes in physiological state. *Scandinavian Journal of Work, Environment and Health, 14,* 189–196.

3

*Martin M. Greller, Charles K. Parsons, and
Debora R. D. Mitchell*

Additive Effects and Beyond: Occupational Stressors and Social Buffers in a Police Organization

Stress has destructive potential. This is true both for individuals and for the organizations that depend on their reliable participation (Sauter, Murphy, & Hurrell, 1990). As in other areas of psychology, when industrial/organizational practitioners have examined the subject of stress, they have viewed it as an interaction between external circumstances (e.g., stressors) and personal characteristics (e.g., coping style and resilience) that determines the individual's experience ("strain"; Newman & Beehr, 1979; Rodin & Salovey, 1989).

Some researchers have focused directly on the health effects of stress, using manifestations of disease as the criteria (Holmes & Rahe, 1967). But, for organizational research, these indicators appear too late. Stress needs to be addressed before the worker's health is sacrificed and productivity is lost. Because the workplace itself is the source of some stressful events, these events represent areas in which the organization can take action and may exercise control over at least some of the sources of stress.

The effects are not always negative, however. A certain level of arousal may facilitate performance. Stress may produce the optimal level of arousal for some people, resulting in increased effectiveness. For others, the same amount may be excessive, leading to decreased effectiveness.

Organizations have an interest in reducing stress when it results in diminished performance. Conditions in the work environment associated with such reactions would make good targets for change. But, there are two potential problems. First, some sources of stress are an integral part of the job and are not subject to change by the organization, regardless of the amount of strain they produce (House, 1981). For example, although physical assault by a criminal may be stressful for a police officer, the organization is not in a position to prevent such attacks as part of a stress reduction program. The work of a commodities trader is by its very nature fast paced and uncertain, with very high consequences of error. In such cases, the

The authors wish to thank Richard Kopelman and Charles Spielberger for their suggestions and advice in the preparation of this chapter. The data reported here were collected while the senior author was with Rohrer, Hibler & Replogle, Inc., New York.

best an organization can do is hope to mitigate the consequences deleterious to performance and employee health.

The second problem is one of the field's own making. Organizational researchers have not always operationalized their variables in ways that readily facilitate action. Among the most studied stress variables are task ambiguity and role conflict. These have a demonstrated relation to a wide range of distresses (Ganster, Fusilier, & Mayes, 1986; Jackson & Schuler, 1985; Kahn, Wolfe, Quinn, Snoek, & Rosenthal, 1964; Rizzo, House, & Lirtzman, 1970). However, the constructs themselves merge environmental conditions with personal evaluations. A series of conditions that appears ambiguous and ill-defined to one person may be crystal clear to another.

A similar problem appears in another current method for measuring stressors that involves asking workers about their attitudes and beliefs concerning potential stressors. Specific job elements or experiences are used, but they are evaluated in terms of the degree of distress they cause rather than the extent to which they are present. This is the basis of the "hassles" approach, which asks how much of a problem ("hassle") a given event was during a specified period of time (Houlahan & Moos, 1990; Lazarus, 1984). A series of items corresponding to potentially stressful job events is listed, and employees rate their stressfulness (Spielberger, Westberry, & Greenfield, 1981).

Given the current state of theory, combining personal and situational factors may be conceptually sound. This procedure captures all elements needed to describe the phenomenon, but it does not help to target the intervention for those who would act on the organization (versus those interested in coping or treatment).

Considered from the framework described earlier in this book, occupational risk factors native to the situation are confounded with individual responses. Combining situational and personal factors provides no clear measure of the organizational risk factors, although it may provide a good indicator of subsequent health risks.

Recent thinking has made the role of external, organizationally managed events more critical. As the cost of stress-related maladies increases, representing a large portion of workplace disabilities, policymakers are becoming more interested in the ways employers can reduce this cost (Hatfield, 1990; Pattison & Varca, 1991; Sauter et al., 1990) as researchers direct their attention to job factors (Karasek, 1979; Landy, 1990). But, acting on the situation requires measuring the presence of the potentially strain-causing conditions in a particular work environment. This means knowing the frequency with which the events occur—particularly if their occurrence can be demonstrably related to adverse outcomes. The organization may act to alter the frequency of some stressful events.

Event frequency has been used as a successful measure of stress (Wheeler & Reis, 1991). The incidents selected are often powerful, acute stressors (e.g., Holmes & Rahe, 1967). Typically, these are major life events. They are useful clinically, but they do not represent the broad range of potentially stressful events, especially those that most often occur in the context of work. The present study attempts to capture a broad range of events that might contribute to the stressfulness of a particular environment.

Cumulative Effects—Are They Additive?

An underlying notion in the previously described methods of measurement is that stressors have an additive effect. In the cases of the stressful life event's effect on health (Holmes & Rahe, 1967), this is demonstrably true. Spielberger et al. (1981) looked at a broad range of events occurring in the police environment and found that their effects were cumulative. Russell, Altmaier, and van Velzen (1987) showed burnout to be a function of different elements that, when added together, affected teachers. These research findings have an analogue in daily experience, where the pressure of individual events add up. The last event may be no more stressful than any of the preceding ones; however, all the events taken together cause it to be "the last straw."

Stressors are not straws. They are discrete events of differing intensities occurring in different parts of one's life. These events not only happen in the same life but also may create the context in which other events are experienced. Considered in this light, the increment of strain produced by an event may be greater when it occurs in a situation that is already stress filled. In such cases, stressful events would be interactively related to strain. The presence of one stressor would magnify the effect of another.

Examples of interactive effects of stress have been shown. Greller and Parsons (in press) found that the strain attributable to negative feedback from one source was a function of the sort of feedback received from other sources. Cobb and Rose (1973) found that among air-traffic controllers there was an interaction effect for attentional demands and working in high-density traffic areas (suggesting a higher consequence of error). Martin and Wall (1989) found an interaction between attentional demand and cost of responsibility on anxiety, depression, and mental health among production workers. Reports from the National Center for Post-Traumatic Stress Disorder suggest that acute stress experiences produce posttraumatic stress syndrome that may result in long-term physiological effects so that reactions to new stressors are heightened (Charney cited in Goleman, 1990). Birnbaum and Sotoodeh (1991) have demonstrated that judgments of stress depart from linearity.

Therefore, our first hypothesis (H1a) is that stress sources will be directly related to strain. In addition, we hypothesize (H1b) that stress sources will interact in their relation to strain such that the strain associated with the occurrence of each stressful event will be increased when other stressful events are present.

Buffers—Compensatory Effects Versus Moderators

Research has shown that social relations can reduce the strain of a stressful environment. In this respect, social support factors are buffers—circumstances altering the extent to which a stressor affects the individual. As such, they have a nonadditive effect. Buffers are traditionally not seen as independent sources of stress but as factors diminishing the impact of stressful events (LaRocco, House, & French, 1980). Such amelioration would be of considerable practical value in situations in which the precipitating event cannot be addressed directly.

Social support is perhaps the most frequently identified buffer of stress (Cobb, 1976). Houlahan and Moos (1990) found that family support helped people use more effective coping strategies when confronted by severe stress, as well as encouraging them to grow when confronted by moderate stress. DeLongis, Folkman, and Lazarus (1988) found emotional support (from a broad range of sources) buffered future health from the effects of daily hassles. DiMatteo and Hays (1981) found that support facilitated recovery from strain-related illness. Yet, often there is some caveat to the effectiveness of social support as a buffer. A review by Cohen and Wills (1985) concluded that the most consistent social support buffers were those that could provide esteem-type support (e.g., make a person feel worthwhile) and information-type support (e.g., helps the individual understand or respond to stressful demands). Etzion (1984) found that social support buffered stress but that men were buffered from work stress only by support in the work environment, whereas women were buffered by social support from outside of work. Smith, Smoll, and Ptacek (1990) showed that social support buffered adolescent athletes from experiencing injury subsequent to stress, but the effect was noticeable only for those people with limited coping skills. Although one study even showed that casual conversation with one's supervisor could provide buffering (Beehr, King, & King, 1990), another could find scant evidence of any social buffering (Ganster et al., 1986).

On balance, the research gives evidence of some social buffering. But who buffers whom under what circumstances is less clear. The previous research is also limited in that it aggregates the potentially stressful events into one monolithic index of environmental stressfulness. So, it is unclear whether different sources of stress might be offset by different types of social support. As Kaufman and Beehr (1989) observed, under some circumstances, increased interaction with an individual may simply mean increased exposure to the source of stress. For example, when a supervisor criticizes a subordinate, the subordinate's level of strain increases (Greller & Parsons, in press).

Social support may also have a direct effect on strain. If support is associated with less strain (e.g., a supportive family life may result in fewer health problems than average), it may simply compensate for the negative effects of other events. Taken to the extreme, statistical evidence of an interaction may appear when deficient social relationships are such sources of strain that they limit the range available for further reactions. It was just such an effect for instrumental social support that led to Kaufman and Beehr's (1989) explanation of reverse buffering. Others have found significant buffers that also have a direct effect on strain (Etzion, 1984; Greller & Parsons, in press). And, some efforts to use social support have found only a main effect on the measures of distress used (Ganster et al., 1986; LaRocco & Jones, 1978).

Thus, in the literature, the term *buffer* has referred to a variable that may operate in two ways. Buffers may have an additive effect, compensating through their presence for other, stressful events, rather like sugar added to make lemonade palatable. Alternatively, they may change the way the stressful event is experienced but have no direct effect on the level of strain. Finally, a buffer may do both: have a salutary, independent effect on strain and also reduce the relation between a typically stressful event and strain.

Therefore, we hypothesize (H2a) that social support variables will be negatively related to strain. In addition, we hypothesize (H2b) that social support variables from the work environment, but not from the home environment, will interact with stress sources to produce a "moderator" effect. Workplace support offers the possibility of both informational and situationally relevant self-esteem enhancement, giving it an advantage over social support from nonwork sources.

Method

Data for this study were collected as part of a survey of stress in police work. A questionnaire was developed and distributed to a large metropolitan police department. A total of 1,638 questionnaires with usable data were returned and available for analysis. The present study is based on those participants who responded to every stressful event question ($n = 728$).

This was a conservative approach given that it eliminated participants who failed to answer only one of the 89 items. However, it provided a complete data matrix with which to assess the stress environment. The resulting sample was representative of the department. Because of the number of topics covered in the larger survey, collateral questions (i.e., those dealing with family, supervisor characteristics, and co-workers) were only administered to subsamples. The subsamples were designed so that each set of questions was paired with every other set of questions in one of the subsamples. This enabled each of the scales to be correlated with every other scale. It also meant that each of the collateral measures was based on a sample composed of different people, with samples ranging in size from 265 to 801. The demographic compositions of the various subsamples used in our analyses were very similar. The mean age ranged from 39.0 to 40.7 years, the proportion of men ranged from 95.6% to 97.9%, the proportion of Whites ranged from 88.2% to 90.7%, the proportion of Blacks ranged from 5.7% to 7.6%, the mean education ranged from 14.2 to 14.5 years, and mean department tenure ranged from 15.1 to 16.1 years.

Stressful Events and Strain

The measure of stressful events was developed by interviewing a cross section of officers about stressors that they experienced at work. The list was edited for clarity and to eliminate redundancy. This resulted in 89 items that were used in the questionnaire. Participants were asked to rate the frequency with which they had experienced each event in the past year. The response options ranged from 0 to 25 or more occurrences.

To simplify the data, responses to the 89 items were analyzed using a principal

Table 1. First 10 Eigenvalues from 89 Stress Source Frequency Items

Component	Eigenvalue
1	26.1
2	4.4
3	4.0
4	2.3
5	2.0
6	1.8
7	1.6
8	1.6
9	1.5
10	1.4

Table 2. Rotated Component Loadings for Selected Stress Frequency Items

| Stressful event | Components of police work | | | |
	Routine work	External	Management	Extreme work
Change from day to night shift	.39	.29	.08	.11
Exposed to death of civilians	.58	.30	.08	.14
Deliver a death notification	.49	.11	.24	.37
Court appearances on day off or day following night shift	.47	.18	.05	.27
Issue summons	.67	−.13	.19	.03
Deal with family dispute/crisis	.81	.11	.13	.05
High-speed chase	.62	.09	.19	.37
Confrontations with aggressive crowds	.67	.23	.14	.27
Respond to felony in progress	.85	.15	.03	.07
Receive personal insult from citizen	.61	.29	.22	.18
Situation requires use of force	.69	.34	.13	.25
Exposed to adults in pain	.76	.32	.10	.30
Exposed to battered or dead children	.49	.31	.07	.32
Run risk of minor injury on the job	.64	.32	.10	.14
Involved in large civilian disturbance	.58	.21	.13	.34
Court lenient with criminals	.33	.43	.17	.27
Experienced political pressure from outside the department	.16	.44	.33	.28
Come across distorted or negative press accounts of police	.31	.58	.22	.02
Experienced ineffectiveness of judicial system	.39	.62	.11	.24
Experienced ineffectiveness of correction system	.26	.53	.17	.27
Assigned increased responsibility	.05	.54	.37	.13
Read about police incident in newspaper	.32	.54	.17	−.07
Demands for high moral standards are made on me	.18	.46	.25	.14
Court decisions unduly restrict my police action	.47	.51	.19	.25
Experience public apathy toward police	.32	.53	.10	.12
Have to use personal property for police business	−.02	.58	.16	.21
Observed plea bargaining and technical rulings leading to case dismissal	.38	.46	.03	.35
Excessive paper work	.20	.54	.30	−.02
See other city workers making more money than they should relative to my salary	.23	.51	.26	.08

Table 2 (*Continued*)

Stressful event	Components of police work			
	Routine work	External	Management	Extreme work
Work with civilian in job that used to belong to police officer	−.02	.37	.24	−.02
Request to work overtime turned down	.17	.14	.40	.24
Fellow officers not doing their jobs	.26	.47	−.02	
Strained relations with nonpolice friends	.17	.19	.43	.16
Inadequate support by supervisor	.04	.30	.63	.26
Inadequate support by department	.17	.32	.48	.32
Supervisor puts you down	.03	−.01	.64	.26
Difficulty getting along with boss	.11	.07	.67	.18
Second guessed by someone higher up	.19	.38	.54	.17
Lack of recognition for good work	.10	.35	.61	.10
Excessive or inappropriate discipline	.21	.11	.48	.24
Not allowed participation in policy-making decisions	.04	.37	.46	.19
He/she is goofing off	.26	.31	.60	.01
Experience poor/inadequate supervision	.11	.28	.60	.09
Obligated to work with people who are not competent	.12	.36	.58	−.01
Supervisor does not listen when I try to tell him/her about a problem	.02	.27	.64	.18
Incapacitated by physical injury on job	.25	−.02	.20	.47
Defendant in departmental trial	.12	.01	.10	.66
Promoted or received commendation	.14	.20	.10	.47
Investigated following use of gun	.12	.11	.04	.68
Accident in patrol car	.20	−.03	.15	.71
Physical attack on one's person	.46	.20	.19	.56
Exposed to press accounts of event in which I was involved	.19	.28	.06	.51
Kill someone in the line of duty	.00	−.02	.04	.75
Interviewed in integrity investigation	.20	.08	.15	.49
Shot at in line of duty	.09	−.05	.17	.60

components analysis, followed by a varimax rotation of the components with ei-genvalues that were both greater than 1.0 and appeared meaningful through use of a scree plot (Cattell, 1966). The first 10 eigenvalues appear in Table 1. The first four components, accounting for about 42% of the total variance, appeared to be above the inflection point and were rotated. The loadings from 55 items that were primarily identified with one component are presented in Table 2. The first component represents events that are commonplace in police work. Issuing summons, settling domestic disputes, and so on are normal parts of the job; therefore, this component was labeled *routine (police) work*. The second component represents events that are external to the police organization. These are events such as negative press reports or perceived ineffectiveness of the criminal justice system. This component was called *external*. The third component consists of items related to supervision and administration. For example, items such as "receive inadequate support from supervisor" and "request for overtime turned down" loaded on this factor. This component was called *management*. The final component represents work events that occur less frequently but are certainly a part of the job. Examples are "incapacitated by physical injury on job" and "defendant in departmental trial." This component was called *extreme work*.

The items that are indicated in Table 2 were summed according to the factor on which they loaded highly, forming scales representing the relative frequency of stressful events from each source. The internal consistency (coefficient alpha) for each scale was routine work, .92; external, .88; management, .89; and extreme work, .81.

The measure of strain was a psychosomatic complaints scale (for a full report on the development and psychometric properties, see Greller & Parsons, 1988). The scale consists of 31 items relating physical and psychological stress symptoms and has a coefficient alpha of .91. Sample items are "difficulty falling asleep" and "have bad dreams."

Measures of Support

The measures of social support can be divided into three groups: family support, co-worker support, and supervisor/departmental support. Family support was measured using a family cohesiveness scale, which consisted of five items and had an internal reliability (alpha) of .90. The items were "we respect each others' feelings," "in our home we feel loved," "there is a sense of belonging in our family," "ours is a reliable, dependable family," and "we enjoy being a family." Family cohesiveness was rated on a 5-point scale (1 = does not fit our family at all; 5 = fits our family well).

Co-worker support was measured with two scales. The first measured co-worker cohesiveness and consisted of 10 items with an alpha of .67. Typical items on this scale were "I know I can always go to friends in the Department if I have a problem," "the people I work with are very open," and "you do not let others know your weak points in this group." Team work consisted of four items with an alpha of .55. The items were "we are able to work in unison," "most of the work is accomplished by an individual doing things on his/her own," "I find myself alone even when I could use the support of others," and "even when we have the opportunity we do not work as a team." (Negatively worded items were reversed coded.) These items were rated on a 5-point scale (1 = does not describe at all; 5 = describes very well).

Departmental and supervisory support was indicated by five measures. Consideration was based on seven items with an alpha of .82 (Szylagi & Sims, 1974). Consideration indicated emotional support and caring. Hierarchical influence used six items with an alpha of .61 to indicate the degree to which the supervisor could influence things in the department (Herold, 1974; Wigdor, 1969). Influence was included as it reflected the instrumental value of the supervisor's input. Positive hierarchical feedback was based on eight items with an alpha of .72 (Herold & Greller, 1977). Such feedback offers support both to self-esteem and provides instrumental information. A scale measuring participation consisted of eight items with a reliability of .75 (e.g., "I have a chance to voice my ideas to the supervisor on the way things should be done," "when I point out a problem the supervisor acts on it," and "we do not know a decision is being made until after it is done"). Departmental concern was shown through two items with a reliability of .73: "the department has concern for our well being" and "the department is on the side of its employees in things that matter."

Results

The correlation matrix for all variables appears in Table 3. As expected, there were significant positive correlations between the four stress sources and strain. The largest correlation was between the management stress factor and strain ($r = .37$). Thus, we have support for H1a that the reported frequency of stress events is related to strain. In addition, there were significant correlations between many of the social support variables and strain. The largest correlations were for co-worker cohesiveness, which correlated $-.28$ with strain. Also worth noting in Table 3 is that the

Table 3. Correlation Between All Stress Sources, Buffers, and Strain

Variable	1	2	3	4	5	6	7	8	9	10	11	12
1. Strain	—											
2. Routine work	.24*	—										
3. Extreme work	.19*	.53*	—									
4. Management	.37*	.52*	.48*	—								
5. External	.28*	.68*	.49*	.73*	—							
6. Family cohesiveness	−.18*	−.01	.02	−.08*	.06	—						
7. Work group cohesiveness	−.28*	−.25*	−.12*	−.42*	−.29*	.25*	—					
8. Team work	−.28*	−.14*	−.18*	−.41*	−.25*	−.14*	.58*	—				
9. Positive hierarchical feedback	.10*	.04	.14*	−.02	.12*	.19*	.28*	.17*	—			
10. Consideration	−.17*	−.21*	−.19*	−.49*	−.29*	−.05	.46*	.48*	.26	—		
11. Participation in decisions	−.20*	−.28*	−.13*	−.47*	−.28*	.00	.39*	.45*	.30*	.79*	—	
12. Supervisor influence	−.18*	.18*	−.11*	−.35*	−.22*	.06	.39*	.41*	.18*	.59*	.60*	—
13. Departmental support	−.26*	−.19*	−.09*	−.29*	−.28*	.12*	.27*	.21*	.22*	.32*	.39*	.34*

Note. $N = 265$ to 801.

*$p < .05$.

median correlation among the stressful events scales is .52, suggesting that individuals who report experiencing stressful events of one sort also report experiencing others.

A hierarchical multiple regression was used to test H1b, that stress sources interact statistically in their effect on strain. Four stress source variables were entered in the first step, followed by the six cross-product terms representing all possible two-way interactions among the stress source variables. Table 4 shows that in the first regression step, including only the linear effects of stressful events, there was a single significant main effect for management (beta = .30, $p < .001$). The multiple correlation for the linear model was .35. Adding the first-order interactions created a significant increase in the variance explained (.024, $F = 3.33, p < .01$). There were two significant interactions: Routine Work × External and Extreme Events × External. These interactions appeared in the context of a much-altered regression model. The independent role of management events decreased. The strain of routine police work is made worse by encounters with the judicial system and press. The negative interaction between external and extreme work may reflect a boundary condition. At low levels of extreme work, exposure to external events may result in more strain, but as the amount of extreme police work increases, there is less room for increased strain to be experienced. It appears that stress sources do interact in their effect on stress symptoms, supporting H1b.

The next analysis used a three-step hierarchical regression in which the four stress-source factors were entered first, then one of the social support factors and, finally, the cross-product terms for the social support factor with each of the four stress-source factors. A separate hierarchical analysis was done for each social support factor. The test of the hypothesis concerning a main effect for each social support factor (H2a) was whether or not there was a significant increase in the variance explained when the linear effect of the support factor was included. The

Table 4. Hierarchical Regression to Test for Interactions Between Stress Sources

Factor entered	R^2	R^2 change	Beta linear	Beta interactions
Step 1				
RW			.03	−.54*
M			.30*	.31
EW			.03	.58*
E			.04	.21
	.125*	.125*		
Step 2				
RW × M				−.30
RW × EW				.64
RW × E				.63*
M × EW				−.18
M × E				.37
EW × E				−1.26*
	.149*	.024*		

Note. $N = 728$. RW = routine work, M = management, EW = extreme work, E = external.
*$p < .05$.

Table 5. Proportion of Variance Explained by Interaction of Social Support Variable With Police Events Regressed on Strain

Social support variable	R^2 change police events linear effects	R^2 change variable linear	R^2 change variable interaction	N
Family cohesiveness	.143*	.045*	.007	256
Family financial stability	.144*	.076*	.010	258
Family organization	.140*	.027*	.011	256
Work group cohesiveness	.104*	.085*	.003	297
Team work	.108*	.031*	.027	299
Positive hierarchical feedback	.166*	.044*	.072*	285
Supervisor consideration	.125*	.000	.037*	300
Participation in decisions	.127*	.001	.036*	294
Supervisor influence	.125*	.001	.025	300
Departmental concern	.125*	.049*	.035*	303

*$p < .05$.

test for the buffering hypothesis (H2b) was whether the incremental variance due to the four cross-product terms was significant.

The results for the hierarchical regressions appear in Table 5. The family and the co-worker factors showed significant main effects, but not interaction effects, suggesting that these sources played additive roles in their effect on stress symptoms. That is, they can add to (or subtract from) strain, but they do not fundamentally alter the effect of work stress sources. Both hierarchical positive feedback and departmental concern also showed significant main effects on stress symptoms. Therefore, H2a was supported for the most part.

In the final step of the hierarchical regression analysis, statistically significant incremental variance was explained by the interaction terms for positive hierarchical feedback, .072; supervisor consideration, .037; participation in decision making, .036; and departmental concern, .035. The strongest effect was for positive hierarchical feedback, accounting for 7.2% additional variance. Thus, there is support for H2b. However, there was no evidence of buffering from co-worker or family support. The hierarchical sources accounted for all instances of buffering observed.

The most impressive result was for the main effect and interaction terms of positive hierarchical feedback, which combined to account for 12% additional variance in stress symptoms. In looking at regression weights for specific interactions, the highest weight was for the interaction of management as a source of stress with positive hierarchical feedback.

Discussion

Social support may serve as either a palliative or an ameliorative. Where social support factors act as buffers (or moderators), they ameliorate—reducing the strain that would otherwise be experienced more severely. However, when one observes a main (or additive) effect for social support factors, there is a compensatory effect on strain: A palliative is present. For example, in the present study, a particularly supportive home life was associated with less stress.

But, should such additive effects be described as "buffers" at all? An unrewarding, personally draining home life would be associated with greater strain regardless of what occurred on the job. Thus, a favorable home life does not reduce the adverse effects of stressful events on the job; it simply avoids the addition of yet add another set of stressful events (Coyne & Downey, 1991; Weissman, 1987). Viewed in a positive light, a particularly good home life may be compensatory— keeping the aggregate level of strain below deleterious levels even if the job is stress filled.

Social support from the supervisor was the only true buffer found in this study, and it operated differently than other so-called buffers. The presence of such support ameliorates, altering the impact of otherwise strain-producing events so that they have a weaker association with strain. This is consistent with Russell et al.'s (1987) finding that supervisor support interacted with job-related stress in explaining burnout among teachers.

The supervisor is uniquely positioned as a source of support. Cohen and Wills (1985) proposed three factors that contribute to buffering: information, support, and esteem. In the work situation, the supervisor can provide all three. Positive feedback from above offers information and fosters esteem. Support may be either material or emotional—both are evident in the buffers studied here. Participation in decisions allows greater control over events (Rodin, 1986). Supervisor consideration and positive feedback offer the emotional component. Taken together, information, support, and esteem may help the individual alter the stress-producing situation—or at least hold out the possibility of so doing. Support from external sources do not offer such a promise. One caveat here is that the sample was primarily male, and earlier research has shown men more responsive to work-related social support than women (Etzion, 1984; Marshall & Barnett, 1990).

If stressful events within the family are considered, there may be similar moderating factors that accelerate (or reduce) the strain produced by family events and conditions. These may be more pronounced for women—or for homemakers of either gender who identify more with home and family than with employment.

The results of the present study directly contradict a similarly intentioned study conducted by Ganster et al. (1986). With a sample size similar to that used in our analysis of social support factors, they found only linear effects on strain. Considering their most directly comparable measure of strain (an adhoc symptoms measure), the differences are evident from the very outset. They found only 6% of the variance explained by stressors. In the present study, 14.9% of the variance was explained by the stressors, and 3.3% was explained by interactions involving supervisory support.

We believe the method of assessing work environment stressors may explain the differences in outcome. Ganster et al. (1986) used aggregated measures describing reactions to the job's ambiguity, variety, and lack of stimulation. These measures were most closely associated with job satisfaction.

We avoided such measures in this study, as explained in the Introduction, because they do not offer clear guidance for action. However, use of more specific, event-based measures of stressors, grounded in the experience of respondents, may provide a more powerful link between stress and strain—one that permits the relation both to be demonstrated and possible moderating effects to be tested.

When considering social buffers, investigators of stress in the workplace should also be mindful of earlier efforts examining the ways people in organizations and groups manage anxiety (Bion, 1961; Miller & Rice, 1967). Much of this literature examines the role that organization structure plays in meeting members' needs for psychological defense in a stress-filled environment (Menzies, 1975). Although researchers in this tradition are more apt to address the phenomenon in terms of coping or defense, the result is moderation of the relation between the stressfulness of one's environment and the strain experienced. Similar to the conclusions from this study, authority figures are viewed as critical in shaping the (often covert) mechanisms by which organizations and groups allow members to defend themselves against anxiety.

For those interested primarily in workplace stress, the results suggest that employers are in a particularly powerful position to influence the effects of stress in their organizations. Effective management may permit employees to work comfortably in environments that would otherwise produce high levels of strain. Conversely, managed badly enough, employees can experience high levels of strain in situations that would otherwise be quite bearable. The results support Russell et. al.'s (1987) recommendation that intervention programs focus on supervisors and ways to reassure individuals of their worth and acknowledge their skills and abilities.

Approaching stress management by improving the quality of supervision to ameliorate the effects of stressful events has implications for the way stress research is conducted. The occurrence of a stressful event and the individual's evaluation of it need to be kept separate given that the approach requires measurement of and intervention on the events themselves. The strategy should be to change the nature of supervision—not to alter the way employees think about it.

The method used in the present study asked people to rate the frequency of a range of events. This offered a relatively objective indicator of the environment. Other approaches might be fruitfully explored. Having independent judges evaluate work environments would be another approach. Of course, if it is the supervisors whose behavior is to be influenced, one might profitably explore how they assess the stressfulness of their subordinates' environments and how those perceptions could be sharpened.

Efforts to manage stress and its consequences in the workplace may take many different tacts. One fruitful avenue is a variation on a traditional theme in stress research—seeking buffers. There appear to be real buffers—ones that alter the effects of other stress factors rather than just compensating for them. Supervisor behaviors offer rich potential for helping workers deal with particularly stressful environments.

References

Beehr, T. A., King, L. A., & King, D. W. (1990). Social support and occupational stress: Talking to supervisors. *Journal of Vocational Behavior, 36,* 61–81.

Bion, W. R. (1961). *Experiences in groups.* New York: Basic Books.

Birnbaum, M. H., & Sotoodeh, Y. (1991). Measurement of stress: Scaling the magnitude of life changes. *Psychological Science, 2,* 236–243.

Cattell, R. B. (1966). The scree test for the number of factors. *Multivariate Behavioral Research, 1,* 140–161.

Cobb, J. (1976). Social support as a moderator of life stress. *Psychosomatic Medicine, 38,* 300–314.

Cobb, S., & Rose, R. M. (1973). Hypertension, peptic ulcer and diabetes in air traffic controllers. *Journal of the American Medical Association, 224,* 489–492.

Cohen, S., & Wills, T. A. (1985). Stress, social support and the buffering hypothesis. *Psychological Bulletin, 98,* 310–357.

Coyne, J. C., & Downey, G. (1991). Social factors and psychopathology: Stress, social support and coping processes. *Annual Review of Psychology, 42,* 401–425.

DeLongis, A., Folkman, S., & Lazarus, R. S. (1988). The impact of daily stress on health and mood: Psychological and social resources as mediators. *Journal of Personality and Social Psychology, 54,* 486–495.

DiMatteo, M. R., & Hays, R. (1981). Social support and series illness. In B. G. Gottlieb (Ed.), *Social networks and social support in community mental health* (pp. 117–147). Newbury Park, CA: Sage.

Etzion, D. (1984). Moderating effects of social support on the stress–burnout relationship. *Journal of Applied Psychology, 69,* 615–622.

Ganster, D. C., Fusilier, M. R., & Mayes (1986). Role of social support in the experience of stress at work. *Journal of Applied Psychology, 71,* 102–110.

Goleman, D. (1990, June 12). A key to post-traumatic stress lies in brain chemistry. *The New York Times,* pp. C1, C12.

Greller, M. M., & Parsons, C. K. (1988). Psychosomatic complaints scale of stress: Measure development and psychometric properties. *Educational and Psychological Measurement, 48,* 1051–1065.

Greller, M. M., & Parsons, C. K. (in press). Feedback and feedback inconsistency as a source of strain and self evaluation. *Human Relations.*

Hatfield, M. B. (1990). Stress and the American worker. *American Psychologist, 45,* 1162–1164.

Herold, D. M. (1974). Interaction of subordinate and leader characteristics in moderating the consideration–satisfaction relationship. *Journal of Applied Psychology, 59,* 649–651.

Herold, D. M., & Greller, M. M. (1977). Feedback: The definition of a construct. *Academy of Management Journal, 20,* 142–147.

Holmes, T. H., & Rahe, R. H. (1967). The social readjustment rating scale. *Journal of Psychosomatic Research, 11,* 213–218.

Houlahan, C. J., & Moos, R. H. (1990). Life stressors, resistance factors and improved psychological function: An extension of the stress resistance program. *Journal of Personality and Social Psychology, 58,* 909–917.

House, J. S. (1981). *Work, stress, and social support.* Reading, MA: Addison-Wesley.

Jackson, S. E., & Schuler, R. S. (1985). A meta-analysis and conceptual critique of research on role ambiguity and role conflict in work settings. *Organizational Behavior and Human Decision Processes, 36,* 16–78.

Kahn, R. L., Wolfe, D. M., Quinn, R. P., Snoek, J. R., & Rosenthal, R. A. (1964). *Organizational stress: Studies in role conflict and ambiguity.* New York: Wiley.

Karasek, R. A., Jr. (1979). Job demands, job decision latitude, and mental strain: Implications for job redesign. *Administrative Science Quarterly, 24,* 285–308.

Kaufman, G. M., & Beehr, T. A. (1989). Occupational stressors, individual strains, and social support among police officers. *Human Relations, 42,* 185–197.

Landy, F. J. (1990, November). *Work design and stress.* Paper presented at the meeting of American Psychological Association/National Institute for Occupational Safety and Health Conference on Work and Well-Being, Washington, DC.

LaRocco, J. M., House, J. S., & French, J. R. P. (1980). Social support, occupational stress and health. *Journal of Health and Social Behavior, 21,* 202–218.

LaRocco, J. M., & Jones, A. P. (1978). Co-worker and leader support as moderators of stress–strain relationship in work situations. *Journal of Applied Psychology, 68,* 629–634.

Lazarus, R. S. (1984). Puzzles in the study of daily hassles. *Journal of Behavioral Medicine, 7,* 375–389.

Marshall, N. L., & Barnett, R. C. (1990, November). Work related support among women in caregiving occupations. Paper presented at the meeting of the American Psychological Association/National Institute for Occupational Safety and Health Conference on Work and Well-Being, Washington, DC.

Martin, R., & Wall, T. D. (1989). Attentional demand and cost responsibility as stressors in shop floor jobs. *Academy of Management Journal, 32,* 69–86.

Menzies, I. E. P. (1975). A case-study in the function social systems as a defense against anxiety. In A. D. Coleman & W. H. Baxton (Eds.), *Group relations reader* (pp. 281–312). Sausalito, CA: GREX.

Miller, E. J., & Rice, A. K. (1967). *Systems of organization: The control of task and sentient boundaries.* London: Tavistock.

Newman, J. E., & Beehr, T. A. (1979). Personal and organizational strategies for handling job stress: A review of research and opinion. *Personnel Psychology, 32,* 1–44.

Pattison, P. A., & Varca, P. E. (1991, August). *Psychological stress in employment: Legal and managerial implications.* Paper presented at the meeting of the American Business Law Association, Portland, ME.

Rizzo, J. R., House, R. J., & Lirtzman, S. I. (1970). Relation of job stressors to affect, health, and performance outcomes: A comparison of multiple sources. *Administrative Science Quarterly, 15,* 150–163.

Rodin, J. (1986). Aging and health: The effects of the sense of control. *Science, 233,* 1271–1276.

Rodin, J., & Salovey, P. (1989). Health psychology. *Annual Review of Psychology, 40,* 533–579.

Russell, D. W., Altmaier, E., & van Velzen, D. (1987). Job related stress, social support and burnout among classroom teachers. *Journal of Applied Psychology, 72,* 269–274.

Sauter, S. L., Murphy, L. R., & Hurrell, J. J. (1990). Prevention of work-related psychological disorders. *American Psychologist, 45,* 1146–1158.

Smith, R. E., Smoll, F. L., & Ptacek, J. T. (1990). Conjunctive moderator variables in vulnerability and resiliency research: Life stress, social support, and coping skills, and adolescent sport injuries. *Journal of Personality and Social Psychology, 58,* 360–370.

Spielberger, C. D., Westberry, L. G., & Greenfield, G. (1981, Fall). closer look at police stress. *Florida Fraternal Order of Police,* pp. 31–43.

Szylagi, A. D., & Sims, H. D. (1974). Cross-sample stability of the supervisory behavior description questionnaire. *Journal of Applied Psychology, 59,* 767–770.

Weissman, M. M. (1987). Advances in psychiatric epidemiology: Rates and risks for depression. *American Journal of Public Health, 77,* 445–451.

Wheeler, L., & Reis, H. T. (1991). Self-recording of everyday life events: Origins, types and uses. *Journal of Personality, 59,* 339–354.

Wigdor, L. (1969). *Effectiveness of various management and organizational characteristics on employee satisfaction and performance as a function of employees needs for independence.* Unpublished doctoral dissertation, Bernard M. Baruch College, City University of New York.

4

Karl W. Kuhnert and Robert J. Vance

Job Insecurity and Moderators of the Relation Between Job Insecurity and Employee Adjustment

Threats to the job security of workers have proliferated in recent years. Plant closings, foreign competition, downsizing, corporate mergers, and skill obsolescence have all been cited as factors adversely affecting job security (Cameron, Sutton, & Whetten, 1988; Whetten, 1980). However, the evidence that security is a salient issue for many Americans is mostly circumstantial. Little research has actually examined individual perceptions of security and insecurity as they relate to personal and organizational outcomes.

Greenhalgh and Rosenblatt (1984) responded to the deficit in attention to job security by producing a model of the causes, effects, and organizational consequences of perceived job insecurity. According to this model, a message concerning an objective threat of job loss is transmitted to the individual by means of intended and unintended cues from the organization and through rumors. The individual attends to the message and may react to it with decreased effort expenditure at work, increased resistance to change, and greater likelihood of leaving the organization. For the organization, these reactions mean lower productivity, higher employee turnover, and lower adaptability to a changing environment. The Greenhalgh and Rosenblatt model also proposed a variety of potential moderators of the linkages between messages regarding security and perceptions of insecurity and between perceptions of insecurity and reactions to these perceptions.

Ashford, Lee, and Bobko (1989) developed a measure of job insecurity based on the Greenhalgh and Rosenblatt (1984) theoretical formulation. They used it to test hypotheses about the antecedents and consequences of job insecurity for 183 employees of three organizations. Following Greenhalgh and Rosenblatt, they calculated an insecurity score for each subject as a multiplicative combination of importance and threat of loss of job features, importance and threat of loss of the job itself, and sense of powerlessness to prevent a loss. Hypotheses regarding potential antecedents of insecurity, including anticipated organizational change, role ambiguity, and locus of control, were supported. A hypothesis regarding role conflict as an antecedent was not supported. As predicted, job insecurity was related to such

We thank Mary Anne Lahey for her comments on an earlier version of this manuscript and Mark Urban and Marie Waung for their help with data processing and analysis.

outcomes as intentions to quit, organizational commitment, trust in the organization, and job satisfaction. Contrary to expectations, however, perceptions of insecurity were found to be unrelated to number of somatic complaints or to supervisory ratings of job performance.

The finding of Ashford et al. (1989) that job insecurity is not related to individual health is inconsistent with other on-going research on job security. Using a multidimensional measure of job security (Lahey, 1984; Lahey & Kuhnert, 1988), Kuhnert, Sims, and Lahey (1989) found that, for a sample of 201 employees in two manufacturing firms, job insecurity was significantly related to increased symptoms of ill health as measured by the SCL-90 (Derogatis, Lipman, & Covi, 1973), a self-report clinical rating scale. Specifically, perceptions of job insecurity were related to increased depression, interpersonal sensitivity (difficulties in interpersonal relationships), and somatic complaints. Another study by Kuhnert and Palmer (1991) using a sample of state government employees found that workers' perceptions of job insecurity contributed additional unique variance to employee health beyond that explained by such intrinsic and extrinsic job factors as job challenge, intrinsic motivation, job involvement, extrinsic job aspects, and pay satisfaction.

Thus, contrary to the Ashford et al. (1989) findings, perceptions of job insecurity have been found in other contexts to adversely affect employee health and adjustment. As the extensive literature on stress and the health of workers attests (e.g., Bhagat, 1983; Cooper & Marshall, 1976; Cooper & Payne, 1988; Hendrix, Ovalle, & Troxler, 1985; Karasek, 1990; Roskies & Louis-Guerin, 1990), physical and psychological health problems of workers directly cost employers billions of dollars each year. These costs are seen directly in employee health insurance as well as indirectly in absenteeism and reduced quantity and quality of performance. Contradictions in findings, as well as the potential for detrimental effects on employees and employers, make the relation between job security and worker adjustment a topic in need of further research.

One explanation for the inconsistencies in the relations between job security and employee health outcomes may lie in the role of individual difference and situational moderator variables (cf. Quinn, 1972). We investigated two moderators proposed by Greenhalgh and Rosenblatt (1984)—occupational mobility and work orientation. Occupational mobility was operationalized in two ways. First, it was defined as the perceived likelihood of finding a comparable job in another firm or the ease with which the employee could find a similar job if a layoff occurred. This concept was termed *employment security*. Second, occupational mobility was operationalized as employee age. In spite of the illegality of age discrimination, older employees were expected to feel that their ability to change jobs would be diminished as compared with younger employees. Work orientation was operationalized as organizational commitment.

Based on Greenhalgh and Rosenblatt's (1984) discussion of dependence on one's present job for economic security, it was expected that employees who perceived limited occupational mobility (either in the form of decreased employment security or as older age) would have more severe reactions to the threat of job loss than those who have perceived mobility. Similarly, it was expected that employees with strong work orientation (in the form of organization commitment) would be more threatened at the prospect of having to leave their job. To examine these aspects of the Greenhalgh and Rosenblatt model, we tested three specific hypotheses:

Hypothesis 1. Job and employment security interact in their effects on psychological well-being and adjustment in the following manner. Employees who report high employment security would report themselves as having few adjustment problems regardless of perceived amount of job security; however, those who report low employment security would report fewer adjustment problems if they perceived themselves as high in job security and more adjustment problems if they perceived themselves as low in job security.

Hypothesis 2. Job security and age interact to affect adjustment. It was expected that younger employees would report less severe adjustment reactions to the threat of job loss than would older workers regardless of their levels of job security, whereas older employees who felt job insecurity would report more adjustment problems than would older workers whose jobs were not threatened. This hypothesis stems from Greenhalgh and Rosenblatt's (1984) discussion of economic security as well as occupational mobility as moderators of the job security–outcome relation. Our assumption was that older workers would tend to have more invested in their present job due to family obligations, pensions, and so on, as well as fewer options on the job market, and therefore would react more negatively to the threat of job loss than would younger workers. Similarly, we expected blue-collar workers to report more adjustment problems than white-collar workers because blue-collar workers have less occupational mobility.

Hypothesis 3. This hypothesis was derived from the Greenhalgh and Rosenblatt (1984) proposition that work orientation moderates the job security–outcome relation. Individuals for whom the work situation is more important should show stronger adverse reactions to threats to security. This hypothesis was tested using both job security (Hypothesis 3a) and employment security (Hypothesis 3b) as the security construct. In the latter, it was expected that job security and organizational commitment would interact to affect psychological well-being and adjustment in a manner so that employees who felt insecure in their present jobs and who were committed to the organization would report more adjustment problems than would employees who felt insecure and who were less committed; employees who felt secure would report fewer adjustment problems regardless of degree of commitment to the organization. Conversely, Hypothesis 3b predicted that employment security and organizational commitment would interact to affect psychological well-being and adjustment so that employees low in employment security (who believed that they would have a difficult time finding employment elsewhere) and who were *not* committed to their present employer would report more adjustment problems than would employees with low commitment who were confident of their ability to find another job or than would employees with high commitment.

Method

Setting and Sample

Data were gathered by questionnaire from a stratified random sample of employees of a large union-free midwestern manufacturing organization (about 1,000 employees) that produces products for materials removal applications (e.g., grinding, polishing, drilling). Sales in the 3-year period from 1984 to 1986 did not meet expectations, resulting in substantial cutbacks in the workforce. Senior management of the firm were also replaced during this time period, and the new management team adopted a radically different approach to running the business. Their efforts were quite successful; sales increased during 1987 and 1988. Data were collected in the summer of 1988.

Surveys were sent through company mail to a stratified random sample of 430 employees (about 43% of the total). Stratification was on the basis of broad job categories, including exempt, technical and clerical, and production and maintenance workers. Surveys were returned in sealed envelopes by company mail to a mail slot reserved for the study. Usable surveys were returned by 262 employees (61%).

Table 1 summarizes relevant demographic information about respondents. Data are reported separately for the total sample and for blue-collar ($n = 151$) and white-collar ($n = 66$) subsamples, although hypotheses were not explicitly formulated in

Table 1. Descriptive Statistics for Study Variables

Variable	Alpha	Total sample M	SD	Blue-collar M	SD	White-collar M	SD
Demographics							
Age[a]		3.76	1.00	3.81	0.93	3.63	1.06
Tenure[b]		2.96	1.05	2.77	1.05	3.29	1.02
Education[c]		2.80	0.91	2.54	0.76	3.42	0.98
Number of layoffs		1.32	1.71	1.62	1.74	0.38	0.78
Attitudes toward work							
Employment security[d]	.80	2.97	0.72	2.88	0.67	3.26	0.76
Job security[d]	.81	3.51	0.57	3.53	0.55	3.55	0.59
Organization commitment[e]	.81	5.70	0.90	5.69	0.95	5.80	0.83
Adjustment							
Somatization	.81	1.24	0.30	1.25	0.30	1.21	0.27
Depression	.87	1.36	0.40	1.37	0.42	1.31	0.37
Anxiety	.82	1.24	0.31	1.24	0.31	1.21	0.32
Anger/hostility	.78	1.27	0.39	1.27	0.39	1.23	0.32
Obsessive–compulsive	.77	1.42	0.36	1.45	0.38	1.37	1.29
Interpersonal sensitivity	.77	1.36	0.40	1.40	0.41	1.29	0.32

Note. Total sample, $n = 262$; blue-collar subsample, $n = 151$; white-collar subsample, $n = 66$.
[a]$3 = 30–39$ year-old age range.   [b]Tenure: $2 = 1–5$ years tenure; $3 = 6–10$ years tenure.   [c]Education: $2 =$ high school graduate; $3 =$ some college.   [d]5-point scale: $1 =$ very insecure; $5 =$ very secure.   [e]7-point scale: $1 =$ not committed; $7 =$ highly committed.   [f]4-point scale: $1 =$ no symptoms; $4 =$ extreme symptoms.

terms of these subgroups.[1] Eighty-six percent of the participants were men, and 84% were married. On average, respondents were in their late 30s, had worked for the company for about 5 years, and had experienced job layoff an average of 1.3 times during their working lives. Blue-collar employees tended to be somewhat older than did white-collar employees, although the difference was not significant. White-collar employees, however, tended to have longer tenure in the organization, $t(215) = 3.37, p < .001$; to be better educated, $t(215) = 7.16, p < .001$; and to have experienced substantially fewer job layoffs than did blue-collar workers, $t(213) = 5.47, p < .001$.

Instruments

Attitudes toward work. Perceived job security was assessed using the 12-item job permanence subscale of the Job Security Survey (Lahey & Kuhnert, 1988). The subscale measures employees' beliefs that they could keep their present jobs indefinitely. Employment security was measured by six items developed for use in this study. These items assess whether employees believed that they could easily get comparable jobs elsewhere in the event of loss of their present jobs. A 5-point agree–disagree response scale was used for both job and employment security, with higher values representing greater security. Organizational commitment was assessed by a 9-item scale described by Cook, Hepworth, Wall, and Warr (1981).

Adjustment. Psychological adjustment was measured by the SCL-90, a 9-dimension self-report symptom checklist produced by Derogatis et al. (1973). Six SCL-90 dimensions were used: psychological depression, anxiety, anger–hostility, interpersonal sensitivity, obsessive–compulsive tendencies, and somatization (the latter being physical symptoms such as headaches, other aches and pains, numbness or weakness). A 4-point response scale asked participants to indicate how much they were bothered by each complaint (1 = not at all, 4 = extremely). Thus, higher scores indicate greater maladjustment.

Analyses

The three hypotheses were tested by means of hierarchical moderated regression analyses (Cohen & Cohen, 1983). In the first step, adjustment scores were regressed on the two predictors specified by the hypothesis; the product of the two predictors was entered as the second step. Significance of the regression coefficients associated with the product terms indicated support for the interaction predictions, provided that they took the expected form.

---

[1]Forty-five respondents were not classified because of unique job titles or missing demographic information.

Results

Table 1 summarizes the means, standard deviations, and internal consistency reliabilities (Cronbach, 1951) for summated variables for the total sample and for the blue- and white-collar subsamples. ("Other" respondents were included in the total sample but not in subsample analyses.) Internal consistency reliabilities for summated variables were acceptably high.

Inspection of means and standard deviations revealed that, on average, employees reported themselves to be secure in their jobs and committed to the organization. The mean scores for job security were somewhat above the midpoint of the scale for both blue-collar and white-collar groups. The mean score on employment security was just below the scale midpoint for blue-collar workers and above the midpoint for white-collar workers. Tests of differences between these groups revealed a significant difference only for employment security, $t(215) = 3.73, p < .001$.

Psychological adjustment as measured by self-reports of adverse symptoms on the SCL-90 indicated a relatively well-adjusted workforce. All of these distributions were positively skewed, with relatively few employees reporting serious adjustment problems and no significant differences between blue-collar and white-collar subsamples. The highest occurrence of reported symptoms was for obsessive–compulsive tendencies; however, these scores were still comparatively low. Nevertheless, there was substantial variability in the adjustment scale scores, with standard deviations ranging from .27 to .42.

Table 2. Intercorrelations of Study Variables

| | Security | | | | | |
| | Total sample | | Blue-collar | | White-collar | |
	Job	Employment	Job	Employment	Job	Employment
Attitudes toward work						
Employment security	.11*		.01		.32**	
Organization commitment	.51**	− .08	.44**	− .16*	.58**	− .03
Adjustment						
Somatization	.18**	− .16**	− .17**	− .10	− .20	− .13
Depression	− .31**	− .11*	− .33**	− .11	− .35**	− .12
Anxiety	− .25**	− .13**	− .22**	− .12	− .39**	− .13
Anger/hostility	− .17**	− .15**	− .21**	− .21**	− .07	− .09
Obsessive–compulsive	− .31**	− .03	− .32**	− .07	− .33**	− .07
Interpersonal sensitivity	− .23**	− .05	− .19**	− .01	− .37**	− .15
Demographics						
Age	.25*	− .29**	.28**	− .21**	.14	− .38**
Tenure	.16**	− .11*	.19**	− .11	.06	− .31**
Education	− .10*	.24**	− .06	.14*	− .16	.06
Number of layoffs	− .03	− .15**	− .12	− .09	.14	− .10

$*p < .10.$ $**p < .05.$

Table 3. Proportions of Variance Associated With Significant Interaction Terms in Moderated Regression

	R^2		
	Total sample	Blue-collar	White-collar
Hypothesis 1:			
Job Security × Employment Security			
Depression	1.4%*	1.5%*	ns
Anxiety	ns	1.9%**	ns
Hypothesis 2:			
Job Security × Age			
Somatization	ns	1.8%*	ns
Anxiety	ns	4.2%**	ns
Anger/hostility	ns	1.8%*	ns
Interpersonal sensitivity	ns	ns	3.6%*
Hypothesis 3a:			
Job Security × Commitment			
Obsessive–compulsiveness	ns	ns	5.8%**
Hypothesis 3a:			
Employment Security × Commitment			
Depression	ns	3.9%**	ns
Anxiety	ns	3.5%**	ns
Anger/hostility	ns	2.9%**	ns
Obsessive–compulsiveness	ns	3.5%**	ns
Interpersonal sensitivity	ns	3.6%**	ns

*$p < .10.$ **$p < .05.$

Table 2 shows the correlations among job security, employment security, and the adjustment measures. Several points are noteworthy. First, job and employment security were significantly and positively correlated only for white-collar employees. Second, job security correlated positively with organizational commitment for all employees, whereas employment security did not. Third, job security showed a stronger relation to adjustment than did employment security. Job security was significantly and negatively correlated with all adjustment variables for the total sample and for the blue-collar subsample. For the white-collar subsample, 4 of 6 of the adjustment variables showed similar correlation. In other words, employees who believed their jobs to be more secure reported better adjustment (lower scores) than did those who perceived job insecurity.

The relation between job and employment security and biodemographic measures is also shown in Table 2. In the total sample, job security was significantly correlated with age and with tenure; older and longer term employees reported greater job security. Employment security was negatively correlated with age and number of layoffs in the total sample but positively correlated with education. Consistent with the premise of Hypothesis 2, younger employees reported greater perceptions of job mobility (employment security) than did older employees.

In the blue-collar subsample, job security was significantly related to age and

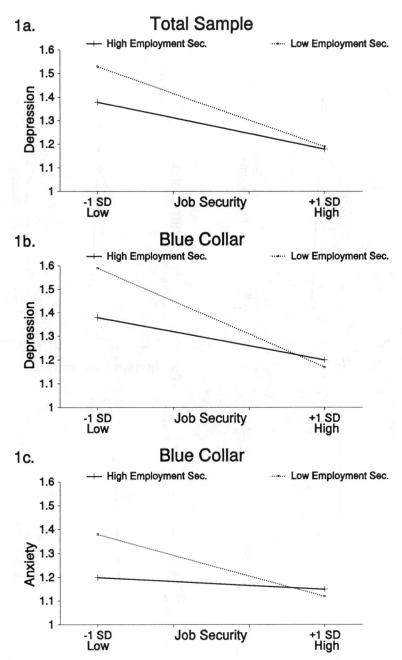

Figure 1.   Interaction of job and employment security on employee adjustment.

tenure; workers who were older or who had longer job tenure reported greater job security than did younger or less tenured employees. Neither age nor tenure was significantly correlated with job security in the white-collar sample. Employment security was significantly and negatively correlated with age in both subsamples and with tenure in the white-collar subsample.

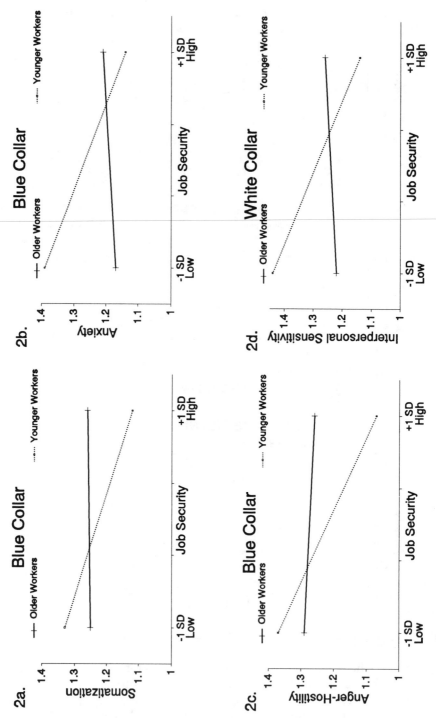

Figure 2.   Interaction of job security and age on employee adjustment.

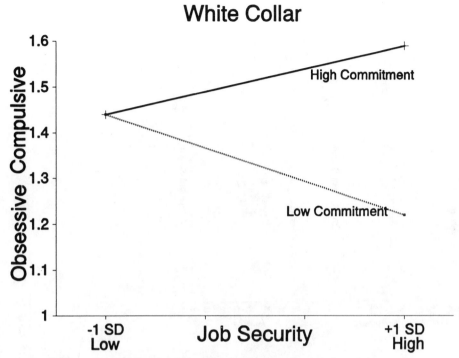

Figure 3.   Interaction of job security and organizational commitment.

Table 3 summarizes the results of the moderated regression analyses used to test the three hypotheses described above. Because the hypotheses were stated in terms of significant interactions, the table shows the percentage of variance and significance levels for all significant interaction terms.

Hypothesis 1

The prediction that job and employment security would interact in their effects on adjustment received some support. For the total sample, the interaction was significant only for the measure of depression; in the blue-collar subsample, the interaction was significant for depression and anxiety. Interactions between job and employment security did not affect adjustment for white-collar employees. The forms of the interactions were generally as expected (see Figures 1a, 1b, 1c). That is, employees who felt secure in their jobs reported fewer adjustment problems regardless of perceived employment security, whereas those who felt job insecurity reported more adjustment problems, particularly if they also felt employment insecurity.

Hypothesis 2

This prediction stated that perceptions of job security should interact with employee age to affect adjustment so that older employees who feel insecure would report

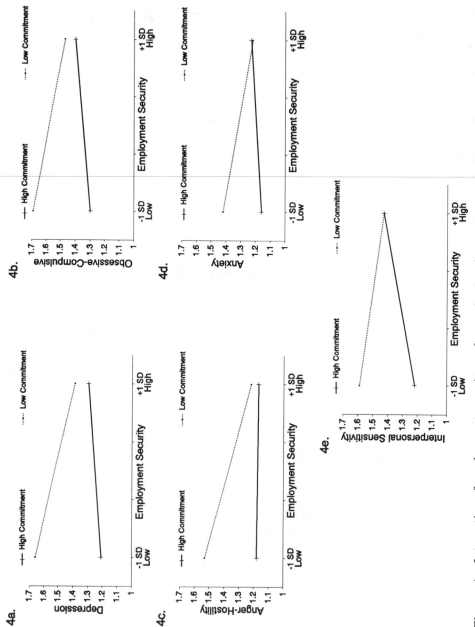

Figure 4. Interaction of employment security and organizational commitment for blue-collar employees.

more adverse reactions than would older employees who feel secure or would younger employees. Table 3 shows that for blue-collar employees, the Job Security × Age interaction was significant for the dimensions of somatization, anxiety, and anger/hostility. For white-collar employees, the interaction was significant for the dimension of interpersonal sensitivity. Figure 2 shows the forms of these interactions, which were opposite to predicted. Older employees were equally well adjusted regardless of perceived threats to job security. Younger employees who felt their job security was threatened reported greater adjustment problems that did younger employees who felt secure in their jobs.

Hypothesis 3

Hypothesis 3a predicted that job security and organizational commitment would interact so that employees higher in commitment would react more strongly to feelings of job insecurity than would employees lower in commitment. As indicated in Table 3, no support was obtained for this hypothesis for blue-collar employees. For white-collar employees, the hypothesis was partially supported. Consistent with our expectations, highly committed employees who felt that their job security was threatened reported more obsessive–compulsive symptoms than did committed employees who felt job security. Employees with low levels of organizational commitment, however, showed a pattern opposite to that expected (see Figure 3). Lower commitment employees reporting the highest levels of job security were highest on the obsessive–compulsive dimension, whereas lower commitment employees reporting low job security were lower on obsessive–compulsiveness.

Hypothesis 3b predicted that employment security and organizational commitment would interact so that employees lower in commitment and lower in employment security would report more adjustment problems than would employees higher in commitment or higher in employment security. This hypothesis was supported for blue-collar employees on five of the six adjustment dimensions: anxiety, depression, anger/hostility, obsessive–compulsiveness, and interpersonal sensitivity. As shown in Figure 4, the interactions took the expected form. Employees with low commitment to their present organization who felt that it would be difficult to get a comparable job elsewhere were more distressed than were low commitment employees who felt employment security or were high in commitment.

Discussion

The results of this study provide support for Greenhalgh and Rosenblatt's (1984) model of job insecurity by substantiating the relation between perceived job security and employees' reactions. Although the direction of the results were not always consistent with the proposed hypotheses, these data do demonstrate a moderating effect of occupational mobility and work orientation. It is clear, however, that the relation between job security and health is complex and that a clear understanding of the nature of the relation may have to await the inclusion of a broader range of moderating variables and influences as well as study of other populations.

This study extends the Greenhalgh and Rosenblatt (1984) model by corroborating other research that includes employee health outcomes among reactions to job insecurity. Although they do not specifically reference psychological and physical health in their model, Greenhalgh and Rosenblatt do note that "workers ... psychologically withdraw from ... the job" in anticipation of job loss and that the anticipation of job loss can produce the same reactions as can anticipated death. The growing literature on stress also suggests that employees confronted with a stressful environment will suffer from a variety of health-related problems (Frese, 1989; Karasek & Theorell, 1990; Winefield, Winefield, Tiggemann, & Goldney, 1991).

Although this study specifically tested two moderators proposed by Greenhalgh and Rosenblatt (1984), it appears that job type is also an important determinant of the relation between job security and employee health. In both the univariate and the multivariate analyses presented here, the patterns of relations were different for blue-collar and white-collar workers. Although the workers did not differ in their reported levels of job security, the correlation between job security and employment security was much higher for white-collar workers, relations between job security and demographic characteristics were significant only for blue-collar workers, and the pattern of correlations between job security and adjustment scores was different for the two subsamples. Also noteworthy is the fact that many of the hypothesized interactions were clearly different for the two groups of workers.

A striking example of these differences was found in the test of Hypothesis 3. Hypothesis 3a examined the relation among job security, organizational commitment, and employee health. In light of past research findings (e.g., Reichers, 1985), we had expected that employees higher in commitment would react more strongly to feelings of job insecurity than would lower commitment employees. The rationale was that the more committed the worker, the greater were the perceived stakes associated with losing one's job. This prediction did not hold true for blue-collar workers. On one of the adjustment dimensions, white-collar workers demonstrated a different pattern: Although highly committed but insecure workers did report more symptoms than did highly committed secure workers, the greatest obsessive–compulsiveness was reported by low commitment workers who were secure in their jobs. One possible explanation is that employees were disturbed by the organization's apparent commitment to them, expressed by high job security, which they failed to reciprocate (they were low in commitment). It is not clear why this concern would be expressed in terms of thought disturbances (the hallmark of obsessive–compulsiveness), however, and complete explanation awaits further study.

Hypothesis 3b predicted that those individuals low in employment security and low in organizational commitment would experience the greatest adjustment problems. In fact, for blue-collar workers, this result was found for five of six adjustment dimensions. No significant results were found for white-collar workers.

These results on the whole suggest that reactions to job-related stress may differ for blue-collar and white-collar workers. Job-type differences may partially account for the seemingly discrepant findings of past research as well. Previous research studies that demonstrated a job insecurity–adjustment relation (e.g., Fisher, 1985; Kornhauser, 1965; Kuhnert et al., 1989; Kuhnert & Palmer, 1991; Strange,

1977) were based on samples composed primarily (although not exclusively) of blue-collar or lower level employees. Ashford et al. (1989) collected data from a variety of workers including auditors, nurses, students, and industrial hygienists and did not examine potential differences among these samples. The results of our research suggest that more attention should be given to the differences between blue-collar and white-collar samples when examining the construct of job security. It may be that differences between blue-collar and white-collar workers in their explicit or implicit employment contracts with employers can account for the differences in results found in this study.

Another surprising finding from this study was the moderating effect of age on the relation between job security and adjustment. It was predicted that older employees would perceive themselves as having less occupational mobility than would younger employees and therefore would react more negatively to threats to their current jobs. In fact, older employees did report that they would be less likely than their younger counterparts to find a similar job elsewhere; however, they reported fewer adverse symptoms than did younger employees who were job insecure. In other words, older employees seemed to be much more resilient to the stress of job insecurity than did their younger counterparts. A few researchers such as Rhodes (1983) and Pond and Geyer (1987) have noted that the values, needs, and expectations of employees change as they traverse different developmental stages in their lives and careers. If employees in different career stages differ with respect to values, needs, and expectations, it is likely that they value job security and occupational mobility differently. Obviously, the present results provide a challenge for future research in the area.

It should be noted that the actual levels of job insecurity and the degree of physical and psychological distress reported by employees were quite low; employees were generally healthy and felt secure in their current jobs. Even though the amount of variability available in the measures was modest, some of the expected relations between security and adjustment surfaced. If such relations are evident in relatively secure environments, negative reactions in more acutely distressed organizations may be even more severe. It is also important to note that causality cannot be determined from correlational data such as these. However, the security to adjustment directional interpretation is consistent with theory, and interactions such as those found between job and employment security would be difficult to explain if one assumed that adjustment problems cause perceptions of insecurity, rather than the other way around. If maladjustment causes perceptions of insecurity, one would expect maladjusted employees to report high levels of both job and employment insecurity. This was not the case here.

It is clear from these results, however, that further research is needed in organizations facing greater risk and that longitudinal research on the duration and causality of the effects is needed. In addition, future research would benefit from linking job security to more general models of stress and coping, such as models for occupational mental health promotion and distress prevention outlined in this volume. In particular, the relations between job security and other work-related constructs need further clarification if we are to fully understand job security's role within the organization and in peoples' mental health and well-being.

References

Ashford, S. J., Lee, C., & Bobko, P. (1989). Content, causes, and consequences of job insecurity: A theory-based measure and substantive test. *Academy of Management Journal, 32*, 803–829.

Bhagat, R. S. (1983). Effects of stressful life events on individual performance effectiveness and work adjustment processes within organizational settings: A research model. *Academy of Management Review, 8*, 660–671.

Cameron, K. S., Sutton, R. I., & Whetten, D. A. (Eds.). (1988). *Readings in organizational decline.* Cambridge, MA: Ballinger.

Cohen, J., & Cohen, P. (1983). *Applied multiple regression/correlation analysis for the behavioral sciences.* New York: Wiley.

Cook, J. D., Hepworth, S. J., Wall, T. D., & Warr, P. B. (1981). *The experience of work: A compendium and review of 249 measures and their use.* San Diego, CA: Academic Press.

Cooper, C. L., & Marshall, J. (1976). Occupational sources of stress: A review of the literature relating to coronary heart disease and mental ill health. *Journal of Occupational Psychology, 49*, 11–28.

Cooper, C. L., & Payne, R. (1988). *Causes, coping and consequences of stress at work.* New York: Wiley.

Cronbach, L. J. (1951). Coefficient alpha and the internal structure of tests. *Psychometrica, 16*, 297–334.

Derogatis, L. R., Lipman, R. S., & Covi, L. (1973). SCL-90: An outpatient psychiatric rating scale—Preliminary report. *Psychopharmacological Bulletin, 9*, 13–28.

Fisher, S. (1985). Control and blue collar work. In C. Cooper & J. Smith (Eds.), *Job stress and blue collar work* (pp. 19–48). New York: Wiley.

Frese, M. (1989). Theoretical models of control and health. In S. Sauter, J. Hurrell, & C. Cooper (Eds.), *Job control and worker health* (pp. 107–128). New York: Wiley.

Greenhalgh, L., & Rosenblatt, Z. (1984). Job insecurity: Toward conceptual clarity. *Academy of Management Review, 9*, 438–448.

Hendrix, W. H., Ovalle, N. K., & Troxler, G. R. (1985). Behavioral and physiological consequences of stress and its antecedent factors. *Journal of Applied Psychology, 70*, 188–201.

Karasek, R. J. (1990). Lower health risk with increased job control among white collar workers. *Journal of Organizational Behaviour, 11*, 171–185.

Karasek, R., & Theorell, T. (1990). *Healthy work: Stress, productivity and the reconstruction of working life.* New York: Basic Books.

Kornhauser, A. (1965). *Mental health of the industrial worker.* New York: Wiley.

Kuhnert, K. W., & Palmer, D. (1991). Job security, health, and the intrinsic and extrinsic characteristics of work. *Group and Organizational Studies, 16*, 178–192.

Kuhnert, K. W., Sims, R. R., & Lahey, M. A. (1989). The relationship between job security and employee health. *Group and Organizational Studies, 14*, 399–410.

Lahey, M. A. (1984). *Job security: Its meaning and measure.* Unpublished doctoral dissertation, Kansas State University, Manhattan.

Lahey, M. A., & Kuhnert, K. W. (1988). The meaning and measure of job security. In R. Sims (Chair), *Technological innovation and its impact on today's employees.* Symposium conducted at the National Meeting of Operations Research Society of America/The Institute for Management Science, Washington, DC.

Pond, S. B., & Geyer, P. D. (1987). Employee age as a moderator of the relation between perceived work alternatives and job satisfaction. *Journal of Applied Psychology, 72*, 552–557.

Quinn, R. P. (1972). *Locking-in as a moderator of the relationship between job satisfaction and mental health.* Ann Arbor: University of Michigan, Institute for Social Research.

Reichers, A. E. (1985). A review and conceptualization of organizational commitment. *Academy of Management Review, 10*, 465–476.

Rhodes, S. R. (1983). Age-related differences in work attitudes and behavior: A review and conceptual analysis. *Psychological Bulletin, 93*, 328–367.

Roskies, E., & Louis-Guerin, C. (1990). Job insecurity in managers: Antecedents and consequences. *Journal of Oranizational Behavior, 11*, 345–359.

Strange, W. G. (1977). *Job loss: A psychological study of worker relations to a plant closing in a company town in Southern Appalachia.* Unpublished doctoral dissertation, Cornell University, Ithaca, NY.

Whetten, D. A. (1980). Sources, responses, and efforts to organizational decline. In J. R. Kimberly, R. H. Miles, & Associates (Eds.), *The organizational life cycle* (pp. 342–374). San Francisco: Jossey-Bass.

Winefield, A. H., Winefield, H. R., Tiggemann, M., & Goldney, R. D. (1991). A longitudinal study of the psychological effects of unemployment and unsatisfactory employment on young adults. *Journal of Applied Psychology, 76*, 424–431.

5

David M. Corey and Gordon D. Wolf

An Integrated Approach to Reducing Stress Injuries

Reflecting an awareness that psychological health issues in the workplace "are approaching crisis proportion" (Ilgen, 1990, p. 282), researchers have focused increasing attention on the impact of work on workers (Cooper & Payne, 1978, 1980; Keita & Jones, 1990; Shipley, 1987). This has occurred for several reasons that are succinctly summarized by Levi (1990): (a) a humanistic–idealistic desire for a good society and a good working life; (b) a drive for health and well-being; (c) a belief in worker participation, influence, and control at the individual level; and (d) economic interest in competitiveness and profits of business organizations and the economic system. All of these reasons represent legitimate motives underlying scientific and applied efforts in the new and expanding field of "occupational health psychology" (Raymond, Wood, & Patrick, 1990), and all of these reasons lay at the heart of a comprehensive intervention we describe in this chapter.

Perhaps the most significant reason for our efforts in this area has been the desire to reduce stress-related injuries among workers and thereby promote economic, health, and humanistic-idealistic interests. Employment can be a rich source of personal assets, contributing to psychological well-being (Baruch & Barnett 1987), socioeconomic improvement, and physical health (Repetti, Matthews, & Waldron, 1989). Stress injuries also can be expensive and capable of producing devastating costs both for the injured person and for the constituents that must carry the financial burden for those injuries.[1] This fact has led Sauter, Murphy, and Hurrell (1990) to conclude that "data on workers' compensation provide a particularly striking indicator of the magnitude of psychological disorders as an occupational health issue" (p. 1148).

The California Worker's Compensation Institute (CWCI, 1990) reported that during the 10-year period between 1979 and 1988, the frequency of mental stress claims for every 1,000 covered workers in California increased 540% whereas the incidence of all disabling injuries declined 8%. The highest incidence of stress claims originated from public sector employees (e.g., law enforcement personnel, firefighters, teachers, and other employees of state and local government). In 1986, there were 1.7 stress claims filed for every 1,000 public sector employees, nearly six times the frequency for employees in the private sector. The total cost of stress

---

[1]Our references to *stress injuries* are intended to include a broad range of psychological and physiological disorders that may also properly be referred to as *stress illnesses*.

claims in California was $263 million in 1985 and $383 million in 1987. For stress-disability retirements of firefighters, police officers, and deputy sheriffs—who benefit from a state law that provides substantially more generous compensation for public safety officers—estimates of stress-related retirements range from $350,000 to $2.7 million per claim (Corey 1988). In short, "mental stress claims are a significant—and growing—segment of the California's worker's compensation program" (CWCI, 1990, p. 6).

Levi (1990) has pointed out that the list of 10 leading work-related diseases or injuries published by the National Institute for Occupational Safety and Health (NIOSH, 1988) reflected health outcomes that "are not only stress-related but are also of human origin and are thereby preventable in the sense that their etiology, pathogenesis, course, treatment, and prevention depend heavily on human action, reaction, and lack of reaction" (p. 1142). Attempts to intervene in this occupational health issue have consisted largely of efforts both clinical (i.e., interventions that focus on individual change, including prevention and treatment) and organizational (i.e., interventions that target group change within the workplace). Despite mounting indications that both clinical and organizational efforts are useful, and possibly necessary, to produce substantive improvements in long-term measures of occupational health and performance, we have found no evidence in the literature that these efforts have been integrated in any coherent and systematic way to produce a measurable impact on stress injuries.

Numerous authors (e.g., Ilgen, 1990; Keita & Jones, 1990; Levi, 1990; Sauter et al., 1990) recently have urged the blending of approaches traditionally used in clinical and organizational psychology. Virgil (1986) has suggested that organizational development (OD) and employee assistance programs (EAPs) are complementary services with the same goals, which include the retention of valuable employees and the improvement of productivity and profit. Virgil has encouraged OD and EAP providers to work cooperatively in a "holistic approach" (p. 35) to problem solving in client organizations.

Argyris (1958) offered an early analysis of "the psychological health of organizations," attributing such traditional organizational concerns as reduced growth and union grievances to failures of employees "to grow, develop, and feel an inner sense of worth" (p. 107). Here, Argyris understood organizational factors to be capable of influence by clinical approaches.

Similarly, in 1983 a journal devoted to exploring "new directions for mental health services" explicated the role of the "occupational psychiatrist" (McLean, 1983) and the "occupational clinical psychologist" (Manuso, 1983). These two clinical roles were urged by their proponents to adopt organizational perspectives and to attend to corporate needs that extend far beyond the usual clinical concerns related to employee health and adjustment.

Hall (1986) reasoned in his work on stress among Australian executives that efforts to achieve greater perceived autonomy, reduced work hours, and other desirable changes in organizational practice could have direct effects on executives' health and, by extension, on the health of subordinate workers. He focused his attention, in large part, on the "feelings" of managers. Here was an example of classic organizational interventions being proposed as a means of producing results that heretofore had been the primary domain of clinicians.

Organizational development specialists, expounding on the "contemporary trends" in their field in 1988, described activities in the area of instrumentation and measurement, job redesign, participation, and quality circles, as well as stress and burnout (Head & Sorensen, 1989). Golembiewski, Hilles, and Daly (1987) also detailed an organizational development effort to reduce individual job burnout and psychological distress. Like Hall (1986), these authors recognized the benefits of focusing organizational strategies on clinical targets and did not restrict their attention to only the traditional concerns of organizational consultants.

The growing concern around the costs of worker stress claims has spurred recent research that analyzes how companies with low incidences of stress claims differ from those with higher claims incidences. Shalowitz (1991) described the results of a study of factors affecting work stress injury claims by a large workers' compensation insurance carrier. She reported that its research showed that "stress-related illnesses were far less likely among workers at companies with supportive work and family policies, effective management communication, health insurance coverage for mental illness and chemical dependency and an employee assistance program" (p. 3), perhaps reflecting the influence of another, primary variable: an employer's value placed on employee wellness. Although this research points to the empirical value of both organizational and clinical interventions in achieving occupational health, these respective approaches still continue to be applied largely independent of one another.

An Integrated Organizational–Clinical Approach

We have proposed elsewhere (Wolf & Corey, 1989) that a significant proportion of stress injury claims result from what we regard as a breakdown in the "mutual accommodation process" between a worker and the employing organization. The mutual accommodation process defines the normal and nonpathologic interaction between an employee and an employer (or manager/supervisor). When this interaction is healthy, both the worker and the employer support one another and make allowances for one another in an effort to reduce conflict and support the achievement of shared and respective goals. As either the worker or the employer deviates far from established patterns of mutual accommodation, the relationship between the two parties becomes pathogenic and serves to alienate the two from their shared interests. The resulting alienation is expressed in stress claims, consumer complaints of poor service, various forms of employee theft, overusage of the medical system because of tension-related complaints, and other analogues of worker–employer estrangement.

There are three components to the mutual accommodation process: (a) the individuals (including both the supervisor's and the worker's skills, behaviors, personalities, aptitudes, etc.), (b) the relationship between the individuals, and (c) the environment or context in which they both work (including the actual job that each performs, the structure or hierarchy of power, the culture of the organization, and the systems for supporting both worker and manager). We assert that it is in the management of the mutual accommodation process—and its three components— that occupational health is nurtured or impeded. Martin (1987) similarly categorized interventions into personal strategies attempting to change the individual, interpersonal strategies aimed at changing the relationships between individuals, and external strategies for affecting the environmental or organizational situation.

Attention to each of these three components can take the form of clinical or organizational activities, or both. Organizational efforts can be used to change individual behavior and relationships, and clinical strategies can be used to effect collective changes in organizational culture and group behavior. But even when clinical and organizational approaches are both used, as Virgil (1986) suggested, the clinical services do not typically come with a particular view of how work per se is related to the presenting problems (Keita & Jones, 1990), and organizational activities often ignore (at least in practice, if not in theory) the relevance of individual problems and issues.

We describe here an integrated strategy for promoting occupational health. This approach dynamically combines clinical and organizational strategies in a way that attends carefully to the process of adjustment between the individual (worker and supervisor) and the environment and to the three components of that process. The key elements of the program include (a) development of a shared system of management that holds managers accountable for being a resource to their subordinates; (b) implementation of a proactive EAP chartered to solve problems rather than merely provide services and with open access throughout the organization; (c)

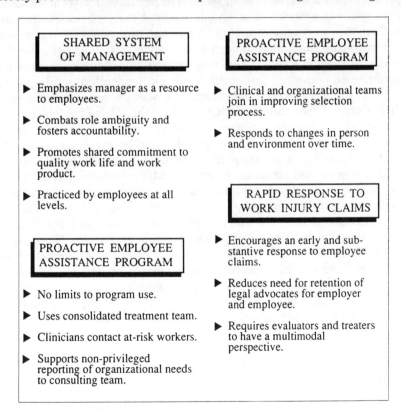

Figure 1. Key features of the four components of the integrated organizational–clinical approach to stress injury reduction.

a focus on person–environment fit in all hirings and promotions; and (d) early, aggressive responses to worker claims of job-related injuries. These program components are outlined in Figure 1 and discussed in greater detail below.

Shared System of Management

Sauter et al. (1990) identified six psychosocial risk factors that pose a threat to psychological well-being among workers: (a) work load and work pace, (b) work schedule, (c) role stressors, (d) career security factors, (e) interpersonal relations, and (f) job content. Indeed, management is traditionally responsible in most organizations for managing these risk factors in a way that enhances productivity and profit while also protecting the health of its workers. That the behavior of management in an organization has a powerful, if not direct, effect on the health of employees is not a matter of professional dispute. In recognition of this effect, we developed a model or system of management that managers in any organization, public or private, could collectively endorse and practice and that would serve to promote employee productivity and reduce psychosocial risk factors. Key features of this element of the integrated approach are summarized in Figure 1.

The need for such a shared system seemed important for several reasons. First, existing management systems (e.g., management by objectives, management by results, performance management, etc.) lacked the philosophical foundations necessary for stimulating fundamental cognitive change as well as behavioral change among managers. Second, each system emphasized a particular aspect of management behavior (e.g., planning, targeting, feedback, leadership) while giving short shrift to other key behaviors. The management model we developed (Corey & Wolf, 1986; Wolf & Corey, 1988), called MBR,[2] accomplishes these two objectives by establishing and reinforcing the primary role of the manager as a resource to the employees in carrying out their respective roles and by giving equal emphasis to the full range of functions a manager must fulfill (i.e., planning, role clarity, task management, resource and obstacles management, and nondelegated tasks).

Each aspect of a manager's training in this system incorporates relevant literature on the relation between job design and occupational health. For example, research evidence suggesting that factors of worker control and participation significantly affect worker health (e.g., Spector, 1986) is used in the MBR training. In addition, such knowledge is used to help managers design communication systems, feedback systems, and planning processes that optimize participation and control.

Another feature of the shared management system is the accountability component. Managers are taught the importance of, and skills in, developing role clarity for themselves and their employees based not only on evidence that supports the value of role clarity in promoting productivity but also on data that demonstrate a link between role clarity and freedom from job tension and dissatisfaction (e.g., Jackson & Schuler, 1985). The written clarification of roles—which, for managers, includes responsibility for maintaining productive and healthy relationships with

---

[2]MBR is a proprietary, trademarked name for a management system that we have developed titled "Management By Resource." The name reflects the emphasis placed on the role of management as a resource to employees.

their subordinates—is used as the basis for a formal performance appraisal system. In this way, managers are held accountable for carrying out their roles as resource or helper to the employees in addition to fulfilling the more technical aspects of their job functions. Finally, accountability is further supported through the education of all employees, including first-line workers, in the basic tenets of MBR. This provides employees with information about what to legitimately expect of their managers in terms of support and role fulfillment, as well as tools for effectively and cooperatively working with management.

The adoption of management systems that reject the traditional role of the boss (i.e., to plan, organize, implement, and measure) are cropping up elsewhere as well. We do not believe that MBR possesses a formula of practices that is intrinsically superior to other models that stress the supportive role of managers in an employee's work life. General Electric, for example, is undergoing a transformation of its management models that calls for managers to counsel groups, provide resources for them, and help them think for themselves (Stewart, 1991). Any management system that emphasizes these points, is founded on human worth and dignity, and incorporates sound principles of worker health as well as worker productivity and quality production can likely produce results similar to MBR.

Proactive Employee Assistance Program

Perhaps the most commonly used tool in American business to reduce the worksite impact of substance abuse and other personal problems is the EAP. Recent estimates suggest that between 2,500 and 8,000 EAPs are currently providing services to 12–15% of the American work force (Farcas, 1989).

Sauter et al. (1990) have listed the key organizational characteristics that EAP mental health services should offer, including joint management–labor input to program planning and administration, a formalized policy for referrals, health awareness and development programs, and access to the EAP by employees at all organizational levels. In addition, they have recommended that EAPs "should evolve to a higher state of awareness and practice, recognizing both occupational and nonoccupational factors as influential to health, and offering opportunities for both organizational and individual interventions to improve mental health" (p. 1156). They have also expressly urged that mechanisms be established for periodic feedback to the organization in ways that protect confidentiality and that help identify and resolve organizational problems.

Our approach to EAP services follows the recommendations of Sauter et al. (1990). We go beyond their recommendations, however, in two particular areas: (a) limits of program utilization and (b) provider development. Figure 1 lists the primary features of the proactive EAP component.

Inasmuch as the goal of our integrated approach is to manage the occupational psychological health of the organization's workers, we do not set arbitrary limits on the number of self-referred EAP sessions an employee can have. Instead, we are committed to helping the employee resolve the problem regardless of the number of visits needed. Certainly, the vast majority of presenting problems in an EAP are capable of being treated within the context of a brief therapy model. Others, however, require a greater investment of therapy as well as different forms of intervention (i.e., when treating chemical dependency or addiction, major depression, etc.).

Sauter et al. (1990) criticized EAPs for aiming "primarily at reducing personnel and productivity problems, alcoholism, and chemical dependency problems" (p. 1155) rather than encompassing family and community issues and organizational issues such as management style and environmental policies. We share their concern. EAPs that provide a mere basic service (i.e., a certain number of visits per employee per year) are not positioned to promote in-depth change in the workplace or in the work force. Consistent with the urging of Moriarty and Field (1990), utilizing a "proactive" approach to EAP services, in which employees who are identified as at-risk for developing adverse health conditions (as evidenced by behavior on the job or by exposure to noxious work conditions) are referred to the EAP, can promote work-force psychological health better than a passive program. The proactive EAP is an adjunct to self-referral, not a replacement for it, and can include a more active role for the EAP provider by personally contacting employees who are known to be facing a major stressor (either personal or work-related).

An illustration of this active therapeutic role is seen in the case of Anne,[3] one of our clients whose child had drowned in the swimming pool of her home. The tragedy was well-known at Anne's workplace, and her supervisor and several co-workers called the EAP to alert us to her trauma. One of the clinical psychologists called Anne at home to offer supportive counseling, which she accepted after an appropriate delay. Anne shared months later that she likely would not have sought counseling on her own, wracked as she was with guilt and self-blame, and her work performance and health both would possibly have been impaired longer by her presumably more-enduring depression, social isolation, and preoccupation.

The selection and development of EAP providers is also an integral component of our approach. We do not contract with community clinicians to provide independent services to covered workers. Rather, we employ and contract clinicians who provide services at our facility, receive our training, attend peer supervision, and work cooperatively with our collective clinical staff to ensure the highest level of care for the worker. Because our fee for the integrated services (both clinical and organizational) is a flat annual fee not based on actual utilization, the clinicians are able to use each other's skills without increasing charges to the worker or the employer.

A common setting for providing clinical services helps to assure a depth of communication about the types of problems that workers are revealing about the organization. At weekly staff development meetings, specific concerns about the employing organization are discussed by the clinicians, and the organizational psychologists are also present to receive and share nonprivileged information. The staff members discuss at these meetings what resources (e.g., information, skills, consultation, etc.) they need to help address client problems, and resources are subsequently provided on the basis of those identified needs.

During the course of a 7-month period, the Public Works Department[4] of one of our municipal clients was showing a significant increase in EAP utilization. Many of the employee/clients were complaining of management practices that were

---

[3]The details of case illustrations, although drawing on actual people and events in our practice, have been altered to protect the confidentiality of clients.

allegedly contributing to union–management grievances. In turn, some managers who were reportedly personalizing the union actions began to "make life difficult" for their subordinates by delegating tasks widely regarded as punitive reprisals. Out of a belief that additional grievances would only lead to more reprisals, the employees submitted to the assignments, only to find themselves feeling increasingly angry, vindictive, and anxious. Home life was also deteriorating for many of them; they reported increased marital conflict, insomnia, and alcohol abuse.

The EAP clinicians expected worker's compensation claims to be filed eventually. In the interim, they gained permission to share the nature of their concerns (without communicating names of employees, supervisors, or work unit) to the organizational consultants. The consultants, with their awareness raised, began to attend to the work environment of the Public Works Department, offering their resources to management—who had themselves grown weary over the relentless tension. No quick solutions, team building, or conflict mediations ensued. But over the course of the next 4 months, management did participate in a planning and problem-solving session, facilitated by one of the organizational psychologists, that led to self-identified, relevant changes in practice and structure—changes experienced by rank-and-file workers as substantive.

Focus on Person–Environment Fit

Cox (1987) has noted that occupational stress is a function both of environmental demands on a worker and of that person's perceived inability to cope with those demands. Thus, personal competency vis-à-vis a job function plays a significant role in defeating the effects of organization stress. Everly (1989) asserted that

> the key to understanding occupational stress and illness depends largely upon an appreciation for the manner in which the needs, expectations, motives, personality, and so on of an individual is matched in a positive, health-promoting manner to the job description he or she is asked to assume. (p. 298)

Clinical and organizational psychologists bring distinctly unique contributions to this aspect of the integrated approach to occupational health. Clinical psychologists, from the knowledge they gain from the EAP of the actual problems that real workers have in coping with specific aspects of their work, are able to identify salient individual traits to use in preemployment or prepromotional decisions. Likewise, organizational psychologists are able to use their expertise in assessment, test construction, and validation procedures to develop appropriate screening methods. Together, the two approaches help to promote person–environment fit through better selection. Selection procedures are designed, after all, both to identify functional or job-content skills, abilities, and aptitudes and to detect the individual traits necessary to successfully facilitate the mutual accommodation process.

Once the right employees are hired, proper orientation of those employees to the organization is important for maintenance of person–environment fit. New workers become part of the group by learning about the organizational culture (i.e., the values that are emphasized by others in the workplace). For example, some organizations prize creativity, whereas others stress sticking to established procedures to maintain process integrity. Either direction can be appropriate depending on the organization's needs. It is vital that managers develop an empirically based training program from the onset of an employee's work experience to ensure proper orientation to work expectations. It takes time for employees to understand their new roles fully and to develop the coping skills necessary to work effectively in the job and with their coworkers, and managers must guide the process to assure success.

Even the achievement of the ideal goal of zero error selection combined with effective orientation cannot ensure person–environment fit over time. Well-suited and trained employees can be faced with changes in organizational leadership, management styles, job functions, and technology that effectively undo the person–environment fit that may have been attained initially. The Independent Commission on the Los Angeles Police Department (1991), commonly known as the Christopher Commission, noted the relevance of this fact when it observed that "officers may enter the force well suited psychologically for the job, but may suffer from burnout, alcohol-related problems, cynicism, or disenchantment, all of which can result in poor control over their behavior" (p. 10). For this reason, on-going training and other interventions are needed to bolster individual deficits in coping and job-content skills and abilities. In this way, person–environment fit is maintained across time.

In our own work with police and sheriff departments, we have addressed the deleterious potential of many high-risk assignments by promoting policies that require periodic debriefing and reevaluation of at-risk personnel. Undercover narcotics officers, for example, are known to be vulnerable to the unusually stressful and life-altering influences of their work, and we meet with them at least once every 6 months to assess changes in behavioral and emotional patterns. Although this procedure alone cannot necessarily reveal the deteriorating officer who wants to avoid detection, it does offer at least a limited strategy for identifying at-risk employees. Through this procedure, some officers have been alerted to their own early signs of impairment, and many of these have sought assistance to prevent the rapid decline they have seen in other undercover officers.

One of the integrative features of our approach is the use of both the MBR and the EAP to facilitate person–environment fit. MBR training is used to help bring about changes in both the individual managers and the organization as a whole, whereas the EAP promotes individual change in the short run and more global organizational change in a collective or additive way. The EAP also helps identify person–environment fit problems that go beyond individual deficits and reflect broader problems with selection, orientation, training, job design, and supervision. Feedback from the EAP's clinical psychologists (in ways that do not violate individual rights to confidentiality) to the organizational psychologists provides the necessary information for designing needs-based interventions for the organization. We emphasize that the clinical and organizational psychologists are both considered part of the "treatment team" because the work of each is designed to support the same objectives, and the integration of their efforts is essential to achieving those objectives.

Rapid Response to Work Injury Claims

The EAP is designed, in part, to help keep workers' psychological problems from becoming compensable claims of injury or disability. Nevertheless, some employees will utilize the worker's compensation system to report an injury, gain specialized treatment, or seek financial compensation. Whether the claim is for a stress-related injury or a purely physical one, *how* the employer responds to the employee claim can significantly, if not terminally, affect the mutual accommodation process between that worker and the employer.

In our integrated approach, as Figure 1 shows, we encourage an early and aggressive approach to work injury claims. By "early," we mean that the employer's claims administrator responds to the employee's claim quickly, carrying the message that the employee—whether or not he or she is suffering a compensable injury— is important to the organization. By "aggressive," we imply that the response must be substantive (i.e., designed to produce understanding of the condition and its treatment), initiated and maintained by the employer without a need for the employee to seek legal assistance to stimulate action, and specific to the concerns of the injured worker.

Once a claim has been made, it is critical to have the case evaluated in its medical, psychological, social, cultural, and legal aspects, using providers who share this multimodal perspective of treatment (Wolf & Corey, 1989). Under this viewpoint, medical problems are caused by life style, personality, and sociocultural and organizational factors, not just by accidents, viruses, and bacteria. Organizing a team of professionals that will work with all of these aspects of the case offers an opportunity for integrated treatment and offers the best chances for an early and successful return of the worker to the workplace.

Implementation and Outcome

Despite the fact that public sector workers claim nearly six times the incidence of stress injuries compared with workers in the private sector (CWCI, 1990), most occupational health programs remain focused on white-collar workers in the private sector (Sauter et al., 1990). As psychologists who began our professional practice careers providing occupational health services (e.g., preemployment psychological screening, critical incident debriefing, management development, and confidential personal and family psychotherapy) to police departments, we found the marketing of our integrated organizational approach to other municipal organizations to be a natural extension of our work. Surprisingly, we found these public employers to be enthusiastic supporters of the underlying concepts and remarkably open to having "outsiders" inspect their operations and policies, advise them on job design issues and management practices, train their managers, and provide confidential counseling services to the entire range of workers.

We will describe below the implementation of our organizational approach in five public sector organizations (three cities, one police department, and one county sheriff's department). Each of these organizations is in Northern California. Two of the three municipal corporations have a constituent population of approximately 65,000 residents and have employees numbering nearly 450 in each of the two city organizations; the other serves a population of about 40,000 residents and has an employee work force of nearly 300. The police department is in a city of about 60,000 residents and has approximately 75 employees, and the sheriff's department serves a population of nearly 340,000 and has around 400 employees.

At the time we began these interventions, there were a total of 13 stress injury claims in all five organizations (approximately 1,675 employees), equaling a rate of 7.76 per 1,000 workers. The statewide average at that time was approximately 1.7 claims per 1,000 public sector workers (CWCI, 1990).

Implementation Strategy

Each of the four components of the integrated organizational approach described above is intended to be implemented simultaneously. The course of intervention occurs over multiple consecutive years and is meant to be a permanent, recurrent part of the organization's risk management program. Implementation in the case of the five municipal organizations that are the focus of this chapter began in 1985 for three of the employers and in 1987 for the other two; the programs continue at present.

The management training program is best initiated from the top down: Only when the chief executive (i.e., city manager, police chief, or sheriff) was demonstrably competent in the tenets of MBR and related skills were subordinate employees included in the training. The content of that training varied depending on the employees' roles and levels (e.g., executive or midmanager, supervisor, rank-and-file employee) within the organization.

In practice, we found that we were not always able to provide the training that we felt needed to be provided in the order or timing that we judged to be best. In the real world of the workplace, the experience of the work force determined what we did, when we did it, and who was involved. For example, in one instance our training plan and schedule called for teaching performance evaluation skills, but the organization's needs dictated that we postpone such training in deference to a hiring crisis. The latter required numerous hours of facilitating meetings between departmental administrators, personnel officials, and employee groups to determine the nature of the problem and to identify and evaluate solutions. The need to reduce employee overtime and related stressors (which resulted from the staffing crisis) outweighed the need to improve performance appraisals at that time. In addition, it was important to pace the introduction of new information and training given that the interventions themselves could have served to overburden the workers. As Rosen (1989) noted, "excessive, poorly managed change can make people sick" (p. 1139). Thus, although neither the process nor the actual content of our organizational interventions was identical in each of the five organizations, in all cases our focus remained on the activities needed to bring about effective change in the workplace.

Outcomes

The average utilization rate of EAPs throughout the nation is estimated to be 5.7% of the work force in any given year (Abbot, 1990). The utilization rates during the years of program implementation in the five organizations described here averaged 18.3%. This substantially higher level of utilization was the result, we believe, of provider exposure in nonthreatening and nonclinical forums (such as on-site "brown bag" sessions during lunch periods when practical lectures were given on subjects such as stress management, smoking cessation, single parenting, etc.) and of provider identity (as the employees learned about the reputation of certain clinicians by word-of-mouth and had the opportunities to select a particular therapist). In addition, employees met the therapists at their work site during particularly distressing periods following, for example, a work-related death, a shooting, or a bomb scare. Finally, the organizational psychologists' recommendation of the EAP to particular managers for specific interpersonal and personal problems also helped to promote utilization. The organizational psychologists enjoyed high visibility and credibility, and their referrals were typically met with little resistance.

In mid-1990, 3 years after initiation of the most recent program implementation among the five organizations and 5 years after the earliest, the total number of stress injury claims totaled two employees for the 12-month period preceding the count. As shown in Figure 2, this represents a postintervention rate of 1.190 claims per 1,000 workers, compared with a preintervention rate of 7.76 claims per 1,000 workers.

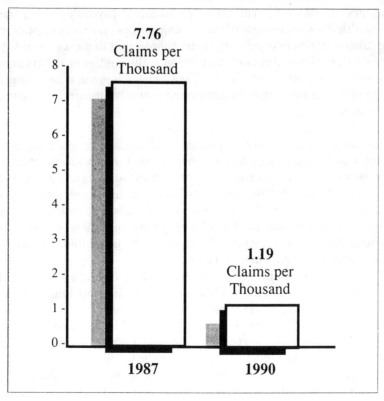

Figure 2. Proportion of stress injury claims per 1,000 reported by study subjects (municipal organizations) pre- and postintervention.

Conclusions and Implications

We believe that the integrated organizational approach we describe is effective in reducing stress injuries and improving occupational health. Certainly, other factors may also have contributed to the observed reduction in stress claims during the period of study described here. These factors might include the independent efforts of the chief executives of the respective organizations, particularly when one considers that these executives demonstrated considerable innovativeness and human concern to invite such large-scale attention to occupational health issues. They might also include changes produced by other members of the organizations who, in response to initial interventions, introduced ideas and creative solutions within their own areas of the workplace. The mere fact that workers' compensation claims were being closely looked at by the organizations may have led to greater reluctance by workers to file claims, whether spurious or not.

One cannot rule out the influence of the Hawthorne effect: Workers may feel enthusiastic and optimistic as a result of virtually any innovation that shows interest in them. Recognition of this effect makes the evaluation of any organizational intervention difficult, but the factors of change introduced into the workplace by the integrated organizational approach have tremendous face validity as well as broad support in the literature (e.g., Sauter et al., 1990).

The integrated use of clinical and organizational psychologists to improve occupational health does not come without its challenges and risks. Cooperative practice among subspecialties in psychology is neither taught in most graduate programs nor is there much real-world opportunity to learn the subtleties of this nexus. What follows are four of the most significant discoveries we made concerning this relationship. Psychologists interested in attempting a similar integrated approach would do well to take heed.

1. It is not enough merely to protect confidentiality; what *appears* to be a compromise of privilege has at least as much effect as an actual violation. For this reason, we learned to keep clinical and organizational staff roles separate: Although they cooperate and coordinate services, they must not substitute for one another or take on dual roles. Psychologists who perform EAP functions should not later be seen entering the boss's office to provide organizational consultation. The visit may be unrelated to clinical matters, but it will likely appear nefarious.

2. Clinical psychologists and organizational psychologists tend to think differently from one another. They also use a different language. Therefore, integrating their contributions, unless managed well, can be laden with professional turf battles. This risk is reduced by employing or contracting psychologists who, by virtue of their life experience or academic training, value the contributions of their counterparts.

3. As an adjunct to the point above, avoid the mistake of thinking that any one component of the intervention program is more important than another. Likewise, no single aspect of any of the components should be viewed as cardinal to the program's success. The utility of the integrated approach

comes, we believe, from its flexibility, responsiveness, and its absence of orthodoxy. Once it becomes inviolate, it becomes impotent.

4. Process consultation (Schein, 1987) is a valuable framework for working in organizations, whether as a clinician or as an organizational consultant. Moreover, because the process consultation model "lies in how the consultant structures the relationship, not in what the client does" (p. 29), it is especially useful as a tool for integrating the approaches of disparate subspecialties. The key benefit of Schein's model, as he explains it, is that the client owns the problem and continues to own the problem throughout the consultation process. Whenever this perspective is lost or confused, organizational change is no longer a viable objective for the psychologist, whatever his or her specialty.

Time will tell if the blending of organizational and clinical psychological services, as we describe it here, will continue to support occupational health as measured by stress injury claims. In the meanwhile, we remain convinced—as do the organizations benefiting from this approach—that the dynamic contribution made by this blending produces an outcome superior to either approach used independently.

References

Abbot, T. E. (1990, May). Buena Park tackles the emotional issues that impede productivity. *Western City*, pp. 15–18.

Argyris, C. (1958). The organization: What makes it healthy? *Harvard Business Review, 36*, 107–110.

Baruch, G. K., & Barnett, R. C. (1987). Role quality and psychological well-being. In F. J. Crosby (Ed.), *Spouse, parent, worker: On gender and multiple roles* (pp. 91–108). New Haven, CT: Yale University Press.

California Worker's Compensation Institute. (1990, June). Mental stress claims in California worker's compensation: Incidence, costs and trends. *CWCI Research Notes*. (Available from CWCI, 120 Montgomery Street, Suite 1300, San Francisco)

Cooper, C. L., & Payne, R. (1978). *Stress at work*. New York: Wiley.

Cooper, C. L., & Payne, R. (1980). *Current concerns in occupational stress*. New York: Wiley.

Corey, D. M. (1988). The psychological suitability of police officer candidates. *Dissertations International, 49*, 3433B. (University Microfilms No. 8821055)

Corey, D. M., & Wolf, G. D. (1986). *Manager as resource: Removing the obstacles to employee performance*. Unpublished manuscript.

Cox, T. (1987). Stress, coping and problem solving. *Work & Stress, 1*, 5–14.

Everly, G. S., Jr. (1989). *A clinical guide to the treatment of the human stress response*. New York: Plenum Press.

Farcas, G. M. (1989). The impact of federal rehabilitation laws on the expanding role of employee assistance programs in business and industry. *American Psychologist, 44*, 1482–1490.

Golembiewski, R. T., Hilles, R., & Daly, R. (1987). Some effects of multiple OD interventions on burnout and work site features. *Journal of Applied Behavioral Science, 23*, 295–313.

Hall, K. (1986). Tight rein, more stress. *Harvard Business Review*, January/February, 160–166.

Head, T. C., & Sorensen, P. F. (1989). Contemporary trends in OD: 1988. *Organizational Development Journal, 7*, 13–24.

Ilgen, D. R. (1990). Health issues at work: Opportunities for industrial/organizational psychology. *American Psychologist, 45*, 273–283.

Independent Commission on the Los Angeles Police Department. (1991). *Report of the Independent Commission on the Los Angeles Police Department: Summary*. Los Angeles: Author.

Jackson, S., & Schuler, R. (1985). A meta-analysis and conceptual critique of research on role ambiguity and role conflict in work settings. *Organizational Behavior and Human Decisions, 36,* 16–28.

Keita, G. R., & Jones, J. M. (1990). Reducing adverse reaction to stress in the workplace: Psychology's expanding role. *American Psychologist, 45,* 1137–1141.

Levi, L. (1990). Occupational stress: Spice of life or kiss of death? *American Psychologist, 45,* 1142–1145.

Manuso, J. S. (1983). Health promotion through psychological services. *New Directions for Mental Health Services, 20,* 49–56.

Martin, E. V. (1987). Worker stress: A practioner's perspective. In L. R. Murphy & T. F. Schoenborn (Eds.), *Stress management in work settings* (pp. 149–172). Cincinnati, OH: National Institute for Occupational Health and Safety.

McLean, A. A. (1983). The psychiatrist's role in occupational mental health. *New Directions for Mental Health Services, 20,* 57–63.

Moriarty, A., & Field, M. W. (1990). Proactive intervention: A new approach to police EAP programs. *Public Personnel Management, 19,* 155–161.

National Institute for Occupational Safety and Health. (1988). *A proposed national strategy for the prevention of work-related psychological disorders.* Cincinnati, OH: Author.

Raymond, J. S., Wood, D. W., & Patrick, W. K. (1990). Psychology doctoral training in work and health. *American Psychologist, 45,* 1159–1161.

Repetti, R. L., Matthews, K. A., & Waldron, I. (1989). Employment and women's health: Effects of paid employment on women's mental and physical health. *American Psychologist, 44,* 1394–1401.

Rosen, R. (1989). Healthy people, healthy companies: Striking the critical balance. *Advances, 6,* 8–11.

Sauter, S. L., Murphy, L. R., & Hurrell, J. J. (1990). Prevention of work-related psychological disorders: A national strategy proposed by the National Institute for Occupational Safety and Health (NIOSH). *American Psychologist, 45,* 1146–1158.

Schein, E. H. (1987). *Process consultation: Vol. 20: Lessons for managers and consultants.* Reading, MA: Addison-Wesley.

Shalowitz, D. (1991, May 20). Another health care headache. *Business Insurance,* pp. 3–5.

Shipley, P. (1987). The management of psychosocial risk factors in the working environment: UK law compared. *Work & Stress, 1,* 43–48.

Spector, P. E. (1986). Perceived control by employees: A meta-analysis of studies concerning autonomy and participation in decision making. *Human Relations, 39,* 1005–1016.

Stewart, T. A. (1991, August 12). GE keeps those ideas coming. *Fortune,* pp. 41–49.

Virgil, L. D. (1986). The EAP movement and organizational development: Working together for mutual benefit. *Employee Assistance Quarterly, 1,* 35–48.

Wolf, G. D., & Corey, D. M. (1988, February). How to turn technicians into effective managers. *Western City,* pp. 12–31.

Wolf G. D., & Corey, D. M. (1989). *The organizational approach to reducing worker's compensation cost.* Unpublished manuscript.

6

Beryce W. MacLennan

Stressor Reduction: An Organizational Alternative to Individual Stress Management

Current theory indicates that stress overload results from an imbalance between inner psychological states and psychosocial coping skills, on the one hand, and environmental stressors and support deficits, on the other, and that this imbalance is demonstrated in a range of physical, psychological, and behavioral problems.

Although theoretical recognition is given to both sides of the equation (personal and organizational), in practice most emphasis seems to be placed on increasing individual stress tolerance and capacity to cope with stressors through training in problem solving, assertiveness, relaxation methods, improved capacity to communicate, and time management and through referral of those with severe problems for counseling or treatment. Indeed, Everley and Feldman (1984) went so far as to write, "The goal of stress management is to have the participant learn to avoid/minimize excessive stress regardless of its source . . . stress management must focus on the individual" (p. 9). Kobasa, Maddi, Ouccelli, and Zola (1985) emphasized the increase in individual "hardness." Hurrell (1987) disagreed. He wrote, "Job redesign and organizational change approaches focus on reducing or eliminating the sources of stress at work and, hence, are preferred solutions" (p. 39), and Pearlin (in Sargent, 1980), at a conference in 1980, went so far as to state that "it is a cruel and cynical act to place the burden of coping on individuals when organizational changes are required to reduce stress" (p. 4). Although not negating the importance of individual approaches, there are many ways in which the working environment, organization, and climate can be altered to eliminate excessive stress.

Categorization of Organizational Stress

Writers on stress in the workplace have categorized stressors in a number of different ways. Cooper and Davidson (1987) identified four areas of potential stress: the individual, the home, the social environment, and the work arena. In the last, they included factors intrinsic to the job such as job fit and satisfaction, equipment and training, shift work, work overload, work underload, physical danger, work-related self-esteem, the worker's role in the organization (including present and future role ambiguity and role conflict), responsibility for people, organizational boundaries, career development, over and under promotion, status congruency, remuneration, relationships with colleagues (including supervisors and subordinates), organizational structure and climate, politics, consultation communication, participation in decision making, restriction on behavior, and rigidity of departmental policies. Karasek and Tores (1990) emphasized the issue of control over work as being a critical element in work stress, including control over the pace of work and input into decision making. Moos (1981) identified three major areas in his Work Environmental Scale: relationships including involvement, peer cohesion, supervisor support; personal growth including autonomy, task orientation, and work pressure; and systems maintenance and change including clarity, control, innovation, and physical comfort.

Singer, Neale, and Schwartz (1987) in their categorization of stressors and relevant interventions identified three interventions that essentially relate to the personal life and functioning of the individual worker and consider interpersonal dimensions such as marriage, family, and psychological and biological conditions. One intervention measures sociocultural stressors related to events such as racism/sexism, ecological shifts, economic downturns, political changes, and military crises. They include three work-related categories: (a) organizational factors such as hiring policies, plant closings, layoffs, relocation, automation, market shifts, retraining, and organizational priorities; (b) work-setting factors such as task supervision (time, speed, autonomy, and creativity), co-workers relationships, ergonomics, participation in decision making; and (c) physical environmental factors including air quality, climate, noise exposure, toxic substance exposure, lighting quality, radiation exposure, and equipment design and architecture factors.

I identify three major stressor areas. The first is the condition of the physical environment, which includes sensory and perceptual factors such as outlook, light, noise, spatial proportions, temperature, humidity and safety considerations such as clean air, toxic exposure, and equipment design and appropriateness. A second is the organizational/managerial area, which includes such factors as clarity of role functions and promotional policies, opportunities for staff development, rate of work flow and pace, availability and functionality of human and physical resources, quality of benefits and leave policies, flexibility of hours of work, and fairness of salary scales. The third area is concerned with interpersonal relationships and the climate of the organization. This includes such factors as atmosphere, management, supervisory and peer relations, toleration of discrimination and harassment, and prestige of the occupation and organization. Empowerment of workers, including control over some aspects of decision making and problem solving (e.g., involving working hours and work pace) and of suggestions for improvement of work conditions are considered to be important in reducing stress. Policies related to personal conduct such as dress codes, substance use and abuse and smoking also affect the climate of the organization.

Differences in Stressors Between Occupations and Industries

There are broad differences between normally stressful conditions in different occupations and in the stress tolerance or "hardness" of individuals. One person's stressor is another person's stimulant, and to some extent, individuals select occupations with a stress level suited to their temperament and coping capacity. Different occupations and levels in organizations will have intrinsically different stressors. Aviation pilots and air-traffic controllers take major responsibility for the lives of others. Workers in chemical factories have to contend daily with issues of safety and toxic contamination. Senior executives have major responsibilities for correct decision making and the survival of their organizations, whereas middle-level managers may be caught between the demands from above and the capacity of their subordinates to perform. Blue-collar workers in factories are affected by the pacing of machines, the quality of monitoring, and the strains of shift work. Office workers may have to respond to the competing requirements of many different bosses, may be affected by long hours at computer screens, or may resent the barriers placed on advancement to executive or administrative levels. Women and minorities may face racism, sexism, and harassment and the invisible walls between them and the inner circles of information, decision making, and advancement. Age-related stressors are common. Beginning workers are anxious about entry into a field and holding their first job. Middle-aged workers worry about peaking in their careers, and older workers are concerned about obsolescence, redundancy, and extrusion.

Although normally stressful conditions differ greatly among occupations, there are many work settings in which acute or chronic organizational problems create dysfunctional stress reactions in a high percentage of the workers. When organizations encounter increased symptoms among workers such as alienation, high rates of turnover, absenteeism, accidents, or sickness, organizational problems should be suspected, a situational analysis should be undertaken, and problem-specific organizational remedies undertaken. I will describe several problem situations related to one or more of these stressor dimensions and discuss remedial actions. The first set of examples involves two types of stressors experienced in banks in 1990. One of these was alienation and boredom resulting from feelings of lack of self-worth and involvement in the bank and sometimes from lack of opportunity for career advancement. Another stressor occurred because a high percentage of employees were women who experienced many work/family conflicts. Two other examples are drawn from the federal government. One explores the extent of sexual harassment among federal employees in the Washington metropolitan area and discusses changes in policy that defined sexual harassment as inadmissible job discrimination, created channels for complaints, and provided training in the identification and management of this problem. The other describes some work-flow problems in a federal agency and employees' reactions and ways in which the agency attempted to relieve the stress. The third set of examples is drawn from transportation and includes stressors felt by air-traffic controllers, long-distant truckers, and AMTRAK engineers.

Stressors in Banking Institutions in 1990

At the beginning of the 1990s, banking institutions were under pressure. Financial problems had resulted from deregulation and from the high inflation and interest rates of the early 1980s, and many banks and savings and loan associations had

gone bankrupt or were having to downsize their workforce. Banks and other financial institutions were forced to become more competitive. To survive, they became
more efficient and actively promoted their services. There had been a shortage of
educated, competent personnel to work in banks, and recent technological change
had required banks to undertake large-scale training and retraining. Today, banks
are both caught between the need to reduce the numbers in their work force and
the need to recruit and retain their most competent employees. Employee turnover
has been high in the banking industry, which becomes costly when there has been
an investment in training. Seventy-five percent of bank employees are women,
which creates some special stressors.

Two major stressors that banks have attempted to alleviate have been identified
in the banking literature. One of these is alienation and boredom, particularly
among the lower echelons of workers. The second is work/family conflict among
women of all ages and young parents.

Alienation in the Workforce

Several banks have reported combatting alienation and boredom through developing
training and opportunities for advancement and through encouraging and rewarding employees for making suggestions. For instance, J. P. Morgan has created a
staff administrative department to train secretaries and create career ladders for
them along executive, managerial, and paraprofessional tracks ("Employers Now
Provide," 1990). Banks are expanding their encouragement of employee suggestions.
Sovran Bank has developed an ideabank for involving employees ("How to," 1989).

To involve its employees in decision making and to reduce environmental stress,
a large southwest banking corporation consulted its employees when planning a
new branch. The employees had many suggestions. Adequate lighting and reduced
noise, for example, were important to them. They wanted ventilation and temperature control in the offices. They opted for a nonsmoking rule and wanted higher
quality furniture and carpeting and fully equipped work stations (MacLennan &
Birkel, 1991).

The First American Bankcorp of Nashville, Tennessee, which has 150 banks
and over $7 billion in capital, had problems with low productivity, high turnover
(50% teller turnover each year), and a high rate of sick days ("Performance Action,"
1990). Job dissatisfaction, boredom, and alienation were identified as major problems, and management considered changing the bank culture to promote quality
service and recognize personnel as valued. They developed performance action teams
(PATs) consisting of three to four individuals from each operations area and trained
them in problem identification and problem solving. (PATs were originally started
at the head office and, when they were found to be useful, were extended into the
branches.) The teams met after work to identify and solve problems and in so doing
gained prestige in the eyes of other workers. Workers rotated on and off the teams
so that over time many people were trained and had the opportunity to participate
on the teams. In the first year, turnover was cut from 50% to 25%. Management
also initiated a certification program for tellers and platform personnel based on
service quality and accounts knowledge as a means for basing salary increases and
promoting quality service. Although currently the bank is engaged in downsizing

its workforce and turnover per se is not such a concern, the PATs have been retained because they create networks across operations areas for information sharing, mutual support, and problem solving and improve morale among the workers (personal communication, K. Geiger, NCBC, July 16, 1990).

Work/Family Conflicts

Work hours, leave policies, and needs for child and eldercare are all potential sources of conflict for parents, particularly working mothers on whom most of the responsibility for the family generally falls. In October 1990, the magazine *Working Mothers* (Moskowitz & Townsend, 1990) conducted a survey to identify the 75 best companies for working mothers. Given that 75% of the work force in banking institutions are women, one would expect that banks would be represented, and indeed several were. The surveyors reported that the American Bank Insurance Group provided one on-site day-care center and one on-site public school for Grades K–2, which was open before and after school, and used one near-site day-care center. Maternity leave, job protection for 30 days, and a few part-time jobs were also offered. Citibank, the largest U.S. bank operated one on-site day-care center and paid 80% of the cost for one near-site center. It also provided vouchers or discounts for child-care in some locations. The bank also offered 12 family sick days, 12 weeks of unpaid maternity leave, and 4 weeks of unpaid personal leave. There were opportunities for flextime, part-time work for returning mothers and fathers, job sharing, and work at home. A resource and referral service was offered to help workers with elder care. Dominion Bankshares provided 5 family sick days, 6 weeks of maternity leave at full pay after 5 years of service, and up to 10 weeks of unpaid leave. This bank also offered flextime and had a large part-time program. Both these banks offered some aid with adoption. The South Shore Bank in Chicago provided excellent opportunities for women to advance in the bank and provided loans to 40% of the child-care centers in the community. It welcomed children in the bank after school and provided unpaid maternity leave for up to 6 months.

The American Bankers Association polled 370 banks and found that half had a family leave policy, and 64 provided child care benefits ("A Growing Number," 1989). The National Westminster Bank, USA was one of seven companies that had emergency child care. Chase Manhattan Bank in New York City had an EAP corporate counseling service with 24-hr access to discuss problems of elder relatives, help search for nursing homes, draw up wills, fill out Medicaid applications, and arrange for Meals on Wheels—all of which would otherwise take time away from work and create stress for the employees ("Chase Elder Care," 1989). The service is nationwide because the elderly relatives may live anywhere in the United States.

The North Carolina National Bank was concerned with the attendance and advancement of parents in the bank and with child care and elder care. The bank had a system of flexible work schedules that allowed workers to move from full-time to part-time work and back again depending on their personal needs. The bank was even able to accommodate part-time executives and had one part-time vice president ("Career Planning," 1989). The bank provided 6 weeks of paid parental leave when a baby is born and 5,000 hr of unpaid leave that individuals can use to care for spouses, elderly parents, or children. There was a day-care benefit of $35 a week for anyone earning less than $24,000 a year. The bank was working on developing day care close to bank sites. Morale was reported to be high, and employees were loyal to the bank (Alpin, 1990).

Organizational Stressors in the Federal Government

Most federal workers enter the government as a career and expect to spend many years in their chosen agency. Neither managers nor staff have the same freedom to choose their colleagues as they might have in nontenured organizations. Some personality conflicts may be hard to avoid, and political appointees to executive positions may change an agency's climate in a radical way. Both career managers and workers are consequently vulnerable to the climate of the agency and the conditions of work that they encounter. This section examines the effect of changes in the management of sexual harassment in the federal government over a period of 5 years and some work-flow problems in one division of a federal agency.

Sexual Harassment in the Federal Government

All forms of discrimination, including sexism, racism, ageism, and discrimination with regard to religion and against the handicapped, are sources of stress, particularly when the victims are subject to harassment. When employees are sexually harassed on the job, they may be placed in a very difficult position if they cannot gain support from their superiors. Some victims are able to deal directly with the harasser, but often they are in a vulnerable position and may be unable to avoid persistent harassment. Some victims become very anxious or depressed. Some become physically ill. Others quit their jobs or seek a transfer. Still others take undue amounts of personal and sick leave, report late and leave early from the job, or just become unproductive. A few make formal complaints and may end up with a court case that drags on for years and is itself extremely stressful. Harassment is an organizational problem that needs firm organizational remedies. As the following indicates, however, even with legal and administrative requirements, discrimination and harassment are likely to persist if senior executives and managers are not determined to eradicate the problem.

In 1976, the court decision *Williams v. Saxbe* (1976) determined that sexual harassment is a form of sex discrimination within the meaning of Title VII of the Civil Rights Act of 1964 and that, consequently, victims may file Equal Opportunity complaints. In the fall of 1979, the Subcommittee on Investigations of the House Committee on Post Office and Civil Service held hearings on the prevalence of sexual harassment and its management in the federal government (Subcommittee on Investigations, 1980). At the request of the subcommittee, Donald Campbell, then director of the Office of Personnel Management (OPM) distributed a policy statement and definition of sexual harassment to all heads of departments and independent agencies (Campbell, 1979). This memorandum stated that "sexual harassment is a prohibited personnel practice when it results in discrimination, for or against an employee, on the basis of conduct not related to performance, such as the taking or refusal to take a personnel action, including promotion of employees who resist or protest sexual overtures" (p. 1). It defined sexual harassment as "deliberate or repeated unsolicited verbal comments, gestures, or physical contact of a sexual nature which are unwelcome" (p. 1) and stated that OPM's policy is that sexual harassment is unacceptable in the workplace and would not be condoned. The memorandum also stated that complaints would be considered under Title VII of the Civil Rights Act (1964).

The Equal Employment Opportunity Commission (EEOC) also clarified the definition of sexual harassment in an amendment to its guidelines *Discrimination Because of Sex* and held that an employer is responsible for acts of sexual harassment in the workplace when an employer, its agents, or supervisory employees know or should have known of the conduct. Furthermore, the commission determined that federal employees could also seek redress through the Special Council of the Merit Systems Protection Board, which is empowered to use a stay of personnel actions to protect complainants from reprisals (Civil Service Reform Act, 1978).

To provide testimony for the subcommittee hearings, Federally Employed Women (FEW; MacLennan, 1986) circulated a questionnaire on sexual harassment experienced on the job to the 1,000 female members employed in federal agencies and the Armed Forces in the Washington, DC, metropolitan region. Although the time in which the members were to respond was short (3 weeks), 191 members responded. Of these, 123 had experienced some form of sexual harassment at least once.

The most common forms of sexual harassment reported were the least offensive. Ninety-four women reported sexual remarks and jokes, 65 reported patting and touching, and 56 reported unwelcome sexual propositions without conditions. However, some of the women who refused propositions to which no conditions were attached did in fact experience reprisals, such as poor performance ratings or loss of promotions or transfers, as a consequence. One woman reported obscene phone calls. Less common were sexual propositions with rewards, which were reported by 21 women, sexual propositions with threats reported by 18 women, and sexual assault reported by 12 women.

The subcommittee had been concerned that few complaints of sexual harassment were made. Consequently, FEW included in their questionnaire questions regarding how the women had dealt with sexual harassment. Only eight women made formal complaints. Three of these tried an informal approach first. Twenty-seven others complained informally. Seventy-two stopped the harassment themselves. Thirty endured it or did nothing to stop it. Six women resigned or transferred. The results of formal or informal complaints were as follows:

Formal complaints: 6 women experienced reprisals
                    1 harasser was reprimanded
                    1 case was still pending
Informal complaints: 2 harassers were transferred
                    5 harassments ceased
                    2 harassments lessened
                    7 women experienced reprisals
                    3 women were transferred
                    1 harasser moved to a better job
                    1 harasser was promoted

The harassers were drawn from all ranks: 51 supervisors, 19 managers, 52 colleagues, 32 people outside the immediate work setting, and 6 others. Of these others, one was an instructor, one a member of a state agency, a third a contractor's representative. One harasser was a woman.

As a result of these hearings, sexual harassment was not only clearly defined as a forbidden activity in the federal government and channels for grievances and complaints established with formal protection against reprisals, but OPM also developed a 3-hr training module to be included in all supervisory courses to train managers and executives. The EEOC also designed a training module on sexual harassment for EEO personnel and requested Federal Women's Program officers to include sexual harassment information in their programmatic initiatives (Subcommittee on Investigations, 1980).

Five years later, FEW was interested in obtaining information on how these initiatives had affected sexual harassment in the Washington, DC, metro region. In January 1985, they sent the questionnaire to a random sample of 500 members of the FEW in the Washington, DC, metro region (MacLennan, 1986). This time, the members had 2 months in which to respond, and 256 (51.2%) responses were received. Two questions were added to this second questionnaire. One differentiated between harassment experienced before and after January 1, 1980, and the second requested information on training offered by the agencies in which the women were employed. In 1979, 123 women had experienced sexual harassment of one kind or another. This was 12.3% of the total sample and 64.4% of those returning the questionnaire. In 1985, 127 had experienced sexual harassment at some time during their federal employment. This was 25.4% of the total sample and 49.6% of those returning the questionnaire. However, only 67 or 13.4% of the total sample had experienced sexual harassment since January 1, 1980.

FEW compared these 67 with the 123 who had reported experiencing harassment in the first questionnaire. The percentages of those making sexual remarks and jokes were roughly the same (77% vs. 78%). However, all other forms of harassment appeared to have declined: patting and touching from 52.8% to 11.9%, propositions without conditions from 45.5% to 31.3%, propositions with conditions (either rewards or threats) from 31.7% to 20.8%, and sexual assault from 1.2% (12 cases) to .2% (1 case).

However, it was disappointing to find that a smaller percentage of women had made use of either formal or informal complaint mechanisms (28.5% vs. 17.3%) and that the results of complaining had not improved. In fact, 78.6% as opposed to 70.6% of the women reported unfavorable consequences. Between 1980 and 1985, 53% and 82%, respectively, did not complain. Most handled the harassment personally (76%). Moreover, 11% in 1980 and 20.8% in 1985 still stated that they were afraid of reprisals. Some women commented that, because the initial complaints had to go through the agency, when managers and supervisors were not supportive, complaining increased their problems and usually was not effective. They would have liked to have seen complaints channelled through an outside independent agency.

The rank of harassers had not changed appreciably: 13.9% were managers, 30.6% supervisors, 48.6% colleagues, and 6.9% from outside the work area or other people. Of the 67 women complaining of harassment between 1980 and 1985, 47 stated that some training was provided by the agency, 9 stated that none had been provided, and 11 did not know. The targets of training were managers and supervisors only in 15 cases, all staff in 32 cases, and there was additional training for women in how to cope with being harassed in 6 cases. Some of the women commented that the training was a farce because the managers did not take it seriously. In other situations, the women responded that managers were supportive, efforts were made to eliminate all sexual harassment, and the training did appear to be effective.

Although these surveys told nothing about individual agencies, FEW was able to gather, through discussions in the metro region chapters and through the complaints that were made to FEW by its members, that most of the problems were in the more conservative, male-dominated agencies and the Armed Forces and that newer agencies, such as the Environmental Protection Agency and agencies with higher percentages of women at all levels such as the Department of Health and Human Services, had fewer problems. The commitment of the head of the agency and of the President were both seen as important. Independent channels for complaints were viewed as necessary if the process was to work effectively, and FEW concluded that all ranks should be included in training to prevent discrimination and harassment. Although sexual harassment had by no means been eliminated from the federal government by 1985, it was clear that the more serious forms of harassment were less prevalent than before the subcommittee hearings.

A survey by the U.S. Merit Systems Protection Board in 1988 (Sandroff, 1988) found that over a 2-year period, 42% of female workers and 14% of male workers reported that they had experienced persistent, unwelcome sexual attention. However, only about 5% had actually filed a formal complaint or requested an investigation.

In a survey of sexual harassment in Fortune 500 companies, Sandroff (1988) reported in *Working Woman* that, although 76% of the companies had formal policies banning sexual harassment, 90% had had at least one complaint in the past year, and 25% had received six or more complaints in the past year. Moreover, a specialist who worked on the survey stated that every attitude survey that she had conducted in the private sector had shown that at least 15% of the female employees had been sexually harassed in the past year. In Sandroff's *Working Woman* survey, 26% of the complaints filed involved touching, leaning over, or cornering, and 29% cited unwelcome pressure for dates or sexual favors. Actual or attempted assault was involved in 1% of the cases. The ratio of complaints to incidents continued to be low because the victims feared retaliation.

Fortune 500 companies are finding sexual harassment expensive not only because employers are held responsible for the behavior of their employees and can be fined by the courts but also because, if victims quit, the company loses money spent in training and in the time and costs involved in recruiting and training replacements.

Sandroff (1988) also concluded that commitment from top policymakers is critical in the prevention of sexual harassment and that training needs to be extended throughout the companies rather than for management only. It is also cost effective for businesses to make sure that incidents are promptly recognized, reported, and dealt with so that companies do not become involved in expensive liability suits and workplace friction that can cost them millions of dollars annually and create high stress among their employees.

Work Flow Problems in a Federal Agency

Following an employee death from a heart attack during a period of intense work pressure, a division management in a government agency decided to assess the extent and causes of work-related stress and to analyze the potential for stress reduction and management (personal experience, 1989). Interviews were conducted by an in-house consultant with division employee councils and a representative sample of employees. The interviews covered whether the employees felt stressed, what stressors were most critical to them, how they coped with problems, and what they knew about stress management. The results were reported both to managers and staff, and ideas about how to solve the problems were solicited from both. The study made clear that many employees, managers, supervisors, and staff experienced high stress at work. Some of the staff did not know how to reduce their own level of stress and said that they could use stress education and training. This was provided through information in the division newsletter, presentations at staff meetings, tapes that staff could take home, and better publicity from the agency counseling service. However, the major problems appeared to be organizational. Some of these problems were felt by all the staff; others were specific to entry staff, supervisors, middle managers, and some senior managers.

The division's functions consisted of investigating, analyzing, and evaluating federal policies and programs and reporting on the findings. Work flow was a major problem. Pressures from top management and outside the agency required division management to take on more jobs than the staff could reasonably handle and, particularly, to react positively to emergency demands. Deadlines were set to fulfill executives' performance-appraisal goals and were hard to meet if delays occurred. Middle management and project staff became particularly stressed when other emergency work was accepted that drew off staff and delayed completion of the primary project. When this resulted in missed target dates, staff became anxious about their own performance appraisals. Emergencies often necessitated evening and weekend overtime work for employees to catch up, and the additional work created work/family conflicts, particularly for families with small children. Although some staff were stimulated by the challenge of these pressures, others were turned off and sought transfer, left the agency, or accommodated to little prospect of advancement in the future and began to make greater commitments to interests outside the agency.

A second work-flow problem was caused by excessive layers of oversight. If senior managers were busy and could not give their approval, work was delayed, and staff remained idle until decisions could be reached. The tension resulting from the "rush, rush, stop, go" work flow was very stressful to some workers.

A third work-flow problem related to report production because reports were also required to pass through several managerial levels of review, comment, and agreement before they could be released for publication. Sometimes, documents were caught in disagreements between reviewers, and deadlines were missed. Staff were held responsible although they did not have final responsibility. Staff also complained that they rarely received positive feedback and felt that they were penalized for not having expert writing ability if they made use of available editorial talent.

Senior managers were discontented because they felt under pressure to complete more jobs than their staffs could reasonably handle. They also felt that they were insufficiently recompensed for the amount of work and overtime that they undertook. Project officers and middle managers also felt under great pressure because of the inconsistent and increasing amounts of work with which they had to deal. Advancement was very competitive, and workers were anxious about their prospects for promotion. Junior staff, particularly entry-level staff, were concerned because annual appraisals for promotion did not coincide with their rotations from one supervisor to another so that some appraisals were made by supervisors who did not know them well. Junior staff and project officers also believed that if they went to supervisors with problems, they were likely to be penalized in their appraisals.

Several actions were taken on the basis of this report. Although outside pressure still remained on managers to accept more emergency work than available staff could realistically accomplish, they were encouraged to improve their negotiating skills to delay, reorganize, or combine work and thus economize staff time. Flexibility was built into management contracts so that deadlines could be more easily changed without penalty. Planning conferences, which all project staff and managers attended, were held once the first report draft was completed so that all could agree on the report structure, conclusions, and recommendations to be made, thus reducing the likelihood of later disagreement. More editorial assistance was provided, which staff were encouraged to use, and reviewers were discouraged from making unnecessary editorial changes.

Managers and supervisors were provided with training in developing a more supportive environment, team building, and recognizing good work. Staff were encouraged to work as a team and to seek expert assistance as needed without being made to feel incompetent. Attention was paid to the relations between job transfers and appraisals for promotion so that, if the timing did not coincide, at least the former supervisor's evaluation was included in an appraisal.

All staff came to recognize that, because of outside pressures and the relative unpredictability of emergency demands, the work would continue to be inherently stressful. Work/family conflict would continue but could be recognized and minimized to some extent. Nevertheless, within the agency, priority still appeared to be given to work over family requirements. However, organizational changes could be made to improve the environment on the job, set goals more flexibly, manage emergencies and job flow more effectively, and eliminate bureaucratic bottlenecks. Supervisors could improve their skills in giving recognition for good work and in dealing with problems more sympathetically. Finally, an effort was made to leave as much responsibility for decision making with the staff who actually performed the work.

Organizational Stressors in Transportation

Some jobs in transportation have been cited as very stressful, and organizational factors can make a considerable difference as to whether there are health consequences from stress overload. The U.S. Bureau of Labor Statistics (1991) reported that in 1985, there were 4.5 million people employed in the transportation and material moving industry, that two thirds were between 18 and 44 years of age, and that 91.8% were male. Over 60% had at least a high school education, and 40% earned $25,000 or more a year. Some categories of transportation workers were among the highest for such health risks as cardiovascular diseases (particularly high blood pressure), eschemic heart disease and hemorrhoids, deafness, and visual impairments (National Center for Health Statistics, 1989). About 30% were reported to suffer from gastric disorders. In this section, I discuss three examples: stress among long-distance truckers, Amtrak engineers, and air-traffic controllers (ATCs).

Long-Distance Truckers

In 1989, according to the Bureau of Labor Statistics, there were 1,836,000 people employed in the trucking industry and 452,000 truck and trailer equipment operators. Truckers have received considerable attention in recent years because the National Safety Council (1988) reported that trucks have been involved in 20% of all road accidents. The National Transportation Safety Board (1989) in a study of road accidents in which truck drivers were killed found that fatigue was the major problem (31%) followed by substance abuse (29%) in these fatal accidents. In 1989, the Regular Common Carrier Conference (1990) conducted a Motor Carrier Safety Survey that included 1,285 interviews at three truck inspection stations in Northern Florida. Drivers came from across the United States and Canada. Many more accidents were reported by inexperienced than experienced drivers. Five percent of accidents reported involved fatalities, 55% involved injuries, and the remainder involved no injuries. Driver fatigue was considered by two thirds of the respondents to be a major factor in accidents. The major causes of fatigue were considered to be tight trip schedules and the requirement that the driver load and unload the truck. Turkel (1972), in his interview with an interstate trucker, graphically described the problems of having to load and then drive and unload at the other end. Additional problems could be created if mistakes were made in loading and the weight had to be rechecked or the weight was found to be too great at some inspection station. In the survey, 37% of the drivers also mentioned that road congestion and having to travel at peak traffic hours were sources of fatigue, and 27% reported that the hours of service conflicted with their normal wake/sleep rhythms.

Turkel's (1972) trucker described the stress caused by the irregular hours, hassles over loading and unloading, and the long hours of boredom on the road. Truckers today also mention dangerous driving by other drivers on the road. Problems related to eating adequately, getting sufficient exercise and regular sleep, and maintaining a family life are all still problems today. In 1972, many truckers were reputed to take "Bennies" (amphetamines) to keep themselves awake. Today, drug abuse is still a problem. In the National Transportation Safety Board's (1989) study, 33% of the fatally injured drivers tested positive for alcohol and other drugs of abuse. These substances included alcohol, marijuana, amphetamines, and other stimulants and to a small extent codeine and PCP.

Some organizational changes have occurred to make the truckers' lives less stressful. Some states and companies regulate the hours that truckers are expected to drive. However, this too may be a source of stress in that if there are delays on the road, the drivers may push their vehicles and exceed the speed limit to reach their destination on time. Permissible driving time may also not include loading and unloading time. Drivers would like to be freed from the responsibility of loading and unloading. Although there are many more freeways today, the truckers would still like more bypasses, truck lanes, and improved roads. There is some debate about speed limits on highways, the trucking companies preferring the 55 mph speed limit and the truckers 65 mph. However, the National Safety Council (1988) reported many truck-related accidents on rural highways where the speed limit has been increased.

Although drug abuse and alcoholism are problems with some truckers, most approve of drug testing, at least before employment and after accidents to aid in determining cause. The American Trucking Association supports a ban on the sale of alcohol at truck stops, and the National Association of Truckstop Operators have a campaign titled Operation Roadblock to declare truckstops drug-free zones (National Association of Truckstop Operators, 1990). In at least one truck stop, there is a medical clinic and a drug-testing unit. Some truck stop operators are now developing the sale of healthier food at truck stops. There are facilities for resting, and there is discussion about the provision of exercise facilities.

Truckers would like to see improved driver education for the public so that they do not find cars cutting in in front of them with too short a distance for them to stop. The evidence for the value of truck driver training is not clear according to the Motor Carrier Safety Survey (Regular Common Carrier Conference, 1990). However, the authors of the survey consider that this lack of clarity is the result of averaging effective and ineffective training rather than identifying training that makes a difference.

Attention is being paid to the organization and conditions of work for long-distance truckers to reduce fatigue and make driving easier, the hours of work more reasonable, and rest stops healthier. However, long-distance trucking probably will always remain a stressful and boring way of life selected by a limited number of people.

AMTRAK Engineers

In recent years, high-speed trains have been developed in most parts of the world. France and Japan are particularly famous for their fast trains, and a few studies have been undertaken to identify whether there are any special problems for the drivers. The evidence has been inconclusive up to this time.

AMTRAK runs high-speed trains as well as local trains along its Eastern corridor, and several years ago the management decided to reduce the number of engineers driving these fast trains from two to one. Many of the drivers were middle aged and had been used to working as couples throughout their adult life. They and their union (the Brotherhood of Railroad Engineers) complained that this change was causing high stress among the engineers (U.S. Government Accounting Office, 1986).

At the time when the change was initiated, no ergonomic studies were undertaken to identify what alterations might be needed, for instance, in the placement of instrumentation or seating in the cab to increase the comfort and efficiency of a driver working alone. The drivers missed the companionship of their partners. They felt that having a second person added to their capacity to perceive danger early enough for them to stop, and they pointed out that there was no relief available if they should suddenly be taken ill on route.

The union hired consultants to survey the engineers, and stressors were identified that varied between routes and between depots but that, if eliminated, could reduce the stress of the drivers. Supervisory relationships were clearly poorer in some depots than in others. Some engineers complained that train inspectors allowed trains to depart with defects such as faulty breaks. Some also found that the inspectors were arbitrary and disrespectful. There were differences between those who operated diesel and electric trains. Diesel trains were dirtier, and some engineers complained about dirty windows that impeded their vision. Drivers on the east–west route indicated that their vision was impaired by the sun in the afternoons. Vandalism on some parts of the track created anxiety because these fast trains could not stop quickly in a short distance, and fencing to protect the railway lines was insufficient. Fewer engineers meant more emergency returns to duty, consequently disrupting family and social life and increasing fatigue. All these problems seemed amenable to managerial intervention, which could reduce some stress of driving high-speed trains without a backup engineer.

Air-Traffic Controllers

The work of ATCs has generally been considered to be quite stressful. However, the degree to which ATCs suffer from stress overload has been a matter of dispute. ATCs are carefully selected for their work both physically and psychologically and may be more stressor resistant than the average employee. In a 10-year review of the literature, coupled with a study of ATCs at several air-traffic facilities on psychological and physiological variables, Smith (1980) concluded that most ATCs were satisfied with their work. He found that most did not suffer from stress overload or from psychosomatic illness to a greater extent than did the general public.

Questions had been raised over the years of whether different shift arrangements affect the health of ATCs. Melton and Bartanowicz (1986) concluded that there was little evidence that any particular shift arrangement was less stressful than any other. However, there was evidence that arbitrarily imposed shift arrangements were stressful and that ATCs valued some freedom of choice.

Maxwell (1986), in a large study of ATCs in England, while recognizing that the occupation did carry high stress, found that most ATCs were well suited for their profession and not overloaded. He did not find that they suffered from hypertension and other psychosomatic illnesses to a greater extent than did the general population. He did find that most operators experienced at least one period of psychological problems during their work life, although not necessarily requiring treatment. Quite a number did suffer from anxiety and depression, particularly when life stresses coincided with work stresses. He also found that approximately 50% of the ATCs were heavy drinkers. He found the following four elements to be most stressful: work overload, fear of equipment failure, poor ability of other ATCs, and poor operating procedures by pilots.

Maxwell's (1986) findings are significant in the light of current ATC conditions in the United States. The U.S. General Accounting Office (1987), in testimony before Congress, reported that, although in 1981 prior to the ATC strike there were 16,244

ATCs, in June 1987, with increased traffic, there were only 13,632 ATCs. In 1981, 13,205 ATCs were fully trained, whereas in 1987, only 9,617 held that status. This would indicate that in 1987, many ATCs were working under conditions in which they were overloaded, were training other workers, or were working alongside relatively inexperienced workers. Because of the shortage of personnel, ATCs were also having to work excessive overtime, and it was difficult for them to take annual leave. Critical shortages in maintenance technicians also increased the likelihood of equipment failures. All of these factors, organizational in nature, were likely to raise the level of stress among ATCs and create stress overload in some.

Discussion

External stressors affecting employed workers can be of many kinds but can be classified as resulting from three different sources: (a) the physical environment, (b) organizational management, and (c) interpersonal relationships. Different industries and organizations experience these stressors to varying degrees.

In banking, an industry that employs a high percentage of women, management issues related to work empowerment, such as involvement in problem solving and decision making and interpersonal concerns related to work/family conflicts (e.g., working hours, leave benefits, and dependent care) were found to be most critical. Changes in these two areas were reported to have had considerable effect on morale, productivity, and turnover. Stressors for executives in banking appear to be more closely related to the condition of the economy (Driscoll, 1988).

In both federal government examples, interpersonal relationships of caring and fairness were seen as important. Recognition and definition of sexual harassment, the development of a no-tolerance policy for discrimination and harassment, and staff training to implement the policy appeared to have reduced the amount and degree of serious harassment of federally employed women in the Washington metropolitan area.

Managerial issues related to work flow and levels of decision making were of primary importance in the second example. The elimination of "bottlenecks" and the reduction in the number of emergency work demands coupled with enhanced supervisory training went some way to reduce worker stress.

In transportation, a largely male-dominated industry, the nature of the work carries many intrinsic stressors such as long hours in confined spaces, prolonged vigilance, and life-and-death responsibility, particularly for drivers of high-speed trains and ATCs. However, managerial problems related to work flow and lack of trained employees seemed to be major factors in ATC stress. For AMTRAK, lack of ergonomic studies that analyzed physical environmental requirements in changing from two drivers to one, poor maintenance in some depots, and a perceived lack of concern for the engineers by managers and supervisors added to normal stress. In the trucking industry, employers, state officials, and trucker associations have combined to develop policies and resources that will provide more manageable hours, adequate rest and exercise facilities, and improved nutrition for truckers on the road.

Although there are many accounts of high stress experienced by workers in particular organizations and of attempts to reduce stressors, there are relatively few studies that evaluate interventions. Among the examples described in this chapter, there were no controlled evaluations. One bank did monitor the effects of its changing policies on worker turnover and morale, in both federal government examples, there was worker feedback, and in transportation, there have been a number of studies of ATC working conditions over the years.

Individuals vary greatly in their capacity to endure stressful situations, and there is, undoubtedly, self-selection in the kinds of jobs and stressors that individuals choose. However, organizational remedial measures that address environmental, organizational/managerial, and interpersonal problems contribute to stress and organizational remedial measures have been able to reduce the pressures on overstressed workers. It is suggested that whenever there are indications of a raised stress level in an organization (e.g., increased turnover, absenteeism, sickness, reduced productivity), a situational analysis and stress study should be undertaken to identify the causes of trouble and to seek organizational remedies. Improved management can be a potent force in stressor reduction.

References

A growing number of banks now offer a family leave policy (1989, May). *Bank Personnel Report*, p. 7.

Alpin, S. (1990, May–June). One bank's approach to caregiving programs. *Banker's Magazine*, pp. 69–72.

Campbell, A. K. (1979). *Policy statement and definition of sexual harassment*. Washington, DC: U.S. Office of Personnel Management.

Career planning: NCNB offers employees a temporary break from the fast track. (1989, February). *Bank Personnel Report*, pp. 3–4.

Chase elder care program helps employees balance work and family needs. (1989, July). *Bank Personnel Report*, pp. 2–3.

Civil Rights Act, 1964. Title VII, Section 77 Sub. 703-42 U.S.C. 2000C-16.

Civil Service Reform Act, 1978. Title V U.S.C. 2301 *Merit system principles* and U.S.C. 2302 *Prohibited personnel practices*.

Cooper C. L., & Davidson, M. (1987). Sources of stress at work and their relation to stressors in non-working environments. In R. Kalimo, M. A. El Batawi, & C. L. Cooper (Eds.), *Psychosocial factors at work: Their relation to health* (pp. 99–108). Geneva, Switzerland: World Health Organization.

Driscoll, J. (1988). Stress management. *Commercial West, 32*, 10–14, 40.

Employers now provide career ladders for secretaries. (1990, May). *Bank Personnel Report*, pp. 7–8.

Everley, G. S., & Feldman, R. H. L. (1984). *Occupational health promotion*. New York: Wiley.

How to make an employee suggestion program work for a bank. (1989, January). *Bank Personnel Report*, pp. 1–2.

Hurrell, J. J. (1987). An overview of organizational stress and health. In L. M. Murphy & T. F. Schoenborn (Eds.), *Stress management in work settings* (pp. 31–39). Cincinnati, OH: National Institute for Occupational Health and Safety.

Karasek, R., & Tores, T. (1990). *Healthy work, stress, productivity and the reconstruction of working life*. New York: Basic Books.

Kobasa, S. C., Maddi, J., Ouccelli, M., & Zola, M. C. (1985). Effectiveness of hardiness, exercise and social support as resources against illness. *Journal of Psychosomatic Research, 29*, 525–533.

MacLennan, B. W. (1986). *Two surveys of sexual harassment experienced by federally employed women in the Washington metro region, 1979, 1985*. Unpublished manuscript.

MacLennan, B. W., & Birkel, R. (1991). *Health promotion in banking 1990*. Washington, DC: Washington Business Group on Health.

Maxwell, V. B. (1986). Stress in air traffic control. *Stress Medicine, 2*, 27–36.

Melton, C. E., & Bartanowicz, R. S. (1986). *Biological rhythms and rotating shift work*. Washington, DC: Office of Aviation Medicine.

Moos, R. (1981). *Work Environment Scale*. Palo Alto, CA: Consulting Psychologist Press.

Moskowitz, M., & Townsend, C. (1990). The 75 best companies for working mothers: 5th annual survey. *Working Mother, October*, 31–33, 36, 38, 42, 46.

Murphy, L. M., & Schoenborn, T. F. (1987). *Stress management in work settings*. Atlanta, GA: National Institute for Occupational Safety and Health.

Murphy, L. R. (1984). Occupational stress management: A review and appraisal. *Journal of Occupational Psychology, 57*, 1–15.

National Association of Truckstop Operators. (1990). *Operation roadblock*. Alexandria, VA: Author.

National Center for Health Statistics. (1989). *Viral and health statistics: Health characteristics by occupation and industry, United States 1983–85* (PHS No. 90-1598). Washington, DC: Author.

National Safety Council. (1988). *Accident Survey, 1987*. New York: Author.

National Transportation Safety Board. (1989). *Safety study: Fatigue, Alcohol, Other Drugs and Medical Factors in Fatal-to-the-Driver Heavy Crashes* (Vols. 1 & 2). Washington, DC:

Performance action teams. (1990, April). *Bank Personnel Report*, pp. 1–3.

Regular Common Carrier Conference. (1990). *Motor carrier safety survey, 1989*. Alexandria, VA: Author.

Sandroff, R. (1988, December). Sexual harassment in the Fortune 500: Survey results. *Working Women*. pp. 69–73.

Sargent, M. (1980). Stress on the job: Coping skills help less than changes in work situation. *ADAMHA News, 10*, 1.

Singer, J. A., Neale, M. S., & Schwartz, G. E. (1987). The nuts and bolts of assessing occupational stress. In L. R. Murphy & T. E. Schoenborn (Eds.), *Stress management in work settings* (Vol. 5, pp. 87–111). Atlanta, GA: National Institute for Occupational Health and Safety.

Smith, R. C. (1980). *Stress, anxiety and air traffic control: Some conclusions from a decade of research*. Washington, DC: Federal Aviation Administration, Office of Aviation Medicine.

Subcommittee on Investigations of the House Committee on Post Office and Civil Service, 96th Congress, 2nd Session. (1980). *Sexual harassment in the federal government*. Washington, DC: U.S. Government Printing Office.

Turkel, S. (1972). *Working*. New York: Ballantine Books.

U.S. Bureau of Labor Statistics. (1991). *Employment and earnings* (Report No. 391). Washington, DC: Author.

U.S. General Accounting Office. (1986). *AMTRAK: Northeast corridor locomotive engineer stress* (GAO/RCED-37-1). Washington, DC: Author.

U.S. General Accounting Office. (1987). *FAA air traffic controller staffing and related issues: Testimony before the Subcommittee of Investigators of the House Committee on Post Office and Civil Service* (GAO/T-RCED-87-42). Washington, DC: Author.

Williams v. Saxbe, 1976. No. 74-156 (D.D.C., August 1).

7

Holger Luczak

"Good Work" Design: An Ergonomic, Industrial Engineering Perspective

Many different disciplines, such as psychology, engineering, ergonomics, and physiology, have individual approaches to the problem of work design. Campion (1988) reported a test of four approaches to work design and concluded that different approaches influence different outcomes, each approach having its own costs and benefits. Therefore, trade-offs may be needed, and both theory and practice can benefit from interdisciplinary perspectives.

This chapter proposes a conceptual approach to the design of work that is best labeled *anthropocentric*, as opposed to *technocentric*, and is based on an industrial engineering perspective. The chapter is organized into five major sections. The first section outlines the basic responsibilities of production engineering in the design of work. The second section addresses the human aspects of flexibility, automation, and integration. The third section examines the avoidance of unfavorable working conditions through the notions of practicability, endurability, acceptability, and satisfaction. The fourth section examines the dimensions of "good" work with respect to the aforementioned human considerations. The concluding section presents a brief argument for combining the concepts of Computer Integrated Manufacturing (CIM) and Human Integrated Manufacturing (HIM).

Responsibilities of Production Engineering

As the applied science of matter and motion, engineering is concerned with the modification of the world through a variety of techniques. In particular, production and industrial engineers may modify the shape of a landscape, the traffic system of a town, economic structures, and, presently unspecific, the design of work and the work environment as it affects the worker physically and psychologically. Production and industrial engineers also affect ecological systems by the choice of production processes and the development of new products.

In planning a new plant, the work of production and industrial engineers represents an intervention in and an infringement on existing structures that may lead to some irreversible results (or at least long-lasting ones). Presuming a crucial interference with the environment and society, generally a question arises: What do industrial and production engineers need to know and to master beyond production technology?

Whether they are alone or in a team, engineers must connect a wide spectrum of professional and interdisciplinary problems when planning, implementing, and operating manufacturing technology. To address aspects of production and "mentofacturing," technology alone is not enough for the engineer (Forward, Beach, Gray, & Quick, 1991). Mentofacturing is an approach to making (*factus*) products that emphasizes the mind (*mento*) as opposed to the hand (*manus*). An interdisciplinary approach is required instead that focuses on the planning process and its consequences.

In the process of planning, engineers must take law, ecology, and democratic decision mechanisms (e.g., the German system of codetermination of unions) into account. In addition, knowledge of the fundamentals of production technology, the organization of production, and the division of labor will also require consideration. New technologies are more likely to be successfully implemented when there is a comprehensive understanding of the planning process from a variety of perspectives. This understanding includes the anticipation of difficulties in the implementation process of new technologies and, therefore, avoids complications in future production processes. Hence, the engineer must think in terms of the "design of work" generally (i.e., What is work? What are all of the components that affect it?) and not only in terms of the design of the technological aspects of the work. Furthermore, the engineer must engage in *anticipatory thinking* in terms of processes and their consequences. This is a basic philosophy of successful plant engineering and operation.

In a recent study (Wildemann, 1990), approximately 60% of the sampled firms that were examined with respect to CIM-introduction strategies implemented technological innovation. However, it was only later in the process that organizational and personnel problems with regard to CIM-implementation were considered. Clearly, this does not exemplify anticipatory thinking. The application of anticipatory thinking would most likely result in discovery of work design deficiencies as well as objections from workers prior to the completion and implementation of the design.

In this context, anticipation means that one is aware of the consequences of one's actions. If the consequences are negative, they can be a permanent burden. It can be said that the "sins" of production engineers are "original sins" in the theological sense in that they cause further sorrow. This is especially true for the consequences of decisions that production engineers make concerning human work. The purpose of this chapter is dual: (a) to obtain attention to possible problems caused by engineers in plant operation with respect to human work and (b) to provide recommendations about ways to overcome these potential problems.

Human Aspects of Flexibility, Automation, and Integration

There are three key concepts that emerge from the literature on plant operation, design, and manufacturing engineering: flexibility, automation, and integration. Engineers and manufacturing experts attempt to achieve flexibility, automation, and integration through the introduction of new technologies such as the use of computers. When inquiring about areas that should become more flexible, automated, and integrated, the answers are largely universal: all work systems, manufacturing processes, and aspects of plant operations without exclusion. An explanation for this reply can be explained by the increased national and international economic competitiveness that is achieved through the enhanced design process.

There are, then, both economic and technological reasons for these new concepts of plant operation. This new approach can be termed as the *technocentric* approach of innovation in plant operation. In the technocentric design philosophy, human resources become peripheral and too often of secondary importance. Thus, human labor is seen only as a potential for savings in an economic context. Organizational adaption in manufacturing with respect to human needs, abilities, and behavior generally runs far behind technological development.

The alternative to the technocentric approach of innovation is the *anthropocentric* approach, which is basically human oriented (Brödner, 1990). The anthropocentric approach is based on flexibility, automation, and integration that enables those who design work to account for the human aspects of work design. What, then, is meant by flexibility, automation, and integration in this context?

Flexibility is now a fashionable manufacturing virtue. At the end of the 20th century, customers are demanding faster response and a wider variety of updated products. Correspondingly, competitors are achieving levels of performance well above what was considered feasible a few years ago. Flexibility, above all other measures of manufacturing performance, is cited as a solution. More flexibility in manufacturing operations means an increased ability to adapt to customer needs, to respond to competitive pressures, and to function "closer" to the market (Slack, 1990). Abilities, responsiveness, and closeness are characteristic features of humans. Therefore, the highest flexibility standards in manufacturing operations can be delivered by working people, not just by advanced technology. In the production process, this natural ability to adapt to new situations has always been, and still is, the basis of flexible manufacturing.

Automation means the design of a technical process in which humans work in neither a permanent nor a forced rhythm (REFA, 1987). It is one of the ironies of automation that human tasks in an automated factory become not superfluous but more important (Bainbridge, 1982). Monitoring the automated process, as well as undertaking and stabilizing it in the case of faults, requires even greater diagnostic and cognitive skills on the part of the human operator. Additionally, a greater knowledge base as well as enhanced manual control skills are now more critical than they ever were prior to automation. Thus, the concept of the completely automated "factory of the future" must be replaced by the concept of the factory that uses highly skilled human work.

Integration is the third key concept in the anthropocentric approach. Integrated production systems include all kinds of production facilities, with complementary singular functions in tool manufacturing and assembly, as well as in material flow and information handling. For the most part, material and information processing proceeds automatically. A basic feature of integrated production systems is the connection of the system elements by information technology (REFA, 1987). The task of integration requires a holistic view in which the "which, what, who, and where" can be integrated; this task is undoubtedly largely a human function.

If the anthropocentric approach is implemented into work design, questions such as the following inevitably arise: What aspects of human nature must be considered in the design process? What are the dimensions of work that need to be taken into account?

Avoiding Unfavorable Working Conditions

A hierarchical approach to the evaluation of human work was developed some years ago (Luczak & Rohmert, 1984; Rohmert, 1983). In this context, *hierarchy* means that the lower levels of evaluation have to be realized before the next higher levels are taken into account. The hierarchical approach evaluates under which technical, organizational, and ergonomic conditions human work is practicable, endurable, acceptable, and satisfactory (see Figure 1).

Practicability and endurability can be evaluated ergonomically by measurements from the natural sciences, whereas acceptability and satisfaction are subject to changes that are connected to economic and sociopolitical conditions (e.g., perceptions of unions and employer's associations or a labor market in which there is either a shortage of labor or high rates of unemployment). There can be no doubt that societal values and individual, subjective estimations together determine what is acceptable or satisfactory.

Concerning the acceptability of working conditions, the methods and criteria for the evaluation of practicability and endurability are the basis of and prerequisites for collective bargaining in the assessment process of human work. These are the classical domains of the natural and technical sciences. The hierarchical classification from practicability to satisfaction implies that an employee or an

Scientific Approaches of Labour Sciences	Levels of Evaluation of Human Work	Problem Areas and Assignment to Disciplines
view from natural science; primarily oriented to individuals / primarily oriented to groups; view from cultural studies	PRACTICABILITY	technical, anthropometrical and psychophysical problem (ERGONOMICS)
	ENDURABILITY	technical, physiological and medical problem (ERGONOMICS & OCCUP. HEALTH)
	ACCEPTABILITY	economical and sociological problem (OCCUP. PSYCHOLOGY & SOCIOLOGY, PERSONNEL MANAGEMENT)
	SATISFACTION	socio-psychological and economical problem (OCCUP. SOCIAL-PSYCHOLOGY, PERSONNEL MANAGEMENT)

Figure 1. Hierarchical model of criteria for the evaluation of human work.

employer (or both) may risk his or her health when high satisfaction is expected. In this context, people with high motivation to work are particularly likely to neglect limits of endurability and, for instance, expose themselves to the risk of a heart attack.

The concept of "minimal" standards (widely accepted by German scientists, practitioners, unions, and employers associations) must be achieved with respect to practicability and endurability and also should be achieved with respect to acceptability and satisfaction.

Practicability

The first and basic condition of work design is the practicability of the task. Generally, the anthropometric conditions of workplaces have to be congruent with the bodily stature of the worker. Furthermore, conditions of information processing should not exceed the perceptual limits of the sensory organs and the cognitive capacities of the worker. Some decades ago, a human resource-oriented work group of engineers analyzed the use of a variety of machine tools for drilling, lathes, milling-machines, and so forth with respect to anthropocentric conditions (Schulte, 1952). The result was catastrophic. The "ideal operator," as depicted with a good dose of British humor, was the so-called Cranfield man (the research was done at the University of Technology in Cranfield). This Cranfield man, designed in accordance with the present body frame of people working with machine tools at that time, is a "homunculus" with extremely long arms and short legs. This ideal operator would have no difficulty in reaching all the various knobs, switches, cranks, and so on of the machinery studied and could simultaneously scan the manufacturing process itself.

There is no doubt that the anthropometric design of machine tools has improved, but we must ask ourselves continually the following question: What are the pitfalls in the design of currently used machinery? The current situation with computer-assisted manufacturing of machine tools can be characterized by a certain task spectrum ranging from the qualified operator to the unskilled worker as an assistant/helper. A considerable amount of time is spent on process survey and on control. Monitoring machine tools and manufacturing processes seems to be a problem area in computer-aided manufacturing. Numerical control does not perceive disturbances because it lacks sensors and processes information only in a feed-forward mode. Moreover, deviations in algorithms cannot be recognized and included for further processing. In contrast, control loops use feedbacks and smooth deviations.

The processing of feedback and adaptation to changing conditions is a specifically human task. Thus, process inspection and control is still a task for human operators in computer-aided manufacturing. However, is it possible to conclude that this task is really "practicable" for human beings? Unfortunately it is not. Instead, three conclusions can be drawn.

First, the layout of complex production systems is frequently designed in such a way that machine tools are grouped around a conveyor belt. This grouping diminishes the clarity of the layout of the system because of the elimination of the simple sequential ordering of tasks. Additionally, only individual processes and machines obtain special attention from the operator.

Second, the manufacturing processes are surrounded by protective constructions such as doors, fences, exhaustion devices, and so on. A direct view of the process is impossible for the operator; the spectrum of auditory signals and noise is reduced and transformed in frequency, and odors cannot be detected. Because of the complex arrangement of different signal characteristics, direct sensory perception and evaluation of the situation in the manufacturing process become impossible.

Third, the speed of the manufacturing process is augmented to a level at which sensory perception becomes difficult. In addition, the anticipation of deviations from a change in signal characteristics before a break-down or damage often exceeds the reaction time of the operator.

With respect to the criterion of practicability of work, it can be concluded that the problems in manufacturing have shifted from anthropometrical failures in the manner of the Cranfield man to problems in information handling in process control. In several cases, elements of the job are simply not practicable.

Endurability

A second basic condition for the evaluation of human work is the endurability of a job or working condition. *Endurability* means that a worker can fulfill a job and withstand working conditions over a shift, a week, or a total working life without getting overly tired or worn out and without risking his or her health. Occupational physiology and medicine as well as ergonomics play a dominant role in the work system design with respect to this criterion.

Can conditions that cause such severe results actually occur in manufacturing systems? With regard to unskilled employees and the distribution of their duties over time, almost 50% of the working hours are dedicated to materials handling and cleaning. This is obviously a physical aspect of the workload that may cause weakening of the spine in the lumbar region. Statistics on back pain indicate that such working conditions are common in industry. Although there might be good reasons to be skeptical with respect to the criterion of endurability in most workplaces in machine tool manufacturing, this is especially the case in manual assembly.

By applying sophisticated electro-physiological measurement techniques that identify one-sided muscular workload and fatigue as well as deficiencies in sensory motor coordination, the occupational physiologist and ergonomist can derive evaluation models for endurability. Under such conditions of strain, principles of linearity of input/output functions in organic segments of the human body or the whole organism are no longer valid, which means that an equilibrium between organic functioning and recreation processes can no longer be maintained. In those cases, the following two conditions are most likely to be found: short cycles in manual assembly and high muscular strain for specific groups of muscles. A way to overcome such problems has been impressively demonstrated by the Daimler Benz Corporation in their Bremen plant, where a specific new manual assembly concept for the manufacture of the 190 and Roadster models has been designed. The seven basic requirements to be fulfilled by this concept are as follows: (a) high flexibility with respect to different types and variants in car production as well as in production output, (b) new forms of work organization, (c) appropriate ergonomical design, (d) partial mechanization and automation, (e) reduced inventory stocks, (f) reduced process times, and (g) high productivity.

These requirements were addressed by an assembly design known as *box assembly* or *star assembly*. Only assembly operations that are equal for all cars within a particular type are performed in a conventional assembly line. Electrical and other equipment, which differs considerably from car to car, is assembled independently in a so-called box by a team of four workers. The assembly operations now take 60–180 min and comprise a set of operations for the working group that avoids problems of endurability with respect to the individual strain reactions of each worker.

Acceptability

The third notion, that of acceptability, is heavily influenced by cultural and societal values. In the Charlie Chaplin film *Modern Times*, a working person is performing a certain handgrip on objects located on a conveyor belt during a high-speed operation. This work might be endurable, but it would not be acceptable by most societies because of the mistreatment of the worker.

Technical innovations and their introduction in work organizations enforce a new division of labor, a restructuring of job design and organizational change. The functional efficiency of such changes will depend to a large extent on their acceptance by those directly or indirectly affected. Hence, attention should be directed toward the individual and group-oriented preference structures of employees. In this process of preference development, economical categories of extrinsic motivation interfere undoubtfully with job design categories of intrinsic motivation. A study on trade-off functions and quantities between economic and organizational factors determining "acceptability" was recently performed by Ruiz-Quintanilla (1988). The preference structure between pay and two conditions of job design was analyzed through a pair-wise comparison test on almost 6,000 employees in seven industrialized countries. The first condition was autonomy, and the second condition consisted of autonomy, skill use, and interesting work in relation to an increase in pay of 10%, 30%, and 50%, respectively. The first question focused on whether workers prefer constant pay for different jobs within a job design. With slight differences between countries, the replies were clearly affirmative. Especially in Germany (West Germany at the time) job design with a constant pay rate was preferred. Because of the autonomy aspect, Japanese employees preferred the alternative in this area when compared with workers from other nations.

The second question addressed the trade-off between two levels of job condition with respect to acceptability and an alternative pay raise. The study indicated that a pay raise of 10% motivated only 5% to 10% of employees to give up the option of autonomy, skill use, and interesting work. Even a pay raise of 50% did not crucially change the results, which means that only 20% of the employees changed their minds in the direction of getting financial compensation for barely acceptable working conditions. These surprising results lead to the following conclusions for personnel management and job design: It is trivial to state that most people work to receive a material basis for their living; money is a fundamentally important reason to accept work. Reaching an income that yields a relatively comfortable living standard, however, causes the monetary incentive to lose a lot of its existential value, whereas the noninstrumental qualities of a job acquire increasing importance. In other words, acceptability standards are often more significant than are remunerative standards. Autonomy, the application of skills, and the meaningfulness of work seem to be the directions of design that should be considered to use the potential of new technologies in human-centered workplaces. Additionally, this will have a beneficial effect on worker satisfaction.

Identifying the Dimensions of Humane Work

In a manner of speaking, "good, humane work" should provide for degrees of freedom to attain goals. If presetting of goals is necessary, individual methods to forming approaches to these goals should be possible. In an ideal world of quality work life, the goals would be chosen by the individual in a self-determining process. However, the ideal of self-set goals in human work settings obviously meets with organizational limits and restrictions.

Figure 2 illustrates the different levels of human work by dividing them into structural and procedural levels of work processes. For example, on Level S3 of Figure 2, goal-oriented actions are combined with the individual's functional means. That is, tasks require qualifications. An illustration of the process is the example of a university professor in Germany. The position requires the worker to conduct research, to teach, to administrate, to direct an institute, and to accomplish other varied tasks. Work is found to be satisfying if changing tasks have to be performed with different requirements (see Figure 3). These tasks should offer chances to learn new things; the development of functional abilities for various tasks can be seen as a characteristic of good work on this level. When passing from Level S3 to Level V3 (Figure 3), tasks are executed on the individual and motive-oriented level. The central word in this context is *motivation*. Studies about the motivation of German professors and scientists, for example, indicate that motivation is only marginally caused by money but caused more by so-called scientific reputation. For instance, social feedback in the form of acknowledgment by colleges after the publication or recognition of a book or after completion of a research project can be perceived as more important than financial incentives. Motivation theories also indicate that purely financial incentives are inadequate. A number of incentives should also stem from the work process itself, the opportunity to intervene and influence the dynamics of the task and its estimation by society. Additionally, surrounding groups appear to be crucial; loops for positive feedback must be open.

At Level S4 (Figure 3) a worker's complete span of activity is examined. An individual job with all its characteristics, including the technical and organizational components, is analyzed. Using the example of a German university professor again, it appears that good work on this level means personal freedom in the choice of things to accomplish. Additionally, it includes a comfortable office for thinking, writing, discussing, and reading (with a variety of books immediately available), a secretary and co-workers with whom one can interact in an open style (and whom one respects as individuals), readily available laboratory equipment and computers, and so forth. Beyond this material and social environment, the professor treasures

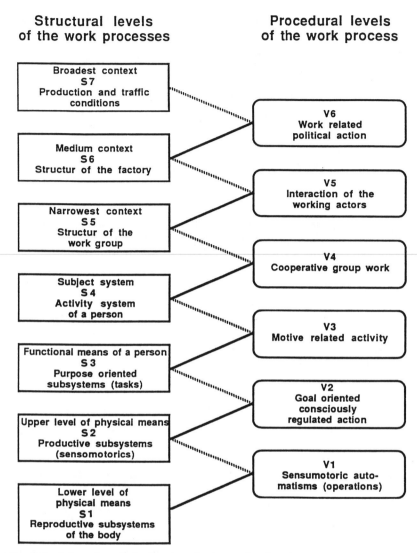

Figure 2. Principles of work design in relation to levels of work sciences.

the ability to freely dispose of his or her time. Although another individual might have other criteria for good work, personal freedom in disposition over work content, an appropriate social and material environment, and a degree of control over one's time are clearly universal elements of a good job.

The structural and functional components on Levels V4/S5, V5/S6, and V6/S7 are so closely related that it becomes difficult to differentiate characteristics of good work between the corresponding Levels S and V.

On Level V4/S5, the perspective widens from the individual to the social context (Figure 4). Clearly, most work is done in groups, and labor partition has to take place to achieve an outcome. If cooperative groups succeed, then the organizational context in which these groups function must form a decisive set of criteria for good work. During the past 15 years, the German Federal Minister of Research and

S 1:   Principle of "healthy" working conditions respecting
             limits of tolerability and safety

V 1:   Principle of using reflexes in complex movement cycles

S 2:   Principle of practicability of a task,
             principle of control of a situation

V 2:   Principle of degrees of freedom in goal-setting and
             individual paths of performance

S 3:   Principle of variety of tasks and qualifications

V 3:   Principle of reachable incentives

S 4:   Principle of disposition over work content, social and
             material environment, and over time

Figure 3.   Principles of work design for the individual. (S = structural level; V = procedural level.)

Technology has financed programs that have focused on the "humanization of work" and that have been centered on the structure of work. The basic outcomes of this program demonstrate that cooperative group activities should (a) initiate discussions to improve working conditions and work results (e.g., "quality circles," which are small groups of volunteers who meet to solve problems pertaining to their work and should indicate essential contributions and responsibilities of each individual), (b) avoid frictions and misunderstandings between people through discussions, and (c) replace struggles in the organizational relation between individuals through coherent group activities with reciprocal subsidies and the balancing of failures. The composition of the work group and the organizational integration of the department can be improved through the desired results when the program is realized because cooperation and communication are better as organizing principles than are unquestioned instructions or imperatives. Therefore, essential conclusions for good work can be drawn from this discussion (Pornschlegel, 1986).

Proceeding to Level V5/S6, the implications of industrial and administrative plant management and services on human work have to be identified. Today, it is commonly accepted that enterprises develop a distinct culture. These sociocultural traits are related to the working atmosphere in that institution. In addition, the organization's culture is characterized through certain interacting interest groups. These interests reflect the concerns of the capital owners and the personnel representatives. For example, collective bargaining takes place between union representatives and managers on working conditions and salaries. The resultant dialectic might be compared with that of a crew in one boat, all of whom represent different positions and different interests in the direction and the steering strategy of the boat. The way in which this conflict can be resolved may be helpful in the design

V 4 / S 5:   Set of principles of organizational development with respect to

- information handling/communication by discussion and discurses

- reciprocal subsidies of individuals

- feedbacks of contributions and responsibilities

V 5 / S 6:   Set of principles of collective bargaining with respect to

- overcoming conflicts

- participatory work design

- direct information on technological and economical change

V 6 /S 7:   Set of principles of legal regulations and infrastructural investments with respect to

- stable work contracts and income

- chances of the labour market

- educational systems and qualification

- social networks and insurances

- traffic systems and

- ecological interventions

Figure 4. Principles of work design for groups (or the labor force). (S = structural level; V = procedural level.)

of good work at this level. To summarize, participation, or at least substantial participatory elements in the leadership style of a company, appears to be a criterion for good work (see Endruweit, Gaugler, Staehle, & Wilpert, 1985). When implementing this strategy, basic principles of the company's technological and organizational development can be discussed at various levels and formed into concrete designs that respect employees' interests. If these principles are established through flat hierarchies characterized by direct interactions, contacts, and influences among concerned people, a further feature of good work is identified.

Proceeding to Level V6/S7, there is no doubt that governmental actions crucially influence good work. The government legislates the conditions for economic growth and development, for legal regulations in the sociopolitical and contractual sphere, and for the infrastructure and global investment strategies of the national economy. What can employées expect from these global work-related political actions with respect to their own personal evaluations of good work? First, good work should be expected to have a certain degree of stability regarding the length of contracts and the readiness of income. Because work affects the stability of a person's entire life, being permanently and safely employed in an economically prospering branch or section of one's national economy is a fundamental criterion of good work. If, in addition to this, the labor market offers opportunities for development for any qualified person to improve his or her work situation, another criterion of good work is identified. Good work also means qualified work and, when referring to Germany, it is a governmental responsibility to present possibilities for qualification processes by providing an appropriate educational system with variants for individual biography and life-style. It is certainly an advantage (and, therefore, a criterion of good work) if a social net is available in a national economy that prevents people from falling into a "black hole" if a job is lost because of age, illness, or economic reasons. Governmental structures influence good work in setting priorities with respect to the development of traffic systems, housing areas, and industrial regions in the landscape. If this arrangement fulfills the requirement that the workplace is accessible from the living area in a short time, a large portion of nonwork time can be devoted to leisure activities, and good work can be further diagnosed.

Evolution Theory and Biological Considerations

In most cases, humans have forgotten that they are an element of nature (really a product) that has developed to its current status by processes of selection and evolution. Another important consideration in this context seems to be that humans are a part of nature themselves in the sense that they are biological systems with strong connections to other biological systems in material, informational, and social terms.

Recently, a very enlightening and far-reaching concept of work design for humankind (with a considerable philosophical and anthropological background) was published by Volpert (1990). Volpert's examination of the evolutionary theory in terms of human beings, biological implications, and social theory led him to develop a series of demands for human engineers and design engineers for the technological development of work processes.

Evolution and self-organization are basic principles of the development of many organisms, and, thus for humankind, too. Theories of human personality, human action, and human learning refer to these principles. Additionally, these principles are addressed in theories of individual human action and work, as well as in models of work/motivation and appropriate organizational design. Several philosophical and anthropological roots can be identified to formulate the principles of the design of work, which then, if applied, should guarantee something like the possibility of autonomous development, action, and mental reflection by any working person within his or her sociocultural context.

According to Volpert's (1990) evolutionary theory, nine guidelines apply for the development of an individual worker. Following are the first four guidelines; the remaining will be introduced on the next pages: (1) generating tasks with freedom of activities to improve personal development; (2) giving workers autonomy in controlling their time; (3) creating tasks that offer possibilities to structure individual ways of performance; and (4) avoiding frictions in task execution by technical or organizational constraints. These four guidelines are derived from the common principle of evolution of "own ways of development."

Another set of implications arises from the fact that humans have a physical existence with biological needs and purposes arising from physiological functions and ecological interactions with the environment. The common principle of "physical existence in a real world" leads to a necessity for real movement of limbs and includes the active engagement in the environment with modification to changes of the real world. Multimodal perception and realistic thinking patterns form a substantial part of human existence. We exist only by our bodies and perceive the world only by organismic systems.

The five additional guidelines are biological and social implications with respect to the physical and bodily existence of humans in the real world: (5) creating tasks that involve sufficient amounts and diversity of physical activity; (6) assuring that tasks provide multiple stimuli to different sensory organs; (7) taking concrete action to provide real material and direct social interaction; (8) incorporating into tasks the feature of "centralized variability" (i.e., different conditions or ways of performing equally structured tasks); and (9) assuring that tasks make possible and improve cooperation and contact between workers.

If one compares Volpert's (1990) approach with the systematic approach, many comparable requirements become apparent. There is no doubt about additional hints acquired from the evolution theory and from the biological concept, especially when considering realistic interaction with the world. Researchers, who perceive the essentials of their work in abstract information handling and process planning, often forget these aspects of "concrete material handling," "multiple stimuli," or the idea of "freedom," freedom of activities, freedom in time disposition, and freedom in task structuring.

Self-Report, Empirical Evidence

Beyond theoretical considerations of human nature, evolution, and biological existence and beyond systematic consideration of what aspects of human work are important for determining the criteria of good work, there have been empirical studies on the meaning of work. These studies show that for most people in industrialized countries, work is of central importance in their lives (Ruiz-Quintanilla 1988). These studies, using representative samples of subjects in Belgium, Holland, Israel, Japan, Yugoslavia, Great Britain, (West) Germany, and the United States, indicated that criteria for the evaluation of human work actually exist in a specific ranking order: In these multicultural, multinational studies, the subjective importance of "interesting work" ranked first and did not depend on age. If work is to keep its central importance, design engineers and managers in plant operations should first attempt to create jobs and tasks that will be perceived as "interesting" by the employees.

The second rank of "good salary" should not seduce employers into compensating for dull work with high wages. Other factors, such as secure employment, can be related to wage aspects as well. For example, it is no wonder that for a German civil servant (a professor belongs in this category in Germany), a "steady position" (with minimal danger of being fired) is of high importance as well, with a certain bias with respect to age. All the criteria that have fundamental importance for personality development (e.g., human relations, the variety of task allocation, the chance for learning while performing) rank in the upper part of the list.

It is perhaps hard for an engineer, whose training is characterized by basic biophysiological influences stemming from ergonomics and natural sciences, to notice and to conclude that working time and physical conditions of work rank low. Moreover, the balance of capabilities and demands that represent the common known problem of stress rank only slightly higher.

Another surprising finding was the low ranking of "career opportunities." It appears that many firms have overestimated the importance of this area in their personnel development concepts. This conclusion may be important if design proposals that imply a reduction of hierarchical levels, flexible task allocation with flat hierarchies, and decentralized production structures with a low stimulation of personnel with respect to motivation by career incentives are implemented. Most advanced corporations have recognized this direction in development and are beginning to implement these concepts in plant operation. Because of the positive results that, at least in the minds of employees, can apparently be obtained, I recommend a comprehensive application of these ideas.

Computer Integrated Manufacturing and Human Integrated Manufacturing

Recently, in production engineering, terms like *computer integrated manufacturing*, *logistics*, and *just-in-time* have been broadly discussed as strategic approaches to improve service ability and to reduce lead or through-put time in production. In the meantime, the average lifetime of many products on the market has become shorter than the average time for the development of a product that is a new problem for plant operations. Apparently, the reduction in lead time in production alone is no longer sufficient to master this problem. Therefore, the scope of observations and thoughts has to be broadened. To improve a company's position in the competitive world, two methods can be applied: The first approach is characterized by the development of computer-aided methods to reduce the time span from the first concept of a product to its complete implementation in the market by information processing. The basic approach is to parallel the sequential operations of the production process, to build the production facilities, to develop production software, to prepare market strategies, and, finally, to begin production.

The second approach concentrates on the labor force, or aspects of the personnel and human resource management of the company. This approach is an alternative to the first approach and can be applied as a complement to it. The connection and interactions of CIM and HIM are indicated in Figure 5.

Process analysis will be necessary if computer functions or job functions are

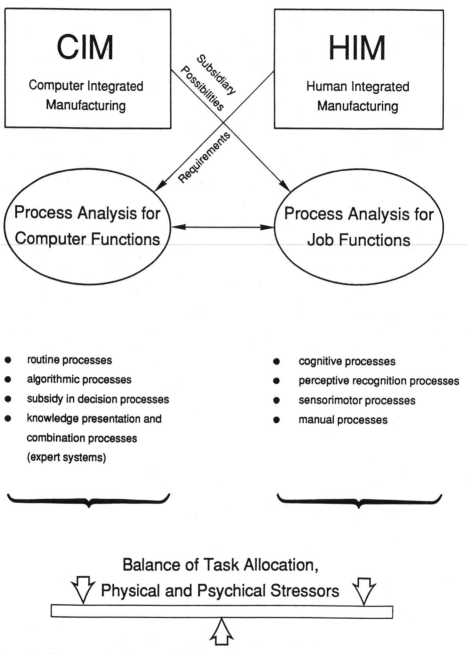

Figure 5.   Concepts of technocentric and anthrocentric work.

defined for individuals. Human-integrated manufacturing means the establishment of networks that preview an allocation of functions between humans and computers following the principles of good work. By balancing the results of such designs, several changes in production, organization, and employees have been recommended

Table 1. Changes in Production, Organization, and Employees by HIM Concepts

Production
Improvement of product quality
Increase of production output
Reduction of lead times
Increase of flexibility
Reduction of absenteeism
Reduction of fluctuation
Increase of company's attractiveness to the labor market

Organization
Decrease of hierarchical positions
Change in roles of superior staff
Change in control spans
Shift of tool setting and quality control activities to productive people
Diminished requirements for improvisation
Redefinition of jobs
Alteration of concepts of salary

Employees
Decrease of one-sided workload
Decrease of stress using mental aides
Change in the structure of work satisfaction
Shift from extrinsic to intrinsic motivation
Improvement of qualifications
Increase of individual task-flexibility
Improvement of leisure activities

by projects in the humanization of work in Germany (Ulich, Conrad-Betschart, & Baitsch, 1989; see Table 1).

Even if only one of these effects can be found and all other conditions are stable, there is no doubt that the improvement will have an impact on the performance of the company. Humanization efforts will lead to improved productivity and cost-effectiveness, as studies with new forms of economic calculations indicate. Thus, organizations should enter paths in technological, organizational, and personnel development that offer options of good work. Design must stress systems that overcome the weaknesses of humankind and that support its specific strengths.

References

Bainbridge, L. (1982). Ironies of automation. *Proceedings of the International Federation of Automation and Control (IFAC) Conference Analysis Design and Evaluation of Man–Machine Systems*, 129–135.

Brödner, P. (1990). Technocentric–anthropocentric approaches: Towards skill based manufacturing. In M. Warner, W. Woobe, & P. Brödner (Eds.), *New technology and manufacturing management* (pp. 101–111). New York: Wiley.

Campion, M. A. (1988). Interdisciplinary approaches to job design: A constructive replication with extensions. *Journal of Applied Psychology, 73*, 467–481.

Endruweit, G., Gaugler, E., Staehle, W., & Wilpert, B. (1985). *Handbuch der Arbeitsbeziehungen* [Handbook of work relationships]. Berlin, Germany: deGruyter.

Forward, G. E., Beach, D. E., Gray, D. A., & Quick, J. C. (1991). Mentofacturing: A vision for American industrial excellence. *Academy of Management Executive, 5,* 32–44.

Luczak, H., & Rohmert, W. (1984). Stand der Arbeitswissenschaft [Situation of the science of work]. *Zeitschrift für Betriebswirtschaft* (Journal for Business Management), *1.*

Pornschlegel, H. (1986). Perspektwen Arbeitswissenschaftlicher Forschung in Forderprogramm: Humanisierung des Arbeitslebens der Bunderegierung [Perspectives of research in work science in the advancement program: Humanization of life of work in the German government]. *Zeitschrift fur Arbeitswissenschaft* [Journal for Science of Work], *40,* 1–6.

REFA. (1987). *Verband für Arbeitsstudien und Betriebsorganisation: Planung und Gestaltung Komplexer Produktionssysteme* [Association for the studies of work and the organization of companies: Planning and design of complex systems of production]. Munich, Germany: C. Hanser Verlag.

Rohmert, W. (1983). Möglichkeiten und Grenzen Menschengerechter Arbeitsgestaltung durch Ergonomie [Possibilities and limits of adequate human design of work through ergonomics]. In F. Fürstenberg (Ed.), *Menschengerechte Gestaltung der Arbeit* [Adequate human design of work] (pp. 39–76). Mannheim, Germany.

Ruiz-Quintanilla, A. (1988). Work values and new technologies. In V. de Keyser, T. Qvale, B. Wilpert, & A. Ruiz-Quintanilla (Eds.), *The meaning of work and technological options* (pp. 45–57). New York: Wiley.

Schulte, B. (1952). *Arbeitserleichterung durch Anpassung der Maschine an den Menschen* [Facilitation of work through the adaptation of machines on humans]. Unpublished doctoral dissertation, Munich University of Technology, Germany.

Slack, N. (1990). Flexibility as managers see it. In M. Warner, W. Wobbe, & P. Brödner (Eds.), *New technology and manufacturing management* (pp. 33–48). New York: Wiley.

Ulich, E., Conrad-Betschart, H., & Baitsch, C. (1989). *Arbeitsform mit Zukunft: Ganzheitlich-Flexibel Statt Arbeitsteiling* [Forms of work with future: Entire flexible instead of work splitting]. Bern, Germany: Verlag P. Lang.

Volpert, W. (1990). Welche Arbeit ist gut für den Menschen? Notizen zum Menschenbild und Arbeitsgestaltung [What kind of work is good for humans? Notes about humans and the design of work]. In F. Frei & I. Udris (Eds.), *Das Bild der Arbeit* [The view of work] (pp. 27–40). Bern, Germany: Verlag H. Huber.

Wildemann, H. (1990). *Einführungsstrategien für die computerintegrierte Produktion (CIM).* [Introduction strategies for computer-integrated production]. Munich, Germany: GFMT.

Part III _____

Individual Stress Responses and Early Warning Signs

Introduction

In keeping with the basic theme for this book presented in Chapter 1, the eight chapters in this section are concerned with individual stress responses and early warning signs of distress. The chapters are clearly diverse in nature, consisting of descriptions of empirical investigations as well as more conceptual works. As we have noted earlier, and as is evident in these chapters, distinguishing between early warning signs and outright distress is not always easy. Yet, when early warning signs can be identified, they can be addressed through secondary prevention efforts that are aimed at modifying and enhancing individuals' responses to risks. Four of the eight chapters in this section are largely assessment oriented, and four are largely intervention oriented.

Assessment Chapters

Chapter 8, by Fitzgerald, represents a departure from what might be expected in a volume concerned with occupational mental health in that its major focus is on musculoskeletal disability. However, Fitzgerald argues that all work-related disabilities have a psychosocial component. To label a disability as either *musculoskeletal* or *psychological*, according to Fitzgerald, merely reflects the relative importance of that factor in the presumed etiology of the injury or illness. He maintains that subtle psychological reactions to work, such as work attitudes and symptoms of mild depression, are often significant predictors of disability. After reviewing four models of musculoskeletal disability, he concludes that common pathways mediate a series of responses that increase the likelihood of a disability outcome. Recommendations concerning the assessment of the individual stress response and its risk factors are made.

Chapter 9, by Tetrick, discusses a study of perceived role stress in over 800 individuals in three organizations. While acknowledging the impact of the objective work environment, this study emphasizes the importance of individual perceptions of the work environment. In particular, the perception of role stress was found to influence perceived anxiety as well as perceptions of one's job, leader, and work group. Tetrick's results suggest that stress management techniques need to focus on interpersonal aspects of the work environment.

Chapter 10, by McKee, Markham, and Scott, reports a study of job stress and employee withdrawal among some 733 sewing machine operators working in five apparel manufacturing plants. The authors found a significant positive relation between job stress and intention to leave the job. This relation was higher for those without dependents than for those with dependents living at home. The latter finding underscores the need to consider variables outside the work setting to gain a comprehensive understanding of individual stress responses.

Chapter 11, by Nelson and Hitt, reviews the literature on gender differences in work stress and describes a study of stress among 248 male and 195 female personnel professionals. In this study, like other studies of gender difference in job stress, men and women were found to differ in their perceptions of what factors are stressful. In particular, female personnel professionals, unlike their male counterparts, found political exchanges and games in the workplace to be stressful. Based on their review of the literature and this study, Nelson and Hitt offer numerous recommendations to eliminate distress among women at work.

Intervention Chapters

Chapter 12, by Kirschman, Scrivner, Ellison, and Marcy, describes three successful mental health service delivery programs for police officers. Although distinctly different in composition, each is an on-site program that is involved with the structure and operation of a police agency. The success of these programs is attributed, in part, to accurate diagnosis of organizational and community cultures and an understanding of the dynamics operating within law enforcement subcultures.

In chapter 13, Robbins, using her experiences as a psychologist involved in a university health and safety structure, discusses the role of joint labor–management health and safety committees in dealing with job stress issues. Although it is clear that the great majority of employees in the United States are not unionized and that the university setting may be atypical, Robbins concludes that health and safety committees offer a workable means for identifying certain occupational stress problems.

Chapter 14, by Martin, represents a synthesis of the author's experiences in developing stress training programs. He asserts that stress training for works at all levels is essential and feasible and proposes a model of stress training. The purpose of the model is to help practitioners increase the power of trainees to make intentional changes in their stress situations. The model is cyclic in nature and allows for revision and refinement to reflect advances in theory and experiential learning.

Chapter 15, by Gehlmann, reports an empirical study of the effects of workspace characteristics and personality traits on symptoms of stress and levels job satisfaction in 87 college employees. The results indicate a significant relation between stress and type of office space, with people in more open office spaces reporting more stress. No significant relation was found between job satisfaction and type of office space. Measures of personality traits were not consistently related to either stress or satisfaction.

8

Terence E. Fitzgerald

Psychosocial Aspects of Work-Related Musculoskeletal Disability

The central premise of this chapter is that disability prevention strategies should be guided by robust conceptual models that can describe an individual worker's progression from normal functioning to disability and from disability to rehabilitation and safe return to work. The following discussion will primarily focus on issues that relate to musculoskeletal disability. After a brief review of its prevalence and consequences, hypothesized determinants of disability will be advanced in the context of relevant conceptual models of coping and behavior change. Finally, relevant findings from the review of mechanisms of musculoskeletal disability will be abstracted as recommendations for the surveillance and prevention of occupational psychological disorders.

Conventional wisdom argues that disabled workers can be typically classified into two mutually exclusive groupings: (a) those afflicted with chronic, debilitating medical conditions and (b) outright malingerers whose behavior is reinforced by disability benefit payments (cf. Weighill, 1983). Epidemiological investigations, however, have failed to substantiate either of these conditions. Medical conditions clearly affect work disability but only to the extent that they engender physical impairment relative to specific job demands (Luft, 1978). Instead, demographics and work-related psychological and social factors account for most of the variance in disability outcomes, relegating level of replacement income to a minor role in most studies involving American workers. Work attitudes, perceived control over job tasks, psychological demands at work, flexibility of work rules, and symptoms of depression have been identified as significant predictors of disability (Yelin, 1986; Yelin, Nevitt, & Epstein, 1980).

Two recent directives from the National Institute for Occupational Safety and Health (NIOSH) recommended surveillance of threats in the work environment that may contribute to job stress, impairment, and disability. The first initiative (NIOSH, 1986) addressed the early detection of risk factors for musculoskeletal impairment, the primary cause of work-related disability in the United States. Musculoskeletal injuries are likely to remain a prominent component of worksite surveillance programs because of their high frequency of occurrence, the severity of their psychosocial impact, and their presumed amenability to prevention efforts. A separate statement (NIOSH, 1988) outlined a national strategy for the prevention of work-related psychological disorders. Primarily concerned with the monitoring of affective disturbance, maladaptive health behaviors, and substance abuse, it did not target chronic mental disorders for intervention. Although both NIOSH statements acknowledged the potential for interaction between personal and occupational risk factors, the articulation of separate prevention strategies appears to imply that the etiological pathways of occupational disabilities may be qualitatively different depending on the nature of the presenting complaint. Although the issue has yet to be examined prospectively, psychological appraisals do seem to play an important role in the acquisition and maintenance of disability-related behaviors following occupational injury or illness.

The Scope of Work-Related Musculoskeletal Disability

Accidental injuries are sustained by 11 million workers each year, over 10% of whom can expect to be disabled at any given time (U.S. Public Health Service, 1988). In the case of low-back trauma, it has been observed in one population that although the annual incidence of work absence is 1.4%, the majority of injured workers return to work within 1 month of onset of symptoms. The 7% with activity-related spinal disorders who remain disabled after 6 months account for 76% of compensation-related costs (Spitzer, LeBlanc, & Dupuis, 1987). The long-term effects of back injury on return to work are equally compelling. In a study of industrial workers, McGill (1968) found that those out of work for more than 6 months had a 50% chance of return; absence greater than 1 year occasioned a 25% return to work rate, whereas a 2-year absence virtually obviated the possibility of work reentry.

The American Academy of Orthopaedic Surgeons has estimated that the total direct and indirect costs of all musculoskeletal injuries exceeds 27 billion dollars annually (Holbrook, Grazier, Kelsey, & Stauffer, 1984). Average disability payments related to back injuries in the workplace have been estimated at approximately $7,000 for each injured employee, with 60% of the cost attributable to lost work time and 40% to medical and rehabilitation expenses (Federspiel, Guy, Kane, & Spengler, 1989; Webster & Snook, 1990). Relatedly, upper-extremity cumulative trauma disorders (UECTDs), although generally not permanently disabling, have resulted in average worker's compensation claims of $5,670 in the mid-Atlantic region of the United States (Fletcher, 1990).

Determinants of Disability

Although the societal cost of musculoskeletal injuries is significant, projections of health-care costs, compensation payments, and lost productivity do not take into account the impact of functional impairment on personal suffering and the unnecessary prolongation of disability. Indeed, continued unemployment has been associated with increased somatic complaints, anxiety, depression, and utilization of health-care services (DeFrank & Ivancevich, 1986; Linn, Sandifer, & Stein, 1985). For disabled individuals with minimal opportunities for social support and self-esteem enhancing activities outside the workplace, the resumption of employment may serve to improve perceptions of health and quality of life independent of level of objective physical impairment (Kutner, 1984; Nathanson, 1980).

Typically, disability claims are adjudicated on the basis of neurologic, structural, and radiological examinations; yet, there exists no empirical support for an unequivocal link between physical and biomedical measures and postinjury functional capacity (Gallagher et al., 1989; Murphy, Sperr, & Sperr, 1986). Although the poor correlation between pain report and objective signs of disease is well documented (e.g., Nachemson, 1983), the reason for this discordance remains elusive. Recent conceptualizations of pain, however, may help to clarify this problem. Feuerstein, Papciak, and Hoon (1987), for example, defined pain as the "total experience of some noxious stimulus which is influenced by current context of the pain, previous experiences, learning history, and cognitive processes" (p. 244). This perspective on pain appears to be validated by research that shows that pain perception can occur in the absence of overt tissue damage or pathophysiology (International Association for the Study of Pain, 1979).

A transactional view of pain-related disability now serves as an alternative to an artificial dichotomy of disability as either organic or psychogenic. Moving beyond simple stimulus–response models of behavior, operant schemes focus instead on the reinforcing consequences of disability. For instance, "pain behaviors" may be maintained by social reinforcement long after nociceptive stimulation has ceased (Fordyce, 1976). Broadly defined, pain behaviors include anxiety, attention seeking, pain complaints, medication use, general verbal complaints, distorted posture and mobility, fatigue, insomnia, and depressive mood (Turk, Wack, & Kerns, 1985).

Cognitive processes may reciprocally determine pain perception (cf., Turk, Meichenbaum, & Genest, 1983) in that fear of a pain exacerbation may lead to avoidance of activities that are expected to produce pain. For the worker with prolonged disability, the belief that pain is a signal for reinjury may foster gross inactivity, muscular deconditioning, muscle tension, perceived stress, and maladaptive cognitions. Moreover, stress-related thoughts may induce muscular arousal that can precipitate pain stimulation (Flor, Turk, & Birbaumer, 1985).

Although much of disability research has used cross-sectional or retrospective methods from which causation can not be inferred, certain relational patterns have emerged, with the following implications.

Implication 1: Although most demographic variables have proven to be poor predictors of work disability, age is a notable exception. A stable age-related association has been demonstrated for work loss. For the 35–44 year-old cohort, estimates of disability range from 7.1% to 7.5%, increasing to 11–12.3% for those 45–54 years old and to 22.2–24.1% for those 55–64 years old (Kraus & Stoddard, 1989; McNeil, 1982). Projecting a significant decline in economic productivity, Bowe (1983) estimated that half of the population of the United States will be physically disabled, chronically ill, or beyond retirement age by the year 2000. The reasons for the relation between age and increased disability have not been explicated; however, older workers and those with low incomes, low levels of education, and decreased physical fitness appear to be at increased risk (Andersson & Pope, 1991).

Several studies have demonstrated a link between advancing age and increased injury and illness (e.g., Biering-Sorenson, 1982; McPherson, 1984), although the notion of inevitable pathophysiological decline during the working years has not been proved. Although age has been implicated in various musculoskeletal changes such as reductions in muscle and bone mass, joint flexibility, tendon capillary blood flow, and tissue elasticity, these biological changes are remarkably similar to those associated with prolonged physical inactivity (Bortz, 1982; Shephard, 1978). Relatedly, physically active older adults do not appear to show significantly greater incidence of tendinitis and stress fracture than do active younger people (Matheson, MacIntyre, Taunton, Clement, & Lloyd-Smith, 1989).

Implication 2: Musculoskeletal "injury" may be precipitated by a mismatch between the physical capabilities or work style of the individual and the biomechanical demands of the job. In some worksites, low isometric strength and overall fitness have been shown to be significant contributors to risk of back pain–related disability (e.g., Biering-Sorenson, 1984). Conversely, findings from a recent prospective study have failed to support a link between spinal flexibility or aerobic capacity and subsequent report of low-back pain in an industrial setting (Battie et al., 1990). Physical problems secondary to chronic cigarette smoking also may be associated with future report of back problems and greater pain severity in epidemiological surveys (Battie et al., 1989; Frymoyer et al., 1983). Although coughing has been implicated as the causal agent (Biering-Sorenson & Thomsen, 1986), nicotine has been hypothesized to constrict vertebral-body blood circulation, affect disc metabolism, and increase disc vulnerability to mechanical stress (Urban, Holm, Maroudas, & Nachemson, 1977).

Furthermore, ergonomic factors in the workplace have been implicated in both low-back and upper-extremity injuries. Prolonged sitting and standing, twisting motions, highly repetitive lifting, and unassisted lifting of heavy loads have been associated with onset of low back pain (Pope, Andersson, Frymoyer, & Chaffin, 1991). The pervasive view of back injury as an acute phenomenon, however, does not accurately reflect the observed natural history of work-related back pain, which is characterized by frequent, recurring symptoms (e.g., Troup, Martin, & Lloyd, 1981). This suggests that a chronic mismatch between capabilities or work style and occupational demands may set the stage for dysfunction.

The etiologies of upper-extremity disorders, particularly those thought to involve cumulative trauma, remain even less clear. Speculation has focused on repetitive motion and exertion of the affected joint, although high force and vibration have also been suggested as "traumatogens" (Armstrong, Fine, Goldstein, Lifshitz, & Silverstein, 1987; NIOSH, 1986; Silverstein, Fine, & Armstrong, 1987). In a case control study of sign-language interpreters, Feuerstein and Fitzgerald (1991a) exposed subjects to an analog work task and assessed potential biomechanical factors that may contribute to UECTD symptoms. In comparison to a pain-free control group, those reporting pain and fatigue while working exhibited fewer rest breaks, more frequent hand/wrist deviations from a neutral posture, more frequent lateral excursions from an optimal work envelope, and more frequent finger/hand movements during the interpreting task. These findings suggest a work style characterized by heightened behavioral expressivity to physical and psychosocial job demands. Decreasing risk for UECTDs may, therefore, involve training workers to cope effectively with work-related stressors as well as incorporating ergonomic task modifications to limit exposure to excessive physical demands.

Implication 3: Mood-related appraisals and behaviors may inhibit adaptive coping and prolong musculoskeletal disability. It remains open to question whether negative affect states associated with musculoskeletal pain such as depression and anxiety are primarily reactive, coexisting, or dispositional (Romano & Turner, 1985). Although it is difficult to reliably determine the temporal relation between negative mood and the multiple manifestations of pain-related disability, depression has been viewed as an overlearned response to inadequate coping efforts (e.g., Seligman, 1975) and as a consequence of an imbalance in central nervous system biogenic amines (Walsh, 1983). Alternatively, Barsky and Klerman (1983) made a case for dispositional factors in the etiology of musculoskeletal-related psychopathology. They identified three interactive characteristics—(a) amplication of bodily sensations, (b) misinterpretation or overinterpretation of normative bodily sensations, (c) and signs of emotional arousal—and a proclivity to experience the world in physical and concrete terms rather than make subjective and emotion-based judgments. In this way, abnormal illness behavior, disease conviction, and overutilization of medical consultation are seen as outward manifestations of a perceptual/cognitive defect. These individuals are likely to experience little control over their functional decline given that causal attributions are external and disease related.

Largely supporting the latter view, Watson and Pennebaker (1989) provided extensive evidence that negative affectivity is a general "somatopsychic" trait characterized by chronic self-report of distress bridging a range of emotions and health complaints. The authors argued that the distinction between psychological and physical complaining is artificial and confounding. Systematic research is needed to articulate relations among negative affectivity, objective physical impairment, and perceived work disability. A study of chronic pain treatments, however, suggests that high pretreatment levels of negative affectivity and pain behavior do not necessarily engender poor outcomes following multidisciplinary interventions (Kleinke & Spangler, 1988).

Implication 4: Perceptions of the work environment may influence the likelihood of disability. Using established "social climate" measures such as Moos's (1986) Work Environment Scale, investigators have explored putative links between various aspects of the social milieu and protracted disability. Svensson and Andersson (1983) examined vocational stress in 40–47 year-old male industrial workers. Occurrence of low-back pain was linked to a perception of a lack of control over the method and pace of job tasks, less concentration required at work, reduced job satisfaction, high perceived monotony of work, and frequency of lifting demands. Comparing ambulatory low-back pain subjects with healthy matched controls, Feuerstein, Sult, and Houle (1985) found that work environment measures predicted affective and evaluative dimensions of pain but not the sensory dimension that is more dependent on neural input. Less co-worker cohesion, less physical comfort, and less job clarity were correlated with increased pain but not with distress. Interestingly, higher ratings of work pressure were related to decreased levels of depression and pain. The authors concluded that pain modulation in the workplace may be mediated by factors associated with job dissatisfaction and by an adaptive distraction effect whereby higher job pressure provides a constructive diversion from pain and negative moods.

Bigos et al. (1991) reported the results of a longitudinal, prospective investigation of the influence of work perceptions on report of back injury in an industrial setting. Other than extant back problems at time of evaluation, perceived enjoyment of job tasks was the strongest single predictor among all potential physical and nonphysical correlates of recurrent report of acute back injury. Although psychosocial influences, as currently measured, seem to lack the necessary power to be used as sole predictors of disability, the utility of evaluations that exclude these variables is questionable.

Implication 5: Work-related musculoskeletal disability is most likely a multivariate phenomenon maintained by interactions among physical, ergonomic, and psychosocial factors. It is axiomatic that older workers are less likely to return to full-time employment following an injury (e.g., Sandstrom, 1985), although explanations for this finding have been largely speculative. A recent prospective study, however, may offer some guidance. Gallagher et al. (1989) compared two groups of low-back pain patients (pain clinic attendees and Social Security Disability Insurance applicants) and found that between-groups physical and biomechanical differences disappeared after the confounding effects of age and length of time out of work were partialed out.

Evidence that comprehensive, multidisciplinary treatment approaches are successful in the rehabilitation of chronic musculoskeletal disability (Mayer et al., 1987) also may support current conceptualizations of the problem as multiply determined. The effectiveness of these efforts may be due to their focus on several components of disability (e.g., mood, fitness, self-regulation and coping skill deficits, lack of easily transferable job skills, inappropriate use of narcotic analgesics, and general overutilization of health-care providers). It is important to note that successful outcome does not support causality. Only multivariate, prospective analyses can confirm the actual determinants of disability and the efficacious components of a treatment program.

In summary, all of the findings suggest that prolonged musculoskeletal disability cannot be explained by physical findings alone. It appears that the predictive validity of objective indexes of impairment could be enhanced by the inclusion of measures that tap subjective judgments about the cause of pain, its meaning in the individual's life, and one's capabilities to cope and execute appropriate courses of action. It is important that the use of a conceptual framework of how people alter maladaptive beliefs and behaviors may also facilitate the development of a multidimensional assessment of vulnerability to physical and psychological stress at work as well as guide treatment and prevention efforts. Such a model should be able to explain relations among functional, ecological, motivational, and dispositional factors in the tradition of a biopsychosocial approach to illness (Engel, 1977).

Conceptual Models of Health-Related Behavior Change

The following review will address the potential utility of four dynamic models that may advance our understanding of disability-related mechanisms: the Glasgow illness model, the Rochester model, the self-regulatory model, and the transtheoretical model.

Glasgow Illness Model

Similar to findings in the area of cognitive modulation of pain perception (e.g., Melzack & Wall, 1982), it may be that heightened appraisal of pain and disability differentiates those who remain disabled from those who return to more adaptive functioning. This hypothesis appears to be supported by the work of Waddell and his colleagues, who have investigated the impact of psychological factors on recovery from various surgical procedures to relieve chronic low back pain. Summarizing their research to date, Waddell and colleagues (Waddell, Main, Morris, DiPaola, & Gray, 1984; Waddell, Morris, DiPaola, Bircher, & Finlayson, 1986) concluded that psychological distress develops secondary to physical trauma and is typically manifested as depression, increased body awareness, and abnormal illness behavior. They viewed disability as a function of the interaction between physical impairment and psychological distress and argued that indicators of illness behavior should be clearly differentiated from those of physical disease. Using factor analytic procedures, Waddell and Main (1984) have developed indices of behavioral disability (e.g., restrictions in lifting, sitting, and social life) and physical impairment (e.g., anatomic pattern, root compression signs, and previous surgery). They have advanced the Glasgow illness model to explicate the relative contributions of physical and psychological factors to the etiology of disability.

This model has been validated by two clinical investigations. The first, an exploratory study, demonstrated that although physical impairment alone explained 40.3% of the variance in low-back pain disability, psychological distress (depression, 13.4%; bodily awareness, 9.1%) and magnified illness behavior (inappropriate symptoms and signs, 8.4%) also made significant contributions (Waddell et al., 1984). In the second investigation, a prospective study of 185 low-back pain patients, surgical outcome was almost entirely predicted by physical factors such as accuracy of diagnosis, operative findings, and avoidance of complications. Level of emotional distress and abnormal illness behavior, however, was predicted by self-reports of low-back pain, disability, and, ultimately, return to work (Waddell et al., 1986). It is important that psychological distress and abnormal illness behavior were better predictors of disability than were sex, age, demographic characteristics, and measures of personality.

Rochester Model

Feuerstein (1991) has advanced a multidimensional heuristic of pain-related disability to aid in the understanding of mechanisms that appear to exacerbate or maintain disability and decrease the likelihood of work reentry following the onset of an occupational musculoskeletal disorder. Currently, this framework is being applied in an ongoing program of research on the mechanisms and management of work disability with individuals with UECTDs and low-back pain. As Figure 1 illustrates, the model incorporates the worker's medical status, as it affects work

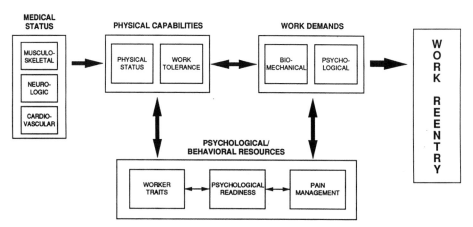

Figure 1. The Rochester model: A multidimensional heuristic for understanding musculoskeletal work disability.

capacity, and physical capabilities, as measured by objective indicators of trunk and upper-extremity strength and endurance and observed work tolerance (e.g., lifting, carrying, and reaching). These factors may interact with work demands and the psychological behavioral resources that the worker brings to bear on any discrepancy between physical capabilities and work demands.

The model proposes that physical capabilities should be contrasted with actual work demands to identify a discrepancy that may reduce the likelihood of work reentry. Although preparedness to return to work may be simply measured as a ratio of physical capabilities to actual job demands, the "psychological readiness" component of the model suggests that self-appraisals of pain and ability, degree of psychopathology, and social support should be assessed, particularly with individuals whose work disability exceeds 6 months (Feuerstein, 1991).

A recent investigation of factors that mediate job stress underscored the importance of a multidimensional approach to understanding musculoskeletal disability. Feuerstein and Fitzgerald (1991b) explored the relation between anticipatory anxiety prior to exposure to typical work demands in sign-language interpreters, an occupational group with a reportedly high prevalence of UECTDs. A step-wise regression analysis revealed that occupational anxiety was related to catastrophic thinking, perceptions of a low degree of management control, and significant fatigue following an interpreting task. Two groups were then formed using a median split based on reported UECTD symptoms (Putz-Anderson, 1988). High- and low-symptom groups frequently were significantly discriminated by a combination of psychosocial and biomechanical measures. Interpreters with three or more UECTD symptoms demonstrated significantly less perceived supervisor support and job pressure, greater anticipatory anxiety, and a faster pace of finger/hand movement while interpreting than did peers who reported fewer symptoms. Interestingly, no significant group differences were observed for demographic or physical strength and endurance measures. These findings illustrate a complex interaction among perceived job stress, anxiety, and biomechanical risks as factors contributing to the exacerbation or maintenance of pain and disability.

Self-Regulatory Model

One approach to articulating cognitive mediators of disability is outlined in Bandura's (1977, 1986) program of research on self-efficacy. In social cognitive theory, self-efficacy serves as the central factor in self-regulatory mechanisms that govern motivation and action. According to Bandura, self-efficacy is the perception that one has the capability to perform necessary behaviors that will produce a desired outcome. These beliefs determine whether an activity will be attempted, as well as the amount and duration of effort expended in the face of aversive stressors. Optimal functioning seems to require both skills and the perception of high personal efficacy. Conversely, low self-efficacy (i.e., the perception that situational demands exceed coping resources) may exacerbate disability by negatively affecting performance appraisals, level of activity, distress, and pain.

The role of self-efficacy in predicting disability-related behaviors has been examined in studies on motor performance (Feltz & Albrecht, 1985), physical stamina (Gould & Weiss, 1981), exercise compliance (Kaplan, Atkins, & Reinsch, 1984), affective distress (Davies & Yates, 1982), and the self-regulation of health habits (Fitzgerald & Prochaska, 1990, in press). Self-efficacy has been shown to predict the resumption of an active lifestyle and greater workload performance on a treadmill exercise test following myocardial infarction (Ewart, Taylor, Reese, & DeBusk, 1983), pain tolerance (Bandura, O'Leary, Taylor, Gauthier, & Gossard, 1987; Litt, 1988; Manning & Wright, 1983), and treatment outcome following rehabilitation (Dolce, 1987). A recent investigation has demonstrated both that self-efficacy can be reliably manipulated in a clinical setting using positive feedback and verbal persuasion and that this approach improves behavioral coping with an aversive medical examination (Gattuso, Litt, & Fitzgerald, 1992).

Self-efficacy is situation specific and, therefore, is likely to be a good predictor of behavior in a stressful encounter such as a functional capacity evaluation following injury. Although the construct has been examined with a variety of activities that may influence disability, no previous investigation has examined the impact of efficacy judgments on subsequent performance of people coping with work-related musculoskeletal disabilities. To that end, Fitzgerald and Feuerstein (1992) developed the Physical Capabilities Scale (PCS), which was administered during a pilot study of 40 disabled workers undergoing a functional capacity evaluation following occupational low-back injury. The PCS is composed of eight efficacy judgments related to expected performance on a standardized evaluation of isokinetic strength, range of motion, and endurance using a computer-interfaced dynamometer. The scale demonstrated adequate reliability (Cronbach's alpha = .85).

Correlational analyses revealed that preevaluation efficacy judgments for flexion and extension, full range of motion, ease of performance, and need for a rest break were significantly associated with all objective measures of subsequent dynamometer performance. Additionally, the validity of this measurement approach was supported by significant correlations between several PCS items and standard measures of pain and behavioral disability obtained prior to the evaluation. Greater perceived ability to remain calm during the exam was related to lower average pain ratings as was expected ease of performance. Pain management efficacy was inversely related to average pain ratings and behavioral disability (e.g., hours of daily "down time" and narcotic analgesic use). Confidence in flexion and extension of the trunk was negatively correlated with total observed pain behaviors and reported control over pain. Finally, expected degree of calmness and comfort during the exam was inversely related to fear of reinjury (10-cm visual analog scale). The latter finding, in particular, supports the potential utility of a brief measure to monitor self-efficacy percepts over the course of rehabilitation efforts. For fearful individuals, clinical manipulation of perceptions of coping self-efficacy may be a useful alternative to performance-based enhancement (e.g., systematic desensitization), resulting in better estimates of functional capacity and level of physical deconditioning.

Transtheoretical Model

An alternative method of assessing risk and preventing disability involves the naturalistic measurement of a worker's motivation to change and use of cognitive and behavioral strategies that may decrease the likelihood of musculoskeletal impairment or reinjury following rehabilitation. This approach dates to seminal efforts by Hunt and Bespalec (1974) and others to understand the process of relapse in addictive behaviors. After reviewing treatment outcome research to date, they concluded that readiness to change was a primary mediator of a successful outcome. Building on this finding, Simon (1979) suggested that models of behavior change move beyond grouping people on the basis of demographic or individual difference variables alone. He suggested that motivational or developmental constructs be used as marker variables to maximize the understanding of person–problem interaction patterns.

A fourth conceptual framework, the transtheoretical model (DiClemente & Prochaska, 1985; Prochaska & DiClemente, 1983, 1984) incorporates the latter recommendation using an organizational schema whereby stages and processes of change (covert or overt coping techniques) and cognitive decision-making constructs (e.g., self-efficacy) interact as people alter problem behavior patterns. Integrating the terminology of Simon (1979) and Prochaska (Prochaska & DiClemente, 1983, 1984), a problem-solving strategy (process of change) acts as a critical intervening variable between the motivational environment (stage of change) and a behavioral production (e.g., adhering to a physical conditioning regimen following injury).

The transtheoretical model has been well validated with self-changing smokers (Prochaska & DiClemente, 1983) and patients attempting cardiovascular risk reduction following coronary bypass surgery (Fitzgerald, Prochaska, & Pransky, 1991), as well as with individuals seeking professional consultation for psychological distress and weight reduction (Prochaska & DiClemente, 1985). In this model, the stages of change (precontemplation, contemplation, preparation, action, and maintenance) follow each other in an invariant linear progression unless relapse occurs. Stages represent distinct periods of time when certain types of change can occur. Each stage is characterized by a relative willingness to engage in certain intentional activities—the processes of change.

As with other developmental models, an individual must engage in stage-specific coping strategies to move to the next stage. Most people do not move linearly through the stages of change but rather demonstrate a cyclical pattern as they modify a health-related behavior. Relapse, the result of unsuccessful action, typically necessitates a reappraisal of an individual's readiness to modify a problem behavior. Relatedly, self-efficacy judgments appear to be more powerful predictors of change status in the later stages (e.g., action or relapse) when behavior modification has been initiated (Fitzgerald & Prochaska, 1990).

The processes exemplify an intermediate level of abstraction between theory-level postulates and the techniques presumed to affect change. The processes of change are covert or overt coping operations that individuals use as they modify a problem behavior such as psychological distress. In prospective studies, 10 processes of change have been identified, each receiving differential application depending on stage of change (Prochaska & DiClemente, 1986). Stage-specific frequency of change process use tends to be fairly consistent across a broad range of health promotion activities including self-control over addictions; fitness and exercise; risk-reduction for acquired immune deficiency syndrome (AIDS), skin cancer, and heart disease; psychological distress; and *Diagnostic and Statistical Manual of Mental Disorders* (3rd ed., rev.; American Psychiatric Association, 1987) syndromes (Prochaska & DiClemente, in press).

Summary

By way of a preamble to programmatic surveillance of worksites and, ultimately, prevention of musculoskeletal impairment and disability, it has been suggested that cognitive, perceptual, and behavioral factors may contribute to the continuance of functional limitation following occupational injury. Measurement of these nonorganic factors may serve to guide secondary prevention efforts (i.e., prevention of reinjury and prolonged disability) and recommend primary prevention interventions such as the identification of person–job interactions that may promote injury, illness, or disproportionate disability. Each of the models offers a unique vantage point from which to investigate occupational disability.

The Glasgow illness model provides a holistic perspective on perceived disability and its relation to level of physical impairment, thus improving the predictive validity of extant objective assessments. The Rochester model allows for a comprehensive evaluation of personal and workplace factors that contribute to injury, as well as offering significant potential in the identification of efficacious components of occupational rehabilitation programs. The transtheoretical model may be especially useful in the articulation of a development-stage approach to recovery from musculoskeletal disability. Adaptation of the cognitive and behavioral process measures to different health-related problems can be done with relative ease and reliability, so that tracking an important factor such as exercise adherence should be straightforward. Finally, self-efficacy, the centerpiece of the self-regulatory model, appears to be a unifying construct consistent with all of the frameworks.

Future prospective research could track changes in disability perceptions, illness behavior, and change process use over time, both in the work environment and as an adjunct to clinical interventions designed to enhance self-efficacy and recovery of function. Additional investigations might involve cross-sectional analyses of cognitive mediators and psychosocial factors that are presumed to influence differential patterns of impairment and disability that have been observed anecdotally. For example, using the Glasgow illness model method, individuals could be assigned to one of four conditions: low impairment/low disability, low impairment/high disability, high impairment/low disability, and high impairment/high disability.

Implications for Worksite-Based Mental Health Promotion

It has been demonstrated that individual differences in age, mood, previous social learning history, work environment perceptions, and complex interactions among these factors may be important contributors to the initiation and unnecessary prolongation of work disability following musculoskeletal injury. Arguably, all work-related disabilities have a psychosocial component. This suggests that common pathways mediate a series of responses that increase the likelihood of a disability outcome. To label a disability, for example, "musculoskeletal" versus "psychological" is merely to reflect the relative importance of that factor in the presumed etiology of the injury or illness. From a clinical or public-health perspective, individual disabilities become especially problematic when impairment and observed functional disability are highly discrepant. In the case of work-related psychological disorders, the determination of impairment is complicated further by recent relaxation of worker's compensation award criteria coupled with the increasing use of nonobjective standards for assessing occupational stress (DeCarlo & Gruenfeld, 1989).

Several recommendations for occupational mental health promotion can be drawn from the previous discussion of musculoskeletal impairment and disability. First, definitional and measurement issues need to be clarified with respect to the operationalization of individual stress responses (personal outcomes) and job characteristics (risk factors). Because observed associations among negative affectivity, health complaints, and measures of stress suggest an underlying somatopsychic distress factor (e.g., Watson & Pennebaker, 1989), unrelated measures (e.g., stress-related behaviors or psychophysiological responses) could be included in outcome assessments to enhance interpretation of findings. In any event, it is advisable to include a valid measure of trait-negative affectivity in a surveillance battery to control for its influence.

Second, the notion of a chronic "mismatch" between job demands and the physical and psychological resources of the worker should be explored with respect to onset of psychological complaints. Given that ergonomic influences are not easily dichotomized into physical and psychological dimensions, personal factors such as strength, endurance, cardiovascular fitness, anthropometric considerations, and cognitive skills should be assessed to the extent that they could affect level of job task performance and, therefore, individual stress. Should a significant mismatch exist, secondary prevention strategies could include performance and distress monitoring and, if necessary, recommendation for transfer or vocational retraining.

Third, although secondary prevention strategies to reduce psychological distress typically target the individual worker for surveillance and education or treatment, integrative models that incorporate microlevel (individual-based, clinical research methodology) and macrolevel (population-based, public health–epidemiologic approach) domains offer promise for identifying important interactions between the individual and the larger social environment that may enhance or impede change.

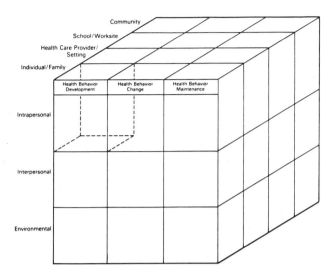

Figure 2. A health-enhancement planning model. (From Weiss, 1991. Copyright 1991 by Lawrence Erlbaum. Reprinted by permission.)

Weiss (1991) presented a useful schema (Figure 2) that acknowledges complex interactions between "functional levels," situational contexts, and stages of health behavior change. Use of an integrative approach to stress reduction at the workplace allows for the manipulation of a wider range of social and environmental factors that may affect occupational mental health. It also sets the stage for fostering generalization of adaptive practices based on evolving workplace norms.

Finally, subjective appraisals of the social milieu at work should be tracked using instruments with demonstrated psychometric properties. The occupational health literature strongly supports the influence of perceptions of job satisfaction, supervisor support, pressure, autonomy, and control on certain work-related disabilities. High levels of dissatisfaction, for example, in a small subgroup of workers might suggest individual-level interventions. Large-scale negative perceptions of the workplace might call for macrolevel solutions. In keeping with a multidimensional approach to assessment and treatment, pathogenic interactions between subjective appraisals and objective measures of the pace, quality, and content of work should be identified. In this way, causal pathways for psychological disability can be isolated, and remedies can be instituted to promote and maintain change on individual and organizational levels.

References

American Psychiatric Association. (1987). *Diagnostic and statistical manual of mental disorders* (3rd ed., rev.). Washington, DC: Author.

Andersson, G. B. J., & Pope, M. H. (1991). The patient. In M. H. Pope, G. B. J. Andersson, J. W. Frymoyer, & Chaffin, D. B. (Eds.), *Occupational low back pain: Assessment, treatment and prevention* (pp. 132–147). St. Louis, MO: Mosby.

Armstrong, T. J., Fine, L. J., Goldstein, S. A., Lifshitz, Y. R., & Silverstein, B. A. (1987). Ergonomic considerations in hand and wrist tendinitis. *Journal of Hand Surgery, 12A,* 830–837.

Bandura, A. (1977). Self-efficacy: Toward a unifying theory of behavioral change. *Psychological Review, 84*, 191–215.

Bandura, A. (1986). *Social foundations of thought and action: A social cognitive theory.* Englewood Cliffs, NJ: Prentice-Hall.

Bandura, A., O'Leary, A., Taylor, C. B., Gauthier, J., & Gossard, D. (1987). Perceived self-efficacy and pain control: Opiod and nonopiod mechanisms. *Journal of Personality and Social Psychology, 53*, 563–571.

Barsky, A. J., & Klerman, G. L. (1983). Overview: Hypochondriasis, bodily complaints, and somatic styles. *American Journal of Psychiatry, 140*, 273–283.

Battie, M. C., Bigos, S. J., Fisher, L. D., Hansson, T. H., Nachemsonm, A. L., Spengler, D. M., Wortley, M. D., & Zeh, J. (1989). A prospective study of the role of cardiovascular risk factors and fitness in industrial back pain complaints. *Spine, 14*, 141–147.

Battie, M. C., Bigos, S. J., Fisher, L. D., Spengler, D. M., Hansson, T. H., Nachemson, A. L., & Wortley, M. D. (1990). The role of spinal flexibility of back pain complaints within industry: A prospective study. *Spine, 15*, 768–773.

Biering-Sorenson, F. (1982). Low back trouble in a general population of 30-, 40-, 50-, and 60-year-old men and women. *Danish Medical Bulletin, 29*, 289–299.

Biering-Sorenson, F. (1984). Physical measurements as risk indicators for low back trouble over a one-year period. *Spine, 9*, 106–119.

Biering-Sorenson, F., & Thomsen, C. (1986). Medical, social and occupational history as a risk indicator for low-back trouble in a general population. *Spine, 11*, 720–725.

Bigos, S. J., Battie, M. C., Spengler, D. M., Fisher, L. D., Fordyce, W. E., Hansson, T. H., Nachemson, A. L., & Wortley, M. D. (1991). A prospective study of work perceptions and psychosocial factors affecting the report of back injury. *Spine, 16*, 1–6.

Bortz, W. M. (1982). Disuse and aging. *Journal of the American Medical Association, 248*, 1203–1208.

Bowe, F. (1983). *Demography and disability: A chartbook for rehabilitation.* Fayetteville: University of Arkansas Press.

Davies, F. W., & Yates, B. T. (1982). Self-efficacy expectancies versus outcome expectancies as determinants of performance deficits and depressive affect. *Cognitive Therapy and Research, 6*, 23–35.

DeCarlo, D. T., & Gruenfeld, D. H. (1989). *Stress in the American workplace: Alternatives for the working wounded.* Fort Washington, PA: LRP Publications.

DeFrank, R., & Ivancevich, J. (1986). Job loss: An individual level review and model. *Journal of Vocational Behavior, 28*, 1–20.

DiClemente, C. C., & Prochaska, J. O. (1985). Processes and stages of self-change: Coping and competence in smoking behavior change. In S. Shiffman & T. Willis (Eds.), *Coping and substance use* (pp. 319–341). San Diego, CA: Academic Press.

Dolce, J. J. (1987). Self-efficacy and disability beliefs in behavioral treatment of pain. *Behavior Research and Therapy, 25*, 289–299.

Engel, G. L. (1977). The need for a new medical model: A challenge for biomedicine. *Science, 196*, 129–136.

Ewart, C. K., Taylor, C. B., Reese, L. B., & DeBusk, R. F. (1983). Effects of early post-myocardial infarction exercise testing on self-perception and subsequent physical activity. *American Journal of Cardiology, 51*, 1076–1080.

Federspiel, C. F., Guy, D., Kane, D., & Spengler, D. (1989). Expenditures for nonspecific back injuries in the workplace. *Journal of Occupational Medicine, 31*, 919–924.

Feltz, D. L., & Albrecht, R. R. (1985). The influence of self-efficacy on approach/avoidance of a high-avoidance motor task. In J. H. Humphrey & L. Vander Velden (Eds.), *Current research in the psychology/sociology of sport* (Vol. 1). Princeton, NJ: Princeton Book.

Feuerstein, M. (1991). A multidisciplinary approach to the prevention, evaluation, and management of work disability. *Journal of Occupational Rehabilitation, 1*, 5–12.

Feuerstein, M., & Fitzgerald, T. E. (1991a). *Biomechanical factors affecting upper extremity cumulative trauma disorders in sign language interpreters. Journal of Occupational Medicine, 34*, 257–264.

Feuerstein, M., & Fitzgerald, T. E. (1991b). *Job stress and UECTD symptom severity: The role of anticipatory anxiety, work style, and environment.* Manuscript submitted for publication.

Feuerstein, M., Papciak, A. S., & Hoon, P. (1987). Biobehavioral mechanisms of chronic low back pain. *Clinical Psychology Review, 7*, 243–273.

Feuerstein, M., Sult, S. C., & Houle, M. (1985). Environmental stressors and low back pain: Life events, family and work environment. *Pain, 22,* 295–307.

Fitzgerald, T. E., & Feuerstein, M. (1992, March). *Self-efficacy, physical performance, and pain behaviors following musculoskeletal injury.* Paper presented at the meeting of the Society of Behavioral Medicine, New York.

Fitzgerald, T. E., & Prochaska, J. O. (1990). Nonprogressing profiles in smoking cessation: What keeps people refractory to self-change? *Journal of Substance Abuse, 2,* 87–105.

Fitzgerald, T. E., & Prochaska, J. O. (in press). Longitudinal typologies of self-change of smoking behavior: Implications for intervention and education. In R. H. Feldman & J. H. Humphrey (Eds.), *Advances in health education: Current research* (Vol. 3, pp. 1–25). New York: AMS Press.

Fitzgerald, T. E., Prochaska, J. O., & Pransky, G. S. (1991, March). *Health risk reduction and psychosocial adaptation in coronary artery bypass graft surgery patients.* Paper presented at the annual meeting of the Society of Behavioral Medicine, Washington, DC.

Fletcher, M. (1990, September 10). Cumulative trauma disorders: Repetitive motion cases cost billions annually. *Business Insurance,* pp. 3–6.

Flor, H., Turk, D. C., & Birbaumer, N. (1985). Assessment of stress-related psychophysiological responses in chronic back pain patients. *Journal of Consulting and Clinical Psychology, 53,* 354–364.

Fordyce, W. E. (1976). *Behavioral methods for chronic pain and illness.* St. Louis, MO: Mosby.

Frymoyer, J. W., Pope, M. H., Clements, J. H., Wilder, D. G., MacPherson, B., & Ashikaga, T. (1983). Risk factors in low-back pain. *Journal of Bone and Joint Surgery, 65,* 213–218.

Gallagher, R. M., Rauh, V., Haugh, L. D., Milhous, R., Callas, P. W., Langelier, R., McCallen, J. M., & Frymoyer, J. (1989). Determinants of return-to-work among low back patients. *Pain, 39,* 55–67.

Gattuso, S. M., Litt, M. D., & Fitzgerald, T. E. (1992). Coping with gastrointestinal endoscopy: Self-efficacy enhancement and coping style. *Journal of Consulting and Clinical Psychology, 60,* 133–139.

Gould, D., & Weiss, M. (1981). Effect of model similarity and model self-talk on self-efficacy in muscular endurance. *Journal of Sport Psychology, 3,* 17–29.

Holbrook, T. L., Grazier, K., Kelsey, J., & Stauffer, R. (1984). *The frequency of occurrence, impact, and cost of selected musculoskeletal conditions in the United States.* Chicago: National Academy of Orthopaedic Surgeons.

Hunt, W. A., & Bespalec, D. A. (1974). An evaluation of current methods of modifying smoking behavior. *Journal of Clinical Psychology, 30,* 431–438.

International Association for the Study of Pain. (1979). Pain terms: A list and notes on usage. *Pain, 6,* 249–252.

Kaplan, R. M., Atkins, C. J., & Reinch, S. (1984). Specific efficacy expectations mediate exercise compliance in patients with COPD. *Health Psychology, 3,* 223–242.

Kleinke, C. L., & Spangler, A. S. (1988). Predicting treatment outcome of chronic back pain patients in a multidisciplinary pain clinic: Methodological issues and treatment implications. *Pain, 33,* 41–48.

Kraus, L. E., & Stoddard, S. (1989). *Chartbook on disability in the United States: An info use report.* Washington, DC: National Institute on Disability and Rehabilitation Research.

Kutner, N. G. (1984). Women with disabling health conditions: The significance of employment. *Women and Health, 9,* 21–31.

Linn, M. W., Sandifer, R., & Stein, S. (1985). Effects of unemployment on mental and physical health. *American Journal of Public Health, 75,* 502–506.

Litt, M. D. (1988). Self-efficacy and perceived control: Cognitive mediators of pain tolerance. *Journal of Personality and Social Psychology, 54,* 149–160.

Luft, H. (1978). *The economic causes and consequences of health problems.* Cambridge, MA: Ballinger.

Manning, M. M., & Wright, T. L. (1983). Self-efficacy expectancies, outcome expectancies, and the persistence of pain control during childbirth. *Journal of Personality and Social Psychology, 45,* 421–431.

Matheson, G. O., MacIntyre, J. G., Taunton, J. E., Clement, D. B., & Lloyd-Smith, R. (1989). Musculoskeletal injuries associated with physical activity in older adults. *Medicine and Science in Sport and Exercise, 21,* 379–385.

Mayer, T. G., Gatchel, R. J., Mayer, H., Kishino, N. D., Keeley, J., & Mooney, V. (1987). A prospective two-year study of functional resporation in industrial low back injury. *Journal of the American Medical Association, 258,* 1763–1767.

McGill, C. (1968). Industrial back problems: A control program. *Journal of Occupational Medicine, 10,* 174–178.

McNeil, J. M. (1982). *Labor force status and other characteristics of persons with a work disability.* Washington, DC: U.S. Government Printing Office.

McPherson, B. D. (1984). Sport, health, well-being, and aging: Some conceptual and methodological questions for sport scientists. In *The 1984 Olympic Scientific Congress Proceedings* (Vol. 5, pp. 3–24). Champaign, IL: Human Kinetics Publishers.

Melzack, R., & Wall, P. D. (1982). *The challenge of pain.* New York: Basic Books.

Moos, R. H. (1986). *The Work Environment Scale manual* (2nd ed.). Palo Alto, CA: Consulting Psychologists Press.

Murphy, J. K., Sperr, E. V., & Sperr, S. J. (1986). Chronic pain: An investigation of assessment instruments. *Journal of Psychosomatic Research, 30,* 289–296.

Nachemson, A. (1983). Work for all. *Clinical Orthopedics and Related Research, 179,* 77–85.

Nathanson, C. A. (1980). Social roles and health status among women: The significance of employment. *Social Science and Medicine, 14,* 463–471.

National Institute of Occupational Safety and Health. (1986). *Proposed national strategy for the prevention of musculoskeletal injuries.* Washington, DC: U.S. Department of Health and Human Services.

National Institute of Occupational Safety and Health. (1988). *Proposed national strategies for the prevention of leading work-related diseases and injuries: Psychological disorders.* Washington DC: U.S. Department of Health and Human Services.

Pope, M. H., Andersson, G. B. J., Frymoyer, J. W., & Chaffin, D. B. (Eds.). (1991). *Occupational low back pain: Assessment, treatment and prevention.* St. Louis, MO: Mosby.

Prochaska, J. O., & DiClemente, C. C. (1983). Stages and processes of self-change of smoking: Toward an integrative model of change. *Journal of Consulting and Clinical Psychology, 51,* 390–395.

Prochaska, J. O., & DiClemente, C. C. (1984). *The transtheoretical approach: Crossing traditional boundaries of therapy.* Chicago: Dow Jones/Irwin.

Prochaska, J. O., & DiClemente, C. C. (1985). Common processes of change for smoking, weight control, and psychological distress. In S. Shiffman & T. Wills (Eds.), *Coping and substance use* (pp. 345–363). San Diego, CA: Academic Press.

Prochaska, J. O., & DiClemente, C. C. (1986). Toward a comprehensive model of change. In W. R. Miller & N. Heather (Eds.), *Treating addictive behaviors: Processes of change* (pp. 3–27). New York: Plenum Press.

Prochaska, J. O., & DiClemente, C. C. (in press). Stages of change in the modification of problem behaviors. In M. Hersen, R. M. Eisler, & P. M. Miller (Eds.), *Progress in behavior modification.* Newbury Park, CA: Sage.

Putz-Anderson, V. (Ed.). (1988). *Cumulative trauma disorders.* New York: Taylor & Francis.

Romano, J. M., & Turner, J. A. (1985). Chronic pain and depression: Does the evidence support a relationship? *Psychological Bulletin, 97,* 18–34.

Sandstrom, J. (1985). Clinical and social factors in rehabilitation of patients with chronic low back pain. *Scandinavian Journal of Rehabilitation Medicine, 18,* 35–43.

Seligman, M. E. P. (1975). *Helplessness: On depression, development, and death.* San Francisco: Freeman.

Shephard, R. J. (1978). *Physical activity and aging.* Chicago: Year Book Medical Publishers.

Silverstein, B. A., Fine, L. J., & Armstrong, T. J. (1987). Occupational factors and carpal tunnel syndrome. *American Journal of Industrial Medicine, 11,* 343–358.

Simon, H. (1979). Information processing models of cognition. In M. Rosenweig & L. Porter (Eds.), *Annual review of psychology* (Vol. 30, pp. 363–396). Palo Alto, CA: Annual Reviews.

Spitzer, W. O., LeBlanc, F. E., & Dupuis, M. (1987). Scientific approach to the assessment and management of activity-related spinal disorders: A monograph for clinicians. Report of the Quebec task force on spinal disorders. *Spine, 75* (Suppl.), 3–59.

Svensson, H. O., & Andersson, G. J. (1983). Low back pain in 40–47 year old men: Work history and work environment factors. *Spine, 8,* 272–276.

Troup, J. D. G., Martin, J. W., & Lloyd, D. C. (1981). Back pain in industry: A prospective study, *Spine, 6,* 61–69.

Turk, D. C., Meichenbaum, D., & Genest, M. (1983). *Pain and behavioral medicine: A cognitive-behavioral perspective.* New York: Guilford Press.

Turk, D. C., Wack, J. T., & Kerns, R. D. (1985). An empirical examination of the "pain-behavior" construct. *Journal of Behavioral Medicine, 8,* 119–130.

Urban, J. P. G., Holm, S., Maroudas, A., & Nachemson, A. (1977). Nutrition of the invertebral disc: An in vivo study of solute transport. *Clinical Orthopaedics, 129,* 101–114.

U.S. Public Health Service (1988). *National health survey.* Washington, DC: Author.

Waddell, G. (1987). A new clinical model for the treatment of low-back pain. *Spine, 12,* 632–644.

Waddell, G., & Main, C. J. (1984). Assessment of severity in low-back disorders. *Spine, 9,* 204–208.

Waddell, G., Main, C. J., Morris, E. W., DiPaola, M., & Gray, I. C. M. (1984). Chronic low-back pain, psychologic distress, and illness behavior. *Spine, 9,* 209–213.

Waddell, G., Morris, E. W., DiPaola, M. P., Bircher, M., & Finlayson, D. (1986). A concept of illness tested as an improved basis for surgical decisions in low-back disorders. *Spine, 11,* 712–719.

Walsh, T. D. (1983). Antidepressants in chronic pain. *Clinical Neuropharmacology, 6,* 271–295.

Watson, D., & Pennebaker, J. W. (1989). Health complaints, stress, and distress: Exploring the central role of negative affectivity. *Psychological Review, 96,* 234–254.

Webster, B. S., & Snook, S. H. (1990). The cost of compensable low back pain. *Journal of Occupational Medicine, 32,* 13–15.

Weighill, V. E. (1983). "Compensation neurosis": A review of the literature. *Journal of Psychosomatic Research, 27,* 97–104.

Weiss, S. M. (1991). Health at work. In S. M. Weiss, J. E. Fielding, & A. Baum (Eds.), *Perspectives in behavioral medicine: Health at work* (pp. 1–10). Hillsdale, NJ: Erlbaum.

Yelin, E. (1986). The myth of malingering: Why individuals withdraw from work in the presence of illness. *Milbank Quarterly, 64,* 622–649.

Yelin, E., Nevitt, M., & Epstein, W. (1980). Toward an epidemiology of work disability. *Milbank Memorial Fund Quarterly/Health and Society, 58,* 386–415.

9

Lois E. Tetrick

Mediating Effect of Perceived Role Stress: A Confirmatory Analysis

Role stress has been investigated either implicitly or explicitly in terms of the effects of insufficient, excessive, or conflicting information; conflicting expectations; and time or resource constraints (Beehr & Bhagat, 1985; Beehr & Newman, 1978; Cooper & Payne, 1988; Kahn, Wolfe, Quinn, & Snoek, 1964; Miles & Perreault, 1976; Van Sell, Brief, & Schuler, 1981). Since Kahn et al. (1964) published their compendium on organizational stress, most of the research has focused on the manifestations of stress: role ambiguity, conflict, or overload.

After a quarter of a century, or more, of such investigations of stress, what do we know about occupational stress? It would appear that the one fact that has become evident is that stress is a perceptual phenomenon. In fact, most definitions of stress are perceptual in nature (Caplan, Cobb, French, Harrison, & Pinneau, 1975; McGrath, 1976). Consistent with these perceptual definitions, the research findings have noted considerable variability among individuals in their perceptions of stress and the consequences of such perceptions. That is, individuals who are presumably in the same job in the same organization experience their work environment differently. Some report the experience of stress, whereas others do not. Some individuals appear to suffer strain as a result of these perceived stressors; others do not.

How can we explain this body of research and the theoretical underpinnings of the data obtained? I suggest that first it is necessary to clearly differentiate perceptions from the more "objective" work environment, and second, our investigations must recognize the interrelatedness of perceptions of the work environment. Drawing on role theory, psychological climate theory, interactional psychology, and cognitive information processing, the model presented in Figure 1 is proposed as one that integrates much of what we know about the experience of stress at work. At the heart of this model are the perceptions of one's job, leader, and workgroup as well as perceived role stress and anxiety. The proposed structure denotes that anxiety and perceived role stress are reciprocally related. That is, not only does stress cause anxiety, but anxiety mutually and simultaneously causes stress. Furthermore, perceptions of stress are posited to be reciprocally related to perceptions of the job, leader, and workgroup. Thus, perceived role stress functions as a mediator among the perceptions of the work environment and concern for one's organizational well-being.

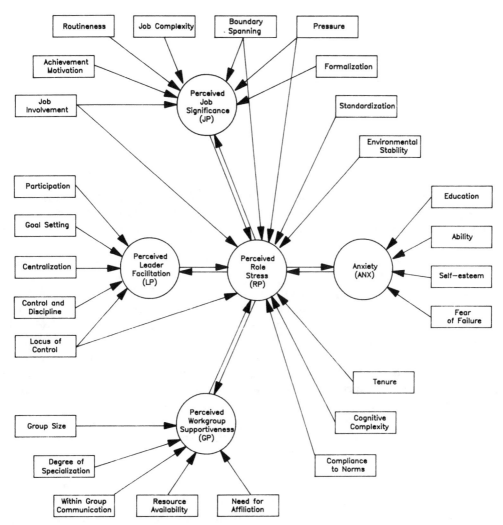

Figure 1. Model reflecting the hypothesized relations among anxiety, role stress, higher order perceptions of the work environment, and characteristics of the individual and work environment.

General Theoretical Framework

Stress has been defined in several ways. McGrath (1976) conceptualized stress as the result of environmental demands exceeding the person's capabilities and resources under conditions in which the consequences of meeting or not meeting the demands are expected to result in a substantial difference in rewards or costs. Another definition of stress comes from the general model advanced by the person–environment fit theorists (Caplan et al., 1975; Harrison, 1978). According to this position, stress results from demands that the individual cannot meet or from insufficient resources in the environment to meet the individual's needs. A distinction is made between the objective and the subjective person–environment fit. By subjective fit, these authors mean the perceived environmental fit with the individual's self-appraised needs.

It is the theoretical position of the person–environment fit theorists that the subjective or perceived environment is the more powerful determinant of an individual's behavior given that the cognitive or perceptual process is the means by which an individual attributes psychological meaning to the events occurring in the work environment (James & Jones, 1980; Lazarus, 1982). This position is congruent with role theory and psychological climate theory, both of which have their foundations in Lewin's (1951) work positing that it is one's perceptions or cognitions of the environment that influence one's behavior rather than the objective environment itself.

According to role theory (Biddle, 1979), one's role is composed of the conceptions of one's environment that engender certain patterns of behavior. By conception, Biddle is referring to covert processes through which one integrates past experiences (personal attributes) and observations of environmental events (situational attributes). Thus, one comes to know one's role through this interaction between situational and personal events.

The construct of conception as used by Biddle (1979) is similar to the construct of psychological climate. Joyce and Slocum (1979) define climate as a multidimensional, descriptive, perceptual abstraction of the work environment. Individuals process information about other individuals and events to form summary perceptions of the work environment centered on the job itself, the leader, the workgroup, and one's role in the organization. These summary perceptions, or higher order cognitive schemata, represent general and abstract rules concerning regularities and relations among events, reflected by beliefs about situations (James, Hater, Gent, & Bruni, 1978). It is these higher order schemata that integrate information from one's past experiences with that observed in the work environment.

Both role theory and psychological climate theory incorporate the position of interactional psychology (Endler & Magnusson, 1976) and social learning theory (Bandura, 1978). One's behavior is a result of the person, the situation, and the interaction between the person and the situation. This interaction results in the cognitive interpretation one gives to environmental events (James & Sells, 1981). The cognitive interpretation or psychological meaning one assigns to the dimensions of the work environment are related in that one strives to maintain cognitive consistency among one's beliefs about the environment (James & Sells, 1981).

Therefore, role stress is defined in this study as a perception indicated by ambiguity, conflict, and overload and arising from both the characteristics of the individual and the work environment. It is hypothesized that perceived role stress, as a part of the interpretation of one's role in the organization, is a mediating variable through which one assimilates and accommodates the cognitive interpretations of one's job, leader, and workgroup thereby preserving cognitive consistency among one's beliefs about the work environment.

The empirical literature supports as sources of role stress attributes of the individual, job, leader, workgroup, and organization (Beehr & Newman, 1978; McGrath, 1976; Miles & Perreault, 1976; Randolph & Posner, 1981; Van Sell et al., 1981). On the basis of the cognitive information processing approach, one theoretically would propose that it is actually the perceptions of self, job, leader, and workgroup that are the determinants of role stress. Although these perceptions are related to objective characteristics of the work environment, the literature on organizational and psychological climate supports the position that the objective environment is not isomorphic with the perceptions of the environment (Hellriegel & Slocum, 1974; James, Hater, Gent, & Bruni, 1978).

Stress as a Function of Perceptions of the Work Environment

According to psychological climate theory, perceptions of one's job, leader, and work-group are higher order cognitive interpretations of the work environment. Role theory specifies that one's role is a set of expectations arising from the task, the role-sender or leader, and co-workers. In psychological climate terms, perceptions of one's role would be a higher order schema that is a function of the experienced psychological meaning attached to the job, leader, and workgroup as well as one's beliefs, values, and needs.

Role perceptions have been defined as role ambiguity, conflict, and overload (Abdel-Halim, 1981a; Kahn et al., 1964; Mossholder, Bedeian, & Armenakis, 1981). It has been suggested that these indicators of one's role perceptions reflect a single underlying construct—role stress—although there may be differential relations among other variables and these three indicators of role stress (Bedeian, Armenakis, & Curran, 1982; Jackson & Schuler, 1985; Netemeyer, Johnston, & Burton, 1990; Tracy & Johnson, 1981). Therefore, it is hypothesized that role stress is a function of the psychological meaning one assigns to the job, leader, and workgroup.

One's higher order perception of the job—perceived job significance—is indicated by the extent to which it is perceived to be varied, challenging, autonomous, and important (Abdel-Halim, 1981a; James & Jones, 1980; Jones & James, 1979). It has been demonstrated that jobs perceived to be complex require more information processing on the part of the incumbent than simpler, less complex jobs (Leavitt, 1951; Tushman, 1978; Van de Ven & Ferry, 1980). These higher information processing demands, however, do not reflect greater uncertainty (Daft & Macintosh, 1981). The perceived discretion in dealing with job demands and the active participation in deciding how the job should be done actually serve to increase the amount of information processed and reduce the perceived uncertainty in the environment (Daft & Macintosh, 1981; Lee & Schuler, 1982).

One's perception of the leader—perceived leader facilitation—is indicated by the perceived degree of supportiveness, goal emphasis, work facilitation, and interaction facilitation (Bedeian & Armenakis, 1981; Jones & James, 1979). The leader functions to facilitate the accomplishment of one's role in the organization by providing necessary information and resources (House, 1971; Tetrick, 1989). To the extent that the leader is perceived as facilitating by providing the necessary information, the more uncertainty in the environment will be reduced and the less one will perceive role stress in the work environment.

The higher order perception of the workgroup—perceived workgroup supportiveness—is indicated by the extent to which the workgroup is perceived to be cohesive, cooperative, and friendly. The workgroup serves as a source of information and support (Cohen & Wills, 1985; A. P. Jones & James, 1979; Randolph & Posner, 1981; Schriesheim & Murphy, 1976; White, Mitchell, & Bell, 1977). The more cohesive and supportive one perceives the workgroup to be, the less uncertainty and equivocality of information will be apparent in the environment, thus reducing perceived role stress.

Reciprocal Causation Among One's Higher Order Perceptions

It is predicted that perceived role stress serves as a central construct in the cognitive processes involved in assigning psychological significance to events in the work environment. E. E. Jones and Gerard (1967) stated that these cognitive processes are geared to the construction of a subjective reality, which is compatible with one's beliefs, values, and attitudes. This cognitive appraisal process may result in changes to the psychological meaning assigned to the three facets of the work environment—job, leader, and workgroup—and may be a function of role stress (Lazarus & Folkman, 1984). The reconstruction, redefinition, and reinterpretation of the environment occurs rapidly to achieve cognitive consistency among one's higher order perceptions of the work environment. Therefore, it is hypothesized that the perception of role stress is reciprocally related to one's perceived job significance, perceived leader facilitation, and perceived workgroup supportiveness.

Information arising from one's higher order perception of the job as significant, the leader as facilitating, and the workgroup as supportive may be equivocal or conflicting and result in the perception of stress. As McGrath (1976), Beehr and Newman (1978) and Van Sell et al. (1981) indicated, organizational events not related to one's task, leader, or workgroup also may directly affect the perception of stress. An increase in role stress may change the psychological meaning assigned to the job, causing one to interpret it as less significant or involving less discretion, challenge, and variety. This increase in role stress may result from organizational factors, from decreases in the perceived facilitation provided by one's leader or from the perceived supportiveness of the workgroup. Likewise, role stress can reduce one's perception of the leader as facilitating or the workgroup as supportive. Equivocal information resulting in an increase in role stress may reduce one's perceptions of the leader as facilitating because the needed clarity is not perceived in the environment. Similarly, an increase in role stress can cause one to reconstruct or redefine the degree of perceived support provided by the workgroup.

Relation Between Anxiety and Stress

Anxiety is an affective, emotional response to the perception of stress (Bedeian & Armenakis, 1981; Beehr & Newman, 1978; Brett, 1982; House & Rizzo, 1972; Miles & Perreault, 1976; Van Sell et al., 1981). Emotional responses result from a cognitive appraisal of the situation. This appraisal process mediates the relations between the person and the environment (Lazarus, 1982). Because perceived role stress is essentially an appraisal of the information in the generalized abstractions of one's perception of the work environment, it serves to mediate the effects of one's perceptions of the job, leader, and workgroup on one's sense of well-being or anxiety.

The relation between affect and cognition is hypothesized to be one of reciprocal causation (James & Tetrick, 1986; Lazarus, 1982; Zajonc, 1980). Interactional psychology and social learning theory state that there is a continuing reciprocal interaction between people and their environments (Bandura, 1978; Endler & Magnusson, 1976; James et al., 1978; James & Sells, 1981). One knows the situation through the cognitive construction of the situation. Therefore, the reciprocal relation is actually between the cognitions or higher order perceptions of the work environment and affect (James et al., 1978; Lazarus, 1982; Zajonc, 1980).

Because perceived role stress is hypothesized to mediate one's perceptions of the work environment, it also is hypothesized to mediate the relation among the higher order perceptions of the job, leader, workgroup, and affective response of anxiety. Not only does role stress in the work environment cause anxiety, but anxiety causes the perception of role stress in the work environment, as depicted in Figure 1. The more apprehensive one is concerning one's organizational well-being, the less efficient one is in processing information (Organ, 1981). The less efficient one is in processing information, the greater the perception of role stress as indicated by greater ambiguity and conflict.

In summary, the process whereby the cognitive interpretations of the work environment are brought into congruence with each other and with one's beliefs, needs, and experienced anxiety is hypothesized to be mediated by perceived role stress. This process occurs almost simultaneously with perception and does not necessarily involve conscious effort (Lazarus, 1982). It is hypothesized that the perception of role stress is the focal construct mediating one's perceptions of the job, leader, and workgroup as well as experienced anxiety. Furthermore, a reciprocal causal relation is hypothesized to exist between the perception of role stress and the perception of the job, leader, and workgroup, as well as between stress and anxiety.

Other Determinants of Work Environment Perceptions

At this stage, a theoretical rationale has been presented concerning the interrelatedness of perceptions of the work environment, perceived role stress, and anxiety. However, it is necessary to link these perceptions to more "objective" characteristics of the work environment as well as individual characteristics. Previous research findings from the literature on job characteristics, leadership, group behavior, stress, and anxiety have identified aspects of the work environment that are related to one's perceptions of the work environment as shown in Figure 1. Congruent with psychological climate theory, it is hypothesized that situational attributes characterizing the job directly affect one's perceptions of the job, those characterizing the leader affect one's perceptions of the leader, those characterizing the workgroup affect one's perceptions of the workgroup, and those characterizing the organization affect one's role perceptions. Several individual attributes also are included to reflect personal characteristics that differentially affect one's interpretation of environmental events and the experience of anxiety. An abbreviated theoretical rationale for these exogenous variables is presented below.

Consistent with the literature on information processing and psychological climate theory, it is hypothesized that job complexity, routineness, pressure, boundary spanning, and formalization of work and role activities directly affect the perceived significance of one's job (Aldag, Barr, & Brief, 1981; Daft & Macintosh, 1981; Hackman & Oldham, 1980; Hage & Aiken, 1969; Miles, 1980; Sutton & Rousseau, 1979). Formalization, standardization of personnel procedures, pressure, boundary spanning, and stability of the organizational environment are hypothesized to directly affect the perception of role stress (Dieterly & Schneider, 1974; Graen, 1976; Miles, 1980). Goal setting, participatory management, centralization of authority, and attempts to influence or control the incumbent by the leader are hypothesized to directly affect the perceived facilitation of the leader (French & Caplan, 1972; House, 1971; House & Dessler, 1974; Latham & Yukl, 1975; Lee & Schuler, 1982; Mossholder, 1980; Posner & Randolph, 1980; Tetrick, 1989; Van Sell et al., 1981). Size of workgroup, the degree of specialization within the workgroup, the frequency of communication among members of the workgroup, and the availability of resources are hypothesized to directly affect the perception of the workgroup as supportive (Bridger, 1978; LaRocco & Jones, 1978; Payne, 1980; Posner & Randolph, 1980; Randolph & Posner, 1981; Schriesheim & Murphy, 1976; Shaw, 1976; White et al., 1977).

In addition, it is proposed that individual characteristics such as higher order needs, self-concepts, and beliefs serve as learned cognitive predispositions that affect perceptions of the job, leader, and workgroup as well as role stress and anxiety (James & Jones, 1980; Mischel, 1973). It is predicted that individuals will perceive their jobs to be more significant to the extent that they have high achievement motivation and are involved in their jobs (Batlis, 1980; Rabinowitz & Hall, 1977; Revelle & Michaels, 1976). Perceptions of one's leader are predicted to be affected by one's locus of control (Boal & Cummings, 1981; Mossholder, 1980; Organ, 1981; Phillips & Lord, 1980). Need for affiliation is predicted to influence the psychological meaning one attributes to the workgroup (Bedeian, 1980; Keller, 1975). Position tenure, compliance to norms, and cognitive complexity are predicted to influence role stress, in addition to job involvement and locus of control (Beehr & Newman, 1978; A. P. Jones & Butler, 1980; Kahn et al., 1964; McMichael, 1978; Randolph & Posner, 1981; Tetrick & LaRocco, 1987; Van Sell et al., 1981). Lastly, it is hypothesized that self-esteem, fear of failure, education, and experienced competence will directly affect anxiety (Caplan et al., 1975; Fisher, 1978; Harrison, 1978; Kahn et al., 1964; Mossholder et al., 1981).

At this stage, a theoretical rationale has been presented explicating the causal hypotheses represented in Figure 1. Consistent with the theoretical position underlying the model, the central constructs are the result of the assimilation of situational events into existing perceptions so as to preserve cognitive consistency with one's perceptions, beliefs, and needs. The literature provides little consistent support for the existence of moderator effects on the relations of interest (Abdel-Halim, 1981b; Batlis, 1980; Bedeian, 1980; Fisher & Gitelson, 1983; Jackson & Schuler, 1985; Posner & Randolph, 1980; Tetrick, 1989; Tetrick & LaRocco, 1987). Therefore, it is not hypothesized that the personal variables moderate the relations between the constructs, and the functional relations are assumed to be linear and additive.

Furthermore, given that perceptual or cognitive processes tend to occur rapidly (James et al., 1978) and that the hypothesized reciprocal causal relations are described as occurring almost simultaneously, only a very short period of time would be required for the effects of a change in one variable to work its way through the causal model. With such a short causal interval, the assumption that the variables are in equilibrium can be considered to have been reasonably satisfied. Thus, the full model, as presented in Figure 1, may be considered to meet the conditions for confirmatory analysis, and the adequacy of the model can be tested.

Method

Sample

Nonsupervisory employees of three organizations were selected for participation in this study to represent a heterogeneous sample with respect to their work environments. The total sample included 746 employees, 446 unique job types, and 173 separate workgroups. The first subsample included 179 employees of an information systems group of a large, private health-care program. The second subsample consisted of 288 firefighters from a large metropolitan fire department in the Southwest, and the third subsample was composed of 279 production workers of a paper products manufacturing organization located in four plants across the United States. A complete description of the sample is reported in James and Jones (1980). Only individuals who completed all the data on the nonsupervisory questionnaire and whose supervisor completed the supervisory questionnaire were included in the data analysis ($N = 675$).

Data Collection

Each respondent voluntarily answered a questionnaire containing items designed to measure work environment perceptions and personal attributes. Situational attributes were obtained from the respondents' supervisors and organizational records in an attempt to reduce or avoid confounding measures of situational characteristics and the perceptions of those characteristics. All items used 5-point response scales (1 = to a very great extent; 5 = not at all).

Endogenous Variables

The manifest indicators of the endogenous variables representing the psychological meaning of the work environment were measured using A. P. Jones and James's (1979) psychological climate scales: job challenge and variety; job autonomy; job importance; leader trust and support; leader goal emphasis and work facilitation; leader interaction facilitation; workgroup cooperation, friendliness, and warmth; workgroup pride; role ambiguity; role conflict; and role overload. In cases in which fewer than four scales were used as indicators of a latent variable, subscales were created so that each latent variable had at least four manifest indicators. Furthermore, because causal analysis is sensitive to measurement error, anxiety was treated as a latent variable manifestly indicated by individuals' responses to the five items of the anxiety scale that were taken from Spielberger, Gorusch, and Luschene's (1968) job-related tension scale.

Exogenous Variables

Personal attributes. The personal characteristics were obtained by questionnaire at the same time as the endogenous variables. The items used for measures of achievement motivation, cognitive complexity, compliance to norms, job involvement, locus of control, need for affiliation, self-esteem, and fear of failure are described in James and Jones (1980) and A. P. Jones and James (1979) and are based on similar scales reported in the literature (Crutchfield, 1955; Hermans, 1970; Hunt, Singer, & Cobb, 1967; James & Jones, 1980; Lawler & Hall, 1970; Levenson, 1974; Rosenberg, 1965; Steers & Braunstein, 1976). Education was measured by a self-report of the number of years in school, and past academic ability was measured by the response to six biographical items addressing performance in school. Position tenure was measured by self-report as to the length of time the individual had been in the present position.

Situational characteristics. Situational characteristics were obtained from workgroup supervisors at three levels of analysis. The scales reported in A. P. Jones and James (1979) were used to assess the situational attributes. Job characteristics (job complexity, routineness, boundary spanning, and pressure) were obtained from supervisors' responses for each job type within their workgroup. Leader behaviors (goal setting, participation, and control and discipline) were measured at the individual level by requesting the supervisor to respond to the items for each subordinate. The remaining situational variables (standardization, formalization, resource availability, stability of the workgroup environment, centralization, use of control and discipline, and workgroup communication) were assessed by asking the supervisors to respond to the items for their workgroup as a whole (see James & Jones, 1980, for further description of the scales). Specialization was measured by counting the number of unique job types in each workgroup. Workgroup size was the number of individuals assigned to each workgroup as specified in organizational records.

Results

Table 1 presents the number of items and indicators of internal consistency for each of the variables. All scales with the exception of locus of control, need for affiliation, and fear of failure had acceptable estimates of internal consistency. These three variables were excluded from all further analyses and are not shown in Table 1.

Test of the Hypothesized Measurement Model

A confirmatory factor analysis, using LISREL VI (Jöreskog & Sörbom, 1983), was performed to assess the overall fit of the hypothesized measurement model. First, the covariance matrix among the multiple indicators of perceived job significance, perceived leader facilitation, perceived workgroup supportiveness, perceived role stress, anxiety, and all of the personal attributes with the exception of education, past academic ability, and position tenure, which were treated as manifest variables,

Table 1. Means, Standard Deviations, and Reliability Estimates for Endogenous and Exogenous Variables

Variable	Number of items assessed	Internal consistency indicators	Observed variable	
			M	SD
Perceived job significance				
Job challenge and variety	6[a]	.76	17.97	2.46
Job autonomy	5	.68	14.47	3.30
Job importance	3	.64	5.96	2.15
Perceived leader facilitation				
Leader trust and support	8[a]	.87	21.45	3.58
Leader goal emphasis and work facilitation	10[a]	.86	27.03	3.77
Leader interaction facilitation	4	.72	11.88	2.32
Perceived workgroup supportiveness				
Workgroup cooperation, friendliness, and warmth	7[a]	.78	16.18	2.06
Workgroup pride	4	.67	9.79	2.92
Perceived role stress				
Role ambiguity	10[a]	.78	32.84	3.30
Role conflict	8[a]	.70	24.40	2.61
Role overload	5	.57	16.90	3.03
Anxiety	5[a]	.87	18.58	1.01
Person variables				
Achievement motivation	9[a]	.65	21.78	1.92
Cognitive complexity	10[a]	.65	25.88	2.06
Compliance to norms	9[a]	.71	17.29	1.45
Job involvement	4[a]	.69	12.64	1.02
Self-esteem	5[a]	.54	19.21	.82
Past academic ability	6	.66	15.80	3.72
Postion tenure	1	na	5.40	1.99
Education	1	na	12.78	2.09
Situation variables				
Job complexity	3	.52	10.94	2.35
Job routineness	1	na	3.44	1.03
Boundary spanning	2	.29[b]	5.36	1.94
Pressure	2	.48[b]	6.55	1.53
Formalization	4	.50	13.72	2.66
Standardization	3	.74	6.52	1.79
Type of environment	4	.69	12.27	3.22
Centralization	5	.54	10.01	2.19
Leader goal setting	2	.49[b]	5.30	1.70
Leader participation	2	.50[b]	4.78	1.76
Control and discipline	8	.71	12.58	3.11
Resource availability	3	.53	6.34	1.69
Workgroup communication	3	.56	8.91	2.14
Degree of specialization	na	na		
Group size	na	na		

[a]Subscales were constructed to provide multiple indicators in subsequent analyses.   [b]Interitem correlation.

was computed. All the hypothesized latent variables were allowed to covary with each other while restrictions were placed on the relations between the observed indicators and the latent variables, as hypothesized. Results of this analysis yielded a chi-square of 3016.43 with 729 degrees of freedom, a ratio of 4:1, which is in the acceptable range (Marsh & Hocevar, 1985). The goodness-of-fit index (GFI) was .78, and the adjusted goodness-of-fit index (AGFI) was .73. All hypothesized factor loadings were significant based on the criterion that the t value was greater than 2.00 (Jöreskog & Sörbom, 1983), and the squared multiple correlations (SMC) for all observed indicators exceeded .20. Although the hypothesized measurement model did not account for all the covariance among the observed variables, it was deemed adequate to continue to test the structural relations. Modification of the measurement model to improve the fit prior to testing the hypothesized structural relations would be logically inconsistent because one would be, in effect, redefining the latent variables on which the model is based.

One further confirmatory factor analysis that included the above as well as the situational attributes and the demographic variables for which there were not multiple indicators was performed to obtain a standardized covariance matrix among the latent and manifest variables adjusted for measurement error. The diagonal elements of the phi matrix containing the covariance parameters among all latent and manifest variables were fixed to 1.0, thus standardizing the variances on the latent variables. This correlation matrix among the 28 variables in Figure 1, as shown in Table 2, was used in all subsequent analyses (Anderson & Gerbing, 1988).

Test of the Proposed Structural Model

The test of the overall fit of the hypothesized structural model as shown in Figure 1 yielded a chi-square of 432.22 with 81 degrees of freedom (GFI = .96; root AGFI = .80; RMS = .03), and the normed fit index (NFI) and parsimonious fit index (PFI) were .63 and .44, respectively, indicating that more of the covariance among the variables could be explained. (Note that the null model used in calculating the NFI and PFI allowed all the exogenous factors to be correlated but constrained all other relations to zero.) The total coefficient of determination for the system of structural equations was .89 with the respective coefficient of determination values for perceived job significance, leader facilitation, workgroup supportiveness, role stress, and anxiety being .40, .43, .42, .50, and .37, respectively, indicating that the model did account for a significant amount of the variance in the endogenous variables.

The structural coefficients for the proposed model, which one can interpret as one would a regression coefficient, are presented in Table 3 so that each column represents the structural equation for a specific endogenous variable. For example, the first column indicates that perceived job significance was found to be a function of role stress ($\beta = -.54$), achievement motivation ($\beta = .14$), job involvement ($\beta = .17$), job complexity ($\beta = -.21$), and boundary spanning ($\beta = -.06$). Although most of the hypothesized structural coefficients were significant, there were some hypothesized relations that were not supported. Furthermore, testing of sequential, nested models as recommended by Bentler and Bonett (1980) indicated that some of the paths that were hypothesized to be zero were, in fact, significantly different from zero. Therefore, the proposed model was disconfirmed.

Table 2. Phi Matrix of Correlations Submitted to Test the Proposed Structural Model

Variable	1	2	3	4	5	6	7	8	9	10	11	12	13	14	15	16	17	18	19	20	21	22	23	24	25	26	27	28
1. Job significance	—																											
2. Leader facilitation	63	—																										
3. Workgroup supportiveness	50	62	—																									
4. Role stress	-49	-65	-61	—																								
5. Anxiety	-22	-32	-44	-49	—																							
6. Achievement motivation	28	11	09	-09	-17	—																						
7. Cognitive complexity	-02	-05	-16	16	19	48	—																					
8. Compliance to norms	13	18	21	-25	-17	41	33	—																				
9. Job involvement	50	41	33	-29	-17	44	19	29	—																			
10. Self-esteem	-27	-16	-21	27	47	-61	03	-30	-24	—																		
11. Academic ability	-01	01	-02	03	-11	39	04	02	07	-38	—																	
12. Position tenure	-06	-04	-18	06	-01	11	-01	-15	-09	-12	28	—																
13. Education	-01	-04	01	-09	13	-05	25	13	21	-36	-03	-30	—															
14. Job complexity	-33	-20	-14	10	07	00	25	09	-17	-03	-03	09	16	—														
15. Job routineness	-20	-25	-14	04	01	05	07	05	-10	07	-11	-04	17	20	—													
16. Boundary spanning	-22	-15	-05	03	10	00	20	09	-16	01	-05	-00	15	41	14	—												
17. Pressure	-22	-21	-16	11	08	07	19	08	-07	-03	03	14	00	47	23	37	—											
18. Formalization	03	07	-05	-02	-11	-07	-09	-08	01	-09	04	02	-17	-13	-16	-06	-20	—										
19. Standardization	18	02	-04	10	-00	04	-14	-02	03	-14	06	03	-21	-16	-16	-10	-04	25	—									
20. Type of environment	02	06	-14	10	-01	05	-11	-08	06	-01	09	19	-31	-17	-14	-22	-02	24	10	—								
21. Centralization	-10	-20	-34	15	05	16	13	-04	-03	-07	12	25	-02	14	09	-09	18	13	10	-06	—							
22. Leader goal setting	21	22	10	-11	-07	04	-12	-05	08	-04	-01	-00	-05	-25	-12	-19	-21	04	-15	01	-03	—						
23. Leader participation	22	19	10	-05	00	03	-11	-03	10	01	-06	-08	-03	-31	-14	-27	-24	14	-06	09	-01	67	—					
24. Control and discipline	22	17	36	-10	-18	-02	-32	04	08	-13	-03	-21	-12	-25	-10	-18	-21	04	19	-06	-30	-07	16	—				
25. Resource availability	11	11	19	-13	-08	-17	-17	-03	-01	-01	-02	-11	-08	-18	-03	-05	-15	02	04	04	-12	01	-06	15	—			
26. Workgroup communication	13	15	37	-16	-04	-00	-06	05	09	01	-02	-26	19	-15	-08	-01	-15	-17	-14	-23	-33	10	13	31	04	—		
27. Degree of specialization	31	28	38	-14	-14	-06	-29	-05	15	-12	04	-14	-32	-41	-31	-26	-20	07	17	-06	-31	16	35	24	15	38	—	
28. Group size	28	19	42	-15	-13	-07	-26	03	12	-05	-07	-37	-01	-23	-14	-23	-30	02	03	-14	-41	12	16	54	10	38	53	—

Table 3. Parameter Estimates of the Proposed Model and the Best Fitting, Most Parsimonious Model

Variable	Proposed Model					Revised Model				
	1	2	3	4	5	1	2	3	4	5
Endogenous variables										
1. Job perceptions				ns					ns	
2. Leader perceptions				ns					−.19	
3. Workgroup perceptions				−.25					−.14	
4. Role perceptions	−.54	−.81	−.84			.42	−.56	−.23	−.78	.41
5. Anxiety				.21					.30	
Exogenous variables: Personal characteristics										
6. Achievement motivation	.14					.28				.14
7. Cognitive complexity				.11					.15	
8. Compliance to norms				−.11		−.20			.12	
9. Job involvement	.17			−.19		.21	.30		−.12	
10. Self-esteem					.38					.44
11. Position tenure				ns		−.14			ns	
12. Education					.09				−.08	.09
13. Past academic ability					.09					ns
Exogenous variables: Situational characteristics										
14. Job complexity	−.21					−.16				
15. Job routineness	ns					−.10	−.18			
16. Boundary spanning	−.06			ns		−.07			−.06	
17. Pressure				ns					ns	
18. Formalization	ns			ns		ns			ns	
19. Standardization				ns		.16			.07	
20. Type of environment				.05					.08	
21. Centralization		−.07					−.10			
22. Leader behavior: Goal setting		.08					.13			
23. Leader behavior: Participation		ns					ns			
24. Leader behavior: Control and discipline		ns					.08			
25. Resource availability			.06					.06		
26. Within-group communication			.17					.17		
27. Degree of specialization			.11					.13		
28. Group size			.11					.14		

Note. Each column represents the coefficients in the structural equation for that endogenous variable.

In an attempt to improve the fit of the model, exploratory analyses were performed. The parameter with the largest modification index, as provided by LISREL VI (Jöreskog & Sörbom, 1983), was freed to be estimated. The fit of this less-restricted model was evaluated, the parameter associated with the largest modification index was identified, and the process repeated if the parameter to be freed was reasonable from a theoretical perspective until the chi-square value was not significant at the .05 level. Examination of the PFI indicated the point at which further relaxation of the model was not warranted given the loss in degrees of freedom.

The best fitting, most parsimonious model obtained from this exploratory analysis yielded a total coefficient of determination of .89 (GFI = .98; AGFI = .90; RMS = .02; NFI = .86; PFI = .54). The coefficient of determination for the five endogenous variables—perceived job significance, perceived leader facilitation, perceived workgroup supportiveness, perceived role stress, and anxiety—were .51, .45, .46, .55, and .38, respectively. Therefore, this model accounted for more of the variance in the endogenous variables than did the hypothesized model.

The structural coefficients for this best-fitting, most parsimonious model are presented in Table 3 along with those from the proposed model. Based on these results, perceived job significance was found to be a function of perceived role stress, achievement motivation, compliance to norms, job involvement, position tenure, job complexity, job routineness, boundary spanning, and standardization. Perceived leader facilitation was influenced by perceived role stress, job involvement, job routineness, centralization, leader goal setting, and leader controlling and disciplinary behaviors. Perceived workgroup supportiveness was influenced by perceived role stress, resource availability, within-group communication, degree of specialization within the workgroup, and size of the workgroup. Perceived role stress was a function of perceived leader facilitation, perceived workgroup supportiveness, anxiety, cognitive complexity, compliance to norms, job involvement, education, boundary spanning, standardization, and stability of environment. Anxiety was influenced by perceived role stress, achievement motivation, self-esteem, and education.

Discussion

This study represents an attempt to explain the relations among the major facets of the perceived work environment and anxiety. As in any causal analysis, alternative models may be developed that explain the covariance structure equally well if not better. However, particular attention was given in this study to meeting the conditions for causal analysis. Although not all of these conditions were tested, or for that matter testable, the development of theoretical rationales for the predictions was considered of key importance in lessening the effects of incomplete satisfaction of the conditions. Furthermore, it should be kept in mind that the results of this study are dependent on the measurement model used and on a revised model developed through exploratory, theory-trimming procedures. This revised model, although not extremely different from the proposed model, has not been tested or confirmed. It therefore serves only as a guide for further theory building, hypothesis generation, and future causal analyses.

It was hypothesized that the perception of role stress is reciprocally related to the emotional, affective response of anxiety. The results between cognition and affect are consistent with those postulated by James and Jones (1980), James and Tetrick (1986), Lazarus (1982), and Zajonc (1980). It was shown that not only did perceived role stress increase anxiety, but anxiety mutually and simultaneously increased the perception of role stress. Furthermore, none of the situational attributes were directly related to anxiety. The influence of situational characteristics on anxiety was completely mediated by the perceptions of the work environment consistent with James and Tetrick (1986) and Lazarus (1982).

It also was hypothesized that perceived role stress is reciprocally related to one's perceived job significance, perceived leader facilitation, and perceived workgroup supportiveness and mediated the relations among one's other perceptions and anxiety. Smith (1982) suggested that the relations among cognitive variables are not adequately described by unidirectional relations and proposed that all cognitive constructs are probably reciprocally related. Although it was found that perceived role stress was reciprocally related to perceived leader facilitation and perceived workgroup supportiveness, the data suggest a unidirectional relation between perceived role stress and perceived job significance.

Perceived job significance was not found to have a direct effect on perceived role stress. Perceived job significance as manifestly indicated by challenge and variety, autonomy, and importance is closely aligned with the motivating potential of the job (Hackman & Oldham, 1980). Influences on this motivational state such as anxiety, leader perceptions, and workgroup perceptions were found to be mediated by perceived role stress, but this motivational state did not reciprocally affect perceived role stress. Therefore, as perceptions of leader facilitation increased based on the leader's behavior toward the individual, role stress was reduced and perceived job significance or motivation improved. Likewise, perceptions of workgroup supportiveness reduced the perception of role stress and resulted in increased perceptions of job significance. These results seem to clarify how factors other than the characteristics of one's job may influence motivation as well as perceived role stress.

Because leader facilitation and workgroup supportiveness were both found to be reciprocally related to perceived role stress, increases in leader facilitation also can increase perceived workgroup supportiveness by reducing role stress and vice versa. To the extent that leaders provided information to clarify ambiguity about what was expected, anxiety was reduced, the workgroup was perceived as more supportive, and the job was perceived as more significant. All these effects, however, were mediated by perceived role stress.

Perceived role stress was found to have a stronger impact on perceived workgroup supportiveness than vice versa, whereas the effect of perceived role stress on leader facilitation and vice versa were roughly equal. The pattern of structural coefficients among the central constructs suggests that perceived role stress contributed more to one's perceptions of the job, leader, and workgroup than these perceptions contributed to perceived role stress. These results may be explained, at least in part, by social attribution theory (Heider, 1958; E. E. Jones & Davis, 1965; Kelley, 1967) and implicational molecule theory (Wyer & Carlston, 1979). According to these theoretical perspectives, there is a self-serving bias, a tendency to attribute negative behaviors to external factors, to enhance or maintain one's self-esteem. Role stress, generally considered a negative perception, was found to be reciprocally related to anxiety, which is a function of self-esteem. Attribution theory thus would lead one to expect the perception of role stress to result in attributions about external factors, one's job, leader, and workgroup. Thus, the preservation of cognitive consistency among one's beliefs about the work environment may stem from a desire to maintain one's self-concept.

Conclusions and Implications

This study provides evidence that one's role in the organization, specifically the perception of role stress, is a key variable influencing one's perceptions of other aspects of the work environment. Perceived role stress appears to mediate the influence of anxiety on these perceptions as well as one's other perceptions of the work environment on one's psychological well-being. It would appear that individuals do interpret events in the work environment so as to preserve cognitive consistency among their higher order perceptions, beliefs, and needs. That is, as more role stress is perceived in the work environment, resulting from changes in situational events, anxiety, or changes in perceptions of leader facilitation or workgroup supportiveness, the lower the perceived job significance, perceived leader facilitation, and perceived workgroup supportiveness and the higher the experienced anxiety.

Beyond the complexity of the experience of role stress demonstrated by this study is the importance of the social aspects of the work environment. It would appear that the actual tasks one performs at work have less impact on the experience of role stress than does the social milieu. There was no evidence suggesting that characteristics of the job per se influenced the perception of role stress. However, both characteristics of the leader and the workgroup, as mediated by perceived leader facilitation and workgroup supportiveness, did affect the perception of role stress. These results suggest that stress management techniques need to incorporate issues of job design from a broader perspective and focus on interpersonal relationships within the work environment rather than on just the characteristics of the tasks performed or the individual who is experiencing role stress.

References

Abdel-Halim, A. A. (1981a). Effects of role stress–job design–technology interaction on employee work satisfaction. *Academy of Management Journal, 24*, 260–273.

Abdel-Halim, A. A. (1981b). A reexamination of ability as a moderator of role perceptions-satisfaction relationship. *Personnel Psychology, 34*, 549–561.

Aldag, R. J., Barr, S. H., & Brief, A. P. (1981). Measurement of perceived task characteristics. *Psychological Bulletin, 90*, 415–431.

Anderson, J. C., & Gerbing, D. W. (1988). Structural equation modeling in practice: A review and recommended two-step approach. *Psychological Bulletin, 103*, 411–423.

Bandura, A. (1978). The self system in reciprocal determinism. *American Psychologist, 33*, 344–358.

Batlis, N. C. (1980). Job involvement and locus of control as moderators of role-perception/individual-outcome relationships. *Psychological Reports, 46*, 111–119.

Bedeian, A. G. (1980). Personality correlates of role stress. *Psychological Reports, 46*, 627–632.

Bedeian, A. G., & Armenakis, A. A. (1981). A path-analytic study of the consequences of role conflict and ambiguity. *Academy of Management Journal, 24*, 417–424.

Bedeian, A. G., Armenakis, A. A., & Curran, S. M. (1982). The relationship between role stress and job-related, interpersonal, and organizational climate factors. *Journal of Social Psychology, 113*, 247–260.

Beehr, T. A., & Bhagat, R. S. (Eds.). (1985). *Human stress and cognition in organizations.* New York: Wiley.

Beehr, T. A., & Newman, J. E. (1978). Job stress, employee health, and organizational effectiveness: A facet analysis, model, and literature review. *Personnel Psychology, 31*, 665–699.

Bentler, P. M., & Bonett, D. G. (1980). Significance tests and goodness of fit in the analysis of covariance structures. *Psychological Bulletin, 88*, 588–606.

Biddle, B. J. (1979). *Role theory: Expectations, identities, and behaviors.* San Diego, CA: Academic Press.

Boal, K. B., & Cummings, L. L. (1981). Cognitive evaluation theory: An experimental test of processes and outcomes. *Organizational Behavior and Human Performance, 28*, 289–310.

Brett, J. M. (1982). Job transfer and well-being. *Journal of Applied Psychology, 67*, 450–463.

Bridger, H. (1978). The increasing relevance of group processes and changing values for understanding and coping with stress at work. In C. L. Cooper & R. Payne (Eds.), *Stress at work* (pp. 241–258). New York: Wiley.

Caplan, R. D., Cobb, S., French, J. R. P., Jr., Harrison, R. V., & Pinneau, S. R., Jr. (1975). *Job demands and worker health: Main effects and occupational differences* (USGPO Catalog No. HE 20.7111:J57. USGPO Stock No. 1733-00083). Washington, DC: U.S. Government Printing Office.

Cohen, S., & Wills, T. A. (1985). Stress, social support, and the buffering hypothesis. *Psychological Bulletin, 98*, 310–357.

Cooper, C. L., Payne, R. (Eds.). (1988). *Causes, coping and consequences of stress at work.* New York: Wiley.

Crutchfield, R. S. (1955). Conformity and character. *American Psychologist, 10*, 191–198.

Daft, R. L., & Macintosh, N. B. (1981). A tentative exploration into the amount and equivocality of information processing in organizational work units. *Administrative Science Quarterly, 26*, 207–224.

Dieterly, D. L., & Schneider, B. (1974). The effect of organizational environment on perceived power and climate: A laboratory study. *Organizational Behavior and Human Performance, 11*, 316–337.

Endler, N. S., & Magnusson, D. (1976). Toward an interactional psychology of personality. *Psychological Bulletin, 83*, 956–974.

Fisher, C. D. (1978). The effects of personal control, competence, and extrinsic reward systems on intrinsic motivation. *Organizational Behavior and Human Performance, 21*, 173–188.

Fisher, C. D., & Gitelson, R. (1983). A meta-analysis of the correlates of role conflict and ambiguity. *Journal of Applied Psychology, 68*, 320–333.

French, J. R. P., Jr., & Caplan, R. D. (1972). Organizational stress and individual strain. In A. J. Marrow (Ed.), *The failure of success* (pp. 30–66). New York: AMACOM.

Graen, G. (1976). Role-making processes within complex organizations. In M. D. Dunnett (Ed.), *Handbook of industrial and organizational psychology* (pp. 1201–1245). Chicago: Rand McNally.

Hackman, J. R., & Oldham, G. R. (1980). *Work redesign.* Reading, MA: Addison-Wesley.

Hage, J., & Aiken, M. (1969). Routine technology, social structure, and organizational goals. *Administrative Science Quarterly, 14*, 266–276.

Harrison, V. R. (1978). Person–environment fit and job stress. In C. L. Cooper & R. Payne (Eds.), *Stress at work* (pp. 175–208). New York: Wiley.

Heider, F. (1958). *The psychology of interpersonal relations.* New York: Wiley.

Hellriegel, D., & Slocum, J. W., Jr. (1974). Organizational climate: Measures, research, and contingencies. *Academy of Management Journal, 17*, 255–280.

Hermans, H. J. M. (1970). A questionnaire measure of achievement motivation. *Journal of Applied Psychology, 54*, 353–363.

House, R. J. (1971). A path goal theory of leader effectiveness. *Administrative Science Quarterly, 16*, 321–338.

House, R. J., & Dessler, G. (1974). The path-goal theory of leadership: Some post hoc and a priori tests. In J. G. Hunt & L. L. Larson (Eds.), *Contingency approaches to leadership* (pp. 29–59). Carbondale: Southern Illinois Press.

House, R. J., & Rizzo, J. R. (1972). Role conflict and ambiguity as critical variables in a model of organizational behavior. *Organizational Behavior and Human Performance, 7*, 467–505.

Hunt, S., Singer, K., & Cobb, S. (1967). Components of depression identified from a self-rating depression inventory for survey use. *Archives of General Psychiatry, 16*, 441–447.

Jackson, S. E., & Schuler, R. S. (1985). A meta-analysis and conceptual critique of research on role ambiguity and role conflict in work settings. *Organizational Behavior and Human Decision Processes, 36*, 16–78.

James, L. R., Hater, J. J., Gent, M. J., & Bruni, J. R. (1978). Psychological climate: Implications from cognitive social learning theory and interactional psychology. *Personnel Psychology, 31*, 783–813.

James, L. R., & Jones, A. P. (1980). Perceived job characteristics and job satisfaction: An examination of reciprocal causation. *Personnel Psychology, 33*, 97–135.

James, L. R., & Sells, S. B. (1981). Psychological climate: Theoretical perspectives and empirical research. In D. Magnusson (Ed.), *Toward a psychology of situations: An interactional perspective* (pp. 275–295). Hillsdale, NJ: Erlbaum.

James, L. R., & Tetrick, L. E. (1986). Confirmatory analytic tests of three causal models relating job perceptions to satisfaction. *Journal of Applied Psychology, 71*, 77–82.

Jones, A. P., & Butler, M. C. (1980). Influences of cognitive complexity on the dimensions underlying perceptions of the work environment. *Motivation and Emotion, 4*, 1–19.

Jones, A. P., & James, L. R. (1979). Psychological climate: Dimensions and relationships of individual and aggregated work environment perceptions. *Organizational Behavior and Human Performance, 23*, 201–250.

Jones, E. E., & Davis, K. E. (1965). From acts to dispositions: The attribution process in person perception. In L. Berkowitz (Ed.), *Advances in experimental social psychology* (Vol. 2, pp. 219–266). San Diego, CA: Academic Press.

Jones, E. E., & Gerard, H. B. (1967). *Foundations of social psychology*. New York: Wiley.

Jöreskog, K. G., & Sörbom, D. (1983). *LISREL: Analysis of linear structural relationships by the method of maximum likelihood*. Chicago: National Educational Resources.

Joyce, W. F., & Slocum, J. W., Jr. (1979). Climates in organizations. In S. Kerr (Ed.), *Organizational behavior* (pp. 317–336).

Kahn, R. L., Wolfe, D. M., Quinn, R. P., & Snoek, J. D. (1964). *Organizational stress: Studies in role conflict and ambiguity*. New York: Wiley.

Keller, R. T. (1975). Role conflict and ambiguity: Correlates with job satisfaction and values. *Personnel Psychology, 28*, 57–64.

Kelley, H. H. (1967). Attribution theory in social psychology. In D. Levine (Ed.), *Nebraska symposium on motivation* (pp. 192–240). Lincoln: University of Nebraska Press.

LaRocco, J. M., & Jones, A. P. (1978). Co-worker and leader support as moderators of stress-strain relationships in work situations. *Journal of Applied Psychology, 63*, 629–634.

Latham, G. P., & Yukl, G. A. (1975). A review of research on the application of goal setting in organizations. *Academy of Management Journal, 18*, 824–845.

Lawler, E. E., III, & Hall, D. T. (1970). Relationships of job characteristics to job involvement, satisfaction, and intrinsic motivation. *Journal of Applied Psychology, 54*, 305–312.

Lazarus, R. S. (1982). Thoughts on the relations between emotion and cognition. *American Psychologist, 37*, 1019–1024.

Lazarus, R. S., & Folkman, S. (1984). *Stress, appraisal, and coping*. New York: Springer Publishing.

Leavitt, H. J. (1951). Some effects of certain communication patterns on group performance. *Journal of Abnormal and Social Psychology, 46*, 38–50.

Lee, C., & Schuler, R. S. (1982). A constructive replication and extension of a role and expectancy perception model of participation in decision making. *Journal of Occupational Psychology, 55*, 109–118.

Levenson, H. (1974). Activism and powerful others: Distinctions within the concept of internal–external control. *Journal of Personality Assessment, 38*, 377–383.

Lewin, K. (1951). *Field theory in social science*. New York: Harper.

Marsh, H. M., & Hocevar, D. (1985). Application of confirmatory factor analysis to the study of self-concept: First and higher order factor models and their invariance across groups. *Psychological Bulletin, 97*, 562–582.

McGrath, J. E. (1976). Stress and behavior in organizations. In M. D. Dunnette (Ed.), *Handbook of industrial and organizational psychology* (pp. 1351–1395). Chicago: Rand McNally.

McMichael, A. J. (1978). Personality, behavioural, and situational modifiers of work stressors. In C. L. Cooper & R. Payne (Eds.), *Stress at work* (pp. 127–148). New York: Wiley.

Miles, R. H. (1980). Boundary roles. In C. L. Cooper & R. Payne (Eds.), *Current concerns in occupational stress* (pp. 61–96). New York: Wiley.

Miles, R. H., & Perreault, W. D., Jr. (1976). Organizational role conflict: Its antecedents and consequences. *Organizational Behavior and Human Performance, 17*, 19–44.

Mischel, W. (1973). Toward a cognitive social learning reconceptualization of personality. *Psychological Review, 80*, 252–283.

Mossholder, K. W. (1980). Effects of externally mediated goal setting on intrinsic motivation: A laboratory experiment. *Journal of Applied Psychology, 65*, 202–210.

Mossholder, K. W., Bedeian, A. G., & Armenakis, A. A. (1981). Role perceptions, satisfaction, and performance: Moderating effects of self-esteem and organizational level. *Organizational Behavior and Human Performance, 28*, 224–234.

Netemeyer, R. G., Johnston, M. W., & Burton, S. (1990). Analysis of role conflict and role ambiguity in a structural equations framework. *Journal of Applied Psychology, 75*, 148–158.

Organ, D. W. (1981). Direct, indirect, and trace effects of personality variables on role adjustment. *Human Relations, 34*, 573–587.

Payne, R. (1980). Organizational stress and social support. In C. L. Cooper & R. Payne (Eds.), *Current concerns in occupational stress* (pp. 269–298). New York: Wiley.

Phillips, J. S., & Lord, R. G. (1980). Determinants of intrinsic motivation: Locus of control and competence information as components of Deci's cognitive evaluation theory. *Journal of Applied Psychology, 65*, 211–218.

Posner, B. Z., & Randolph, W. A. (1980). Moderators of role stress among hospital personnel. *Journal of Psychology, 105*, 215–224.

Rabinowitz, S., & Hall, D. T. (1977). Organizational research on job involvement. *Psychological Bulletin, 84*, 265–288.

Randolph, W. A., & Posner, B. Z. (1981). Explaining role conflict and role ambiguity via individual and interpersonal variables in different job categories. *Personnel Psychology, 34*, 89–102.

Revelle, W., & Michaels, E. J. (1976). The theory of achievement motivation revisited: The implications of inertial tendencies. *Psychological Review, 83*, 394–404.

Rosenberg, J. M. (1965). *Society and the adolescent self image*. Princeton, NJ: Princeton University Press.

Schreisheim, C. A., & Murphy, C. J. (1976). Relationships between leader behavior and subordinate satisfaction and performance: A test of some situational moderators. *Journal of Applied Psychology, 61*, 634–641.

Shaw, M. E. (1976). *Group dynamics: The psychology of small group behavior*. New York: McGraw-Hill.

Smith, E. R. (1982). Beliefs, attributions, and evaluations: Nonhierarchical models of mediation in social cognition. *Journal of Personality and Social Psychology, 43*, 248–259.

Spielberger, C. D., Gorusch, R. L., & Luschene, R. (1968). *Self-evaluation questionnaire*. Palo Alto, CA: Consulting Psychologists Press.

Steers, R. M., & Braunstein, D. N. (1976). A behaviorally-based measure of manifest needs in work settings. *Journal of Vocational Behavior, 9*, 251–266.

Sutton, R. I., & Rousseau, D. M. (1979). Structure, technology, and dependency on a parent organization: Organizational and environmental correlates of individual responses. *Journal of Applied Psychology, 64*, 675–687.

Tetrick, L. E. (1989). The motivating potential of leader behaviors: A comparison of two models. *Journal of Applied Social Psychology, 19*, 947–958.

Tetrick, L. E., & LaRocco, J. M. (1987). Understanding, prediction, and control as moderators of the relationships between perceived stress, satisfaction and psychological well-being. *Journal of Applied Psychology, 72*, 538–543.

Tracy, L., & Johnson, T. W. (1981). What do the role conflict and role ambiguity scales measure? *Journal of Applied Psychology, 66*, 464–469.

Tushman, M. L. (1978). Technical communication in R & D laboratories: The impact of project work characteristics. *Academy of Management Journal, 21*, 623–645.

Van de Ven, A. H., & Ferry, D. (1980). *Measuring and assessing organizations*. New York: Wiley-Interscience.

Van Sell, M., Brief, A. P., & Schuler, R. S. (1981). Role conflict and role ambiguity: Integration of the literature and directions for future research. *Human Relations, 34*, 43–71.

White, S. E., Mitchell, T. R., & Bell, C. H., Jr. (1977). Goal setting, evaluation apprehension, and social cues as determinants of job performance and job satisfaction in a simulated organization. *Journal of Applied Psychology, 62*, 665–673.

Wyer, R. S., Jr., & Carlston, D. E. (1979). *Social cognition, inference, and attribution*. Hillsdale, NJ: Erlbaum.

Zajonc, R. B. (1980). Feeling and thinking: Preferences need no inferences. *American Psychologist, 35*, 151–175.

10 ⸻

Gail H. McKee, Steven E. Markham, and K. Dow Scott

Job Stress and Employee Withdrawal From Work

Occupational stress as it relates to employee health is an important work-related issue. Workers in blue-collar jobs appear to be at particular risk for stress (Cooper & Smith, 1985). In a major comparative study of 23 different occupations completed during the 1970s, Caplan, Cobb, French, Van Harrison, and Pinneau (1980) found that "assemblers and the relief workers on the machine paced lines clearly stand out as being high in stress" (p. 192). A study by House, Wells, Landerman, Mc-Michael, and Kaplan (1979) provided evidence that for blue-collar workers, there is a significant relation between job stress and mental health (e.g., psychosomatic disorders). After a review of several studies examining the effects of repetitive work on employees' perceptions of their health, Cox (1985) reported support for the hypothesis that stress caused by repetitive work can be damaging to employees' mental and physical well-being. Shostak (1980) predicted that throughout the 1980s, the stress level of blue-collar workers would probably increase because of more media coverage of health and safety concerns resulting from the discovery of new health risks on the job.

Blue-collar workers who are paid on a piece-rate basis also experience stress as a result of that type of incentive system (Levi, 1984). House (1980) found that employees in the tire and rubber industry perceived piecework as a primary source of their workload pressure. Perrewe and Ganster (1989) used the term *quantitative overload* to define the situation in which the amount of work "exceeds what an individual can accomplish in a given period of time" (p. 214). Because this chapter is concerned with the job of the sewing machine operator, a blue-collar job emphasizing fast-paced piecework production at a low-base rate, the type of stress investigated in this study is that of quantitative work overload. Furthermore, "experienced" or "perceived stress" is examined because how individuals perceive a demand and react to it is a determinant of the stressfulness of a situation (McGrath, 1976; Parasuraman & Alutto, 1984).

The apparel industry continues to be characterized by labor intensive and repetitive jobs despite some automation. Production is still the primary responsibility of individual sewing machine operators, even though there has been growing interest in approaches using employee involvement (Howell, 1990) and teamwork (Bailey, 1990). The current design of the sewing machine operator's job is one that may contribute to considerable job stress. Although operators may be able to set their own pace, they are pressured by the flow of work from the preceding operation and by the piece-rate wage system. Subramanian (1987) found in a recent study of textile manufacturers in India that the mental health of those industrial workers engaged in mechanized and assembly-line technology was lower than the mental health of those engaged in either handicraft or automated technology.

Both absenteeism and turnover have been characterized as ways employees can withdraw from work. Gupta and Jenkins (1983) noted that both might be considered an "escape" from aversive conditions in the organization. Rosse and Miller (1984) believed that both absence and turnover share common roots. This conceptualization has resulted from attempts at explaining the positive relation that is sometimes found between the two variables (Rhodes & Steers, 1990). Thus, it seems appropriate to investigate further whether job stress might be related to both absenteeism and turnover. The apparel industry traditionally has experienced absenteeism of over 6% and turnover ranging from 50% to over 100% annually. Although absenteeism and turnover could be indicative of a number of factors, job stress could very well be one of the antecedents.

More specifically, the relation between job stress and absenteeism might be expected, given the increasing evidence that stress is related to cardiovascular disease (see Carruthers, 1980; Chesney & Rosenman, 1980) and to psychosomatic disorders (see House et al., 1979). Hedges (1973) found absence to be higher on jobs considered to be more stressful (assembly-line work). Frankenhaeuser and Gardell (1976) likewise found that the relation between perceived stress and absence was higher for jobs requiring less skill and with less autonomy. A study by Samoilova in the Soviet Union (cited by Cox, 1985) found that "workers engaged in repetitive tasks were absent from work for medical reasons up to 5 times as often as those with less repetitive jobs" (p. 104). Fitzgibbons and Moch (1980) reported that job stress contributed to the prediction of unexcused absence. Given that the evidence appears weak, albeit supportive of a positive relation between perceived stress and absence from work, we proposed the following hypotheses:

> *Hypothesis 1*. The greater the perceived stress, the higher will be an employee's absenteeism rate.

Some research indicates that perceived stress is related to turnover (Brief & Aldag, 1976; Gupta & Beehr, 1979; Parasuraman & Alutto, 1984). Finding a relation between turnover and stress would not be surprising in that one widely recognized method of coping is avoidance (Edwards, 1988). Leaving a job is certainly one means of solving the problem of job stress. On the other hand, Hellriegel and White (1973) studied the relation between role pressures and turnover for accountants and found no significant relations. Kraut (1975) also found no significant relations between the amount of work and turnover of salespeople. Mobley (1982) concluded that the "conceptual and empirical linkages between stress and turnover have been inadequately researched" (p. 182).

In their literature review of the employee turnover process, Mobley, Griffith, Hand, and Meglino (1979) reported six studies in which turnover intentions by employees were consistently related to actual turnover. A meta-analysis by Steel and Ovalle (1984) of the relation between turnover intentions and actual departure found that the weighted average correlation between the two variables was .45.

This provides further support that the decision to leave progresses from an intention to actual departure. Mobley, Horner, and Hollingsworth (1978) suggested that turnover intentions might represent employees' evaluation of different alternatives. It this was the case, then the intention of employees to stay or leave a job would be an important outcome of job stress because, even if employees could not actually withdraw from the workplace, turnover intention would assess the relation between job stress and a desire to withdraw. This led to the second hypothesis:

> *Hypothesis 2.* The greater the perceived stress, the stronger will be an employee's intention to leave the job.

Although job stress originates at the workplace, there is growing interest in what happens outside the workplace. Wallace, Levens, and Singer (1988) noted social epidemiologists' desire to study how such social variables as marital status, ethnic background, or gender might affect one's perception of stress.

In their review of studies examining social support and stress, Cohen and Wills (1985) noted that "significant interpersonal relationships such as marriage sometimes show main effects and/or buffering interactions" (p. 320). Googins and Burden (1987) reported increased stress in the lives of employees with children under 18 years of age when compared with employees with no children. Thus, we made the following hypothesis:

> *Hypothesis 3.* Employees with dependents at home will have higher levels of stress than those employees without dependents at home.

The demands of raising children have fallen primarily on women. Thus, a child's illness has frequently resulted in absence of the mother from work. It follows logically that those women with more dependents would be absent more frequently than would those women with fewer or no dependents. The research, however, is mixed. Although two studies found a positive relation for women between absence and family size (Garrison & Muchinsky, 1977; Naylor & Vincent, 1959), a subsequent study found no such relation (Johns, 1978). A more recent study provided additional support for a positive relation between the number of dependents and absenteeism for both men and women (Scott & McClellan, 1990). Rhodes and Steers (1990) reported on the results of three national surveys of employers providing child-care services. The percentage of employers responding that such child-care services lowered absenteeism was 72% in one study and 53% in another study. In a third study, lower absenteeism was ranked as one of the top three benefits of child-care services. An additional study by Goff, Mount, and Jamison (1990) found that "employees who were more satisfied with the quality of their child's care, regardless of location, experienced less work/family conflict. In turn, lower levels of work/family conflict were found to be related to lower absenteeism" (p. 804).

Women have also frequently entered, left, and returned again to the work force after giving birth to a child or responding to other family demands. A study by Shaw (1985) found that for married women, the presence of young children caused gaps in employment. In another study, Gronau (1988) used information on approximately 1,900 women (married and nonmarried from the 1976 Panel Survey of Income Dynamics) and found that "being married, having children (particularly

young ones), having a husband with a high income, and changes in family circumstances (getting married, separating, or having another child), all increased women's
tendency to leave the labor force" (p. 284). Thus, although economic forces might
encourage a woman with dependents to stay on the job, it appears that the coun-
tervailing forces mentioned above push her to periodically leave. It was also found
in the three national surveys conducted and reported by Rhodes and Steers (1990)
that the presence of child care also had a strong positive impact on turnover prevention. In the first study, 57% of the employers responded that the job-turnover
rate was lowered, and in the second study 65% responded so. In the third study,
lower turnover was ranked as the fourth major benefit of child-care services. Thus,
we developed the following two hypotheses for this study (the sample of which was
almost entirely composed of women and in which the employer provided no child-
care services):

> *Hypothesis 4.* Employees with dependents at home will have higher absenteeism
> than will employees without dependents at home.

> *Hypothesis 5.* Employees with dependents at home will have higher intention to
> leave their jobs compared with employees without dependents at home.

The last set of hypotheses considers the relations between perceived stress and
both absenteeism and turnover intention for those employees with and without
dependents. Because it was expected that employees with dependents would perceive
more stress (see Hypothesis 3) and would have higher absenteeism and intention
to leave their jobs (see Hypotheses 4 and 5), it was also expected that the relation
between perceived stress and both measures of employee withdrawal from work
would be higher for those with dependents. This is because absenteeism and turnover
may provide a means of coping with aversive conditions through escape (Gupta &
Jenkins, 1983). Because employees with dependents at home would have a greater
range of possible escape behavior measured by higher absenteeism and intention
to leave the job, the relation between the variables was also expected to be stronger.
The last two hypotheses were thus similar to Hypotheses 1 and 2 but extended those
hypotheses by investigating whether having dependents at home serves as a boundary condition for the relation between job stress and employee withdrawal from
work.

> *Hypothesis 6.* The relation between perceived stress and absenteeism will be
> stronger for those employees with dependents at home.

> *Hypothesis 7.* The relation between perceived stress and employee intention to
> leave the job will be stronger for those employees with dependents living at home.

Method

Setting and Data Collection

The research locations included five nonunion apparel manufacturing plants of the
same organization located in the Virginia/North Carolina region. Plants ranged in

size from approximately 150 to 350 employees. Questionnaires were used to survey all production employees at the five plants. There were a total of 1,271 production employees on the payroll at the time the survey was administered. Operations were halted by management while employees completed the questionnaires. Absence, illiteracy, and missing or incomplete data reduced the number of usable question- naires to 1,146. Thus, the response rate was 90.2%. For purposes of this study, only responses of sewing machine operators (N = 733) were studied to control for possible effects of occupation. Sewing machine operators were paid on a piece-rate basis. Women accounted for 97.7% of the operators. The average age was 35.8 years (SD = 11.6). The average tenure was 5.3 years (SD = 5.5). The absence policy at this organization was stringent. Perfect attendance was expected. There were no paid sick days. Employees would be terminated for excessive absenteeism.

Measures

Individual attendance records were collected for the 6-month time period prior to the administration of the questionnaire. *Absence rate* was calculated by dividing the number of days absent by the number of days an employee could have worked (excluding time off for vacation, personal leave, or layoffs). The average absent rate was 4.15% (SD = 4.8%). *Absence frequency* was calculated by counting the number of absence incidents, regardless of the number of days in each incident. The average absence frequency was 3.2 incidents (SD = 2.8).

Job stress was measured by a scale consisting of three items (α = .72) based on Kahn, Wolfe, Quinn, Snoek, and Rosenthal's (1964) scale of job-related tension. The items were "A feeling that the amount of work you have to do interferes with how well it gets done," "A feeling that job pressures are too much for anyone," and "A feeling that the job makes you very nervous." Employees were asked to indicate whether they ever had the feelings expressed in each question. Possible responses were never occurs, sometimes occurs, undecided, often occurs, and always occurs.

Turnover intention was operationalized by a scale consisting of four items (α = .80). The following two items were from the Michigan Organizational Assessment Questionnaire (Cammann, Fichman, Jenkins, & Klesh, 1979): "I often think about quitting" and "I will probably look for a new job in the next year." The third item was a reversal of the second item: "I will probably remain with this company for at least the next 12 months." The fourth item was adapted from Hrebeniak and Alutto's (1972) Organizational Commitment Scale: "I would change jobs if I could make a little extra money." Employees were asked to indicate the degree to which they disagreed or agreed with the item. A 6-point rating scale was used ranging from *strongly disagree* to *strongly agree*.

Analytical Techniques

Pearson product moment correlations were used to investigate the relation of stress with employee absenteeism and turnover intention. After dividing the sample into two subgroups on the basis of whether employees had dependents living at home, an analysis of variance (ANOVA) was used to assess mean differences for stress, absenteeism, and turnover intention of those employees with and without dependents. Next, correlations were calculated for each subgroup. Finally, an analysis of covariance (ANCOVA) was used to determine whether having dependents at home was a boundary condition affecting the relation between stress and employee absence or turnover intention. A homogeneity-of-slopes model was used to test for differences between the regression lines of each subgroup.

Results

No relation was found between employee perceptions of stress and either their absence rate ($r = -.03$, ns) or their absence frequency ($r = .02$, ns). Thus, no support was found for the first hypothesis.

A significant positive relation was found between the amount of stress employees perceived and their intention to leave their jobs ($r = .45$, $p < .0001$); thus, the second hypothesis was supported.

To investigate further the relation between employee withdrawal and perceived stress, the sample was divided into those sewing machine operators who had dependents (children or nonworking adults) at home ($n = 503$) and those who did not have dependents at home ($n = 230$). Those operators reporting dependents at home had an average age of 35 years ($SD = 10.3$) and an average tenure of 4.8 years ($SD = 5.1$). Those operators reporting no dependents at home had an average age of 37.5 years ($SD = 13.8$) and an average tenure of 6.5 years ($SD = 6.2$). The mean differences between the two subgroups for both age, $F(1,731) = 7.52$, $p < .01$, and tenure, $F(1,707) = 14.70$, $p < .001$, were statistically significant.

Next, an F test was used to assess whether the two subgroups differed significantly in their perception of stress. No significant difference, $F(1,731) = .37$, was found between the perceived job stress of employees with dependents ($M = 2.13$) and those employees without dependents ($M = 2.10$). Consequently, the third hypothesis was not supported.

The fourth hypothesis investigated whether there were significant differences between the two subgroups on each measure of absenteeism (absence rate and absence frequency). No significant difference, $F(1,704) = 1.27$, was found between the absence rate of those employees with dependents ($M = 4.29\%$) and those without dependents ($M = 3.85\%$). However, there was a significant difference, $F(1,704) = 6.33$, $p < .05$, for the absence frequency of those employees with dependents ($M = 3.35$ incidents) in contrast with those without dependents ($M = 2.78$ incidents). Thus there was partial support for the fourth hypothesis.

The fifth hypothesis investigated whether significant differences existed between the two subgroups regarding their intention to leave their jobs. Turnover intention was significantly, $F(1,717) = 4.46$, $p < .05$, higher for those employees with dependents ($M = 3.52$) in contrast with those employees without dependents ($M = 3.33$). Thus, the fifth hypothesis was supported.

The sixth hypothesis investigated whether having dependents at home was a boundary condition affecting the relation of perceived job stress with employee absenteeism. No relation was found between perceived stress and absence rate for either employees with dependents ($r = -.05$) or without dependents ($r = .01$) nor was there a relation found between perceived stress and absence frequency for employees with dependents ($r = .03$) or without dependents ($r = .00$). The sixth hypothesis was not supported.

The last hypothesis examined whether having dependents at home was a boundary condition affecting the relation of perceived stress with employee turnover intention. A significant positive relation was found between perceived job stress and intention to leave the job for those employees with dependents ($r = .41, p < .0001$) as well as for those without dependents ($r = .51, p < .0001$).

The test of homogeneity-of-slopes for the two subgroups indicated that the slopes were different from each other. As can be noted from the correlations just reported, the relation between employee perception of job stress and turnover intention was stronger for those employees without dependents at home than for those employees with dependents at home. Because the seventh hypothesis had suggested the opposite (i.e., that the relation would be stronger for those with dependents at home), the seventh hypothesis was not accepted.

By way of further exploration, a full ANCOVA model was performed, which showed highly significant results. When predicting intention to leave one's job, the addition of the categorical variable of dependents with the variable of job stress produced an R-square of 21%, $F(3, 715) = 61.75, p < .0001$. The interaction was

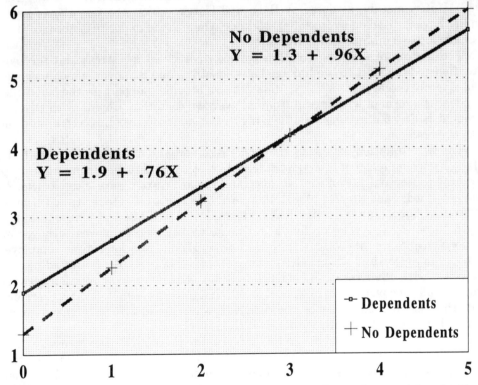

Figure 1. Regression lines of stress on turnover intention for employees with and without dependents. (X axis = perceived job stress; Y axis = intention to leave job. Grand means for dependents condition = [2.13, 3.51]. Grand means for no-dependents condition = [2.10, 3.53].)

not significant. For employees with dependents, perceived job stress predicted 17% of the variation in turnover intentions, whereas for employees without dependents, perceived job stress predicted 26% of the variation.

Notice in Figure 1 that employees with dependents reported higher intentions to leave their job when job stress was low. At high levels of perceived job stress, both groups reported about the same levels of intention to leave their jobs.

Discussion

The lack of relation between perceptions of job stress and absenteeism may be a result of situational constraints, such as family responsibilities, that limit the possibility of free choice (Steers & Rhodes, 1978). For example, even though employees experience stress and would like a day off from work, there may be financial obligations prohibiting them from acting on their desires. Therefore, employees may not really be free to choose whether to attend work. This would probably be especially true in the organization studied, where employees were not paid when absent. At the same time, there is some support that although absence is positively related to stressors in a job's context, it is not related to stressors involving job content (Arsenault & Dolan, 1983; Gupta & Beehr, 1979; Tellenback, Brenner, & Lofgren, 1983). Unfortunately, as noted by Baba and Harris (1989), the majority of stress studies have focused on white-collar workers, whereas the majority of absence studies have focused on blue-collar workers.

The finding of a strong relation between perceived job stress and turnover intention adds support to the linkage between stress and turnover, which has been inadequately researched (Mobley, 1982). It also provides support for the belief that turnover is a form of withdrawal from an aversive condition. Coping with stress is accomplished by fantasizing about leaving the job and thus avoiding a confrontation with the problem.

The weak relation between perceived stress and absence (in contrast with the relatively strong relation between perceived job stress and turnover intention) supports the conceptualization that absence and turnover are separate constructs. As noted by Rhodes and Steers (1990), other variables affect absenteeism and turnover differently. For instance, having a short-term illness will affect absence more than it will turnover. The relation found in this study between employee turnover intention and absence rate was not significant ($r = .01$); the relation between employee turnover intention and absence frequency was ($r = .11, p < .01$). Both findings are consistent with other research evidence that has shown either no relation between absence and turnover or a weak positive relation (Mobley, 1982). It may, therefore, still prove best to study absence and turnover as two distinctive phenomena—even though both have to do with withdrawal from work.

The lack of a significant difference between the perception of job stress by those with dependents and without dependents was surprising. However, it may be that although some employees with dependents are stressed by the demands of their dependents, others receive social support from them. Maslach and Jackson (1985) found that employees who were married and employees who had children experienced less burnout. Thus, the average perception of job stress by those with dependents could be a mixture of two opposite forces. Further study appears necessary to determine how the quality of the relations employees have with their dependents and other significant people (inside as well as outside of the workplace) affects their withdrawal from the workplace.

The lack of a significant difference between the absence rates of those with and without dependents living at home was also surprising given that other studies have shown significantly higher absence rates for those employees with children. However, the finding in this study could have occurred because of this organization's absence policy. Because there were no paid absences, financial obligations could more strongly affect whether employees would be absent. The finding of a significant difference between the absence frequency of those with and without dependents provides further support for the interpretation of absence frequency as a measure of occasional absence (e.g., the unexpected brief illness of a child). Again, the strength of the relation might have been constrained because of this organization's practice of not paying for absence.

The finding that turnover intentions were higher for those with dependents is consistent with other studies (Mobley, 1982). It may be that those with dependents think more about leaving their job because they are trying to improve their financial situation. It would also be useful to study the marital status of those with and without dependents given that the financial support of a partner might provide the security for an employee (especially one who is experiencing job stress) to change jobs. Of course, the spouse's job might also trigger turnover should there be a job transfer.

The discovery that the relation between perceptions of job stress and turnover intention was weaker for those employees with dependents was not expected. Close examination of the regression lines (see Figure 1) indicates that only at low levels of perceived job stress did having dependents at home make a difference. An explanation for this finding is that those employees low in stress and with dependents have the lowest average age (M_1 = 34.8 years) and tenure (M_2 = 4.4 years) of the four groups. (The four groups were: low stress with dependents, M_1 = 34.8 years, M_2 = 4.4 years; high stress with dependents, M_1 = 35.4 years, M_2 = 5.4 years; low stress without dependents, M_1 = 38.1 years, M_2 = 6.5 years; and high stress without dependents, M_1 = 36.3 years, M_2 = 6.4 years.) It could be that employees in this first group think more about leaving their job not because of job stress but because of family pressures requiring them to leave (e.g., having more children while they are at a younger age). Therefore, there may be two very different reasons for turnover—one that is related to job pressure and the other that is related to family pressure. This would help explain why the relation between perceived job stress and turnover intention would be stronger for those without dependents. Being older and a more senior member of the organization may also affect employee perception of stress. This was evidenced by the third group (low stress, no dependents), who had the highest average age and tenure.

In conclusion, the finding of a significant relation between perceived stress and turnover intention may be a red flag to management indicating that a change is required. If the work is perceived as excessive—beyond the capabilities of a single individual—then perhaps the move toward modular designs and teamwork approaches is justified. A continuous-process technology may also help to provide jobs "characterized by more freedom, control and meaningful involvement" (Subramanian, 1987, p. 79). In any case, a cooperative effort between management and employees to improve job design and identify ways for employees to cope with perceived stress on the job would help provide a more lasting and satisfying solution for both parties.

Withdrawal from work has multiple causes. The workplace may not always be an aversive condition nor job stress the only response. This study is a reminder of the importance of assessing boundary conditions (such as the presence of dependents) in trying to understand job stress and employee turnover. It may be that other family challenges and personal interests lead to withdrawal from work. Understanding job stress and its relation to employee withdrawal from work appears to require going outside the immediate work setting. It requires paying attention to the demands of the work situation, as well as to the demands of the family situation, so that unnecessary turnover can be avoided.

References

Arsenault, A., & Dolan, S. (1983). The role of personality, occupation, and organization in understanding the relationship between job stress, performance, and absenteeism. *Journal of Occupational Psychology, 56,* 227–240.

Baba, V. V., & Harris, M. J. (1989). Stress and absence: A cross-cultural perspective. *Research in Personnel and Human Resources Management,* Suppl. 1, 317–337.

Bailey, T. (1990). Facing the labor shortage crisis. *Bobbin, 32,* 82–88.

Brief, A. P., & Aldag, R. J. (1976). Correlates of role indices. *Journal of Applied Psychology, 61,* 404–409.

Cammann, C., Fichman, M., Jenkins, D., & Klesh, J. (1979). *The Michigan organizational assessment questionnaire.* Ann Arbor: University of Michigan Press.

Caplan, R. D., Cobb, S., French, J. R. P., Jr., Van Harrison, R., & Pinneau, S. R., Jr. (1980). *Job demands and worker health.* Ann Arbor: University of Michigan Press.

Carruthers, M. (1980). Hazardous occupations and the heart. In C. L. Cooper & R. Payne (Eds.), *Current concerns in occupational stress* (pp. 3–22). New York: Wiley.

Chesney, M. A., & Rosenman, R. (1980). Type A behavior in the work setting. In C. L. Cooper & R. Payne (Eds.), *Current concerns in occupational stress* (pp. 187–212). New York: Wiley.

Cohen, S., & Wills, T. A. (1985). Stress, social support, and the buffering hypothesis. *Psychological Bulletin, 98,* 310–357.

Cooper, C. L., & Smith, M. J. (1985). Introduction: Blue-collar workers are at risk. In C. L. Cooper & A. J. Smith (Eds.), *Job stress and blue-collar work* (pp. 1–4). New York: Wiley.

Cox, T. (1985). Repetitive work: Occupational stress and health. In C. L. Cooper & A. J. Smith (Eds.), *Job stress and blue collar work* (pp. 85–112). New York: Wiley.

Edwards, J. R. (1988). The determinants and consequences of coping with stress. In C. L. Cooper & R. Payne (Eds.), *Causes, coping and consequences of stress at work* (pp. 53–76). New York: Wiley.

Fitzgibbons, D., & Moch, M. D. (1980). Employee absenteeism: A multivariate analysis with replication. *Organizational Behavior and Human Performance, 26,* 349–372.

Frankenhaeuser, M., & Gardell, B. (1976). Underload and overload in working life: Outline of a multidisciplinary approach. *Journal of Human Stress, 2,* 35–46.

Garrison, K. R., & Muchinsky, P. M. (1977). Attitudinal and biographical predictors of incidental absenteeism. *Journal of Vocational Behavior, 10,* 221–230.

Goff, S. J., Mount, M. D., & Jamison, R. L. (1990). Employer supported child care, work/family conflict, and absenteeism: A field study. *Personnel Psychology, 43,* 793–809.

Googins, B., & Burden, D. (1987). Employees look to the work place for help with job–family problems. *Business and Health, 4,* 58.

Gronau, R. (1988). Sex-related wage differentials and women's interrupted labor careers—the chicken or the egg. *Journal of Labor Economics, 6,* 277–301.

Gupta, N., & Beehr, T. A. (1979). Job stress and employee behaviors. *Organizational Behavior and Human Performance, 23,* 373–387.

Gupta, N., & Jenkins, D. G., Jr. (1983). Tardiness as a manifestation of employee withdrawal. *Journal of Business Research, 11*, 61–75.

Hedges, J. N. (1973). Absence from work—A look at some national data. *Monthly Labor Review, 96*, 24–31.

Hellriegel, D., & White, G. E. (1973). Turnover of professionals in public accounting: A comparative analysis. *Personnel Psychology, 26*, 239–249.

House, J. S. (1980). *Occupational stress and the mental and physical health of factory workers*. Ann Arbor: Survey Research Center Institute for Social Research, University of Michigan.

House, J. S., Wells, J. A., Landerman, L. R., McMichael, A. J., & Kaplan, R. H. (1979). Occupational stress and health among factory workers. *Journal of Health and Social Behavior, 20*, 139–160.

Howell, A. (1990). Working on our work force. *Bobbin, 32*, 68–72.

Hrebeniak, L. G., & Alutto, J. A. (1972). Personal and role-related factors in the development of organizational commitment. *Administrative Science Quarterly, 17*, 555–573.

Johns, G. (1978). Attitudinal and nonattitudinal predictors of two forms of absence from work. *Organizational Behavior and Human Performance, 22*, 431–444.

Kahn, R. L., Wolfe, D. M., Quinn, R. P., Snoek, J. D., & Rosenthal, R. (1964). *Organizational stress: Studies in role conflict and ambiguity*. New York: Wiley.

Kraut, A. I. (1975). Predicting turnover of employees from measured job attitudes. *Organizational Behavior and Human Performance, 13*, 233–243.

Levi, L. (1984). *Stress in industry*. Geneva, Switzerland: International Labour Office.

Maslach, C., & Jackson, S. E. (1985). The role of sex and family variables in burnout. *Sex Roles, 12*, 837–851.

McGrath, J. E. (1976). Stress and behavior in organizations. In M. D. Dunnette (Ed.), *Handbook of industrial and organizational psychology* (pp. 1351–1395). New York: Wiley.

Mobley, W. H. (1982). *Employee turnover: Causes, consequences, and control*. Reading, MA: Addison-Wesley.

Mobley, W. H., Griffith, R. W., Hand, H. H., & Meglino, B. M. (1979). Review and conceptual analysis of the employee turnover process. *Psychological Bulletin, 86*, 443–522.

Mobley, W. H., Horner, S. O., & Hollingsworth, A. T. (1978). An evaluation of precursors of hospital employee turnover. *Journal of Applied Psychology, 63*, 408–414.

Naylor, J. C., & Vincent, N. L. (1959). Predicting female absenteeism. *Personnel Psychology, 12*, 81–84.

Parasuraman, S., & Alutto, J. A. (1984). Sources and outcomes of stress in organizational settings: Toward the development of a structural model. *Academy of Management Journal, 27*, 330–350.

Perrewe, P. L., & Ganster, D. C. (1989). The impact of job demands and behavioral control on experienced job stress. *Journal of Organizational Behavior, 10*, 213–229.

Rhodes, S. R., & Steers, R. M. (1990). *Managing employee absenteeism*. Reading, MA: Addison-Wesley.

Rosse, J. G., & Miller, H. E. (1984). Relationship between absenteeism and other employee behaviors. In P. S. Goodman & R. S. Atkin (Eds.), *Absenteeism: New approaches to understanding, measuring, and managing absence* (pp. 194–228). San Francisco: Jossey-Bass.

Scott, K. D., & McClellan, E. L. (1990). Gender differences in absenteeism. *Public Personnel Management, 19*, 229–253.

Shaw, L. B. (1985). Determinants of the increasing work attachment of married women. *Work and Occupations, 12*, 41–57.

Shostak, A. B. (1980). *Blue-collar stress*. Reading, MA: Addison-Wesley.

Steel, R. P., & Ovalle, N. D., II. (1984). A review and meta-analysis of research on the relationship between behavioral intentions and employee turnover. *Journal of Applied Psychology, 69*, 673–686.

Steers, R. M., & Rhodes, S. R. (1978). Major influences on employee attendance: A process model. *Journal of Applied Psychology, 63*, 391–407.

Subramanian, S. (1987). Mental health of the industrial workers in different technological operations and their innovativeness. *Indian Journal of Industrial Relations, 23*, 72–79.

Tellenback, S., Brenner, S., & Lofgren, H. (1983). Teacher stress: Exploratory model building. *Journal of Occupational Psychology, 56*, 19–33.

Wallace, M., Levens, M., & Singer, G. (1988). Blue-collar stress. In C. L. Cooper & R. Payne (Eds.), *Causes, coping and consequences of stress at work* (pp. 53–76). New York: Wiley.

11

Debra L. Nelson and Michael A. Hitt

Employed Women and Stress: Implications for Enhancing Women's Mental Health in the Workplace

Women who work outside the home constitute a growing segment of the U.S. labor force. It has been estimated that 90% of women in the age range of 18–49 years held jobs in 1986 (Stipp, 1988). Although multiple roles for women produce a number of positive outcomes, it has been determined that certain work conditions are deleterious to women's health. Many scholars have called for the integration of these research findings into organizational programs and public policies aimed at promoting women's health in the workplace (Matthews & Rodin, 1989; Rodin & Ickovics, 1990; Russo & Denmark, 1984).

To develop programs and policies to accomplish this goal, it is necessary to have an understanding of the stressors and strains that working women experience. Scholars have proposed that working women experience not only the same stressors as their male counterparts but also unique stressors by virtue of their entry into traditionally male-dominated, patriarchal organizations (Jick & Mitz, 1985; Nelson & Quick, 1985). The purpose of this chapter is to propose a set of recommendations for enhancing women's mental health in the workplace by examining research on working women and stress.

We begin with a discussion of the beneficial effects of work for women. Next, we review the research on gender differences in work-related stressors, strains, and organizational resources available for managing stressors. We then describe our study of male and female personnel professionals, which provides evidence for gender differences and patterns of the linkages between stressors and strain outcomes for the women. Finally, we conclude with a set of recommendations for organizational programs and public policies to address women's well-being at work.

The Health Benefits of Work for Women

Examination of the association between work and well-being among women suggests that work has beneficial as well as distressful outcomes. Most of the research regarding the beneficial nature of work focuses on both paid employment and multiple role occupancy.

Several correlational studies have demonstrated significant relations between women's employment and physical and mental well-being; that is, employed women are comparatively healthier than nonemployed women (LaCroix & Haynes, 1987; Verbrugge, 1989). A review of the empirical evidence concluded that employment improved the health of both married and unmarried women who had positive attitudes toward employment (Repetti, Matthews, & Waldron, 1989). Several explanations for these findings have been proposed, including the opportunities for challenge, control, structure, social support, financial rewards, and self-esteem (Baruch, Biener, & Barnett, 1987; Rodin & Ickovics, 1990). Similarly, associations between women's occupancy of multiple roles (e.g., worker, parent, spouse) and well-being have been documented (Waldron & Jacobs, 1989). However, most studies have ignored role quality. Baruch and Barnett (1986) found that the quality of roles occupied by women were more strongly associated with physical and mental health than were the number of roles held. It has been suggested that roles with low control, time pressures, and variable schedules are threats to health (Verbrugge, 1986).

Thus, both paid employment and the occupancy of multiple roles are related to positive health outcomes for women with the presumption that there is high quality among the roles held. What is unclear from these studies, however, is the direction of causality. Healthier women may self-select into multiple roles and employment, rather than the reverse. More rigorous studies are needed to address the causal dilemma.

Although employed women are healthier on average than are nonemployed women, specific work situations can be stressful for women. Job stressors can extract health costs from women that outweigh the health benefits of working. One question that arises in this regard is whether women's experience of work stress differs from that of men. In the following section, we review the literature on work stress and gender differences.

Sex Differences in Work Stress

Interest in gender differences in work stress has increased in recent years in both theory building (Jick & Mitz, 1985; Nelson & Quick, 1985) and empirical research (Davidson & Cooper, 1983; Zappert & Weinstein, 1985). The research in this area has focused on stressors and strain symptoms and to a lesser extent on organizational resources for managing work stress.

Stressors

The conceptual literature on stressors suggests that working women are prone to the same stressors as are working men. However, they also face several potentially unique stressors such as discrimination, stereotyping, social isolation, and work/home conflicts (Nelson & Quick, 1985).

The empirical research has examined sex differences in specific work stressors. Davidson and Cooper (1983) surveyed 884 British managers and found a number of significant differences. Female managers reported more external, discriminatory-based stressors and more stress from the home/social arena than did men. In a study of male (n = 50) and female (n = 73) MBA graduates, Zappert and Weinstein (1985) found that women reported inflexible schedules, low control over workflow, boring work, difficulty in accepting criticism, and work/home conflict as stronger stressors than did the men.

Other studies have also found work/home conflicts to be problematic for working women. Although women have adapted to share the provider role with their partners, men have not adapted as well in sharing the domestic responsibilities (Duxbury & Higgins, 1991; Voydanoff, 1988). Greenglass (1985) found in a study of Canadian managers that work/home conflicts are more stressful for women. In another study, male and female managers rated conflicts between family and job responsibilities to be a more consistent cause of poor job performance for women than for men (Wiley & Eskilson, 1988). Thus, women are more likely to experience work/home conflicts because of their multiple roles (and the unwillingness of men to share the domestic role), and such conflicts serve as stronger stressors for women than for men.

Another stressor that has been suggested to plague working women is politics, which involves behaviors individuals engage in for the purpose of gaining power. Because women often are relegated to the lower ranks of male-dominated occupations, they possess limited opportunities to develop political skills because of lack of access to role models and influential managerial jobs (Schein, 1978). And, in the instances in which women hold responsible managerial positions higher in the corporate hierarchy, they sometimes find themselves excluded from the informal social interactions enjoyed by their male peers, where many political transactions take place (Bhatnagar, 1988; Nelson & Quick, 1985). When women attempt to enter into the informal social networks, their contributions frequently are ignored or denigrated (Bernard, 1976; Voydanoff, 1988). Davidson and Cooper (1983) found office politics to be a major source of stress for junior women managers.

A predominant source of organizational power is the position held by an individual. In a longitudinal study of 10,317 working men and women, Wolf and Fligstein (1979) found that women were less likely to hold power positions than were men. In addition, women have been found to possess less authority in organizational decision making (Sherman, Ezell, & Odewahn, 1987) and are rated as less influential than men by other managerial and nonmanagerial personnel (Brass, 1985). Thus, it may be expected that working women experience politics as stressful.

Another source of stress for working women is career progress. Although men also face this stressor, it is particularly demanding for women because they remain clustered in the lower levels of the hierarchy. For example, only 2% of senior management positions are held by women, and only 5% of corporate board members are women (Friedman, 1988). One explanation for this finding is that stereotypes and biases of male decisionmakers prohibit women's career advancement. This is exemplified in the research of Hitt and Barr (1989) who found sex to have both main and interactive effects on decision models used to select middle- and upper-level managers. The barrier formed by these biases that limit women's career advancement has been referred to as the "glass ceiling" (Morrison, White, & Van Velsor, 1987).

The Framingham studies showed that limits on women's career progress may affect their health (Haynes & Feinleib, 1980). For example, decreased job mobility was found to be a major predictor of coronary heart disease among female clerical workers. Additionally, women reported more job changes but fewer promotions than did men. Thus, the upward mobility for women may be severely constrained.

The preceding review suggests that women experience different and more stressors at work than men. In addition, sex differences in symptoms of strain have been shown.

Symptoms of Distress/Strain

Sex differences in symptoms of distress or strain have been more widely addressed. Women report greater overall levels of psychological distress symptoms than do men (Davidson & Cooper, 1983; Jick & Mitz, 1985). Specifically, women report more anxiety (Defares, Brandjes, Nass, & van der Ploeg, 1984), depression (Cleary & Mechanic, 1983; O'Neill & Zeichner, 1985), and sleep disturbances (Cox, Thirlaway, & Cox, 1984; Zappert & Weinstein, 1985).

Physical symptoms of distress or strain have also been the focus of sex differences research, although the pattern of results is less clear. Studies have indicated that men report more symptoms such as hypertension (Defares et al., 1984), poor physical condition (Cooper & Melhuish, 1984), and upset stomach (Davidson & Cooper, 1985) than do women. Other studies have found that women report poorer overall physical health, poorer physical fitness, and more upset stomachs (Cox et al., 1984; Zappert & Weinstein, 1985), and more headaches (Davidson & Cooper, 1985) than do men.

Behavioral strain symptoms often are associated with stress and have been the focus of sex differences studies. Female executives have been found to smoke more than their male counterparts in some studies (Cooper & Davidson, 1982; Jacobson, 1981), yet other studies have found no gender differences in smoking behavior (Defares et al., 1984; Gottleib & Green, 1984). Smoking rates among women have increased, whereas smoking rates among men have decreased substantially in recent years (Rodin & Ickovics, 1990). Although alcohol abuse among women is rising, this behavioral symptom is more prevalent among men (Kilbey & Sobeck, 1988; Wilsnack, Wilsnack, & Klassen, 1984). Cooper and Melhuish (1984) found that 30% of the male managers in their study used tranquilizers or antidepressants for relieving tension, whereas Cooper and Davidson (1982) found that 40% of a comparable sample of female managers took these drugs.

Psychological, physical, and behavioral symptoms of distress have been examined for gender differences. Although the results of these studies are unclear, it can be concluded that men and women report different symptoms. These differences may be understated because few inventories include distress symptoms that are unique to women. Premenstrual syndrome, amenorrhea, infertility, and anorexia are seldom included in distress symptom measures, yet women are at risk for these stress-related disorders (Witkin-Lanoil, 1984).

Organizational Resources

The recognition of the costs of distress to individuals and, in turn, to the organizations that employ them have sparked organizational interest in providing resources to help individuals manage stress. Yet, research has not examined the effects of the provision of parental leave, daycare, and alternative work scheduling as resources for preventively managing stress (Freedman & Phillips, 1988). Many scholars of working women and stress have called for programs such as flextime and staff support (Friedman, 1988), mentoring (Noe, 1988; Sherman et al., 1987), and goal-setting activities (Voydanoff, 1988). Research is needed to examine the relations between organizational resources and the stressors at which they are targeted and between the resources and symptoms of distress. Gender differences in the provision and efficacy of these resources should also be explored.

The Personnel Professionals Study

Our own work on sex differences in work stress broadens and complements the previous research. Detailed presentation of the study's theoretical background, hypothesis development, method, and results is published elsewhere (Nelson, Quick, & Hitt, 1989; Nelson, Quick, Hitt, & Moesel, 1990). The discussion that follows is a brief summarization of our findings that pertain to gender differences in work stress and the relations among stressors, strains, and organizational resources for working women.

Our study examined gender differences in stress among personnel professionals. Personnel managers have not often been the subject of previous studies of work stress, with a single exception. Glogow (1986) examined burnout among personnel managers and concluded that these individuals must take responsibility for managing their own stress. In addition, personnel managers are seen as the guardians of health and well-being in the organization. Personnel managers experience considerable stress as a result of their boundary-spanning roles, role conflict, and status incongruence. This group of managers also represents an interesting sample to study because the personnel profession was one of the first to accept and encourage women's careers within its ranks.

Questionnaires were mailed to 2,000 personnel managers. Our sample consisted of 443 personnel professionals (248 men and 195 women) from the Southwest United States, resulting in a 22% response rate. The industries represented by the respondents included oil and gas, finance, banking, advertising, manufacturing, and real estate. Demographics suggested that the sample was representative of the Association of Human Resource Management membership in the United States.

We first examined the data for potential sex differences in work stressors, distress symptoms, and preventive stress-management strategies. Our hypotheses suggested that women would report more work/home conflict and greater use of social support than would men, whereas men would report greater use of exercise as a prevention strategy. Results indicated that the sole stressor on which women and men differed was organizational politics ($t = 2.06, p < .05$). The politics measure in this study consisted of four items: people taking credit for other's achievements, exchanging favors with people of higher rank, game playing to obtain power/authority, and getting ahead by knowing the right person.

Other interesting results emerged from this study. Men did report greater use of exercise as a prevention strategy, but women did not report greater use of social support. Women did report higher levels of distress symptoms both of a psychological and physical nature, as expected.

These findings indicate that female personnel professionals find political exchanges and games in the workplace stressful. Furthermore, these results suggest that women continue to be at a power disadvantage, even in personnel management.

The lack of significant differences in work/home conflict was unexpected. It may reflect a process of accommodation occurring within dual career couples. It may also be a product of our pool of respondents; that is, personnel managers, as targets of substantial management literature, are well informed about the potential distress from work/home conflicts and therefore take early actions to manage this stressor.

An important finding was that female personnel professionals reported more distress than did male personnel professionals. It may be that the higher activity level in exercise and sports for men was associated with their lower levels of symptoms. However, it also may suggest the need to help women develop more effective stress-coping mechanisms.

We further analyzed the data within the group of female respondents. Specifically, we were interested in the associations between three particular stressors (politics, lack of career progress, and work/home conflicts) and the health-related outcomes (satisfaction and distress/strain symptoms). We found that politics and lack of career progress were associated with greater strain symptoms and reduced satisfaction, and organizational resources were associated with lower levels of these stressors. The pattern for work/home conflict was different. Work/home conflicts were associated with greater strain symptoms but were unrelated to satisfaction and organizational resources. Thus, politics and lack of career progress were perceived as related to the work situation and resolvable or preventable by the organization.

These results indicate that stressors have differential effects and should not be treated as equivalent. For instance, work/home conflicts may have significant, dysfunctional effects on women's health but be independent of other organizational stressors and unrelated to job satisfaction. Women may see these conflicts more as products of the domestic situation than of the work situation. As a result, work/home conflicts may not be resolvable (or preventable) by traditional organizational resources. In contrast, politics and lack of career progress may be better targets on which organizations should focus. The increased commitment of organizational resources was associated with significant reductions in the adverse effects of politics and lack of career progress as stressors ($-.29, p < .05; -.21, p < .05$, respectively).

The findings take on added significance given the women in the study. Even in a progressive profession such as personnel management, politics and lack of career progress have adverse associations with women's job satisfaction. This suggests that there are still discriminatory attitudes, stereotypes, and a potential glass ceiling for women. And the problems may be magnified for women who work in traditionally male occupations.

Summary

Sex differences in the experience of work stress have been demonstrated in terms of stressors encountered and distress/strain symptoms reported. The results of our study of personnel professionals, along with the previous work on gender differences, provide evidence that working women's experience of stress differs from that of men. The research, then, suggests that working women should be considered a population at risk and that therefore programs should be developed to enhance women's well-being at work. Prevention programs are particularly important with the increased number of women in the workforce and in professional and managerial positions.

Implications for Organizational Programs and Public Policy

Psychologists and organizational scientists can play key roles in influencing public policy that encourages women's well-being at work. There are four specific areas that public policy and organizational programs should emphasize to help women deal with the stress nature of their multiple roles.

Equity in Pay, Benefits, and Education

Although efforts to achieve pay equity have made strides in the recent past, the wage gap continues to exist. Women's earnings persist at the level of 60% of men's earnings (Ferraro, 1984). The wage gap continues to be a significant problem and even more so given the number of single working women in the labor force. The problem is magnified because many benefits received by employees often fluctuate with their level of direct compensation (Russo & Denmark, 1984).

Benefits are of special significance to female workers for several reasons. The majority of women's illnesses produce symptoms that are long term, disability producing, and require continuous care (Verbrugge, 1989). Women are also prescribed drugs more often and are more likely to be candidates for surgery (Rodin & Ickovics, 1990). It is estimated that 50% of women's mortality is linked to maladaptive behavior intended to cope with stress. Such dysfunctional coping responses including smoking, alcohol consumption, and prescription drug abuse (Hamburg, Elliot, & Parron, 1982). Insurance and other health-care benefits are essential for working women.

Women continue to live longer than do men, although this life-span advantage is declining in part because of changes in labor-force participation. Women thus face high prospects of widowhood and potential poverty in their advanced ages. Retirement and pension plans are also of primary importance to working women.

When benefits such as income protection programs and health care are tied to compensation levels, women lose advantages of employment, which they need to an even greater extent than do men. Bridging the pay equity gap thus means not only gains in terms of direct compensation but also gains in important benefits for women.

Related to the issue of pay equity is occupational segregation. Ferraro (1984) noted that women are selected into the lowest paying occupations and are confined to jobs that are female dominated, undervalued, and undercompensated. This segregation results in women occupying jobs that are more health threatening because they are jobs with high demands, low autonomy, and low control (Baruch et al., 1987). These are precisely what Karasek (1979) referred to as high-strain jobs, that is, jobs with the most potential destructive effects on well-being (physical and psychological).

Solutions to occupational segregation and the wage gap lie in both public policy and organizational efforts. Sex-based employment discrimination and wage discrimination are illegal under Title VII and the Equal Pay Act. However, employers have created ways to circumvent these laws such as altering job content in women's positions (Ferraro, 1984). What is needed is vigorous enforcement of existing laws to prohibit discrimination. Where gains in pay equity have been achieved, they have often resulted from job evaluation systems. Organizations should institute bias-free job-evaluation programs to analyze and eliminate wage discrimination.

Furthermore, the research suggests that managers use decision models that systematically discriminate against women in access to managerial jobs and in the compensation paid to women in these jobs (Hitt & Barr, 1989). Thus, programs must target current decision-makers to change their subjective decision models. National programs targeted toward employers emphasizing the potential gains in performance that can be made from fully utilizing human resources may also offer potential advantages. Particular attention should be given to equity in starting salaries of men and women in the same job because even if men and women are treated equally in subsequent pay decisions (e.g., merit decisions), the gap remains (Hitt & Barr, 1989). The only way to eliminate an inequitable pay gap is to provide unequal increases in favor of women.

Related to the issue of occupational segregation is educational equity. Russo and Denmark (1984) noted that women's right to higher education was only won in this century. Men continue to occupy most policy-making positions; therefore, most public policy is addressed from a male viewpoint and is designed to meet male needs. For women to have an impact on policy making, it is essential that they have access to quality education to prepare themselves for policy-making roles. Increased educational opportunities can also reduce occupational segregation. Public programs that permit women greater access to educational opportunities are necessary. Organizations can also provide assistance to working women by encouraging continued education by means of tuition refund programs and flexible work schedules.

Job Redesign for Flexibility

Because women continue to be viewed as the primary caretakers of home life, organizations must design jobs to allow women and men the flexibility of dealing with the problems that arise in their domestic situations. In addition, organizations could encourage men to take on more of the responsibilities for resolving work/home conflicts through internal communications and programs. The problem does not reside with working women or work organizations alone for that matter; rather, it is a larger, societal stereotype that places a larger share of this burden on women. Men must be included in the solution. Research has indicated better mental health among women whose husbands share family responsibilities and home upkeep (Baruch et al., 1987).

The effective administration and design of flexible jobs will require organizations to discard another stereotype: that physical absence from the workplace equates with lost productivity. Arrangements such as telecommuting demand a leap of faith from organizations that employees' performance will remain high when they are given greater discretion over scheduling of their work and are released from the vigilance of superiors. Flexible work arrangements alone will not relieve women of the stress of their caretaker roles. Programs to assist women in caring for others must be the focus of efforts of policymakers and organizational providers.

Childcare and Eldercare

Russo and Denmark (1984) noted that child care will become an increasingly important policy issue as the baby boomers reach their peak childbearing years. In addition, women whose earnings exceed the limits of qualifying for publicly funded daycare often cannot afford quality daycare or full-time household help. Companies should be encouraged to consider providing corporate daycare facilities, sponsoring daycare centers within the community, or providing financial assistance to working women for private daycare.

A problem of growing concern is that women find themselves part of the "sandwich generation"; that is, they are expected to care for two classes of dependents: their children and their elderly parents. Companies have been less responsive to the needs of women in caring for aged parents. This dual caretaker role is a stressful one and most often falls to daughters, who report economic strain as well as diminished mental and physical health (Brody, Kleban, Johnsen, Hoffman, & Schoonorer, 1987). The national policy agenda must address the issue of parent care.

Finally, organizations should be encouraged to develop comprehensive programs that focus jointly on individuals and their work situations. The work environment can be made more conducive to health through equity issues, job redesign, childcare, and eldercare. Individuals need assistance such as stress counseling to understand their own stressors and the unique ways that they respond to stressful situations. It has been found, for example, that women place higher expectations on themselves to excel in every role than do men (Zappert & Weinstein, 1985). The need to be everything to everybody has been referred to as *Type E behavior* (Braiker, 1986). Stress counseling, using cognitive restructuring, can help women develop more realistic expectations. In combination with efforts to alter the work situation, gains can be made in preventively managing working women's stress.

Earlier, it was noted that our research showed that politics and lack of career progress may have more dysfunctional effects on women than work/home conflicts. Childcare and eldercare programs should somewhat ease work/home conflicts. Furthermore, programs to achieve more equity in types of jobs and in pay for women may enhance career opportunities. However, other efforts may be required to enhance womens' skills in dealing with managing and reacting to organizational politics.

Programs on Managing Organizational Politics

In one of the few studies on political behavior in work organizations, it was reported that political behavior occurred frequently (Madison, Allen, Porter, Renwick, &

Mayes, 1980). Furthermore, political behavior was more prevalent at high levels in the managerial hierarchy. In fact, almost 25% of the managers in the study perceived that political behaviors were important in promotion, salary, and transfer decisions. Given the prevalence of political behaviors among managers and the amount of distress that politics cause among professional women (Nelson et al., 1990), programs to enhance women's skills in dealing with organizational politics are important.

Organizational politics are designed to acquire and use power for the accomplishment of personal gain (Mintzberg, 1984). Thus, the organization should be interested in eliminating or containing the use of political behaviors. Mintzberg (1985) and Ralston (1985) both referred to a number of political "games" that are often used. Sponsorship and alliance building may not always have negative consequences, whereas insurgency and ingratiation may be more debilitating political behaviors (Middlemist & Hitt, 1988). Jones (1985) developed a set of recommendations for controlling and managing political behavior in organizations. Thus, a development program could be designed to inform women of typical political behavior and games. Furthermore, the program could entail strategies for effectively controlling and managing such behavior (Jones, 1985).

This seems particularly critical as women break through the glass ceiling and move into top executive ranks. For example, Mintzberg, Raisinghani, and Theoret (1976) argued that most decisions made by top executives (i.e., strategic) are unstructured and fraught with ambiguity. The strategic decision-making process involves the use of mutual adjustment (March & Simon, 1958) and negotiated outcomes (Murray, 1978). Therefore, Finkelstein (1988) concluded that most strategic decisions were influenced by power and politics among the top executive team and other key players (e.g., board of directors).

Formalized training programs may focus on understanding political game playing and the bases of power in organizations. Participation in these programs should begin early in a person's managerial career. Furthermore, and perhaps more importantly, the firm may sponsor a formal mentorship program for women whereby men and women in higher ranks would mentor female managers and professionals at lower ranks (Kram, 1983; Kram & Isabella, 1985). At the very least, the firm could promote informal mentoring through development programs and special "linkage" programs (i.e., assignments to special task forces and project teams).

Research on Working Women and Stress

Psychologists and organizational scholars can also affect public policy and organizational assistance to working women by their roles as researchers. Research results from studies of working women and stress must be more effectively disseminated among those who make decisions and policy. Lobby efforts for greater institutional funding of research on health issues that affect working women must be emphasized. In addition, women must be included in more studies of work and health. The absence of women as subjects in health research has been highlighted in a review by Rodin and Ickovics (1990), who noted that although women are given more stress-related prescriptions, they are often excluded from the research studies on stress-related drugs. By advocating increased attention to the unique problems of women in the workforce, researchers can become part of the solution for a population at risk and help to encourage women's mental health.

Conclusions

Research has shown that men and women differ in the stressors experienced as well as in the physical and psychological consequences of stress. In fact, some research (e.g. Nelson et al., 1990) suggests that women at work experience more dysfunctional stress consequences than do men. Thus, for a number of reasons, policies to institute actions to prevent or manage stress-related problems for women at work are important.

Women are becoming an increasingly important part of our workforce. Perhaps more importantly, women represent a primary resource for professional and managerial positions. We have yet to fully take advantage of this resource. Given the current and potential future problems of strategic competitiveness among U.S. firms (Hitt & Hoskisson, 1991), more effective use of this resource becomes even more critical.

Herein, we recommended several actions necessary to eliminate distress among women at work and more effectively take advantage of the rich resource available to organizations.

- Promote equity in pay and benefits for women
- Promote benefit programs of special interest to women
- Eliminate occupational segregation
- Produce bias-free job evaluation programs and equal starting salaries on jobs of equal value
- Support educational opportunities for women
- Educate men regarding importance of sharing responsibilities outside of work
- Provide more job flexibility for women and men to better manage work/home conflicts
- Promote childcare and eldercare options in the community or in the organization
- Support programs to educate and develop skills among women for managing and controlling organizational politics
- Develop programs for effective dissemination of research on stress and working women
- Support increased funding for research on health issues related to working women
- Promote more research on the effects of stress among working women

Therefore, although substantive gains in our knowledge of stress and its consequences have been made, more work is required. In effect, we *must* know more about the stressors and strains experienced by working women. Furthermore, policies to direct behavior to help preventively manage distress among working women are critical.

References

Baruch, G. K., & Barnett, R. C. (1986). Role quality, multiple role involvement, and psychological well-being in mid-life women. *Journal of Personality and Social Psychology, 3*, 578–585.

Baruch, G. K., Biener, L., & Barnett, C. R. (1987). Women and gender in research on work and family stress. *American Psychologist, 42*, 130–136.

Bernard, J. (1976). Where are we now? Thoughts on the current scene. *Psychology of Women Quarterly, 1*, 21–37.

Bhatnagar, D. (1988). Professional women in organizations: New paradigms for research and action. *Sex Roles, 18*, 343–355.

Braiker, H. B. (1986). *The type E woman.* New York: Dodd, Mead.

Brass, D. J. (1985). Men's and women's networks: A study of interaction patterns and influence in an organization. *Academy of Management Journal, 28*, 327–343.

Brody, E. M., Kleban, M. H., Johnsen, P. T., Hoffman, C., & Schoonover, C. B. (1987). Work status and parental care: A comparison of four groups of women. *The Gerontological Society of America, 27*, 201–208.

Cleary, P., & Mechanic, D. (1983). Sex differences in psychological distress among married people. *Journal of Health and Social Behavior, 24*, 111–121.

Cooper, C. L., & Davidson, M. J. (1982). The high cost of stress on women managers. *Organizational Dynamics*, Spring, 44–53.

Cooper, C. L., & Melhuish, A. (1984). Executive stress and health. *Journal of Occupational Medicine, 26*, 99–104.

Cox, T., Thirlaway, M., & Cox, S. (1984). Executive stress and health. *Ergonomics, 27*, 499–510.

Davidson, M., & Cooper, C. (1983). *Stress and the woman manager.* Oxford, England: Martin Robertson.

Davidson, M., & Cooper, C. (1985). Women managers: Work, stress, and marriage. *International Journal of Social Economics, 12*, 17–25.

Defares, P. B., Brandjes, M., Nass, C. H., & van der Ploeg, J. D. (1984). Coping styles and vulnerability of women at work in residential settings. *Ergonomics, 27*, 527–545.

Duxbury, L. E., & Higgins, C. A. (1991). Gender differences in work–family conflict. *Journal of Applied Psychology, 76*, 60–74.

Ferraro, G. H. (1984). Bridging the wage gap: Pay equity and job evaluations. *American Psychologist, 39*, 1166–1170.

Finkelstein, S. (1988). *Managerial orientations and organizational outcomes: The moderating roles of managerial discretion and power.* Unpublished doctoral dissertation, Columbia University, New York.

Freedman, S. M., & Phillips, J. S. (1988). The changing nature of research on women at work. *Journal of Management, 14*, 231–251.

Friedman, D. E. (1988). Why the glass ceiling? *Across the Board, 7*, 33–37.

Glogow, E. (1986). Burnout and locus of control. *Public Management, 15*, 79–83.

Gottlieb, N. J., & Green, L. W. (1984). Life events, social network, life-style, and health: An analysis of the 1979 National Survey of Personal Health Practices and Consequences. *Health Education Quarterly, 11*, 91–105.

Greenglass, E. R. (1985). Psychological implications of sex bias in the workplace. *Academic Psychological Bulletin, 7*, 227–240.

Hamburg, D., Elliot, G., & Parron, D. (Eds.). (1982). *Health and behavior: Frontiers of research in the biobehavioral sciences.* Washington, DC: National Academy Press.

Haynes, S. G., & Feinleib, M. (1980). Women, work, and coronary heart disease: Prospective findings from the Framingham Heart Study. *American Journal of Public Health, 70*, 133–141.

Hitt, M. A., & Barr, S. H. (1989). Managerial selection decision models: Examination of configural cue processing. *Journal of Applied Psychology, 74*, 53–61.

Hitt, M. A., & Hoskisson, R. E. (1991). Strategic competitiveness. In L. W. Foster (Ed.), *Advances in applied business strategy* (pp. 1–36). Greenwich, CT: JAI Press.

Jacobson, B. (1981). *The lady killers: Why smoking is a feminist issue.* New York: Pluto Press.

Jick, T. D., & Mitz, L. F. (1985). Sex differences in work stress. *Academy of Management Review, 10*, 408–420.

Jones, R. E. (1985). Internal politics and the strategic business plan. *Journal of Small Business Management, 23*, 31–37.

Karasek, R. A., Jr. (1979). Job demands, job decision latitude, and mental strain: Implications for job redesign. *Administrative Science Quarterly, 24*, 285–308.

Kilbey, M. M., & Sobeck, J. P. (1988). Epidemiology of alcoholism. In C. B. Travis (Ed.), *Women and health psychology: Mental health issues* (pp. 91–107). Hillsdale, NJ: Erlbaum.

Kram, K. E. (1983). Phases of the mentor relationship. *Academy of Management Journal, 26*, 608–625.

Kram, K. E., & Isabella, L. A. (1985). Mentoring alternatives: The role of peer relationships in career development. *Academy of Management Journal, 28*, 110–132.

LaCroix, A. Z., & Haynes, S. G. (1987). Gender differences in the health effects of workplace roles. In R. C. Barnett, L. Beiner, & G. K. Baruch (Eds.), *Gender and stress* (pp. 96–121). New York: Free Press.

Madison, D., Allen, R., Porter, L., Renwick, P., & Mayes, B. (1980). Organization politics: An exploration of managers' perceptions. *Human Relations, 33*, 79–100.

March, J. G., & Simon, H. A. (1958). *Organizations*. New York: Wiley.

Matthews, K. A., & Rodin, J. (1989). Women's changing work roles: Impact on health, family, and public policy. *American Psychologist, 44*, 1389–1393.

Middlemist, R. D., & Hitt, M. A. (1988). *Organizational behavior*. St. Paul, MN: West.

Mintzberg, H. (1984). Power and organization life cycles. *Academy of Management Review, 9*, 207–224.

Mintzberg, H. (1985). The organization as a political arena. *Journal of Management Studies, 22*, 135–154.

Mintzberg, H., Raisinghani, D., & Theoret, A. (1976). The structure of unstructured decision processes. *Administrative Science Quarterly, 21*, 246–275.

Morrison, A., White, R. P., & Van Velsor, E. (1987). *Breaking the glass ceiling*. Reading, MA: Addison-Wesley.

Murray, E. A. (1978). Strategic choice as a negotiated outcome. *Management Science, 26*, 960–972.

Nelson, D. L., & Quick, J. C. (1985). Professional women: Are distress and disease inevitable? *Academy of Management Journal, 10*, 206–218.

Nelson, D. L., Quick, J. C., & Hitt, M. A. (1989). Men and women of the personnel profession: Some differences and similarities in their stress. *Stress Medicine, 5*, 145–152.

Nelson, D. L., Quick, J. C., Hitt, M. A., & Moesel, D. (1990). Politics, lack of career progress, and work/home conflict: Stress and strain for working women. *Sex Roles, 23*, 169–185.

Noe, R. A. (1988). Women and mentoring: A review and research agenda. *Academy of Management Review, 13*, 65–78.

O'Neill, C. P., & Zeichner, A. (1985). Working women: A study of relationships between stress, coping, and health. *Journal of Psychosomatic Obstretics and Gynaecology, 4*, 105–116.

Ralston, D. A. (1985). Internal politics and the strategic business plan. *Academy of Management Review, 10*, 477–487.

Repetti, R. L., Matthews, K. A., & Waldron, I. (1989). Employment and women's health. *American Psychologist, 44*, 1394–1401.

Rodin, J., & Ickovics, J. R. (1990). Women's health: Review and research agenda as we approach the 21st century. *American Psychologist, 45*, 1018–1033.

Russo, N. F., & Denmark, F. L. (1984). Women, psychology, and public policy: Selected issues. *American Psychologist, 39*, 1161–1165.

Schein, V. E. (1978). Sex role stereotyping, ability and performance: Prior research and new directions. *Personnel Psychology, 31*, 259–268.

Sherman, J. D., Ezell, H. F., & Odewahn, C. A. (1987). Centralization of decision making and accountability based on gender. *Group & Organization Studies, 12*, 454–463.

Stipp, H. H. (1988). What is a working woman? *American Demographics, 10*, 24–27.

Verbrugge, L. M. (1986). Role burdens and physical health of women and men. *Women and Health, 11*, 47–77.

Verbrugge, L. M. (1989). The twain meet: Empirical explanations of sex differences in health and mortality. *Journal of Health and Social Behavior, 30*, 282–304.

Voydanoff, P. (1988). Women, work, and family: Bernard's perspective on the past, present, and future. *Psychology of Women Quarterly, 12*, 269–280.

Waldron, I., & Jacobs, J. A. (1989). Effects of multiple roles on women's health: Evidence from a national longitudinal study. *Women and Health, 15*, 3–19.

Wiley, M. G., & Eskilson, A. (1988). Gender and family/career conflict: Reactions of bosses. *Sex Roles, 19*, 445–465.

Wilsnack, R. W., Wilsnack, S. C., & Klassen, A. D. (1984). Women's drinking and drinking problems: Patterns from a 1981 national survey. *American Journal of Public Health, 74*, 1231–1238.

Witkin-Lanoil, G. (1984). *The female stress syndrome.* New York: Berkely Books.

Wolf, W. C., & Fligstein, N. D. (1979). Sex and authority in the workplace: The causes of sexual inequality. *American Sociological Review, 44*, 235–252.

Zappert, L. T., & Weinstein, H. M. (1985). Sex differences in the impact of work on physical and psychological health. *American Journal of Psychiatry, 14*, 1174–1178.

12

Ellen Kirschman, Ellen Scrivner, Katherine Ellison, and
Carol Marcy

Work and Well-Being: Lessons From Law Enforcement

In 1963, a Los Angeles police officer stood in an isolated onion field and watched his partner be brutally murdered. The surviving officer had been forced to surrender his own gun and narrowly escaped with his life. It took 7 years to bring the perpetrators to justice, during which time the surviving officer suffered great emotional distress despite the efforts of department personnel to assist him. Later, in light of the officer's personal deterioration, department personnel wondered whether their methods unwittingly contributed to his decline and added to his trauma (Reese, 1987).[1] The case dramatically demonstrated that a badge and gun cannot protect a police officer from the psychological consequences of trauma and in 1968 led to the establishment of the first formal program of psychological intervention in law enforcement.

The Contribution of Psychology to the Occupational Well-Being of Law Enforcement Professionals

Initially, the concept of psychological services seemed to threaten the image that police had of themselves and their mission in the community: to serve and protect; to do a job others cannot do; to be reliable, dependable, and tough; to solve problems, not have them. Police worried that the advent of psychological interventions would change this image, raise concerns about their stability and reliability, and turn first-line defenders into emotional invalids, suitable only for the "rubber-gun squad." On the contrary, law enforcement and psychology developed a productive partnership, achieving success in spite of a population traditionally resistant to outside intervention. In fact, police organizations may be structured so that they are actually more amenable to psychological interventions in the workplace than is the private sector: Police organizations are, after all, narrow authoritarian systems with a clear-cut mission.

The bottom line in police work is not profit but the lives of citizens and officers.

---

[1]This incident and its impact on the officer, his career, and his family was popularized by author/officer Joseph Wambaugh in the book and film *The Onion Field* (1973).

There is great liability in police work, and liability can be a powerful motivator of change—stronger perhaps than that attached to profit or altruism. A strong consumer-advocacy movement, developed in the 1960s, led to a sharp increase in civil suits against police officers. There was also a dramatic rise in the number of stress-related disability claims filed by the police themselves (Kirschman, 1983). The expense and trauma of all this liability forced police managers to develop standards for the psychological suitability of police candidates and to use psychologically sound principles in the training, supervision, and management of police employees.

The partnership of police and psychology was significantly influenced by the 1965 Watts riots in Los Angeles. This event led police to seek out psychologists for assistance in human relations training. This training eventually expanded to include crisis intervention skills and department-wide training in stress management (Ellison & Genz, 1983). Educational psychologist Martin Reiser headed the first formal implementation of psychological services in 1968 for the Los Angeles Police Department. The program included direct services to individuals (personal counseling and referral), pre-employment selection and career guidance, training, consultation to middle- and top-level management, specialized consultation (e.g., internal affairs, community relations, homicides, etc.), and research (Reiser, 1972).

On the East Coast, the partnership of law enforcement and psychology took a different turn. In a push to reduce their response time, New York City police began to arrive at crime scenes while the crime was still in progress, and perpetrators began seizing hostages as collateral for escape. The police required a technology to safely contain and defuse those situations. Thus, the field of hostage negotiation was initiated, spearheaded by police officer and psychologist Harvey Schlossberg (Schlossberg & Freeman, 1979). There is now a solid knowledge base concerning hostage negotiation (a cross-pollination between psychological principles and police tactics) and the training and selection of hostage negotiators. Psychologists are often consulting members of the negotiating team and also help debrief hostages.

Law Enforcement Assistance Administration discretionary grants in the 1970s opened still another door for psychologists in law enforcement, enabling research on the use of psychological tests in the pre-employment screening of police applicants. The research goal was to establish valid norms for tests for police candidates and to encourage screening for emotional stability prior to employment. Subsequent applications of psychological testing have extended to selection for specialty assignments such as SWAT (special weapons and tactics) teams, undercover narcotics work, hostage negotiation, and management positions. Several states now mandate pre-employment psychological screening, and it has become a standard requirement for police department accreditation by the Commission on Accreditation for Law Enforcement Agencies.

In 1975, the National Institute for Occupational Safety and Health (NIOSH) sponsored one of the first conferences specifically focused on police stress. This symposium delineated sources of stress for police officers, offered possible solutions, and developed recommendations for future research (Kroes & Hurrell, 1975). A prevalent conference theme addressed a pernicious source of job stress—perceived lack of administrative support and poor supervision—thus exposing the need for management and organization consultation services.

The evolution of psychological services from the 1960s to the 1990s has produced a body of scientific knowledge grounded in behavioral research, as well as a core of intervention strategies including, but not limited to, counseling services, training services, pre-employment applicant selection, posttraumatic support services, hostage negotiation, and specialized applications such as the psychological profiling of criminals. Behavioral scientists continue to expand on these now basic services with management consultation and organizational development interventions (Kirschman, 1987).

There is much discussion about job design in the study of work and well-being. Police psychologists have not really redesigned police jobs, although such an intervention may now be timely given the widespread implementation of community policing and the impact of high technology on communications, field services, evidence collection, and records management. For the past two decades, the emphasis has been on building support systems and altering the environment. In 22 years, not a long time in the history of psychology, police psychology has been identified as a separate, specialized section within Division 18 of the American Psychological Association, and police psychologists have become a basic resource to law enforcement organizations and to individual officers.

Cultural Considerations in Creating Intervention Strategies That Work

With over 150,000 police and sheriff's departments and 555,000 police officers in the United States, it is unrealistic to suggest the provable existence of a unified police culture or a singular police personality type. The profession of law enforcement is actually a collection of professions, each with its own purpose and character. The daily life and concerns of a body crimes detective in a municipal police agency is as different from his or her peer in the patrol division as is the sheriff's deputy guarding prisoners in the county jail, the undercover Drug Enforcement Administration agent working in a foreign country, the secret service officer guarding a prominent politician, the FBI agent researching forensic anthropology, the parking monitor writing parking citations, or the dispatcher answering all calls. Yet, all these individuals are part of law enforcement, and to one degree or another, they identify with one another. Intervention services must consider the following aggregate elements of law enforcement culture.

Societal Values

Part of law enforcement culture reflects societal notions of masculinity and youth, exaggerated symbols of which abound in the media and make police work appear more exciting and dangerous than it actually is. The symbolic officer who is young, White, and male raises issues of self-esteem, identity, and belonging for officers who fit none of these categories. Although there is some evidence that such stereotyping is beginning to change, for many years the preponderance of research in law enforcement was done with academy recruits, who make poor analogues for older, experienced officers (Kirschman, 1983). This reliance on rookies as subjects suggests a collusive (and unconscious) denial of aging that is a cultural hallmark of the patrol subculture and perhaps the industry itself given that policing appears to be a young person's occupation. In California, for instance, some departments mandate retirement at age 55 years.

Subcultures

Group size is a particularly critical variable in organizational culture. Ninety percent of American police agencies have 10 or fewer employees. The larger the department, the more numerous and differentiated the subcultures. Subcultures may be based on rank and cemented by antagonism, like the universal and ongoing antipathy between patrol officers and administrators, or they may be lateral in structure and interdependent, like squads or shifts. Behaviors, norms, loyalties, and attitudes toward the total agency are highly influenced by the subculture to which one belongs. Failure to traverse the subcultural terrain wisely can embroil a consultant in the irrational, emotional undercurrent of organizational life (Walima & Kirschman, 1988). A thorough grounding in systems thinking and group relations theory is extremely useful.

Patrol officers are the most highly visible, numerically strong subculture in a police department, and the patrol function is the cornerstone of most municipal police departments. But unless the agency is very small, patrol is only one of many interdependent elements responsible for the operation and survival of the department. A consultant must become familiar with as many subunits as possible because each will form its own temporary culture, particularly those specialty units that are separated from the organizational mainstream by task, such as undercover, SWAT, and canine units, or by caste, such as civilian employees. Although there is collaboration and teamwork in policing, there are also turf problems, conflicts over loyalty, and competition for resources. In an authoritarian culture, rank determines territory, and, as one is promoted, there are significant changes in group loyalties and a resocialization to norms of the new rank. However, these internal differentiations virtually disappear when police close ranks against hostile outsiders or those they perceive to be hostile.

Selection and Training

Screening procedures and the applicant pool on which police organizations draw determine organizational culture. Some agencies are so desirable in terms of locale, pay, and benefits that they can screen prospective employees for compatible values. Other departments have to go to great lengths to attract and retain applicants. The screening procedure, training program, and systems of discipline and dismissal are all vehicles for incorporating cultural values in the workplace and socializing new officers to both overt and covert norms of the agency.

The Individual

Police work demands a strong occupational persona, a mask of competence under the worst of circumstances. Conflict over the etiology of the occupational persona ranges along the familiar continuum between the dispositional and the situational (Vastola, 1978). Without a thorough grounding in law enforcement culture, behavioral scientists can confuse psychological and cultural variables, classifying behavior according to the impulses that appear to inspire it (Bateson, 1972). Regarding authoritarianism, for example, some researchers have mistakenly assumed that all police work involves violence and aggression and that officers who use necessary force in the course of their duties are aggressive by nature and have selected police work as a sanctioned outlet. The abuse of authority is a complex phenomenon with many causes. Personality is only one factor, and further research is needed.

By and large, law enforcement professionals, particularly at the line level, have been taught to think on their feet, make fast decisions with the data at hand, resolve situations quickly and practically, and then move to the next situation. The police culture is a dependent culture taught to give and take orders (Bion, 1975). Police are, by necessity, responsive to the unpredictable ebb and flow of human activity in their community, and although the content and pace of this activity vary greatly from large to small and urban to rural settings, it is the driving force behind field operations. How an officer manages time and data gathering varies according to his or her task or subcultural work unit; detectives and higher ranking personnel have more opportunity and time to plan in advance or conduct in-depth investigations than do patrol officers responsive to all calls.

Humor

Gallows humor is an important, often misunderstood element of the police culture. Police see so much conflict, emotion, and vulnerability in their work that they often use humor to deny or avoid vulnerability, conflict, and emotion in their personal lives. It is also clear that as professional helpers and protectors, many officers experience enormous anxiety when they feel helpless, passive, or remorseful. Humor provides temporary relief.

The Culture Clash Between Psychology and Law Enforcement

Behavioral scientists working with law enforcement have noted various cultural differences between the two professions and how these differences can negatively affect their collaborative efforts. Scrivner (1987), Berg (1982), and Stratton (1982) charted these differences from various perspectives, all agreeing that there are mine fields of misunderstanding inherent in language, norms, and values. Stratton observed that, in general, police come from working-class backgrounds and authoritarian homes, are politically conservative, often have had military experience, adhere to a philosophy of strict law and order, begin their careers and marriages at an early age, and learn best through experience. Psychologists on the other hand, often come from middle- or upper-class, child-centered families, are politically liberal, have infrequent military experience, postpone marriage in favor of education, and enter careers at a much older age. The latter groups are likely to be academic learners, to hold more varied lifestyles, and to favor emotional expression over emotional control.

Berg (1982) observed that differences in values manifest in language and implied that police and mental health professionals need to define terms carefully when speaking to each other; for example, what one group would call emotional sensitivity, the other might refer to as naivety; one's bleeding heart could be another's empathy. For a mental health professional, introspection or reflection are positive actions. For some law enforcement professionals, they signify inaction and indecision. Control for one means brutality to another, action is interpreted as impulsivity, suspicion as paranoia, and persistence is seen as stubbornness.

On the other hand, Scrivner (1987) found significant parallels between law enforcement and mental health professionals. For example, both groups work within managed structures and use problem solving in their work with people. The target populations and techniques greatly differ, of course. Law enforcement responds, whereas mental health reflects. Law enforcement contains a situation; mental health explores it. One is bound by fact; the other uses fantasy, and the like.

Perhaps the most significant differences between law enforcement and psychology have to do with control and emotional expression. Police are taught from academy onward to stay in control of the situation and their emotions, to respond professionally and objectively in spite of their own feelings or provocations from the environment. They are warned that loss of control may lead to death, injury, lawsuits, complaints, internal affairs investigations, or disciplinary action. Psychology, on the other hand, places a premium on self-expression.

Value differences between law enforcement and psychology notwithstanding, police frequently appreciate the different perspective of a trusted outsider and value feedback from a competent, empathetic source that is uncontaminated by the law enforcement persona. Nevertheless, the psychologist should be cautious, because some of the differences between law enforcement and behavioral science may exert a subtle, yet persistent pull on the consultant. There is the seduction of youth, the illusion of safety, and the feeling of power associated with being even temporarily admitted into the closed culture of police. For any psychologist working with police, positive as well as negative transference is a compelling force to manage and balance.

Programs That Work

The following programs demonstrate the variety of ways that a range of services can be delivered to law enforcement. Although the agencies cited are municipal police departments, they serve communities of varying sizes and varying financial resources. With the exception of a time-limited external intervention, the programs considered here have been in place for at least a decade. Their consistent use, continued financing, and administrative support are the soundest practical measures of their positive impact on the workplace.

The Health Resources Coordinator Program (HRC)—Palo Alto Police Department, Palo Alto, California: A Program of Contractual Organizational Consultation

Background. Palo Alto is an affluent university town 50 miles south of San Francisco. The police department is of moderate size, with 100 sworn and 60 civilian employees. The HRC was implemented in 1980 following a series of costly, stress-related disability retirements. Rather than focus solely on the troubled individuals, the agency adopted a systems approach. First, a consultant undertook a detailed organizational analysis of stress in the workplace. Her final report included a list of familiar organizational ills: poor communication, ambiguous and poorly circulated information, insufficient acknowledgment, poorly delivered performance evalua-tions, and insufficient opportunity or motivation to participate in decision making and problem solving (Walima & Kirschman, 1988). As a result of this analysis, the Palo Alto City Council approved a plan to hire an organizational consultant to design, implement, and evaluate an 18-month trial program.

The hiring process was itself a model of shared decision making. Nearly a third of the agency, sworn and civilian, helped design the assessment process and choose the consultant. Candidates for the work were recruited from a wide spectrum of professional disciplines. When it was apparent that no one applicant could meet the department's multiple needs, a cross-disciplinary pair of consultants, an orga-nizational development specialist and a psychologist, were chosen. In the decade following, the program has been modified to reflect changing organizational needs, changes in consultants, and increased budget reductions. The current program op-erates with one half-time consultant psychologist; an in-house, multirank advisory board of civilian and sworn staff; and a predoctoral intern in organizational psy-chology.

Range of services. The HRC program is a radical departure in practice and philosophy from most employee assistance programs (EAPs) that emphasize indi-vidual coping and usually intervene after a problem has occurred. The HRC em-phasizes the relationship between the organization and the individual and focuses on prevention. The program is also radically different from most external consulting arrangements in that the HRC coordinator maintains an office in the police station and is available to talk to people in patrol cars, restaurants, or locker rooms or by phone. Being an internal part of the organization allows the consultant to share the daily pace and pressure of the agency; thus, interventions are immediate and grounded in empirical data—literally customized to fit the need. Because the or-ganization is continuously involved in feedback with the HRC coordinator through surveys and through the Health Resources Advisory Group, the program is respon-sive to the changing needs of the agency. The program consists of a 14-point work plan with the following objectives:

1. To provide voluntary, confidential counseling and/or make referrals for individuals under stress. All employees and their dependents are also entitled to free, short-term counseling with an independent, off-site em-ployee assistance program, or they may apply a portion of their major medical benefits to counseling with a therapist of their own choosing. (For ethical and practical reasons, fitness-for-duty evaluations are conducted by an outside provider.)
2. To provide conflict resolution for individuals and groups.
3. To identify sources of organizational stress and consult with work units and individual managers to resolve them. These issues range from the

specific (i.e., an individual manager and his or her style) to more global, long-standing issues such as the promotional process and ways to acknowledge the contributions of career officers who fail to get promoted or do not seek promotion.

4. To monitor organizational change to ensure involvement and information for all those who will be affected. For example, the HRC program has been involved in the agency-wide implementation of computer technology and in the agency-wide participation in hiring a new chief.

5. To monitor management decisions with regard to their stressful impact, search for implementation methods that minimize that impact, and advise management staff.

6. To train field-training personnel in communications, problem solving, conflict resolution, and supervisory skills that can minimize stress and optimize learning for new officers. This has involved stress-inoculation seminars for new recruits and their families, psychological assessment to match trainers and new officers, and attention to the special needs of women and minorities.

7. To advise individual managers on the development of productive management techniques and leadership skills. As a consequence, the Palo Alto Police Department has "graduated" 20 police chiefs in the past 20 years.

8. To educate all police personnel in the range of stress reduction/health enhancement techniques available in the Palo Alto area and encourage their use.

9. To design and facilitate team-building and problem-solving meetings for managers and their work units. In addition to working with small work groups or teams of work groups, the HRC helps plan and facilitate annual 2-day, off-site meetings for the entire management group of 16 and for a mixed group of approximately 24 managers and supervisors.

10. To teach personnel how to design and facilitate problem-solving and team-building meetings.

11. To sponsor special events and workshops related to personal and organizational health (e.g., stress management training, substance abuse prevention, and AIDS awareness).

12. To assist in program evaluation, the HRC submits quarterly reports on the number of hours spent and type of service used and includes remarks on current system-wide issues. These reports are posted for the entire organization to read. In addition, consultants have systematically surveyed the entire agency twice in 10 years concerning program utilization, future direction, and general concerns.

13. To maintain a health-related bulletin board and a library of health-related materials.

14. To provide career counseling and life-assessment guidance.

In addition to the goals listed above, the HRC serves as consultant and professional back-up to the peer counseling program, offers support during hostage negotiation and SWAT team call-ups, conducts critical incident and postshooting debriefings, selectively participates in activities involving the community, and occasionally provides crime-specific consultation.

Office of Stress Management (OSM)—Montgomery County Police Department, Rockville, Maryland: An Internal, Clinically Based Program

Background. Montgomery County is an affluent, suburban community north of Washington, DC. The police department employs 850 sworn officers and 200 civilians. The OSM was created in 1981 following a Law Enforcement Assistance Administration–sponsored stress survey that found a need to improve the functioning of the organization and its employees and to relieve distress through education and support.

Since its inception, the OSM program has received the support of the Fraternal Order of Police and has tripled the rate of client utilization. Current staff includes one full-time and one half-time psychologist, a volunteer who assists with research and monitors the pre-employment screening contract, and pre-doctoral interns who provide occasional assistance.

Range of services. The OSM uses a variety of programs to promote the emotional, mental, and physical well-being of sworn and civilian employees (both current and retired) and their families. To ensure confidentiality, the OSM office is located away from police headquarters and district stations, although service providers are visible through ride-alongs and through their participation in various aspects of the police department.

Psychotherapy and counseling services provide free long-and short-term psychotherapy and counseling for individuals, couples, families, and groups. Employees may have administrative leave to use OSM services for up to eight visits, or they can use sick leave, annual leave, or days off for their appointments. All OSM services and records are confidential, and self-referral is encouraged.

The Traumatic Incidents Program has been developed to reduce the acute and cumulative impact of such incidents by providing psychological and educational support, including counseling and information on universal responses to trauma and coping methods for individuals and their families.

The Diversion Program is offered as an alternative to disciplinary action or termination for the employee who has job performance problems with psychological roots or substance abuse. The troubled employee is offered an alternative intervention that focuses on correcting work performance problems and restoring an acceptable level of functioning. Referrals to this program are initiated by the chief of police.

Training programs (recruit, in-service and supervisory) educate officers and acquaint them with OSM personnel and services. For recruits, the OSM psychologist minimizes current and future stress by discussing the myths and realities of the police officer's role and by offering training in stress management, communication skills, team building, alcoholism education, and coping skills applicable to critical incidents and the excessive use of force. In-service training is offered to the ranks of sergeant and below, with particular emphasis on stress management, health education, and methods of handling anger and cynicism. Supervisors receive training to increase their effectiveness in recognizing and responding to the troubled employee.

The Specialized Services and Research Department consults with the Hostage Negotiation Team, the SWAT team, the Youth Division, the Personnel Unit, and others in the role of observer and advisor. The OSM also conducts research that can directly influence work-related stress. Current projects include a rotating shift proposal, exit interviews, research in field training, and the psychological impact of child sexual-abuse interviews on investigators.

Although the police department contracts with an outside vendor for pre-employment screening, the OSM monitors this contract through testing sessions, quality control, validation factors, and billing verification. Such a liaison enhances the ability of the external contractor to serve the needs of the contracting agency.

External Time-Limited Consultation Model: Police Layoffs—A Secondary Prevention Program

Background. In the Spring of 1989, citing financial considerations, a medium-sized city in the northeastern United States laid off approximately 70 of 225 police officers. Layoffs were by seniority, and some laid-off officers had as much as 6 years of service. "Outplacement," the provision of services to help laid-off workers obtain new employment is common in the private sector but virtually unknown in the public domain, especially in policing, where job security is an important benefit. Because the city failed to offer services and left laid-off officers to fend for themselves, the police union established an informational hot line. Union members were unsure of what specific services to provide and believed that they lacked adequate skills to deal with their distressed colleagues. Their concern was exacerbated by calls from laid-off officers indicating serious coping problems. At this point, the police union contacted crisis intervention consultants.

Range of services. Consultants met with the union to identify needs and worked with department members to produce the booklet *When You Are Laid Off: A Survival Manual for Police Officers* (Ellison & Munnings, 1990), which included sections on what to expect in terms of common emotional reactions and what to do, including psychological coping methods such as cognitive restructuring and practical information about credit counseling, resume writing, and job-hunting skills. In addition, the consultants planned sessions on crisis intervention strategies for hot-line staffers who were providing officers with critically needed information about the status of ongoing negotiations.

Fortunately, the city rescinded the planned layoffs and there was no further need for this program. However, a contingency plan of this nature is a cost-effective model to have ready, especially in light of the uncertainty of the current economy, shrinking financial resources of local governments, and ample evidence that laid-off employees who are later rehired may take months or years to return to their former level of motivation (Dooley, Catalano, & Rook, 1988). Anxiety, distrust, and a sense of betrayal appear to affect workers long after the issue of employment status is resolved, with probable consequences to the workplace and the work itself (Iverson & Sabroe, 1988; Miller, 1990).

The program consultants recommended that the union bear the costs for underwriting a limited external consulting contract to plan for possible layoffs. In a setting less adversarial than the one for which they consulted, it is conceivable that the costs for such a plan could be undertaken jointly by labor and management.

Psychological Services Division (PSD)—Prince George's County Police Department, Prince George's County, Maryland: A Multiservice, In-House Approach

Background. Prince George's County Police Department, serving a community that adjoins Washington, DC, has a total of 1,500 sworn and civilian police employees. The community consists of a broad range of socioeconomic groups, a diverse population, and a rich, active community life. Major law enforcement challenges are crimes associated with drug abuse and a fluctuating homicide rate.

In October 1980, under a grant from the Governor's Commission on Law Enforcement, the department established a psychological services unit to provide a full range of behavioral science technology for the organization and its employees. The unit was designated as a division in 1988 and consists of two full-time and one part-time licensed psychologists and one administrative assistant.

Range of services. The Psychological Services Division provides for the emotional well-being of police personnel and contributes to enhancing the delivery of professional police services to the community with the following programs.

The Administrative Referral Service responds to referrals initiated by supervisors concerned with performance-based problems. In these instances, a supervisor determines that an officer might need counseling rather than disciplinary action to correct a performance problem and generally consults with the Psychological Services staff to determine if a referral is appropriate. Short-term counseling may be conducted by division staff, or referrals may be provided for long-term therapy or fitness-for-duty evaluations.

With the Critical Incident Service, a psychologist responds to the Criminal Investigation Division following all shooting incidents. The major focus of this program is to help the officer adjust to trauma and return to work as a productive employee, free of stress symptoms and preoccupations.

The 24-hour Emergency Response Service responds to such emergencies as barricade–hostage situations, police emergencies regarding mental health crises of personnel, and departmental emergencies such as police personnel injuries or fatalities. In this program, the psychology staff is deployed either to an on-scene situation or to a hospital and consults with on-scene commanders or affected personnel.

With the Exposure to Communicable Disease Counseling Service, an officer is scheduled for a pretest counseling session following a potential exposure. If an officer is identified as having sustained a significant exposure, this service then assists the officer during the testing process and stores all test records in confidential files. Officers are scheduled for posttest counseling sessions to discuss their results. The service combines health interventions with preventative information and attempts to reduce anxiety about dealing with future suspects and victims. In 1988, this program service was the recipient of a National Association of Counties Award.

The Situational Counseling Service provides all officers involved in investigations of excessive force complaints, irrespective of the outcome, with individual, confidential counseling to examine all elements of the complaint, including coping with the stress of the investigation. This service also collects and categorizes data on the specific incidents themselves and uses such data to enhance in-service and recruit training.

Prince George's Psychological Services Division also offers several voluntary (nonmandated) programs. The EAP provides direct treatment and preventative individual, couple, or family counseling services. The EAP also responds to police personnel who present symptoms related to substance abuse and facilitates the necessary referral for chemical-dependency treatment. In these situations, the EAP monitors employee progress while in treatment and then assists with the employee's return to the work setting.

The Biofeedback Treatment Service responds to police personnel who present psychological symptoms that manifest physiologically. When symptoms are considered remedial, a biofeedback psychologist initiates a treatment program.

Training programs include formal classes in stress management, postshooting reactions, crisis intervention skills, abnormal psychology, hostage negotiations skills, crisis communication, alcohol education, adult learning, coaching and counseling employees, and management stress—each integrated into schools developed by the Training Division. Psychological Services also responds to training requests initiated by district stations or specific units. For example, it has created a 2-hr roll call training program designed to alleviate the stress of workload demands and staffing shortages.

A research service can be initiated by any division or command in the police department. To date, Psychological Services has developed surveys on varied shift plans, the need for peer-counseling programs, development of a community questionnaire, and a management-development needs survey.

The Management Consultant Program includes formal presentations to the command staff on management issues related to human resource development, as well as the implementation of organizational development interventions. To date, interventions have been initiated in the Records Division, the Drug Lab, and designated district stations. The focus of this service attempts to provide management and managers with a means to improve overall organizational performance.

In addition to these structured program services, Psychological Services sponsors other activities not defined as specific programs; for instance, it responds to requests to address community groups, provides media interviews, and consults with other agencies on program development. Crime-specific consultation is also provided to the Criminal Investigation Division, and all exit interviews are conducted by the division. Finally, the director, as a member of the command staff, actively participates in a number of organizational committees and represents the department at designated interagency and community meetings.

Summary

The models described in this chapter exemplify only a few of the unlimited possibilities for tailoring mental health services to fit the needs and resources of a variety of law enforcement organizations.

Palo Alto's Health Resources Coordinator Program in California is grounded in organizational development, systems thinking, and group relations theory. Its primary mission is to address the needs of both agency and individual and the relation between the two. Its basic blueprint is a 14-point work plan that also serves as the coordinator's contract. Program activities include personal counseling; conflict resolution; monitoring of organizational changes, management decisions, and leadership development; training in communications, supervisorial behavior, problem solving, and stress management; and services to the field-training division.

The HRC coordinator is an independent contractor who reports directly to the chief. The coordinator works 2 days per week, 11 months per year, and adjusts hours to fit emergencies and special needs. The program cost is absorbed in triplicate with the prevention of one stress-related disability retirement.

Montgomery County's Office of Stress Management in Maryland sees clients with a variety of presenting problems, including issues of individual growth, self-fulfillment, and job stress. It serves as an agent for positive change within the department, reducing organizational stress through research and through active participation as consultants for various law-enforcement tasks.

The OSM program includes consultations over traumatic incidents; interventions that may substitute for disciplinary action; training programs for recruit, in-service, and supervisory positions; and pre-employment screening. These services engage one full-time and one half-time psychologist, one volunteer who assists with research and monitoring of pre-employment screening contracts, and occasionally a pre-doctoral intern.

An external time-limited consultation model is also discussed. It deals with the economic, emotional, and health consequences of unemployment, in particular involuntary job loss or layoffs within the law enforcement profession.

There are no data about the effects of layoffs on police officers, although it may be hypothesized that they are especially stressful given the unofficial industry norm that less than a 20- or 25-year career represents a failure. Retirement plans and other benefits are generally structured to support lengthy careers. A premature layoff can be ruinous on many levels.

The program engaged two consultants who designed a self-help manual for laid-off officers, which detailed what to expect in terms of emotional responses and what to do in terms of coping psychologically as well as financially. A crisis intervention strategy was also designed for a telephone hot-line program. A contingency plan, the availability of similar support for the potential victim of future layoffs, is highly recommended.

Prince George's County Police Department Psychology Services Division in Maryland exists to help the department deliver problem-free police service insofar as possible. To this end, the PSD addresses the department as well as its officers, making formal management consultation presentations on issues related to human resources and organizational development. This program employs two full-time and one part-time psychologists who conduct individual counseling per administrative referrals, respond to crises, and intervene in special situations such as exposure to communicable diseases or the investigation of complaints against an officer. In addition, the PSD offers voluntary programs to law-enforcement personnel including individual counseling, biofeedback treatment, and a full range of training programs. There is also a research arm that responds to specific requests for information from divisions or command.

What these different programs share is their own on-site physical presence and their involvement with the structure and operation of the workplace, not just the workers. That they are all successful is, in part, based on an accurate diagnosis of organizational and community cultures, a sophisticated understanding of the dynamics operating within various law enforcement subcultures, and a comprehension of the complexities of forming and maintaining a productive partnership between law enforcement and psychology.

References

Bateson, G. (1972). Steps to an ecology of mind. New York: Ballentine Books.

Berg, P. (1982, April). Resistances: Clinicians' concerns about cops. Paper presented at the conference Psychotherapy and Law Enforcement: Issues and Techniques, sponsored by the University of California at San Francisco (Department of Psychiatry, Langley Porter Psychiatric Institute) and the San Francisco Police Department, San Francisco.

Bion, W. (1975). Selections from "experience in groups." In A. Colman & W. Bexton (Eds.), Group relations reader (pp. 11–20). Sausalito, CA: Grex.

Dooley, D., Catalano, R., & Rook, K. (1988). Personal and aggregate unemployment and psychological symptoms. Journal of Social Issues, 44, 107–124.

Ellison, K. W., & Genz, J. L. (1983). Stress and the police officer. Springfield, IL: Charles C Thomas.

Ellison, K. W., & Munnings, R. (1990). When you are laid off: A survival manual for police officers. Unpublished manuscript.

Iverson, L., Sabroe, S. (1988). Psychological well-being among unemployed and employed after a company closedown: A longitudinal study. Journal of Social Issues, 44, 144–152.

Kirschman, E. F. (1983). Wounded heroes: A case study and systems analysis of job related stress and emotional dysfunction in three police officers. Dissertation Abstracts International, 44, 1279B. (University Microfilms No. 83–19, 921).

Kirschman, E. F. (1987). Buddha in search of the barrel. In H. More & P. Unsinger (Eds.), Police managerial uses of psychology and psychologists (pp. 85–106). Springfield, IL: Charles C Thomas.

Kroes, W., & Hurrell, J. J. (1975). Job stress and the police officer. Washington, DC: U.S. Government Printing Office.

Miller, S. (1990, November). Styles of coping with threat: Implications for adaptation and well being at work. Paper presented at the NIOSH/APA Conference on Work and Well-Being, Washington, DC.

Reese, J. T. (1987). A history of police psychological services. Washington, DC: U.S. Department of Justice, Federal Bureau of Investigation.

Reiser, M. (1972). The police department psychologist. Springfield, IL: Charles C. Thomas.

Schlossberg, H., & Freeman, L. (1979). Psychologist with a gun. New York: Carward, McCann & Goeghegan.

Scrivner, E. (1987). Culture clash. Paper presented at the conference "Development and promoting comprehensive mental health program for law enforcement personnel," University of Miami, FL.

Stratton, J. (1982, April). Cross cultural influences: Police and psychologist. Paper presented at the conference "Psychotherapy and law enforcement: Issues and techniques," University of California, San Francisco.

Vastola, A. (1978). The police personality: An alternative explanatory model. *Police Chief.* 50–52.

Walima, S., & Kirschman, E. (1988). Health resource coordinators: Organization consultation services. *Police Chief, 15,* 78–81.

Wambaugh, J. (1973). *The onion field.* New York: Delacorte.

13

Lillian Robbins

Health and Safety Committees as a Means of Relieving Psychological Stress

Although there has long been interest in improving workplace safety, especially in high-risk occupations such as mining, the 1970 passage of the Occupational Safety and Health Act (OSHAct) marked the beginning of such widespread and systematic efforts in the United States (Kochan, Dyer, & Lipsky, 1977). Historically, organized labor had been involved in attempts to ameliorate working conditions, chiefly because the serious risks connected with certain jobs were most evident in industries in which unions were strong. The early efforts aimed at passing legislation that would provide both standards and the potential of enforcement while protecting whistle blowers. In time, it became clear that joint labor–management health and safety committees were an ideal vehicle for translating specific problems recognized in the field into more general policies and for monitoring ongoing incidents and their implications. At the heart of the conceptualization of joint committees has been recognition of the differences that exist between the adversarial relationship in such activities as collective bargaining and the collaboration so essential where health and safety are concerned.

This chapter will briefly review the history and traditional functions of health and safety committees and the problems that have been noted in their operation and effectiveness. My decade of experience as chair of a faculty health and safety committee at a large university will then be used to illustrate psychological benefits to faculty, staff, and students that have been essentially ignored by other writers. The predominance of engineers and other technocrats in the health and safety field has led to greater emphasis on thresholds and wipe samples than on helping employees to identify legitimate concerns and allay fears in a responsible and supportive manner. Finally, recommendations will be made for enhancing the general effectiveness of health and safety committees.

I would like to thank Jeffrey Katz, librarian at Rutgers' Institute of Management and Labor Relations, and the staff of Rutgers-Newark's Dana Library for their help with obtaining references. I would also like to acknowledge the ongoing support of Chris Berzinski, Miles Galvin, and Wells Keddie of the Rutgers AAUP who contributed so amply to my understanding of Health and Safety issues. Most of all, I would like to thank Edwin Robbins, who has shared my concerns in every way, and has served consistently and lovingly as chief sounding board and technical advisor.

Provisions of OSHAct

The OSHAct is widely recognized as having been the spur for renewed efforts to improve health and safety in the workplace. According to Factor and Uehlein (1991), the labor movement was the driving force behind the act. Until then, union approaches to health and safety had included lobbying for legislation that would set standards and regulations for enforcement, negotiating provisions to protect workers and give indemnification for work-related injuries, and developing committees to monitor ongoing efforts. All these were implemented in the OSHAct on a federal basis, with health and safety committees mandated in 1980 rather than remaining voluntary as before. The law made plant safety a higher priority for management while at the same time giving unions greater involvement and the potential for enforcement.

Since 1970, more collective bargaining contracts contain health and safety provisions. Ruttenberg (1989), stated that only 28% of the collective bargaining contracts surveyed by the U.S. Bureau of Labor Statistics in 1951 had clauses related to health and safety. Of the 345 contracts that mentioned the topic, the majority gave committees limited scope in contrast to management. Kochan et al. (1977) cited figures collected by the U.S. Bureau of National Affairs showing that 85% of contracts surveyed in 1975 had health and safety provisions as compared with 65% in 1970. By the time of Ruttenberg's 1989 report for the U.S. Department of Labor, there were thousands of health and safety committees in the United States, many in work settings considered nonhazardous. She reported a range from a low of 10% in the construction industry to 100% in rubber manufacturing. However, the law applied only to large firms involved in interstate commerce and not to small companies, which employ the majority of workers in the United States. Furthermore, public employees were initially exempt, although a number of states now protect them with the Public Employee Safety Act (P-OSHA; Eaton & Egarian, 1991).

Standard setting has been a slow process, because of pressures from different constituencies (Greenwood, 1984). Management, primarily concerned with the costs of implementation, has argued for waiting until full and incontrovertible evidence is available. Labor, more concerned with injuries and illnesses, has pushed for standards that err on the side of caution. In addition, OSHA and the National Institute for Occupational Safety and Health (NIOSH), the agencies mandated with developing standards and overseeing their implementation, have had a multitude of directors, all political appointees with differing degrees of technical expertise. There has also been a good deal of turnover in their scientific and technical staffs (Greenwood, 1984). As a result, the conceptualization of health and safety legislation has been far ahead of its tangible accomplishments.

Scope and Functions of Health and Safety Committees

According to Bryce and Manga (1983) and Ruttenberg (1989), there has been no single formula for health and safety committees' structure. They vary in size and in the proportion of employers and employees. Several patterns have emerged, ranging from committees that meet rarely and have limited functions to active groups that have the authority to review all plant accidents and injuries and make recommendations for change.

There have been several basic types of committees: those that consist only of labor representatives who have to find means of bringing problems to the attention of management and the more successful joint committees, which have the potential of greater and more constructive impact on the workplace (Egarian, 1989; Ruttenberg, 1989). On the management side, they consist primarily of people involved in employee relations and safety, many with technical expertise. Egarian and Ruttenberg both believe that even a well-functioning joint committee requires a union-also group as a counterpart to management's health and safety staff.

The committee functions highlighted include making recommendations; reviewing accident and injury records (although this typically is a problematic area for management); identifying hazards, such as fumes, dust, poor lighting, and leaks; making recommendations for alleviation; and making periodic inspections, including accompanying government inspectors (Bryce & Manga, 1983; Eaton & Egarian, 1991; Egarian, 1989; Ruttenberg, 1989). The primary focus has been on end results such as reducing the number of accidents and injuries in specific worksites or on instituting training programs. Attention to more subtle aspects, such as improving morale or reducing stress in the workforce are scarcely mentioned, possibly because few of the writers and activists in this area have been psychologically trained or inclined.

Ruttenberg (1989) pointed out that involving the people most affected by hazards and solutions is a particularly effective way for committees to operate. She cited the example of a company that recognized problems with the lighting and ergonomic features of equipment at video display terminal stations. Inviting the computer operators to choose the chairs they preferred and make suggestions regarding lighting proved to be a far more satisfactory and cost-effective approach than other companies' arbitrary selection of equipment. More generally, involving employees in the identification of problems and suggested remedies is helpful in ensuring greater compliance in such aspects as the use of protective equipment and other work practices. In addition, improving health and safety by such collaborative means reduces company costs by lowering insurance rates and the number of work days lost (Ruttenberg, 1989).

Kochan et al. (1977) felt that both OSHA and Equal Opportunity legislation have had a dramatic impact on workplace policies and practices. However, although advertisements for jobs often pay at least lip service to being an "equal opportunity employer," there is generally silence regarding health and safety protection. It may well be that employers would rather downplay risks and hazards. This would explain their tendency to shun publicity for efforts at improvement.

It is puzzling that health and safety have been combined when the two are really distinct in terms of their connection to workplace conditions. Safety is much simpler to document and remedy. If someone is injured by unshielded machinery or by building materials that fall off a poorly loaded truck, cause and effect are relatively easy to establish. Although worker carelessness might be invoked as a factor in either of these examples, a strong union can generally demonstrate that technological improvements and training can reduce accidents and be cost-effective as well as humane. Work-related health problems are far more difficult to substantiate. First, they may not manifest themselves immediately but after a lag, which sometimes may be years, nor do they necessarily present with the same symptoms or degree of severity. Second, unless there is excellent on-site medical coverage, used exclusively by all employees, identifying a cluster is virtually impossible. The fact that company physicians may have a stake in minimizing health problems (Cromer, 1991; Leslie, 1991) is another deterrent to the identification of work-related health conditions. Concerns about confidentiality may also rule against identifying cases and finding patterns. More important, however, is the reluctance of management to take responsibility for illnesses (Bryce & Manga, 1983; Leslie, 1991) or for the correction of underlying problems that tend to be far more expensive than adding machine guards or improving truck-loading practices.

Under the law, employers retain the ultimate responsibility for providing a healthy and safe workplace (Ruttenberg, 1989). If the top levels of management are genuinely committed to improving health and safety, they will collaborate in the development of an organizational structure with the expertise, authority, and financial means to deal with safety problems, a reward structure providing incentives for increasing health and safety, and the appropriate training of workers (Kochan et al., 1977). To these functions, Ruttenberg recommends adding full access to records and data, joint planning, the ability to hire and fire safety and medical personnel, the authority to immediately stop the use of dangerous equipment, and an atmosphere of mutual trust.

Positive Features of Health and Safety Committees

Kochan et al. (1977) and Ruttenberg (1989), among others, have pointed out that health and safety is one area in which common goals and collaboration between management and labor are likely. However, although effective collaboration is necessary, it is not sufficient to improve workplace safety. Kochan et al. interviewed representatives of both unions and management associated with a broad range of occupations in a high-risk industry to assess the impact of health and safety committees. They recognized the problems inherent in studying an ongoing process only by retrospective and cross-sectional methods. Their findings indicated that there was a general lack of systematic records or minutes, so that little is known about what transpires during health and safety committee meetings. In addition, they could not obtain adequate long-term information on accidents and illnesses to assess the tangible outcome of committee efforts because of management concern about confidentiality and liability. Not surprisingly, they found that there were different perceptions and expectations by labor and management, with each essentially overstating its contribution and minimizing the other's. Management reported a greater commitment to health and safety on its part than was acknowledged by union representatives.

Kochan et al. (1977) pointed out that there are several possible models of health and safety committees. The most popular choice, adopted by 60% of firms they surveyed, especially in larger plants, consists of several labor representatives who meet in a joint committee with management. Two equally popular choices, each accounting for 15% of worksites surveyed, involve having a single representative meet periodically with management safety staff or a union health and safety committee, which provides data that its leadership can discuss with management. The remaining industries still did not have any formal health and safety committees at the time of the study.

Regardless of the organizational features, a viable commitment to health and safety requires sensitizing employees to recognize and identify problems and to perceive their representatives as people who will take their concerns to management in a responsible fashion. Furthermore, there must be both the commitment and capacity to achieve solutions in terms of being able to consult with experts to discover appropriate remedies and facilitate their implementation.

Although the grievance process is available for dealing with health and safety issues, Kochan et al. (1977) and Ruttenberg (1989) indicated that it is rarely used. Instead, problems are resolved by making suggestions, many of which are implemented. This is an important way in which job-related stress is relieved given that people have immediate and tangible ways of seeing that their perceptions matter. Feedback in the form of reports at staff meetings, newsletter inserts, and the like is essential to sustain interest (Beaumont, Coyle, Leopold, & Schuller, 1982; Eaton & Egarian, 1991).

Problems Associated With Health and Safety Committees

Kochan et al. (1977) pointed out that employees need a strong commitment to health and safety, both in terms of contract provisions and their responsibility for monitoring situations on an ongoing and regular basis. Unions need to develop procedures for identifying hazards and working out solutions that involve feedback from the rank and file (Factor & Uehlein, 1991). One major difficulty is that employees typically engage in health and safety work as volunteers. Although most contracts specify that union members are to receive salaries for the time spent on inspections or committee meetings, there are no provisions for making up the work that they miss during these activities, an issue that may be more relevant to some occupations than others. It is hard for volunteers to sustain interest in health and safety on a preventive rather than a crisis-response basis. Furthermore, workers may be reluctant to press management for information on accidents and illnesses if they fear retaliation, particularly if they are not union members with explicit protection. Finally, general economic problems may increase reluctance to raise health and safety issues, especially those that might be costly to remedy, out of concern for job security (Beaumont et al., 1982).

In practical terms, well-placed subordinates can sabotage management commitment if they are defensive about defects found or unwilling to remedy them. Sometimes, this may be the result of a perceived disparity between the stated commitment of top management to health and safety and actual attempts to keep problems submerged. If the safety staff perceives that its jobs are dependent on minimizing problems, they will do so, jeopardizing their credibility with employees and delaying both discovery and remediation. In addition, if the safety staff has limited resources, it is hard for them to implement change. For instance, a number of states now require implementation of right-to-know legislation, which involves making inventories of hazardous substances and monitoring their use. If there is no budget to provide staff for the development and maintenance of inventories and no money for buying locked cabinets or safe transport equipment, implementation of the law becomes in part an illusion. This is exacerbated by the fact that the legislation makes no distinctions between substances that are toxic in minute doses and ones that are more generally hazardous. Needing to keep track of literally thousands of substances becomes a daunting task.[1]

There are also practical problems in terms of what constitutes the appropriate training of workers to minimize risks of exposure to hazardous substances. One common approach is to provide a slide show supported by written material to employees whose signature demonstrates their presence at the training session. However, although this complies with the letter of the law, there are major loopholes. In populations such as custodians, who are often at the front lines of exposure to hazardous substances, little effort is made to ascertain what language is spoken by work crews or their reading level. Furthermore, recommendations made in written documents can easily be undermined if personal protective equipment is unavailable in the proper sizes or if necessary tools such as wet vacs are scarce or nonfunctional.

Egarian's case studies (1989) showed additional reasons for the difficulties in obtaining valid data on health and safety improvements as a result of committee work. She pointed out that the number of reported problems went up in groups such as New York State's Public Employee Federation, which had an elaborate and well-funded health and safety structure. Her explanation was that this reflected more accurate record keeping and greater awareness by workers that people are interested in documenting what previously were private concerns. However, there may be other reasons that have little to do with the presence or absence of committees. For instance, greater reliance on part-time and relatively inexperienced workers could be associated with an increased number of accidents. The recent waves of staff layoffs may also result in greater stress and overload on the remaining workers.

In practical terms, there is a lack of both outcome and process data about health and safety committees. It is hard to determine what the committees do and what difference, if any, their presence means for health and safety in objective terms. None of the studies reviewed make it possible to ascertain the extent to which morale might be improved because the committees exist or the extent to which some accountability is better than none in ensuring workplace safety. This is why the literature reviewed, despite some attempts at methodological sophistication and ambitious ranges of occupations surveyed, consists of essentially illustrative case studies (e.g., Egarian, 1989; Leslie, 1991; Ruttenberg, 1989).

One problem has been that joint committees may be seen as a threat to management prerogatives. This requires delicate handling on the part of all concerned. Management often wants to emphasize the purely advisory role of health and safety committees, whereas labor organizers are eager to use their results as demonstration of interests that transcend monetary considerations. As a result, although joint committees can have a superficially good working relationship, there may also exist complex interlocking health and safety structures designed to retain a top hand for

---

[1]It would be interesting to study both stress level and turnover in safety staffs faced with meeting contradictory and overwhelming demands so to remain employed.

management if it feels threatened by limits to its discretion and wishes to encourage lengthy delays in implementation.

There has also been controversy with regard to the inspections mandated by the OSHAct. In addition to the fact that sometimes management has been fore-warned and has been able to clean up in preparation for inspections—an approach that would not be so abhorrent if inspections were frequent—there have also been accusations that inspectors are closer to management than to unions. Bryce and Manga (1983) cited a California nuclear plant that worked out an arrangement with OSHA guaranteeing no inspections if a health and safety committee was established. Management, in turn, has accused inspectors of raising trivial issues (Greenwood, 1984; Kochan et al., 1977). Regardless, chronic shortages in staff mean that inspections, especially those unsolicited by either side, are relatively rare.

Although joint committees are generally regarded as the ideal, virtually all agree on their fragility. Kochan et al. (1977) recalled the disbanding of war plant safety committees soon after World War II. Such waxing and waning in interest may be a natural feature of groups. Although it is good to ensure continuity, it may be that too ardent following of a formula (e.g., regular meetings, whether or not concerns have been expressed) may favor disinterest. In many circumstances, a shadow committee, available for immediate responsiveness if there is an outbreak of injuries or major changes in equipment or materials used, would seem more realistic. How to maintain momentum while at the same time not be overwhelmed by details is a challenge for all such committees.

The Rutgers Experience

Universities are not usually thought of as high-risk employment settings in terms of employee safety and health. However, to the hazards associated with other work-places, such as air circulation for copying machines or food spills in the cafeteria, can be added others hazards of varying degrees of severity.

First, there may be unusually poor ventilation in sealed buildings. Fears of vandalism and student takeovers, coupled with concern over energy costs, have inspired a style of architecture in which buildings resemble fortresses, with no openable windows. Because public institutions, in particular, are expected to award contracts to low bidders, there is often skimping on fail-safe mechanisms such as back-up fans, and thermostats must each control several rooms. Reduced budgets, inflationary costs, and a commitment to classroom teaching rather than deferred maintenance increasingly mean that filter replacements and duct cleaning become rare events. Finally, the continuous use of many rooms, many of them windowless, by large classes may mean that air quality deteriorates between Monday morning and Friday afternoon.[2]

Second, there are multiple opportunities for exposure to chemicals, with spotty enforcement of right-to-know legislation. Even in the computer age, the rapid pace at which supplies come and go requires additional personnel to keep track of storage and use patterns. The scope of the problem becomes evident when one recognizes

---

[2]This may be exacerbated by the frequent practice of converting space (e.g., from storage areas to classrooms or classrooms to laboratories) because retrofitting tends to be expensive.

that chemicals are not only used in teaching and research laboratories but also in darkrooms and art department studios, as well as other classes. Furthermore, although science faculty presumably are aware of the risks incurred by the materials they work with, each semester brings a new crop of undergraduate and graduate students who must be educated and supervised. The large concentration of foreign students in science and engineering may also involve language barriers. Finally, researchers faced with time pressures to complete work and apply for new grants may be tempted to keep on working even when malfunctions in hoods and other protective equipment would suggest otherwise, unwittingly exposing students and colleagues to hazards.

Third, exposure to animal wastes and zoonotic transmission of disease is possible, especially when large animal facilities are improperly located and maintained. If animal colonies are housed on the top floors of buildings because of economies in venting odors, there is always the possibility that material failures or insufficient and poorly supervised maintenance staffs may cause leaks. In facilities where animal laboratories coexist with other departments, it becomes possible for people whose work does not require contact with animals to nevertheless be exposed to dander, viruses, and bacteria. This problem may be particularly acute where buildings are sealed and even a partial amount of air is recirculated. People may develop allergies to dust and animal products, as well as more serious illnesses.

Rutgers is unique among universities in having an active health and safety committee since 1980. In large part, this occurred because the leadership of the American Association of University Professors (AAUP), which serves as both faculty union and professional association, has long been supportive of the recognition and amelioration of workplace hazards. In part, the discovery of some major environmental problems made it necessary to mount a strong and sustained response. Although the illustrations in this section will be drawn from a particular university, they should be taken as exemplars of the types of situations and responses that occur more generally when health and safety issues are considered in settings that are not usually considered sufficiently hazardous to warrant a committee's existence.

At a structural level, the initial committee, which lasted for 2 years, was joint and co-chaired by a member of the AAUP and the university's personnel director. Because it also included senior levels of the administration, with the authority to allocate funds for necessary repairs and improvements, it was extremely effective. One major advantage was the direct access of faculty representatives knowledgeable about problems to senior staff who were able and willing to make changes. In 1982, the structure was changed unilaterally when the administration appointed faculty members to represent its positions in meetings with the AAUP. It took an arbitration case to determine that this no longer constituted a "joint" faculty–administration committee. Losing the opportunity to meet with management stymied the committee, even though there was unanimous agreement as to the seriousness of certain environmental problems. It is interesting that the observation made in some of the literature (e.g., Beaumont et al., 1982; Ruttenberg, 1989) regarding management's devaluation of the suggestions made by employees applied even when the participating union was composed of faculty, virtually all PhDs.

As a result of another arbitration case, the AAUP won the right to participate in joint inspections of a problematic worksite with management representatives for a 2-year period. These inspections were successful in uncovering a number of violations, many of which were fairly easily resolved. No joint inspections have since taken place. However, the AAUP has occasionally hired industrial hygienists to walk through facilities about which concerns have been expressed. The intervention of outside agencies, such as the New Jersey Department of Health, P-OSHA and NIOSH, has been extremely helpful in alleviating stress because personnel trust their objectivity more than that of administration representatives.

The current structure, in force since 1983, is one in which the AAUP has its own committee, which responds when members raise issues. The chairperson, along with several other members of the executive council and staff, meets three or four times a year with administration representatives. However, problems can no longer be communicated directly to the head of physical plant or the university's Department of Radiation, Environmental Health and Safety (REHS). Instead, requests for attention can only be funneled through the administrative chain of command. In addition, responses to requests for information that were once virtually immediate now are given in writing at the joint meetings. This gives no time for consultation or careful review and in effect delays serious consideration of problems to interim correspondence and the next meeting. All of this requires great patience and determination. Interestingly, other university union workers are still functioning on a joint committee basis, but all have been denied access to accident and illness data.

The AAUP has worked collaboratively with the unions representing secretaries and custodians on a number of projects, as well as with student groups when appropriate. This has been very useful for a number of reasons. Tenured faculty can speak out with less fear of intimidation than can other groups. Professors with the requisite expertise can usually be located and their knowledge is effective in countering misinformation. For their part, the secretaries and custodians are likely to have more direct facts about workplace hazards. The elimination of status barriers where health and safety are concerned has been useful in improving lines of communication in other contexts as well.

The AAUP Health and Safety Committee has not worked extensively with community groups, although we have given some support to the coalition working toward the implementation of HELP (hazard elimination through local participation) in New Jersey (Jeffrey, 1991). Other activists at Rutgers have also joined forces in connection with such issues as the siting of hazardous waste facilities.

At times, the hierarchic university structure has created some ludicrous situations. When a reading room opened with glass doors adjacent to a post, the AAUP pointed out to the administration that this might lead to student injuries when classes changed and large groups rushed in and out. We recommended putting decals on the doors and painting the post to reduce the risk of accidents. The response was that the students were not part of our bargaining unit. When we rephrased the concern to one of faculty being hurt by the invisible doors, decals and paint were quickly deployed. On another occasion, when serious leaks from the cage washing apparatus in an animal laboratory required evacuation of a classroom directly below, the professor was advised to obtain samples of the liquid. Collection cups and lids were obtained from the student cafeteria next door. When analysis by an outside laboratory, retained by the AAUP, showed evidence of avian fecal material, the administration tried to cast doubts on the findings by saying that the cups were not sterile and that the sample collector was an experimental physicist rather than a bacteriologist. This example also illustrates the need for the AAUP's allocation of modest sums for independent tests and consultations in addition to in-house responses.

The AAUP Health and Safety Committee and the AAUP Executive Council are concerned about the potential for increased delays because deferred maintenance must compete for increasingly scarce funds with other priorities. In addition, fiscal practices that once might have been appropriate now encourage inefficiency. Thus, apportioning money for specific purposes each year may mean that it is more feasible to do patch-up work than to dip into capital funds for long-term solutions. It is cheaper to mop up leaks than to fix pipes and to repair deteriorating air conditioners than to replace them. Although physical plant directors may earn administrative praise for their frugal management, the long-term costs may be greater than if problems were addressed adequately the first time. At the psychological level, the people who work in affected areas experience stress not only because limited maintenance results in poor working conditions but also because their discomfort confirms that they do not matter.

Another issue to which the Health and Safety Committee has repeatedly drawn attention is that of regarding incidents as isolated, with no prior history and no connection to other environmental events. When a secretary developed a severe allergic response to the daily accumulation of dust in her office, the floors and furniture were cleaned thoroughly. However, it was deemed too expensive to clean the air-conditioning ducts, and her symptoms became so severe that she had to be relocated to another department. Although faculty down the hall reported similar problems with dust, the response continued to be local rather than broad based. Furthermore, despite repeated requests to identify the allergens, the official response was to clean without testing. In another instance, after weeks of inaction in response to reports of water in front of the blackboard in a windowless classroom, the committee was contacted. Its chairperson recognized the problem might be related to severe air-conditioning leaks in offices two floors above. The separate reporting of incidents to physical plant and the reluctance of top management to make on-site inspections had not led others to make the connection. When the leaks were repaired, the classroom problems ended. However, the next summer, the underlying deterioration of the cooling plant was so severe that there was no air conditioning for 2 months, and these same classrooms were not usable.

When the remedy is relatively inexpensive to put in place and maintain, administrative response has been rapid. For instance, after a student was trapped for several hours in a locked stairwell and had to break a window to summon help, the Health and Safety Committee formally requested that a phone connected to the university police be installed. This was done with dispatch. However, it has been difficult to generalize to other settings in the absence of precipitating incidents. When inspection of a new building disclosed that the exit sign arrows were 180 degrees off, these were promptly changed, just as the committee's observations that fire extinguishers were misleadingly labeled led to adoption of a more accurate method of signaling when service was needed.

However, in situations in which capital expenditures are involved, solutions take time, and the concerted effort of many individuals and groups has been necessary. A good case in point was a library, which for years had been plagued by a heavy fall-out of dust. Staff members complained repeatedly about the coating on shelves and books and expressed their concern about breathing the powder. Administrators maintained that the tests performed by the REHS showed that no asbestos was present and that the condition of other buildings was far worse. When P-OSHA was called by a coalition of the three unions and students, custodians were asked to clean the library especially carefully before the inspection, even though they routinely removed bags of debris before staff and students arrived. Near the end of the inspection, it was mentioned that several shelves had been left as they were found that morning. Tests by the state confirmed the presence of asbestos, and the library was closed for major renovations. Until budgetary constraints became prevalent in the last few years, the committee was periodically apprised of ongoing asbestos removal in university buildings. The committee continues to be informed of abatement efforts in areas where moisture or construction have led to damage.

At times, it has seemed absurd for a psychologist to spend time on such matters, especially as a volunteer. However, the Health and Safety Committee has been seen by many faculty and staff members as an essential tool in providing a forum for legitimizing health and safety complaints and working out solutions. People throughout the university have come to recognize that their complaints are more likely to be heard and remedial action considered if the committee intervenes. People who have felt diminished by the seeming unresponsiveness of physical plant or REHS feel they have an alternate channel for being heard. In addition, when the committee investigates a complaint and follows it up, it legitimizes what might initially have been perceived as individual idiosyncrasy. For lower status employees, in particular, this has been essential in empowering them to do something tangible about poor working conditions. Because of union support and the formal designation of the committees in all three contracts, there has also been some protection to whistle blowers, who might otherwise jeopardize their future.

From the administration's standpoint, having faculty and staff observe and report problems is of enormous value in assisting the understaffed REHS to monitor the environment, even if such help is not always graciously acknowledged.

Over time, it has also become evident that there are several modes of coping with continuing and severe environmental stresses. A surprisingly common approach, also commented on by Factor and Uehlein (1991) is to deny that problems exist and to minimize their impact. This has the advantage of not requiring recognition of one's vulnerability and is the preferred style of employees who are afraid of the consequences of "making waves." Thus, a researcher whose reprints were discolored by frequent leaks of fecal matter from an animal laboratory directly overhead was reluctant to object, lest his promotion be delayed. He preferred to ignore the matter but found means of working in other locations as much as possible—a solution that is not so easily available to secretaries or staff. A similar pattern was shown by the personnel of a physics lab, who were concerned about the seemingly high incidence of early deaths but were reluctant to confront the work and pain that a thorough investigation would entail. However, when people do complain, the committee has learned that some supervisors can make their lives difficult by such means as writing negative letters for their personnel files or firing them if they have not completed their probationary period.

What the committee has achieved has been the development of a structure whereby environmental incidents can safely be reported. Our track record in objectively assessing situations has enhanced credibility, so that the administration responds promptly to most requests. This has helped faculty and staff immeasurably given that it contrasts markedly with the indifference with which so many other environmental problems are treated when the committee is not involved. It has also helped at a personal level because people recognize that they have support and that persistence and follow-up are part of the package. Developing procedures for identifying problems and for credible follow-up has proved helpful in alleviating individual and group stress. Working in concert with others to deal with these issues serves as a powerful tool for improving self-esteem and collegiality over and above the goal of ameliorating the work environment.

Occasionally, the committee has been able to work in a preventive mode. It was able to question the wisdom of saving money by incinerating laboratory wastes in the university heating plant before it was begun and to stop the temporary relocation of animal cages in hallways of classroom buildings during laboratory renovations. We also co-sponsored a well-attended conference on cancer and the workplace, emphasizing strategies for support and survival in conjunction with community groups and the local medical school AAUP. Although the impact on health of students and employees is not easy to assess, and although much more remains to be achieved, there is no question that the Health and Safety Committee has performed useful functions.

Recommendations and Conclusions

Both the literature and institutional experience have pointed to the importance of well-functioning health and safety committees. Their common tasks of identifying hazards, making recommendations for alleviation, and developing sound training programs are enhanced if certain characteristics prevail: (a) joint management–employee committees, based on mutual respect and with sufficient authority to implement change; (b) collaborative inspections, including technically appropriate representation; (c) access to workplace accident and injury records, reviewed periodically to identify patterns if any; and (d) publicity for problems and solutions to increase awareness of health and safety issues and encourage preventive measures.

This chapter has been written from the perspective that it is desirable to draw on the expertise of people on an assembly line, in an office, or in a classroom who are often the first to recognize the presence of hazards. Serving as useful adjuncts to management, safety specialists have the advantage of inexpensively increasing the scope of observations. The presence of an effective health and safety committee ensures that fears about exposure to toxic materials or possible reasons for clusters of illnesses will be addressed supportively and substantively.

In all fairness, it should be stated that some people believe that health and safety concerns among employees are stressors in their own right. Research is needed to establish how management and personnel at different occupational levels view this issue and whether the stressor is the underlying anxiety or powerlessness to even attempt amelioration.

It should also be noted that because health and safety committees typically exist in association with unions, only a minority of the working population enjoys their protection. As of 1991, only 16% of U.S. workers were unionized, with 10% membership in the private sector and 38% among the public employees (L. Troy, personal communication, December 1991). These figures have been decreasing each decade and are likely to continue to diminish as the nature of the work force changes in terms of type of work and part- or full-time status. However, better attention to health and safety issues can improve conditions for a broader constituency than union members. In schools, for instance, students' health is enhanced if teachers and staff work for better ventilation and the removal of deteriorating asbestos.

Recent disasters have demonstrated that good will and common sense may be more important for improving workplace and general safety than the use of high technology. Some New York subway passengers were killed because of a drunken motorman whose erratic behavior was evident prior to the fatal accident, and workers burned to death in a chicken processing plant in North Carolina because exits were locked.

In the ideal setting, health and safety committees should be unnecessary. Tests would be performed in a timely fashion, and those responsible for maintaining the work environment would ensure that optimal conditions prevail. Requests for assistance would be handled promptly. Stonewalling and resistance would be replaced by openness, and employee fears would be treated with respect. However, until such model conditions exist, health and safety committees will remain a good means for identifying problems and for persevering until they are satisfactory resolved. Overcoming the isolation of individuals and providing support for constructive amelioration of working environments seems a particularly apt focus for continued collaboration between the American Psychological Association and NIOSH.

References

Beaumont, P. B., Coyle, J. R., Leopold, J. W., & Schuller, T. E. (1982). *The determinants of effective joint health and safety committees*. Glasgow, Scotland: Centre for Research in Industrial Democracy and Participation, University of Glasgow.

Bryce, G. K., & Manga, P. (1983). *Changing the power relationship in the workplace: Joint labour–management occupational health and safety committees in Canada*. (Working Paper 83–23). Ontario, Canada: University of Ottawa.

Cromer, L. (1991). Plucking Cargill: The RWDSU in Georgia. In *Organizing for health and safety* (Labor Research Review No. 16, pp. 15–23). Chicago: Midwest Center for Labor Research.

Eaton, A., & Egarian, M. (1991). *Guide to effective joint labor/management safety & health committees*. Trenton: New Jersey Department of Health, Public Employee Occupational Safety and Health Program.

Egarian, M. (1989). *Effective public sector labor–management health and safety committees: Five case studies*. Trenton: New Jersey Department of Health, Occupation Health Service.

Factor, D., & Uehlein, J. (1991). Organizing for safe work in a safe world. In *Organizing for health and safety* (Labor Research Review No. 16, pp. 1–13). Chicago: Midwest Center for Labor Research.

Greenwood, T. (1984). *Knowledge and discretion in government regulation*. New York: Praeger Special Studies.

Jeffrey, E. K. (1991). HELP in New Jersey: From right-to-know to right-to-act. In *Organizing for health and safety* (Labor Research Review No. 16, pp. 51–57). Chicago: Midwest Center for Labor Research.

Kochan, T. A., Dyer, L., & Lipsky, D. B. (1977). *The effectiveness of union–management safety and health committees.* Kalamazoo, MI: W. E. Upjohn Institute for Employment Research.

Leslie, M. (1991). Stalking a killer: UAW 735's cancer watch. In *Organizing for health and safety* (Labor Research Review No. 16, pp. 91–96). Chicago: Midwest Center for Labor Research.

Ruttenberg, R. (1989). *The role of labor–management committees in safeguarding worker safety and health.* Washington, DC: U.S. Department of Labor.

14 ⎯⎯⎯⎯⎯⎯⎯⎯⎯⎯⎯⎯⎯⎯⎯⎯⎯⎯⎯⎯⎯⎯⎯⎯⎯⎯

Eugene V. Martin

Designing Stress Training

My initial interest in occupational stress was to find in the literature a design for a relatively brief workshop that could be adapted, if necessary, and used as part of a course on occupational safety and health for workers. My client, an international labor union, wanted to help its members protect themselves at work; at the same time, they did not want the course to contradict the legal and ethical obligation of employers to provide a safe and healthy workplace. The designs and materials for stress training I found seemed to reinforce this concern; the stress training available had little relevance to occupational issues and almost always "blamed the victim" of stress by focusing on the need for individuals to be different, without any attention to the need for change to eliminate unnecessary stress due to, say, work rules, supervisory practices, lack of benefits, the work environment, or the employing organization.

Still, the challenge remained: What training would enable workers to protect themselves and their occupational interests in dealing with stress? As I worked with that problem and a variety of other change and stress issues, I came to see stress training for large numbers of workers, regardless of whether they worked in the executive penthouse or on the shop floor, as essential, feasible, and providing professionals with some of their most appropriate and effective roles for preventing psychological disorders in the workplace.

This chapter addresses that challenge and presents a partial and preliminary model for designing stress training as an effective prevention intervention. The model is, necessarily, a work in progress. The issues are complex, the concerns are interdisciplinary, the stress field itself is relatively new, and its basic concepts are still evolving. This chapter is not a research report; it is an overview and summary of my work on stress training.

The views presented are a synthesis of my experience as a change agent and consultant designing, initiating, assisting, and evaluating a wide range of planned change projects and programs, in public and private sectors, in the United States and abroad. In addition to designing and presenting stress programs for several national and international organizations, my work experience includes joint labor–management efforts, occupational safety and health programs, substance-abuse assistance activities, training to support the entry of women into nontraditional employment, the use of radio and television broadcasting as educational strategies, and socioeconomic development projects in Africa, Asia, and Latin America.

In this work with colleagues and clients, I have come to see model-based stress training as an essential requisite for people to better manage the psychological aspects of enlightened self-interest in their social, economic, or political situations. It follows that the nature of the stress training available can be a central and critical determinant in the evolution of democratic institutions and in the manner by which society approaches issues of economic equity and social justice.

At a personal level, this chapter is an effort to initiate and expand a collegial dialogue to accelerate our evolution of stress training. I hope to hear from others whose purpose is helping people increase their own skills for intentional change and who might want to apply, test, correct, or elaborate these ideas.

Context: Stress Training in the Workplace

This section provides a context for my conclusions about workplace stress training. First, I identify the most important assumptions on which my ideas for stress training are based, other than those commonly dealt with in the literature. Second, I identify references that position my work in relation to the voluminous literature on stress. Finally, I sketch the case for asserting that workplace stress training is essential, feasible, and should be different from prevailing efforts.

Basic Assumptions About Stress Training

Although stress is a complex phenomenon, any discussion of it is necessarily framed in a specific, usually limited context. In designing occupationally appropriate stress training, we need a range of perspectives varying from the individual/subjective to a societal/objective point of view. Indeed, the physical reality of the individual stress response, with its cascading physiological, psychological, and behavioral effects as mediated by the presence and role of others, underlines the objective reality of our mental and physical interdependence on each other. Thus, dealing with stress inevitably requires dealing with self, others, and an external world beyond relationships.

Given this view of stress, the pivotal issue for stress training is the way a person learns, especially from her or his own experience, and applies these learnings to competently deal with her or his situation. This puts the focus of stress training on experiential learning, the primary means by which almost all of us learn about ourselves and develop our skills for managing self and situation.

As opportunities permitted I worked to increase the experiential nature of my stress training. I developed or found exercises by which participants could explore their own experiences and draw their own conclusions about their stress situations, their individual and collective strengths, the dynamics of stressors and strains, and practical next steps to improve their situations. Participants liked these exercises, said so, and seemed to make good use of them. As I increased the proportion of experientially derived information compared with presented information, I also heard increasing concerns about whether the workshop offered sufficient information. These concerns seemed largely allayed when I included an exercise to increase awareness of the experiential process and of participants' past learnings from their own experiences. Yet, when I explicitly asserted that one's own experience and

2915

judgment were inevitably and appropriately the basis for increasing stress competencies, I encountered dismay and disagreement.

I began to notice that people are little aware of and do not consciously value their experiential learning. Parents, schools, religions, and civic authorities all encourage people to accept revealed truths vastly more than they encourage people to trust discoveries formed from their own perceptions and judgment. I concluded that most people are learning impaired as experiential learners.

(This conclusion may seem overstated; I mean it quite literally. I think there is ample reason to recognize that even the best and most loving of conventional parenting teaches children, even that fortunate minority, to have basic doubts about their own judgment and, even more fundamentally, about their own goodness or rightness. However, let me acknowledge that this conclusion about experiential learning disability deserves discussion beyond the scope of this chapter.)

For me, this conclusion moved experiential learning from being the preferred learning process in stress training into the content area of the training. I found it necessary to introduce exercises by which people could reconsider their ways of knowing and learning. Of course, viewing the dynamics of an individual's learning process as a valuable and improvable set of skills began to add specificity to the outcomes that the training is intended to achieve.

This perspective also shifts training outcomes from being focused on participants' motivations to their skills. For example, participants need to know and apply operational aspects of the psychology of individual change. They need (a) increased ability to examine their own subjective experience, (b) to know that they can and do change and how they can change intentionally, (c) unqualified validation of who they are now.

Their understanding of themselves in the context of change also requires that they understand some general aspects of the process of planned change. For example, they need to appreciate change as a process of ongoing exploration and learning rather than as a triumph or failure of will. And, they need to know how to apply a simple next-step action learning model that will evoke reflection on experience.

Moreover, they need to know that their occupational stress has an entirely nonsubjective aspect that is interactive with self and situation. They need ways of putting work issues into an appropriate nonpersonal perspective with an analytic framework that will support the continuing development of their critical thinking. And, they need an understanding of the dynamics of stress mediation that balances personal and impersonal factors.

Linkage to the Literature

Although humans have long known, written, and sung about the personal, social and work effects of events and conditions in our lives, the concept of stress as a focus for systematic and scientific inquiry is relatively recent and is usually credited to Selye (1956). Work to clarify the conceptual foundations of the field continues (Hobfoll, 1988), and much, if not most, of the current research on occupational stress appears to focus on describing its origins, dynamics, and effects (Karasek & Theorell, 1990), especially on health (Klitzman, House, Israel, & Mero, 1990). Few researchers have examined the effectiveness of training and technical assistance interventions to reduce or remediate stress effects (Murphy, 1984), and I know of few efforts to systematically design and refine such interventions (Israel, Schurman, & House, 1989; Martin, 1989).

Stress Training in the Workplace

Stress is variously a cause, concomitant, and consequence of change. In a rapidly changing world that is arguably increasing the levels of stress that people experience on the job and off, stress is more than a health issue. It is an aspect of productivity and of the effectiveness of managing public and private sector activities; a factor in intragroup, intergroup, community, national, and international tensions; a parameter in the levels of political participation as well as psychological powerlessness and depression; and socioeconomic determinant that requires more than coping skills in response.

Although more legislative and organizational attention is needed to address occupational stress, appropriate training for workers—at all levels of the employer hierarchy—must also be a central aspect of any successful strategy to prevent psychological disorders in the workplace. The professional literature on individual change and the history of industrial labor both provide ample justification for requiring and combining social and legal regulation with self-help efforts.

The following outlines my reasons for thinking that stress training for workers is essential, feasible, and should be significantly different from much of what is currently offered.

Stress training for workers is essential. One way to classify interventions intended to help people deal with problematic situations is to consider the control available to the intervener. A surgeon, for example, relies on his or her patient for little beyond a decision called informed consent; the surgeon defines the intervention, and his or her skill largely controls its outcome. A fitness coach, on the other hand, may be a highly valuable resource well able to provide expertise, encouragement, and support; however, the client rather than the coach controls what use is made of the opportunity and what happens as a result.

What about interventions to improve stress situations? I suggest that, in our efforts to help people deal with stress, we are much more likely to be coaches than surgeons. By the very nature of the stress response, the occurrence and consequences of stress are highly individualized. Moreover, the strategies for dealing with either stressors or strain outcomes are inextricably interwoven with the individual's situation and perception of interests in that situation. Even collective action to achieve changes in environmental and organizational conditions ultimately requires individual awareness, commitment, knowledge, and participation.

The point that the utility of stress knowledge and related skills ultimately rests in the hands of individuals who are stressed and in their ability to apply that knowledge and skill to their own specific situation, does not imply any less need for professional practitioners to expand their knowledge. It would also be a mistake, I believe, to continue to pose training for individuals as an alternative to labor and management action to expand stress abatement efforts and to increase collective problem solving.

Stress training for workers is feasible. In the mid 1970s, the Occupational Safety and Health Administration (OSHA) initiated a New Directions program that funded labor unions and nonprofit organizations working jointly with labor and management to develop industry-specific programs to train workers in essential occupational safety and health skills. Many of the training programs and products produced with federal funding assistance have now been incorporated into sustaining activities in a wide variety of ways. To be sure, there were false starts and problems with the program and variations in use and impact among the various grantees. Although this effective approach to reducing the human consequences and dollar costs of occupational health and safety hazards did not survive the federal withdrawal of attention in the 1980s, the lessons learned from it include the feasibility of reaching the national work force and of increasing individuals' abilities to protect themselves through occupationally relevant training in the context of institutional action and controls.

Stress training for workers will be different. Stress training already has a meaning for many people. I hasten to differentiate the stress training I envision from many of the workshops now available. As I see it, stress is a broader issue than health promotion, and stress training must go beyond teaching "coping" or "tips to live by." This requires that stress training move beyond a psychological framework for the issues of power and responsibility and train participants, not simply exhort them. Appropriate stress training deserves attention in its own right and will be less trivial when it is offered in conjunction with stress-abatement efforts.

Much of the stress training now available is brief, introductory, and rarely has follow-up; it is focused solely on life-style issues and encourages coping and individual and sometimes interpersonal change but pays little attention to organizational or environmental change. NIOSH research does not encourage us to assume that the current approaches to designing and presenting stress workshops will enable interested and conscientious learners to initiate and achieve sustaining, intentional improvements in their stress situations. Indeed, Murphy's (1984) work suggests that these workshops can have harmful effects when they encourage coping strategies more appropriate to personal than to work-related situations.

Coping skills are certainly necessary and appropriate, but they are, at best, a partial response to major stressor issues like racial, gender, and ethnic discrimination; economic insecurity; fear of crime; and the like. The suggestion that stress can be adequately dealt with by coping makes stress trivial and blames the victims by implying that it is their responses to reality that are inadequate no matter what calamity or injustice they encounter.

The existence of widespread and significant psychosocial stressors such as poverty, injustice, and economic insecurity supports the observation that issues of power and responsibility cannot be dealt with in a purely psychological context without significant possibility of confusing and misinforming participants in a manner that contradicts the professional, ethical, and legal obligations of the workshop presenter. For example, it may be useful—in a purely therapeutic context—to urge people to "take responsibility for everything that happens to you." In a workshop in the workplace, this statement is highly inappropriate at best. In such a setting, the need for organizational and social action to change working conditions as requisites for prevention raise the issue of power and how individuals can learn to increase and apply it. Appropriate stress training must focus on changes beyond coping, such as efforts to abate unnecessary or inappropriate stress in the immediate workplace.

Such stress training will be more than the peripheral activity it usually is now. Typically, strategies to prevent or remedy workplace problems focus on activities that are professionally or expertly controlled and centrally organized to deliver a specified solution to a so-called target or at-risk population. In this context, training, as a means for changing individual behavior, is usually seen as only a peripheral aspect of the solution. Even when training is recognized as necessary, its function is often limited to obtaining acceptance of and support for the centralized strategy from the work force. Thus, for example, the stress training now offered by most firms' Employee Assistance Programs (EAPs) or labor unions' Members Assistance Programs (MAPs) is usually intended to increase participants' awareness and use of the sponsoring program. It is supportive of, rather than central to, the program's success.

Stress training can—and should—offer professionals a way to help increase individual workers' skills for and exercise of control in their own situations and on their own behalfs. When stress abatement efforts are linked to stress training, the training design can provide participants with an opportunity to consider their individual objectives within the larger situation and others' efforts. Training will then be more intentional, less mystical, and will help people examine their assumptions about and use of their implicit psychosocial analysis of their situation.

Having identified my working hypotheses about stress training and the limitations of our prevailing models, I will offer some suggestions for improvement.

Characteristics of Effective Training

This section lists some of the characteristics that I believe training must have to be effective in preventing psychological disorders in the workplace.

Training Will Focus on Stress

Hollister (1977) recommended stress-model strategies for designing primary prevention programs in mental health to the 1976 National Institute of Mental Health Conference on Primary Prevention. Asking, What can we prevent? he saw this question as suggesting an appropriately humble set of objectives. Furthermore, he called attention to the added benefit that, with this conceptualization, many commonsense services of mental health and other helping agencies can be identified and publicly acknowledged as prevention. Although the source of such services has, at least temporarily, shifted toward private providers like EAPs, the benefit remains. Hollister considered the four major strategies of primary prevention to be stressor management, stressor avoidance, stress-resistance building, and stress-reaction management.

I prefer a different taxonomy of strategies, but I agree with his focus on stress. I like the fact that the stress model can help maintain a focus on the interaction between individual and environment; I fear our widely prevailing, even institutionalized, tendencies to exclude consideration of socioeconomic forces and to view psychological issues only in terms of individual dynamics and pathology. Moreover, I think that approaching prevention issues from a stress perspective is most likely to permit and encourage the widest possible participation of those affected. My professional experience indicates that although stress is somewhat stigmatized, people find it easier to talk about stress than "psychological issues," "mental health," or such. Employers and employees generally view stress as related in some way both to work and to nonwork life. The question, What stress do you experience? is meaningful and relevant for adults in every demographic and occupational category. Given an appropriate setting, many if not most adults are interested in considering whether their stress situation could be improved.

Certainly, the concept of stress is sufficiently broad to provide a framework for training to develop the individual knowledge, skills, and attitudes necessary, if not sufficient, for preventing psychological disorders in the workplace.

Training Will Be Relevant to Widely Varied Audiences

The training must be relevant to audiences that are widely varying in their situations, needs, and opportunities with respect to stress, occupation, status, and security. One paradoxical aspect of this requirement is that, as we note and honor the range of individual differences and requirements, we become better able to recognize and respond to the commonalities.

Training Will Occur During and in the Context of Stress-Abatement Efforts

Competent and appropriate training in occupational safety and health assumes and supports efforts to abate—remove or reduce—identifiable physical hazards. For maximum effectiveness, stress training should be presented in the context of visible and institutionalized efforts—optimally, an explicit program—for stress abatement. Adult learning theory strongly links effectiveness to relevance. Thus, stress training should specifically address the learner's immediate situation, objective as well as subjective, and thus help the worker identify, examine, and deal with the highest risk stress hazards in his or her working situation.

People's individual learning and change can be greatly facilitated by a formal and visible stress-abatement program. These simultaneous and supportive efforts in the worker's immediate environment encourage belief that change is possible, increase the likelihood that others will assist, and foster synergistic activities between the individual and organizational levels. Conversely, asking people to change their stress situations when their employer or union is doing nothing to abate organizational and environmental stress hazards is an inadequate and possibly illegal response that innately blames the victims, contributes to learned powerlessness, and further increase unnecessary and inappropriate stress.

Training Will Be Model-Based, Evaluated, and Progressively Improved

As a relatively new focus for study and application, even the best of current stress training should be viewed as preliminary, first approximations of what is needed. We can increase the possibility of systematically improving stress training by making it more replicable and amenable to systematic evaluation of content relevance, process effectiveness, and workshop impact. This requires stress-training designs based on an explicit model and the evolution of the model as well as its use in designing and delivering training.

Explicit training models are a key aspect of a strategy to improve stress training by fostering convergence of research and practice to clarify both stress-training goals and what is required to achieve them. Two factors may constrain this strategy. First, effective and affordable assessment of training for other than cognitive learning objectives is itself innovative. Second, the market dynamics for selling stress training seem to inhibit rather than encourage assessment and open discussion of the effects of stress training.

Ultimately, Stress Training Is About Power and Change

One way to identify the function of stress training is as "helping people discover within themselves the courage and ability to confront reality and to collectively change it" (the quote is largely Bill Moyers's phrase from another context.) I like this formulation because it recognizes that people inherently have the resources of courage and ability required to confront change and to work together in enlightened self-interest to achieve their self-help requirements. In its original context, Moyer was describing the skill of an organizer devoted to increasing economic justice and social equity. Self-help is required in every aspect of our lives; it is not solely a health issue. I believe that stress training must focus on individual power and proactive response to change.

The role of stress training is to help learners claim and apply their resources to enhance their functioning in pursuit of complex, interrelated changes in the personal, interpersonal, and societal aspects of their individual situations. Because of the ubiquity of stressors and the nature of the stress response, adequate and appropriate ways of dealing with stress require no less. Power is an inescapable aspect of stress training—from the goal to which the training contributes to the dynamics by which the training design is implemented.

Training Will Be Reoccurring and Cyclic

Rather than a single "course" or program of study, I see stress training as a multicomponent workshop that an individual learner might return to at various times in her or his life. Stress training will be reoccurring because the information and skills to be learned exceed what is likely to be achieved in any single workshop or series; most people study stress to learn how to improve their immediate situation. Although some may discover or develop a larger interest in stress as an issue, most will return to learn more only later when their perceived needs again increase.

I suggest the use of a cyclic model because growth and maturation, in general, seem based on cyclic dynamics. Also, a natural advantage of a cyclic model is that each replication taught offers reexposure to critical aspects of both theory and practice with the opportunity for the learner to re-view issues from additional perspectives and to adapt and adopt ideas and practices when they are perceived to be relevant and useful.

I do not see the need for differentiating in name or design between the initial training and successive workshops. In fact, there are important reasons not to foster the suggestion that some work on the self is "elementary," whereas other topics are "advanced." People tend to accept these distinctions that can undermine the achievement of essential learning objectives such as affirming self-esteem and fostering empowerment. I can see the need for other stress workshops focused on different, specialized outcomes.

Training Content and Process Will Be Congruent

When training is internally congruent, content and process are mutually reinforcing for the achievement of training outcomes. Many training practices undermine the objective of empowering learners. A prime example is the implicit assumption by the trainer that because the participant came to training, he or she has consented to make those personal changes recommended by the trainer. Instead, when change strategies and techniques are introduced, they must be presented with their risks and counterindications clarified so that learners are able to give informed consent to learning and using them. Otherwise, we are subtly yet significantly controlling learners' behavior in the name of empowering them.

Most critically, the selection and use of strategies and techniques for dealing with stress must be entirely learner controlled. Stressors occur in every aspect of life, and change strategies have to be congruent with both the individual situation and the origin of the stressor. No stress expert can provide a solution to such a multiplicity of concerns and issues. There is little realistic likelihood that our prescriptions for how others should live will be useful, let alone accurate; nor will a competent adult generally accept significant intervention and control from another.

In prevailing stress programs that ignore this reality, single parents with minimum wage jobs are advised to job or to delegate authority; a battered spouse is advised to try "open and leveling" communication. Such advice is as inadequate as suggesting that every underpaid worker can organize a union. This does not imply the exclusion of the trainer as a resource for learners. It does mean that the trainer's role is primarily facilitative rather than prescriptive.

Training Will Be Tied to Support Groups and Change Projects

Stress training is most likely to be sustained in effect when it is tied directly to participation with others in specific group activities intended to provide support or foster change. The training experience should, among other outcomes, lead individuals to better understand their needs and take steps to obtain either ongoing support or participation with others in change projects related to their stress concerns.

I want to emphasize that stress training that focuses only on personal change blames the victim. Even more, I want to increase recognition of the need for collaborative action to achieve change—personal, interpersonal, or societal.

An Empowerment Model for Stress Training

This section proposes a model of stress training (see Figure 1). The purpose of this model is to help practitioners design and deliver stress workshops that increase participants' power to make intentional changes in their stress situation. The model is intended to provide a framework for determining the content to be covered in training, for choosing the processes that will be used to help participants learn, and to anticipate the time required for the major activities. Training designed from the model is intended to provide participants ways of initiating and sustaining behavioral changes as an intentional learning process—changes that are freely chosen and supportive of individual growth and interdependent functioning. The model is also intended to suggest testable hypotheses so that it can be revised and refined to reflect advances in theory and the lessons learned from the experience of applying it.

The generic purpose of stress training based on this model is to enable learners to change their stress situations intentionally and systematically. Although this design views stress training as a prevention intervention, relevance requires that it focus on stressors of greatest concern to participants. Thus, it may sometimes seem like a tertiary intervention (i.e., a way of dealing with immediate problems).

This model has three components: pretraining needs assessment, training, and posttraining. In practice, they may be conducted as distinct phases or in overlapping activities. The three seem to me to be a formalization of an experiential stress learning process that many people already experience, albeit not consciously. That is, when the perception of need to deal with stress becomes of sufficient importance, or perhaps exceeds one's sense of competence, then curiosity and receptiveness to learning more about stress are triggered and are likely to last until the initial sense of need is fulfilled. After training, the individual continues, at least episodically, to be involved with some form of group support or change activity, and there is a continuing assessment of stress competence against demand.

Pretraining Needs Assessment

Although some part of a workshop participant's assessment of need has already occurred before the workshop begins, one can only presume that the decision was to see what the workshop might offer. I believe that this decision is often considerably less than a wholehearted commitment from participants to making specific and profound changes in themselves, their relationships, or their situations. This may seem obvious, but many exercises in stress workshops seem to implicitly assume that workshop participants have such a commitment or are more ready to examine their psychological situation than may be the case.

Another reason for conducting a needs assessment is that few people, in my

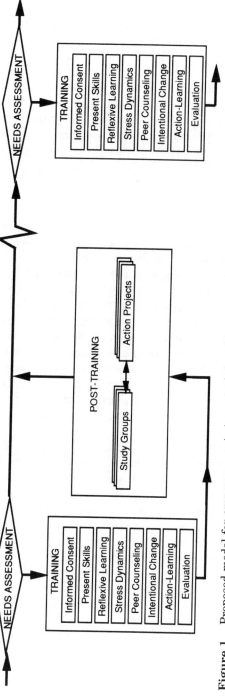

Figure 1. Proposed model for empowerment stress training designs.

experience, really appreciate their existing stress skills, their capacity for learning, and the effectiveness of their own judgment in many circumstances. We are most likely to be able to help people learn to enhance or use these capacities when we begin with an affirmation of the learner and his or her existing stress abilities.

Needs assessment, in this case, means the individual's initial clarification of the stress competencies that they already have and what additionally they seek. I vastly prefer to design for the use of experiential exercises rather than pencil-and-paper instruments. I find that it generally allows me to increase the situational relevance of the workshop to participants and that self-appraisal and naming one's concerns are a vastly more important and useful learning experience than getting a test score, especially in this context. I am also concerned about the many people for whom literacy skills and educational procedures are or were significant stressors.

Posttraining

Why should stress training include activities to encourage and help participants begin or find support groups and change activities? Although some people have adequate support networks or the ability to augment their support when they need to, others do not, especially when specific and intense problems occur. The support groups I envision are "self-owned" (i.e., they belong to their members) and, in most cases, do not require ongoing professional facilitation following an initial period. Their generic purpose is to provide their members with a safe and supportive environment for discussing personal experience. It may be useful and appropriate during the stress training to help people develop group and peer-support related skills, identify others with shared interests and concerns, and explore forming support groups, even scheduling a first posttraining meeting. However, the training designer should remain aware that the generic function of these groups makes it inappropriate for an employer or other outsider to have ongoing access to or a continuing relationship with the group.

Change activities as well as support groups are needed. At some point, training that deals seriously with stress must encourage people to look critically at the models they have for the institutional and environmental forces affecting them, as well as their interpersonal and personal situation. Some participants will seek external changes (e.g., in specific aspects of their work, social organizations, or environment). Empowerment stress training helps participants with political and social agendas as well as those with psychological objectives. Such help need not put a stress workshop sponsor in the position of recruiting volunteers for a specific cause (e.g., either to join the antiwar movement or to enlist in the National Guard). The idea is to enable participants to link the training to their next steps.

Will considering or taking an active role in external or social change issues in itself be stressful? Certainly, the answer can be yes. However, attempting personal or interpersonal change is not necessarily less stressful. Some people find it easier to deal with objective situations than with subjective ones. There are a great many change-focused activities that people join depending on their interests and outlook. Tough's work (1982) suggests that voluntary, highly intentional change is a common feature of life and usually focuses on the areas of job, career, training, residential location, and enjoyable activities as well as the realm of human relationships, emotions, and self-perception. Still more people might address their overall stress situation by undertaking social-change action if they have a clearer picture of the range of opportunities available, understand the need for their involvement and their skills, or are more able to access an interesting sector of activity.

I hope it is clear that I view training follow-on in both the areas of personal and social change as going well beyond and as separate from the training itself. Indeed, some people will not choose to consciously identify their change goals. Still, stress training will be incomplete and ineffectual without some tie-in to its primary areas of application.

Training

I term this an empowerment model because its purpose is to enable the design of stress training content and process focused on increasing participants' own capability to affect their stress situation rather than on delivering a specific body of knowledge about stress. Stress-training designs based on this model will have seven components, some of which may well be combined: informed consent, assessment of and affirmation for present skills, augmentation of reflexive learning skills, stress dynamics information, peer counseling skills, intentional change skills, an action-learning approach to personal planning, and evaluation. Moreover, training activities will be linked to or initiate optional activities occurring after training.

Informed consent. In this model, training must offer learners an opportunity to decide consciously whether they want to make changes in themselves. The learner's presence, perhaps motivated only by a desire to know more about the course and the presenter, should not be taken as tacit consent for the trainer to attempt significant life change efforts. Without informed consent, stress training, no matter what its cognitive content, can undercut the individual's confidence in and capacity for self-directed change. Moreover, the trainer is likely to be operating without the degree of cooperation and participation needed from learners. Learners need time, and perhaps structured assistance, to consider, What is my stress situation now, what kinds of changes can and do I want to make in my situation, and am I ready and willing to start now?

Assessment of an affirmation for present skills. Recognizing the skills one has is part of a rational strategy for assessing new learning needed and for building on the foundation of skills present. But, possibly even more significant than such a rational strategy is the stimulating positive effect that affirmation has for enabling learning. In my experience, affirmation from self and others is a powerful and necessary force that reduces, at least temporarily, doubts about one's judgment and thus promotes experiential learning.

Augmentation of reflective learning skills. By *reflexive learning,* I mean learning about one's own learning practices and preferences with the purpose of knowing how to use and appropriately trust this capacity. I believe that the skills for reflexive learning are the crux of empowering stress training. People need to know more about how they learn so that they can understand and take control of the processes involved. In particular, people need to understand, in a suitable context, basic concepts of motivation, the dynamics of experiential learning, and distinctions between perception and judgment functions. Most specifically, people need to know the effects of stress on learning so that they can better attend to and appreciate their own experiences.

Stress dynamics information. Stress training must provide some basic information about stress dynamics that is essential for participants' understanding and formulating their own ways of dealing with stress. The most important categories of this basic information include the concept of stressors; the physical nature of the individual stress response; the concepts in a "perceptually triggered, individual, nonspecific response"; the concept of mediators, and the variety of possible strains and their consequences. Although this chapter does not fully define the boundaries of the basic cognitive content or how to match the selection of this content to the specific training group, I do want to offer some observations about this material and its presentation.

I find that few adults ask for a definition of stress; the concept is virtually universally understood at the conversational level. Instead of generic definitions, people need to explore and name their stressors for themselves; there seems to be some compelling requirement and validation involved. I learned to take the time required by small group exercises in which people list their stressors and later the strains they experience "or have seen others experience."

Many people, especially men, are socialized to desensitize themselves to the experience of stress and need help in redeveloping appropriate levels of self/stress awareness. The exercises that facilitate participants' (re)discovery of their own stress dynamics are an essential first step in recreating awareness as well as providing a basis for developing conscious response or remediation strategies. Such exercises impart a sense of power, help clarify and demystify stress as a phenomenon, and establish stress as a shared human experience rather than as an individual failing.

I also concluded it is important to describe the sequence of cascading events that make up the stress response. Few people seem aware that the stress response is involuntary and has physiological and behavioral as well as psychological components. The realization that stress is a physical reality, not "just a psychological weakness," helps people take their own stress concerns seriously and starts to move the issue of what to do about stress beyond "being tough" and "staying in control." Moreover, clarifying the dynamics of the stress response provides the framework for introducing stress mediators or resources.

Peer-counseling skills. The fifth component is the acquisition of peer counseling skills for use in self-owned groups to obtain on-going affirmation and support. During the formal portion of stress training, learners work in a variety of small groups. It is important that each learner become a member of a relatively small, fixed group that works together periodically throughout training. This support groups provides the learner with social support and specific assistance for dealing with the stress of the learning process itself. Also, this group becomes a source of data for experiential learning about support in general and peer-counseling skills specifically. As trust levels increase, the group becomes a natural focus for learning about and practicing the skills needed in a self-owned support group.

Learners will also learn peer counseling skills appropriate to their context; these may range from simple, active-listening skills to more complex strategies for helping others deal with recurring problems. The groups continuing to function after training may or may not be the support groups that function during it.

Intentional change skill. Because stressors originate in social conditions—the changing global, national, community, organizational, group, and interpersonal environments—people need an appropriate array of change-agent skills to use in working with others on projects to achieve intentional change. In fact, people already have some level of competence as change agents. They probably have not, however, recognized their communication, persuasion, and observational skills or understood them in this light. The purpose of this training component is not to provide professional-level change skills so much as to have learners clarify their understandings of basic change models, to more fully appreciate the change capabilities they now have, to identify some of the skills that will support their efforts in the near term, and to see how they can begin to build on their existing skills in the course of working with others on actual change projects.

One set of change agent competencies that I think should be explored with learners is now primarily applied to international development programs and projects as the Team Planning Methodology (TPM) developed initially for the Technical Assistance Division of the Office of International Cooperation and Development of the Department of Agriculture and extensively applied by the Agency for International Development.

An action-learning approach to planning and managing change. This component derives from my belief that stress trainees need a framework for analyzing their stress situation in a larger context, including understanding change as an ongoing process. Recent work on adult learning calls attention to the essential role of critical thinking (Brookfield, 1987) and critical reflection (Mezirow & Associates, 1990) in experiential and transformative learning. Planning and change management models also rest on analysis, assuming that the user will apply a consistent and valid form of analysis for interpreting and applying "data." Yet, people often need to bring their interpretive assumptions and deciding processes into consciousness for examination and, possibly, reconstruction.

The task of stress training is to help participants identify the individual analyses they are currently using, to clarify the underlying beliefs and implicit values they hold, and to facilitate their reflection on and possible reframing of these values and beliefs. This component of training is not intended to prescribe for learners what their value assumptions and de-facto analytic framework should be. We can expect learners' frameworks to range anywhere from fundamental orthodoxies to highly eclectic ways of organizing and understanding experience. We can also expect learners to exhibit a full range of maturational stages and degrees of mental health and clarity.

As trainers, I believe we need to respond to any and all of these points of view respectfully, without insincerity or the implicit violence of manipulation. This provides the basis for helping learners: clarify and articulate how they now understand their situation and themselves (i.e., by what means they now observe, assess, and choose); begin to appreciate that others operate with different frameworks, aspects of which they can consider and accept or reject; and identify alternate ways they can continue to clarify and evolve their own operational axioms.

The most effective dynamic for this I know is *action learning*, sometimes called *action research*, which is a paradigm for organizing both learning and action so that each activity provides the field of attention for the other. It is made up of a basic cycle of three steps that are repeated in order: Assess one's current situation and objectives, prepare to act by choosing a next step from considered alternatives, and act in an exploratory manner. It is especially suited to learning how to do things that the learner/actor has not done before and to achieve objectives that are initially unclear and require learning new skills and the application of the new skills in an unstable environment. Descriptions of the theory and application of action research are available in texts on organizational development (e.g., French & Bell, 1984).

The team-planning methodology referred to above is a specific implementation of the generic action-learning model applied to international development activities and, unfortunately, is less easy to access (D. Levine, personal communication, 1989). I have found Argyris's (1985) theories of action a useful complement to and extension of these action and learning models.

Evaluation. Evaluation of stress training is an essential foundation for both the continuing education of the trainer/facilitator and for the improvement of subsequent training delivery and the progressive refinement of the empowerment model itself. It is easier to call for evaluation than it is to conduct an assessment that is actually useful for such outcomes. I think we will need some very creative work to operationalize models of empowerment and thus support evaluation that is more useful than identifying what participants feel or recall after the training.

Posttraining Activities

The phase that is explicitly training should set the stage for learners to continue with either or both of two follow-on phases; either of these may lead the learner to the other or to seek additional training. The posttraining activities that will support the change processes initiated by the learner include self-owned study/support groups and change projects.

Self-owned study/support groups. Learners who finish the course with a personal change agenda need and often want continuing support. The purpose of organizing one or a variety of small groups is to assist these individual efforts and to do so in a manner that affirms the value and necessity of collaborative and cooperative work. A group might consist entirely of learners who were together in a group during training, or it may be made up of one or several learners and others they invite who were not in the training. The trainer(s) may or may not have a role to play in helping the training participants identify potential foci of attention for follow-on groups.

Similarly, there are a range of ways that these groups may need or want assistance in their initial series of meetings to develop their internal guidelines and group-maintenance capabilities. These dynamics and decisions must be based on the nature of the learners, their group skills, the competencies of the trainer(s), the trust/safety levels that evolve during training, and the occupational context of the situation.

The essential aspect of the process by which these groups are created is that they are owned by their participants, who set the purpose and process to meet their needs and determine the life of the group. The women's movement provided us with thousands of examples that people can creatively and successfully use small-group dynamics to reconstruct the potentials of their lives. The relatively unsuccessful efforts of men's groups to apply this process persuaded me that we need to better understand this learning model to apply it to the wide variety of differing groups and needs. One challenge professionals face is increasing our capacity to launch and assist learner-designed and learner-controlled support groups. I suspect that we will do better to rename support groups and reconsider them as study groups, focusing attention on the self in both social and psychological contexts.

Change projects. Following the course, other learners will give priority to action to change some aspect of their occupational or socioeconomic situation; their objectives may range from seeking work elsewhere or modifying work rules and working conditions to becoming active in union, church, political, or other volunteer activities. As was the case with study groups, such activities offer some learners a suitable means to apply and continue their learning. Depending on what is appropriate to the specific training program, suitable follow-on project options can be a brief and relatively theoretical presentation or a topic of group discussion or can be integrated into the consideration of action learning, including extensive individual and group work on action plans and how these will be enacted. The trainer's purpose with respect to the change project follow-on is to design the training so that learners are most able and likely to apply what they have learned on their own behalf.

Challenges for Trainers

I think that stress training poses a variety of challenges for trainers. Some issues and problems posed for the trainer by stress training are general to training but are not less difficult and significant for having been noted for some time. The issues I consider especially significant for stress training include the following.

Some limitations we confront derive from our skills. Stress trainers are often more knowledgeable about and comfortable with psychological-change activities than with social-change dynamics; we need both. We must extend the professional practicum to deal with will and motivation so that training can replace exhortation and learners are functionally more able to enact their skills. We must also help obtain and then use innovative evaluation tools to improve stress training.

At another level, training for empowerment requires the trainer to have unusual clarity about his or her own power needs and how to manage them so that we are able to facilitate and not impair learners' experimenting with and acquiring the skills of power. Indeed, stress-training participants often exert great pressure in seeking solutions from us for their different problems. Dealing with our own stress and staying helpful and clear in the midst of stress training can be extraordinarily challenging.

Another set of limitations we encounter flow from the market for stress training. The most widespread demand is for quick, low-cost training that quiets employees' complaints, if not their stress. Such training may not change anything, but who evaluates noncognitive changes anyway? This conflict between need and demand suggests a number of practical and ethical issues about the services we can and should sell. How do we accurately represent what we can and cannot accomplish within our clients' time and cost limits? How do we balance the demand from employers to change workers with the need to change the workplace? Will market forces alone support the necessary research and development needed to evolve stress training and provide professionals with an appropriate and highly needed role in the prevention of psychological disorders in the workplace?

Finally, I want to conclude this list of challenges with the hope that others will be interested in collegial work to further elaborate, test, and correct this model and training designs derived from it. I would like to see and be part of a network or have available a clearinghouse that will specifically facilitate the systematic improvement of empowering stress training.

References

Argyris, C. (1985). *Strategy, change and defensive routines*. Boston: Pitman.

Brookfield, S. D. (1987). *Developing critical thinkers*. San Francisco: Jossey-Bass.

French, W. L., & Bell, C. H., Jr. (1984). *Organization development* (3rd ed.). Engelwood Cliffs, NJ: Prentice Hall.

Hobfoll, S. E. (1988). *The ecology of stress*. New York: Hemisphere.

Hollister, W. G. (1977). Basic strategies in designing primary prevention programs. In D. C. Klein & S. E. Goldston (Eds.), *Primary prevention: An idea whose time has come. Proceedings of the Pilot Conference on Primary Prevention, April 2–4, 1976* (DHEW Publication No. [ADM] 77–447, pp. 41–47). Washington, DC: U.S. Government Printing Office.

Israel, B. A., Schurman, S. J., & House, J. A. (1989). Action research on occupational stress: Involving workers as researchers. *International Journal of Health Services, 19,* 135–155.

Karasek, R., & Theorell, T. (1990). *Healthy work: Stress, productivity, and the reconstruction of working life*. New York: Basic Books.

Klitzman, S., House, J. S., Israel, B. A., & Mero, R. P. (1990). Work stress, nonwork stress, and health. *Journal of Behavioral Medicine, 13,* 221–243.

Martin, E. V. (1989). Worker stress: A practitioner's perspective. In L. R. Murphy & T. F. Schoenborn (Eds.), *Stress management in work settings* (pp. 135–156). New York: Praeger.

Mezirow, J., & Associates. (1990). *Fostering critical reflection in adulthood*. San Francisco: Jossey-Bass.

Murphy, L. R. (1984). Occupational stress management: A review and appraisal. *Journal of Occupational Psychology, 57,* 1–15.

Selye, H. (1956). *The stress of life*. New York: McGraw-Hill.

Tough, A. (1982). *Intentional changes: A fresh approach to helping people change*. Chicago: Follett.

15

Sheila C. Gehlmann

Individual Differences in Employee Stress as Related to Office Environment and Individual Personality Factors

Stress in the United States has been steadily increasing for quite some time. In fact, the 1980s were frequently referred to as the *stress decade* in countless newspaper articles on the subject. Excessive worker compensation claims, work-related deaths and injuries, and costs to companies in terms of absenteeism and health care have resulted in a national interest in examining the causes and prevention of stress in the workplace. One federal agency, the National Institute for Occupational Safety and Health has developed a national strategy for the prevention of work-related psychological disorders (Sauter, Murphy, & Hurrell, 1990).

The term *stress* as used in this chapter is defined as the various levels of mental and physical strain experienced by employees at work. As levels of stress increase, individuals may become distressed and exhibit certain responses or early warning signs of illness. The present knowledge of what causes work-related stress is incomplete. Many variables interact to cause stress-related injuries, and more knowledge is needed in regard to these variables and other sources of stress.

This study investigates the effects of work-space characteristics and individual personality traits (extroversion and sensation seeking) on job satisfaction and employee symptoms of stress.

Previous research on employee reactions to work-space characteristics has examined the effects of noise and distraction on performance and stress levels. The results of this research indicate that the level of job complexity plays a role in how much privacy is required in a work space. Generally, for employees performing mundane, repetitive tasks, it is beneficial to work in an open environment where interaction with others is possible. However, in more complex jobs, social interaction is distracting, and more privacy is needed (Sundstrom, Burt, & Kamp, 1980). Results of a study by Zalesny and Farace (1987) on traditional versus open office space showed that professional and managerial-level employees reported dissatisfaction, perception of crowding, and lack of privacy when working in an open space. However, clerical and secretarial staff were comfortable and satisfied with the open space in their work areas.

As Oldham and Fried (1987) noted, "research is needed on the impact of individual differences on the relations between workspace characteristics and employee responses" (p. 79). The results of Oldham and Fried's study indicated that the physical characteristics of the work environment have an impact on employee behavior and attitudes. Employees reacted in an adverse manner to social density, room darkness, few enclosures, and close proximity to others. This supports overstimulation theory, which argues that features of a physical environment can contribute to excessive stimulation, leading to stimulus overload. Employees experiencing stimulus overload have difficulty concentrating on their work and are thus dissatisfied and stressed. Oldham and Fried suggested that certain types of people may be more suited to working in a distracting environment than may others, and it would be helpful to determine the individual differences among those groups.

According to the optimal level of arousal theory, every individual strives to maintain his or her own optimal level of arousal; once the level is surpassed, further stimulation is uncomfortable and has adverse effects. The optimal level of arousal varies among individuals and has biological and psychological bases.

It has been suggested that the optimal level of arousal is the basis for sensation-seeking behavior. Duffy's general arousal theory, for example, holds that "individuals with fast alpha rhythm in the EEG (high arousal) are characterized as quick, impulsive, and variable in behavior, whereas those with slow alpha are rated as cautious and steady" (Zuckerman, 1979, p. 26).

Sensation seeking is defined by Zuckerman (1979) as "a trait defined by the need for varied, novel, and complex sensations and experiences and the willingness to take physical and social risks or the sake of such experience" (p. 10). Determining individual employees' levels of sensation seeking can be helpful for hiring and placement purposes if it is determined that there is a correlation between job satisfaction and the sensation-seeking trait. However, the problem with using a sensation-seeking scale in employment testing is that job applicants may fear that if they are viewed as sensation seekers, they may be disqualified from certain jobs.

As discussed in Zuckerman (1979), previous research supports the correlation between sensation seeking and occupational preference. The findings indicate that those higher on the sensation-seeking scale have a more extroverted temperament, are attracted to the social sciences, and have higher divorce rates (as compared with low sensation seekers in the physical sciences). Research has demonstrated that women scoring low in sensation seeking tend to choose such occupations as home-making and elementary school teaching. Police officers scored higher on sensation-seeking scales that did jailers. This relation between an individual's level of sensation seeking and choice of occupation suggests that sensation-seeking scales can be very useful in vocational testing. A high sensation seeker will choose an occupation that is adventurous and sometimes even dangerous (e.g., police work). A low sensation seeker will instead prefer a "safe" occupation (e.g., homemaking). A woman who chooses to stay at home will not have to struggle with outside pressures of the business world. On the other hand, a high sensation seeker who finds himself or herself in a less exciting role (e.g., homemaking) might be dissatisfied and miserable.

Another important variable to consider in the relation between office environment and stress is that of introversion/extroversion. In 1963, H. J. Eysenck and S. E. G. Eysenck proposed that the extrovert had a higher optimal level of stimulation that did the introvert. Thus, low levels of stimulation are perceived as pleasant by the introvert and unpleasant by the extrovert, whereas high levels of stimulation are uncomfortable for the introvert but still positive for the extrovert. In neurophysiological experiments, Zuckerman (1979) concluded that "introverts would be expected to show greater physiological response to low intensities of stimulation, and extroverts should show stronger responses at high intensities of stimulation" (p. 45).

The following hypotheses were formulated:

Hypothesis 1. The nature of the work interacts with the physical characteristics of the work environment to influence perceived stress and job satisfaction. Specifically, among employees performing tasks that require high concentration, the openness of the office will be associated with more symptoms of stress and less job satisfaction. For employees performing tasks that require moderate amounts of or no concentration at all, no relation between office space and stress or job satisfaction will be found.

Hypothesis 2. Personality traits of sensation seeking and introversion/ extroversion will interact with the physical work environment to affect employee stress and job satisfaction. Employees located in open offices who are high sensation seekers and introverts will experience more symptoms of stress and less job satisfaction in an open-space office environment than will low sensation seekers and extroverts. Employees located in closed offices who are high sensation seekers and introverts will experience less stress and higher job satisfaction than will low sensation seekers and extroverts.

Method

Research Setting and Subjects

The research was conducted in all offices of a small, private northeastern college. Data were collected from 87 full-time employees at all levels in both academic and nonacademic departments. The categorical breakdown was as follows: 31 professional staff (department heads, managers, directors, deans, etc.); 15 professors and research assistants; 20 secretaries and administrative assistants; and 21 unidentified. Educational levels were as follows: 15 high school graduates; 12 with "some college"; 56 college graduates; and 4 unidentified. The mean length of employment was 7 years. The sample worked in a variety of office environments at the college.

Procedure

A research questionnaire was distributed to groups of employees through interoffice mail. The questionnaire included questions that measured the subjects' levels of job stress, type of office space they work in, level of job satisfaction, and concentration required. A total of 300 questionnaires were distributed at a rate of 60 per week over a 5-week period because of limitations of resources. The response rate averaged 25 per week for 3 weeks then dropped to 5 per week in the last 2 weeks in which the questionnaires were returned. The respondents were very representative of the population under study.

The first page of the questionnaire explained the purpose of the study. A blank was provided for the employee's name, but this item was optional. Although it was emphasized that all data would be kept confidential, only 39 participants signed their name, and the majority (48) remained anonymous. Out of the 39 respondents who signed their names, 19 were male and 20 were female.

It is noteworthy that at the same time the questionnaire was distributed, the college was experiencing budget cuts and a reduction of staff. This created an overall lowering of morale, and the fear of losing jobs created a climate of distrust and paranoia. Under the circumstances, many people were afraid to answer the personal questions about their jobs and objected to those questions regarding illegal behaviors. Others claimed that the 7-page questionnaire took too much time to fill out. Some subjects suggested the response rate would have been greater had the questionnaire been shorter and less threatening. This attitude was confirmed by the fact that in the 3 weeks prior to the layoffs, 15–30 questionnaires per week were returned, and in the 2 weeks following the layoffs, less than 10 questionnaires were returned. (Recall that the same number of questionnaires were distributed each week over the 5-week period.)

As part of the questionnaire, the subjects completed a sensation-seeking scale consisting of 36 questions that measured each individual's level of sensation seeking. Zuckerman's (1979) sensation-seeking measure was used because its construct validity has been demonstrated in other research: "The results are consistent with prior conceptions of the sensation seeker as one who is independent, unconventional, and low in social values or conformity, needs variety, and does not value order or routine" (Zuckerman & Link, 1968, p. 424). Zuckerman found the internal reliability of the sensation-seeking scale to be as high as .86 in some sections. This study used the shorter of two versions, the internal reliabilities of which ranged from .83 to .86 using coefficient alpha.

After the sensation-seeking scale, the subjects completed a 27-item version of H. J. Eysenck's and S. E. G. Eysenck's (1963) introversion/extroversion scale. Coefficient alpha was used to test for internal consistency, resulting in a reliability of .97. The construct validity of Eysenck's scale has been demonstrated in other research (S. G. Eysenck & H. J. Eysenck, 1969).

When using these types of measures, there is always a possibility that subjects' responses on the first scale could bias their responses on the second scale. Because the sensation-seeking measure was of greater importance to the study than was the introversion/extroversion measure, it was administered first.

Measures

Workspace characteristics. Subjects rated their office space on a 4-point scale as "other" (1), open (2), semi-private (3), or private (4). All cases of either missing data or an office space rating of 1 were eliminated from the study, reducing sample size to 80.

Features of the job. Subjects rated the amount of concentration required by their jobs. Scores ranged from 1 to 5 (5 = *highest amount of concentration*).

Reactions. Subjects indicated their symptoms of stress and the frequency of the symptoms on an 8-item psychophysiological stress scale developed by the author. This measure contained similar items as other, more standard stress scales that are longer, more comprehensive, and more time consuming. In standard stress scales, psychological and physiological symptoms are generally listed in separate sections of the instrument. However, for the purpose of this study, only certain job-related symptoms were targeted. Those symptoms included headaches, backaches, occasional emotional outbursts, drinking more than usual, smoking more than usual, overall fatigue, not wanting to come to work, and have considered quitting. The stress measure was tested for internal consistency, using coefficient alpha, resulting in a reliability of .92.

Each subject's level of stress was calculated by summing up the points assigned to the answers given. The level of stress was rated on a 3-point scale (3 = *highest amount of stress*).

The questionnaire also included a measure of job satisfaction derived from the Job Diagnostic Scale (Oldham & Hackman, 1980). The 14-item scale was tested for internal consistency, using coefficient alpha, resulting in a reliability of .97. Subjects were asked to rate the 14 items on a 7-point scale ranging from 1 (*extremely dissatisfied*) to 7 (*extremely satisfied*). The points were then added together and divided by the total number of questions answered to determine the level of job satisfaction.

Personality characteristics. Sensation seeking was measured by scoring the subjects' responses to Zuckerman's (1979) sensation-seeking scale. The higher the score, the higher the level of sensation seeking.

A 27-item version of H. J. Eysenck and S. E. G. Eysenck's (1963) introversion/extroversion scale was scored to provide the measure introversion/extroversion. High scores indicated extroversion, and low scores indicated introversion.

Statistical Analyses

Work-space type percentages were calculated, the distribution of which was as follows: 50% of the sample (40 people) worked in private office space, 23.8% (19 people) worked in semiprivate office space, and 26.3% (31 people) worked in open office space.

To test the hypotheses, two types of analysis were used. To test Hypothesis 1, zero-order correlations between all variables for the entire sample were examined, and the means and standard deviations were calculated. Then, the sample was divided into two groups determined by the amount of concentration required in the job. Scores of 4 were placed in the high-concentration group, and scores of 1, 2, and 3 were placed in the low-concentration group. Zero-order correlations between all variables were examined, and the means and standard deviations were calculated for each group separately.

The second type of analysis used a multiple regression. Two stepwise regression analyses were calculated to examine the variance explained by the interactions among the variables. The first stepwise regression predicted stress by introducing the variables space, concentration, and Cross1 (Space × Concentration interaction). The second stepwise regression predicted satisfaction by introducing the variables space, concentration, and Cross1.

To test Hypothesis 2, four stepwise regression analyses were calculated. The first one used stress as the dependent variable and introduced the independent variables space, sensation seeking, and Cross1; the second one used stress as the dependent variable and introduced the independent variables space, extroversion, and Cross2 (Space × Extroversion interaction). The third and fourth stepwise regression analyses were conducted in the same way, only substituting job satisfaction as the dependent variable in the equation.

Results

Table 1 shows the correlations between variables or all subjects in the sample. In general, the correlations were both positive and negative and were statistically

Table 1. Means, Standard Deviations, and Intercorrelations Among All Variables for All Subjects

Variable	M	SD	1	2	3	4	5	6
1. Satisfaction	4.7	1.0	—					
2. Space	3.2	0.8	.01	—				
3. Concentration	3.3	0.9	−.24*	.21*	—			
4. Sensation seeking	12.8	5.7	−.13	.26*	.19	—		
5. Extroversion	13.4	6.4	.25*	.06	.00	.22*	—	
6. Stress	1.2	0.5	−.43*	−.21*	.13	.01	−.13	—

Note. $N = 80$. The sample included 29 professional staff, 15 professors and research assistants, 18 secretaries and administrative assistants, and 18 unidentified. Fourteen were high school graduates, 11 had "some college," 51 were college graduates, and 4 were unidentified. The mean length of employment was 6.5 years.
*$p ≤ .05$.

Table 2. Means, Standard Deviations, and Intercorrelations Among All Variables for the High-Concentration Group

Variable	M	SD	1	2	3	4	5	6
1. Satisfaction	4.6	1.0	—					
2. Space	3.4	0.8	−.05	—				
3. Concentration	4.0	0.0	.00	.00	—			
4. Sensation seeking	13.3	5.1	−.14	.21	.00	—		
5. Extroversion	14.8	6.4	.19	.10	.00	.33*	—	
6. Stress	1.1	0.5	−.40*	−.20	.00	−.05	−.18	—

Note. $N = 37$. The sample included 18 professional staff, 6 professors and research assistants, 4 secretaries and administrative assistants, and 9 unidentified. Four were high school graduates, 4 had "some college," 27 were college graduates, and 2 were unidentified. The mean length of employment was 6.5 years.
*$p ≤ .05$.

Table 3. Means, Standard Deviations, and Intercorrelations Among All Variables for the Low-Concentration Group

Variable	M	SD	1	2	3	4	5	6
1. Satisfaction	4.8	0.9	—					
2. Space	3.0	0.8	.16	—				
3. Concentration	2.6	0.8	−.29*	.06	—			
4. Sensation seeking	11.9	5.8	−.01	.24	.15	—		
5. Extroversion	12.1	6.1	.38*	−.04	−.34*	.14	—	
6. Stress	1.1	0.4	−.43*	−.29*	.29*	−.04	−.06	—

Note. $N = 43$. The sample included 11 professional staff, 9 professors and research assistants, 14 secretaries and administrative assistants, and 9 unidentified. Ten were high school graduates, 7 had "some college," 24 were college graduates, and 2 were unidentified. The mean length of employment was 6.5 years.

*$p \le .05$.

significant. There were significant negative correlations between stress and satisfaction and between stress and space. This provides partial support for Hypothesis 1. The correlation between satisfaction and space was not significant and therefore does not support the hypothesis.

Table 2 shows the correlations among all variables in the high-concentration group. As shown, the correlations were generally insignificant. There was a significant negative correlation between stress and satisfaction, but the correlations between stress and space and between satisfaction and space were not significant. These findings do not support the hypothesis.

Table 3 shows the correlations among all variables in the low-concentration group. Although the correlations were generally low, there were some significant relations. There were significant relations between stress and satisfaction and between stress and space. This does not support the hypothesis.

The findings were not consistent with what was expected. Although the subjects in open offices experienced higher stress than did those in closed offices, this was more true of people in the low-concentration group than in the high-concentration group.

Stepwise Regression Analyses (Hypothesis 1)

The first stepwise regression analysis was performed on the independent variables space, concentration, and Cross1 to predict the dependent variable stress. The significance level was set to .15 for all stepwise regressions. The variables space and concentration met the significance level for entry into the model, which explained 5% and 8% of the variance, respectively. Space was marginally significant, and concentration was not significant in the model.

The second stepwise regression analysis was performed on the same independent variables space, concentration, and Cross1 to predict the dependent variable satisfaction. The only variable that met the significance level for entry into the model was concentration, which explained 6% of the variance in job satisfaction. These results provided partial support for Hypothesis 1.

Stepwise Regression Analyses (Hypothesis 2)

Four stepwise regression analyses were performed to test the contributions of the interactions of the personality variables sensation seeking and extroversion to the amount of stress or job satisfaction experienced.

For the model Stress = Space × Sensation Seeking × Cross1, only the variable space entered the model, and it explained 5% of the variance in stress.

For the model Stress = Space × Extroversion × Cross2, only the variable space entered the model, and it explained 5% of the variance in stress.

For the model Satisfaction = Space × extroversion × Cross2, only the variable extroversion entered the model, and it explained 6% of the variance in satisfaction.

In the fourth stepwise procedure, no variables met the significance level for entry into the model Satisfaction = Space × Sensation Seeking × Cross1. The results of these analyses provide only partial support for Hypothesis 2.

Ideally, to test Hypothesis 2, the data should be broken down into another subset containing only those subjects who fell into the categories of high sensation seeking/introvert and low sensation seeking/extrovert. However, the sample size for this group was too low to derive any significant conclusions. Only 4 subjects in this group were in the high sensation seeking/introvert category, and this finding supports Zuckerman's (1979) theories on the sensation-seeking trait. High sensation seeking usually corresponds to extroversion as opposed to introversion, because risk takers generally have outgoing, "extroverted" personalities. Extroverts also have a higher optimal level of arousability than introverts, which corresponds to a higher level of activity in the nervous system.

Discussion

The results of this study support previous studies in finding that more open office space was associated with higher reported stress levels (Hypothesis 1). Moreover, when the low-concentration and high-concentration groups were examined separately, the results were not significantly different, indicating that the openess of the office contributes to stress regardless of the level of concentration required by the job. This implies that there were other factors contributing to individual stress levels of the subjects. For example, in this study, the uncertainty of employment conditions in the organization could have accounted for some of the employee stress. Keita and Jones (1990) stated that "poorly managed organizational change can be hazardous to the physical and psychological health of workers, whether they are blue-collar workers or corporate executives . . . excessive, poorly managed change can make people sick, especially when unpredictability and uncertainty become the norm" (p. 1139).

Previous research has also found the issue of individual control over workload to be a contributing factor in employee stress. In this study, on an exploratory basis, the subjects rated the amount of control they had over their daily work schedules. A stepwise regression analysis of these data was performed, which showed a significant negative relation between control and stress ($r = .03$, $p < .05$). That is, the more control over daily work schedule, the lower the stress experienced. This finding supports a good deal of previous research on control.

The results of this study support the findings of population-density studies as well. Positive correlations have repeatedly been found between perceptions of crowding and higher incidence of mental illness and alcoholism. For example, in a study by Kamal (1988), 200 people from both densely populated and sparsely populated areas were interviewed and evaluated for psychiatric symptoms. A positive correlation was found between high feelings of crowding and high frequency of mental illness. In comparison, open-style, or "bullpen," office environments are often very crowded, with limited personal space. Because there is a positive correlation between open offices and high stress levels, it is possible that crowding may be a factor.

Because the sample size was too small to properly test the second hypothesis, the study needs to be replicated in other organizations. From the results of this study, I can conclude only that there is a significant relation between stress and space and that extroverts experience higher job satisfaction than do introverts.

The interaction of individual personality characteristics and job placement should not be overlooked. As concluded by the U.S. National Academy of Science's Institute of Medicine (Levi, 1990)

> if a mismatch exists between the worker and the job, if the worker is (or feels) unable to control his or her work conditions, or if he or she copes ineffectively or lacks social support, then pathogenic reactions may occur. These reactions may be emotional, cognitive, behavioral, and physiological. Under some conditions of intensity, frequency, and duration, and in the presence of some and absence of other interacting variables, these reactions might lead to disease—physical, mental, or both (p. 1143)

Drug and alcohol abuse are also cited as problems experienced as a result of "displacement." Zuckerman, (1979) said it well: "One thinks of the millions of workers performing repetitive and minimal manual operations on a production line, the deadening monotony of the 'paper shuffling' of the clerical worker, and the rows of IBM card punchers. Whereas such jobs may be satisfactory to low sensation seekers, one would guess that even moderate-level sensation seekers would find such work aversive" (p. 251).

The absenteeism and alcoholism among production-line workers is an index of the severity of the restriction of their operations. For these workers, their work is most definitely not "play" (Zuckerman, 1979). Thus, high sensation seekers in a clerical role are displaced to begin with, and that is part of the reason for their distress. The other part comes from the noise and distraction they invariably experience from being in an office environment, which decreases their productivity.

As reported in Table 1, the correlation between extroversion and job satisfaction was .25, a significant and surprising finding. There was, however, no significant relation between introversion/extroversion and concentration, nor between personality and amount of stress experienced.

Additional research is needed on individual differences in employee stress as related to office design. This study indicates a potential relation between personality characteristics (sensation seeking and extroversion) and level of stress experienced depending on what type of office space is occupied. To explore this possibility, larger sample sizes are needed.

Certain people and types of jobs may be better suited to an open-style office than others. Another factor to consider is that of the ability to screen out noise and distraction. Some individuals are able to screen out what is going on around them enough to get the job done, whereas others find that the activity around them actually interferes with their job performance. If this is so, the office environment can be changed to suit the job demands or needs of the individuals performing the jobs. Making these types of adjustments can lower turnover, increase productivity and job satisfaction, and lower stress.

References

Eysenck, H. J., & Eysenck, S. E. G. (1963). *Eysenck Personality Inventory.* San Diego, CA: EDITS.

Eysenck, S. G., & Eysenck, H. J. (1969). *Personality structure and measurement.* San Diego, CA: Robert A. Knapp.

Kamal, P. (1988). Feelings of crowding and mental illness. *Indian Psychological Review, 33,* 32–40.

Keita, G. P., & Jones, J. M. (1990). Reducing adverse reaction to stress in the workplace. *American Psychologist, 45,* 1137–1141.

Levi, L. (1990). Occupational stress: Spice of life or kiss of death? *American Psychologist, 45,* 1142–1145.

Oldham, G. R., & Fried, Y. (1987). Employee reactions to workspace characteristics. *Journal of Applied Psychology, 72,* 75–80.

Oldham, G. R., & Hackman, J. R. (1980). *Work redesign.* Reading, MA: Addison-Wesley.

Sauter, S., Murphy, L. R., & Hurrell, J. J. (1990). Prevention of work-related psychological disorders: A national strategy proposed by the National Institute for Occupational Safety and Health. *American Psychologist, 45,* 1146–1157.

Sundstrom, E., Burt, R. E., & Kamp, D. (1980). Privacy at work: Architectural correlates of job satisfaction and job performance. *Academy of Management Journal, 23,* 101–117.

Zalesny, M. D., & Farace, R. V. (1987). Traditional versus open offices: A comparison of sociotechnical, social relations, and symbolic meaning perspectives. *Academy of Management Journal, 30,* 240–259.

Zuckerman, M. (1979). *Sensation seeking: Beyond the optimal level of arousal.* Hillsdale, NJ: Erlbaum.

Zuckerman, M., Buchsbaum, M. S., & Murphy, D. L. (1980). Sensation seeking and its biological correlates. *Psychological Bulletin, 88,* 187–214.

Zuckerman, M., & Link, K. (1968). Construct validity for the sensation-seeking scale. *Journal of Consulting and Clinical Psychology, 32,* 420–426.

Part IV

Distress in the Workplace

Introduction

The six chapters in this section focus on expressions of individual and organizational distress that require some type of treatment. In reference to the stages of prevention as described in the model presented in Chapter 1, this section of deals with tertiary prevention. The types of distress addressed in the four assessment chapters include accidents, employee theft, depression, and sick building syndrome. The intervention chapters deal with tertiary prevention strategies, namely, posttraumatic crisis intervention and a broad-based employee assistance program.

Assessment Chapters

In Chapter 16, Jones and Boyce review the literature linking stress to employee counterproductivity, an underresearched outcome in occupational stress studies. Most of the research reviewed deals with employee theft, although studies on violence and alcohol abuse are also discussed. Beyond demonstrating a relation between perceived job stress and counterproductive behaviors, the authors suggest that perceived job stress interacts with employee attitudes (e.g., tolerance of theft) to predispose employees to engage in counterproductive behavior. Implications for organizational stress management programs are offered.

Guastello uses data collected from 290 bus operators to test a nonlinear model of employee ill-health and occupational accidents in Chapter 17. Postulating that accidents and stress-related disorders share a common underlying dynamic, Guastello demonstrates how catastrophe theory provides a more accurate prediction of accidents and stress-related disorders than do linear regression models. The author also finds support for the proposition that stress plays a key role in the epidemiology of accidents and, accordingly, for the view that stress and accidents can be studied from a common theoretical framework.

Chapter 18, by Schonfeld, examines methodologic problems inherent in stress studies that use a self-report methodology for gathering stressor and health information. Focusing on elementary school teachers, Schoenfeld reviews prior stress research and identifies methodologic problems, such as the confounding among stressor and strain measures and the inadequacies of stress/burnout measures. He then elaborates alternative assessment strategies that bypass these methodological problems. One such alternative, neutral self-reports of working conditions coupled with independent assessments of depressive symptoms, was used by the author in a longitudinal study of graduates from the City University of New York. Analyses of the data revealed that neutral self-reports of job conditions, more so than preemployment levels of depressvie symptomatology, were significantly related to reported depression.

In Chapter 19, Hedge addresses a prevalent workplace problem: "sick building syndrome." Questionnaire data on indoor air climate were obtained from 3,155 workers from 18 office buildings in the Eastern U.S.A. Questionnaires measuring boredom, job stress, concentration, job satisfaction, and health complaints were obtained from a sample of 30 workers. Analyses indicated that, although measures of indoor air quality did not correlate with health complaints, measures of job stress, job satisfaction, and hours of video display terminal use were significant predictors. The authors speculate that physiological stress reactions mediated the effects of ambient environmental conditions on workers.

Intervention Chapters

The intervention chapters in this section focus on tertiary prevention strategies. Chapter 20, by Braverman, describes a crisis intervention model for dealing with psychological trauma (e.g., posttraumatic stress disorder) in the workplace. The crisis intervention model seeks to foster the emotional well-being of both managerial and nonmanagerial workers. Braverman includes case studies to illustrate the problem of workplace trauma and to discuss aspects of the intervention model. The proposed model includes four elements: crisis readiness, management consultation, group meetings with affected employees, and follow-up. Finally, Braverman integrates the crisis intervention model with findings from mainstream job stress research.

Philips and Muchinski describe the employee assistance program (EAP) at Metropolitan Life Insurance Company in Chapter 21. A history of "employee services" at MetLife is presented, beginning in 1919 as a pioneer EAP. The program's relation with the National Committee on Alcoholism and Alcoholics Anonymous in the 1960s, and its recent upgrade in 1989, provides valuable insights for the reader. The variety of services provided to employees, including assessment, referral, and crisis intervention are presented, as well as the program philosophy, the relationship with management, and the multidisciplinary composition of the EAP staff. MetLife's program is not offered as a prescription for other companies but rather as one example of EAP structure and function within one organizational setting.

16

John W. Jones and Michael W. Boye

Job Stress and Employee Counterproductivity

Occupational stress can be thought of as job-related discomfort or illness that people experience because of their work situations (Beehr, 1991). This discomfort may manifest itself in a variety of ways, including coronary heart disease, headaches, restless sleep, fatigue, other somatic symptoms, and decreases in individual performance on the job (Boye, 1990; Cooper & Marshall, 1976; Friend, 1982; Hendrix, 1985; House, 1974; Jamal, 1984; Jones, Barge, Steffy, Fay, Kuntz, & Wuebker, 1988; Quick & Quick, 1984; Spector, Dwyer, & Jex, 1988). The symptoms of job stress may be psychological, psychophysiological, or behavioral in nature (Quick & Quick, 1984). Individual and organizational costs associated with job stress include low worker morale, high job turnover, employee alcohol and drug misuse, and interpersonal conflicts, to name a few (Jones, 1980a, 1980b, 1980c, 1980d; Maslach, 1976). These and other job stress–related costs are specified in Table 1.

Researchers have begun to examine the relation between job stress and employee counterproductivity (Jones, 1980e, 1980f, 1991). This chapter examines the relation of job stress to three types of employee counterproductivity—on-the-job violence, alcohol misuse, and theft—with major emphasis given to the job stress–employee theft relation.

Job Stress, Violence, and Alcohol Misuse

Much of the early research on the job stress–employee counterproductivity relation was conducted with police personnel. Increased feelings of job stress have been found to correlate significantly with various forms of counterproductive behavior among police officers, especially on-the-job violence and alcohol misuse (cf. Keating, 1979; Powers & Kutash, 1980; Schlesinger & Revich, 1980).

Using a valid and reliable stress scale for police personnel, Jones (1980h) found that increased job stress levels significantly correlated in the predicted direction with the number of times an officer felt like criminally assaulting a suspect (see Jones, 1991 for a review of instruments that assess levels of job stress). This violence criterion measure was shown to be important given that it correlated significantly with the number of times an officer used his or her weapon (e.g., gun, club) on a suspect ($r = .60$, $p < .05$). Additionally, job stress levels significantly correlated

Table 1. The Personal and Organizational Effects of
Occupational Stress

Effects	
Personal	
Alcohol abuse	Anxiety
Drug abuse	Psychosomatic diseases
Emotional instability	Eating disorders
Lack of self-control	Boredom
Fatigue	Mental illness
Marital problems	Suicide
Violence	Insecurity
Depression	Health breakdowns (cardiovascular, etc.)
Insomnia	Irresponsibility
Frustration	
Organizational	
Thefts	Inflated health-care costs
Accidents	Unpreparedness
Reduced productivity	Lack of creativity
High turnover	Increased sick leave
Increased errors	Premature retirement
Absenteeism	Organizational breakdown
Disability payments	Disloyalty
Sabotage	Job dissatisfaction
Damage and waste	Poor decisions
Replacement costs	Antagonistic group action

with the number of times an officer shouted at, pushed, or shoved a suspect ($r = .28$, $p < .05$). Jones (1991) postulated that the unavoidable physical and psychological discomfort that accompanies ongoing job stress predisposes afflicted police officers to engage in violent on-the-job behavior. This hypothesis on the stress–aggression relation is consistent with the pain–aggression models formulated by Berkowitz (1978) and Ulrich (1966).

Regarding the relation between job stress and alcohol misuse, Jones (1980b) also found that police officers' scores on a job stress scale significantly correlated with the number of alcoholic drinks they consumed during paid work hours ($r = .31$, $p < .05$). Overall, the more stressed an officer perceived himself or herself to be, the more drinking in which he or she was likely to engage. On-the-job alcohol use during paid work hours was considered delinquent behavior because it lowers a worker's effectiveness, vigilance, and ability to perform (Hegarty, 1979). Whenever police officers are under the influence of alcohol during work hours, they are "at risk" to jeopardize their own lives, as well as the lives of civilians and their fellow officers.

Jones's (1980b) findings support other research on the job stress–alcohol misuse relation (e.g., Jones, 1980c, 1980d). Possibly, the more stress an officer perceives himself or herself to be under at work, the more likely he or she is to use alcohol as a "coping drug," especially if he or she has learned to drink to reduce feelings of distress.

The job stress–violence and job stress–alcohol misuse relations are not re-stricted to police officers. Jones (1981c) found similar significant correlations be-tween job stress and both violence and alcohol misuse in the workplace in samples of customer-service and retail workers. These correlations tended to range from .30 to .50 (ps < .05). The relation of job stress to many forms of employee counterpro-ductivity (e.g., high absenteeism, serious on-the-job mistakes, medical malpractice) has been documented (Edelwich & Brodksy, 1980; Jones, 1980c, 1980d; Jones et al., 1988; Pines & Aronson, 1981), but additional research is warranted.

Job Stress and Employee Counterproductivity

A body of research is evolving that examines the relation of job stress to employee counterproductivity (cf. Jones, 1985). Employee counterproductivity is widespread and rapidly growing in the United States (Slora, 1991). Morgernstern (1977) esti-mated that 30% of all business failures each year are due to employee theft and dishonesty. A recent estimate reported that losses incurred from various forms of employee counterproductivity were as much as $50 billion in 1986 and that this figure is growing at a rate of 15% annually (Kuhn, 1988). The relation of job stress to employee theft has been documented in five studies summarized below. All of these studies used the Employee Attitude Inventory (London House, 1980a) to obtain a valid and reliable measure of job stress.

Employee Attitude Inventory

ALl subjects anonymously completed the Employee Attitude Inventory (EAI) in the five studies reviewed below. The EAI is a valid and reliable organizational climate survey that is given to current employees. It includes a Dishonesty or Theft Attitudes scale, a Violence scale, a Drug-Abuse scale, a Job Satisfaction scale, and a Job Stress scale (cf. London House, 1980b, 1980c). Only the Dishonesty scale and the Job Stress scale were included in the analyses in the five studies examined below.

Dishonesty scale. The Dishonesty scale includes test items that measure em-ployees' attitudes, values, perceptions, and opinions toward theft. Attitudes and cognitions toward theft have significantly correlated with employees' actual ad-missions of theft (e.g., Jones, 1980a, 1981a; Jones & Terris, 1991; McDaniel & Jones, 1986; Terris, 1979; Terris & Jones, 1980). Higher scores on the Dishonesty scale indicate that an employee has more tolerant attitudes and cognitions toward em-ployee theft and is more prone to steal when both the need and opportunity to steal are present. For instance, an employee who scores high on this scale (a) is less punitive toward theft, (b) engages in many of the common rationalizations for theft, (c) exhibits more interthief loyalty, (d) suspects more employees of stealing at work, (e) projects more theft in others, (f) tends to be more vulnerable to peer pressure to steal, (g) is aware of more theft among co-workers, and (h) ruminates more often over theft as compared with an individual who scores low on this scale (cf. Jones & Terris, 1991). The Spearman-Brown split-half reliability of the EAI Dishonesty scale is .88.

Job stress scale. The EAI Job Stress scale was designed to measure the job stress and burnout syndrome as defined by Maslach (1976, 1978), Pines and Aronson (1981), and Jones (1980b, 1980c, 1980d, 1981c, 1982). The Job Stress scale was designed to assess stress levels in employees who have constant exposure to customers, clients, patients, co-workers, and so on in the course of their work.

Parenthetically, Jones (1981b) found that each item on the EAI Job Stress scale significantly correlated with the total score of the Staff Burnout scale for health professionals ($ps < .01$). Both the reliability and the validity of the burnout scale have been thoroughly established and presented elsewhere (Jones, 1980g, 1980h, 1982). The total EAI Job Stress scale scores were correlated with the total scores from the Burnout scale to establish the construct validity of the former measure. The relation was highly significant, $r(87) = .75, p < .001$.

The EAI Job Stress scale assesses adverse cognitive reactions (e.g., "How often do you think to yourself that this company is a bad company to work for?"), affective reactions (e.g., "How often do you feel frustrated and really bored at work?"), behavioral reactions (e.g., How often do you find that you try to avoid talking with customers?"), and psychophysiological reactions (e.g., "How often do you get headaches on the job?") that are associated with employees perceiving continuous high levels of job stress. The Job Stress scale also tends to measure (a) extreme disgruntlement with work and the resulting anger toward management (e.g., "Has this company treated you unfairly?"; "How often do you become frustrated and angry by the stupid mistakes made by management?"); (b) psychological and interpersonal tension (e.g., "Is your job causing problems for you with your spouse or family?"; "Does worrying about your job cause you to lose sleep?"); (c) physical illness and distress (e.g., "How often have you had to stay home from work because of colds, flu, and other illnesses?"; "Do you often feel tired at work?"); and (d) unprofessional and discourteous relationships with customers or clients (e.g., "Do you find that you have a tendency to treat customers in a detached and almost mechanical fashion?"; "How often do you become irritated and angry with customers or clients?"). Higher scores on the Job Stress scale indicate greater perceptions of stress by respondents (cf. Jones, 1982). The Spearman-Brown split-half reliability of this scale is .87.

The Job Stress–Employee Counterproductivity Relation

In the first study conducted by Jones (1985), the EAI was administered to 248 current employees in 74 convenience stores in eight regional areas. Job stress ($r = .68, p < .05$) and more tolerance-related attitudes toward theft ($r = .67, p < .05$) were significantly correlated in the expected direction, with average inventory shortages in the eight regions. Management from the convenience store chain acknowledged that they were having more loss-control problems in the convenience stores that were classified by EAI scores as being high-stress stores. Hence, the relation between job stress and inventory shortages was established in this initial study.

In the second study (Lavelli, 1986), 507 current retail employees anonymously completed the EAI and a comprehensive criterion checklist that measured different types of counterproductivity (e.g., theft, rule breaking, poor performance). Results showed that the Dishonesty scale scores were significantly related to theft admissions ($r = .38$, $p < .01$), illegitimate absenteeism ($r = .22$, $p < .01$), and misuse of company materials and time ($r = .34$, $p < .01$). The Job Stress scale scores were significantly related to theft admissions ($r = .38$, $p < .05$), illegitimate absenteeism ($r = .33$, $p < .01$), and emotional outbursts during the work day ($r = .35$, $p < .01$). The interaction between dishonesty and job stress was not studied.

Social facilitation theory. The following research not only assists in the assessment of the effects of job stress on employee counterproductivity but also provides partial support for Zajonc's (1965) social facilitation (SF) theory, which postulates that the presence of others has a distinct effect on an individual engaging in any given activity. This effect of the presence of others simultaneously engaging in the same activity as the given individual is that within the individual, a state of arousal is brought about. The individual's arousal state increases the probability that well-learned responses will be elicited. These responses can either facilitate or be detrimental to performance in regard to the activity. Thus, this theory can be viewed as consisting of two distinct components: (a) A state of arousal is brought on within the individual as a result of the presence of others simultaneously engaging in the same activity, and (b) well-learned responses are likely to be made by the individual as a result of this state of arousal.

Partial support for the SF theory would be obtained by results lending support for either of these two components of the theory. The following research partially supports Zajonc's (1965) theory by supporting the second component listed above, that arousal tends to elicit well-learned responses from individuals. Job stress was the variable theorized to function as the source of arousal in the following research. The measure of job stress in this research was the EAI Job Stress scale, as previously described.

Job stress–employee counterproductivity research supportive of SF theory. In a third study, Jones (1981a) found that EAI Job Stress scale scores significantly correlated with nurses' anonymous theft admissions (cf. Jones, 1980e, 1980f). Nurses who were seriously stressed reported more theft of general hospital supplies, medical supplies, and drugs or medication than did nonstressed nurses. (The correlations ranged from .20 to .30 and were all statistically significant at the .05 level or less.) On the partial basis of SF theory, Jones (1981a) also examined the interactive effects of (a) the nurses' attitudes toward theft, (b) their job stress levels, and (c) their anonymous admissions on an employee theft questionnaire. Based on SF theory, it was suspected that increased arousal (in this case, brought on by job stress), functions so as to solidify a person's response hierarchy, making well-learned responses more dominant than less well-learned ones. Therefore, SF theory implies that employees with favorable attitudes toward theft who are experiencing heightened levels of job stress should steal significantly more cash and merchandise than should nonstressed employees with equally favorable attitudes toward theft. However, workers with intolerant attitudes toward theft who are experiencing high stress levels should not greatly differ in their theft behavior from workers with equally unfavorable attitudes toward theft who are not experiencing high levels of job stress.

As hypothesized, Jones (1981a) found that the high stress/high dishonesty group made significantly greater theft admissions for a 6-month period than did the high stress/low dishonesty group, the low stress/high dishonesty group, or the low stress/low dishonesty group. The latter three groups did not significantly differ in their theft admissions. These results, which provide preliminary support for Zajonc's (1965) SF theory, are presented in Figure 1.

In a fourth study, Jones (1981b) examined the relation of job stress and dishonesty with employee theft using a more heterogeneous sample of 89 hospital workers. This study was an attempt to replicate the results of the Jones (1981a) research. The sample obtained by Jones (1981b) included 58 nurses, 13 social workers, 7 physicians, 3 clerical workers, and 8 "unspecified" cases. Subjects anonymously completed the EAI and a criterion checklist. This checklist asked respondents for the estimated dollar amount of all hospital supplies, medical supplies, drugs or medications, and other miscellaneous items they had taken without authorization from their hospitals in the past 3 months.

Results indicated that both job stress ($r = .39$, $p < .05$) and attitude toward theft ($r = .45$, $p < .05$) were significantly related to employee theft admissions among hospital workers. These results were similar to the Jones (1981a) findings. Jones (1981b) pointed out that the job stress–employee theft relation suggests that employee thieves on the average tend to be more discouraged about their work and more often think about quitting than do more honest employees. Employee thieves also tend to experience more emotional or physical exhaustion because of the pressures of their jobs and tend to feel more anger toward and frustration with customers, co-workers, and supervisors compared with more honest employees. An in-depth explanation of the dishonesty–employee theft relation has been given elsewhere (cf. Jones & Terris, 1991; Terris, 1979).

To further test Zajonc's (1965) SF theory, Jones (1981b) computed median splits on both the Dishonesty scale scores and the Job Stress scores. Four groups of hospital workers were delimited for this post-hoc analysis. They were the low stress/low dishonesty group ($n = 27$), the high stress/low dishonesty group ($n = 17$), the low

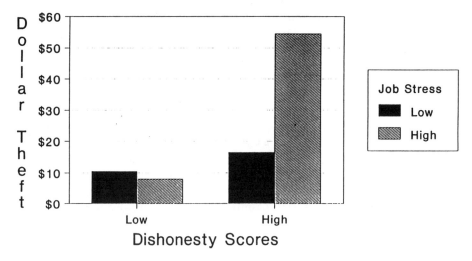

Figure 1. Employee theft as a function of dishonesty and stress (average theft admissions reported for a 6-month period).

stress/high dishonesty group (n = 17), and the high stress/high dishonesty group (n = 28). In addition, total theft disclosures greater than $10 per 3-month period were operationally defined as *serious theft admissions*.

Jones (1981b) found that 39% of the high stress/high dishonesty group made serious theft admissions compared with 12% of the low stress/high dishonesty group, 6% of the high stress/low dishonesty group, and none of the low stress/low dishonesty group. Testing the difference between these proportions, Jones found that the high stress/high dishonesty group statistically differed at the .05 level of confidence or less from the other three groups. The latter three groups did not statistically differ regarding the proportion of employees who made serious theft admissions. The relation found by Jones is presented in Figure 2.

Jones's (1981b) findings shown in Figure 2 replicate previous research (Jones, 1981a) and support Zajonc's (1965) SF theory. Job stress conceivably acted as a form of arousal that activated and facilitated dominant theft responses. Therefore, among groups of dishonest workers who had very tolerant attitudes toward theft, dishonest workers who experienced relatively high stress levels admitted to more theft than did dishonest employees who experienced relatively low levels of stress. Conversely, job stress apparently did not serve to "ignite" and "fuel" theft behavior among workers with low theft dispositions. This pattern of results was found among employees who admitted to theft admissions greater than $10 in a 3-month period.

Jones and Boye (1990) conducted yet another study to confirm Jones's previous research, using a much larger sample. In this study, the EAI was again used to explore relations among job stress, attitudes toward theft, and employee theft admissions (cf. Jones, 1985; London House, 1980a). Again, on the basis of Zajonc's (1965) SF theory, one can infer that increased arousal solidifies a person's response hierarchy, making well-learned, dominant responses more probable than those responses that are not as well-learned. On the basis of this theory, employees with tolerant attitudes toward theft who are experiencing excessive job stress should report stealing significantly more cash and merchandise than should employees not

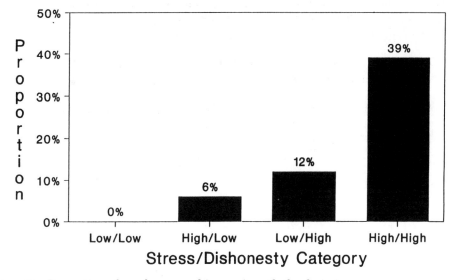

Figure 2.   Proportion of employees making serious theft admissions.

suffering from stress but who hold equally tolerant attitudes toward theft. However, workers with intolerant attitudes toward theft who are perceiving high levels of stress would not be expected to differ greatly in their theft admissions from workers with equally intolerant theft-related attitudes who are not overly stressed. That is, an interaction between theft tolerance and job stress would be predicted.

In the fifth study, 3,468 retail employees completed the EAI. Dishonesty scores and Job Stress scores were computed. Stanine scores were analyzed. Employees were grouped into one of three categories based on their Dishonesty scale stanine scores: (a) low theft tolerance (stanine = 1, 2, 3); (b) medium theft tolerance (stanine = 4, 5, 6); or (c) high theft tolerance (stanine = 7, 8, 9). Employees were also grouped into one of three categories on the basis of their Job Stress stanine scores: (a) low job stress (stanine = 1, 2, 3); (b) medium job stress (stanine = 4, 5, 6); and (c) high job stress (stanine = 7, 8, 9).

The dependent variable was the total dollar amount of all employee theft an employee admitted to for the past three years. On a research questionnaire, the employees estimated the total dollar amount of cash and merchandise they stole, including the cost of all company merchandise they gave to their families and friends without authorization. An overall theft estimate was then computed. Approximately 33% of the total sample made theft admissions that ranged from $25 to $3,500 ($M$ = $181.90, SD = $333.50). These estimates are consistent with other research (cf. Slora, 1991).

The Jones and Boye (1990) results are summarized in Table 2 and Figure 3. Inspection of these analyses reveals that the main effects (i.e., Job Stress and Dishonesty scale groupings) were statistically significant, yet the three levels of Dishonesty scores yielded a much higher F ratio than did the three levels of Job Stress scores. Additionally, the eta statistic for the Dishonesty variable equaled .30, whereas eta for the Job Stress variable equaled .19. The multiple correlation equaled .32.

As predicted, a statistically significant Job Stress × Theft Tolerance interaction was obtained. Inspection of Figure 3 shows that employees were more likely to steal significant amounts of company assets when they were both stressed and tolerant of on-the-job theft. These findings provide further support for Zajonc's (1965) SF theory and replicate and extend previous research by Jones (1985).

Job stress–employee theft relation: A preliminary explanation. Overly stressed workers experience a great deal of anger, resentment, frustration, and disappoint-

Table 2. Analysis of Variance: Effects of Job Stress and Theft Tolerance on Average of Employee Theft in Past 3 Years

Source of Variation	df	F	p
Main effect	4	98.983	.000
Job Stress	2	24.408	.000
Theft Tolerance	2	126.820	.000
Stress × Tolerance	4	4.644	.001
Explained	8	51.814	.000
Residual	3,459		
Total	3,467		

Note. From Jones and Boye (1990).

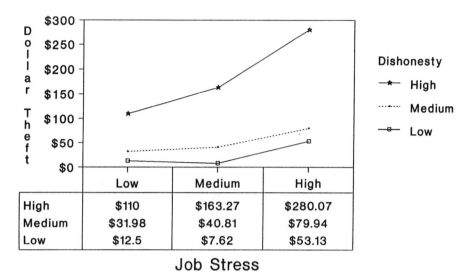

	Low	Medium	High
High	$110	$163.27	$280.07
Medium	$31.98	$40.81	$79.94
Low	$12.5	$7.62	$53.13

Job Stress

Figure 3.   Job stress, theft tolerance, and employee theft (average theft for the past 3 years).

ment toward their employer and company. These feelings can be consciously or unconsciously experienced (Haack & Jones, 1981). Research suggests that overly stressed workers are also more disloyal toward their company than are unstressed workers (Techman & Jones, 1981). These stress-related feelings of anger, frustration, and disloyalty may build up over time and can result in counterproductive activity against the company. This may be especially likely when employees perceiving high job stress levels project blame for their resultant feelings onto management. It is possible, therefore, that some highly stressed workers steal as a form of revenge and as a way to release pent-up feelings of anger and frustration.

Terris and Jones (1981) found that revenge is a major motivation for employee theft. Excessive feelings of job stress can provide a powerful predisposition to steal. Stress-related motivations to steal can conceivably weaken, erode, and eventually override the cognitive controls that prevent theft, especially if an employee already has tolerant attitudes toward theft activity (cf. Jones, 1981b). Schlesinger and Revich (1980) presented case studies that support this tentative hypothesis. Moreover, if employee theft by workers experiencing high job stress levels is an aggressive act of revenge against management, then the job stress–employee theft relation can be partially explained using Berkowitz's (1978) pain–aggression model. That is, job stress is a form of emotional pain, and employee theft is an act of aggression.

Implications and Conclusions

This review chapter has presented research demonstrating that higher levels of job stress are associated with higher levels of on-the-job counterproductive behaviors. The findings from the aforementioned studies suggest that offering organizational stress management programs to distressed workers might aid security professionals in better controlling employee theft. By helping workers to cope effectively with job stress, organizations may reduce the tendencies of theft-tolerant employees to act out their frustrations in dishonest or counterproductive ways. These findings also have implications for the use of preemployment integrity testing (cf. Jones & Terris, 1991). That is, if applicants who are highly tolerant of theft can be identified prior to hiring, this identification would hold promise for the hiring of employees who are much less likely to engage in employee theft, regardless of their level of stress. Research is needed to determine the viability of these recommendations.

A number of studies highlighted in this chapter indicate that job stress levels and specific attitudes (e.g., tolerence of theft) interact to predispose employees to engage in a variety of counterproductive on-the-job behaviors. These results suggest the possibility that job stress levels may interact with a number of attitudinal variables to increase the likelihood that employees may also become involved in a wide variety of other activities leading to many other negative personal and or-ganizational outcomes. For example, an individual who has an attitudinal predis-position toward on-the-job illicit drug or alcohol use may indeed engage in this type of behavior when experiencing continuing high levels of job stress. Research indi-cates that high levels of job stress are associated with lower levels of job performance (e.g., Boye, 1990; Friend, 1982; Jamal, 1984; Jones et al., 1988; Spector et al., 1988). Research also shows that certain individuals in the population may be more sus-ceptable to a variety of negative outcomes as a result of certain attitudinal predis-positions (e.g., Brown & Joy, 1985; Joy, 1988). Additionally, it has been empirically demonstrated that a number of other variables, including leadership sensitivity, feedback from others, education, and personality type, may interact with job stress to bring about a variety of negative outcomes (e.g., Arsenault & Dolan, 1983; Be-night & Kinicki, 1988; Vredenburgh & Trinkaus, 1983). These outcomes include absenteeism and reduced job performance. Thus, there is reason to suppose that attitudinal variables may also interact with job stress to predispose employees to act in ways that bring about personal and organizational costs, although future research is needed to determine the extent of this interaction.

It may well be that a large number of attitudinal variables interact with job stress to predispose individuals to engage in behavior (e.g., violence, theft, high accident risk behavior) that results in negative individual and organizational out-comes (e.g., damage to company property, theft-related losses, accidents and inju-ries). In the Jones and Boye (1990) study, those who admitted to the highest amounts of dollar theft were those who were experiencing high job stress levels and who also possessed attitudes of high tolerance toward theft. Boye (1989) found that job stress and attitudes toward on-the-job illicit drug and alcohol use interacted to predict those who were likely to engage in on-the-job drug or alcohol use or to come to work hungover from illicit drugs or alcohol. Those experiencing higher job stress levels and who were more tolerant of the use of illicit drugs or alcohol in the workplace engaged in more frequent illicit drug- or alcohol-related behavior in the workplace than did other respondents.

Future research might also focus on the interrelations among job stress, atti-tudes toward safety, and on-the-job accidents. Much has been written regarding the relation of job stress to accidents (e.g., Murphy, DuBois, & Hurrell, 1986; Steffy, Jones, Murphy, & Kunz, 1986). The direct and indirect costs of on-the-job accidents to employers is often phenomenal. In 1989 alone, the cost of work accidents was estimated at $48.5 billion (National Safety Council, 1990). An application of the job stress–attitudes interaction theory discussed above and derived from the research reviewed in this chapter is the prevention of on-the-job accidents.

A number of studies have indicated that on-the-job accident frequency can be predicted by safety-related attitudinal factors (e.g., Boye, Joy, Slora, & Jones, 1990; Rafilson & Rospenda, 1988). Individuals possessing specific safety-related attitudes (e.g., "There is nothing I can do to prevent accidents") have been shown to be more likely than others to become involved in accidents on the job.

It is likely that job stress and safety-related attitudes interact to predispose high-risk employees (i.e., those who are stressed and lack safety consciousness) to become involved in on-the-job accidents. Research is needed to determine the extent of this interaction because an interaction of this type would hold significance for accident reduction. That is, to reduce workplace accidents, this research application would suggest that job applicants be assessed to determine their attitudinal predispositions toward on-the-job accident involvement. Once this attitudinal predisposition is known, the organization can act accordingly regarding accident prevention. If high accident risk applicants are hired, they can be placed in positions that do not expose incumbents to higher job stress levels, thus potentially greatly reducing organizational risk exposure.

Research has indicated that an employee perceiving high stress levels is at risk to prematurely quit, misuse alcohol or drugs during paid work hours, and heatedly argue with customers, co-workers, and supervisors (Jones, 1980a, 1980b, 1980c, 1980d). By identifying these severely stressed workers, interviews may be conducted with them to determine the extent of their stress-related problems, as well as to possibly develop and implement an intervention to reduce their perceived stress levels. Psychological research on job stress and employee counterproductivity is needed to document the costs of stress to organizations and businesses. This research could provide the impetus for sufficient resources to be allocated to identify, reduce, and eventually prevent job stress in organizations.

References

Arsenault, A., & Dolan, S. (1983). The role of personality, occupation and organization in understanding the relationship between job stress, performance and absenteeism. *Journal of Occupational Psychology, 56*, 227–240.

Beehr, T. A. (1991). Stress in the workplace: An overview. In J. W. Jones, B. D. Steffy, & D. W. Bray (Eds), *Applying psychology in business: The handbook for managers and human resource professionals* (pp. 709–714). Lexington, MA: Lexington Books.

Benight, C. C., & Kinicki, A. J. (1988). Interaction of Type A behavior and perceived controllability of stressors on stress outcomes. *Journal of Vocational Behavior, 33*, 50–62.

Berkowitz, L. (1978). Whatever happened to the frustration–aggression hypothesis? *American Behavioral Scientist, 32*, 691–708.

Boye, M. W. (1989). [Job stress and substance use-related attitudes: Their effects upon on-the-job substance use and hangover.] Unpublished raw data.

Boye, M. W. (1990). [Job stress and job performance]. Unpublished raw data.

Boye, M. W., Joy, D. S., Slora, K. B., & Jones, J. W. (1990). *The relation of the Employee Safety Inventory to driving accidents and related costs at a national trucking company* (ESI Technical Report No. 13). Park Ridge, IL: London House.

Brown, T. S., & Joy, D. S. (1985). *The predictive validity of the Personnel Selection Inventory in the grocery industry* (PSI Technical Report No. 48). Park Ridge, IL: London House.

Cooper, C. L., & Marshall, J. (1976). Occupational sources of stress: A review of the literature relating to coronary heart disease and mental health. *Journal of Occupational Psychology, 49,* 11–28.

Edelwich, J., & Brodsky, A. (1980). *Burn-out: Stages of disillusionment in the helping professions.* New York: Human Sciences Press.

Friend, K. E. (1982). Stress and performance: Effects of subjective work load and time urgency. *Personnel Psychology, 35,* 623–633.

Haack, M., & Jones, J. W. (1981, November). *Projective drawings as aids in diagnosing burnout.* Paper presented at the First National Conference on Burnout, Philadelphia.

Hegarty, C. (1979). *Alcoholism today: The progress and the promise.* Minneapolis, MN: CompCare.

Hendrix, W. H. (1985). Factors predictive of stress, organizational effectiveness, and coronary heart disease potential. *Aviation, Space, and Environment Medicine, 56,* 654–659.

House, J. S. (1974). Occupational stress and coronary heart disease: A review and theoretical integration. *Journal of Health and Social Behavior, 15,* 12–27.

Jamal, M. (1984). Job stress and job performance controversy: An empirical assessment. *Organizational Behavior and Human Performance, 33,* 1–21.

Jones, J. W. (1980a). Attitudinal correlates of employees' deviance: Theft, alcohol use, and non-prescribed drug use. *Psychological Reports, 47,* 71–77.

Jones, J. W. (1980b, November). *Correlates of police misconduct, violence and alcohol use on the job.* Paper presented at the 6th Annual Conference of the Society of Police and Criminal Psychology, Atlanta, GA.

Jones, J. W. (1980c, October). *Diagnosing and treating staff burnout among health professionals.* Paper presented at the American Medical Association's 4th National Conference on Medical Care and Health Services in Correctional Institutions, Chicago.

Jones, J. W. (1980d, September). *A measure of staff burnout among health professionals.* Paper presented at the 88th Annual Conference of the American Psychological Association, Montreal, Quebec, Canada.

Jones, J. W. (1980e). *Preliminary manual: The Staff Burnout Scale for Health Professionals.* Park Ridge, IL: London House.

Jones, J. W. (1980f). *The Staff Burnout Scale for Health Professionals.* Park Ridge, IL: London House.

Jones, J. W. (1980g, May). *The Staff Burnout Scale: A validity study.* Paper presented at the 52nd Annual Conference of the Midwestern Psychological Association, St. Louis, MO.

Jones, J. W. (1980h). *The Staff Burnout Scale for Police and Security Personnel.* Park Ridge, IL: London House.

Jones, J. W. (1981a). Attitudinal correlates of employee theft of drugs and hospital supplies among nursing personnel. *Journal of Nursing Research, 30,* 349–351.

Jones, J. W. (1981b, August). *Dishonesty, staff burnout, and employee theft.* Paper presented at the 89th Annual Conference of the American Psychological Association, Division of Industrial Psychology, Los Angeles.

Jones, J. W. (1981c). *Is employee violence contagious?* Unpublished manuscript.

Jones, J. W. (1982). *The burnout syndrome: Current research, theory, interventions.* Park Ridge, IL: London House.

Jones, J. W. (1985). Dishonesty, staff burnout, and employee theft. In W. Terris (Ed.), *Employee theft: Research, theory and applications* (pp. 67–80). Park Ridge, IL: London House.

Jones, J. W. (1991). Assessing stress in the workplace. In J. Jones, B. Steffy, & D. Bray (Eds.), *Applying psychology in business: The handbook for managers and human resource professionals* (pp. 741–749). Lexington, MA: Lexington Books.

Jones, J. W., Barge, B. N., Steffy, B. D., Fay, L. M., Kunz, L. K., & Wuebker, L. J. (1988). Stress and medical malpractice: Organizational risk assessment and intervention: *Journal of Applied Psychology, 73,* 727–735.

Jones, J. W., & Boye, M. W. (1990, November). *Job Stress and employee counterproductivity.* Paper presented at the meeting of the American Psychological Association in conjunction with the National Institute for Occupational Safety and Health, Washington, DC.

Jones, J. W., & Terris, W. (1991). Personnel selection to control employee theft and counterproductivity. In J. Jones, B. Steffy, & D. Bray (Eds.), *Applying psychology in business: The handbook for managers and human resource professionals* (pp. 851–861). Lexington, MA: Lexington Books.

Joy, D. S. (1988). *Reliability and validity of a pre-employment honesty test.* Manuscript submitted for publication.

Keating, J. P. (1979). Environmental stressors: Misplaced emphasis. In I. G. Saranson & C. D. Spielberber (Eds.), *Stress and anxiety* (Vol. 6, pp. 55–66). New York: Wiley.

Kuhn, R. (1988). Psychological tests reduce counterproductive acts by employees. *Assets Protection, 9,* 9–12.

Lavelli, M. (1986). *Psychological predictors of employee counterproductivity.* Unpublished master's thesis, DePaul University, Chicago.

London House. (1980a). *The Employee Attitude Inventory.* Park Ridge, IL: Author.

London House. (1980b). *The Personnel Selection Inventory.* Park Ridge, IL: Author.

London House. (1980c). *Test administration and analysis instruction manual: The London House Personnel Selection Inventory.* Park Ridge, IL: Author.

Maslach, C. (1976). Burned-out. *Human Behavior, 5,* 16–22.

Maslach, C. (1978). Job burnout: How people cope. *Public Welfare 1978, 36,* 56–58.

McDaniel, M. A., & Jones, J. W. (1986). A meta-analysis of the validity of the Employee Attitude Inventory theft scales. *Journal of Business and Psychology, 1,* 31–50.

Morgernstern, D. (1977). *Blue collar theft in business and industry.* Springfield, VA: National Technical Information Service.

Murphy, L. R., DuBois, D., & Hurrell, J. J. (1986). Accident reduction through stress management. *Journal of Business and Psychology, 1,* 5–18.

National Safety Council. (1990). *Accident facts* (1990 ed.). Chicago: Author.

Pines, A., & Aronson, E. (1981). *Burnout: From tedium to personal growth.* New York: Free Press.

Powers, R. J., & Kutash, I. L. (1980). Alcohol abuse and anxiety. In I. Kutash & L. Schlesinger (Eds.), *Handbook on Stress and Anxiety* (pp. 329–343). San Francisco: Jossey-Bass.

Quick, J. C., & Quick, J. D. (1984). *Organizational stress and preventive management.* New York: McGraw-Hill.

Rafilson, F., & Rospenda, K. (1988). *Concurrent validation study of the Safety scale* (ESI Technical Report No. ESI-S005). Park Ridge, IL: London House.

Schlesinger, L. B., & Revich, E. (1980). Stress, violence and crime. In I. Kutash & L. Schlesinger (Eds.), *Handbook on Stress and Anxiety* (pp. 174–188). San Francisco: Jossey-Bass.

Slora, K. B. (1991). An empirical approach to determining employee deviance base rates. In J. W. Jones (Ed.), *Preemployment honesty testing: Current research and future directions* (pp. 21–38). Westport, CT: Greenwood.

Spector, P. E., Dwyer, D. J., & Jex, S. M. (1988). Relation of job stressors to affective, health, and performance outcomes: A comparison of multiple data sources. *Journal of Applied Psychology, 73,* 11–19.

Steffy, B. D., Jones, J. W., Murphy, L. R., & Kunz, L. (1986). A demonstration of the impact of stress abatement programs on reducing employees' accidents and their costs. *American Journal of Health Promotion, 1,* 25–32.

Techman, C., & Jones, J. W. (1981). *Executive burnout and corporate loyalty.* Unpublished manuscript.

Terris, W. (1979). Attitudinal correlates of employee integrity: Theft-related admissions made in preemployment polygraph examinations. *Journal of Security Administration, 2,* 38–39.

Terris, W., & Jones, J. W. (1980). Attitudinal and personality correlates of theft among supermarket employees. *Journal of Security Administration, 3,* 65–78.

Terris, W., & Jones, J. W. (1981, October). *Psychological factors related to employee theft in the convenience store industry.* Paper presented at the 7th Annual Conference of the Society of Police and Criminal Psychology, Baton Rouge, LA.

Ulrich, R. E. (1966). Pain as a cause of aggression. *American Zoologist, 6,* 643–662.

Vredenburgh, D. J., & Trinkaus, R. J. (1983). An analysis of role stress among hospital nurses. *Journal of Vocational Behavior, 22,* 82–95.

Zajonc, R. A. (1965). Social facilitation. *Science, 149,* 269–274.

17

Stephen J. Guastello

Accidents and Stress-Related Health Disorders Among Bus Operators: Forecasting With Catastrophe Theory

There is a growing awareness among accident specialists that accidents can be studied as if they were diseases (Bertazzi, 1989; Kemp, 1967; Leigh, 1986, Vilardo, 1988; Waller, 1987). By doing so, epidemiological modeling concepts that work for diseases can be used to predict and control accidents as well. To some writers, the accident–disease crossover amounts to "collecting carefully controlled observations, formulating hypotheses, and designing studies capable of proving or disproving these hypotheses" (Coleman, 1981, p. 91). Others focus attention on the spread of occupational or public health hazards caused by industrial safety considerations (Bertazzi, 1989; Leigh, 1986). A third point of view is concerned with the development of mathematically defined models that can be applied to both accident and disease investigations (Kemp, 1967). The three views are better thought of as compatible rather than as mutually exclusive.

Efforts in mathematical modeling of disease functions, which has been an active pursuit since Farr (1840), can be summarized into four major classes of ideas: specification of (a) background variables, (b) trigger variables, (c) a mechanism of contagion, and (d) mathematical models that tie everything together. This chapter describes the use of epidemiological concepts to predict accidents and stress-related medical disorders for 290 bus operators from a large midwestern metropolitan area. The qualitative variables involved will be described first, then the mathematical model. The model was used to forecast accidents as well as stress-related medical disorders.

The Occupational Hazards Survey

The Occupational Hazards Survey (OHS) is a tool for diagnosing the causes of accidents, usually in manufacturing settings (D. D. Guastello & S. J. Guastello, 1987a, 1987b; S. J. Guastello & D. D. Guastello, 1988). Accident control strategies based on OHS recommendations have been successful in reducing accident rates by an average of 30% by the end of a 6-month period (S. J. Guastello, 1989). In this

Portions of this work were completed under a Marquette University Summer Faculty Fellowship grant.

study, the OHS and the diagnostic paradigm were adapted for use with bus operators. Predictor variables were safety management, danger ratings, transit experience and age, stress from physical sources, stress from social sources, anxiety,
environmental hazards, and transit hazards. Transit hazards included assaults to
and insults on the operator and the need to reprimand passengers for various infractions of bus rules. Criterion variables were transit accidents and medical disorders that are generally thought to be somewhat stress related (cf. Quick & Quick,
1984): heart disease, high blood pressure, kidney disorder, cancer, nervousness,
insomnia, carpal tunnel syndrome, and ulcers.

Two lines of logic suggest that stress-dependent effects, notably accidents, are
subject to a contagionlike escalation process (S. J. Guastello, Ikeda, & Connors,
1985). One view addresses individual stress buildup; the other addresses transpersonal stress buildup. With regard to the within-person view, stress is thought to be
a predictor of accidents, on the one hand (Levenson, Hirschfeld, Hirschfeld, & Dzubay, 1983; McCarron & Haakonson, 1982), and a consequence of them, on the other
(Ersland, Weisaeth, & Sund, 1989; Weisaeth, 1989a, 1989b, 1989c). It follows that
each successive accident predisposes a person to greater amounts of risk for future
calamities. With regard to transpersonal buildup, Holmes and Rahe (1967) showed
that an individual's stress level can accumulate as a result of illness, accidents, or
deaths of family members and friends.

Catastrophe Theory

Catastrophe theory is a general systems theory for describing and predicting discontinuous changes in events (Poston & Stewart, 1978; Stewart & Peregoy, 1983;
Thom, 1975; Zeeman, 1977). Its central proposition is the classification theorem,
which holds that, given certain constraints, all discontinuous changes of events can
be modeled by one of seven elementary topological forms. The forms are hierarchical
and vary in the complexity of the behavior spectrum they encompass. The cusp
model (Figure 1) is the simplest catastrophe model that describes the change in
behavior of a system between two equilibrium states. The cusp model has two control
parameters. The bifurcation parameter (b) describes how large the difference (e.g.,
in accident rate) is between the two stable states. The asymmetry parameter (a)
describes the proximity to a set of points in the system where a sudden and dramatic
change takes place.

The cusp surface is three-dimensional and features a two-dimensional manifold
(unfolding). At low values of b, change between the two stable states of behavior is
smooth; at high values of b, it is discontinuous. At low values of a, changes occur
around the lower mode and are relatively small in size. At middle values of a,
changes occur between models and are relatively large. At high values of a, changes
occur around the upper model and are again small.

The potential function for the cusp model is

$$f(y) = y^4/4 - by^2/2 - ay. \tag{1}$$

Taken together, the surface is a set of points where

$$df(y)/dy = y^3 - by - a. \tag{2}$$

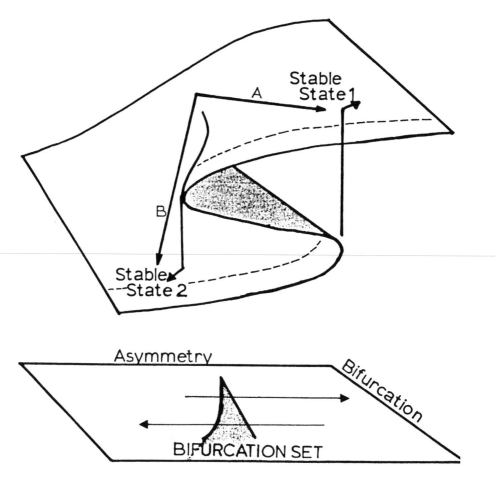

Figure 1. The canonical cusp model showing two stable states of behavior, asymmetry and bifurcation axes, gradients from the cusp point (A and B), and repeller region (shaded). (The path of the control point [explained in text] is shown in two dimensions by the horizontal arrows on the bifurcation set and in three dimensions by the dotted line on the response surface.)

The cusp surface appears in the upper portion of Figure 1. Change in the behavior of the subject is denoted by the path of a control point over time (dotted line). The point begins at some high level of a behavior, or behavior of one type, and is observed in that model for a period of time. During that time, its coordinates on a and b are changing until suddenly it reaches a fold line and drops to the lower value of the behavior, which is qualitatively different, where it remains. Reversing direction, the point is observed in the lower mode until coordinates change to a critical pair of values, at which moment the point jumps back to the upper mode. There are two thresholds for behavior change, one ascending and one descending. The shaded area of the surface is the region of inaccessibility in which very few points fall. The cusp and higher order models also have a control surface on which the bifurcation set is drawn, mapping the unfolding of the surface in (for the cusp) two dimensions. When highlighted on the response surface itself, the cusp bifurcation set induces two diverging response gradients, which are joined at a cusp point. The diverging gradients are labeled A and B on the cusp surface in Figure 1. Behavior at the cusp point is ambiguous; a classic example is the dog who sits in one position rather than attacking or running away from a threatening stimulus (Zeeman, 1977). The diverging gradients represent varying degrees of probability that the dog might attack or run away. Statistically, one would observe an antimode between the two stable states that would correspond to the shaded region of the surface (Cobb, 1978). The cusp point is the *point of degenerate singularity* and is the most unstable point on the surface. Analogous points exist in other catastrophe models as well.

For theorists in many scientific disciplines, catastrophe theory offers a qualitative theory of discontinuous change, equilibria, and stability. For the applied scientists, it offers a systematic methodology for the prediction of change. Thom's (1975) theorem and the models themselves are powerful theoretical tools because they reduce a potentially large class of change functions to a mere few prototypes. Furthermore, catastrophe theory contributes to efficient psychological theories because catastrophe models invoke principles that are already known to describe a wide range of physical and social science phenomena (S. J. Guastello, 1987c).

The Accident Model

Occupational accidents are interpreted as oscillations between two stable states: one with high risk where accidents occur and one with low risk where accidents do not occur. The asymmetry parameter is composed of hazard and danger variables. The bifurcation parameter is composed of safety management, stress, anxiety, and related variables. Asymmetry and bifurcation parameters are analogous to background and trigger variables, respectively (S. J. Guastello, 1988a, 1989). As ambient hazards increase, the outcome (to an individual worker or a group of workers) does not change until a critical point is reached. At that moment, risk increases suddenly and dramatically. The disparity of the difference in risk depends on the strength of the bifurcation parameter, which is a collection of stress indicators in the accident model. If the hazard and danger levels are now allowed to decrease, no change in risk level is observed until a different critical point is reached, at which time risk returns to its lower modal value.

The mechanism for contagion is best shown on the bifurcation plane by the zigzag path (Figure 2). The occurrence of an accident increases stress levels in the individual in question and in the immediate work group. Thus, with each successive accident, the control point veers further and further out along the manifold, instead of returning to the lower mode by following a path defined by a constant level of b.

Trajectories between the cusp point and the modes form gradients which can be defined behaviorally. If one observes the process underlying a single accident, the surface modalities represent either an accident or a lack of one. The gradients, then, represent underlying subcritical risk, perhaps expressed as the number of near-miss accidents. When one observes a distribution of group accident rates, the gradients are observed as low and sometimes zero-level accident rates.

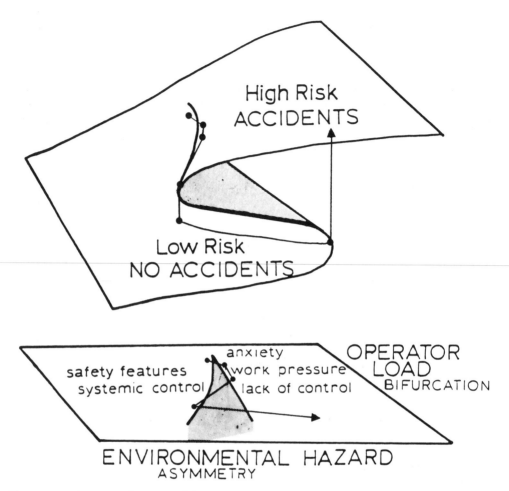

Figure 2. The general cusp model for the accident process as a function of hazard and load (or stress) levels. (Systematic control and safety features, or lack thereof, are characterized as gradients on the cusp surface. The zigzag paths on the bifurcation set and response surface represent an escalating process produced by the inherent contagion mechanism [Hopf bifurcation].)

Validity of the Cusp Model

The validity of the cusp catastrophe for modeling accident processes has been observed in three studies. The evaluation of the accident control strategy using the OHS, described earlier, was supplemented with catastrophe analysis. Initial levels of hazard or danger did not affect rates of improvement. The squared multiple correlation .44 was obtained for the cusp model of the accident process, which compared favorably to the squared multiple correlation .17 for the best log-linear alternative (S. J. Guastello, 1989). The stress and anxiety variables, which cause human error to occur, also predispose the group to strong improvements once a control procedure is initiated.

In another application, the cusp model was used to assess change in group accident rates at a large steel mill (over 9,500 workers represented) as a function of organization subgroup size (bifurcation) and specific work location (asymmetry). Group accident rates were changing *ad libitum* rather than as a result of a control program. Once again the squared multiple correlation for the cusp model was between 42% and 562% greater than those obtained for comparable linear models (S. J. Guastello, 1988a).

Cusp manifolds have been observed in morbidity statistics for people employed in 9 out of 10 industrial classes from an insurance database representing 23 million years of life exposed (S. J. Guastello, 1987b). The exceptional class was financial services, where accidental deaths and injuries are rarely the result of differential occupational exposures. It was also found that, when accidental deaths and all other claims were considered as separate dependent measures, the geometry of accident risks expanded to the six-dimensional mushroom catastrophe model.

Hypothesis Testing

The hypothesized cusp catastrophe function for transit accident is stated statistically as

$$z_2 - z_1 = B_0 + B_1 z_1^3 + B_2 z_1^2 + B_3 b z_1 + B_4 a, \tag{3}$$

$$z_1 = (y_i - \lambda)/\tilde{\sigma} \tag{4}$$

in which, y is a raw score for accident frequency, λ is the estimate of the location parameter, $\tilde{\sigma}$ is the estimate of the scale parameter, z_2 is number of bus accidents, z_1 is number of car accidents, b is the bifurcation parameter, and a is the asymmetry parameter (S. J. Guastello, 1982, 1987a, 1988a). Several survey variables may contribute to a parameter, each with its own weight. Also, a research variable may contribute to both parameters; such a variable would be interpreted as a gradient.

The location parameter is a constant subtracted from y to center the data in the range of the function. This manipulation has the effect of improving the fit of the theoretical model and, to some extent, reducing the correlation between polynomial terms in the regression equation (Darlington, 1990). Imperfections in the estimations of λ are accounted for, again to an extent, by the inclusion of z_1^2 in Equation 3.

The scale parameter is the variation around a statistical mode rather than the variation around the mean. The division of $\tilde{\sigma}$ in Equation 4 converts y to a common scale, the statistical moment. Although correlations involving linear variables are impervious to transformations of location and scale, the same is not true for polynomial or other multiplicative functions (Darlington, 1990; Evans, 1991).

The squared multiple correlation for the cusp hypothesis (Equation 3) is calculated then compared against two linear models involving the same survey variables:

$$z_2 - z_1 = B_0 + B_1 b + B_2 a \tag{5}$$

and

$$z_2 = B_0 + B_1 z_1 + B_2 b + B_3 a \tag{6}$$

Because the cusp hypothesis involves evaluating and comparing theoretical models, the forward entry method of multiple regression is usually preferred (Darlington, 1990; Graybill, 1976; S. J. Guastello, 1982, 1987a, 1988a). The following applications use a variation of the forward entry procedure that allows researchers to test the alternative hypotheses that variables originally thought to contribute to the b parameter also contribute to a and vice versa.

Analysis for Bus Operators

Subjects were 290 bus operators from a midwestern city. Of that number, 238 subjects completed all the measures needed for these analyses. The variable that was most often missing was the subject's age. Each subject received a letter explaining the purpose of the study and a statement that the confidentiality of all responses were ensured. All data were collected on a voluntary and anonymous basis. Union assistants were available to assist operators in the completion of the survey.

All variables under study were contained in the OHS for transit operators, which contained the OHS variables described earlier, plus transit hazards (e.g., assaults on the operator or other passengers and the need to reprimand passengers for various rule infractions), and vehicle crashes, which were the dependent measures.

Criteria were measured on the basis of frequency using the same scale that was used for transit hazards (0 = none, 1 = once in 3 years, 2 = twice, 3 = three times, 4 = four or more times). The two accident measures were the number of times the operator was involved in a traffic accident while driving the bus during the previous 3 years and the number of times the operator was involved in an accident while driving his or her personal auto during the previous 3 years. An accident was interpreted as harm to the bus, to the operator, or to another vehicle.

The dependent measure for the catastrophe analysis was the difference in accident scores (bus minus personal automobile). This is a variation from other applications of the catastrophe model in which the same accident rate is measured at two points in time. In this instance, there were two points in time represented: all time on the job and all time off the job. The operator is thus viewed as oscillating between two stable and disparate levels of risk, and one would surmise that accident rate would fluctuate accordingly.

Equation 4 was applied to each y_i within separate points in time. The location parameter was set equal to the lower limit of y, which was zero. The scale parameter was the estimated variation around the modes, which was calculated as follows. The two conceptual modalities were no accident and the presence of at least one accident. For the distribution of scores for the Time 1 and Time 2 health measures, the calculation of scale was

$$\tilde{\sigma} = \frac{\sqrt{\sum\sum (y_{m-}^{m+} - m_i)^2}}{N - 1} \tag{7}$$

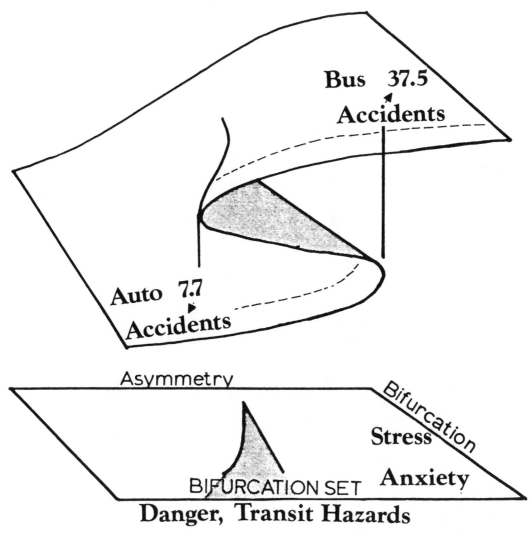

Figure 3. Cusp model obtained for traffic accidents. (Accident rates are expressed in incidents per 100 person years of exposure.)

where m_i is the modal value of y, which was either 0.00 or 1.00 for this problem. y_{m-}^{m+} is the range of y in the neighborhood of m_i. For this problem, $y = 0$ for all cases in the neighborhood of $m_i = 0$, and $1 < y < 8$ in the neighborhood of $m_i = 1.00$. The sums of squares were summed over cases within modes, then summed over modes.

Physical stressors, social stressors, and anxiety were the hypothesized bifurcation variables. Age and experience, danger, environmental hazards, and transit hazards were tested as asymmetry variables.

The cusp catastrophe model was built in a four-stage process that constituted a hierarchical stepwise regression analysis. First, all variables from the hypothesized model were entered in a forward (or simultaneous) order: the cubic potential,

Table 1. Summary of Regression for Cusp and Linear Control Models for Transit Accidents

Independent measure	Stepwise R	Shrunken R^2	Weight t	Model F
	Linear difference control model, $R^2 = .20$			
Transit hazards	.38	.14	6.29****	39.57****
All variables	.45	.17	na	6.25****
	Pre–post linear control model, $R^2 = .26$			
Transit hazards	.43	.18	5.45****	na
Car accidents	.45	.20	2.24**	na
Anxiety	.47	.21	2.10**	20.82****
All variables	.51	.23	na	7.89****
	Cusp model, $R^2 = .63$			
Transit hazards	.21	.05	7.32****	na
z_1^2	.71	.50	-8.64****	na
z_1^* Social Stress	.74	.55	-3.19***	na
z_1^3	.80	.63	7.56***	na

Note. z_1 = auto accidents transformed for locomotion and scale.
*$p < .10$.   **$p < .05$.   ***$p < .01$.   ****$p < .001$.

Table 2. Bivariate Correlations Among OHS Variables and Number of Accidents

Variable	1	2	3	4	5	6	7	8	9
1. Age, experience	—								
2. Safety management	-.09	—							
3. Danger	.25**	-.23**	—						
4. Anxiety	-.08	-.15**	.31**	—					
5. Social or job-related stress	-.08	-.10	.15*	.42**	—				
6. Physical stressors	.07	-.19**	.33**	.32**	.23**	—			
7. Environmental hazards	.01	-.12*	.12**	.21**	.13*	.45**	—		
8. Transit hazards	-.04	-.22**	.25**	.41**	.27**	.38***	.31**	—	
9. Car accidents	-.11	-.01	-.11	.00	.04	-.05	.09	.09	—
10. Bus accidents	.02	-.00	.04	.24**	.06	.16*	.15*	.44**	.18**

*$p < .05$.   **$p < .01$ (two tailed).

the quadratic term, the bifurcation variables, and then the asymmetry variables. Second, all variables that did not have a significant weight in the model at $p < .10$ were eliminated. Third, more variables were entered to test the alternative hypotheses that the variables first thought to function as bifurcation variables would contribute to the asymmetry parameter and that the variables first thought to function as asymmetry variables would contribute to the bifurcation parameter. Variables were once again entered in a forward order: those that remained at the second stage, the new bifurcation variables, followed by the new asymmetry variables. At the fourth stage of the analysis, variables that did not have a significant weight at $p < .10$ were removed.

The multiple correlation for the cusp model for transit accidents was .80 F (4, 251) = 237.05, $p < .001$. Statistics for the bifurcation variables suggested that social (and job) stress was the primary bifurcation variable. Transit hazards made a significant contribution to the asymmetry parameter (as described in Figure 3 and Table 1).

In the linear pre–post analysis, the number of transit accidents was optimally predicted by three variables: transit hazards, auto accidents off the job, and operator anxiety, $R = .47$, F (3, 252) = 20.82, $p < .001$. The addition of the remaining survey variables into the regression models increased the correlation to .51, F (10, 245) = 7.89, $p < .001$.

In the linear difference analysis, the difference in the number of transit accidents compared with personal auto accidents was optimally predicted by transit hazards only the correlation .38, F (1, 254) = 39.57, $p < .001$. The addition of the remaining survey variables into the regression model resulted in an increase in the correlation to .45, F (10, 245) = 6.25, $p < .001$. In summary, the cusp model accounted for 37% more criterion variance than did the best linear alternative. Bivariate correlations among OHS and accident measures are listed in Table 2.

Stress-Related Medical Disorders

In light of the proposed similarity between accident and disease functions mentioned at the outset of this chapter, a direct application of the cusp model is warranted. Two independent lines of support for the cusp hypothesis should be briefly mentioned. The first pertains to animal and plant disease or pest functions that follow repeated cycles of outbreak and remission. Casti (1982) discovered that these could be accurately interpreted as cusp functions.

The second line of reasoning was developed in the context of general systems theory with respect to security subsystems (Bosserman, 1982; S. J. Guastello, 1988b). Three analogous butterfly catastrophe models were logically determined for organismic, organizational, and national-level systems. The organismic model is of concern here. The butterfly catastrophe has a five-dimensional response surface. It describes motion among three stable attractor equilibria and two repeller forces as a function of four control parameters. Three stable states of system functioning were identified so that the system is (a) unprotected, (b) protected from external disease sources only, or (c) protected from both external disease sources and internal organ malfunctions. The health of the organism is governed by four control parameters: (a) intensity of the external source of harm, (b) integrity of the organism's immunological system, (c) integrity of the organism's organ functions, and (d) an extruder and decision function by which the organism seeks medical care or takes action to remove or reduce the source of harm (S. J. Guastello, 1988b).

The cusp model for occupational health, tested below, is a simplification of the butterfly model. The simplification was necessary because (a) a detailed medical history of the respondents was not available and, in all likelihood, did not exist for all respondents; and (b) only two levels of system outcome were defined: presence

Table 3. Summary of Regression for Cusp Models and Stress-related Illnesses

Variable	Weight t	Stepwise R	Shrunken R^2
Nervousness, $R^2 = .81, F (8, 229) = 121.89$**			
Transit hazards	2.14	.17	.03
z_1^* Physical stress	-1.71*	.75	.55
Age, experience	2.29**	.75	.55
z_1^3	6.43****	.82	.68
z_1^* Social stress	-2.64***	.85	.72
z_1^* Anxiety	2.15**	.85	.72
z_1^2	-8.68****	.89	.79
Anxiety	-2.88****	.89	.80
Insomnia, $R^2 = .77, F (6, 264) = 148.62$**			
z_1^* Anxiety	2.41**	.60	.37
z_1^3	6.63****	.77	.59
z_1^* Social stress	-3.33***	.81	.66
z_1^2	-9.06****	.87	.75
Anxiety	2.43**	.88	.76
Social Stress	2.08**	.88	.77
Ulcer, $R^2 = .76$ $F (5, 234) = 150.82$**			
Age, experience	2.63***	.09	.01
z_1^* Social stress	-3.25***	.74	.55
z_1^3	5.84****	.83	.68
z_1^2	-8.23****	.87	.75
Physical stress	2.62***	.87	.75
Kidney, $R^2 = .77, F (5, 265) = 175.21$**			
z_1^2	-8.64****	.80	.64
z_1^* Anxiety	3.40****	.82	.67
z_1^* Social stress	-4.27****	.85	.71
z_1^3	6.14****	.87	.76
Social stress	3.11**	.88	.76
Blood pressure, $R^2 = .79, F (5, 230) = 173.53$			
z_1^3	11.7****	.69	.47
z_1^2	-17.95****	.88	.77
Age, experience	3.74****	.88	.78
z_1^* danger	0.34	.88	.78
Anxiety	2.93***	.89	.79
Heart disease, $R^2 = .74$ $F (4, 266) = 190.76$			
z_1^* Social stress	-2.51**	.73	.53
z_1^3	7.61****	.80	.64
z_1^2	-9.85****	.86	.74
Anxiety	1.80*	.86	.74
Carpal tunnel syndrome, $R^2 = .78$ $F (5, 265) = 183.69$			
z_1^* Safety management	-2.81***	.78	.61
Danger	2.14**	.78	.61
Safety management	-1.89*	.79	.62
z_1^3	9.35****	.81	.65
z_1^2	12.08****	.88	.77

Note. z_1 = Preemployment medical illness transformed for location and scale.
*$p < .10$. **$p < .05$. ***$p < .01$. ****$p < .001$.

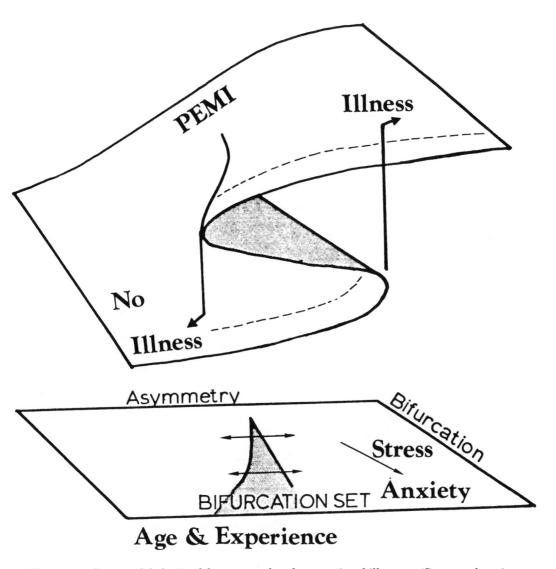

Figure 4. Cusp model obtained for stress-related occupational illnesses. (Stress and anxiety are represented as gradients. PEMI = preemployment medical illnesses.)

or absence of a particular disorder. The asymmetry parameter was defined as the occupational exposure, or the source of potential harm. The bifurcation factor was defined as stress and anxiety variables that are known to have an impact on immunological (Jemmot & Locke, 1984) and organic (Quick & Quick, 1984) functioning. The resulting cusp hypothesis parallels closely the cusp model for the accident process.

Analysis for Bus Operators

In the same survey (the OHS), operators were asked to indicate whether they had sought medical treatment for any of eight listed illnesses prior to their employment

Table 4. Summary of Regression for Linear Control Models for Stress-Related Illnesses

Independent Measure	Stepwise R	Shrunken R^2	Weight t	Model F
Heart disease, $R^2 = .06$				
PEMI	.18	.02	2.59**	6.68
All variables	.24	.02	—	1.69
Blood pressure, $R^2 = .11$				
PEMI	.31	.08	2.36*	8.31***
Age, experience	.20	.04	3.46**	
Anxiety	.27	.07	2.95**	
All variables	.33	.08	—	3.36**
Kidney disease, $R^2 = .07$				
Anxiety	.23	.05	3.63***	13.18**
All variables	.26	.04	—	2.13*
Nervousness, $R^2 = .14$				
Age, experience	.34	.11	2.35*	15.49***
Anxiety	.31	.09	5.21***	
All variables	.37	.10	—	4.33***
Insomnia, $R^2 = .12$				
Anxiety	.27	.07	2.61**	
Environmental hazards	.30	.08	2.17*	
Social stress	.33	.10	2.16*	9.65***
All variables	.35	.09	—	3.86***
Carpal tunnel syndrome, $R^2 = .10$				
Danger	.19	.03	3.05**	9.27**
All variables	.31	.06	—	2.85**
Ulcers, $R^2 = .09$				
PEMI	.26	.06	2.86**	
Age, experience	.18	.03	3.10**	
Anxiety	.30	.08	2.37**	7.51**
All variables	.30	.06	—	2.76**

Note. PEMI = preemployment medical illnesses.
*$p < .05$. **$p < .01$. ***$p < .001$.

with the bus company. Next they were asked whether they had sought treatment for any of the eight illnesses after employment with the bus company. Age and length of service data were collected on a different part of the survey.

The cusp regression model was then applied. The total of preemployment illnesses constituted y_1. Presence or absence of each of the eight illnesses was represented by y_2. Each illness was analyzed separately. The separate analysis for cancer was not performed because the Time 2 incidence was thought to be too low for a sample of this size (.02); the next highest rate for three different illnesses was .07. The estimate of λ was 0.0 for both Time 1 and Time 2. The Time 1 estimate of $\tilde{\sigma}$ was .327 as calculated by Equation 7. The Time 2 estimate of $\tilde{\sigma}$ was the ordinary standard deviation. Physical stressors, social stressors, and anxiety were first hypothesized as bifurcation variables. Age and experience, danger, environmental hazards, and transit hazards were first tested as symmetry variables.

Table 5. Bivariate Correlations Between OHS Variables and Medical Disorders

Variable	PEMI	Disorders						
		1	2	3	4	5	6	7
1. Age, experience	.01	.07	.20**	.02	.12	.07	.14*	.18**
2. Safety management	.09	−.00	−.03	−.05	−.10	−.09	.17**	−.10
3. Danger	−.02	.05	.13*	.16**	.14*	.06	.19**	.12*
4. Anxiety	.01	.08	.17**	.23**	.31**	.27**	.16**	.13*
5. Social or job-related stress	−.04	.04	.12*	.20**	.21**	.24**	.12*	.12*
6. Physical stressors	−.07	−.02	.06	.09	.06	.15*	.08	.14*
7. Environmental hazards	−.08	−.01	.04	.06	.14*	.19**	.13*	.10
8. Transit hazards	−.08	.01	.04	.10	.22**	.12*	.11	.10

Note. PEMI = Preemployment medical illnesses. Disorders: 1 = heart disease; 2 = high blood pressure, 3 = kidney disease, 4 = nervousness, 5 = insomnia, 6 = carpal tunnel syndrome, 7 = ulcers.
$*p < 0.5.$ $**p < 0.1$ (two-tailed).

Results

For all illnesses, large effect sizes were obtained for the cubic and quadratic terms of the model (Table 3). Age and length of service made significant contributions to the onset of high blood pressure, nervousness, and ulcers. Danger levels made significant contributions to the onset of high blood pressure, kidney disorders, and carpal tunnel syndrome. Transit hazards made a significant contribution to nervousness. Physical stressors, social stressors, and anxiety were part of all seven models except that predicting carpal tunnel syndrome. Multiple correlations for the illness cusps ranged from .86 for heart disease to .89 for nervousness and high blood pressure. Figure 4 displays a cusp model depicting a summary for all seven medical conditions.

The summary of regression for the linear comparison models appears in Table 4. For brevity, only the more challenging pre–post linear control model (Equation 6) is reported. Stepwise regression was performed first to identify the most powerful predictors. Remaining variables were then added to the equation to assess the total accuracy of the linear model for purposes of making comparisons with the cusps. Preemployment medical illnesses played a significant role in the models for heart conditions, high blood pressure, and ulcers only. Anxiety played a significant role in the prediction of high blood pressure, kidney problems, nervousness, insomnia, and ulcers. Age and length of service were related to high blood pressure, nervousness, and ulcers. Environmental hazards were specifically related to insomnia. Danger perception was specifically related to carpal tunnel syndrome. Multiple correlation for the linear models ranged from .24 for heart conditions to .37 for nervousness. The cusp models made superior predictions for all stress-related illnesses, accounting for 65% to 70% more criterion variance than their linear counterparts. Stress and anxiety were major contributors to the onset of the medical disorders. The background hazard variables played a less consistent role.

Bivariate correlations between OHS variables and medical disorders appear in Table 5. Unexpectedly, safety management was significantly related to carpal tunnel syndrome ($r = .17$, $p < .05$). Because no bifurcation variable was found for carpal tunnel syndrome, the safety management rating was tested as both an asymmetry and bifurcation variable. It did, in fact, contribute to both parameters.

Discussion

Three major lessons were learned from this research. The first was that stress and related variables play a key role in the epidemiology of accidents and some common medical disorders among bus operators. Second, the cusp mechanism was a powerful explicative model for those phenomena. Third, the view that accidents and illnesses may be studied from a common conceptual framework was strongly supported.

Cusp Model for Accidents

The cusp catastrophe model provided a powerful summary of the relations among stressors, hazards, and operator injuries. A comparison of squared multiple correlation coefficients indicated that the cusp model for operator injuries was 2.42 times as accurate (.63) as the next best linear alternative (.26).

The model offered several useful properties. First, it explained changes in accident rates (from off duty to on duty) as the result of a nonlinear dynamic process. Second, the distribution of accident rates was characterized as biomodal, with one mode near zero and the other at some higher level. Third, changes in accident rates were predicted from four sources: ambient danger and hazard levels, variables that affect human performance, initial accident rates (in this case, auto accidents), and the mathematical function that interrelates those variables.

The mathematical model has properties that allow for causal interference. In the specific case of bus operation, variables that affected human performance were anxiety and multiple forms of stress. Although transit hazards make a situation potentially dangerous, stress impairs the operator's ability to respond effectively to that danger. Because there appears to be a circular, or recursive, relation among stress, anxiety, errors, and accidents (S. J. Guastello et al., 1985), one can only anticipate that operators' capacities to respond to future situations becomes constricted with every negative incident.

Cusp Model for Medical Disorders

The cusp model was effective for describing the onset of seven different stress-related medical disorders and was up to 12 times as accurate as the next best linear comparison. Age and experience played a small role as background (asymmetry) variable. The manifold region of the cusp response surface, on the other hand, played a major role in the observed onset of all disorders. Thus the intensity of the stressful exposure was a critical factor.

Although the overall accuracy level of the illness models was high (average R^2 = .77), some models were qualitatively more complete than others. Treatment seeking for nervousness had the greatest number of variables associated with it: Transit hazards, age, and experience were the asymmetry variables. Physical stressors, social stressors, and anxiety were the bifurcation variables. The weight was positive for anxiety and negative for physical and social stressors. This configuration was interpreted as meaning that it was not so much the amount of stress that triggered the illness but the strength of the individual's reaction to a given amount of stress. The level of transit hazard and age predisposed the operator to increased susceptibility to stress.

A similar stress–anxiety mechanism was observed for kidney disfunction and insomnia. Overall danger level was the asymmetry variable in the kidney model. In the insomnia model, social stress and anxiety contributed to both parameters, suggesting that these variables form gradients on the cusp surface between the cusp point and two equilibria.

Physical and social stressors, age, and experience explained the outbreak of ulcers. Ulcers were triggered by social and job-related stress mostly among people who worked in physically uncomfortable environments, were older, and had been doing the job longer.

High blood pressure was more age related than were some of the other illnesses. It occurred among the more anxious operators and was triggered by danger levels. Both control variables were somewhat related to transit hazards and stressors such as work hours, irregular eating and sleeping schedules (disregulation syndrome), poor job security, and inadequate lavatory facilities. Those who had been treated for nervousness showed similar characteristics.

The effect of danger in the high blood pressure model was not unique like the other effects in the catastrophe models but was retained pending further investigation. Because a significant weight was obtained for the cubic term, a bifurcation variable must exist, according to the classification theorem. Danger had a significant weight until the last step of the variable entry procedure. When the last group of nonsignificant terms was deleted, the weight for danger became smaller.

The model for heart disease showed that cardiac disorders were triggered by social and job-related stress, but as asymmetry variable was not found. Future research on the occupational origins of cardiac disorders might benefit from incorporating medical information that could not be accessed by the OHS/TO.

Danger was a significant background variable in the model for carpal tunnel syndrome. Safety management contributed to both parameters. It was questionable whether the roles of danger and safety management was predictive or the result of hindsight bias on the part of the respondents. If they were the result of hindsight bias, however, they would have been found more pervasively. Instead, danger was associated with only one disorder as an asymmetry variable and one disorder as a weak bifurcation effect.

The model for carpal tunnel syndrome suggested some insights about the disorder that do not appear to have been considered in the past. First of all, carpal tunnel syndrome is the result of prolonged exposure to intense vibration, often to the driver's wrists or seat. OHS/TO did not query vibration discomfort because it was a foregone conclusion that all the buses vibrate. It now appears that operators under greater stress are more susceptible to carpal tunnel syndrome, possibly because of an inclination to grip the steering wheel more tightly than other operators.

Why mathematical modeling?

There are several reasons to pursue catastrophe modeling for the accident process and stress-related disorders. The first is accuracy. Data from this research showed that the cusp model was between 2.42 (accident rate) and 11.33 (heart disease occurrence) times as accurate as the comparable linear alternative explanations for stress outcomes. Similar accuracy advantages have been obtained from other known applications of catastrophe theory in psychology.

Other advantages include the introduction of equilibria and critical points, the descriptive capability of the model, and the theoretical links that are inevitably drawn among very different applications of the general systems theory. Statements concerning equilibria could give a risk assessor an indication of the stability associated with a particular risk level. Although critical points were not of direct concern in the applications presented in this chapter, those techniques could be used with a refined model to give specific values of important variables for which dramatic changes are expected. Equilibria and critical point information would be valuable in the formation of evaluation of control policies. The cusp catastrophe models also offer visual illustrations of important interrelations. Once the models for each of the disorders have been refined further, calibrated graphics would serve as valuable tools for those who rely on research findings for practical decision making.

References

Bertazzi, P. A. (1989). Industrial disasters and epidemiology. *Scandinavian Journal of Work and Environmental Health, 15*, 85–100.

Bosserman, F. K. (1982). The internal security subsystem. *Behavioral Science, 27*, 95–103.

Casti, J. (1982). Catastrophes, control and the inevitability of spruce budworm outbreaks. *Ecological Modeling, 14*, 293–300.

Cobb, L. (1978). Stochastic catastrophe models and multimodal distributions. *Behavioral Science, 23*, 360–374.

Coleman, P. J. (1981). Epidemiologic principles applied to injury prevention. *Scandinavian Journal of Work and Environmental Health, 7*, 91–96.

Darlington, R. B. (1990). *Regression and linear models*. New York: Wiley.

Ersland, S., Weisaeth, L., & Sund, A. (1989). The stress upon rescuers involved in an oil rig disaster: "Alexander L. Kielland." *Acta Psyciatrica Scandinavica, 80* (Suppl. 355), 38–49.

Evans, M. G. (1991). The problem of analyzing multiplicative composits. *American Psychologist, 46*, 6–15.

Farr, W. (1840). Progress of epidemics. *Report of the Registrar General of England and Wales, 2*, 16–20.

Graybill, F. A. (1976). *Theory and applications of the linear model*. Belmont, CA: Wadsworth.

Guastello, D. D., & Guastello, S. J. (1987a). A climate for safety in hazardous environments: A psychosocial approach. *Social and Behavioral Sciences Documents, 17*, 67.

Guastello, D. D., & Guastello, S. J. (1987b). The relationship between work group size and occupational accidents. *Journal of Occupational Accidents, 9,* 1–9.

Guastello, S. J. (1982). Moderator regression and the cusp catastrophe: Application of two-stage personnel selection, training, therapy, and policy evaluation. *Behavioral Science, 27,* 259–272.

Guastello, S. J. (1987a). A butterfly catastrophe model of motivation in organizations: Academic Performance. *Journal of Applied Psychology, 72,* 165–182.

Guastello, S. J. (1987b). Catastrophe modeling of the accident process: Risk dispersions for ten industrial classes. *Social and Behavioral Sciences Documents, 17,* 41.

Guastello, S. J. (1987c). Catastrophe theory: Ten years of progress. *Social and Behavioral Sciences Documents, 17,* 4.

Guastello, S. J. (1988a). Catastrophe modeling of the accident process: Organizational subunit size. *Psychological Bulletin, 103,* 246–255.

Guastello, S. J. (1988b). The organizational security subsystem: Some potentially catastrophic events. *Behavioral Science, 33,* 48–58.

Guastello, S. J. (1989). Catastrophe modeling of the accident process: Evaluation of an accident reduction program using the Occupational Hazards Survey. *Accident Analysis and Prevention, 21,* 61–77.

Guastello, S. J., & Guastello, D. D. (1988). *The Occupational Hazards Survey* (2nd ed.) Milwaukee, WI: Authors. (P.O. Box 92305, Milwaukee, WI 53202)

Guastello, S. J., Ikeda, M. J., & Connors, C. E. (1985). Stress, anxiety, errors, and accidents: A cyclic relationship. *Psychological Documents, 15,* 26.

Holmes, T. H., & Rahe, R. H. (1967). The Social Readjustment Rating Scale. *Journal of Psychosomatic Research, 11,* 213–218.

Jemmott, J. B., III, & Locke, S. E. (1984). Psychosocial factors, immunological mediation, and human susceptibility to infectious diseases: How much do we know? *Psychological Bulletin, 95,* 78–108.

Kemp, C. D. (1967). On a contagious distribution suggested for accident data. *Biometrics, 23,* 241–255.

Leigh, J. P. (1986). Occupational hazards and heart attacks. *Social Science Medicine, 11,* 1181–1185.

Levenson, H., Hirschfeld, M. L., Hirschfeld, A., & Dzubay, B. (1983). Recent life events and accidents: The role of sex differences. *Journal of Human Stress, 9,* 4–11.

McCarron, P. M., & Haakonson, N. H. (1982). Recent life change measurement in Canadian Forces pilots. *Aviation, Space, and Environmental Medicine, 53,* 6–13.

Poston, T., & Stewart, I. (1978). *Catastrophe theory and its applications.* London: Pitman.

Quick, J. C., & Quick, J. D. (1984). *Organizational stress and preventive management.* New York: McGraw-Hill.

Stewart, I. N., & Peregoy, R. (1983). Catastrophe theory modeling in psychology. *Psychological Bulletin, 94,* 336–362.

Thom, R. (1975). *Structural stability and morphogenesis.* New York: Benjamin-Addison-Wesley.

Vilardo, F. J. (1988). The role of the epidemiological model in injury control. *Journal of Safety Research, 19,* 1–4.

Waller, J. A. (1987). Injury as disease. *Accident Analysis and Prevention, 19,* 13–20.

Weisaeth, L. (1989a). The importance of high response rates in traumatic stress research. *Acta Psyciatrica Scandinavica, 80* (Suppl. 355), 131–137.

Weisaeth, L. (1989b). The stressors and the post-traumatic stress syndrome after an industrial disaster. *Acta Psyciatrica Scandinavica, 80* (Suppl. 355), 25–37.

Weisaeth, L. (1989c). A study of behavioral responses to an industrial disaster. *Acta Psyciatrica Scandinavica, 80* (Suppl. 355), 13–24.

Zeeman, E. C. (1977). *Catastrophe theory: Selected papers, 1972–1977.* Reading, MA: Addison-Wesley.

18

Irvin Sam Schonfeld

Assessing Stress in Teachers: Depressive Symptoms Scales and Neutral Self-Reports of the Work Environment

The focal interest of this chapter on teacher stress is methodologic. The purpose is fourfold. First, the chapter enumerates a number of defects in existing measures of job stress in teachers and, concomitantly, other helping professionals. Second, alternative ways of measuring stress in teachers are suggested and evaluated. In the section on these alternatives, the use of depressive symptom scales in concert with more "objective" measures of the work environment is discussed. Third, an application of the proposed alternative measurement strategy is described. Finally, the wider utility of the measurement strategy is briefly described.

Measuring Stress in Teachers

In research on the effects that adverse job conditions exert on the functioning of teachers and other helping professionals, investigators have long used measures of stress and burnout. Typically, research on stress in teachers is cross-sectional, although such designs have many documented weaknesses. However, even if research on teacher stress were longitudinal in design, the defects of stress and burnout measures would still seriously impede an investigator's ability to draw valid conclusions. The problems of stress and burnout measures are manifold.

First, the creators of stress scales often view stress as an overinclusive construct embracing the working conditions that are suspected of provoking distress in teachers, as well as the distress that those conditions are thought to provoke (DeFrank & Stroup, 1989; Dunham, 1984; Dworkin, 1988; Dworkin, Haney, & Telschow, 1988; Farber, 1984; Fimian, 1983; Galloway, Panckhurst, Boswell, Boswell, & Green, 1984; Kyriacou & Sutcliffe, 1978, 1979; Needle, Griffen, & Svendsen, 1981; Pette-

Preparation of this chapter was supported by NIOSH/CDC Grant R01 OH02571 and PSC-CUNY Award Program Grants 667401, 668419, 669416, and 661251. I gratefully acknowledge the cooperation of the individuals who participated in this study. I thank Danqing Ruan for her computer programming and my late friend Jim Johnson for his critical comments on an earlier draft of this manuscript. I extend a special note of appreciation to George Schonfeld.

All correspondence concerning this chapter should be sent to Irvin Schonfeld, EDFN, City College of New York, New York, NY 10031.

grew & Wolf, 1982; Seiler & Pearson, 1984). An example of a commonly used stress questionnaire having such an item structure comes from Kyriacou and Sutcliffe (1978, 1979): "As a teacher, how great a source of stress are these factors? Maintaining discipline; Shortage of equipment . . ."

Without independently measuring job conditions and the distress those conditions are hypothesized to provoke, the investigator forecloses the possibility of testing causal hypotheses that link job conditions to distress. A plausible alternative to the hypothesis that specifiable job conditions cause distress is that individuals who are distressed create (or overreport) the putative stressors, a variety of B. S. Dohrenwend and B. P. Dohrenwend's (1981) event-proneness model. One version of the event-proneness model holds that teachers with preexisting depressive symptoms, because of impaired interpersonal skills, may create classroom environments conducive to student rule breaking, a suspected stressor. Students might, as a consequence of being bored in a class headed by an impaired teacher, rebel or act out aggressive feelings. The impaired teacher would, in turn, be unable to enforce rules of civility. Case study evidence from Schonfeld and Ruan (1991) illustrates the plausibilty of the event-proneness model of teacher stress.

A second problem with stress and burnout measures is that they often fail to provide information on the frequency with which teachers encounter given job conditions. Kyriacou and Sutcliffe's (1978, 1979) item concerning the extent to which maintaining discipline is a "source of stress" does not ask how often the teacher, say, broke up a fight. By the same token, Kyriacou and Sutcliffe's (1978, 1979) item asking the teacher to reveal the extent to which equipment shortages are a source of stress fails to ascertain how often the teacher is actually confronted with equipment shortages. These items are thus useless in ascertaining the frequency with which teachers encounter difficult work-related conditions, factors that may plausibly be viewed as the "independent variable."

A third problem with stress and burnout measures is that they lead the investigator to vacate the role of hypothesis tester. Instead, the subject is cast into that role: The subject is often asked to identify working conditions by the distress that those conditions may promote. Stress items of this type may be well suited for pilot research in which an investigator is attempting to generate hypotheses. They are not, however, well suited for hypothesis testing. Cohen, Karmarck, and Mermelstein (1983) wrote that "there is . . . evidence that people often misattribute their feelings of stress to a particular source when that stress is actually due to another source" (p. 387). For example, a teacher may easily misattribute his or her distress to acting out behavior in one or two children when overcrowding may be a more significant factor (see Worchel & Teddlie, 1976). By the same token, Kasl (1978) pointed out that police officers, in response to questions about job stresses, often identify administrative and court-related work. They rarely mention life-threatening aspects of their jobs.

In stress research on helping professionals such as teachers, *burnout* is a term frequently used to describe a tripartite syndrome consisting of emotional exhaustion, depersonalization, and a reduced sense of personal accomplishment resulting from the task of helping unwilling or ungrateful individuals (Cunningham, 1983; Farber, 1984; Gold, 1984, 1985; Iwanicki & Schwab, 1981; Johnson, Gold, & Knepper, 1984; Malanowski & Wood, 1984; Maslach & Jackson, 1981, 1984; McIntyre, 1984; Pierson-Hubeny & Archambault, 1985). The Maslach Burnout Inventory (MBI; Maslach & Jackson, 1981) is an instrument that has been commonly used in stress research. It has also been a source of items for teacher stress questionnaires (Farber, 1984; Fimian, 1983; Fimian & Santoro, 1983). Exemplary items include: "I feel frustrated by my work" and "Working with people directly puts too much stress on me."

Burnout items are vulnerable to attribution errors (Schonfeld, 1990b). It is possible for a teacher to agree with a Maslach burnout item, asserting that "working with people" is stressful when a teacher has been hounded by an authoritarian supervisor or when a child with conduct difficulties is frustrating well-planned lessons. The burnout literature tends not to identify work-related factors that increase the risk of psychological distress or ill health in teachers.

Schonfeld (in press) adduced evidence for the view that burnout scales largely reflect depressive symptoms. First, he demonstrated with correlational evidence that measures of psychophysiologic symptoms, perceived health, job satisfaction, low self-esteem, and motivation to continue in the teaching profession—factors having known links to burnout scales (Kahill, 1988)—are similarly related to depressive symptoms. Second, he provided rational evidence that two of the three components of burnout, emotional exhaustion and a reduced sense of personal accomplishment, constitute symptoms of depression. He argued that the third component, depersonalization (cynical feelings that helping professionals may direct toward clients), is reflective of the hostility, friction, and aversive control that characterize the interpersonal relationships of depressed individuals (Coyne, Burchill, & Stiles, 1990; Coyne, Kahn, & Gotlib, 1987).

A fourth problem with stress and burnout measures is the absence of clear evidence demonstrating the validity of the constructs. Although sometimes not the purpose of the investigators who conducted the research, they have provided evidence to suggest that burnout and stress measures overlap considerably with depressive symptom scales.

Four studies conducted in different geographic areas illustrate the link between stress or burnout measures and depressive symptoms. First, in a sample of Los Angeles secondary school teachers, Hammen and deMayo (1982) found that a one-item teacher stress measure correlated .63 with the Center for Epidemiologic Studies Depression Scale (CES-D; Radloff, 1977; Weissman, Sholomskas, Pottenger, Prusoff, & Locke, 1977), a validated measure of current depressive symptoms. Had a more reliable, multiitem measure of stress been used, the coefficient would likely have been higher. Second, Belcastro and Hays (1984) compared burned-out and normal Alabama schoolteachers on 12 self-reported illnesses. Although the rate of illness in the burned-out teachers exceeded that of the normal teachers in only 3 of the 12 disorders, depression was the illness in which the rates for the two groups of teachers differed most sharply. Third, Greenglass and Burke (1988) studied 780 Canadian teachers. Greenglass (personal communication, 1990) found that the MBI was significantly related to depressive ($r = .53$), anxiety ($r = .44$), and somatic ($r = .44$) symptoms. Anxiety symptoms and somatic complaints are frequent accompaniments of depressive symptoms (Schonfeld, in press). Fourth, Meier (1984), using a midwestern college faculty sample, found that the MBI, the Meier Burnout Assessment, and a self-rating of burnout correlated with measures of depression about as strongly as the instruments' reliabilities permitted.

The fifth problem refers to an artifact in many burnout and stress measures. Correlations between burnout and stress measures and working conditions are likely to be inflated because many burnout and stress measures refer to difficulties at work. For example, Kyriacou and Sutcliffe's (1978, 1979) measure of stress and Maslach and Jackson's (1981, 1984) measure of burnout refer to job conditions in evaluating distress in teachers and (in the case of the MBI) other helping professionals. Other teacher stress measures (e.g., Fimian & Santoro, 1983) ask the respondents to indicate how bothered or annoyed they are by various school or classroom conditions.

Alternative Avenues to Measuring Stress in Teachers

Paradoxically, one way to measure stress in teachers is to do away with the concept of stress altogether (see Kasl, 1987). Instead of measuring the global concept of teacher stress, I argue that it is preferable to measure hypothesized aversive environmental conditions (the stressors) and depressive symptoms (the distress) independently. The CES-D is a satisfactory depressive symptom scale; however, other depressive symptom scales may do equally well. One advantage of the CES-D is the availability of normative data from unselected general-population samples (Schonfeld, 1990b). Studies of Los Angeles (Hammen & deMayo, 1982) and New York (Schonfeld, 1990a, 1990b) teachers revealed CES-D scores that were elevated in comparison with the normative landmarks that characterize general-population samples. These findings suggest that teaching carries some psychological risk. An epidemiologic survey of Western Australian teachers (Finlay-Jones, 1986) also revealed elevated psychological morbidity using a different general-population measure of psychological distress.

Another advantage of the CES-D is that it makes no reference to working conditions. As described earlier, the wording of many stress and burnout measures increases the likelihood that correlations with working conditions are biased upward. The use of depressive symptom scales like the CES-D, instead of stress/burnout measures, would help to reduce the likelihood of artifactual correlations between workplace stressors and distress.

What Do Depressive Symptom Scales Measure?

Depressive symptoms scales are thought to be reflective of either of two constructs: nonspecific psychological distress or clinical depression. Dohrenwend and his colleagues (Dohrenwend, Levav, & Shrout, 1986; Dohrenwend, Shrout, Egri, & Mendelsohn, 1980) showed that depressive symptoms tend to correlate with a variety of symptom scales about as highly as the scales' reliability coefficients permit. These symptom scales include measures of guilt, anxiety, low self-esteem, poor perceived health, and psychophysiologic symptoms. Dohrenwend and his colleagues (Dohrenwend et al., 1986; Dohrenwend et al., 1980) advanced the view that in the absence of clinical disorder such symptom scales probably measure a construct they called *nonspecific psychological distress* or *demoralization*, after the work of Frank (1973). Nonspecific distress might be thought of as the type of psychological state that motivates many otherwise "normal" people—individuals who do not meet diagnostic criteria for psychiatric illness—to seek help from psychotherapists. Such people suffer from problems with living, although they would not qualify for a *Diagnostic and Statistical Manual of Mental Disorders* (3rd ed., rev.; American Psychiatric Association, 1987) diagnosis.

On the other hand, individuals with high scores on depressive symptom scales like the CES-D are at increased risk for clinical depression (Weissman, Sholomskas, Pottenger, Prusoff, & Locke, 1977). In the psychiatric epidemiology literature, the CES-D has been conceived as a preliminary screening device to improve the efficiency of case finding in follow-up clinical interviews (Boyd, Weissman, Thompson, & Myers, 1982; B. P. Dohrenwend & B. S. Dohrenwend, 1982; Radloff, 1977; Weissman et al., 1977). On the other hand, the extreme distress reflected in high scores on scales like the CES-D in the absence of clinical depression also constitutes a serious mental health problem (Link & Dohrenwend, 1980).

Measures of the Work Environment

Kasl (1978) cogently argued that stress researchers should move away from "the excessive operational circularity in stress and distress measures" (p. 36). He rejected studies that linked measures of perceived job demands to measures of worker unhappiness with those demands. Three alternative measurement strategies for obtaining reasonable information on the work environment are available.

Objective information. First, one can obtain "objective" information on the quality of the work environment. Such a strategy is particularly applicable to studies comparing the health of workers in different occupations. For example, in research linking working conditions to cardiovascular disease, Schwartz, Pieper, and Karasek (1988) obtained independently from one sample (the Quality of Employment Survey [QES; Quinn & Staines, 1979]) ratings of job dimensions like decision latitude and physical exertion that would be used to characterize the jobs of healthy and unhealthy workers in two different samples (the U.S. Health Examination Survey [U.S. Department of Health, Education and Welfare, 1965] and the U.S. Health and Nutrition Examination Survey [U.S. Department of Health, Education and Welfare, 1979]). In a study of work history and schizophrenia risk, Link, Dohrenwend, and Skodal (1986) obtained independent ratings of job dimensions from the *Dictionary of Occupational Titles* (DOT; U.S. Department of Labor, 1965), a document summarizing ratings made by occupational analysts on a great variety of jobs. By using ratings of work dimensions that are external to the study's participants, relations between job dimensions and measures of mental health are uncontaminated by self-report bias (Kasl, 1981).

It is more difficult to study within-occupation variation because objective external measures of job characteristics such as the DOT and the QES provide average values on work dimensions that characterize specific occupations. They do not provide data on within-occupation variability. In my own research on teachers, I attempted to obtain within-occupation, "objective" measures on the quality of the New York City public schools in which many of the study participants have worked. One confidential document that I secured with the help of the local teachers union provided an independent, within-teachers measure of the stressfulness of their work environments. The document provided yearly information on the school-by-school rates at which teachers suffered assaults, robberies, and sexual offenses. One might argue that these statistics index the quality of the teachers' work environments by reflecting the average level of violence in the schools. The data were external to the study participants, who were newly appointed teachers, and were largely compiled before the participants obtained jobs.

This research strategy, however, is not without shortcomings. M. Gillespie, the director of City College's Principals Center and a former New York City public school principal, reported (personal communication, 1990) that principals vary in their willingness to permit such crimes to be aggregated into official records. I have known teachers to be assault victims and under pressure from their principals not report the assaults.

Paired study participants. An alternative within-teachers strategy would capitalize on the circumstance in which two study participants might obtain jobs in the same school. One teacher's report on his or her working conditions could be treated (in, for example, a regression equation) as the working conditions encountered by the other teacher, and vice versa. If sufficient numbers of pairs of teachers at the same level of experience obtain jobs in the same schools, this strategy may prove workable. A strength of such a strategy is that it provides ratings on the school environment that are independent of the teacher reporting distress. A weakness of the strategy is the loss of classroom-level data on the teacher's work environment. Furthermore, approximate matching by grade taught is required: A first-grade teacher's experience does not adequately reflect a fifth-grade teacher's experience even if they work in the same school.

Neutral self-reports. A third type of strategy involves measuring the teacher's immediate work environment with the help of self-report items that minimize the extent to which the teacher projects his or her feelings when responding. Kasl (1987) argued that neutral self-report items that capture the frequency with which workers encounter specifiable conditions are superior to items that ask workers to indicate how bothered or annoyed they are by those conditions. For example, in the longitudinal study of newly appointed teachers, participants were asked to estimate the frequency, within a specified period of time, with which they encountered students engaged in a fight. By contrast, the teachers were *not* asked to rate how annoyed or angered they were by student fighting. The latter type of item is probably confounded with symptoms. A weakness of neutral self-report items is that they probably cannot fully eliminate confounding with symptoms; evidence provided by Schonfeld and Ruan (1991), however, suggests that in scales developed from such items, confounding with symptoms can be kept to a reasonable minimum.

An Application

An ongoing longitudinal investigation of newly appointed teachers began before the teachers entered the work force (Schonfeld, 1991, 1992). The teachers were recruited while they were in their final semesters of college. Preemployment (summer) and postemployment (fall and spring) depressive symptoms were measured with the CES-D. Neutral self-report items were used to obtain information on the teachers' work environments. The data were collected by questionnaires that were pilot tested in two veteran-teacher samples (e.g., Schonfeld, 1990b). The study of newly appointed teachers, which is described in detail in Schonfeld (1992), involved four graduating cohorts, the classes of 1987, 1988, 1989, and 1990, although the findings summarized here are limited to 255 women from the first three cohorts. Men and individuals who did not become teachers were excluded. About 90% of those eligible signed letters of informed consent, and 86% of the women recruited participated in the summer data collection.

Two reliable environmental stressor scales (alpha ≥ .82, fall and spring), the Episodic Stressor Scale and the Strain Scale, were constructed by aggregating neutral self-report items. The Episodic Stressor Scale was a measure of the rate at which the teacher encountered episodically occurring job-related events. An Episodic Stressor Scale score was calculated by computing the teacher's mean on the items assessing the frequency with which she encountered such events (e.g., threat of personal injury, encounter with an insolent student). Each scale item was scored as follows: (0) not at all, (1) once per month, (2) once per week, (3) 2–4 times per week, or (4) daily.

The Strain Scale, which was named for the pioneering work of Pearlin and Schooler (1978), pertained to ongoing types of stressors. A Strain Scale score was calculated by computing the teacher's mean score on items assessing ongoing conditions (e.g., an overcrowded classroom, unmotivated students attending class). Each scale item was scored as follows: (0) not at all, (1) to a minimal extent, (2) to a small extent, (3) to a moderate extent, or (4) to a great extent.

Both the Episodic Stressor Scale and the Strain Scale included (reverse scored) items reflecting positive aspects of the work environment (e.g., "a parent praised you") to counter any tendencies toward response set.

Three sets of analyses were conducted to examine the link between the school environment and depressive symptoms. In the first set of analyses, the sample was arbitrarily divided into three, about equal-sized groups consisting of the lowest, middle, and highest scorers on the fall job environment scales. The purpose of this set of analyses was to evaluate mean group differences on the summer ($n = 247$), fall ($n = 244$), and spring ($n = 210$) CES-D. The findings for the Episodic Stressor Scale, depicted in Figure 1, revealed no summer differences among the sample, but significant differences were found for the fall and spring. Similar findings were obtained with the Strain Scale. It is of interest that the preemployment symptom picture in women who obtained jobs in the best schools improved.

In the second set of analyses, the fall CES-D was regressed on each of the two job environment scales ($n = 238$ with listwise deletion for missing data). In both regression equations, preemployment CES-D, social class of origin, life events, marital status, race, preemployment social support, and age were controlled. The correlation increase associated with the Episodic Stressor Scale was .20. In the full regression equation, only preemployment CES-D and the Episodic Stressor Scale were significantly related to the outcome. The unstandardized regression weight ($B = 8.33$) for the Episodic Stressor Scale indicated that, on average, a unit increase

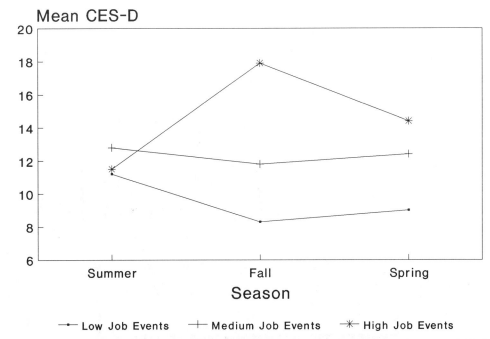

Figure 1. Depressive symptoms in female teachers in the fall low-, medium-, and high-event groups. (Depressive symptoms were measured by the CES-D. The high-event group represents the teachers in the most adverse school environments, and the low-event group represents the teachers in the "best" school environments. Significant group effects were found in the fall [$p < .001$] and spring [$p < .01$] but not the summer. From Schonfeld, 1992. Copyright 1992 by Pergamon Press. Reprinted by permission.)

on the Episodic Stressor Scale was associated with an 8-point increase on the CES-D. A unit increase may be thought of as the difference between a scale score of 1, representing a once-a-month occurrence of a variety of adverse school-related events, and a scale score of 2, representing a once-a-week occurrence of such events. To contextualize this finding, note that the median mean score on the CES-D in general-population samples is about 8 (Schonfeld, 1990b), and 16 is considered to be a marker of clinical significance (Boyd et al., 1982). The results were similar when the Strain Scale replaced the Episodic Stressor Scale in the regression equation.

Despite the inclusion of control variables measured at an earlier point in time (e.g., summer CES-D, social support), the regression procedures constituted concurrent analyses: Fall symptoms were measured at the same time as school conditions. The relatively large effect sizes for the school environment variables did not rule out the hypothesis that preexisting depressive symptoms somehow "caused" the occurrence of the putative environmental stressors (the event-proneness model described earlier). An event-proneness explanation of the findings, however, did not hold because the zero-order correlations between the summer CES-D and the fall and spring school environment measures did not differ significantly from zero.

The third and final set of analyses ($n = 196$) used LISREL software (Jöreskog & Sorbom, 1989) to develop structural equation models (Hayduk, 1987) linking stressors and symptoms during the course of the teachers' first year on the job.

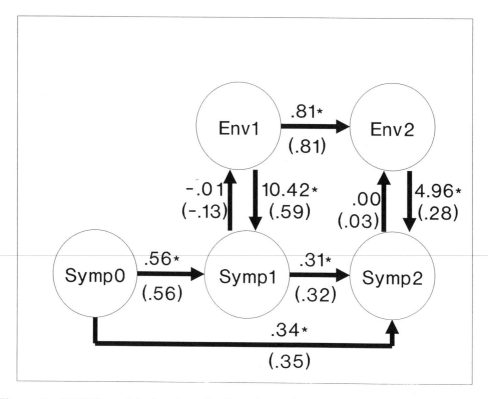

Figure 2. LISREL model of reciprocal effects in newly appointed female teachers. (Env1 and Env2 represent adversity in the school environment in the fall and spring, respectively. Symp1, Symp2, and Symp3 represent depressive symptoms in the summer, fall, and spring, respectively. Unstandardized coefficients are presented above each path, and standardized coefficients are presented below each path in parentheses. Asterisks indicate a significant causal path [$p < .001$]. From Schonfeld, 1992. Copyright 1992 by Pergamon Press. Reprinted by permission.)

Model building was simplified by excluding all control variables except the summer CES-D. This decision was justified in view of the regression analyses, which failed to demonstrate significant effects for control variables other than the summer CES-D. A latent fall (Time 1) school environment variable (Env1 in Figures 2 and 3) was constructed using both the fall Episodic Stressor and Strain Scales as indicators. Similarly, a latent spring (Time 2) school environment variable (Env2 in Figures 2 and 3) was constructed using both the spring Episodic Stressor and Strain Scales as indicators. Env1 and Env2 were forced to assume the same units as the Episodic Stressor Scale. Because both the Time 1 and Time 2 environment factors each had two indicators, LISREL estimated the error terms for each school-stressor indicator.

Summer (preemployment), fall, and spring CES-Ds were used to construct the Time 0, 1, and 2 symptoms measures, respectively. Each Time 0, 1, and 2 symptoms factor was forced to have the same scale as its CES-D indicator. An error term derived from the reliability coefficient (alpha $\geq .89$) for each CES-D indicator was included in the model. Preemployment (Time 0) symptoms constituted an "instrumental" variable required for estimating reciprocal effects (Kenny, 1979). The re-

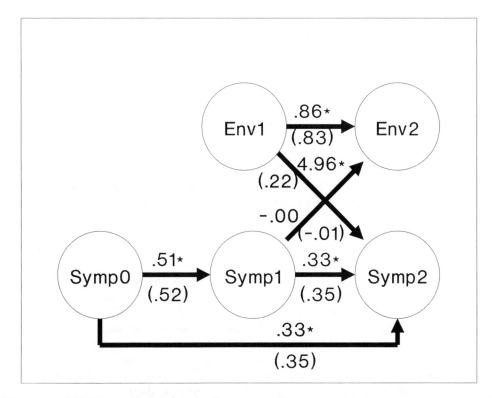

Figure 3. LISREL model of lagged effects in newly appointed female teachers. Env1 and Env2 represent adversity in the school environment in the fall and spring, respectively. (Symp1, Symp2, and Symp3 represent depressive symptoms in the summer, fall, and spring, respectively. Unstandardized coefficients are presented above each path and standardized coefficients are presented below each path in parentheses. Asterisks indicate a significant causal path [$p < .001$]. From Schonfeld, 1992. Copyright 1992 by Pergamon Press. Reprinted by permission.)

ciprocal effects model shown in Figure 2 was consistent with the data. At Time 1 (fall) and again at Time 2 (spring), the model shows reciprocal effects between depressive symptoms and the work environment. The effect from environment to symptoms was at each time considerably greater than the small ("halo") effects from symptoms to environment (*ns*). A rival lagged-effects model was also tested but rejected (see Figure 3).

The three sets of analyses jointly suggest that the effects that working conditions exert on depressive symptoms in newly appointed female teachers is relatively immediate. Adverse effects (and perhaps beneficial effects associated with obtaining a job in low-events schools) begin to appear during the teachers' first year on the job. It would have been too late to have begun a study of the effects of working conditions later in the teachers' careers. A strategic feature of the study, the measurement of depressive symptoms prior to the participants' entry into the work force, afforded an opportunity to evaluate and reject an event-proneness explanation of the findings. An advantage of research designs that follow newly employed, in comparison with veteran, workers is the opportunity that such designs furnish for obtaining preemployment measures of health (see Kasl, 1983; Schonfeld & Ruan, 1991). Preemployment health or symptom measures may constitute instrumental variables that could help to disentangle the effects that develop after individuals enter the work force.

Self-Report Items

An important feature of the study was the creation of job environment variables based on neutral self-report items. This chapter advances the view that carefully worded self-report items can sometimes be as helpful as many "objective" indicators in constructing measures of the work environment. This is not to say there will be no risk of confounding with prior psychological symptoms. The extent to which there will be confounding is an empirical question that should be studied. The issue of which items are likely to be confounded with prior symptoms ought to be resolved in pilot research prior to the substantive study.

I am not arguing for doing away with so-called objective measures. On the contrary, objective indicators of airport noise near a school may be superior to subjective measures (Cohen, Evans, Stokol, & Krantz, 1986). There are, however, occasions when objective measures of the work environment are not objective enough, as in the case of official school-by-school records of assaults against teachers. Alternatively, neutral self-report items may inquire into teachers' exposures to putative stressors (e.g., pupil fighting, vandalism). Coupled with satisfactory longitudinal data, an investigator may examine the independence of postemployment stesssors from preemployment health and the effects of exposures to such stressors on future health.

The Role of the CES-D in Identifying Psychiatric Cases

Depressive symptom scales are one of a number of possible outcome variables. Earlier mentioned advantages of well-standardized measures like the CES-D include normative landmarks from general-population samples and the absence of reference to the work environment. Scales like the CES-D have another advantage absent in traditional stress and burnout measures. Because high scores on scales like the CES-D suggest elevated risk for affective illness and low scores decreased risk, these measures make it possible to add, economically, clinical case-finding procedures to research on occupational stress.

An example of the utility of such a procedure comes from a current pilot study of the 1990 cohort. The purpose of the study is to examine the relation between incident psychiatric disorder and the working conditions of newly appointed teachers. The psychiatric study was put in the field as a "graft" onto the longitudinal study described in this chapter. Because of budget constraints, experienced female diagnosticians conducted telephone interviews with the subjects selected ($n = 69$ female teachers and nonteachers, 61 interviews completed as of the writing of this chapter). Ideally, face-to-face interviews are to be preferred. The use of the telephone interviews, however, was not considered a drawback because participants were accustomed to relatively frequent mail and telephone contact in connection to their participation in the main study.

To qualify for the psychiatric study, a female teacher must have obtained a score on the preemployment CES-D that is below the clinical cutoff (<16). Scores greater than or equal to the cutoff are associated with increased risk of clinical depression, and scores below the cutoff are associated with decreased risk (Boyd et al., 1982; Radloff, 1977; Weissman et al., 1977). Any teacher whose preemployment CES-D was greater than or equal to the cutoff did not qualify for the clinical study because the study's aim was to assess the incidence of disorder after the women obtain jobs of varying quality. This preemployment "gate" reduces the likelihood of identifying individuals with preexisting disorders. Every subject whose (a) preemployment (summer) CES-D was below the cutoff and (b) fall CES-D was greater than or equal to the clinical cutoff was scheduled for a clinical interview after the project's receipt of the completed fall CES-D. These subjects might be aptly called the *low–high group* based on their summer–fall CES-D profile.

Members of a second group, a low–low group consisting of women whose scores on the CES-D were below the cutoff in both the summer and fall, were also scheduled for interviews. Because there were many more low–lows than low–highs, the low–lows were randomly selected and matched to the low–highs for date of the project's receipt of the completed fall CES-D. There are approximately equal numbers of

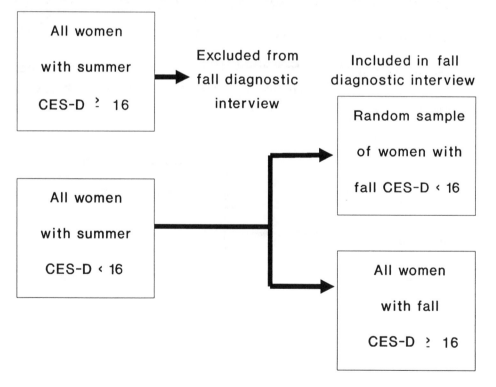

Figure 4. Description of the two-stage research design to ascertain the incidence of affective illness in teachers: fall procedures. (CES-D = Center for Epidemiologic Studies Depression Scale.)

low–highs and low–lows. The clinical interviewers were blind to all information available in the completed questionnaires, including the subjects' scores on both CES-Ds. The study design is depicted in Figure 4.

It was more preferable to sample from the low–low group than to interview every member of that group because depressive illness, the disorder of primary interest, is rare among individuals with low scores on the CES-D. By contrast, it was desirable to interview all low–high subjects because that group was at considerably higher risk than was the low–low group. These twin procedures made for an economy of scale while maximizing the chances of identifying true cases. An extended set of procedures, described in Figure 5, was used for data collected in the spring.

It is important to bear in mind that the CES-D reflects a continuous dimension of psychopathology. Although the CES-D provides good data on this dimension, the scale does not provide sufficient information to diagnose psychiatric disorder (B. P. Dohrenwend et al., 1986). To diagnose psychiatric illness, the second clinical interview stage of data collection is required.

According to B. P. Dohrenwend and B. S. Dohrenwend (1982), in their important article on psychiatric epidemiology, two-stage procedures that combine psychometrically valid screening instruments in Stage 1 with standardized psychiatric interviews in Stage 2 constitute an optimum method for ascertaining "true" incidence and prevalence rates. An advantage that two-stage procedures have over methods

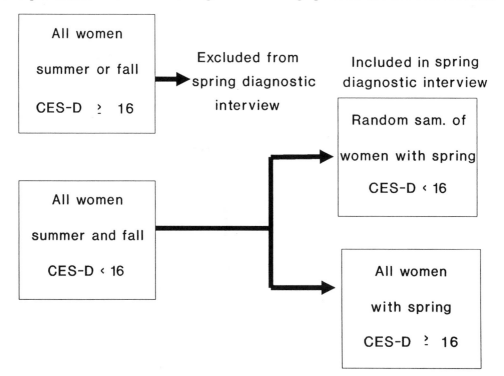

Figure 5. Description of the two-stage research design to ascertain the incidence of affective illness in teachers: spring procedures. (CES-D = Center for Epidemiologic Studies Depression Scale.)

in which entire samples are administered psychiatric interviews in one step without prior screening is that the Stage 1 screening instrument, here the CES-D, serves as a check on the diagnostic information ascertained in Stage 2. With the important control feature of making the Stage 2 diagnosticians blind to the Stage 1 CES-D scores, individuals identified as having a disorder in Stage 2, compared with individuals without a Stage 2 disorder, should have significantly higher scores on the Stage 1 screening instrument.

The diagnostic interviewers used the *Structured Clinical Interview for DSM–III–R* (*SCID*; Spitzer, Williams, Gibbon, & First, 1989). The *SCID* was reorganized slightly for the purposes of this study. To put the interviewee at ease, a number of questions about fairly common "medical" conditions (taken from the section on somatization disorder) were asked before the interviewer turned to the sections on major depression, dysthymia, and a number of anxiety diagnoses. Sections pertaining to psychiatric disorders not relevant to this study (e.g., bipolar illness, schizophrenia) were not included.

Another check on the quality of the data is built into the *SCID*. The *SCID* ascertains the time of onset of severe symptoms. This dating procedure served as a further check on the hypothesis that the diagnoses ascertained reflected incident cases as would be expected when participants with high preemployment CES-D scores were screened out.

References

American Psychiatric Association. (1987). *Diagnostic and statistical manual of mental disorders* (3rd ed., rev.). Washington, DC: Author.

Belcastro, P. A., & Hays, L. C. (1984). Ergo . . . ergophobia . . . ergo . . . burnout? *Professional Psychology: Research and Practice, 15*, 260–270.

Boyd, J. H., Weissman, M. M., Thompson, W. D., & Myers, J. K. (1982). Screening for depression in a community sample: Understanding the discrepancies between depression syndrome and diagnostic scales. *Archives of General Psychiatry, 39*, 1195–1200.

Cohen, S., Evans, G. W., Stokol, D., & Krantz, D. S. (1986). *Behavior, health, and environmental stress.* New York: Plenum Press.

Cohen, S., Kamarck, T., & Mermelstein, R. (1983). A global measure of perceived stress. *Journal of Health and Social Behavior, 24*, 385–396.

Coyne, J. C., Burchill, S. A. L., & Stiles, W. B. (1990). An interactional perspective on depression. In C. R. Snyder & D. O. Forsyth (Eds.), *Handbook of social and clinical psychology: The health perspective* (pp. 327–349). New York: Pergamon Press.

Coyne, J. C., Kahn, J., & Gotlib, I. H. (1987). Depression. In T. Jacob (Ed.), *Family interaction and psychopathology* (pp. 509–533). New York: Plenum Press.

Cunningham, W. G. (1983). Teacher burnout—Solutions for the 1980s: A review of the literature. *Urban Review, 15*, 37–51.

DeFrank, R. S., & Stroup, C. A. (1989). Teacher stress and health: Examination of a model. *Journal of Psychosomatic Research, 33*, 99–109.

Dohrenwend, B. P., & Dohrenwend, B. S. (1982). Perspectives on the past and future of psychiatric epidemiology. *American Journal of Public Health, 72*, 1271–1279.

Dohrenwend, B. P., Levav, I., & Shrout, P. E. (1986). Screening scales from the Psychiatric Epidemiology Research Interview (PERI). In M. M. Weissman, J. K. Myers, & C. E. Ross (Eds.), *Community surveys of psychiatric disorders* (pp. 349–375). New Brunswick, NJ: Rutgers University Press.

Dohrenwend, B. P., Shrout, P. E., Egri, G., & Mendelsohn, F. S. (1980). Nonspecific psychological distress and other dimensions of psychopathology: Measures for use in the general population. *Archives of General Psychiatry, 37*, 1229–1236.

Dohrenwend, B. S., & Dohrenwend, B. P. (1981). Life stress and illness: Formulation of the issues. In B. S. Dohrenwend & B. P. Dohrenwend (Eds.), *Stressful life events and their contexts* (pp. 1–27). New Brunswick, NJ: Rutgers University Press.

Dunham, J. (1984). *Stress in teaching*. Beckenham, Kent, England: Croom Helm.

Dworkin, A. G. (1988). *Teacher burnout in the public schools*. Albany: State University of New York Press.

Dworkin, A. G., Haney, C. A., & Telschow, R. L. (1988). Fear, victimization, and stress among urban public school teachers. *Journal of Organizational Behavior, 9*, 159–171.

Farber, B. (1984). Stress and burnout in suburban teachers. *Journal of Educational Research, 77*, 325–331.

Fimian, M. J. (1983). A comparison of occupational stress correlates as reported by teachers of mentally retarded and non-mentally retarded handicapped children. *Education and Training of the Mentally Retarded, 18*, 62–68.

Fimian, M. J., & Santoro, T. M. (1983). Sources and manifestations of occupational stress as reported by full-time special education teachers. *Exceptional Children, 49*, 540–543.

Finlay-Jones, R. (1986). Factors in the teaching environment associated with severe psychological distress among school teachers. *Australian and New Zealand Journal of Psychiatry, 20*, 304–313.

Frank, J. D. (1973). *Persuasion and healing*. Baltimore: Johns Hopkins Press.

Galloway, D., Panckhurst, F., Boswell, K., Boswell, C., & Green, K. (1984). Mental health, absences from work, stress, and satisfaction in a sample of New Zealand primary school teachers. *Australian and New Zealand Journal of Psychiatry, 18*, 359–363.

Gold, Y. (1984). The factorial validity of the Maslach Burnout Inventory in a sample of California elementary and junior high school classroom teachers. *Educational and Psychological Measurement, 44*, 1009–1016.

Gold, Y. (1985). The relationship of six personal and life history variables to standing on three dimensions of the Maslach Burnout Inventory in a sample of elementary and junior high school teachers. *Educational and Psychological Measurement, 45*, 377–387.

Greenglass, E. R., & Burke, R. J. (1988). Work and family precursors of burnout in teachers: Sex differences. *Sex Roles, 18*, 215–229.

Hammen, C., & deMayo, R. (1982). Cognitive correlates of teacher stress and depressive symptoms: Implications for attributional models of depression. *Journal of Abnormal Psychology, 91*, 96–101.

Hayduk, L. A. (1987). Structural equation modeling with LISREL. Baltimore: Johns Hopkins Press.

Iwanicki, E. F., & Schwab, R. L. (1981). A cross validation study of the Maslach Burnout Inventory. *Educational and Psychological Measurement, 41*, 1167–1174.

Johnson, A. B., Gold, V., & Knepper, D. (1984). Frequency and intensity of professional burnout among teachers of the mildly handicapped. *College Student Journal, 18*, 261–266.

Jöreskog, K. G., & Sorbom, D. (1989). *LISREL 7: User's reference guide*. Mooresville, IN: Scientific Software.

Kahill, S. (1988). Symptoms of professional burnout: A review of the empirical evidence. *Canadian Psychology, 29*, 284–297.

Kasl, S. V. (1978). Epidemiological contributions to the study of work stress. In C. L. Cooper & R. Payne (Eds.), *Stress at work* (pp. 3–48). New York: Wiley.

Kasl, S. V. (1981). The challenge of studying the disease effects of stressful work conditions. *American Journal of Public Health, 71*, 682–684.

Kasl, S. V. (1983). Pursuing the link between stress life experiences and disease: A time for reappraisal. In C. L. Cooper (Ed.), *Stress research* (pp. 79–102). New York: Wiley.

Kasl, S. V. (1987). Methodologies in stress and health: Past difficulties, present dilemmas, future directions. In S. V. Kasl & C. L. Cooper (Eds.), *Stress and health: Issues in research methodology* (pp. 307–318). New York: Wiley.

Kenny, D. A. (1979). *Correlation and causality*. New York: Wiley.

Kyriacou, C., & Sutcliffe, J. (1978). Teacher stress: Prevalence, sources, and symptoms. *British Journal of Educational Psychology, 48*, 159–167.

Kyriacou, C., & Sutcliffe, J. (1979). Teacher stress and satisfaction. *Educational Research, 21*, 89–96.

Link, B., & Dohrenwend, B. P. (1980). Formulation of hypotheses about the true prevalence of demoralization in the United States. In B. P. Dohrenwend, M. S. Gould, B. Link, R. Neugebauer, & R. Wunsch-Hitzig (Eds.), *Mental illness in the United States* (pp. 114–132). New York: Praeger.

Link, B., Dohrenwend, B. P., & Skodal, A. E. (1986). Socio-economic status and schizophrenia: Noisome occupational characteristics as a risk factor. *American Sociological Review, 51*, 242–258.

Malanowski, J. R., & Wood, P. H. (1984). Burnout and self-actualization in public school teachers. *Journal of Psychology, 117*, 23–26.

Maslach, C., & Jackson, S. (1981). *Maslach Burnout Inventory*. Palo Alto, CA: Consulting Psychologists Press.

Maslach, C., & Jackson, S. (1984). Burnout in organizational settings. *Applied Social Psychology Annual, 5*, 133–153.

McIntyre, T. C. (1984). The relationship between locus of control and teacher burnout. *British Journal of Educational Psychology, 54*, 235–238.

Meier, S. T. (1984). The construct validity of burnout. *Journal of Occupational Psychology, 53*, 211–219.

Needle, R. H., Griffen, T., & Svendsen, R. (1981). Occupational stress: Coping and health problems of teachers. *Journal of School Health, 51*, 175–181.

Pearlin, L. I., & Schooler, C. (1978). The structure of coping. *Journal of Health and Social Behavior, 19*, 2–21.

Pettegrew, L. S., & Wolf, G. E. (1982). Validating measures of teacher stress. *American Educational Research Journal, 19*, 373–396.

Pierson-Hubeny, D., & Archambault, F. X. (1985). Role stress and perceived intensity of burnout among reading specialists. *Reading World, 24*, 41–52.

Quinn, R. P., & Staines, G. L. (1979). *The 1977 Quality of Employment Survey: Descriptive statistics with comparison data from the 1960–70 and the 1972–73 surveys*. Ann Arbor: Survey Research Center, Institute for Social Research, University of Michigan.

Radloff, L. S. (1977). The CES-D scale: A self-report depression scale for research in the general population. *Applied Psychological Measurement, 1*, 385–401.

Schonfeld, I. S. (1990a). Coping with job-related stress: The case of teachers. *Journal of Occupational Psychology, 63*, 141–149.

Schonfeld, I. S. (1990b). Psychological distress in a sample of teachers. *Journal of Psychology, 123*, 321–338.

Schonfeld, I. S. (1991). Dimensions of functional social support and psychological symptoms. *Psychological Medicine, 21*, 1051–1060.

Schonfeld, I. S. (1992). A longitudinal study of occupational stressors and depressive symptoms in first-year teachers. *Teaching and Teacher Education, 8*, 151–158.

Schonfeld, I. S. (in press). Burnout in teachers: Is it burnout or is it depression? *Human Stress: Current and Selected Research*.

Schonfeld, I. S., & Ruan, D. (1991). Occupational stress and preemployment measures: The case of teachers. *Journal of Social Behavior and Personality, 6*, 95–114.

Schwartz, J. E., Pieper, C. F., & Karasek, R. A., Jr. (1988). A procedure for linking job characteristics to health surveys. *American Journal of Public Health, 78*, 904–909.

Seiler, R. E., & Pearson, D. A. (1984). Stress among accounting educators in the United States. *Research in Higher Education, 21*, 301–316.

Spitzer, R. L., Williams, J. B. W., Gibbon, M., & First, M. B. (1989). *Structured clinical interview for DSM–III–R: Non-patient edition*. New York: New York State Psychiatric Institute.

U.S. Department of Health, Education and Welfare. (1965). *Coronary heart disease in adults: U.S., 1960–62* (DHEW Public Health Series No. 1000, Series 11). Washington, DC: U.S. Government Printing Office.

U.S. Department of Health, Education and Welfare. (1979). *Plan of operation of the Health and Nutritional Examination Survey, U.S., 1971–73* (DHEW Publication No. 79-1310, Series 1, No. 10b). Washington, DC: U.S. Government Printing Office.

U.S. Department of Labor. (1965). *Dictionary of occupational titles* (3rd ed.). Washington, DC: U.S. Government Printing Office.

Weissman, M., Sholomskas, M., Pottenger, M., Prusoff, B., & Locke, B. (1977). Assessing depressive symptoms in five psychiatric populations: A validation study. *American Journal of Epidemiology, 106*, 203–214.

Worchel, S., & Teddlie, C. (1976). The experience of crowding: A two-factor theory. *Journal of Personality and Social Psychology, 34*, 30–40.

19

Alan Hedge, William A. Erickson, and Gail Rubin

Effects of Personal and Occupational Factors on Sick Building Syndrome Reports in Air-Conditioned Offices

The "sick building syndrome" (SBS) describes a collection of symptoms of general malaise associated with occupancy of certain workplaces. These symptoms have been grouped into five categories: (a) sensory irritation of the eyes, nose, and throat, including dryness, pain, stinging sensations, hoarseness, and changes in the voice and in sounds from the respiratory system; (b) skin irritation, including blushing, pain, stinging or itching sensations, and dry skin; (c) neurotoxic symptoms, such as headache, nausea, drowsiness, tiredness, lethargy, reduced mental capacities, and fatigue; (d) unspecific hyperactivity reactions, such as runny eyes, runny nose, and asthmalike symptoms among nonasthmatics; and (e) odor or taste complaints, including changes in odor or taste and unpleasant odors or tastes (Mølhave, 1989). Researchers repeatedly have shown that the prevalence of SBS symptoms is higher in air-conditioned office buildings than in naturally ventilated office buildings (Mendell & Smith, 1990; Wilson & Hedge, 1987). Consequently, studies of SBS among office workers usually have attributed these symptoms to problems with indoor climate factors, especially poor indoor air quality (e.g., Hedge, 1984; Skov, Valbjørn, & DISG, 1987). However, studies of SBS frequently have failed to show that specific indoor air pollutants alone cause the symptoms reported by workers. In fact, in most investigations of sick buildings, researchers typically have found that the buildings meet current acceptable indoor air quality standards for gaseous pollutants (American Society of Heating, Refrigeration, and Air-Conditioning [ASHRAE], 1989), yet there is a high prevalence of symptom reports among workers.

Four recent intervention studies have tested the effects of increasing ventilation rate on SBS problems. Jaakkola, Miettinen, Komulainen, Tuomaala, and Seppänen (1990) found that the prevalence of SBS symptoms did not increase when 70% of office air was recirculated compared with when no air was recirculated. Menzies (1990) found that increasing the ventilation rate increased SBS symptoms among workers. Nagda et al. (1990) found that doubling the ventilation rate marginally increased complaints about indoor air quality and had no effect on pollutant concentrations in the office air. However, Jaakkola, Reinikainen, Heinonen, Majanen,

Research described in this chapter was conducted under contract to the Center for Indoor Air Research. We thank Susan Ulman and Elizabeth Luke for their assistance with this work.

and Seppänen (1991) reported a marginally beneficial effect of increasing ventilation on reducing the prevalence of SBS symptoms. Thus, the prevailing view that SBS is caused solely by the lack of ventilation in buildings is generally unsupported by the limited research conducted to date.

Epidemiological Studies of SBS

Epidemiological studies of SBS consistently have found a number of organizational and occupational variables that correlate with symptom prevalence (Hedge, Sterling, & Sterling, 1986; Hedge, Wilson, Burge, Robertson, & Harris-Bass, 1987). In a survey of 4,373 U.K. office workers in 46 buildings, workers' gender and occupational factors, such as job stress and video display terminal (VDT) use, correlated with SBS symptom reports (Burge, Hedge, Wilson, Harris-Bass, & Robertson, 1987; Hedge, 1989; Hedge et al., 1987). In a follow-up survey of workers in 6 of these buildings, SBS symptoms correlated with satisfaction with environmental conditions and job stress but not with job satisfaction (Hedge, 1988).

Skov, Valbjørn, Pedersen, and DISG (1989) surveyed 3,507 Danish office workers in 13 municipal buildings. They found that SBS symptoms were correlated with gender, allergy status (hayfever, migraines) and job-related factors (work hours per week, average hours per day, hours of VDT use, handling carbonless copy paper, photocopying, job category), and symptom prevalence varied among the buildings that were studied. However, SBS symptoms did not correlate with any individual indoor air quality measures other than air temperature (Skov et al., 1987). Jaakkola, Heinonen, Majanen, and Seppänen (1989) also reported that SBS symptoms correlated with air temperature and that above 22 °C there is an elevated prevalence of symptoms. Results from a survey of SBS among 7,000 Dutch workers in 61 offices found that gender, job satisfaction, and VDT use were among the most significant correlates of symptom reports (Zweers, Preller, Brunekreff, & Boleij, 1990).

Other research has shown that there are gender differences in perceived job stress, choice of coping response, and long-term mental and physical health problems (Barnett, Biener, & Baruch, 1987). A German study of male blue-collar workers showed that job stress itself may cause psychosomatic complaints (Frese, 1985), some of which are comparable to those used to define SBS, (e.g., headache, irritability, dry throat, chest tightness). Comparable results have been reported in large studies of VDT operators in the United Kingdom (Evans, 1985a, 1985b), in Sweden (Knave, Wibom, Voss, Hedström, & Bergqvist, 1985), and in the United States (Smith, Cohen, & Stammerjoh, 1981) where symptoms similar to SBS reports (e.g., headaches, eye irritation, skin irritation) have been shown to correlate with VDT use. These findings suggest that a broader understanding of the occupational environment may be needed to help unravel the causes of SBS.

However, not all surveys of office workers have confirmed these findings. Nörback, Rand, Michel, and Amcoff (1989) failed to find a correlation between SBS symptoms and either job stress or job satisfaction, although they did confirm a gender difference in symptom prevalence. These negative results may be attributable to the use of single, analog rating scales to measure job stress and job satisfaction rather than the multiple item, 5-point rating scales used in other studies.

Also, Nörback et al. did not define SBS symptoms as being work related (a work-related symptom is one that is alleviated when the worker is away from the building), whereas other studies have investigated work-related symptoms only. Lenvik (1990) studied 764 workers in three offices and found that the prevalence of SBS symptoms did not differ by job type or job satisfaction but did differ by workers gender, with women reporting most symptoms. Men also were found to have greater job satisfaction. However, the lack of multivariate analyses of these data preclude inferring that work factors do not affect SBS reports in offices. On balance, the evidence that gender and job factors affect SBS reports outweighs the evidence to the contrary.

Indoor Environment Risk Factors

In an attempt to integrate the broad array of findings into a common conceptual framework for investigating and understanding the indoor environment, Hedge (1989) developed a multiple risks model of the relations between the diverse factors that have been shown to influence the comfort and health of office workers, either independently or collectively, directly or indirectly, by means of their effects on stress levels. This model suggests that SBS symptoms are caused by exposure to multiple risk factors, only some of which are environmental, rather than by direct exposure to indoor air pollutants in offices alone. These multiple risk factors include direct environmental risks (e.g., exposure to pollutants), indirect environmental risks (e.g., workers' satisfaction with thermal conditions), occupational risks (e.g., job stress, VDT use), and personal risks (e.g., gender, perceived stress). It is hypothesized that these environmental, occupational, and psychosocial factors interact to place a total stress load on a worker that mediates reports of SBS symptoms, depending on the individual's ability to cope.

The model represents these interactions and influences on the worker as three interlocked subsystems of the environment, building, and work. The environmental subsystem represents interrelations between environmental services (ventilation system, lighting system) and ambient conditions (indoor air quality [IAQ], thermal conditions, noise, and vibration). Satisfactory IAQ will be influenced by the outdoor air quality; standards of cleaning and maintenance of the heating, ventilating, and air conditioning (HVAC) system; HVAC system design and operation; and the levels of internally generated pollutants from people, materials, and machines. The following may also contribute to SBS symptoms: HVAC systems, which produce noise and vibrations both from the operations of the plant and the movement of air through the system (Hodgson et al., 1987); thermal conditions, which may affect pollutant emissions (Girman, Alevantis, Kulasingham, Petreas, & Webber, 1987); acoustic ceiling tiles (Hansen, 1989); the design of office lighting systems, which may affect acoustic conditions because luminaries reflect incident sound; lighting fixtures, which can affect IAQ; and volatilized asphalt from malfunctioning fluorescent lamp ballasts (Tavris, Field, & Brumback, 1984). In summary, the environmental subsystem may exert direct and indirect effects on office workers. Direct effects include poor IAQ, poor office lighting, and acoustic and vibration problems. Indirect effects include workers' negative perceptions of office environmental conditions.

The environmental subsystem is affected by the building subsystem. The following characteristics may contribute to SBS symptoms: the building shell, which influences rates of air infiltration; the materials, furnishings, and finishes which may give off gas pollutants; an open-office layout, which may affect office ventilation; open shelving and the area of material surfaces (Skov et al., 1989); and the amount and type of glazing, which will affect office lighting and thermal conditions. The building may also indirectly affect workers' perceptions of environmental quality, patterns of working, and workspace preferences. Also, higher levels of distraction associated with open-office layouts also may be stressful to workers (Dick, Kompart, Reinhartz, Schnadt, & Tossin, 1981).

The work subsystem can influence the environmental subsystem by affecting worker activities that directly affect IAQ. Breathing generates carbon dioxide, to-bacco smoking releases gaseous and particulate air pollutants, and carbonless copy paper may release formaldehyde and other volatile organic compounds (Hedge, 1987). Work activities also influence the building subsystem (e.g., meetings in open office areas may produce bothersome noise for proximate, uninvolved workers) and thus influence SBS reports. Other office technology (e.g., wet photocopiers) also may affect health indirectly releasing air pollutants such as volatile organic compounds (Tsuchiya, Clermont, & Walkinshaw, 1988).

Finally, Hedge's (1989) multiple risks model proposes that in the absence of direct effects of adverse environmental conditions on health (e.g., direct exposure to dangerous levels of indoor air pollutants or bioaerosols), the SBS symptoms reported by a worker will be dependent on internalized comparison of the perceived external state of the environment and the perceived internal state of the body. This comparison process in turn may be influenced by a number of psychobiological factors (e.g., age, personality type, stress status).

SBS and Stress

Most studies of SBS have focused on assessing exposure to indoor air pollutants. These studies have shown that SBS complaints frequently are not simply the result of pollutant exposures at levels judged to be hazardous to health. Personal, occu-pational, and psychosocial factors, however, have been shown to correlate with SBS symptoms. It is likely that these factors act to change a worker's susceptibility to environmental stressors, yet surprisingly, there have been few attempts to inves-tigate the factors that influence a person's susceptibility to manifest adverse health reactions to their indoor environment. Several studies have shown that self-reported stress is highly correlated with negative mood states and with the reporting of physical symptoms, such as nasal congestion, that are similar to those of SBS. The consistency in results has led to the suggestion that these factors may reflect a common psychological state of negative affectivity (Pennebaker & Watson, 1988).

We hypothesized that the development of SBS symptoms would occur when a susceptible person either received a sufficient dose of an air pollutant or combination of air pollutants or perceived that he or she had been exposed to an air pollutant or combination of air pollutants. We further hypothesized that a person's suscep-tibility to developing and reporting SBS symptoms would be influenced by the level of stress that they experienced, whether this stress resulted from the content of their work, from their beliefs and fears about possible exposure to indoor contaminants, or from other indoor environment conditions.

Preliminary support for these hypotheses is found in the path model developed by Hedge, Burge, Robertson, Wilson, and Harris-Bass (1989) to describe the findings from their survey to SBS among 4,373 workers from 46 U.K. office buildings. In this model, job stress, the perception of environmental comfort, and the perception of winter environment conditions all act as mediating factors influencing SBS reports. Unfortunately, IAQ measures were not taken in their study, and therefore it is premature to conclude that the SBS symptoms did not result from exposure to indoor air pollutants.

A Survey of IAQ and SBS

The study described in this chapter was undertaken to extend this earlier work by further testing the multifactorial nature of SBS. The research design systematically investigated the relation among physical environmental variables, personal variables (e.g., gender), work-content variables (e.g., VDT use, job stress, and job satisfaction), and reports of SBS among U.S. office workers. Eighteen office buildings occupied by private sector financial, insurance, sales, and marketing companies were investigated. None of the buildings surveyed was known to have a history of IAQ problems. The main office spaces in all buildings were ventilated by either a variable air volume or a constant air volume system with air recirculation. All buildings studied were located in the Eastern United States: Alabama, Georgia, Indiana, Kentucky, Massachusetts, Michigan, New York, Ohio, and Virginia. Each building was studied for two consecutive workdays in the period from January to June. To ensure that a range of IAQ conditions were studied, the following five smoking policies were investigated: smoking prohibited (3 buildings), smoking restricted to rooms with local filtration (5 buildings), smoking restricted to rooms with no local air treatment (2 buildings), smoking restricted to rooms with separate ventilation (2 buildings), and smoking restricted to the open-plan cubicle workstations and enclosed offices (6 buildings). In effect, smoking policy was used as an experimental treatment to study the effects of different IAQ conditions on SBS reports.

The study used a self-report questionnaire developed from previous research instruments used in SBS investigations (Hedge, 1988; Hedge et al., 1987, 1989). This questionnaire gathered data on employee perceptions of ambient conditions (16 questions), occupational factors (12 questions), work-related health and SBS symptoms (17 questions), and personal information (8 questions). A smoking information section that varied according to the organization's smoking policy (prohibited, restricted to designated areas, or restricted to workstation) was included that contained questions pertaining to smoking history, including amount of and attitude toward tobacco smoke exposure. Answers to the ambient environment questions and the SBS symptom questions consisted of identical scale that asked about the frequency of experience for the previous 1-month period in the building (never, 1–3 times per month, 1–3 times per week, or every day). Jobs were grouped into four categories: managerial, professional, technical, and clerical or secretarial. Only a few jobs did not fit these categories and were thus excluded from subsequent analyses using job type. Hours of VDT use were categorized as follows: never (0 hr); less than 1 hr per day (0.5 hr); 1, 2, 3, 4, 5, or 6 hr per day; or 7 or more hr per day (7.5 hr). Job stress and job satisfaction questions were answered on a 5-point rating scale (strongly agree, mostly agree, uncertain, mostly disagree, strongly disagree). Job satisfaction was measured using a refined set of six items adapted from a short Job Satisfaction Scale (Brayfield & Rothe, 1951). Job stress was measured using five items adapted from a variety of sources. Both the job satisfaction and job stress items had been previously used in SBS surveys (Hedge, 1988).

In each building, IAQ was measured at two sites in the morning and two different sites in the afternoon on each of two consecutive workdays, giving a total of 8 sites per building. Integrating instruments measuring nicotine, formaldehyde, and respirable suspended particles (< 2.5 µm diameter) were housed inside briefcases, one of which was placed centrally at each of the two sample sites for each one-half day sample period. Measures of carbon monoxide, carbon dioxide, respirable particulates (< 3.5 µm diameter), air temperature, relative humidity, and illumination were taken hourly at each site for each sample period. As the indoor climate was being surveyed, approximately 30 questionnaires were individually distributed by the researchers to employees at their workstations in the immediate vicinity of each of the indoor air sample sites in the office areas. In most cases, workers were in open office cubicles. In 3 of the 18 buildings, distribution and collection were done by in-house staff because of the sensitive nature of the work being undertaken in those buildings. The majority of questionnaires were collected by the researchers on the same day. Employees who could not complete the questionnaire on the same day were given a preaddressed return envelope. Less than 2% of the employees who were approached refused to accept a questionnaire, and of the 4,211 questionnaires distributed, 3,155 were returned (75% return rate, range of 60–85% per building).

All data were analyzed on an IBM mainframe computer. Descriptive and multiple regression analyses were performed using SAS (Version 5.18). Multiple regression analysis was used to model the relation of occupational and personal factors with the total number of SBS symptoms. Factor analysis was performed using SPSS[x] (Version 4.0), and the responses to the job stress and job satisfaction questions were analyzed using factor analysis with varimax rotation (Manly, 1986; Rummel, 1970).

Factors Influencing Sick Building Syndrome

Few differences in IAQ were found between the five smoking policies studied; these results have been described in detail elsewhere (Hedge, Erickson, & Rubin, 1991). Except for air temperature ($r = 0.58, p < 0.01$), there were no significant correlations between IAQ measures and the average number of SBS symptoms per building. Temperature variations were small and well within the comfort range.

Job satisfaction and job stress items with negative wording were reversed scored, and responses to these questions were analyzed using factor analysis with varimax rotation. Results confirmed the presence of two orthogonal factors that together explained 55.9% of the common factor variance (Table 1). Six questions were significantly loaded on the job satisfaction factor, and five questions were

Table 1. Factor analysis of job statements

Statement	Job satisfaction	Job stress
My job is usually interesting.	0.84	0.16
I'm happy in my job.	0.89	−0.05
I dislike my job.	−0.83	0.07
I am satisfied with my job.	0.81	−0.04
I'm enthusiastic about my job.	0.84	0.02
My job is rather monotonous.	−0.68	−0.10
My job is not very stressful.	−0.05	−0.51
I usually have to work fast.	0.04	0.66
I often feel stressed at work.	−0.20	0.82
My job demands a lot of concentration.	0.32	0.58
I often feel overworked.	−0.14	0.78
Eigenvalue	4.29	2.41
% common variance	35.80	20.10

Table 2. Prevalence of SBS symptoms (percentages) among 3,155 office workers in 18 air-conditioned buildings

Symptoms	Never	1−3 times per month	1−3 times per week	Every day
Excessive mental fatigue	56.9	22.6	12.5	8.1
Headache across forehead	61.4	22.0	11.6	5.1
Dry eyes	62.9	13.9	11.6	11.6
Irritated, sore eyes	62.0	15.5	13.7	8.7
Nervousness, irritability	63.5	23.0	9.5	4.0
Unusual tiredness lethargy	70.1	18.2	7.1	4.6
Stuffy, congested nose	72.0	11.4	8.3	8.3
Sore, irritated throat	77.8	13.3	5.9	3.1
Runny nose	80.8	10.7	5.2	3.3
Hoarseness	84.7	9.5	4.2	1.6
Dry skin	85.7	4.0	3.8	6.5
Dizziness	89.7	8.0	1.9	0.4
Wheezing, chest tightness	91.5	5.5	1.9	1.0
Nausea	92.3	6.5	1.0	0.3
Skin irritation, rashes	95.5	3.1	0.6	0.8

significantly loaded on the job stress factor. The reliability of each multiple item measure was calculated using Cronbach's alpha, which is a measure of the average interitem correlation (Cronbach, 1970). Values of alpha more than 0.67 indicate acceptable internal consistency (Klitzman & Stellman, 1989). For the job stress items, Cronbach's alpha was 0.70; for the job satisfaction items, Cronbach's alpha was 0.90. In all subsequent analyses, the mean of responses to either the five job stress or six job satisfaction questions for each person was used as the job stress or job satisfaction measures, respectively.

Table 2 summarizes the prevalence and frequency of reporting SBS symptoms and shows that eye problems, fatigue and lethargy, headache, and irritability were among the most prevalent and frequently experienced symptoms. To test the effects of personal and occupational factors on SBS symptoms, a series of multiple regression analyses were used. For these analyses, the total number of SBS symptoms reported by each worker was the dependent variable. The following independent variables were tested: gender, VDT use, job stress, job satisfaction, job type, age, smoking status, and smoking policy. Worker gender, job stress, job satisfaction, and VDT use were significantly associated with the total number of SBS symptoms reported. None of the other variables tested were significantly associated with SBS symptoms. These data were checked for collinearity, and the following tolerances were obtained: gender (0.972), VDT use (0.963), job stress (0.988), and job satisfaction (0.998). These tolerances were all close to unity, which indicates that the independent variables were not collinear (i.e., the variables measured independent aspects). Initial testing showed that separate intercepts for each gender were required to adequately model the data $F(1,2217) = 38.74, p = 0.0001$.

The appropriate regression model for the total number of SBS symptoms has separate intercepts for men and women but a common slope for VDT use, job stress, and job satisfaction, adjusted $R^2 = 0.10$, F (4,2907) = 80.81, $p < 0.0000$. The number of SBS symptoms were calculated as follows.

Men: $(1.27 \pm .32$ [intercept]$) + (0.12 \pm .02$ [VDT use]$) + (0.64 \pm .06$ [job stress]$)$
    $- (0.43 \pm .06$ [job satisfaction]$)$

Women: $(2.02 \pm .32$ [intercept]$) + (0.12 \pm .02$ [VDT use]$) + (0.64 \pm .06$ [job stress]$)$
    $- (0.43 \pm .06$ [job satisfaction]$)$

The adjusted mean number of SBS symptoms for women (3.14 ± 0.06) was higher than that for men (2.39 ± 0.07). The positive coefficients for job stress and VDT use indicate that these variables correspond to increased reports of SBS symptoms. Job satisfaction has a negative coefficient because a low score indicates low satisfaction, which in turn corresponds to reports of more SBS symptoms.

SBS Is a Multifactorial Problem

Of 18 office buildings that were studied, all met current standards for acceptable IAQ (ASHRAE, 1989), yet over 70% of the workers surveyed in these buildings reported at least one SBS symptom. This finding is similar to that reported by Wilson and Hedge (1987), who found that 80% of workers sampled from 46 U.K. office buildings reported at least one SBS symptom.

Comparisons of IAQ measures among buildings failed to uncover significant differences in pollutant concentrations that could account for the SBS symptoms reported by workers. Air temperature was the only physical variable significantly correlated with SBS symptoms, which agrees with the findings of Jaakkola et al. (1989) and Skov et al. (1989). However, only a narrow range of air temperatures was recorded in the present study (averaging around 24 °C with a range of around ± 1 °C), and it seems unlikely that these air temperatures directly caused SBS symptoms. Because many indoor contaminants cannot be consciously perceived by workers, air temperature may be the main sensation that they use to judge the quality of indoor air. We are studying possible relations between perceptions of indoor environment conditions and SBS.

The results show that, in the absence of significant concentrations of indoor air pollutants, gender, job stress, job satisfaction, and VDT use were significantly associated with the total number of SBS symptoms. This finding also is in agreement with those of previous studies (Hedge et al., 1989; Skov et al., 1989; Zweers et al., 1990).

Kjaergaard, Pedersen, and Mølhave (1990) found no differences between women and men in sensitivity of eyes to carbon dioxide or in irritation thresholds to n-decane exposure, which suggests that gender differences in symptom reports may not be attributable to differences in sensitivity to air pollutants. However, women are known to report more health symptoms than men (Pennebaker, 1982) and also have a higher risk for most types of depression (McGrath, Keita, Strickland, & Russo, 1990). Why there should be a gender difference in symptom reporting in so many of the studies of SBS remains a mystery.

Several surveys of office workers have reported that symptoms of eye irritation, fatigue, and skin irritation, similar to those of SBS, are more prevalent among those who work full-time with VDTs (Evans, 1985a, 1985b; Knave et al., 1985; Stellman et al., 1987). Sandström, Mild, and Stenberg (1991) found that the risk of experiencing skin irritation symptoms among VDT workers was significantly elevated for workers exposed to high electromagnetic fields in front of VDT screens and high electromagnetic background fields. We are currently conducting research that suggests that the electromagnetic fields from VDTs may attract irritating fibers and particles to the screen and into the immediate microenvironment of the computer worker. The composition of the materials in the building, such as the types of refractory ceramic and mineral fibers, may determine what potentially irritating fibers and particulates are present. There is also some evidence to suggest that fibers and particulates may be directly transferred to the eyes and the respiratory tract by the fingers whenever they touch dusty surfaces (Schneider, 1986). Franck (1986) reported that complaints of eye irritation correlation with microscopic lesions to the cornea and also to the rapid break-up of the tear film of the eye. Corneal lacerations may be caused by deposits of particulates and mineral fibers on the surface of the eye, and such fibers have been detected in the conjunctival secretions from VDT users reporting eye irritation symptoms (Lob, Guillemin, Madelaine, & Boillat, 1984). The tear film of the eye is normally refreshed by each eye blink, but the blink rate often falls with VDT use, and the heat generated by the VDT may help to locally dry the air, which would also reduce the stability of tear film (Scalet, 1987). VDT work may also increase levels of work stress (Crespy & Rey, 1983), which in turn may have other adverse health effects. To what extent the symptoms of SBS are caused directly by characteristics of VDTs and VDT work and to what extent the symptoms are caused indirectly by the effects of VDT work on stress remains to be thoroughly investigated.

That SBS symptoms did not correlate with job type appears to contradict earlier reports of correlation (Hedge et al., 1989; Skov et al., 1989). However, levels of job satisfaction were not directly measured in either of these studies, and job category may have been acting as a proxy for job satisfaction in these surveys. The present results agree with those of previous research studies that have shown that job stress plays an important role in the etiology of SBS (Skov, et al., 1989; Hedge et al., 1989; Morris & Hawkins, 1987; Norbäck, 1990; Zweers et al., 1990). Several SBS symptoms are similar to symptoms of stress (e.g., headache, chest tightness, irritability), and research needs to be conducted to test how well SBS symptoms correlate with other psychological and physiological stress measures. Intervention studies should be conducted to test whether stress reduction programs may also be effective in reducing SBS complaints. However, the processes that underlie this association await systematic investigation.

We think that it is unlikely that some SBS symptoms (e.g., eye, nose, and throat irritation) are the direct result of job stress or job dissatisfaction. Rather, we suggest that physiological stress reactions may mediate the effects of ambient environmental conditions on individual workers, possibly by changing the body's sensitivity to perceived physical demands. Frankenhauser and Johansson (1986) showed that low perceived control over work demands correlated with increased self-ratings of distress and with increased levels of urinary cortisol. Although the present study did not measure aspects of perceived control, previous studies have found that perceived control over ambient conditions correlates with SBS reports (Hedge et al., 1989). McCann, Warnick, and Knopp (1990) found that perceptions of increased workload and increased stress correlated with behavioral changes such as increased calorie intake, increased intake of total fat, increased percentage of calories from total fat, and increased in total cholesterol levels, even after controlling for caloric intake. Nabiloff et al. (1991) reported that women exposed to a psychologically stressful 12-min mental arithmetic task showed several rapid immunological changes: an increase in the release of CD8 suppressor/cytotoxic T cells and natural killer (NK) cells into the circulation for both young and old women and an increase in the activity levels of the NK cells in young women. Such immunological responses may change the sensitivity of the airways to airborne contaminants.

Several studies have shown correlations between job stress and the development of cardiovascular disease (Johnson & Hall, 1988; Karasek, Baker, Marxer, Ahlbom, & Theorell, 1981). These studies have tested Karasek's demand control model of job stress, which proposes that physiologically aversive strain occurs whenever the psychological demands of work exceed personal resources to control work content (Karasek, 1979). This model has been developed from data on blue-collar workers, and to what extent similar processes may influence the propensity for white-collar workers to develop SBS symptoms requires investigation.

The present study has confirmed an important role for personal and occupational factors in the etiology of SBS, but even though the regression model for these variables is highly significant, it only accounts for 10% of the variation in the number of SBS symptoms reported, which suggests that other variables, as yet untested, influence SBS reports. These results show that, contrary to popular belief, SBS is not caused solely by exposure to indoor pollutants. They show an important role of individual differences and occupational factors in the etiology of SBS. If there is a serious desire to improve the health of office workers, we suggest that future research should focus on unraveling the pathways by which personal and occupational factors affect SBS symptoms.

References

American Society of Heating, Refrigerating, and Air-Conditioning Engineers. (1989). *Ventilation for acceptable indoor air quality.* Atlanta, GA: Author.

Barnett, R. C., Biener, L., & Baruch, G. K. (Eds.). (1987). *Gender and stress.* New York: Free Press.

Brayfield, A. H., & Rothe, H. F. (1951). An index of job satisfaction. *Journal of Applied Psychology, 35*, 307–311.

Burge, P. S., Hedge, A., Wilson, S., Harris-Bass, J., & Robertson, A. S. (1987). Sick building syndrome: A study of 4373 office workers. *Annals of Occupational Hygiene, 31*, 493–504.

Crespy, J., & Rey, P. (1983). *Work on visual display units: Risks for health.* New York: World Health Organization.

Cronbrach, L. J. (1970). *Essentials of psychological testing* (3rd. ed.). New York: Harper & Row.

Dick, C., Kompart, I., Reinhartz, G., Schnadt, H., & Tossin, N. (1981). *Auswirkungen der Tatigkeit in Grossraumburos auf die Gesundheit der Beschaftigten, Pt. II.* Germany: Der Bunderminister für Arbeit und Sozialordnung.

Evans, J. (1985a). Office conditions influence VDU operators' health. *Health & Safety at Work,* December, 33–37.

Evans, J. (1985b). VDU operators display health problems. *Health & Safety at Work,* November, 33–37.

Franck, C. (1986). Eye symptoms and signs in buildings with indoor climate problems ('office eye syndrome'). *Acta Opthalmologica, 64*, 306–311.

Frankenhauser, M., & Johansson, G. (1986). Stress at work: psychobiological and psychosocial effects. *International Review of Applied Psychology, 35*, 287–299.

Frese, M. (1985). Stress at work and psychosomatic complaints: A causal interpretation. *Journal of Applied Psychology, 70*, 314–328.

Girman, J., Alevantis, L., Kulasingham, G., Petreas, M., & Webber, L. (1987). The bake-out of an office building: A case study. *Environment International, 15*, 449–454.

Hansen, L. (1989). Monitoring of symptoms in estimating the effect of intervention in the sick building syndrome: A field study. *Environment International, 15*, 159–162.

Hedge, A. (1984). Suggestive evidence for a relationship between office design and self-reports of ill-health among office workers in the United Kingdom. *Journal of Architectural Planning and Research, 1*, 163–174.

Hedge, A. (1987). Office health hazards: An annotated bibliography. *Ergonomics, 30*, 733–772.

Hedge, A. (1988). Job stress, job satisfaction, and work-related illness in offices. In *Proceedings of the 32nd Annual Meeting, Human Factors Society,* (Vol. 2, pp. 777–779). Santa Monica, CA: Human Factors Society.

Hedge, A. (1989). Environmental conditions and health in offices. *International Review of Ergonomics, 3*, 87–110.

Hedge, A., Burge, P. S., Robertson, A. S., Wilson, S., & Harris-Bass, J. (1989). Work-related illness in offices: A proposed model of the "sick building syndrome." *Environment International, 15*, 143–158.

Hedge, A., Erickson, W. A., & Rubin, G., (1991). The effects of smoking policy on indoor air quality and sick building syndrome in 18 air-conditioned offices. In *Proceedings: Healthy buildings—IAQ '91 ASHRAE Conference* (pp. 151–159). Atlanta, GA: American Society of Heating, Refrigeration, and Air Conditioning Engineers.

Hedge, A., Sterling, E. M., & Sterling, T. D. (1986). Evaluating office environments: The case for a macroergonomic systems approach. In O. Brown, Jr., & Henrick (Eds.), *Human factors in organizational design and management* (Vol. 2, pp. 419–424). New York: Elsevier.

Hedge, A., Wilson, S., Burge, P. S., Robertson, A. S., & Harris-Bass, J. (1987). Environmental, psychological and organizational correlates of employee health in offices: A proposed model. In *Proceedings of the 31st Annual Meeting, Human Factors Society* (Vol. 2, pp. 736–740). Santa Monica, CA: Human Factors Society.

Hodgson, M. J., Permar, E., Squire, G., Cagney, W., Allen, A., & Parkinson, D. K. (1987). Vibration as a cause of "tight building syndrome" symptoms. In B. Siefert, H. Esdon, M. Fischer, H. Ruden, & J. Wegner, (Eds.), *Indoor Air '87: Proceedings of the 4th International Conference on Indoor Air Quality and Climate* (Vol. 2, pp. 449–453). Berlin: Institute for Water, Soil, and Air Hygiene.

Jaakkola, J. J. K., Heinonen, O. P., Majanen, A., & Seppänen, O. (1989). Sick building syndrome, sensation of dryness and thermal comfort in relation to room temperature in an office building: Need for individual control of temperature. *Environment International, 15*, 163–168.

Jaakkola, J. J. K., Miettinen, O. S., Komulainen, K., Tuomaala, P., & Seppänen, O. (1990). The effect of air recirculation on symptoms and environmental complaints in office workers: A double-blind, four period cross-over study. In *Indoor Air '90: Proceedings of the 5th International Conference on Indoor Air Quality and Climate* (Vol. 1, pp. 281–286). Ottawa, Ontario, Canada: International Conference on Indoor Air Quality and Climate.

Jaakkola, J. J. K., Reinikainen, L., Heinonen, O. P., Majanen, A., & Seppänen, O. (1991). Indoor air quality requirements for healthy office buildings: Recommendations based on an epidemiologic study. *Environmental International, 17*, 371–378.

Johnson, J. V., & Hall, E. M. (1988). Job strain, work place social support, and cardiovascular disease: A cross-sectional study of a random sample of the Swedish working population. *American Journal of Public Health, 78*, 1336–1342.

Karasek, R. (1979). Job demands, job decision latitude, and mental strain: Implications for job redesign. *Administrative Science Quarterly, 24*, 285–308.

Karasek, R., Baker, D., Marxer, F., Ahlbom, A., & Theorell, T. (1981). Job decision latitude, job demands, and cardiovascular disease: A prospective study of Swedish men. *American Journal of Public Health, 71*, 694–705.

Kjaergaard, S., Pedersen, O. F., & Mølhave, L. (1990). Common chemical sense of the eyes—Influence of smoking, age, and sex. In *Indoor Air '90: Proceedings of the 5th International Conference on Indoor Air Quality and Climate* (Vol. 1, pp. 257–262). Ottawa, Ontario, Canada: International Conference on Indoor Air Quality and Climate.

Klitzman, S., & Stellman, J. M. (1989). The impact of the physical environment on the psychological well-being of office workers. *Social Science Medicine, 29*, 733–742.

Knave, B. G., Wibom, R. I., Voss, M., Hedström, L. D., & Bergqvist, U. O. (1985). Work with video display terminals among office employees: 1. Subjective symptoms and discomfort. *Scandinavian Journal of Work, Environment and Health, 11*, 457–466.

Lenvik, K. (1990). Comparisons of working conditions and "sick building syndrome" symptoms among employees with different job functions. *Indoor Air '90, Proceedings of the 5th International Conference on Indoor Air Quality and Climate* (Vol. 1, pp. 507–512). Ottawa, Ontario, Canada: International Conference on Indoor Air Quality and Climate.

Lob, M., Guillemin, M., Madelaine, P., & Boillat, M. A. (1984). Collective dermatitis in a modern office. In E. Grandjean (Ed.), *Ergonomics and Health in Modern Offices* (pp. 52–58). London: Taylor & Francis.

Manly, B. F. J. (1986). *Multivariate statistical methods: A primer*. London: Chapman Hall.

McCann, B., Warnick, R., & Knopp, R. (1990). Changes in plasma lipids and dietary intake accompanying shifts in perceived workload and stress. *Psychosomatic Medicine, 52*, 97–108.

McGrath, E., Keita, G. P., Strickland, B. R., & Russo, N. F. (1990). *Women and depression: Risk factors and treatment issues*. Washington, DC: American Psychological Association.

Mendell, M., & Smith, A. (1990). Consistent pattern of elevated symptoms in air-conditioned office buildings: A reanalysis of epidemiologic studies. *American Journal of Public Health, 80*, 1193–1199.

Menzies, R. I. (1990). Sick building syndrome. The effects of changes in ventilation rates on symptom prevelence: The evaluation of a double blind experiment. *Indoor Air '90, Proceedings of the 5th International Conference on Indoor Air Quality and Climate* (Vol. 1, pp. 519–524). Ottawa, Ontario, Canada: International Conference on Air Quality and Climate.

Mølhave, L. (1989). The sick building and other buildings with indoor climate problems. *Environment International, 15*, 65–74.

Morris, L., & Hawkins, L. (1987). The role of stress in the sick building syndrome. In B. Siefert, H. Esdon, M. Fischer, H. Ruden, & J. Wegner (Eds.), *Indoor Air '87, Proceedings of the 4th International Conference on Indoor Air Quality and Climate* (Vol. 2, pp. 566–571). Berlin: Institute for Water, Soil, and Air Hygiene.

Nagda, N., Koontz, M., Lumby, D., Albrecht, R., & Rizzuto, J. (1990). Impact of increased ventilation rates on office building air quality. *Indoor Air '90, Proceedings of the 5th International Conference on Indoor Air Quality and Climate* (Vol. 4, pp. 281–286). Ottawa, Ontario, Canada: International Conference on Air Quality and Climate.

Nabiloff, B., Benton, D., Solomon, G., Morley, J., Fahey, J., Bloom, E., Makinodan, T., & Gilmore, S. (1991). Immunological changes in young and old adults during brief laboratory stress. *Psychosomatic Medicine, 53*, 121–132.

Norbäck, D. (1990). *Environmental exposures and personal factors related to sick building syndrome.* Unpublished doctoral dissertation, Upsala University, East Orange, NJ.

Norbäck, D., Rand, G., Michel, I., & Amcoff, S. (1989). The prevalence of symptoms associated with sick buildings and polluted industrial environments as compared to unexposed reference groups without expressed dissatisfaction. *Environment International, 15*, 85–94.

Pennebaker, J. W. (1982). *The psychology of physical symptoms.* New York: Springer-Verlag.

Pennebaker, J. W., & Watson, D. (1988). Self-reports and physiological measures in the workplace. In J. J. Hurrell, Jr., L. R. Murphy, S. L. Sauter, & C. L. Cooper (Eds.), *Occupational stress: Issues and developments in research* (pp. 184–199). New York: Taylor & Francis.

Rummel, R. J. (1970, June). *Applied factor analysis.* Evanston, IL: Northwestern University Press.

Sandström, M., Mild, K. H., & Stenberg, B. (1991). The office illness project in northern Sweden: The role of ELF and VLF electric and magnetic fields in the office environment for the occurrence of skin symptoms among VDT workers. Paper presented at the 13th Annual Meeting of the Bioelectromagnetic Society, Salt Lake City, UT.

Scalet, E. A. (1987). *VDT health and safety: Issues and solutions.* Lawrence, KS: Ergosyst Associates.

Schneider, T. (1986). Manmade mineral fiber and other fibers in the air and in settled dust. *Environment International, 12*, 61–65.

Skov, P., Valbjørn, O., & DISG. (1987). The sick building syndrome in the office environment: The Danish Town Hall study. *Environment International, 13*, 339–349.

Skov, P., Valbjørn, O., Pedersen, B. V., & DISG. (1989). Influence of personal characteristics, job-related factors and psychosocial factors on the sick building syndrome. *Scandinavian Journal of Work, Environment and Health, 15*, 286–295.

Smith, M. J., Cohen, B. G. F., & Stammerjohn, J. W., Jr. (1981). An investigation of health complaints and job stress in video display operations, *Human Factors, 23*, 387–400.

Stellman, J. M., Klitzman, S., Gordon, G., & Snow, B. R. (1987). Comparison of well-being among non-machine interactive clerical workers and full-time and part-time VDT users and typists. In B. Knave & P. G. Widebäck (Eds.), *Work with display units* (pp. 605–613). New York: Elsevier Science.

Tavris, D. R., Field, L., & Brumback, C. L. (1984). Outbreak of illness due to volatilized asphalt coming from a malfunctioning fluorescent lighting fixture. *American Journal of Public Health, 74*, 614–615.

Tsuchiya, Y., Clermont, M. J., & Walkinshaw, D. S. (1988). Wet process photocopying machines: A source of volatile organic compound emissions in buildings. *Environmental Toxicology and Chemistry, 7*, 15–18.

Wilson, S., & Hedge, A. (1987). *The Office Environment Survey: A study of building sickness.* London: Building Use Studies.

World Health Organization. (1983). Indoor air pollutants: Exposure and health effects. In *EURO Reports and Studies* (Vol. 78, pp. 23–25). New York: Author.

Zweers, T., Preller, L., Brunekreff, B., & Boleij, J. S. M. (1990). Relationships between health and indoor climate complaints and building, workplace, job and personal characteristics. In *Indoor Air '90, Proceedings of the 5th International Conference on Indoor Air Quality and Climate* (Vol. 1, pp. 495–498). Ottawa, Ontario, Canada: International Conference on Indoor Air Quality and Climate.

20

Mark Braverman

Posttrauma Crisis Intervention in the Workplace

The past two decades have witnessed increased interest in the human response to traumatic events. A growing body of research exists on the psychological consequences of military combat, physical and sexual assault and abuse, mass disasters, and the effects of jobs such as law enforcement and emergency response that carry a high risk of exposure to traumatic stress. During the same period, practitioners from a range of fields have begun to view the workplace as an appropriate arena in which to promote the general health and emotional well-being of workers. This work has originated from both public- and private-sector initiatives. Since the establishment in 1971 of the National Institute for Occupational Safety and Health and the continued development in the private sector of technologies for workplace health promotion and stress management, research and program development in these areas has grown considerably, along with a substantial literature on the relation between workplace conditions and stress-related health issues. Investigators and practitioners from a range of disciplines have contributed to this effort. The list includes occupational medicine, occupational safety, organizational development, psychology, social policy, and the law.

This chapter integrates aspects of these diverse fields and describes a model of crisis intervention that focuses on the emotional well-being of managers and employees in the aftermath of traumatic events.

Psychological Trauma in the Workplace

It is only recently that companies have begun to pay attention to the effect of traumatic events in the workplace. Such events arise from many sources. Some jobs, such as law enforcement, emergency response, retail banking, and chemically intensive manufacturing, carry higher than normal risks of exposure to crime or injury. But sudden death or injury, violence, or the threat of violence can strike any work force and can have a profound effect on group and individual functioning,

I gratefully acknowledge the assistance of Susan Braverman, MEd, MSW, for her critical reading of the manuscript and for her collaboration in the development of the ideas and methodologies described herein. I am also grateful for the contributions of David Doepel, who participated in an earlier version of this chapter.

whether the event happens on or off the work site. Other less violent threats to security also affect a work force, such as the threat of job losses brought on by downsizings, restructuring, or relocation. Many companies have developed "disaster plans" for responding to crisis situations, which may include plans for evacuations, policies for public relations, procedures to protect the company from legal action, and policies for death benefits (Truitt & Kelley, 1989). What is often overlooked in any crisis response plan is the profound effect of the event on actual survivors and witnesses—the employees themselves. Despite the concern of individual managers or supervisors, there exist few companies that have developed comprehensive "crisis readiness" plans to directly confront the acute and long-term effects of traumatic events on the health and morale of employees. Equally rare are procedures to identify and treat the employee who, injured at work, may never return to work or to full productivity because of the effects of injury-related posttraumatic stress disorder (PTSD), even after the physical injury is healed. Although some industries, notably law enforcement, have begun to develop methods for avoiding PTSD in employees exposed to psychic injury, essentially no risk assessment of the losses associated with work-related psychological problems exist.

Posttraumatic Stress Disorder

There is a rapidly expanding body of literature on the human response to overwhelmingly stressful events. Growing societal awareness of the pervasiveness and importance of posttraumatic states was confirmed in 1980, when PTSD was recognized in the *Diagnostic and Statistical Manual of Mental Disorders* (3rd ed.; American Psychiatric Association, 1980). Posttraumatic stress affects people who have been exposed to events or conditions that involve a shocking or serious threat to their own security or well-being or that of people close to them. PTSD results when a person's functioning continues to be disrupted as a consequence of the traumatic experience (Paton, 1991). PTSD is characterized by intrusive reexperiencing of the traumatic event, avoidance of activities or situations that are reminders of the trauma, emotional numbing, withdrawal from intimacy and social interaction, disruptions in intellectual and memory functions, and difficulties controlling emotions, especially anger. Clinicians and researchers have understood the seemingly contradictory sets of responses in PTSD, which can alternate within a single individual, as the attempt to master an experience that has overloaded normal mechanisms for coping with stress (Horowitz, 1986).

It is not known precisely why some people develop PTSD as a result of traumatic experiences and some do not. It seems clear that some form of active processing of the traumatic event is important to reduce the risk of long-term psychological impairment, and many forms of individual and group treatment have been advanced (van der Kolk, 1987). Researchers and practitioners agree that the presence of a supportive environment that conveys to survivors that their feelings are legitimate and provides an opportunity to talk about these feelings and reactions is crucial to a positive outcome (Mor-Barak, 1988; van der Kolk, 1987; Wilson, 1989). Without appropriate social or professional supports, traumatized people, unaware that their reactions are normal and overwhelmed by the physiological and emotional response itself, may abandon the effort to process the experience at all. In his landmark article, Lindemann (1944) described the tendency to "wall off" the trauma from consciousness when conscious processing of the event fails. When this active processing does not take place, long-term "posttraumatic decline" can occur. This condition is marked by depression, development of chronic medical problems, progressive social isolation, and the loss of ability to work and maintain relationships (Rosen & Fields, 1988; Titchener, 1986).

Research on PTSD has focused on Vietnam War combat veterans, victims of crime and abuse, and survivors of natural disasters (Rundell, Ursano, Holloway, & Silberman, 1989). There is a substantial body of work on policy stress (Gersons, 1989; Mantell, Dubner, & Lipton, 1985) and a growing body of work on emergency and disaster personnel (Mitchell, 1983; Raphael, 1977). Recently a researcher reported on the long-term psychological adjustment of survivors of a Norwegian oil-rig disaster (Holen, 1990). Beyond this study, there have been no controlled investigations of the effects of traumatic events in the workplace. However, researchers and observers from a range of fields have reported on the variety of posttraumatic conditions observed in individuals who have been injured, have suffered accidents or violence at work, or have witnessed traumatic events in the workplace (Braverman & Gelbert, 1990; Doepel, in press; Dunning, 1985; Hillenberg & Wolf, 1988; Ivancevich, Matteson, & Richards, 1985; Levit, 1989; Raphael, Singh, Bradbury, & Lampert, 1984; White & Hatcher, 1988). Writers in psychology, occupational medicine, sociology, and law, noting the dramatic increase in disability claims relating to mental injury in the past decade, have called emotional stress one of the most important health and human resource issues facing the workplace (LaDoe, 1988; Sauter, Murphy, & Hurrell, 1990; Victor, 1988, 1990). Stress related to traumatic crises and situations is one of the most preventable of job-related health risks.

Crisis Management in the Workplace

The term *crisis management* has most commonly been used in connection with business crises involving financial emergencies or internal "disasters" such as executive crime, product liability, environmental damage, or mergers and acquisitions. Companies employ financial managers, attorneys, public relations professionals, or other business consultants to manage the business aspects of such crises, as well as for "damage control" with respect to the company's public image. In some cases, particularly those involving layoffs or the prospect of takeover or reorganization, this may involve seeking ways to inform or reassure employees about their future with the company. In the vast majority of cases, however, *crisis management* has applied to the company's relation to the public *outside* its boundaries and in particular to the media (Fisher & Briggs, 1989). Few companies respond in an effective, organized manner to the needs of managers, supervisors, security and medical staff, and line employees and their families either during or after traumatic crises. Recently, exceptions to this situation have appeared among several high-risk fields including law enforcement, emergency medical services, and firefighting, many of which have adopted formal protocols for the emotional debriefing of personnel in the aftermath of work-related trauma (Bergmann & Queen, 1986; Mitchell & Bray,

1990). The banking industry has begun to institute procedures to protect employees from the psychological after-effects of robberies (Braverman, 1991).

Traumatic crises, however, are not limited to particular professions. They strike employee groups in workplaces of all kinds (Fisher & Briggs, 1989). Events that are shocking, dangerous, or otherwise traumatic can be especially difficult for people working in settings where they do not expect to confront such events. In most cases, such traumas involve death through suicide or homicide, sudden loss through industrial or motor vehicle accidents or heart attacks, violence or threat of violence, or threats to job security. Employees exposed to such events experience posttraumatic stress reactions similar to those reported by victims of disasters, assaults, and traumatic loss in other settings. Furthermore, such events have an impact not only on individual employees but on the work organization as a whole. It is the responsibility of management to respond with timely and effective action to the challenges posed by these unforeseen, stressful, and frightening events. The following case examples illustrate the kinds of challenges and problems that arise from traumatic crises in the workplace.

Case Examples[1]

The 150 employees of Mutual Finance, a midsized investment company, arrived at work to the news that George Smith, Senior Vice President, had committed suicide by shooting himself in the head at his home. As the shock waves spread throughout the office, questions were raised, fed by both rumor and fact. During the preceding year, the firm had undergone several reorganizations at the highest levels. Rumor held that Smith's performance had been unsatisfactory and that he was about to be fired or "kicked upstairs." Employees wondered if the firm's executives—with a reputation for poor people skills—had mishandled Smith's situation, contributing to his suicide. It was also rumored that Smith had been despondent because of "corporate secrets" that presaged the end of the company. As anxiety spread, fed by these rumors, leadership was increasingly unsure how to respond. Plagued by their own feelings of guilt (however irrational), they felt defensive about how they might be perceived by the work force. How much should they expose to the work force about Smith and the company as a whole? Traumatized by Smith's act, they too were unsure about what it might mean to them at this juncture.

*   *   *

A group of six employees working in a branch office of a bank were held at gunpoint for 30 minutes. Blindfolded and forced to kneel on the floor, they were threatened with death while the bank vault was robbed. Severely traumatized, several of the employees refused to return to work. Morale among other employees suffered, with many expressing fears and resentment about perceived lapses in office security.

*   *   *

---

[1]The following are drawn from the author's practice; incidences are disguised to shield the identities of the companies.

The day after he was fired for poor performance, an employee of a large accounting firm entered the office of the vice president and emptied a pistol at close range, killing the vice president. Scores of horrified employees witnessed the killing.

* * *

International Electronics Corporation had recently built a facility that employed over 2,000 people in the design and manufacture of a new electronic component. One Sunday afternoon, an employee working with hazardous chemicals was fatally injured when a safety system failed. When he was discovered by co-workers, emergency medical personnel and nurses from International were called, and he was taken to the hospital where he was pronounced dead. Representatives from site management and corporate health and safety were on the scene and at the hospital. The corporate medical officer, in consultation with the site manager, convened a meeting with the heads of facilities, corporate communications, and corporate counsel. They considered what to do about employees on the scene as well as the arriving shift. They wanted to avoid a panic and provide reassurance about plant safety, but they were concerned about what they could tell employees at this early stage. How much could they tell people? Should they close the facility?

The Importance of Crisis Management

Faced with these questions, management often founders in its well-meaning attempts to manage a crisis. One typical response is to close the office or plant for a day or two, grant administrative leave to those directly affected, and try to return to normal activities as quickly as possible. Managers may try to deal with their own sense of shock and helplessness in the face of such events by trying to return to "business as usual." Employees, following management's lead, quickly "seal over" or deny the emotional impact of the events. Emotional sealing over is a common reaction to trauma (Horowitz, 1985, 1986; Lindemann, 1944) and is one of the main components that contributes to increased risk of posttraumatic stress reactions. Furthermore, sealing over has consequences for the functioning of the entire work organization. When those in leadership positions try to ignore the trauma, there is a marked disruption in communication, which in turn leads to lowered morale and productivity. Even well-meaning responses can work against recovery from trauma. Temporarily closing down or selecting several individuals for special accommodations can have the effect of blocking communication and separating those affected from needed peer support. The ensuing losses from productivity, increased turnover, and general health problems can be minimized when management initiates a prompt and well-planned trauma response.

The Role of the Workplace in Recovery From Trauma

People exposed to traumatic events in the workplace, like all other traumatized groups, may exhibit a range of reactions. These include emotional numbing, social withdrawal, irritability, fearfulness, depression, sleep disturbances, protracted medical problems, substance abuse, marital disruption, work inhibition, and premature job change. In addition, many people with traumatic experiences in their backgrounds can be seriously affected when a current trauma "rekindles" the pain and upset feelings from a previous loss or exposure to harm (Horowitz, 1986). When a trauma is suffered collectively in a workplace, the importance of group support becomes all the more apparent. Writers in the field of stress have noted the importance of social support as a buffer or moderating variable (Ganster, Fusilier, & Mayes, 1986; Hurrell & Murphy, in press). Group support has been recognized as a critical factor in the outcome of traumatic events (Barrett & Mizes, 1988; Wilson, 1989). Like families, work organizations hold restorative and recovery-promoting attributes that can be activated under conditions of emergency or stress (Mangelsdorff, 1985; Raphael & Middleton, 1987). Under normal circumstances, these intangible connections are maintained daily through the informal communication and support networks that operate within and between work groups. Work organizations owe their ability to be productive and well functioning as much to these often invisible connections and ties as they do to sound operational procedures. The ability of a work organization to mobilize these internal group resources at times of stress will effect general morale as well as individual health. Thus, a primary goal of posttrauma crisis management is to ensure that these resources are mobilized.

Barriers to Workplace Group Recovery

The emergence of group support in the aftermath of a workplace crisis is not always spontaneous. Because of the disruption of normal group processes, management effectiveness, and individual functioning, significant barriers to the mobilization of group support may arise. This can take place at precisely those times when at which support is most crucial for the immediate and long-term recovery of individuals in the workplace. Furthermore, the organizational culture of the particular workplace may mitigate against activation of the support and communication necessary for a resolution of the trauma. Work cultures do not usually permit expressions of fear, vulnerability, or sadness. Where there is also little opportunity for communication about nonbusiness issues, employees will have limited means of expressing their reactions, concerns, and needs for information.

In the absence of explicit permission and sanctioned structures for interpersonal communication about a traumatic event, individuals in a work environment tend to seal over their emotions: Employees, assuming that there is in fact no permission to openly express their reactions to a trauma, will not share their reactions with others at work. Similarly, needs for information may go unmet, increasing the incidence of rumors and the rise in fearfulness among employees. This is especially true in cases of violence or threat of violence when a perpetrator is unknown or believed to be still at large. It can also occur when an industrial accident raises questions about site safety, as happened as soon as news of the fatal accident at the electronics manufacturer spread among employees. Construction sites pose a constant risk of individual and mass fatalities. The affects of these accidents on co-workers and rescuers are only beginning to be recognized. Other situations present threats that are less direct but equally serious psychologically. Heart attacks and suicides prompt fears about work stress or organizational upheaval. In the case of the executive suicide, fears about the firm's stability escalated, along with questions about the leadership's ability to steer away from disaster. In situations like these, ignoring the needs of employees increases the risk of posttraumatic stress reactions in individuals.

Individuals suffering from posttraumatic stress reactions often feel confused, frightened, or ashamed about these reactions. They withdraw from interpersonal contact. Management, unsure of the appropriate response or harboring feelings of irrational (but understandable) guilt or defensiveness, may appear to "stonewall" employees and fail to provide the supportive, visible presence that is needed. In the absence of sanctioned, planned meetings and communications, extreme reactions may prevail. People who have been traumatized feel extremely vulnerable, and their level of emotional arousal is high. People may initially cluster together, but without structures to help them deal with their feelings, these same people become unwilling to talk with one another because of fear of overexposure in their state of heightened emotional arousal (Parson, 1985). Thus, it is imperative that structures be provided to ensure a safe and positive environment in which communication and group support can take place.

The Crisis Response Plan

The key elements of a crisis-response plan provide these structures. Taken together, they are designed to address three areas of primary concern (see Figure 1).

1. Communication. Traumatic events in the workplace inevitably disrupt established communication networks, both formal and informal. Breakdowns in interpersonal and intragroup communication correspond to the sealing over of the individual trauma victim. When employees are unable to talk about what has happened and to have their questions and fears addressed, their ability to carry out usual job functions suffers, both on a team and individual basis.

    I. ESTABLISH COMMUNICATION
- Ally with highest levels, organize crisis team
- Determine relevant information and means of communication
- Inform about plans for meetings and ensure further communication

    II. DETERMINE CIRCLE OF IMPACT
- Extend intervention as broadly as necessary
- Identify appropriate employee groups
- Identify rescuers, witnesses, and other affected groups
- Determine need for services for families

    III. CONVENE AFFECTED GROUPS
- Information
- Education
- Sharing/Normalization
- Referral for individual meetings

    IV. COUNSEL/ASSESS INDIVIDUALS

    V. EVALUATE/FOLLOW-UP

Figure 1. Components of crisis intervention.

2. Support for Management. Traumatic crises present an enormously stressful situation for management. Normal leadership functioning may suffer. During a crisis, those in positions of responsibility and leadership may feel an acute lack of control over operations and the well-being of their employees. They may feel unsure about how to respond effectively when they are struggling with their own feelings of shock, grief, and confusion. However, it is at just such a time that employees will look to management to restore the sense of control, safety, and normalcy that has been shattered.

3. Prevention of Traumatic Stress. Some individual employees will be at risk for posttraumatic stress reactions as outlined above. Posttraumatic stress problems in individuals will affect general workplace morale and the ability of the group to return to normal functioning and productivity within a reasonable period of time.

A Model of Posttrauma Crisis Intervention

The term *intervention* is used to describe the collaborative work of trauma specialists, management, and other key company personnel in response to a traumatic crisis at the workplace. A crisis intervention is composed of the following elements: (1) crisis readiness, (2) consultation with management, (3) meetings with affected groups, (4) assessment and counseling of individuals at risk, and (5) follow-up and recommendations. These elements are described more fully below, and illustrative cases are provided.

Crisis Readiness

When a traumatic event occurs, management must act immediately and decisively on several questions: Should the office or plant be closed and people sent home? What information should be given out, by whom, and to whom? Who needs to be involved in the planning and execution of a response? How can the organization be returned to normal functioning? To ensure such a response it is important to have a set of crisis-readiness procedures in place in advance (Braverman & Gelbert, 1990; White & Hatcher, 1988). A crisis readiness plan should include: (a) guidelines for identifying events and situations that need intervention, (b) procedures that include a chain of response, and (c) education for management and personnel at various levels about traumatic stress in general and the crisis response procedure specifically.

After the takeover at the bank branch, the corporate vice president for human resources researched the frequency of robberies at the bank's branches. He discovered a marked increase in staff turnover and absences at branches that had been robbed. With regional managers of operations and security, he developed a crisis response plan. The plan included identification of serious incidents, designation of human resources representatives responsible for determining the need for intervention, selection of outside resources to provide group and individual services, and guidelines for matching the level of response linked to risk factors (e.g., show of weapons, length of takeover).

Initial Consultation to Management

The decision to initiate an intervention is typically reached within 12 hr after an event. Management and the consultant will then identify a crisis response team (CRT), typically composed of crisis specialists and local and upper management. It may also include representatives from departments of human resources, health services, safety, corporate communications or public relations, employee assistance, security, and union.

Ultimately, the effectiveness of a crisis intervention effort depends on support from the highest levels in the organization. It is important to have senior management from those levels on site to participate in planning and to be visible to employees.

After the fatal accident at International Electronics, the site manager of human resources, in consultation with an outside crisis consultant, quickly assembled a team composed of the medical director, site manager, a representative from corporate communications (a public relations function), and representatives from the corporate legal department. Also included were counselors from International's employee assistance program (EAP), who would work with trauma counselors from the consultant's team. The team decided to organize meetings for every group involved in manufacturing. Special written communications about the tragedy went out to the other groups within the facility.

* * *

The situation at Mutual Investment required an intensive meeting with the top management team before finalizing plans for contact with employees. First, as with most cases of suicide, there was a need to decide how much to reveal to co-workers about the cause of death. Considerations included the wishes of the deceased's family, the impact of the news on the public, and the possible concerns of the Board of Directors. The group decided to state honestly that although the death appeared to have been a suicide, this was not yet official and that information must be kept within the company. This allowed co-workers to begin openly to deal with the difficult issues associated with suicide, while still respecting issues of privacy. Second, the members of this senior management group, who knew Smith well and had struggled with how to deal with his performance problems, needed to resolve any possible feelings of responsibility for his death (as well as feelings of anger at him for his act). Only when this was done could they decide how to answer employee's questions about his death and how to confront the rumors about why he killed himself.

After being briefed by management, the CRT has the following tasks:

Determining the circle of impact. Who are the groups affected, and what are the natural groupings? It is important to extend the "circle of impact" as far as necessary and to not discount or underestimate the impact of an event on related or affiliated groups not seen as directly affected. Management's outreach to all who might be affected is crucial. It is unfortunately not uncommon to miss the after-hours shift, the outside contractors, or the employee out of town on a trip or vacation (Doepel, in press). In the case of International Electronics, an entire work division housed in a connected building was left out of the original intervention effort. Within days, the clamor arising from close to 700 engineers, clerical support staff, and accountants who felt ignored and slighted prompted the CRT to extend the intervention program to them. These employees were found to be experiencing levels of fear and distress equal to those in the manufacturing side of the facility.

It may also be important to identify particular groups who might ordinarily not receive much attention. For example, at International, the small force of security personnel assigned to the facility entrances were under particular stress as a result of dealing with arriving employees who were hungry for information. The "blue shirts," or custodial staff, who felt enormous responsibility for the smooth workings and safety of the facility, needed special meetings and follow-up meetings to deal with the many concerns that arose for them in the wake of the tragedy.

Determination of communications procedures. It is often useful for the entire team to make decisions about how to bring crisis-specific information to the attention of employees. It is crucial that this information come from management. There must be a coordinated process for deciding the method of communication, whether usual electronic or written means, or face-to-face meetings. The outside specialist is often helpful in guiding these decisions. There must be a clear, easily accessible, and consistent means for notifying employees about the intervention, its purpose, and times and places for group and individual meetings. This is also the time for establishing what the facts are, outlining what if any constraints there may be on what information can be shared (including legal issues and issues of confidentiality), and, if necessary, dealing with the media.

Confronting representatives of the media can be stressful for employees as well. Reporters will often approach employees as they enter or leave the workplace or try to reach them over the telephone. Managers can use the initial communication to remind employees of their right *not* to talk to reporters. Employees should be made aware of the appropriate corporate channels to which they can direct reporters.

Identification of individuals at risk. The crisis consultant, in collaboration with the EAP, is responsible for determining who may be particularly affected because of their connection to the event, closeness with victims, or other individual risk factors (e.g., recent personal losses or tragedies, health issues).

Meeting with affected groups. Before groups are convened, it is important to identify the appropriate natural groupings. These can be organized according to shift, location, work task, or proximity to trauma (either emotionally or physically). It is my experience that at having something in common helps to ensure a necessary level of trust. Although the model that follows has been used with groups of 50 people or more, the optimal size is from 10 to 25. The smaller number is particularly important for groups who share a closeness to the event and when strong feelings are likely to be present.

Figure 2 presents the outline for a typical group meeting. These meetings combine an informational, educational, and emotional-sharing approach. Running the meeting is not delegated to the crisis consultants: It must remain very much

    I. Introduction, Framing (*Management*)
- Identification of the event, sharing of feelings
- Introduction of consultants, others, purpose of the meeting

   II. Information (*Management*)
- Update, assurance of continuing information
- Questions and answers

 III. Trauma Education (*Consultant*)
- Theory of posttraumatic stress
- Normalization of signs and symptoms
- Coping strategies

 IV. Group Sharing (*Employees, Management, Consultant*)
- Ground rules, agreements for safety
- Voluntary sharing of reactions, thoughts, concerns

  V. Wrap-up (*Management, Consultant, EAP*)
- Review and reinforcing of group themes and issues
- Information about counseling services

Figure 2.   Posttrauma employee meeting.

the manager's meeting. At the outset, management introduces the crisis consultants and any other unfamiliar people, such as EAP or other corporate personnel, and explains their presence. The first order of business is information. For people in crisis, information is essential, particularly as it pertains to safety. Furthermore, by taking responsibility for providing information, management establishes itself both as being in control and as caretakers. Throughout a crisis, information confers both control and comfort. Although it is important that the managers directing the meeting be connected with the work organizations, in the case of events involving violence or safety issues, it is often important to add the presence of senior management or managers with special information or relevant expertise.

After the murder in the accounting firm, the president of the firm flew in, visiting not only the site of the murder but each of the four other branch offices in the city. Similarly, the division vice president of the bank that was robbed held a special meeting to discuss security issues with the affected employees. It is impossible to overstate the value of this kind of visibility of top leadership. When employees are frightened and shocked, they need the reassuring presence of leaders and are sensitive to their absence. For example, despite recommendations of consultants, the top-ranking vice president for the electronics facility refused to attend meetings with employees, preferring to delegate this to middle management. This created bad feeling, particularly among line supervisors and middle managers. In contrast, the same company's international facilities manager was present at the meetings for each of the half-dozen work organizations at the stricken site to answer questions about the technical aspects of the accident. This was of immense value to employees and managers alike.

During the information section, managers provide facts, address rumors, answer questions, and explain company policy. The crisis consultant then describes the normal range of posttraumatic stress reactions to normalize what people may already be experiencing. It is important to predict what reactions they may experience in the coming days and weeks.

Group Sharing

The consultant then introduces a process through which both management and employees can share their reactions to the event. Confidentiality needs to be agreed to by all because a sense of safety is paramount. Although the expression of strong emotion is allowed, there is no pressure to do so. Again, the presence of management is crucial here. When managers open up discussion of difficult topics and express feelings, employees feel free to follow suit, and group support is activated. In my experience, in companies in which management has called in experts but then withdrawn from the process, essentially turning over their employees to consultants and not attending the meetings, employees have been reluctant to attend the meetings at all.

After the group sharing, the consultant reviews the dominant themes and concerns of the group, taking care to emphasize that they are normal for the event at hand. For example, in a case of suicide, it is important to note the difficulty of resolving the conflicting feelings of anger, sadness, and guilt. In the aftermath of an industrial accident, questions of safety and trust are paramount. It is crucial that these feelings be validated.

At the conclusion of the meeting, employees are offered a variety of ways to access a counselor, taking into account needs for privacy. When EAP counselors are present, they should take the lead in coordinating this process. A feedback questionnaire is distributed asking for a self-report on how each employee is feeling and feedback for management and providing the opportunity to request individual counseling. A follow-up meeting may be scheduled before closing the meeting.

"Isn't This Going to Stir Them Up?": Dealing With Managers' Concerns

Managers are often concerned about the emotional content of such meetings. For many people, expressing emotion and losing control are synonymous. Thus, management is often concerned that a return to order and normalcy will be jeopardized by allowing the expression of feelings. However, under the guidance of a skilled professional, these meetings permit the expression of thoughts and feelings in an atmosphere of control and safety. After such meetings, employees feel relieved and reassured and are able to return to adequate levels of job performance much more quickly. These concerns are also related to fear of reliving the emotional impact of the traumatic event (Horowitz, 1986). It is important to reassure management that by conscious recollection of the traumatic event, mastery of the event is achieved sooner, with a more rapid relief from the unwanted intrusive memories and thoughts of the traumatic event. Therefore, when managers say, as they often do, "Isn't this going to stir people up?" the answer must be, "Your people are already stirred up. These meetings will restore a sense of control to individuals and to your entire organization."

Crisis Counseling for Individual Employees

Once employees are informed that counseling services are available, they will often self-refer for such services. Those who may need such services but who do not self-refer can be contacted tactfully, confidentially, and nonintrusively by counselors. Primary victims and witnesses are always met with, if only for a short "check in" if the employee is unwilling or fearful about such a contact. Typically, employees seek counseling because they feel particularly stressed by their closeness to the event (e.g., direct witnesses to an accident or death, close connection with an injured or dead co-worker, involvement in a rescue attempt) or because the event evokes another event in their lives (e.g., the suicide of a relative or friend, a similar accident, a recent loss, the current illness of a family member). In general, between 10% and 15% of employees participating in a crisis intervention will be seen individually. In cases of severe trauma, such as a murder or disaster witnessed by entire groups within a workplace, a company may mandate individual contact with a counselor for everyone in an office or plant. This was accomplished in the accounting office with almost 100% cooperation on the part of the over 125-member office staff. In these cases, mandating counselor contact with all employees removes the "stigma" of counseling that may inhibit some employees from using the service.

Follow-Up

At the conclusion of the first day of an intervention, and at intervals thereafter for the duration of the intervention, the CRT meets to evaluate and to plan for the future. The consultants provide feedback to management about the state of the organization and offer recommendations for possible future action to ensure the most complete recovery. This information can be quite important in the recovery and healing process; it is always important for a work organization or community to use a trauma as an opportunity for productive change. This may come in the form of improved safety regulations, the implementation of improved intragroup or labor–management communications, or the establishment of a fund or activity in memory of a colleague. At Mutual Investment, in response to overwhelming positive feedback from employees about the response and accessibility of management during the crisis, the firm instituted frequent brown-bag lunches with top management and a new formal meetings structure to improve face-to-face communication with employees. International Electronics considered a high-visibility safety program, emphasizing employee participation. In the case of another company, the fatal heart attack of a sales manager prompted managers to institute a health-promotion program, including a smoking cessation course.

The Relation Between Management and Outside Consultants

Whether outside consultants are engaged to assist with a traumatic crisis, it remains management's job to respond to employee needs. Management should serve as the primary source of information about a crisis or a tragedy, as well as of a model of positive, humane response. Their attitude could be expressed as follows: "We're in this together, and we are doing all we can do to help us pull through." If consultants are present, they are to be seen as a resource brought in by management to support the organization, rather than a replacement for the leadership. The position taken by management could be stated as follows: "Our priority is your well-being. We want to get back to normal as soon as we can, but not by avoiding the impact of this event on all of us. We have invited these experts in to help us accomplish these goals as effectively and completely as possible."

Some models of crisis intervention that emphasize peer support as the primary therapeutic element raise concerns about the effects of outside intervention: Does the presence of experts communicate that the group lacks the skills and resources needed for its own recovery? This is an important question. The value of self-help and restoring a sense of control to a stricken organization is central to the model of intervention presented here. The consultant must not compound the organization's feeling of helplessness by fostering a sense that they lack the ability to recover on their own. The alliance with management is founded on establishing management as in control and as the source of the recovery process. The heart of the group meetings is the normalizing and supportive effect of communal sharing. However, the expertise brought by the consultant is a crucial ingredient in this process. A knowledge of psychological trauma theory is important in demonstrating to management the risks of sealing over and the need for active intervention. Educating employees and managers alike on the effects of trauma is crucial for preventing stress disorders. Therefore, the consultant should not hold back in the initial alliance setting and education phase. A strong, focused approach to helping the leadership face a crisis aggressively, with an emphasis on full visibility for management early on in the crisis, leads to a more rapid return to normal leadership and a sense that the group is back on its feet. Similarly, full attention to the resolution phase of a crisis should allow the consultant to leave the organization with a sense that the experience has begun to be integrated as a meaningful part of the life and history of the group.

Consideration, too, must be given to how the organization will respond to the entry of a consultant. Williams (1991) pointed out that high-risk occupations, such as law enforcement and emergency response, tend to have cultures that emphasize strong peer support. Such organizations rely heavily on internal resources to respond to the relatively frequent occurrence of trauma. These should never be supplanted by outside resources. However, Williams went on to point out that even in organizations with a strongly established internal trauma response capacity, some events, such as the death of a colleague, may require the support of an outside consultant. In such situations it is essential that the consultants be fully familiar to and with the organization (Williams, 1991). When an EAP or other specialized human resource service exists, it is important to assess how its functions will interact with the external resources. An accurate assessment of the limits of internal resources should be conducted so that an adequate and well-coordinated response can be mounted (Queen & Bergmann, in press).

Evaluation of Workplace Trauma Intervention

Researchers have reported on the incidence of posttraumatic morbidity in disaster workers (Ersland, Weisaeth, & Sund, 1980; Raphael et al., 1984), police officers (Gersons, 1989), firefighters (Hytten & Hasle, 1989), and in the general population (Green, 1982; MacFarlane, 1987). Writers in Scandinavia and Australia have proposed research methods for this work and for the evaluation of methods to prevent stress-related problems in responders (Lundin & Weisaeth, 1991; Raphael, Lundin, & Weisaeth, 1989). However, beyond Holen's study (1990) on oil-rig survivors, there are no data on the incidence of stress or health problems in a work force following a workplace trauma. Similarly, no studies have evaluated the effectiveness of workplace posttrauma crisis interventions, either in measures of individual health, organizational functioning, or workplace productivity. As workplace trauma intervention continues to grow as a practice area, so does the need for studies to demonstrate its usefulness and to direct further development, refinement, and applications. Clearly, methodological and ethical problems exist in the design of controlled studies to evaluate workplace interventions. However, useful opportunities exist in quasi-experimental designs such as retrospective studies, record surveys, and naturalistic studies (Hurrell & Murphy, in press; Murphy & Hurrell, 1987). For example, a readily available and rich source of data exists in the personnel records of retail banks. These data could answer some interesting questions. What has happened to employees who have been the victims of robberies? How do their levels of absenteeism, health or disability claims, and length of employment compare with those of other employees? If a robbery response protocol has been instituted, what will a retrospective study of personnel data reveal about its possible effect on employee recovery?

Approaching this research presents an opportunity to integrate the work on traumatic stress with the broader literature on work stress (Hurrell & Murphy, in press). Interest on the part of employers concerning more critical aspects of worker injury and workplace stress is increasing as such critical stressors as restructurings, violence, and serious accidents attract more attention. Many health-promotion, stress-reduction, and trauma-intervention programs are applied in a fashion that takes little account of the characteristics of the population served. They may be poorly suited to the culture of the organization or inappropriate to the prevailing organizational climate. In view of the unique nature of this work, evaluation research should be designed to account for these organizational aspects. By and large, work-stress research has focused on the qualities of the stressor (i.e., job conditions) and the vulnerabilities in the exposed individual or group and how these might interact. Conditions relating to organizational factors have been subsumed into one of these two categories or have been conceptualized as moderating variables of the main stress–health effect. Evaluation research should consider elevating organizational culture and climate from the status of additional or moderating variable to that of a primary variable.[2]

The study of workplace trauma intervention also presents an opportunity to expand knowledge about the relation between group culture and individual health. Working with a group in the throes of a trauma opens a window on the values and culture of a work organization, much as the experience of a trauma presents an individual with a sometimes shattering confrontation with the limits of his or her personal resources. How the group deals with the stressor will reveal much about the underlying beliefs and values of the company, the structure and style of lead-

---

[2]There are problems in the definitions and uses of the terms *culture* and *climate* when applied to the workplace. The research being proposed will have to begin with a review of these terms and adopt working definitions for their applications.

ership, and the characteristics of the individuals that make up the work force. The investigation of these phenomena will require the development of theoretical constructs and practical measures that can begin to describe the complex interaction among organizational, group, and individual factors.

Summary: Crisis to Opportunity

When the members of a company or work group suffer a disaster, a company crisis, or the loss of a colleague, they are faced with an opportunity—one that they certainly did not ask for but that, nevertheless, presents them with a choice. Choosing to deny the effects of a traumatic crisis causes communication to close down and brings a general constriction in the energy and commitment of a company's employees. This results in lowered morale, increased illness, and loss of employees. Most important, however, failure to recognize and respond to a traumatic event represents the loss of an opportunity to expand and deepen communication among employees and between employees and management. Traumatic events threaten one's sense of trust in the world. Temporarily—sometimes permanently—they shatter one's assumptions about safety and predictability. For a workplace in crisis, similar qualities are threatened. These include loyalty to the company, confidence in its leadership, and a sense of mutual support and trust among co-workers. When the leadership of an organization responds actively to a crisis, they acknowledge the importance of these interpersonal bonds for the over-all functioning and well-being of the organization. In so doing, they can take advantage of a powerful opportunity to raise organization functioning to a level even higher than existed before the traumatic event.

References

American Psychiatric Association. (1980). *Diagnostic and statistical manual of mental disorders* (3rd ed.). Washington, DC: Author.

Barrett, T. W., & Mizes, J. S. (1988). Combat level and social support in the development of posttraumatic stress disorder in Vietnam veterans. *Behavior Modification, 12,* 100–115.

Bergmann, L. H., & Queen, T. (1986). Responding to critical incident stress. *Fire Chief,* May, 52–56.

Braverman, M. (1991). Post-robbery damage control: The human factor. *Bottomline, May–April,* 23–25.

Braverman, M., & Gelbert, S. (1990). *Leadership skills for the critical incident.* Beaverton, OR: Great Performance.

Doepel, D. (in press). Crisis management: The psychological dimension. *Industrial Crisis Quarterly.*

Dunning, C. (1985). Prevention of stress. In *Role stressors and supports for emergency workers.* pp. 85–1408. Washington, DC: U.S. Government Printing Office.

Ersland, S., Weisaeth, L., & Sund, A. (1980). The stress upon rescuers involved in oil rig disaster: "Alexander L. Kielland." *Acta Psychiatrica Scandinavica Supplementum, 355,* 38–49.

Fisher, L., & Briggs, W. (1989). Communicating with employees during a tragedy. *IABC Communication World,* February, 32–35.

Ganster, D. D., Fusilier, M. R., & Mayes, B. T. (1986). Role of social support in the experience of stress at work. *Journal of Applied Psychology, 71,* 102–110.

Gersons, B. (1989). Patterns of PTSD among police officers following shooting incidents: A two-dimensional model and treatment implications. *Journal of Traumatic Stress, 2,* 247–257.

Green, B. L. (1982). Assessing levels of psychological impairment following disaster. *Journal of Nervous and Mental Disease, 170,* 544–552.

Hillenberg, J. B., & Wolf, K. L. (1988). Psychological impact of traumatic events: Implications for employee assistance intervention. *Employee Assistance Quarterly, 4,* 1–13.

Holen, A. (1990). A long-term study of survivors from a disaster. Unpublished doctoral dissertation, University of Oslo, Norway.

Horowitz, M. J. (1985). Disasters and psychological responses to stress. *Psychiatric Annals, 15,* 161–167.

Horowitz, M. J. (1986). Stress-response syndromes: A review of posttraumatic and adjustment disorders. *Hospital and Community Psychiatry, 37,* 241–249.

Hurrell, J. J., & Murphy, L. R. (in press). Psychological job stress. In W. N. Rom (Ed.), *Environmental and occupational medicine* (2nd ed.). Boston: Little, Brown.

Hytten, L., & Hasle, A. (1989). Firefighters: A study of stress and coping. *Acta Psychiatrica Scandinavica Supplementum, 335,* 50–55.

Ivancevich, J. M., Matteson, M. J., & Richards, E. P. (1985). Who's liable for stress on the job? *Harvard Business Review,* March–April, 60–72.

LaDou, J. (1988). Cumulative injury in worker's compensation. *Occupational Medicine: State of the Art Reviews, 3,* 611–619.

Lawson, B. Z. (1987). Work-related post-traumatic stress reactions: The hidden dimension. *Health and Social Work, 2,* 250–258.

Levit, H. I. (1989). Post-traumatic stress disorder in workers' compensation cases. *American Journal of Forensic Psychology, 7,* 75–80.

Lindemann, E. (1944). Management and symptomatology of acute grief. *American Journal of Psychiatry, 101,* 141–148.

Lundin, T., & Weisaeth, L. (1991). *Disaster worker's stress and aftereffects: A proposed method for the study of psychological and psychiatric effects on rescue workers and health care personnel.* Unpublished manuscript.

Mangelsdorff, A. D. (1985). Lessons learned and forgotten: The need for prevention and mental health interventions in disaster preparedness. *Journal of Community Psychology, 13,* 239–257.

Mantell, M., Dubner, J., & Lipton, S. (1985). *San Ysidro massacre: Impact on police officers. A report prepared for the National Institute of Mental Health.* Rockville, MD: National Institute of Mental Health.

McFarlane, A. C. (1987). The aetiology of post-traumatic stress disorders following a natural disaster. *British Journal of Psychiatry, 152,* 116–121.

Mitchell, J. (1983). When disaster strikes. The critical incident stress debriefing process. *Journal of Emergency Medical Services, 8,* 36–39.

Mitchell, J., & Bray, G. (1990). *Emergency services stress.* Englewood Cliffs, NJ: Prentice-Hall.

Murphy, R., & Hurrell, J. (1987). Stress measurement and management in organizations: Development and current status. In A. W. Riley & S. J. Zaccaro (Eds.), *Occupational stress and organizational effectiveness.* New York: Praeger.

Parson, E. R. (1985). Post-traumatic accelerated cohesion: Its recognition and management in group treatment of Vietnam veterans. *Group, 9,* 10–23.

Paton, D. (1991). *Assessment of work-related psychological trauma: Methodological issues and implications for organizational strategies.* Unpublished manuscript.

Queen, T., & Bergmann, L. H. (in press). Planning and implementing post-trauma services for employee assistance programs. *Employee Assistance.*

Raphael, B. (1977). The granville train disaster: Psychological needs and their management. *Medical Journal of Australia, 1,* 303–305.

Raphael, B., Lundin, T., & Weisaeth, L. (1989). A research method for the study of psychological and psychiatric aspects of disaster. *Acta Psychiatrica Scandinavica, 80* (Suppl. 353), 1–16.

Raphael, B., & Middleton, W. (1987). Mental health responses in a decade of disasters: Australia, 1974–1983. *Hospital and Community Psychiatry, 38,* 1331–1337.

Raphael, B., Singh, B., Bradbury, L., & Lambert, F. (1984). Who helps the helpers? The effects of disaster on the rescue workers. *Omega, 14,* 9–20.

Rosen, J., & Fields, R. (1988). The long-term effects of extraordinary trauma: A look beyond PTSD. *Journal of Anxiety Disorders, 2,* 179–191.

Rundell, J. R., Ursano, R. J., Holloway, H. C., & Silberman, E. K. (1989). Psychiatric responses to trauma. Annual Meeting of the American Psychiatric Association (1986, Washington, DC). *Hospital and Community Psychiatry, 40,* 68–74.

Sauter, S., Murphy, L. R., & Hurrell, J. J., Jr. (1990). Prevention of work-related psychological disorders: A national strategy proposed by the National Institute for Occupational Safety and Health. *American Psychologist, 45,* 1146–1158.

Titchener, J. L. (1986). Post-traumatic decline: A consequence of unresolved destructive drives. In C. Figley (Ed.), *Trauma and its wake: Vol. 2. Traumatic stress theory, research, and intervention* (pp. 5–19). New York: Brunner/Mazel.

Truitt, R. H., & Kelley, S. K. (1989). Battling a crisis in advance. *Public Relations Quarterly, 34,* 6–8.

van der Kolk, B. (Ed.). (1987). *Psychological trauma.* New York: American Psychiatric Press.

Victor, R. A. (1988). The challenge of occupational stress. In R. A. Victor (Ed.), *Liability for employee grievances: Mental stress and wrongful termination* (pp. 3–6). Cambridge, MA: Worker's Compensation Research Institute.

Victor, R. A. (1990). Major challenges facing worker's compensation systems in the 1990s. In R. A. Victor (Ed.), *Challenges for the 1990s.* Cambridge, MA: Worker's Compensation Research Institute.

White, S. G., & Hatcher, C. (1988). Violence and the trauma response. *Occupational Medicine: State of the Art Reviews, 3,* 677–694.

Williams, T. (1991). *Work-related trauma.* Unpublished manuscript.

Wilson, J. (1989). *Trauma, transformation and healing.* New York: Brunner/Mazel.

21

Sally B. Philips and Margaret H. Mushinski

Configuring an Employee Assistance Program to Fit the Corporation's Structure: One Company's Design

Employee assistance programs (EAPs) are programs set up by companies to aid workers in obtaining help to overcome behavioral or psychosocial problems that undermine work performance. EAPs have proliferated in size, quantity, and scope since their inception in the early 1950s when they were developed principally as an outgrowth of occupational alcoholism programs. They have evolved with changes in society, reflecting a recognition of the impact that substance abuse, family and personal problems, and job-related stress exert on work productivity. Their popularity accelerated during the 1970s and 1980s as increasing numbers of employers realized the efficacy of such programs and understood the potential cost savings of helping and thus retaining valued, yet "troubled," employees.

Currently, more than 80% of Fortune 500 companies have active EAPs in comparison with only around 25% during the early 1970s (Bureau of National Affairs [BNA], 1987). Presently, in excess of 10,000 EAPs are functioning in U.S. companies, whereas less than 100 such programs existed across the country in 1950 (Feldman, 1991). The corporate emphasis has shifted from terminating or punishing the impaired or troubled worker to helping him or her to gain health, well-being, and productivity. Such results have obvious benefits for both the employee and employer.

The EAPs of today have expanded in philosophy and scope, no longer addressing only alcohol and drug abuse problems. They currently provide confidential assistance to employees for a variety of personal difficulties ranging from family, marital, legal, and financial issues to various career problems or other personal, stress-related issues. Through assessment and referrals, EAPs are designed to provide the timely intervention in those problems that, if ignored, could lead to more costly and extensive care. The traditional EAP design has a three-session limit. That is, the clinician is charged with making an appropriate assessment and referral within this time frame (Masi, 1984). The EAP clinician does not provide psychotherapy or long-term counseling but refers those in need of such treatment to appropriate treatment providers.

EAPs continue to grow among public as well as private companies, in part because of the 1988 Drug-Free Workplace Act (PL 100-690, Title V; "Correctional

Information," 1989). As of March, 1989, the act specifically requires primary government contractors (i.e., those receiving federal contracts of at least $25,000 annually) to

1. notify employees in writing that unlawful manufacture, distribution, dispensation, possession, or use of a controlled substance is prohibited in the workplace;
2. establish a drug-free awareness program to inform employees of the dangers of drug abuse, the penalties for violating rules against drugs, and any available EAPs;
3. make sure employees notify them of any criminal drug convictions for actions that occurred in the workplace; and
4. impose sanctions on convicted employees or require them to participate in a rehabilitation program.

Failure to comply with these provisions could result in loss of the contract, the company's suspension from federal work for 5 years and withholding of payments ("Correcting misinformation," 1989). In addition to this powerful motivational force, other reasons to establish and implement an EAP are to

1. help employees find ways to prevent or alleviate personal or family drug abuse or mental health problems that could result in low productivity or excess absenteeism,
2. increase cost savings to employers by decreasing extensive health-care benefits utilization, absenteeism, turnover, and the like; and
3. boost positive employee relations, morale, and loyalty, thus establishing a competitive edge in recruiting efforts and a good public image (Staff, 1991).

Increasingly, companies of all sizes are offering EAPs as part of their health and benefits packages. The programs are being integrated with both indemnity and managed care plans as a means of helping employers contain their spiraling health-care costs—particularly those associated with mental health and substance abuse problems (Staff, 1991). Depending on company size, employers can either establish their own in-house EAP staffed by company employees or contract with one of the ever-increasing numbers of external EAP providers. Many options and program configurations are available, however, and a program can have a single focus, offer a broad array of interventions, be fully staffed and organized by internal professionals, or use outside consultants exclusively or in various combinations.

Anecdotal evidence as well as case reports attest to the cost effectiveness of EAPs. Results of a recent University of Georgia study (Roman & Blum, 1989) on recovery rates indicate that more than two thirds of employees with substance abuse problems had returned to work and were adequately performing within a year, as had almost three fourths of those with nondrug-related problems. Such results are translated into substantial cost savings for companies in terms of reduced job accidents, lowered sick leave and absentee rates, decreased treatment costs per employee, and fewer health insurance reimbursement claims for both employees and dependents (BNA, 1987). Estimates of the savings-to-investment ratio range from

1.5:1 to 15.0:1 depending on the size of the company and the nature and extent of the services offered ("McDonnel Douglas," 1989).

The core of this chapter is a description of one specific, in-house EAP, Employee Advisory Services (EAS) of Metropolitan Life Insurance Company (MetLife), headquartered in New York City. MetLife's experience is presented as a prototype of an internal EAP's delivery of services to employees within a large and complex organization.

History of MetLife's EAS

The unique history of MetLife's internal EAP, EAS, parallels that of the larger EAP movement. MetLife was among the first large corporations to provide some form of counseling to employees with personal problems. From 1919 through the 1940s, employee nonmedical problems were handled by a member of the Personnel Department and later by a "personal advisor" in the Medical Department. MetLife's mental health program expanded during the 1950s as it recognized the importance of emotional well-being and the impact of family problems and stresses on employee productivity and health. Acknowledging alcoholism as a major public health problem, MetLife joined with the National Committee on Alcoholism and Alcoholics Anonymous in 1960 to help address the issue of alcoholism in the workplace (Staff, 1960). In 1961, the Human Resources Department established a counseling unit to provide preretirement and personal advisory counseling services to all employees. Armed forces returnees with drinking problems found much-needed assistance through the program's confidential interventions and personal advising. The unit was renamed *Employee Advisory Services* in 1963 and has continued providing assistance to employees at headquarters as well as at field locations ever since.

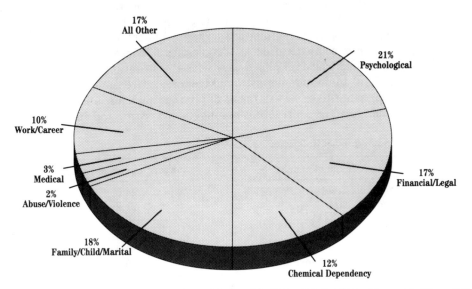

Figure 1. Distribution of assessed problems: MetLife, EAS, 1990. (From Philips, 1991. Adapted by permission.)

The program focus and staff composition changed with the times and was upgraded in 1989 with credentialed mental health professionals and specially trained advisors. An expanded number of problems were attended to by the new EAS staff during 1990, the restructured program's first full operational year. As shown in Figure 1, psychological or emotional issues are the primary problems facing almost one quarter of the clients in 1990. Financial concerns and family problems followed in frequency (Philips, 1991).

Although these statistics reflect the annual EAP activities of one specific program, they are representative of the problems seen by most corporate EAPs across the country. (For a complete description of the 1990 EAS experience, see MetLife Employee Advisory Services, 1991.) Details of EAS services, philosophy, staff, assignment of tasks, and design of service delivery follow.

EAS Services

Assessment and referral. The primary services that any EAP provides are assessments and referrals. Within the first two consultation sessions, the EAS clinician gathers the data necessary to form a diagnostic impression and to recommend a course of action. When appropriate, and if the client wants to use additional assistance, a referral to a fitted service provider is made. Part of this referral process includes an evaluation of various providers in terms of requisite skills, scheduling constraints, convenience of location, and fee structure. These actions are designed to make the best possible match between the client's needs and resources and the provider's expertise and availability. As Table 1 demonstrates, not all referrals made by EAS clinicians are to professional mental health treatment providers.

Education. Inseparable from the recommendation and referral process is the education of the client. An obvious and fundamental goal of this educational process is the client's actual use of the recommended services. A subsidiary goal is to increase the level of the client's sophistication as a consumer of these services. The topics discussed during this educational phase vary with the situation and are tailored to each individual client to include definition of treatment; treatment goals (how the service could help); what to expect in terms of process, outcome, and setting; anticipated time frame; varying contracting arrangements; costs and insurance reim-

Table 1.   1990 MetLife EAS Referrals

Type of service	Percent of closed cases
Reimbursable treatment	24.0
Outpatient care	21.2
Inpatient care	(2.8)
No-cost 12-step program	4.0
Nonreimbursable community resource	33.0
No additional assistance needed/wanted	39.0

Note. N = 618. Nonreimbursable community resources include within-company services such as benefits counseling or the Fitness Center. (For a description of MetLife's fitness program see Corry 1990.) From Philips, 1991. Adapted by permission.

bursement; second opinions; and possible progression of the difficulties if the problem is left "untreated."

Problem resolution/crisis intervention. In those instances in which the EAS clinician is certain that a problem can be resolved in a few more sessions, he or she may contract with the client to work together for a total of six sessions. This flexibility of having client contact beyond the traditional three-session EAP limit allows EAS staff the time necessary to support people through crises that are amenable to brief therapeutic input. Such circumstances are best exemplified by normal reactions to sudden loss.

Debriefing. In some instances, clinicians will travel to other cities to provide on-site services to groups of employees who have all experienced sudden trauma. Such group sessions have been organized in company offices in San Francisco after the 1989 earthquake and in Chicago and Wichita following the destructive tornados of 1990 and 1991.

Advocacy. The guiding philosophy of EAS service is to assist clients in negotiating necessary changes for themselves. The staff frequently contacts third-party payors and managed care providers on the client's behalf when confusion about reimbursements is part of the assessed problem. Knowledge about the proliferation of "cost containment" layers between consumer, payor, and provider and about the continual revamping that these layers undergo is not usually within the purview of the average client. Thus, interceding with these agencies is another one of the services EAS provides.

Management consultation. Managers are entitled and encouraged to consult with EAS staff whenever uncertainty surrounds the appropriate handling of personnel matters. Although managers call about a variety of workplace problems, most of the consultations concern individual employees deteriorating job performances.

Monitoring formal management referrals. When deteriorating performance jeopardizes the employee's job, a recommendation is usually made that the manager formally refer the employee to EAS. Only under these conditions is the manager given limited information about the employee's compliance with the referral, the assessment process, and the recommendations of the EAS clinician. The clinician monitors the employee's involvement in the treatment process for a year and regularly apprises the manager of the employee's continued compliance or withdrawal.

Prevention seminars. To acquaint employees with EAS services and to provide education about various problems encountered in everyday life, EAS arranges seminars and lectures. Among the topics covered are stress management, job relocations, parenting, troubled and normal teen development, bereavement, child and elder care issues, and choosing and using mental health services.

Evaluation. Critical to the success of any EAP is establishing its effectiveness and acceptance with the organization from top levels of management to the lower ranks of employees. Results of evaluations are an essential means of providing feedback to corporate management as well as to the EAP staff itself. To that end, EAS has a number of on-going evaluation activities: (a) Every client is called 2 weeks after the end of the consultation to determine compliance with recommendations and how well the service met expectations; (b) 6 months after the initial contact, the client is mailed an evaluation form with a stamped return envelope; (c) every seminar or presentation ends with a request that the audience complete evaluation forms (on a regular basis, the responses to these polls are tabulated and analyzed); (d) monthly, data on utilization patterns are reviewed (these program statistics are included in a covering report to management along with data on other EAS activities during the month); and (e) a manager's satisfaction survey is conducted (to date, one has been completed and published in MetLife's internal management quarterly; Cerf, 1991).

Program Philosophy

More than a dozen tenets underlie and guide EAS practice. Briefly stated, they are

1. Confidentiality is the keystone of all EAS practice;
2. Any request for service deserves a prompt and respectful response;
3. Every client is entitled to a conscientious and efficient assessment;
4. Client education is a fundamental EAS responsibility;
5. Although contact with EAS may be therapeutic, the staff does not provide psychotherapy;
6. Once a problem or disease has been diagnosed and the individual has been advised and educated, the responsibility for getting and complying with assistance resides with the client;
7. Alcoholism and other addictions are diseases;
8. The power to make or influence beneficial changes is within each individual;
9. Poor job performance is destructive to the individual;
10. Facilitating or allowing poor job performance to continue is destructive to the individual, to the work unit, and to the larger organization;
11. Requiring work performance standards be met is respectful, supportive, and helpful;
12. EAS facilitates but does not make changes for others;
13. EAS may offer opinions to management but does not make or intervene in management decisions;
14. EAS strives to model its recommendations.

EAS Staff

Composition. The EAS staff consists of seven people who combine expertise in mental health, substance abuse diagnosis, community and company resources, career and financial advising, and office management. The four clinicians are licensed or certified to practice independently in New York state and include one full-time psychologist, who also functions as the program manager, and one full-time and two part-time certified social workers. The psychologist and one of the social workers are also certified employee assistance professionals (CEAP). All have previous experience in diagnosing and treating adult problems, mental health disorders, chemical dependencies, and addictions. In addition, they are able to set aside their more passive styles as therapists and to relate as consultants to clients—to interact directively, educationally, facilitatively, and resourcefully.

Another member of the professional team is a human resource generalist who earned an MBA in human resources management and who has a long history of company employment. Among her contributions to program effectiveness is the depth of her corporate knowledge and expertise, particularly in reference to history, departmental relationships, and company procedures and practices. Her ability to identify and locate preexisting company services and resources is instrumental in expediting resolution of many client difficulties.

Somewhat behind the scenes and less intensively involved with direct service to employees are a full-time research assistant and a part-time clerk. Together, all seven members of the team are charged with the timely servicing of all MetLife employees at headquarters and in the field locations across the United States.

Responsibilities. The clinical staff conducts all client assessments. They either help the employee resolve the problem or suggest and facilitate the employee's referral to a community resource.

The responsibilities of the human resource professional overlap with some of those fulfilled by the clinical staff. The human resource professional, too, looks for and evaluates referral resources, most particularly those associated with child- and elder-care providers, financial advisors, and internal company services. As the professional responsible for limited, short-term career advising, she consults about resumes, interviewing skills, and internal job postings. She also brings closure to the clinicians' consultations with 2-week follow-up phone calls during which she asks about the client's follow through with advice and conducts a qualitative evaluation of the services provided.

Any of the five professionals may present seminars, lead discussions, or write articles as part of the preventive and educational services that EAS provides. Monthly activity reports are furnished to corporate management by the team manager.

In addition to the many duties usually associated with an office manager, the research assistant explains the consultation process to and sets up appointments for employees. She also conducts the 2-week follow-up calls, maintains the charts, the chart retrieval system, and the statistical database. She is responsible for collating data from evaluation surveys and for monitoring services provided by the ad hoc clinicians. (See subsequent section "In-person consultation: Ad hoc clinicians.") Assignment of tasks to and monitoring the work completed by the office clerk are additional duties performed by the research assistant.

The Corporation's Structure

MetLife has about 42,000 employees in the United States and, like other large companies, has its corporate headquarters in a major urban center. Its home office has an employee population of several thousand, with seven other U.S. cities contributing more than a thousand MetLife employees each. Many small sales offices also exist, some of which have as few as four or five people on staff, many of whom are frequently on the road. Thus, reaching all MetLife employees with promotional information and EAP services is a complicated undertaking.

In addition to the geographical spread of its employee population, MetLife is divided into approximately one dozen departments. The organizational structure is decentralized, all departments are autonomous, and each (a) is a cost center, (b) is expected to establish and maintain its own budget, (c) has its own recruiting and training sections, (d) has its own human resource professionals, and (e) has it own goals to accomplish. Although two or three departments may be represented in any one city, often they have little intercommunication and few mutual activities.

Further complicating the transmission of promotional materials and a unified EAP educational program is the fact that the corporate human resources department helps other departments draft guidelines and policy but does not originate mandated procedures or training routines. Thus, it is necessary to negotiate independently with each department for any manager training or educational activities. Indeed, at this time, EAP training for managers happens more office-by-office than throughout an entire department.

Methods of Service Delivery

Staff diversity. Just as MetLife has its complexities, its EAP is a complex unit. One of the solutions to supplying EAP services to a company as large and diversified as MetLife is provided by capitalizing on the multidisciplinary nature of the EAS team, with its mix of staff skills and knowledge. Staffing EAS with part-time professionals also adds to the diversity of services provided. MetLife found this staffing arrangement appropriate because of the relatively small size of the EAS unit and because the unit has no career ladder. Consequently, the larger team is composed, in part, of professionals who are developing private therapy and consulting practices. An additional benefit of such staffing practices is a diminution of professional "burnout" and job-related complaints.

Services are provided in a variety of ways and in different settings, as discussed below.

In-person consultation: EAS clinicians. In-person consultations are conducted at corporate headquarters in the EAS suite of offices. A member of the clinical staff is assigned a client and spends a minimum of one 1-hr session identifying and assessing the problem, explaining client rights and clinician responsibilities, defining the confidential nature of the relationship, and discussing possible strategies for problem resolution.

On-site, remote office coverage. A proposal to provide an EAS clincian to a nearby office, outside the corporate headquarters, is being evaluated. The clinician would be on-site for one half or one full day each week, depending on the case load. Hours not scheduled for in-person consultations would be occupied with phone evaluations and referrals as well as chart-entry activities.

In-person consultation: Ad hoc clinicians. Employees in dispersed locations can receive in-person consultations with ad hoc clinicians. These clinicians are credentialed mental health professionals in private practice who agree to consult with MetLife employees in-person in their local offices. Their selection is based on the same criteria that are used for hiring the clinical staff at corporate headquarters. The employee is given the choice of talking with an EAS clinician in corporate headquarters on the phone or of consulting in-person with a locally available ad hoc clinician. If a local clinician is chosen, the employee receives the name and phone number, and an EAS staff member contacts the clinician to authorize the consultation process. It is then the responsibility of the employee to follow through with an appointment for the consultation. EAS receives the ad hoc clinician's chart notes and documentation as well as the bill for the consultation sessions.

Currently, EAS has contracts with two psychologists in two cities, each of which has a large MetLife employee population. The roster of ad hoc clinicians is expected to at least double in the near future.

Telephone consultation: Toll-free number. The same consultation service is available to any employee through a toll-free phone call. A consultation appointment is scheduled with an EAS clinician. The call can be placed from the office, home, or anywhere else in the United States. To protect the employee's privacy, the office call does not become part of the manager's phone bill.

External EAP providers. Two large MetLife facilities have contracted with local hospitals to provide EAPs. An important part of the decision to engage external EAP providers is visibility—the perception of ready accessibility. To ensure comparability of services and quality delivery, EAS provides consultation and quality assurance overview to the facilities' human resource professionals. EAS reviews contracts, suggests revisions of promotional materials, and gives advice about the standards to expect from EAP providers. EAS receives copies of the external EAP provider's program statistics. Completed 6-month mail follow-up forms are sent by their employees to EAS for response tabulation and analysis. A report is returned to the MetLife facility and the local EAP provider.

In addition, it has been agreed that as long as the EAS manager is a licensed or certified mental health professional, his or her access to the charts of the external provider would be permitted. This enables MetLife to ensure delivery of quality clinical service without compromising employee confidentiality.

Other forms of service delivery. Other ways of providing clinical EAP services to employees are summarized in Table 2. Those currently not implemented by EAS for MetLife are not discussed.

Consultation to subsidiaries. Although direct EAS support is not available to employees of MetLife's various subsidiaries, the human resource professionals consult with EAS about implementing independent and individualized EAPs in their dispersed locations. Proposals are being considered whereby subsidiaries will contract with EAS for EAP services in an arrangement similar to one that might be made with an external EAP provider. Currently, fees are quoted on a per case basis,

Table 2. Configurations of MetLife EAP Service Delivery to Individual Employees

Type of delivery	Location
Telephone	
EAS clinicians	Company headquarters
External EAP clinicians	Their firm's offices*
In-person	
EAS clinicians	Company headquarters
	Dispersed company site*
Ad hoc clinicians	Their private offices
	Dispersed company site*
External EAP clinicians	Their firm's offices
	Dispersed company site*

*Method is not currently part of EAS service delivery design.

but it is likely that they will be shifted to a capitated fee once experience is gained and utilization rates become steady.

Intracorporate communication. A robust EAP promotes its activities and services not only to employees but also to management. In a complex organization such as MetLife, it is important to be able to tell management about services, utilization patterns, employee consultation rates, and management referrals. EAS collects demographic data in such a way that each department can be studied independently and separately from the aggregate. In that way, the administration of each department can be informed about the relative awareness of its employees and managers about its EAP.

Comparing Internal and External EAP Providers

Many large companies report substantial cost savings as a result of instituting their own internal EAPs; other companies, both large and small, report similar savings after contracting with an external agency to provide an EAP for their employees. External program providers have flourished since the 1970s, capitalizing on their ability to provide many different types of services in a variety of settings and in a variety of locations.

Internal programs may be more accessible to busy managers and more sensitive to the company's corporate culture. However, they are less likely to be perceived by employees as a benefit or a confidential program than is a program located outside the company. In addition, employees may erroneously view the on-site EAP as yet another method by which upper management can watch the workers or gain access to personal information. Confidentiality remains a major issue for both types of programs, and it is the responsibility of the EAP providers to assure potential clients that all communications (except where mandated by law) are kept strictly private.

The Fitting Configuration

Evaluating an EAP provider can be difficult, particularly if the company has no experience with either the use or provision of such services. The Employee Assistance Society of North America (EASNA) has established standards or measures required for EAP accreditation ("Future Blueprint," 1989; "Mapping the Future," 1989). The one-page reference guide is useful in evaluating the appropriateness of an external EAP for a particular company and location ("Using a Measuring," 1991). Several other sets of guidelines for evaluating EAP providers have been developed: *Standards for EAPs* (Staff, 1990); "Contracting for External EAP Services" (1991); and "Employee Assistance Programs" (Staff, 1991). The confidential nature of the consultation along with the availability of services plus the sophistication of the program statistics and accompanying activity report all play important roles in the decision process. Once the program is decided on, however, whether it is an internal or an external one, it is imperative that it have the active support of top management.

Conclusion

The structure and procedures described in the preceding pages have only recently coalesced. Indeed, it should be clear that EAS is an EAP in the process of developing and evolving. The near future will require procedures for the more comprehensive integration of the ad hoc clinicians with those at headquarters. Other ongoing challenges in this complex organization include maintaining cordial working relationships with human resource professionals, with the Medical Department staff, and with members of the corporate Law Department while continuing to deliver high-quality, confidential, and effective services to increasing numbers of employees.

This chapter has attempted to show how a multidisciplinary team of professionals provides an EAP to employees of a large decentralized and geographically dispersed corporation. Several basic forms of EAP service delivery have been outlined. In addition, job responsibilities and interconnections of staff and duties have been briefly described. We acknowledge, however, that the shape of MetLife's EAP cannot be a prescription for any other organization's EAP: Corporations are as unique as people, and their EAPs will develop to fit them individually.

References

Bureau of National Affairs. (1987). *Employee assistance programs: Benefits, problems, and prospects.* Washington, DC: Bureau of National Affairs Response Center.
Cerf, P. (Ed.). (1991). Who do you call about "people problems"? *Outlook,* Summer, 8–11.
Contracting for external EAP services: Off-the-shelf guidelines and shared experiences. (1991). *EAP Association Exchange, 21,* 37–38.
Correcting misinformation on "drug free workplace." (1989). *The ALMACAN, 19,* 7.
Corry, J. M. (1990). MetLife's experience with fitness and wellness programming. *Statistical Bulletin, 71,* 19–25.
Feldman, S. (1991). Today's EAPs make the grade. *Personnel, 68,* 4.

Future blueprint. (1989). *EmployeeAssistance, 2*, 37–51.

Mapping the future. (1989). *EmployeeAssistance, 2*, 36–42.

Masi, D. A. (1984). *Designing employee assistance programs.* New York: American Management Association.

McDonnel Douglas Corporation's EAP produces hard data. (1989). *The ALMACAN, 19*, 18–26.

MetLife Employee Advisory Services. (1991). *Statistical Bulletin, 72*, 27–35.

Philips, S. B. (1991). *Employee Advisory Services year-end report: 1990.* New York: MetLife, Employee Advisory Services.

Roman, P. M., & Blum, T. C. (1989). Alcohol problem intervention in the workplace: Data on present status and future implications. *Alcohol Health & Research World, 13*, 375–380.

Staff. (1960). *A guide for the family.* New York: Metropolitan Life Insurance.

Staff. (1990). *Standards for EAPs.* Arlington, VA: Employee Assistance Professionals Association.

Staff. (1991). Employee assistance programs (EAPs): Their role and how employers can effectively select one. *Field Release 1991–58 (EAP).* New York: Metropolitan Life Insurance.

Using a measuring stick: A checklist for sizing up EAP vendors. (1991). *EAP Association Exchange, 21*, 39.

Part V

Conclusion

Lawrence R. Murphy, Joseph J. Hurrell, Jr., and
James Campbell Quick

Work and Well-Being: Where Do We Go From Here?

The chapters in this book represent a sample of current research and practice in the area of work and well-being. The book was organized around the prevention model depicted in Figure 1 of Chapter 1, which sets the frame for the three core sections of the book: Occupational Mental Health Risks (part 2), Individual Stress Responses and Early Warning Signs (part 3), and Distress in the Workplace (part 4).

The concern of part 2 is primary prevention, which focuses on organizational/ environmental/psychological risk factors that may have an adverse effect on employee mental health. Three assessment chapters in this section examine stressors such as low job control, social occupational stressors, and the absence of job security. The three intervention chapters in this section describe stressor abatement approaches in a variety of industries and occupations.

Part 3 is concerned with secondary prevention. The five assessment chapters in this section focus on perceptual processes, workplace surveillance, and early response patterns to work stress. The three intervention chapters focus on change strategies to implement before employees are in severe distress.

The concern of part 4 is tertiary prevention (i.e., treatment or therapy) focusing on individuals and groups in distress or crisis. The four assessment chapters identify consequences of mismanaged work stress, whereas the two intervention chapters report treatment approaches for employees in distress.

Where We Have Been

In considering how to approach the theme of this chapter, we felt it useful to examine briefly where we have been to better gauge progress. On December 29, 1971, Elliott Richardson, then Secretary of Health, Education, and Welfare, commissioned an independent task force with the responsibility of examining health, education, and welfare problems in the United States from the perspective of the institution of work. This task force reviewed much of the literature on the subject, interviewed large numbers of blue- and white-collar employees, and solicited papers reflecting expert and practical opinions. Their resulting report, *Work in America* (1973), introduced new perspectives on work and well-being into the national dialogue and provided a rough benchmark for assessing progress in the field over the past 20 years.

At the beginning of the 1970s, according to *Work in America* (1973), significant numbers of American workers were dissatisfied with the quality of their working lives. Dull and demeaning work, work over which the worker has little or no control, and conflict and ambiguity in occupational roles were found to contribute to (i.e., serve as risk factors for) poor mental health, although not necessarily to mental illness. As reflected in the chapters of this book, these themes continue to dominate research in the area of occupational stress.

Germane to public policy, *Work in America* (1973) noted that workers and society appear to be bearing the medical costs that have their genesis in the workplace and that many of these costs could be avoided if preventive measures were taken. A recent survey of American workers by the Northwestern National Life Insurance Company (1991) provides clear evidence that widespread preventive measures have not been forthcoming. In this survey, nearly 72% of the respondents experienced frequent stress-related physical or mental conditions that could increase health costs. Moreover, based on the disability cases managed by Northwestern National Life Insurance Company rehabilitation services, the percentage of stress-related disabilities grew from 6% to 13% over the past nine years.

The redesign of jobs to permit greater worker participation in decisions affecting their lives at work was the keynote of the *Work in America* (1973) report, although the task force decided not to set forth specific recommendations. Not only did worker participation hold the promise to decrease mental and physical health costs, increase productivity, and improve the quality of life, but it would give for the first time a voice to many workers in an important decision-making process. Sadly, efforts to redesign work to reduce or eliminate the sources of stress since the 1970s remain sparse in the published literature (Ivancevich, Matteson, Freedman, & Phillips, 1990).

The present chapter makes general recommendations concerning future directions for research and practice. Following the organization of the chapters in this book, we address issues surrounding assessment first, followed by those concerning intervention. Additionally, a final section of the chapter addresses the need for improved surveillance of worker well-being and methodological improvements in work and well-being research.

In contrast with the general recommendations made in this chapter, a companion volume, *Work and Well-Being: An Agenda for the 1990s* (Keita & Sauter, 1992), sets forth specific action plans for implementing the *National Strategy for the Prevention of Work-Related Injuries and Illnesses* (National Institute for Occupational Safety and Health [NIOSH], 1988). These action plans are outlined in four major areas: surveillance, work design, education and training, and occupational mental health treatment.

Assessment

In the following section, we will address issues pertinent to the assessment of occupational stress. We have restricted ourselves to a limited number of topics that we view as particularly deserving of attention. These include the issues of worker control; objective versus subjective measures of work stressors; stages of career development; selection, maturation, and "drift"; new technologies; influences of stress on infectious diseases; and interactions among work and nonwork factors.[1]

Worker Control

Particular attention has been drawn to low worker autonomy or control as a risk factor for occupational health problems (see Sauter, Hurrell, & Cooper, 1989). Early field studies linking machine-paced work with lack of self-respect, underutilization of abilities, and poor mental health (Caplan, Cobb, French, Harrison, & Pinneau, 1975) and other studies linking low worker control to changes in catecholamine levels (Frankenhauser & Gardell, 1976) announced the importance of this variable for worker health and well-being. A meta-analysis of more recent research found that worker control was associated with high levels of job satisfaction, involvement, commitment, and motivation and with low levels of physical complaints (Spector, 1986).

Degree of worker control also has been found to be an important variable affecting the probability of continued employment in the face of chronic illness and disability. For example, Yelin (1986) demonstrated that among individuals with a chronic illness, those reporting high control at work were twice as likely to continue working than were those with low control. Moreover, among people with some limitation of activity, those with high autonomy at work were more than 20 times as likely to be working, despite their limitations, than were those with low autonomy.

The impact of this rapidly growing body of research on job control is reflected in a recent government pronouncement regarding the importance of job control in protecting worker health. The Swedish Work Environment Act (Ministry of Labor, 1987) stated "The aim must be for work to be arranged in such a way so that the employee himself can influence his work situation" (p. 3). Noting the evidence of the increased tide of work-related psychological disorders in the U.S. workforce, NIOSH made the recommendation that workers "should be given the opportunity to have input on decisions or actions that affect their jobs and their performance of their tasks" (NIOSH, 1988, p. 105).

Increasingly, however, questions are being raised concerning the methods and theory of job control research (Sauter et al., 1989). The need for closer attention to specific dimensions of control is a matter of broad concurrence. In this regard, Landy, Quick, and Kasl (in press) recently emphasized the importance of four aspects of technological and administrative control as they influence worker well-being: job definition; work load and work pace; work scheduling; and rewards, punishments, and performance monitoring.

---

[1]Other important topics not addressed in this chapter, but no less important, include personality factors (Cooper & Payne, 1991), gender differences (LaCroix & Haynes, 1987), aging (Davies, Matthews, & Wong, 1991), and coping (Carver, Scheier, & Weintraub, 1989).

Objective Versus Subjective Assessment Measures

Kasl (1978, 1987) has argued repeatedly and persuasively for a refinement of measures of organizational stress and employee strain and for the need to supplement self-report indicators with more objective measures of job characteristics. Objective measures of job characteristics are needed to validate employee perceptions of objective characteristics and to provide employers with specific guidance for redesigning jobs and changing organizations to improve worker well-being. Progress in this area is noteworthy, as outlined below.

Frese and Zapf (1988) elaborated practical, theoretical, and methodological reasons for using objective measures of job characteristics in future studies of work stress. In one study, The authors compared incumbent, expert-rated, and group-assessed job dimensions in their analysis of objective and subjective assessments of job stress. Frese and Zapf concluded that objective measures of job characteristics tend to underestimate the true correlation between job factors and health outcomes because they do not take into account differences in actual job performance among organizations or organizational differences in work environment factors (e.g., equipment design).

In another view, Shaw and Riskind (1983) used job analysis data taken from the Position Analysis Questionnaire (Mecham, McCormick, & Jeanneret, 1977) aggregated at the occupation level as objective indicators of job dimensions and linked these objective data with independently collected health data. The resulting database was used to identify objective job dimensions associated with mental and physical ill health. This approach was used on a much larger scale more recently by Murphy (1991), and concurrence between the results of these two studies were found for one psychosocial predictor of cardiovascular disease: jobs requiring vigilance plus responsibility (e.g., for the safety of others). Interestingly, these results fit Kasl's (1978) description of work factors associated with the pathogenic process linking stress to disease outcomes, namely, chronic stressors, external pacing of demands, vigilance, and drastic consequences if the job demands are not met.

Finally, Spector and colleagues (J. K. Hall & Spector, 1991; Spector & Jex, 1991) reappraised a basic assumption of causality in work stress research: Objective job characteristics influence employee perceptions, which in turn influence employee affective reactions (e.g., Hackman & Lawler, 1971). Recent studies have questioned the validity of this assumption, and Spector (e.g., J. K. Hall & Spector, 1991) has recommended that researchers consider alternative causal pathways. Moreover, Spector and Jex (1991) recently reported that measures of job characteristics from different sources did not correlate well. The authors compared associations among job characteristics and various outcomes using multiple data sources that included worker self-reports, ratings based on job descriptions, and data from the *Dictionary of Occupational Titles* (U.S. Department of Labor, 1977).

Taken together, the results of studies described in this section argue for the development of alternative measures of job characteristics and the incorporation of objective assessments of job characteristics. For example, in a recent study of 198 nurses, Fox, Dwyer, and Ganster (1991) found that the combined use of objective and subjective assessment measures was important both with regard to demands (stressors) and affective and physiological outcome measures. Specifically, they found significant positive correlations between the objective demand measures and physiological responses (i.e., blood pressure and cortisol levels) as well as significant positive correlations between the subjective demand measures and affective outcomes. However, the objective demand measures were not significantly related to the affective outcomes, nor were the subjective demand measures significantly related to the physiological outcomes. This study suggests two conclusions. First, it is important to incorporate both objective and subjective measures whenever possible in light of the differing results that they may yield. Second, there may be a question as to how accurately individuals are able to self-report stress or strain levels as well as their abilities to make attributions about their subjective experiences of stress.

An earlier study by Nelson and Sutton (1990) raised questions about the amount of variance in strain symptoms that may be explained by dispositional variables. Although the epidemiological model proposed by Kasl (1978) and others encourages focus on the environmental events leading to distress and strain, Nelson and Sutton's (1990) results with 91 newcomers in organizations found that 32% of the variance in symptoms for these newcomers 9 months after entering the organization was explained by their levels of symptoms prior to entering the organizations. Hence, this study strongly suggests the need to incorporate dispositional variables in assessments of stress.

Stage of Career Development

Little empirical research has examined job stressors and stress responses as functions of career development stage. The substantial research efforts devoted to job stress and career development have developed largely as independent endeavors. Thus, job stress studies typically treat age and job tenure (i.e., indicators of career stage) as nuisance variables that are controlled statistically. Studies of career development, on the other hand, define unique views and attitudes associated with career stages but typically do not include health outcome variables, focusing instead on performance, withdrawal behaviors, and job satisfaction (e.g., D. T. Hall & Mansfield, 1975; Schein, 1968). Although some studies in each area acknowledge findings from the other, there has been little cross-fertilization of ideas and theories.

The results of two recent studies of job stress and stage of career development point to a fertile area for future research. Osipow and Doty (1985) reported significant differences in job stress as a function of age and career stage. Older workers reported lower psychological strain than did younger workers, an effect that Osipow and Doty believed to be due to the improved ability among more experienced workers to cope with occupational stressors. Similarly, Hurrell, McLaney, and Murphy (1990) examined job satisfaction, mood state, life events, and perceived health status as functions of three career stages (early, middle, and late). Their results indicated that job stressors associated with health outcomes varied according to career stage, as did the beneficial effects of social support. The findings of these two studies suggest that job stress researchers should abandon the practice of treating age and tenure as nuisance variables in favor of an approach that views stage of career development as a moderator variable.

Several recent developments should provide a stimulus for studies of job stress and career stage. Nelson (1987) integrated findings from job stress studies with the literature dealing with one aspect of career development, organizational socialization, and proposed a Stress of Socialization Model. Also, a recent special issue of *Prevention in Human Services* was devoted entirely to the subject of stress across career stage (Quick, Hess, Hermalin, & Quick, 1990).

Nelson, Quick, and Joplin (1991) have subsequently extended the early socialization model to understand the newcomer's adjustment through a process of adulthood attachment to established organizational insiders. These established insiders provide a range of social resources that enable the newcomer to achieve a sense of psychological intimacy as well as integrated involvement within the organization (Shaver & Buhrmester, 1985). An early test of this theoretical formulation lends some support to this perspective (Nelson & Quick, 1991).

In *Career Stress in Changing Times*, Quick and Quick (1990) set out a life and career cycle framework illustrated through the case of Dr. Otto A. Faust. Within his 64-year career cycle and over 100-year life cycle, they examined the five major career transition points that were sources of stress and through which Dr. Faust achieved accommodation, adjustment, and integration. Other long-term studies of stress and adjustment have been conducted, such as Vaillant's (1977) 35-year followup on a college cohort class. However, the practical and method dilemmas accompanying such longitudinal research are substantial. In addition, there are significant needs for resource commitment and planning in such investigations.

Selection, Maturation, and "Drift"

As Payne (1988) noted, the choices people make about jobs and careers are not random. It seems clear that people, through career choices and job changes, select themselves (or "drift") into occupations where they are better able to cope with the demands. Likewise, workers mature in their work roles, acquiring the skills and coping abilities that allow them to better function in their jobs. Cross-sectional surveys, which represent the most common method used in job stress research, provide no information on such worker adaptational strategies. Moreover, it should be recognized that studies of workers who remain in an occupation in which selfselection occurs are focusing on those who are better able to cope with existing demands. Clearly, the roles of occupational self-selection and drift in occupational stress require greater research attention.

New Technologies

New technologies can be stressful from both an organizational and an individual perspective. Schein (1989) argued that the computer and information technology revolutions have made a significant impact on the nature of organization and managerial interrelations as well. His contention is that organizations are moving from hierarchical to nonhierarchical forms of relationships among people in work environments, for which there are few good models. Hence, this transition created by the information technology revolution needs attention concerning the impact it is having beyond the relationship arena.

Nelson and Kletke (1990) call for cooperative, joint ventures between researchers and practitioners in addressing the stresses and strainers that workers experience as a result of technological innovation and change. They suggest that the stressful aspects of technological change may be eased by developing preventive interventions aimed at facilitating positive adjustment for the individual and the organization. In addressing another aspect of technological innovation, White and Nelson (1990) identified the differing perspectives that individuals and organizations have concerning the process. They advocate training programs designed to ensure transfer of learning for the individual as well as accomplishment of strategic objectives for the organization. However, empirical evaluations of such programs are not readily available, even though they are very much needed.

Stress and Infectious Disease

Recent psychoneuroimmunological studies suggest a role for work stress in the immunological process (e.g., Cohen & Williamson, 1991; Jemmott and Locke, 1984). Increasingly, evidence suggests that immune system responses may mediate some of these relations. A large number of animal studies, for example, have demonstrated that experimentally induced stress increases susceptibility to a variety of infectious agents, as well as the incidence and rate of growth of certain tumors (Borysenko & Borysenko, 1982). Although fewer in number, human studies have shown that psychosocial factors, including stressful life events, are related to diseases that are under immunologic regulation (Jemmott & Locke, 1984).

Other animal and human research provides more direct evidence that stress can affect immunocompetence (i.e., the ability of an organism's immune system to defend against challenge). For example, stress has been linked to changes in levels of circulating antibodies, lymphocyte cytotoxicity, and lymphocyte proliferation (Jemmott & Locke, 1984). Even commonplace stressors (e.g., academic demand, marital separation, divorce, and bereavement) have been shown to produce changes in measures of immunocompetence (Baker, 1987). There is every reason to believe that stressful elements of the work environment also may elicit changes in immunocompetence and thereby influence health status. Technological developments in the quantification of immunocompetence, as well as improved understanding of the nervous–immune systems interconnection, are now beginning to make study of the job stress–immunocompetence relation possible.

Another dimension of the relation between work stress and infectious disease relates to worker fears surrounding occupational transmission of human immunodeficiency virus (HIV) and acquired immunodeficiency syndrome (AIDS). Although the rate of occupational HIV infection is very low (approximately 0.3%; Marcus, 1988), health-care workers often perceive their risk to be substantially higher. In one study, for example, 56% of emergency medical service professionals believed their risk of occupational HIV infection to be "somewhat" or "very high" (Smyser, Bryce, & Joseph, 1990). Another study found that although 80% of residency program house officers knew their chances of acquiring AIDS from contact with AIDS patients (i.e., 1 in 10,000 or less), fully 48% expressed "moderate" or "high" personal concern about acquiring AIDS from patients (Link, Fiengold, Charap, Freeman, & Shelov, 1988).

Interactions Among Work and Nonwork Factors

There is a need for greater assessments of the interactions that occur between the work and nonwork domains of people's lives, especially with the increasing migration of women into the workplace. From a role theory perspective, individuals are "divided" into their various roles and obligations, a process that leads to disintegration as opposed to integration (Lobel, 1991). There is qualitative case data as well as empirical evidence, as mentioned in Chapter 1, that suggest that there are crossover effects from the workplace into the home and vice-versa (Bacharach, Bamberger, & Conley, 1991; Quick, Joplin, Gray, & Cooley, in press). There is a need for (a) designs that are robust enough to capture the breadth and range of the individual's life space and various components and (b) conceptual models that argue for integration of the individual's experience, not disintegration of it. Social identity theory may offer a perspective on the latter. Additionally, Lobel, Quinn, and Warfield (in press) found that psychologically intimate, opposite-sexed relationships in the workplace are quite viable and do not carry with them any necessity for physical or sexual intimacy. This may suggest that the traditional ways of constructing and measuring work and nonwork factors in stress research need to be reconceptualized.

Intervention

In this section, we examine issues concerning organizational and individual programs of prevention and change, including job redesign, stress management interventions, employee assistance programs (EAPs), worker–management collaboration, and occupational mental health services.

Job Redesign and Organizational Change Approaches

Job redesign and organizational change remain the preferred approaches to stress management because they focus on reducing or eliminating the sources of the problem in the work environment. However, job redesign and organizational change approaches require detailed assessment of work factors that generate undue stress and a knowledge of the dynamics of change processes in organizations (Alderfer, 1976) so that potentially undesirable outcomes can be minimized. Moreover, these types of change strategies can be expensive and disruptive interventions, making them less palatable to management than secondary or tertiary prevention strategies.

Three current models offer guidance for designing stress interventions in the workplace: the job characteristics model (Hackman & Lawler, 1971; Hackman & Oldham, 1976), the demand/control model of worker strain (Karasek, 1979), and the person–environment (P–E) fit model (Caplan et al., 1975). Interestingly, each of these models predicts positive health and performance outcomes as the amount of worker control or discretion is increased. For example, the job characteristics model of task design considers autonomy to be a core job dimension that leads to positive affect by means of experienced responsibility for work outcomes. Worker participation in decision making, which presumably increases control (or perhaps perceived control), is a fundamental element of sociotechnical systems theory and quality circles.

Likewise, control is a central feature of P–E fit theory (Caplan et al., 1975), which predicts worker distress as a function of the congruence between objective job demands and subjective worker needs. It follows that workers with more job control can (re)structure jobs to optimize fit with their needs and abilities, thereby reducing job strain.

The most explicit statement of the relation between job control and worker health was offered by Karasek (1979). Karasek hypothesized that psychological strain results from the joint effects of psychological job demands (workload) and the degree of worker control (decision latitude). Worker strain would be reduced as worker control and decision latitude are increased.

As yet, few empirical tests of the predictions from these theories have been made in work settings. A few published reports, however, have produced encouraging results demonstrating decreases in worker strain as the level of worker control over various aspects of work is increased (Jackson, 1983; Karasek, 1990; Pierce & Newstrom, 1983; Wall & Clegg, 1981).

Stress Management Interventions

Reports of "stress management interventions," which typically involve attempts to help employees either modify or control their appraisal of stressful situations (secondary prevention) or cope more effectively with stress reactions (tertiary prevention), are much more frequent in the published literature (Murphy & Schoenborn, 1989). Indeed, recent reviews of the stress intervention literature concur in recommending a wider focus for stress interventions that embraces primary prevention (i.e., strategies to reduce or eliminate the sources of stress at work; DeFrank & Cooper, 1987; Ivancevich et al., 1990; Murphy, 1988; Quick & Quick, 1984).

DeFrank and Cooper (1987), Heaney & van Ryn (1990), and Ivancevich et al., (1990) offered general frameworks for guiding the design and evaluation of stress management interventions. All of these frameworks recommend that stress management interventions be comprehensive, addressing the organizational environment, the individual, and the individual–organizational interface. A collateral need also exists to expand the range of outcome measures in stress intervention studies beyond measures of worker physiological and psychological health to reflect the individual–organization interface. Examples of such measures are absenteeism, turnover, job satisfaction, productivity, health-care costs, disability, and accidents or injuries.

Employee Assistance Programs

As originally designed and operated, EAPs offered tertiary prevention for problem drinkers. Increasingly, however, they are expanding their services to address other problem areas such as drug abuse and employee stress. Because of their access to organizations, EAPs have significant potential for reducing worker distress. For this potential to be realized, EAPs will need to incorporate a primary prevention component and begin providing feedback to organizations with respect to stressful work environment factors. In light of the sensitivity of worker confidentiality, such feedback will have to be provided in a manner that prevents individual worker identification.

Feedback from an EAP in the form of summary statistics would permit organizations to pinpoint high stress departments to establish a starting point for more in-depth stress assessment studies. Other types of feedback could take the form of organizational characteristics that generate worker distress. Of course, EAP counselors would need to become familiar with principles of organizational behavior and the dynamics of work environment–employee health relations. This may mean adding occupational mental health specialists to the EAP staff or providing training to existing staff in these areas.

The scope and content of psychological health programs, whether provided within an EAP context or not, should be adjusted to accommodate such local factors as the nature of the work performed and special needs of the work force. At a minimum, all such programs should offer basic psychological support in areas common to any work force, for example, personal crisis management, alcohol or chemical dependency, marital and family counseling, and stress management. These services should have primary, secondary, and tertiary prevention components. More specialized concerns such as impending retirement, layoffs, relocation, or other job-specific problems may require additional effort and expertise. Mechanisms should be established for input by consultants in occupational mental health.

Mental health services should be integrated into the overall occupational healthcare program, whether on site or external to the organization, and developed in a coordinated fashion with input from all relevant departments (e.g., safety, personnel, risk management, line management).

Confidentiality. The issue of confidentiality is crucial, not only with respect to EAPs but for all types of workplace studies. Some EAPs are tagged "non safe" to report to by employees, especially in the defense industry with security issues at risk. Generally, employees quickly learn whether to "trust" an EAP, and this trust is based largely on employee experiences and impressions regarding confidentiality (Stainbrook & Green, 1989).

Data from insurance claims, medical examinations, EAPs, mental health programs, and health risk assessments are subject to many uses. Some of these may not be in the best interests of employees. For example, there may be fears that such information could secretly be used in decisions about job assignment, promotion, or termination. Also, certain diagnostic labels present more problems than others. For example, drug abuse, alcoholism, and epilepsy are feared to be grounds for not hiring, denying promotions, and forcing early retirement or even dismissal.

Methods of ensuring confidentiality. Several methods can be used to protect the privacy of individual workers, including establishing policies stipulating that only evaluators will have access to information on individuals, sending the results of screening and risk assessments to private physicians or employees' homes, and contracting with outside organizations to provide employers only with aggregate information. The success of these methods depends on the degree of confidence that employees have in them. However, providing only aggregate data precludes further analysis at the individual level.

To provide continued access to individual data and still protect privacy, other methods have been developed. Often, a master list of names along with code numbers is set up. The master list is kept in a secure location, and all data forms are identified only by the code number. This method has been used successfully in the past but has some limitations. Such records could be subpoenaed as a part of a legal proceeding. Because there is no complete guarantee of anonymity, employees may distort responses to questions about alcohol and drug use and other behaviors that may be strongly incriminating or socially unpopular.

Still another way to protect anonymity and possibly reduce response bias on sensitive questions is the use of random response techniques. This approach protects the anonymity of the question rather than the respondent. In one of the simplest models, two questions are presented—the sensitive question and an innocuous question for which the probability of response is already known. Respondents are asked to choose a question by flipping a coin and then to respond without letting the interviewer know which question is being answered. Given prior knowledge of the probabilities of question selection and responses to the innocuous question, the proportions of group responses to the sensitive question can be estimated reasonably accurately. A limitation of the random response techniques is that they require large sample sizes because the obtained variance is a function of the proportion of the sample responding to the sensitive question rather than to the entire sample (Stainbrook & Green, 1989).

In summary, there often is a delicate balance between protecting individual rights and privacy and protecting the best interests of companies. This issue will become more controversial as greater emphasis is placed on screening, risk reduction, and cost containment.

Worker–Management Collaboration: A Process Model

It is important to appreciate that universal solutions to work stress are unlikely to be successful because stress problems often require solutions that are more or less unique to each organization. The intervention process, on the other hand, may be generic and effective. In this regard, Murphy and Hurrell (1987) described a stress intervention involving a marriage of individual stress management and job stressor-focused approaches. In this study, a worker–management "stress reduction committee" was established, containing representatives from various units of the organization. The committee, with the help of outside experts, developed an employee survey using feedback obtained from workers during a "stress management workshop." The sources of stress identified in the survey then were reviewed and prioritized by the committee according to perceived relevance and importance to employee health and well-being and susceptibility to primary prevention. Organizational changes to eliminate or reduce the high-priority stressors then were formulated and presented to management, with recommendations for their implementation and evaluation at annual intervals.

This approach resembles participatory "action research" (Whyte, 1991) and may serve as a useful prototype for stress interventions. Indeed, prior studies attest to the importance of worker involvement in organizational change efforts and the importance of the process, as well as the content, of such interventions (e.g., Dworkin, Hobson, Frieling, & Oakes, 1983; Lawler & Hackman, 1969).

Miscellaneous Intervention Strategies

Other organizational strategies that have potential for preventing or reducing stress include quality circles, which bring bench-level workers into the decision-making process; training programs for workers whose jobs are being altered by the introduction of new technology; redesign of the physical environment on the basis of ergonomic principles; provision of child care (and perhaps elder care) at the workplace, preretirement seminars; lateral promotion schemes to supplement vertical ones; and creation of more psychologically humane evaluation systems to replace ones that are either archaic or monitor employee performance by means of computer monitoring of keystrokes. These interventions have not been subjected to rigorous scientific evaluation, however, perhaps owing to some of the problems mentioned earlier. Evaluation schemes for such interventions should include cost–benefit analyses in addition to assessment of worker satisfaction, job stressors, performance, absenteeism, and health status.

Concluding Issues

If occupational stress research and occupational mental health are to be enhanced in the future, we must come to grips with the lack of national surveillance data as well as at least five methodological problems in the field.

Lack of National Surveillance

Surprisingly, surveillance data do not exist to reliably identify occupations with an increased prevalence of stress-related disorders, the number of workers at risk for stress-related disorders, or whether these numbers are increasing or decreasing. Indeed, surveillance of psychological disorders and their risk factors presents unique problems that are not encountered in traditional occupational safety and health surveillance. For example, psychological disorders do not fit the infectious disease model; there is not a single exposure agent leading to a single disease. Rather, the work environment contains a variety of risk factors or hazards that interact with characteristics of the individual and nonoccupational risk factors to produce health outcomes. In a recent review, Kasl (1992) described these problems and concluded that current occupational health and safety surveillance systems are inadequate for surveillance of job risk factors and psychological disorders. In their present form, however, national data cannot establish causal links between job risk factors and psychological disorders in an unequivocal way.

National surveillance could be accomplished through the establishment of a new data collection mechanism or through modification and better utilization of existing annual and periodic mechanisms. Examples of the latter are the National

Health Interview Survey (NHIS) and the National Health and Nutrition Examination Survey (both conducted by the National Center for Health Statistics), the Census Bureau's Survey of Income and Program Participation, and administrative data on disability collected by the Social Security Administration. A modification of the 1988 NHIS, in the form of a special supplement dealing with occupational health, is a good example, although that supplement did not contain questions on psychological disorders or psychosocial job risk factors (Ehrenberg, 1989).

Indeed, several published studies have used such large health databases to identify occupations and job characteristics associated with health outcomes. Specific health outcomes analyzed in these studies were neuroses, alcoholism, and personality disturbances (Colligan, Smith, & Hurrell, 1977; Hoiberg, 1982), coronary heart disease (Karasek et al., 1988), hypertension (Leigh, 1991), self-reported levels of stress (Shilling & Brackbill, 1987), depressive disorders (Eaton, Anthony, Mandel, & Garrison, 1990; National Center for Health Statistics, 1980), and disability due to various chronic conditions (Fischbach, Dacey, Sestito, & Green, 1986).

Aside from national surveillance systems, data collected at the "shop floor" level may be the most useful for etiological studies. Joint worker or labor and management committees could serve a useful function in the collection of this type of data. In addition to being useful to individual companies for determining the scope of the problem and tracking risk factors and psychological disorders, the data from many different organizations (stripped of personal identifiers) could be archived centrally to form a national surveillance system (Landy, Quick, & Kasl, in press).

Methodological Needs

Occupational stress research must come to grips with at least five methodological problems that hinder advancement (e.g., Kasl, 1978). One major problem is the reliance on retrospective studies to the near exclusion of longitudinal or prospective and follow-up designs. The chapter in this book by Schoenfeld (chapter 18) is refreshing in its longitudinal design and careful distangling of selection versus maturation effects.

Second, more standardized methods are needed for assessing psychosocial risk factors on the job, and standard psychometric instruments in assessing psychological outcomes should be adhered to (see Hurrell, Murphy, Sauter, & Cooper, 1988).

Third, extensive use of collateral measures for assessing working conditions were recommended in an earlier section. These should go beyond self-reports of job incumbents and include assessments by co-workers and managers and objective measurements obtained through job analysis. Likewise, collateral indicators for psychological or health effects might include self-reports, medical and personnel records, psychophysiological measures, performance, and attendance, as well as supervisory and peer evaluations. For example, recent advances in psychoneuroimmunology and relations between stress and infectious disease suggest another set of collateral indicators of job stress (Cohen & Williamson, 1991).

Fourth, representative sampling procedures and replications to assure that the findings will have general application is required. For example, the use of multiple worksites or industries in the investigation of a particular occupation or job dimension is desirable. Finally, increased use of advanced statistical methods, such as structural analysis, to improve the understanding of causal mechanisms and pathways are required.

References

Alderfer, C. P. (1976). Change processes in organizations. In M. Dunnette (Ed.), *Handbook of industrial and organizational psychology* (pp. 1591–1638). Chicago: Rand-McNally.

Bacharach, S. B., Bamberger, P. B., & Conley, S. (1991). Work–home conflict among nurses and engineers: Mediating the impact of role stress on burnout and satisfaction at work. *Journal of Organizational Behavior, 12,* 39–53.

Baker, G. H. B. (1987). Psychological factors and immunity. *Journal of Psychosomatic Research, 31,* 1–10.

Borysenko, M., & Borysenko, J. (1982). Stress, behavior, and immunity: Animal models and mediating mechanisms. *General Hospital Psychiatry, 4,* 59–67.

Caplan, R. D., Cobb, S., French, J. R. P., Jr., Harrison, R. V., & Pinneau, S. R. (1975). *Job demands and worker health* (DHHS [NIOSH] Publication No. 75-160). Washington, DC: U.S. Government Printing Office.

Carver, C. S., Scheier, M. F., & Weintraub, J. K. (1989). Assessing coping strategies. *Journal of Personality & Social Research, 56,* 267–283.

Cohen, S., & Williamson, G. M. (1991). Stress and infectious disease. *Psychological Bulletin, 109,* 5–24.

Colligan, M. J., Smith, M. J., & Hurrell, J. J. (1977). Occupational incidence rates of mental health disorders. *Journal of Human Stress, 3,* 34–39.

Cooper, C. L., & Payne, R. (1991). *Personality and stress: Individual differences in the stress process.* New York: Wiley.

Davies, D. R., Matthews, G., & Wong, C. S. K. (1991). Ageing and work. *International Review of Industrial and Organizational Psychology, 6,* 149–211.

DeFrank, R. S., & Cooper, C. L. (1987). Worksite stress management interventions: Their effectiveness and conceptualization. *Journal of Management Psychology, 2,* 4–10.

Dworkin, J. B., Hobson, C. J., Frieling, E. F., & Oakes, D. M. (1983). How German workers view their jobs. *Columbia Journal of World Business,* Summer, 48–54.

Eaton, W. W., Anthony, J. C., Mandel, W., & Garrison, R. (1990). Occupations and the prevalence of major depressive disorder. *Journal of Occupational Medicine, 32,* 1079–1087.

Ehrenberg, R. L. (1989). Use of direct surveys in the surveillance of occupational illness and injury. *American Journal of Public Health, 79* (Suppl. No. 1), 12–17.

Fischbach, T. J., Dacey, E. W., Sestito, J. W., & Green, J. H. (1986). *Occupational characteristics of disabled workers* (DHHS [NIOSH] Publication No. 86-106). Washington, DC: U.S. Government Printing Office.

Fox, M. L., Dwyer, D. J., & Ganster, D. C. (1991). Stress and control among nurses: Effects on physiological outcomes. In *Best papers proceedings, National Academy of Management* (pp. 267–271). Miami, FL: National Academy of Management.

Frankenhauser, M., & Gardell, B. (1976). Underload and overload in working life: Outline of a multidisciplinary approach. *Journal of Human Stress, 2,* 35–46.

Frese, M., & Zapf, D. (1988). Methodological issues in the study of work stress: Objective vs subjective measurement of work stress and the question of longitudinal studies. In C. L. Cooper & R. Payne (Eds.), *Causes, coping, and consequences of stress at work.* New York: Wiley.

Hackman, J. R., & Lawler, E. E. (1971). Employee reactions to job characteristics. *Journal of Applied Psychology Monograph, 55,* 259–286.

Hackman, J. R., & Oldham, G. R. (1976). Motivation through the design of work: Test of a theory. *Organizational Behavior and Human Performance, 16,* 250–279.

Hall, D. T., & Mansfield, R. (1975). Relationships of age and seniority with career variables of engineers and scientists. *Journal of Applied Psychology, 60,* 201–210.

Hall, J. K., & Spector, P. E. (1991). Relationships of work stress measures for employees with the same job. *Work & Stress, 5,* 29–25.

Heaney, C. A., & van Ryn, M. (1990). Broadening the scope of worksite stress programs: A guiding framework. *American Journal of Health Promotion, 4*, 413–420.

Hoiberg, A. (1982). Occupational stress and disease incidence. *Journal of Occupational Medicine, 24*, 445–451.

Hurrell, J. J., Jr., McLaney, A., & Murphy, L. R. (1990). The middle years: Career stage differences. *Prevention in Human Services, 8*, 179–203.

Hurrell, J. J., Jr., Murphy, L. R., Sauter, S. L., & Cooper, C. L. (Eds.). (1988). *Occupational stress: Issues and developments in research.* New York: Taylor & Francis.

Ivancevich, J. M., Matteson, M. T., Freedman, S. M., & Phillips, J. S. (1990). Worksite stress management interventions. *American Psychologist, 45*, 252–261.

Jackson, S. E. (1983). Participation in decision making as a strategy for reducing job related strain. *Journal of Applied Psychology, 68*, 3–19.

Jemmott, J. B., & Locke, S. E. (1984). Psychosocial factors, immunologic mediation and human susceptibility to infectious diseases: How much do we know? *Psychological Bulletin, 95*, 78–108.

Karasek, R. A. (1979). Job demands, job decision latitude, and mental strain: Implications for job redesign. *Administrative Science Quarterly, 24*, 285–308.

Karasek, R. A. (1990). Lower health risk with increased job control among white collar workers. *Journal of Organizational Behavior, 11*, 171–185.

Karasek, R. A., Theorell, T., Schwartz, J. E., Schnall, P. L., Pieper, C. F., & Michela, J. L. (1988). Job characteristics in relation to the prevalence of myocardial infarction in the U.S. Health Examination Survey (HES) and the Health and Nutrition Examination Survey (NHANES). *American Journal of Public Health, 78*, 910–918.

Kasl, S. V. (1978). Epidemiological contributions to the study of work stress. In C. L. Cooper & R. Payne (Eds.), *Stress at work* (pp. 3–48).

Kasl, S. V. (1987). Methodologies in stress and health: Past difficulties, present dilemmas, future directions. In S. V. Kasl & C. L. Cooper (Eds.), *Stress and health: Issues in research methodology* (pp. 119–146). New York: Wiley.

Kasl, S. V. (1992). Surveillance of psychological disorders in the workplace. In G. W. Keita & S. L. Sauter (Eds.), *Work and well-being: An agenda for the 1990s* (pp. 73–95). Washington, DC: American Psychological Association.

Keita, G. P., & Sauter, S. L. (Eds.). (1992). *Work and well-being: An agenda for the 1990s.* Washington, DC: American Psychological Association.

LaCroix, A. Z., & Haynes, S. G. (1987). Gender differences in the health effects of workplace roles. In R. C. Barnett, L. Beiner, & G. K. Baruch (Eds.), *Gender and stress.* New York: Free Press.

Landy, F. L., Quick, J. C., & Kasl, S. V. (in press). Work and well-being: An agenda for work design, surveillance, education and treatment. *American Psychologist.*

Leigh, J. P. (1991). A ranking of occupations based on the blood pressures of incumbents in the National Health and Nutrition Examination Survey I. *Journal of Occupational Medicine, 33*, 853–861.

Lawler, E. E., & Hackman, J. R. (1969). Impact of employee participation in the development of pay incentive plans: A field experiment. *Journal of Applied Psychology, 53*, 467–471.

Link, R. N., Feingold, A. R., Charap, M. H., Freeman, K., & Shelov, D. D. (1988). Concerns of medical and pediatric house officers about acquiring AIDS from their patients. *American Journal of Public Health, 78*, 455–459.

Lobel, S. A. (1991). Allocation of investment in work and family roles: Alternative theories and implications for research. *Academy of Management Review, 16*, 507–521.

Lobel, S. A., Quinn, R. E., & Warfield, A. (in press). Between genders: An exploration of psychological intimacy in relationships at work. *Academy of Management Journal.*

Marcus, R. R. (1988). Surveillance of health-care workers exposed to blood from patients infected with human immunodeficiency virus. *New England Journal of Medicine, 319*, 1118–1123.

Mecham, R. C., McCormick, E. J., & Jeanneret, P. R. (1977). *Position analysis questionnaire users manual (system II).* Logan, UT: PAQ Services.

Ministry of Labor. (1987). *Swedish Work Environment Act.* Stockholm, Sweden: Ministry of Labor.

Murphy, L. R. (1988). Workplace interventions for stress reduction and prevention. In C. L. Cooper & R. Payne (Eds.), *Causes, coping, and consequences of stress at work* (pp. 301–339). New York: Wiley.

Murphy, L. R. (1991). Job dimensions associated with severe disability due to cardiovascular disease. *Journal of Clinical Epidemiology, 44*, 155–166.

Murphy, L. R., & Hurrell, J. J. (1987). Stress management in the process of organizational stress reduction. *Journal of Managerial Psychology, 2*, 18–23.

Murphy, L. R., & Schoenborn, T. F. (Eds.). (1989). *Stress management in work settings*. New York: Praeger.

National Center for Health Statistics. (1980). *Basic data on depressive symptomatology. Data from the National Health Survey* (DHEW PHS Publication No. 80-1666). Washington, DC: U.S. Government Printing Office.

National Institute for Occupational Safety and Health. (1988). A National Strategy for the Prevention of Psychological Disorders. In *Proposed national strategies for the prevention of leading work-related diseases and injuries*, Part 2, NTIS Publication No. PB89-130348. Cincinnati, OH: Author.

Nelson, D. L. (1987). Organizational socialization: A stress perspective. *Journal of Occupational Behavior, 8*, 311–324.

Nelson, D. L., & Kletke, M. G. (1990). Individual adjustment during technological innovation: A research framework. *Behaviour & Information Technology, 9*, 257–271.

Nelson, D. L., & Quick, J. C. (1991). Social support and newcomer adjustment in organizations: Attachment theory at work. *Journal of Organizational Behavior, 12*, 543–554.

Nelson, D. L., Quick, J. C., & Joplin, J. R. (1991). Psychological contracting and newcomer socialization: An attachment theory foundation. *Journal of Social Behavior and Personality, 6*, 55–72.

Nelson, D. L., & Sutton, C. D. (1990). Chronic work stress and coping: A longitudinal study and suggested new direction. *Academy of Management Journal, 33*, 847–858.

Northwestern National Life Insurance Company. (1991). *Employee burnout: America's newest epidemic*. Minneapolis, MN: Northwestern National Life Insurance Company.

Osipow, S., & Doty, L. (1985). Job stress across career stage. *Journal of Vocational Behavior, 16*, 26–32.

Payne, R. (1988). Individual differences in the study of occupational stress. In C. L. Cooper & R. Payne (Eds.), *Causes, coping, and consequences of stress at work*. New York: Wiley.

Pierce, J. L., & Newstrom, J. W. (1983). The design of flexible work schedules and employee responses: Relationships and processes. *Journal of Occupational Behavior, 4*, 247–262.

Quick, J. C., Hess, R. E., Hermalin, J., & Quick, J. D. (1990). Career stress in changing times. *Prevention in Human Services, 8*, 1–261.

Quick, J. C., Joplin, J. R., Gray, D. A., & Cooley, E. C. (in press). The occupational life cycle and the family. In L. L'Abate (Ed.), *Handbook of developmental family psychology and psychopathology*. New York: Wiley.

Quick, J. C., & Quick, J. D. (1984). *Organizational stress and preventive management*. New York: McGraw-Hill.

Quick, J. C., & Quick, J. D. (1990). The changing times of life: Career in context. In J. C. Quick, R. E. Hess, J. Hermalin, & J. D. Quick (Eds.), *Career stress in changing times* (pp. 1–24). Binghamton, NY: Haworth Press.

Sauter, S. L., Hurrell, J. J., Jr., & Cooper, C. L. (Eds.). (1989). *Job control and worker health*. New York: Wiley.

Sauter, S. L., Murphy, L. R., & Hurrell, J. J., Jr. (1990). A national strategy for the prevention of work-related psychological disorders. *American Psychologist, 45*, 1146–1158.

Scheflin, K. C., Lawler, E. E., & Hackman, J. R. (1971). Long-term impact of employee participation in the development of pay incentive plans: A field experiment revisited. *Journal of Applied Psychology, 55*, 182–186.

Schein, E. H. (1968). Organizational socialization and the profession of management. *Industrial Management Review, 9*, 1–16.

Schein, E. H. (1989). Reassessing the "divine rights" of managers. *Sloan Management Review, 10*, 63–68.

Shaver, P., & Buhrmester, D. (1985). Loneliness, sex-role orientation and group life: A social needs perspective. In P. Paulus (Ed.), *Basic group processes* (pp. 259–288). New York: Springer Verlag.

Shaw, J. B., & Riskind, J. H. (1983). Predicting job stress using data from the Position Analysis Questionnaire. *Journal of Applied Psychology, 68*, 253–261.

Shilling, S., & Brackbill, R. M. (1987). Occupational health and safety risks and potential health consequences perceived by U.S. workers. *Public Health Reports, 102*, 36–46.

Smyser, M. S., Bryce, J., & Joseph, J. G. (1990). AIDS-related knowledge, attitudes, and precautionary behaviors among emergency medical professionals. *Public Health Reports, 105*, 496–504.

Spector, P. E. (1986). Perceived control by employees: A meta-analysis of studies concerning autonomy and participation at work. *Human Relations, 39,* 1005–1016.

Spector, P. E., & Jex, S. M. (1991). Relations of job characteristics from multiple data sources with employee affect, absence, turnover intentions, and health. *Journal of Applied Psychology, 76,* 46–53.

Stainbrook, G. L., & Green, L. W. (1989). Measurement and evaluation methods for worksite stress-management programs. In L. R. Murphy & T. F. Schonfeld (Eds.), *Stress management in work settings* (pp. 101–134). New York: Praeger.

U.S. Department of Labor. (1977). *Dictionary of occupational titles.* Washington, DC: U.S. Government Printing Office.

Vaillant, G. E. (1977). *Adaptation to life.* Boston: Little Brown.

Wall, T. D., & Clegg, C. W. (1981). A longitudinal study of group work redesign. *Journal of Occupational Behavior, 2,* 31–49.

White, M. A., & Nelson, D. L. (1990). Organizational and individual differences in learning perspectives during the technological innovation process. In U. Gattiker & L. Larwood (Eds.), *Studies in technological innovation and human resources* (Vol. 2, pp. 255–276). New York: Walter deGruyter.

Whyte, W. F. (Ed.). (1991). *Participatory action research.* Newbury Park, CA: Sage.

Work in America. (1973). Report of a special task force to the Secretary of Health, Education, and Welfare. Cambridge, MA: MIT Press.

Yelin, E. (1986). The myth of malingering. *Millbank Quarterly, 64,* 622–649.

23 _____

Cary L. Cooper and Roy L. Payne

International Perspectives on Research Into Work, Well-Being, and Stress Management

Our goal in this chapter is to provide an international perspective on stress research as a contrast to the bulk of the work reported in this volume, which has been carried out in the United States. A systematic approach to doing this involves consideration of three basic questions:

1. What has been studied, and does it differ across countries?
2. How has stress been studied, and does it differ across countries?
3. Why might there be differences in the above?

Before considering the first two of these questions in more detail, we offer our impression of the situation. The vast majority of research on stress is derived from work in the United States. Not surprisingly, the methods used to study stress there have also been widely used to study it elsewhere. The great concern of Americans for health and well-being is associated with considerable efforts to remove stress or treat its consequences, and the United States is the world leader in stress prevention and treatment.

Background

Before we begin to explore the differences in orientation between North American and other international approaches to research into work and well-being and the implementation of stress management, it is important to understand the context of the American scene compared with those of other countries. There are, for example, a number of background factors that might directly explain why research and practice in the stress field have developed differently outside the United States. First, unlike the United States, most European and many other countries further afield have some form of national or state-run health service. For example, in Europe almost all countries provide a comprehensive "free-at-source" health service for their populations. Individuals in these countries pay indirectly for their health care needs through taxation, with the state either wholly underwriting the service or substantially subsidizing it. The implications of this from a workplace point of view is that U.S. employers have not had to provide medical insurance coverage for their employees, and employees have not, by lack of necessity, been motivated to instigate disability claims to compensate for medically treated stress-related illnesses (Sutherland & Cooper, 1990). Second, and to some extent related to the first point, is that in Europe and other countries outside the United States, the legal professons have not vigorously pursued occupationally orientated stress-related cases (Earnshaw & Cooper, 1991). This is due in part to the fact that most other countries are not as "litigation conscious" as is U.S. society, as Vice President Quayle himself recently suggested by highlighting the fact that the United States contains 75% of the world's lawyers! In addition, in almost all countries outside the United States, there is no "contingency fee" system for legal renumeration, which means that it is punitively costly for employees to take legal action on stress-related or cumulative trauma cases, and also it is not in lawyers' interests to encourage potential clients to pursue such cases (Bale, 1990). Third, in many countries in Europe and in other parts of the world, there is still a stigma attached to admitting to and being treated for some forms of mental illness. There is a much greater degree of acceptance of mental illness in the United States than almost anywhere else in the West. This has implications in terms of the acceptability of the concept of stress itself in industry and, therefore, of industry's willingness to do something about it through employee assistance programs (EAPs), stress management, wellness programs, and the like.

These background factors have certainly led to differences between the United States and European countries in the implementation of stress prevention and interventions (see Figure 1). We will explore the differences between the United States and Europe in tertiary, secondary, and primary interventions. First, there has been a slower uptake of tertiary forms of stress management, such as EAPs, in countries outside the United States, resulting partly from the litigation-orientated nature of U.S. society and partly from the lack of acceptability of therapy or counseling in other countries. In addition, the whole notion of health promotion in the United States is far more advanced than elsewhere, with mental well-being and stress management adjunct to this movement. The surprising notion from a European point of view, however, is that although EAPs and the like have been around for some time, there is a paucity of research that systematically evaluates their effectiveness. Indeed, in his review of workplace interventions for stress reduction Murphy (1988) claimed that "though EAPs are increasingly prevalent in work settings, well controlled studies are needed to determine their 'active ingredients' and long-term benefits." EAPs in other countries are only in their infancy, with many countries in Europe only dabbling with the concept and others (e.g., the United Kingdom) cautiously beginning to use them. Because of some of the background factors discussed above, many executives in European industry will only use EAPs if they are proven to be effective. One of the consequences of this is a coincidence of stress counseling and evaluation research (Cooper & Sadri, 1991). Many of the early counseling programs in the United Kingdom and in other European countries have been initiated by management with a strong evaluation component to assess the cost–benefit dimension of their implementation (Allison, Cooper, & Reynolds, 1989; Orlans & Shipley, 1983). In addition, these evaluations have usually involved obtaining more objective data (e.g., sickness absence, labor turnover, disciplinary

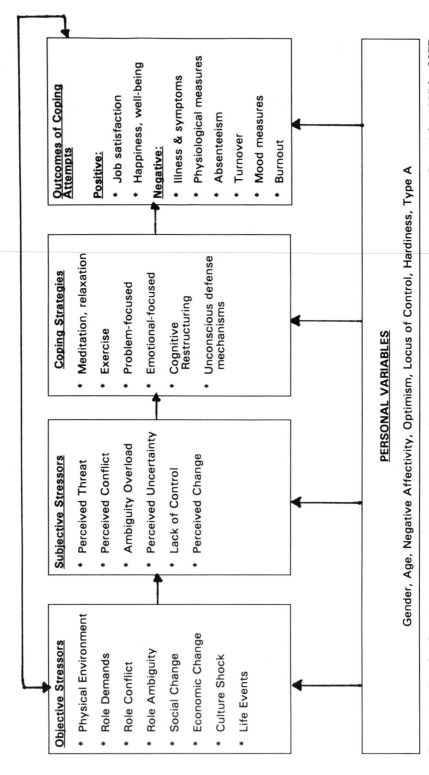

Figure 1. Levels of stress management interventions and outcomes. (From DeFrank & Cooper, 1987. Copyright 1987 by MCB University Press. Adapted by permission.)

events), as well as paper-and-pencil measures (e.g., mental health, self-esteem, job satisfaction), than often found in comparable U.S. studies. European organizations seem to understand the necessity of obtaining "hard evidence" in doing evaluation research and seem more prepared than their counterparts in the United States to allow access to employee data such as sickness absence and disciplinary matters as long as the employee's rights are protected (data provided on a double blind basis). It is also dawning on many European companies that EAPs attract "good publicity," helping to define the employer as a "caring company."

Although countries other than the United States have been involved in secondary forms of interventions in workplace stress, such as stress management training, implementation has started much later but has spread more rapidly than the tertiary EAPs or other counseling approaches. This is because European industry, for example, understands the concepts of training and development (Makin, Cooper, & Cox, 1989), having been exposed to management training, skill training, organizational development, personal development workshops, and the like. As in the United States, however, although these interventions have been widely used, they have not been extensively or adequately evaluated and have other limitations as well.

Reviews of the stress management literature by Murphy (1984) and McLeroy, Green, Multen, and Foshee (1984) drew the following conclusions:

- "Stress management in work settings has been narrowly defined to focus on the individual worker as the target for change. Interventions aimed at modifying stressful aspects of the work environment are rare" (Murphy, 1984, p. 2).
- Programs are preventive and seek to improve worker awareness and recognition of stress. In this sense, the label *stress management* is misleading because neither workers nor organizations with apparent stress problems are solicited.
- Programs are usually offered to workers in white-collar occupations.
- Training typically includes education and some type of relaxation exercise and may additionally include meditation, biofeedback, or a cognition-focused technique.
- Programs have been generic in nature, not targeting specific work stressors or stress symptoms.
- Few studies compared the relative effectiveness of different training techniques. Thus, although doing something appears to be better than doing nothing, the specific technique used may not matter much.
- Evaluations have been based on individual-oriented measures (e.g., anxiety) that have been assessed over short posttraining periods.
- In various studies, stress management has been associated with significant reductions in anxiety, depression, somatic complaints, sleep disturbances, muscle tension levels, blood pressure, and urinary catecholamines.
- The changes observed immediately after training have not always been maintained in follow-up evaluations; regression toward baseline levels has occurred in many studies that contained a follow-up.

As Murphy (1988) suggested, although the number of studies evaluating stress management training have increased since the time of these reviews, the studies in this field have not developed to the extent that they provide data on the comparative effectiveness of different training approaches. In addition, research methodology in this field has been conducted at a relatively basic level, with little pre- and posttraining, few comparative groups, and little objective data (e.g., sickness absence, physiological data). Experiments should be conducted using quasi-experimental designs—randomly assigning participants to different intervention, comparison, and control groups—given that stress management usually involves a training program with some control being exercised by the organization and trainers in terms of who attends and when. There has certainly been more research in this field in the United States than in Europe, where training per se does not need to be justified to the same extent that EAPs would have to be. Even so, the number of studies in toto evaluating stress management training amounts to fewer than 40 reported in the literature, most of which have been carried out in the United States (Murphy, 1988).

In DeFrank and Cooper's (1987) review of stress interventions studies, they found that most of the stress intervention studies (15) were in the secondary and tertiary categories that were aimed or focused on the individual, such as EAPs and stress management training (e.g., relaxation, biofeedback), whereas only 7 studies explored the individual–organizational interface, and only 2 explored organization-oriented interventions. It is in these latter categories, or in the primary intervention area, where there seems to be a major difference in the United States and European approaches. Although there are fewer studies in the primary or stressor-reduction interventions in both the United States and Europe because of the enormous complexities and difficulties of doing such research, the number of interventions at this level is substantially greater in Europe than the United States. Getting at the source of stress in the workplace is by far the most important strategy in terms of producing internalized change, stress prevention, and long-term stress management. However, as Murphy (1988) contended, "Reducing stress through actions aimed at work environment stressors is the most straightforward organisational stress reduction intervention. They also can be costly and difficult to implement in organizations. Stressor reduction requires an identification of the stressors followed by planned changes in organisational structure and function" (p. 322). Because only a minority of any work group experience stress at any one point in time, management is faced with the difficult problem of assessing costs and benefits of organizational interventions.

Although in the United States there have been stressor interventions in terms of work environment factors, these have been usually very focused experiments. They have not tended to be company-wide stressor identification and organizational change projects but rather limited exercises on flex-time or work scheduling (Pierce & Newstrom, 1983) or self-contained participation exercises in decision making (Jackson, 1983) rather than major job redesign experiments (Wall and Clegg, 1981) or large-scale employee involvement experiments such as started in the 1960s and 1970s in many European countries (Cooper & Mumford, 1979). The United States has tended toward individual-oriented stress management strategies, whereas Europe and Japan have attempted to introduce more fundamental diagnostic and job/

organizational redesign projects to get at the primary causes of workplace well-being.

Much of the early work in Europe was derived from the Tavistock Institute in the United Kingdom during the 1950s and 1960s. These action research projects attempted to provide shopfloor workers with more autonomy and control at work. Lack of control at work can be a major source of workplace stress (Sauter, Hurrell, & Cooper, 1990). From these early studies, the tradition has been in Europe, particularly in the United Kingdom and Scandinavia, to identify organization-wide stressors and devise strategies for organizational change. These interventions, and associated research, spread from Olivetti's Ivres plant in Italy (Butera, 1975), to Volvo's and Saab's innovations in Sweden (Norsted & Aguren, 1974; Wilpert & Sorge, 1984), to Phillips in The Netherlands (den Hertog, 1974), to contemporary studies in the brewing industry in the United Kingdom (Bramwell & Cooper, 1991). This approach to stress prevention is also prevalent in Japan as well, where the primary approach, as opposed to the individual-oriented ones, is wide-spread throughout Japanese industry, particularly in the total quality management area (Nakajima, 1988; Shingo, 1986). These programs were not necessarily aimed at reducing work stress, but because of their emphasis on problem solving and social cohesion, they may well have achieved this. There are suggestions, however, that "Japanization" of the workplace actually leads to more sustained rates of work, which could lead to job overload. Such a situation is said to occur in U.S. car assembly plants that have adopted the NUMMI system based on Japanese methods. Such plants are defined by Parker and Slaughter (1990) as "management by stress plants."

The fact is that all organizational or job designs have costs and benefits for the individual and the organization, and there is an inevitable trade-off between these. Striving for a profile that maximizes benefits and minimizes costs is clearly a sensible strategy, but the issues are complex.

If Japanization does increase job overload but ensures long-term security, is this a better outcome for the individual than short-term satisfaction but long-term unemployment? Certainly, there is considerable evidence that unemployment creates psychological distress for a much greater percentage of the population than even the most stressful jobs (Warr, 1987).

So far, we have described the conditions that have led to a vigorous, multidisciplinary interest in stress research and stress prevention in the United States based on the view that U.S. scholars have influenced both what has been studied and how it has been studied (measures and methods). Space prevents a thorough treatment of either topic, but we will expand a little on why we came to the conclusion that the rest of the world (Western and/or English speaking anyway) is an outpost of the United States in stress research. First, we deal with what has been studied.

The Content of Stress Research

Figure 2 presents a conventional "box" model of the stress process and lists the main variables that have been studied.

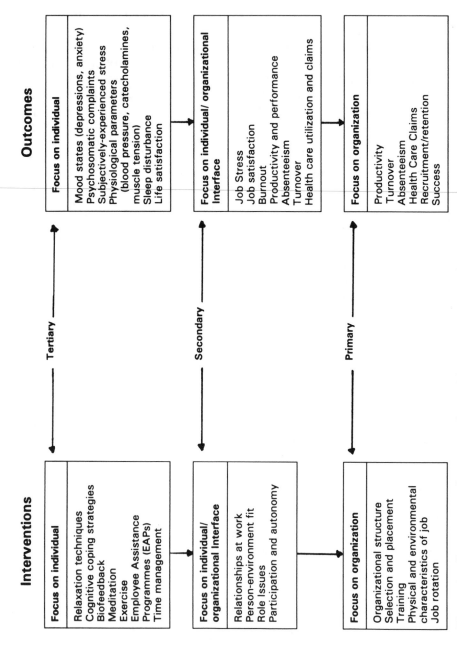

Figure 2. Some commonly measured variables at major stages of the stress process.

Objective Stressors

There are not many actual measures of objective stressors. The life events work initiated by Holmes and Rahe (1967) and the seminal studies of role stress by Kahn, Wolfe, Quinn, Snoeck, and Rosenthal (1964) are exceptions because they rely on reporting of actual events or on using multiple sources of information about the stressed person's role. Most studies of objective stressors have compared people in situations that are "objectively different" (e.g., old vs. modern factories) or have explored universally agreed-on stressful events such as bereavement, disaster, or being a prisoner of war. Given that such events take place worldwide and therefore in different physical and social environments, these studies are less affected by reliance on U.S.-derived measures, at least in terms of the stressors themselves. Earthquakes in California are socially different events from those in Afghanistan.

In contrast, the research on life events as predictors of future illness was started in the United States and copied in many other countries. It is true that studies showed the ratings and rankings of the standard list of life events varied somewhat across cultures (Rahe, 1969), but essentially the same measure was used in many different countries, cultures, and subcultures. Unfortunately, the classic role-set study by Kahn et al. has not been replicated widely, but its effect was on the development of measures of subjective rather than objective stressors.

Subjective Stressors

Perhaps the most widely used measures of stressors in the whole literature are those measuring subjective role conflict, role ambiguity, and role overload. These typically ask the person to rate his or her own situation and conceptually derive from Kahn et al. (1964), although various versions exist. Studies using these measures can be found across the world and across all levels of organizations. Indeed, the most common study in the stress literature, despite its methodological weaknesses (Kasl, 1978), is one involving correlations between self-reported subjective stressors and self-reported physical and/or psychological symptoms.

Studies of control and uncertainty as subjective stressors are common in the stress literature, but they are less obviously rooted in the U.S. research, and there are many more approaches to their measurement than is evident in the role variables. Both have rich traditions in the European literature deriving from their association with cybernetics (Fisher, 1986).

Coping Strategies

The literature on coping strategies has largely developed in the past 20 years, with the exception of the psychodynamic literature, which is, of course, much older. The latter derives from European psychoanalysis, although there is now a huge U.S. literature. Psychodynamic concepts are not commonly used in the traditional stress literature. Stress researchers have relied much more on the work of Lazarus and his colleagues (e.g., Lazarus & Folkman, 1984), although there are several other researchers who have developed coping measures (e.g., Moos & Billings, 1982; Pearlin & Schooler, 1978). The latter have been less well used by others than Lazarus's measures of problem-focused and emotion-focused coping, but we emphasize they are all of U.S. origins.

Studies of exercise and its benefits are more widely dispersed, and much has certainly been done in Eastern Europe, although how closely such work is tied to the stress literature is more difficult to assess. Again, many of the best known studies are from the United States, although because many measures are physiological or performance based, their relevance is less obviously limited to the United States (Masironi & Denolin, 1985).

Although the techniques of meditation and relaxation were developed in India and other Eastern countries, they are widely used to releave stress symptoms and to promote psychological well-being more generally; the empirical study of their effects has again been developed largely in the United States. There is a growing interest in these techniques in other countries too (West, 1987), but the work of Benson (1987) at Harvard University has been particularly influential in bringing these ideas to people interested in stress and its management.

Outcomes of Coping Attempts

There are a number of measures of psychological symptoms that occur regularly in the literature. These include the Langner Scale (Langner, 1962), the Hopkins Symptom Checklist (Derogatis, Lipman, Rickels, Uhlenhuth, & Covi, 1974), the State–Trait Anxiety Inventory (Speilberger, Gorsuch, & Lushene, 1970), and the General Health Questionnaire (Goldberg, 1972). All but the last are American, and the Goldberg measure has been used mainly in the United Kingdom and Australia (Warr, 1987). Although these measures are widely used, this is an area of measurement in which researchers seem willing to develop their own checklists of symptoms so that different lists are found in different countries, although the content tends to be similar (e.g., sleep loss, worry, cognitive errors, etc.). Burnout is a particularly American measure, and the Maslach Burnout Inventory (Maslach & Jackson, 1981) is by far the best known measure for this symptom. Regardless of its U.S. design, it has been used in many other countries.

Most measures of job satisfaction also derive from the United States, but no single one has gained dominance in the field, although the Job Description Inventory (Smith, Kendall, & Hulin, 1969) and Hoppock's scale are well-known (Hoppock, 1935). Again, researchers in different countries have been happy to construct their own lists and rely less on standard measures, although the items have high commonality (e.g., boss, colleagues, the work itself, the environment, pay, etc).

Physiological indicators are used in many countries and generally include catecholamines, cortisol, blood pressure, and a range of other hormones. This area is not U.S. dominated of course, but there is variation in the way assays are carried out to assess the same indicator (e.g., cortisol from blood), and this can make cross-study comparisons difficult.

The detailed way in which absence and turnover are calculated differ from organization to organization, but frequency of absence and total time lost in a given period are commonly used and again cannot be considered unique to U.S. research traditions.

For outcome measures then, the United States has dominated largely in terms of subjective reports of symptoms and job attitudes. Because a large proportion of studies rely on these indicators, there are again grounds for claiming a degree of similarity of work across countries.

Person Variables

The influence of U.S. worker measurements has been enormous. Locus of control and virtually all questionnaire measures of Type A and hardiness are U.S. measures. Negative and positive affectivity measures are both of U.S. origin (Watson & Clark, 1984), although there are other measures of trait anxiety that have been developed outside the United States and used in stress studies. The Eysenck Personality Inventory is the best known (Eysenck & Eysenck, 1964). In summary, across all aspects of the stress process, U.S. research has played a dominant role in influencing what has been studied, even by researchers in different countries and cultures. We now turn to the question of method.

The Methods of Stress Research

In principle, scientific method should be culture free, and should expect to find the same methodological approach in different countries and cultures. This applies less, we suspect, in social science, in which preferences for nomothetic versus idiographic studies differ widely within and across cultures. European social science has been more influenced by interpretative approaches, and that of the United States and the United Kingdom perhaps more by empiricist approaches. Stress research, as opposed to psychotherapy research, has been dominated by empiricism. The "modal" stress study consists of correlating stressors with strains (usually self-report measures). Person variables and coping measures may be incorporated as moderators or mediating variables. The methodological shortcomings of such methods are well-known, and Frese and Zapf (1988) provide an excellent account of these issues for stress research.

Attempts to overcome the weaknesses of such studies have led to useful refinements, such as structural equation modeling, and also to the use of longitudinal studies and cross-lagged correlation. Experimental studies of stress are also numerous but are criticized by some for their low ecological validity. Pseudoexperimental field studies are beginning to include stress and strain measures (e.g., Wall, Kemp, Jackson, & Clegg, 1986). Experimental field studies and longitudinal studies undoubtedly reflect a need to improve methodological rigor in stress research, and given that stress is a process that occurs over time, studies must also be extended over time if the process is to be properly understood (Depue & Monroe, 1986).

Because so much stress research comes from the United States, it is no surprise that it has influenced the methods used in other countries. This is not to say that U.S. research does not include all the approaches listed above. It does, and it is as diverse in its approaches as is any other country, but by virtue of its dominance in measures, it has also tended to influence the way in which those measures have been used. From the point of view of our argument, comparisons of stress research across countries that have had ready access to U.S. ideas would not, we feel, produce very different sets of findings from those in the U.S. literature. This may not be true of Russian or Chinese research. Findings within the United States itself are quite diverse, of course.

We do not wish to imply this U.S. imperialism is necessarily bad. There is a strong argument in favor of developing standard measures and standard methods. In the physical sciences, it would be taken as axiomatic. The question we would like to address is whether other cultures should develop their own measures, if not methods, given that culture is an important determinant of the stress experience. Some studies already indicate interesting possibilities, but they need to be put in the context of Lazarus's (1991) recent *cri de coeur*: "I am constantly dismayed by the absence of cross-cultural research on the process of stress and coping, and indeed on the entire emotion process" (p. 11).

Spradley and Phillips (1972) developed a scale to measure difficulty of readjustment to a new culture. They found differences across cultural groups and between people who has had the experience of adjusting to a new culture versus those who had not. Levine and Bartlett (1984) developed ways of assessing pace of life in six different countries and found large differences in things like the accuracy of clocks, walking speed, and work pace, although there were strong correlations among these measures. They concluded that "when a variety of cultures are considered, the relationship between behaviours such as pace of life and time urgency may not be related to psychological stress and the coronary-prone personality pattern as they are in the United States" (p. 254).

There are cross-cultural studies of health and epidemiology (Dasen, Barry, & Sartorius, 1988) and of psychotherapy and culture (Abel, Metraux, & Roll, 1987), all of which are tangential to the study of stress. However, as Lazarus indicates, there are very few studies on stress per se. In the next section, we create a framework for speculating about how culture might influence the stress process.

Culture and the Stress Process

We start from the assumption that the biological mechanisms that underlie the stress response are universal. This is not to say that different levels of hormones and other body chemicals (e.g., cholesterol) do not exist in different countries. But such differences are most likely due to diet or other environmental factors, and the basic biological processes will be the same throughout the world even if levels do vary and even influence the response to environmental stress.

Given these assumptions, our approach involves conducting a "thought experiment," or speculating about how different cultural variables might influence the stress process. As indicated, we do not mean the physiological process. We mean the process that occurs as a result of the interaction of a person and a stressful environment. The process therefore involves objective stressors, subjective stressors (appraisals of stress), strategies for coping with the stress as appraised, and finally consideration of the outcomes of coping or failing to cope with stress. From these thinking processes, we hope to determine whether cross-cultural studies of stress are worthwhile and what they might concentrate on if they are.

The dimensions of culture that we will use to stimulate our speculations are drawn from Hofstede (1980, 1991). Hofstede helped IBM to design and analyze a questionnaire administered to IBM employees in 40 different countries. The questionnaire contained many questions on values, and because Hofstede found consistent differences across countries, he labeled the measure a *measure of culture.*

Hofstede (1980) originally discovered four cultural factors in the questionnaire he used but based on some work done on values in China (Hofstede, 1991; Hoppe, 1990) added a fifth. The five dimensions are individualism versus collectivism, masculinity versus femininity, power distance (equality vs. inequality), tolerance of ambiguity/uncertainty, and long-term versus short-term gratification of needs.

We plan to consider how two of these dimensions might affect the stress process at each of the four stages described above. The two dimensions we have selected are power distance and masculinity–femininity. We shall consider how a culture high on power distance (with big differences in equality) influences the stress process and how a culture with a strong bias toward femininity does the same. These are chosen because they would appear to offer very different cultural influences.

High Power Distance and Stress

High power distance cultures and objective stressors. According to Hofstede (1991), high power distance cultures produce values concerned with respect for people in authority, obedience to authority; and recognition that differences in rewards, privileges, and status are to be expected and respected, that people in authority know best, and that power should be centralized in the hands of those born and educated to use it.

The countries that Hofstede found to be high on power distance included Malaysia, Panama, Mexico, and Arab countries, with France and Belgium being among the highest European countries. Ignoring the differences in climate and industrialization that exist, and that may themselves lead to differences in stressors, what kinds of stressors would appear common in societies that have such values?

Presumably, stress occurs as a result of transgression of values and norms. Thus, questioning the authority of a superior would be stressful, and failing to meet the obligations placed on one by a superior would create pressure. Transgressing norms of status and the symbols attached to it would be stressful. Not knowing what the rules are would be stressful because in such a society it would be one's duty to know. Being in a position in which innovation and risk taking is required would be very threatening because innovation and unconventionality are distrusted. Being a successful innovator, thereby obtaining rewards to which one is not really "entitled," might be an equally strong source of unpleasant pressure. Even worse in such cultures might be having dependents or subordinates who transgress the values of the society because although they are one's responsibility, one may not be able to control them and thus may live in a state of continuing uncertainty about their future behavior.

Particularly for the inexperienced, the forgetful, or the rebellious, these objective stressors must occur quite frequently in a high power distance culture and cause regular stress. For people who strongly value such a culture and who have internalized the rules and regulations, it might be a relatively safe place, although no doubt many live with the fear that one day they may make a mistake. The degree of fear is presumably related to the severity of the consequences, which obviously vary, even within high power-distance cultures.

High power distance and subjective stressors. In principle, subjectivity must be regarded as a phenomenon relating to the experience of particular individuals in particular situations, so the suggestions that follow assume some generalized other. Given that a person has internalized the values of power distance, however, they are likely to be sensitive to situations involving role conflict and role ambiguity. Role conflict will be particularly stressful because in a well-ordered world there should be a clear answer to problems concerning this issue. Some obligation or person should be more important than another, but if two or more important obligations conflict, then this will produce much uncertainty. Ambiguity will by its nature be stressful in a culture that strives to avoid it. If these issues can be resolved by appealing to higher authority, then all might be well, but the stress involved here entails being sure it is safe to admit one does not know given that this may cause one to be seen as untrustworthy, incompetent, or unreliable.

Subjective stress is likely to be high if the behavior has to take place in public. Speaking before one's superior, answering questions in public, and the like are all threatening, not just because of what one might now know but because of whom one might offend in answering. Thus, ceremonies and important ritual behaviors will be subjectively stressful unless the behavior is highly overlearned.

Power distance cultures and coping strategies. We will assume two basic coping strategies that are consistent with the argument that adjustment involves changing oneself or changing the environment, or doing both (Ackoff & Emery, 1972). Each involves numerous strategies and tactics and bears some similarity to Lazarus and Folkman's (1984) notion of problem-focused and emotion-focused coping. However, in our view, these broad coping strategies are much wider than is implied or contained in the operationalization and conceptual definition of Lazarus's coping strategies.

Attempting to change the world and alter the causes of stress in a power distance culture might be a risky business. Such actions might involve changing the behavior of a superior who may be causing the stress. If one fails to perform a task to the standard required, an action-oriented strategy might entail a request for lowering the standard or for a reduction in the amount of time allocated to the task. If the stressor comes from below, then positive action is much easier in a high power-distance culture given that subordinates are expected to meet the demands of a superordinate. On the other hand, coping tactics involving becoming more dependent on people of lower status can involve loss of face.

A common coping strategy involves acquiring more resources to aid task achievement; this is a good strategy if such resources are in one's control, but it is one that may entail high costs and produce stress itself if the resources have to be obtained from powerful others. It is perhaps not surprising that some of the cultures high on power distance develop specialized roles that use problem-solving action to get rid of a stressor. These involve the use of professionals ranging from lawyers and doctors to astrologists and soothsayers and in the more violent cultures to "hit men" and other sorts of "fixers." Given the potential dangers of trying to change the social environment in high power-distance cultures, it might be safer to use coping strategies involving intraperson coping mechanisms.

Religion offers one method of turning within to deals with stress, although, as Hofstede (1991) pointed out, most high power-distance cultures have highly hierarchical and punitive religions. However, like all religions, they provide comfort and succour to those who have accepted the religion. Other forms of psychological withdrawal involve drugs, and many high power-distance cultures have a history of drug use.

Although in some ways, these strategies of changing the environment or oneself are psychological in nature, both involve behaving and taking action in the outside world. The following are more fully psychological mechanisms that would seem to be consistent with dealing with the stresses of a high power-distance culture:

1. *Splitting and displacement.* The ability to split the world into good and bad objects according to one's own internal standards ought to be helpful in adjusting to the enduring threats of powerful others given that splitting allows one to believe the "good" and doubt the "bad."
2. *Projection.* Defending oneself from the standards imposed by others may involve projecting even higher standards onto others, and these may be conveniently projected onto both superior and subordinate people, enabling oneself to protect one's own integrity.
3. *Rationalization.* The capacity to rationalize that "this is the way the world should be" also enables a person to deal with doubts about the abuse of power both to oneself and by oneself.
4. *Denial.* The capacity to deny what is taking place and to deny that it might even be wrong are again powerful protections for surviving the demands of a high power-distance culture.

It is almost certainly true that any one culture will contain people who use all of the known defense mechanisms. It is our contention that some cultures are more likely to encourage some defense mechanism than others. People in high power-distance cultures no doubt also use sophistication of magical thinking, intellectualization, isolation, reaction formation, and the like, but as an interesting cross-cultural hypothesis, it seems not unreasonable that the four mechanisms highlighted above might be particularly prevalent in aurthoritarianlike societies. These speculations are supported by data in a table by leading British psychiatrist Seaborn-Jones (1968, pp. 219–221). The table presents 11 major philosophical fallacies (e.g., straw man fallacy, fluctuating rigor, behaviorist fallacy, etc.) and indicates how 10 psychodynamic defense mechanisms serve each of the fallacies. It is possible that cultures vary in their people's propensity to commit the philosophical fallacies, but for the moment we shall concentrate on the likely role of defense mechanisms in different cultures.

Outcome Effects in a High Power-Distance Culture. For the sake of simplicity, we assume two outcomes of coping with stressful situations. A positive outcome entails successful coping and continuing sociopsychological well-being. A negative outcome involves psychosocial deterioration, possibly resulting in physical deterioration if the stress is extremely severe or chronic. The question is, How are these two outcomes seen or interpreted in a high power-distance culture?

Positive coping with stress and difficulty is likely to be strongly approved in such societies. People in positions of power receive admiration for coping because they are expected to be strong and capable; this should boost their own view of their strength and leadership qualities. This generalized value put on strength and fortitude presumably also adds to the social approval of people in the lower echelons of the society. This will similarly boost their self-esteem.

Failure to cope with stress consequently has severe penalties, although there may be many relations of dependence in which the "leader" may enjoy the benefits of caring for the weak. Such failures, however, will generally be regarded as signs of weakness and unreliability and result in increased dependence or rejection of a more total kind (e.g., institutionalization or marginalization into the invisible fringes of society). Both outcomes are likely to result in increased stress, creating a nasty downward spiral in both the social and the psychological senses of the phenomenon. Because even the lower ranks of the high power-distance culture show a strong authoritarian streak, the level of social support will be weak, and the general drift downwards of such people does, of course, support the ideology of a culture that believes in inequalities. Because they believe in reincarnation or the importance of spirituality rather than rationality, some religious systems may make it easier to cope with such experiences (e.g., Hinduism or Buddhism vs. Calvanistic versions of Christianity).

Low power-distance cultures are unlikely to be the exact opposite of these suggested patterns, but we will assume they are for the moment, so that we can turn to a different cultural variable and explore its effects on the different stages of the stress process. Again, we will focus on only one end of the dimension.

Masculinity–Femininity and Stress

Another dimension of culture proposed by Hofstede (1991) is masculinity–femininity. To obtain a contrast with power distance, we will focus on the feminine end of the dimension, although strictly speaking the two dimensions are independent. According to Hofstede's findings, another interesting aspect of this dimension is that it is unrelated to economic power; there are strong and weak economies that are high on femininity. High feminine societies are all the Scandinavian countries, Costa Rica, Yugoslavia, Chile, Portugal, and Thailand. Japan, Austria, Venezuela, Italy, Switzerland, Mexico, and Ireland lead the strongly masculine countries.

High feminine societies have the following characteristic values: caring for others and preservation, people and warm relationships are important, modesty is a virtue, both men and women are allowed to be tender, both fathers and mothers deal with facts and feelings, boys and girls are allowed to cry, neither boys nor girls should fight, have sympathy for the weak, to be "average" is to be normal, failing is a minor problem, friendly teachers are encouraged, boys and girls study same subjects, there is a "work in order to live" ethic, managers use intuition and strive for consensus, there is a stress on quality of life, solidarity and equality, and conflict is resolved by compromise and negotiation.

High feminine cultures and objective stressors. Starting from the assumption that transgression of powerful norms and values leads to stress, it must be assumed that behaviors that are aggressive, exploitative, competitive, and tactless lead to social approbation in a "feminine" country or society. Putting people down, trying to be too clever, or showing off will also be regarded as inappropriate behaviors. The interesting question in this culture is how strong the sanctions will be against such socially unacceptable behavior. Because aggression, punishment, and social put-downs are counter to feminine values, those people having to administer the sanctions are themselves put in a difficult situation. One consequence of this is that socially unacceptable behavior is likely to be tolerated for some time. Given the prevailing values, the offending person is likely to be persuaded and counseled before more severe sanctions are administered. Once it has become obvious that the person is a persistent or strongly resistant offender, then the collectivity will no doubt get together to deal with the problem. This collective strength must ultimately put a great deal of pressure on people unless they can escape, find an accommodating niche, or adjust to the social isolation in some other way.

One objective outcome of such a society might be a lack of clarity about what is expected or desired from people, and this ambiguity might itself be a source of stress for relative strangers or members of subcultural groups. Although all societies contain their own stressors, it would appear that a strong feminine culture should produce fewer stressors per unit of time and stressors of less intensity than those of a strongly masculine culture. Because individual stress is a transaction between the person and the environment, there is no doubt that many masculine-oriented people would find a strongly feminine culture a stressful place, although the opposite mismatch might be much more threatening because of the physical and psychological threat inherent in masculine cultures.

High feminine cultures and subjective stressors. Paradoxically, the strong values of "caring and nurturing" are likely to make social situations sources of subjective anxiety. Trying hard not to hurt or offend another person is likely to become a perennial worry. There must also be a problem of worrying about seeming to be too capable. This must make it difficult to decide how to handle stressful situations themselves because jumping in and taking charge, even in a hazardous situation, is very malelike behavior. There must also be a fine balance between being kind, considerate, and supportive and being overprotective or even patronizing. Because nurturance is a strong value, the consequent rejection of nurturing behavior must carry unpleasant implications, and it must be a difficult line to tread particularly in relationships between the sexes.

Again, although it is possible only to generalize to what is likely to be the case for some hypothetical "typical" person in such cultures, anxiety and guilt must be regular features of interpersonal relationships in societies with these values: anxiety about hurting people and guilt if one has because one has failed to deliver equality and fraternity in the nonsexist sense of that word. Fulfiling the demands and expectations of the ideal person in a feminine culture would appear to be difficult, although socially rewarding if the ideals are attained.

As Angyal (1946) pointed out, individuals face two tasks in becoming a mature personality. One involves dealing with one's desire to be an autonomous individual.

The other he calls *heteronomy*, referring to the task of integrating oneself with others while remaining autonomous. The feminine culture stresses the heteronomous challenge, and this must cause conflict with the desire for autonomy. Subjective stress, therefore, is likely to emerge from this conflict and from the high demands of pursuing the feminine ideal of being the caring female, who also provides strength and security. It is possible that this is particularly difficult for men whose sociobiological condition may pull them toward more masculine role models.

As indicated above, the level of objective stressors in a feminine society is likely to be less than in a masculine society, but the psychological stressors indicated in this section do seem to suggest the potential for sustained psychological tension. The stereotype of women is that they do worry more than men, but in analyzing the demands of the culture in this way, it does become apparent that there are both conflicts and ambiguities created by pursuance of feminist values, whether they are pursued by women or men. On the other hand, some of the most successful and satisfied countries in Europe have strong feminist values (Scandinavia), so there must be means of coping with the subjective stressors described here.

High feminine cultures and coping strategies. Changing objective stressors in a feminine culture should be relatively easy given the values of being empathic and supportive. It should be possible to get people to listen well, to understand, and to sympathize with one's needs to change the situation. Thus, gaining both social support and the resources of the community should be much easier than in a male competitive culture. As Gore (1978) has pointed out, not having social support is itself a stressor. This kind of culture should help the problem-oriented coping style.

Another way in which the feminine culture may help is in its concern and use of intuitive problem solving. This may facilitate the production of more creative solutions to problems and less demand for a "rational" set of reasons for trying a solution. Thus, creativity and social innovation are likely to be greater in this sort of culture. Certainly, because failure will not necessarily be seen as a threat, risk taking should be easier to achieve. Being a less competitive society should also make it easier to approach senior people. Indeed, the whole "service" ethic and quality of care is likely to be superior.

Changing oneself, as a coping strategy, will have its distinctive problems, but obtaining help from others to achieve this should also be possible. Help is likely to be available both informally from friends and family but also more formally from the provision of support and welfare services that are prevalent, at least in the European countries holding these values.

The question is, What sorts of psychological defense mechanisms are likely to be developed in dealing with the demands imposed by feminine cultural values? The stress on being average and striving for equality and consensus is likely to give individual initiative negative affective associations. Individualism might, therefore, need to be repressed or denied; thus, denial is likely to be a common defense mechanism. The strong desire to reject masculinity will also be a powerful one, and this might be achieved successfully through the restriction of libido or *noncommitment*, as it is also labeled by Seaborn-Jones (1968). Combined with the following philosophical fallacies, this defense mechanism achieves the following:

Philosophical Fallacy	Psychological Outcome
1. Fluctuating scepticism	Enables the thinker to withdraw at will from unwelcome beliefs.
2. Overextensionism	Withdrawal of libido from insecure no-man's land to well-defended positions.

People holding extremely feminine views (or any other extreme view) are likely to draw on the sophistication of magical thinking. This defense mechanism allows one to commit a whole range of philosophical fallacies achieving the following outcomes: Wish fantasies can be though of as real possibilities; theories can be demolished and reconstructed at will because they are self-produced; mental constructs are attributed the status of the objectively real; pure thinking can settle logical problems independently of science or other disciplines; "truths" are taken as self-evident; one theory can be used to explain everything, or most things.

Defense mechanisms that would seem less likely to work with strong feminine values would be "projection" because it involves setting rigorous standards, blaming others, and so on, and these behaviors would be difficult to achieve given the need to be nurturing and tolerant. Similarly, the close relationships of a feminine value system would militate against the use of isolation to distance one's theories about society from one's feelings of living in it. For similar reasons, intellectualization is unlikely to occur frequently because intellectualizing femininity would involve distancing oneself from the core values of openness and emotional attachment, which is unlikely to work for the person qua person and would certainly cause rejection by other members of the culture. The underlying hypothesis here is that strong cultures influence the ways people cope with stress and that this affects their attempts to use both problem-focused and emotion-focused coping strategies. Any culture will contain myriad coping attempts, but the assumption that we hope we have demonstrated is that culture predisposes individuals and communities to use some styles of coping more readily than others.

Outcome effects in high feminine cultures. Positive coping with stress in feminine cultures is more likely to be taken for granted than publicly admired. Public adulation would involve breaking norms about being average rather than outstanding. Femininity also involves being able to accept one's own vulnerability; thus, "standing on one's own feet" and refusing to give in are in conflict with these values. Indeed, coping by "sharing" and "depending on others" is much more likely to be approved because it reinforces communal values. Interdependence is more important than independence.

Failing to cope with stress, on the other hand, will not involve stigmatization. Vulnerability is a fact of life and the community exists to help people in need. The expectation will be that when one has recovered, the learning and experience one has gained will help one to help others. There is less likely to be blame attached to one as a person in a feminine culture. Stress happens, and people sometimes fail to cope, but that is not their fault, and with appropriate help they will survive.

Conclusion

By speculating about the influence of culture on different parts of the stress process, we believe that we have demonstrated that culture influences all phases of stress. If that argument is accepted, what light does it cast on the question, How does stress research differ across countries/cultures? Our view is that stress research does not differ enough. Researchers have relied too much on measures that have been developed in the United States and other parts of the English-speaking world. If our speculations are even half sound, it becomes obvious that objective stressors in different cultures do vary, but there are few studies that have identified what they are in different cultures. Too often, there is reliance on very general measures such as role conflict or role ambiguity, but surely what is really important is understanding the actual situations that cause ambiguity and conflict. Ambiguity means something very different in a high power-distance culture than in strongly feminine culture, and the conditions that cause ambiguity in one will be very different from those that cause it in the other.

Similarly with subjective stress, the situations that generate anxiety in cultures differ enormously, and the psychological meaning they thus have also differs. Labeling everything as *stress* hides the real nature of the phenomenon, and much needs to be done to get to this level of understanding.

Cultures vary considerably in the sanctions they impose for transgression and failure. What effects does this have? Are thieves in very punitive cultures more stressed? More Japanese students commit suicide for failing examinations than do British students. Are Japanese students in general more stressed, and what are the social, psychological, and physiological implications if they are? And if culture influences peoples' appraisal and coping processes, would we ever find out by measuring them on the same sociopsychological measures? We know from cross-cultural studies of the Holmes and Rahe (1967) measure of life events that people in different countries weight the events somewhat differently (Rahe, 1969). Indeed, there are some differences between urban and rural dwellers within the United States. Marriage was ranked as the 4th most stressful event by the urban sample but 21st by the rural sample (Abel, Metraux, & Roll, 1987). Are not such cultural and subcultural differences likely to occur for many other stressors? And is it not scientifically interesting to then understand why they differ?

Current stress research has also focused narrowly on coping strategies. The bulk of research is Anglo-Saxon in construction, and there must surely be scope for studies that define the parameters of coping within other very different cultures. This is likely to produce a richer picture of coping, improve our understanding of the social and psychological processes that influence the course of the stress process, and enhance the value of comparative studies themselves. The concept of culture has come of age as our introductory quotation implies and so too has the concept of stress as this volume exemplifies. The challenge to our research culture is to integrate them to the mutual benefit of both fields.

References

Abel, T. M., Metraux, R., & Roll, S. (1987). *Psychotherapy and culture.* Albuquerque: University of New Mexico.

Ackoff, R. L., & Emery, F. E. (1972). *On purposeful systems.* London: Tavistock.

Allison, T., Cooper, C. L., & Reynolds, P. (1989, September). Stress counselling in the workplace: The post office experience. *The Psychologist*, 384–388.

Angyal, A. (1946). *Foundation for a science of personality*. New York: Commonwealth Fund.

Bale, A. (1990). Medicolegal stress at work. *Behavioral Science and the Law, 8*, 399–420.

Benson, H. (1987). *Your maximum mind*. New York: Random House.

Bramwell, R., & Cooper, C. L. (1991). *Occupational stress in blue and white collar employees in the brewing industry*. Manuscript submitted for publication.

Butera, F. (1975). Environmental factors in job and organisational design: The case of Olivetti. In L. Davis & A. Cherns (Eds.), *The quality of working life* (pp. 166–200). New York: Free Press.

Cooper, C. L., & Mumford, E. (1979). *The quality of working life in Western and Eastern Europe*. London: Associated Business Press.

Cooper, C. L., & Sadri, G. (1991). The impact of stress counselling at work. *Journal of Social Behaviour and Personality, 6*, 411–423.

Dasen, P. R., Berry, J. W., & Sartorius, N. (Eds.). (1988). *Cross-Cultural Research and Methodology Series: Vol. 10. Health and cross-cultural psychology: Toward applications*. Newbury Park, CA: Sage.

DeFrank, R. S., & Cooper, C. L. (1987). Worksite stress management interventions: Their effectiveness and conceptualisation. *Journal of Managerial Psychology, 2*, 4–10.

den Hertog, F. (1974). Work structuring in Philips. *Industrial Psychology, 10*, 34–57.

Depue, R. A., & Monroe, S. M. (1986). Conceptualization and measurement of human disorder in life stress research: The problem of chronic disturbance. *Psychological Bulletin, 99*, 36–51.

Derogatis, L. R., Lipman, R. S., Rickels, K., Uhlenhuth, E. H., & Covi, L. (1974). The Hopkins Symptom Checklist (HSCL): A self-report symptom inventory. *Behavioural Science, 19*, 1–15.

Earnshaw, J., & Cooper, C. L. (1991). Employer liability for stress on the job. *Employee Counselling Today, 3*, 3–5.

Eysenck, H. J., & Eysenck, S. B. G. (1964). *Manual of the Eysenck Personality Inventory*. London: London Univeristy Press.

Fisher, S. (1986). *Stress and strategy*. Hillsdale, NJ: Erlbaum.

Frese, M., & Zapf, D. (1988). Methodological issues in the study of work stress: Objective vs. subjective measurement of work stress and the question of longitudinal studies. In C. L. Cooper & R. L. Payne (Eds.), *Causes, coping and consequences of stress at work* (pp. 375–412). New York: Wiley.

Goldberg, D. P. (1972). *The detection of psychiatric illness by questionnaire*. Oxford, England: Oxford University Press.

Gore, S. (1978). The effect of social support in moderating the health consequences of unemployment. *Journal of Health and Social Behaviour, 19*, 157–165.

Hofstede, G. (1980). *Culture's consequences: International differences in work-related values*. Newbury Park, CA: Sage.

Hofstede, G. (1991). *Cultures and organizations: Software of the mind*. New York: McGraw-Hill.

Holmes, T. H., & Rahe, R. H. (1967). The Social Re-adjustment Rating Scale. *Journal of Psychosomatic Research, 11*, 213–218.

Hoppe, M. H. (1990). *A comparative study of country elites: International differences in work-related values and learning and their implications for international management training and development*. Unpublished doctoral dissertation, University of North Carolina at Chapel Hill.

Hoppock, R. (1935). *Job satisfaction*. New York: Harper.

Jackson, S. E. (1983). Participation in decision making as a strategy for reducing job-related strain. *Journal of Applied Psychology, 68*, 3–19.

Kahn, R. L., Wolfe, D. M., Quinn, R. P., Snoeck, J. D., & Rosenthal, R. A. (1964). *Organizational stress: Studies in role conflict and ambiguity*. New York: Wiley.

Kasl, S. V. (1978). Epidemiological contributions to the study of work stress. In C. L. Cooper & R. L. Payne (Eds.), *Stress at work* (pp. 3–48). New York: Wiley.

Langner, T. S. (1962). A twenty-two item screening score of psychiatric symptoms indicating impairment. *Journal of Health and Social Behavior, 3*, 269.

Lazarus, R. S. (1991). Psychological stress in the workplace. *Journal of Social Behaviour and Personality, 6*, 1–13.

Lazarus, R. S., & Folkman, S. (1984). *Stress, coping and adaptation*. New York: Springer.

Levine, R. V., & Bartlett, K. (1984). Pace of life, punctuality, and coronary heart disease in six countries. *Journal of Cross-Cultural Psychology, 15*, 233–255.

Makin, P., Cooper, C. L., & Cox, C. (1989). *Managing people at work*. London: Portledge.

Masironi, R., & Denolin, H. (Eds.). (1985). *Physical activity in disease prevention and treatment*. Padua, Italy: Piccin/Butterworth.

Maslach, C., & Jackson, S. W. (1981). Measurement of experienced burnout. *Journal of Ocupational Behavior, 2*, 99–113.

McLeroy, K. R., Green, L. W., Mullen, K. D., & Foshee, V. (1984). Assessing the effects of health promotion in worksites: A review of the stress program evaluations. *Health Education Quarterly, 11*, 379–401.

Moos, R. H., & Billings, A. G. (1982). Conceptualizing and measuring coping resources and processes. In L. Goldberger & S. Breznitz (Eds.), *Handbook of stress: Theoretical and clinical aspects* (pp. 212–230). New York: Free Press.

Murphy, L. (1984). Occupational stress management: A review and appraisal. *Journal of Occupational Psychology, 57*, 1–15.

Murphy, L. (1988). Workplace interventions for stress reduction and prevention. In C. L. Cooper & R. L. Payne (Eds.), *Causes, coping and consequences of stress at work*. New York: Wiley.

Nakajima, S. (1988). *Introduction to total productive maintenance*. Cambridge, MA: Productivity Press.

Norsted, J., & Aguren, S. (1974). *The Saab–Scania Report*. Stockholm: Swedish Employers Federation.

Orlans, V., & Shipley, P. (1983). *A survey of stress management and prevention facilities in a sample of U.K. organisations*. Unpublished manuscript, Birkbeck College, University of London.

Parker, M., & Slaughter, J. (1990). Worked to the limit. *Best of Business, 2*, 42–47.

Pearlin, L. I., & Schooler, C. (1978). The structure of coping. *Journal of Health and Social Behavior, 19*, 2–21.

Pierce, J. L., & Newstrom, J. W. (1983). The design of flexible work schedules and employee responses. *Journal of Organisational Behaviour, 4*, 247–262.

Rahe, R. H. (1969). Multi-cultural correlations of life change sealing: America, Japan, Denmark and Sweden. *Journal of Psychsomatic Research, 13*, 191–195.

Sauter, S., Hurrell, J., & Cooper, C. L. (1990). *Job control and worker health*. New York: Wiley.

Seaborn-Jones, G. (1968). *Treatment or torture: The philosophy techniques and future of psychdynamics*. London: Tavistock.

Shingo, S. (1986). *Zero quality control*. Cambrige, MA: Productivity Press.

Shweder, R. A., & Levine, R. A. (Eds.). (1984). *Culture theory: Essays on mind, self and emotion*. Cambridge, England: Cambridge University Press.

Smith, P. C., Kendall, L. M., & Hulin, C. L. (1969). *The measurement of satisfaction in work and retirement*. Chicago: Rand McNally.

Speilberger, C. D., Gorsuch, R. L., & Lushene, R. E. (1970). *Manual for the State–Trait Anxiety Inventory*. Palo Alto, CA: Consulting Psychologists Press.

Spradley, J. P., & Phillips, M. (1972). Culture and stress: A quantitative analysis. *American Anthropologist, 74*, 518–529.

Sutherland, V., & Cooper, C. L. (1990). *Understanding stress: A psychological perspective for health professionals*. London: Chapman & Hall.

Wall, T. D., & Clegg, C. W. (1981). A longitudinal study of group work redesign. *Journal of Organisational Behaviour, 2*, 31–49.

Wall, T. D., Kemp, H. J., Jackson, P. R., & Clegg, C. W. (1986). Outcomes of autonomous work groups: A long-term field experiment. *Academy of Management Journal, 29*, 280–304.

Warr, P. B. (1987). *Work, unemployment and mental health*. Oxford, England: Oxford University Press.

Watson, D., & Clark, L. A. (1984). Negative affectivity: The disposition to experience aversive emotional states. *Psychological Bulletin, 96*, 465–490.

West, M. A. (Ed.). (1987). *The psychology of meditation*. Oxford, England: Oxford University Press.

Wilpert, B., & Sorge, A. (Eds.). (1984). *International yearbook of organizational democracy*. New York: Wiley.

Index